Rethinking the Pedagogy of Sustainable Development in the AI Era

Caleb Chiidozie Chinedu
Universiti Tun Hussein Onn Malaysia, Malaysia

Nofouz Mafarja
Universiti Malaya, Malaysia

Mahmood H. Hussein
Universiti Tun Hussein Onn Malaysia, Malaysia

Atif Saleem
University of Limerick, Ireland

IGI Global
Scientific Publishing
Publishing Tomorrow's Research Today

Vice President of Editorial	Melissa Wagner
Managing Editor of Acquisitions	Mikaela Felty
Managing Editor of Book Development	Jocelynn Hessler
Production Manager	Mike Brehm
Cover Design	Phillip Shickler

Published in the United States of America by
IGI Global Scientific Publishing
701 East Chocolate Avenue
Hershey, PA, 17033, USA
Tel: 717-533-8845
Fax: 717-533-8661
Website: https://www.igi-global.com E-mail: cust@igi-global.com

Library of Congress Cataloging-in-Publication Data

Names: Chinedu, Caleb Chidozie, 1988- editor. | Mafarja, Nofouz, 1991- editor. | Hussein, Mahmood, 1987- editor. | Saleem, Atif, 1987- editor.
Title: Rethinking the pedagogy of sustainable development in the AI era / edited by Caleb Chinedu, Nofouz Mafarja, Mahmood Hussein, Atif Saleem.
Description: Hershey, PA : IGI Global Scientific Publishing, [2025] | Includes bibliographical references and index. | Summary: "This book seeks to provide a comprehensive analysis of how AI can be integrated into the pedagogy of sustainability, equipping learners with the essential knowledge, skills, attitudes, and values needed to address the complex and interconnected global challenges of our time, such as climate change, resource depletion, and social inequities"-- Provided by publisher.
Identifiers: LCCN 2024055440 (print) | LCCN 2024055441 (ebook) | ISBN 9798369390627 (hardcover) | ISBN 9798369390634 (paperback) | ISBN 9798369390641 (ebook)
Subjects: LCSH: Sustainable development--Study and teaching. | Environmental education. | Artificial intelligence--Educational applications.
Classification: LCC HC79.E5 R48213 2025 (print) | LCC HC79.E5 (ebook) | DDC 338.9/27076--dc23/eng/20250130
LC record available at https://lccn.loc.gov/2024055440
LC ebook record available at https://lccn.loc.gov/2024055441

British Cataloguing in Publication Data
A Cataloguing in Publication record for this book is available from the British Library.

Table of Contents

Foreword xii

Preface xiv

Section 1
Foundations of AI in Sistainable Development Education

Chapter 1
Rethinking the Pedagogy of Sustainable Development in the AI Era: Real-World Applications in Sustainability Education 1
Cynthia Jenny, SRM Institute of Science and Technology, India
V. Kiruthiga, SRM Institute of Science and Technology, India

Chapter 2
Ethical Implications of AI in Sustainable Development Pedagogy 17
Mohanarajesh Kommineni, TEKsystems Global Services LLC, USA
Swathi Chundru, Motivity Labs Inc, USA
Praveen Kumar Maroju, Clientserver Technology Solutions, USA
P. Selvakumar, Nehru institute of Technology, India

Chapter 3
Embracing Cultural Dimensions in AI-Enhanced Sustainability Education: Tailoring Pedagogies for a Global Learner Community 37
Goh Ying Yingsoon, MARA University of Technology, Malaysia
Suyan Zhang, Shandong Jianzhu University, China
Nurul Ain Chua, University Terengganu Malaysia, Malaysia
Yiming Chen, Shenzhen University, China
Tie Xiaoyao, Qilu Institute of Technology, China

Section 2
AI-Driven Learning Strategies and Pedagogical Innovation

Chapter 4
Revolutionizing Education for Sustainable Development Through Adaptive Learning and Artificial Intelligence 63
Jing Wang, Bingtuan Xingxin Vocational and Technical College, China & School of Business and Economics, Universiti Putra Malaysia, Malaysia

Chapter 5
Inbound Learning Active Methodology in Sustainable Development With AI Tools 93
Vitor Lima, Instituto Superior de Gestão e Administração de Santarém, Portugal
Ana Filipa Joaquim, Instituto Superior de Gestão e Administração de Santarém, Portugal

Chapter 6
Integrating AI into a Virtual Learning Environment to Achieve Sustainability and Circularity 111
Anjum Nazir Qureshi, Rajiv Gandhi College of Engineering Research and Technology, India

Section 3
AI Applications in Sustainable Development and Skills Development

Chapter 7
AI in Renewable Energy Education: Teaching the Future of Sustainable Power Systems................. 133
C. Tamilarasi, B.S. Abdur Rahman Crescent Institute of Science and Technology, India
K. Sowmiya, B.S. Abdur Rahman Crescent Institute of Science and Technology, India
G. D. Vignesh, St. Joseph's College of Engineering, India
R. L. Jasmine, College of Engineering Guindy, Anna University, Chennai, India
P. Nehru, B.S. Abdur Rahman Crescent Institute of Science and Technology, India
P. Selvakumar, Nehru Institute of Technology, India

Chapter 8
Predictive Analytics and AI in Sustainability Education: Bridging Data-Driven Insights With Ethical Learning.. 153
Soumya Sankar Ghosh, VIT Bhopal University, India

Chapter 9
Developing Critical Thinking Skills Through AI-Enhanced Science Education for Sustainability .. 173
Nofouz Mafarja, Universiti Malay, Malaysia
Hutkemri Zulnaidi, Universiti Malay, Malaysia
Mimi Mohaffyza Mohamad, Universiti Tun Hussein Onn Malaysia, Malaysia

Chapter 10
Digital Literacy for Sustainability: Preparing Students for the AI-Driven World............................. 197
Mustafa Kayyali, HE Higher Education Ranking, Syria

Section 4
AI in Assessment, Vocational Education, and Workforce Development

Chapter 11
Revolutionizing Educational Assessments With AI Technology 227
Kumar Parmar, Marwadi University, India
Damodharan Palaniappan, Marwadi University, India
T. Premavathi, Marwadi University, India
Rituraj Jain, Marwadi University, India

Chapter 12
ChatGPT as an Automated Essay Scoring System in Comparison With Human Raters in Malaysia 253
Marwan Abd Jal, Universiti Teknologi Malaysia, Malaysia
Si Na Kew, Universiti Teknologi Malaysia, Malaysia
Ghazali Bunari, Universiti Teknologi Malaysia, Malaysia

Chapter 13
The Convergence of Technology and Vocational Pedagogy and Artificial Intelligence for Driving Transformation and Creating a Sustainable Workforce 277
Oladiran Stephen Olabiyi, University of Lagos, Nigeria
Caleb Chiidozie Chinedu, Universiti Tun Hussein Onn Malaysia, Malaysia

Chapter 14
The Role of Artificial Intelligence Autonomy in Higher Education in India 307
Chirag Khandelwaal, Christ University, India
Pankaj Dhaundiyal, Christ University, India
Abhinav Kataria, Christ University, India

Compilation of References 329

About the Contributors 375

Index 383

Detailed Table of Contents

Foreword xii

Preface xiv

Section 1
Foundations of AI in Sistainable Development Education

Chapter 1
Rethinking the Pedagogy of Sustainable Development in the AI Era: Real-World Applications in Sustainability Education 1
Cynthia Jenny, SRM Institute of Science and Technology, India
V. Kiruthiga, SRM Institute of Science and Technology, India

This paper investigates the transformative potential of integrating artificial intelligence (AI) into experiential learning to advance sustainability education. By enriching traditional educational methodologies, AI enables students to engage with real-world environmental challenges, fostering critical thinking and proactive stewardship. Using a qualitative approach, the study synthesizes literature on experiential learning theories, AI technologies, and sustainability education to propose a framework for integrating AI tools in educational settings.

Chapter 2
Ethical Implications of AI in Sustainable Development Pedagogy 17
Mohanarajesh Kommineni, TEKsystems Global Services LLC, USA
Swathi Chundru, Motivity Labs Inc, USA
Praveen Kumar Maroju, Clientserver Technology Solutions, USA
P. Selvakumar, Nehru institute of Technology, India

Educational institutions and policymakers are increasingly incorporating AI into learning environments; addressing the ethical considerations accompanying this technological integration is imperative. Pedagogy lies in its ability to enhance personalized learning experiences, optimize resource management, and foster innovative teaching methods that align with sustainability goals. The deployment of AI technologies aligns with equity, inclusivity, and responsibility principles. One of the primary ethical considerations is the issue of equity and access. AI-powered educational tools have the potential to provide customized learning experiences and resources that cater to individual student needs. However, disparities in access to technology and digital literacy can exacerbate existing educational inequalities. Ensuring the privacy and security of this data is paramount to maintaining trust and safeguarding students' rights.

Chapter 3
Embracing Cultural Dimensions in AI-Enhanced Sustainability Education: Tailoring Pedagogies for a Global Learner Community 37
Goh Ying Yingsoon, MARA University of Technology, Malaysia
Suyan Zhang, Shandong Jianzhu University, China
Nurul Ain Chua, University Terengganu Malaysia, Malaysia
Yiming Chen, Shenzhen University, China
Tie Xiaoyao, Qilu Institute of Technology, China

This chapter explores the integration of cultural dimensions in AI-enhanced sustainability education, emphasizing the need to tailor pedagogies for a diverse global learner community. As sustainability challenges transcend geographical boundaries, it is imperative to develop educational approaches that are inclusive and culturally sensitive. The chapter discusses the potential of Artificial Intelligence (AI) in personalizing learning experiences and addressing the unique needs of learners from various cultural backgrounds. By examining case studies and empirical evidence, we demonstrate how AI can be leveraged to adapt sustainability education to different cultural contexts, fostering a deeper understanding and engagement among students. The chapter also highlights the importance of interdisciplinary collaboration and the role of educators in bridging cultural gaps, ultimately contributing to the development of a more sustainable and equitable global society.

Section 2
AI-Driven Learning Strategies and Pedagogical Innovation

Chapter 4
Revolutionizing Education for Sustainable Development Through Adaptive Learning and Artificial Intelligence 63
Jing Wang, Bingtuan Xingxin Vocational and Technical College, China & School of Business and Economics, Universiti Putra Malaysia, Malaysia

This chapter explores the impact of adaptive learning and AI for sustainable development education (ESD) and reveals its potential to revolutionize the traditional educational model. In the current global context, which is complicated and constantly changing, traditional educational paradigms appear constrained because they only disseminate information in one direction and do not engage learners sufficiently. Therefore, there is an urgent need to transform ESD using system thinking and sustainable development concepts. The role of AI in adaptive learning, personalized platforms, and data-driven evaluation is explained. AI's ability to provide real-time feedback and its application in educational settings are discussed through various case studies. After that, the incorporation of adaptive learning within ESD is explored, with theoretical underpinnings and useful tactics presented. Finally, the chapter concludes with a series of policy recommendations to guarantee educational fairness and accessibility.

Chapter 5
Inbound Learning Active Methodology in Sustainable Development With AI Tools 93
Vitor Lima, Instituto Superior de Gestão e Administração de Santarém, Portugal
Ana Filipa Joaquim, Instituto Superior de Gestão e Administração de Santarém, Portugal

In Portugal, adopting active methodologies has been a growing strategy to engage students and stimulate active participation and autonomy in the educational process. In this context, quality education plays a crucial role in developing sustainable communities, especially with the advancement of AI. AI has the potential to personalize teaching, adapt it to students' individual needs, and facilitate the implementation of methodologies such as Inbound Learning, which focuses on creating relevant and personalized educational experiences. Educational innovation in Portugal seeks to improve the quality of teaching and promote equity and inclusion, ensuring that all students have access to quality educational opportunities. This article presents the IL methodology, which can positively transform teaching-learning. It prepares students to be critical, creative, and adaptable citizens and thus creates the skills and competencies to respond to the challenges of SDG9.

Chapter 6
Integrating AI into a Virtual Learning Environment to Achieve Sustainability and Circularity 111
Anjum Nazir Qureshi, Rajiv Gandhi College of Engineering Research and Technology, India

The popularity of virtual learning environments has transformed learning and teaching practices. AI is a promising technology extensively used to improve the learning experience for those who opt for virtual or online education. AI has enabled many features in the virtual learning system by which the learners enjoy learning at their own pace. AI will make learning more manageable, but the challenges should be handled carefully to increase its adaptability and acceptability. Learning remotely is easily accessible for enthusiastic learners who believe in upskilling themselves to be compatible with the fast-advancing world. It benefits those who work due to weak financial conditions but still want to complete their education. Virtual education has enabled learning from experts around the world. The virtual learning methods have enhanced global and local collaborations. It will bridge the education gaps for those unable to continue education. This will help to achieve sustainability in education by increasing its affordability and accessibility.

Section 3
AI Applications in Sustainable Development and Skills Development

Chapter 7
AI in Renewable Energy Education: Teaching the Future of Sustainable Power Systems................. 133
C. Tamilarasi, B.S. Abdur Rahman Crescent Institute of Science and Technology, India
K. Sowmiya, B.S. Abdur Rahman Crescent Institute of Science and Technology, India
G. D. Vignesh, St. Joseph's College of Engineering, India
R. L. Jasmine, College of Engineering Guindy, Anna University, Chennai, India
P. Nehru, B.S. Abdur Rahman Crescent Institute of Science and Technology, India
P. Selvakumar, Nehru Institute of Technology, India

AI's application in renewable energy education is multifaceted, encompassing areas such as energy management, grid optimization, and predictive maintenance. These simulations enable learners to understand the intricacies of energy systems and develop skills in analyzing data and making informed decisions based on real-time information. In the context of renewable energy education. This implies that students can engage with materials that are specifically designed to address their knowledge gaps and interests, thereby deepening their understanding of complex topics such as solar photovoltaic systems, wind turbine technology, and energy storage solutions. AI-driven platforms can also facilitate interactive learning through virtual labs and simulations, offering students practical experience in designing and testing renewable energy solutions.The integration of AI into renewable energy education also supports the development of critical skills required for the future workforce.

Chapter 8
Predictive Analytics and AI in Sustainability Education: Bridging Data-Driven Insights With Ethical Learning.. 153
Soumya Sankar Ghosh, VIT Bhopal University, India

This study explores how predictive analytics and Artificial Intelligence (AI) can revolutionize sustainability education by fostering personalized learning, ethical reasoning, and inclusivity. Statistical modeling demonstrated significant improvements in sustainability literacy across diverse cohorts, with the greatest gains observed among underperforming students. However, challenges such as algorithmic transparency, bias, and access disparities highlight the need for ethical AI design and infrastructural investments. Combining personalized AI-driven tools with human oversight emerged as essential for meaningful engagement and equity. Recommendations include developing ethical AI systems, fostering digital inclusion, and promoting interdisciplinary research to scale AI-driven sustainability education effectively.

Chapter 9
Developing Critical Thinking Skills Through AI-Enhanced Science Education for Sustainability .. 173
Nofouz Mafarja, Universiti Malay, Malaysia
Hutkemri Zulnaidi, Universiti Malay, Malaysia
Mimi Mohaffyza Mohamad, Universiti Tun Hussein Onn Malaysia, Malaysia

In an era where artificial intelligence (AI) is rapidly transforming every aspect of our lives, the education sector must adapt to equip students with the skills needed to address complex global challenges, particularly in sustainable development. This chapter, titled "Developing Critical Thinking Skills Through AI-Enhanced Science Education for Sustainability," will explore how AI can be integrated into science education to foster critical thinking and problem-solving skills, essential for addressing issues like environmental degradation, renewable energy, and climate change education. This chapter aligns with the overall theme of the book, "Rethinking the Pedagogy of Sustainable Development in the AI Era," by addressing the critical role that AI can play in reshaping science education to better prepare students for the complexities of sustainable development. It highlights the potential of AI to not only enhance educational outcomes but also to empower the next generation of learners to contribute meaningfully to global sustainability efforts.

Chapter 10
Digital Literacy for Sustainability: Preparing Students for the AI-Driven World............................. 197
Mustafa Kayyali, HE Higher Education Ranking, Syria

As the world faces more complex sustainability concerns, the role of digital literacy in influencing students' abilities to contribute to a sustainable future has never been more vital. The rapid breakthroughs in Artificial Intelligence (AI) have created opportunities and difficulties in education, requiring the integration of digital literacy with sustainability education. This article investigates the convergence of digital literacy and sustainability, claiming that preparing students for an AI-driven society is vital for equipping them with the skills necessary to address global concerns. It studies how digital literacy may be harnessed to achieve sustainable development, including the ability to use digital tools, analyze data, and engage critically with technology. The study also explores the pedagogical techniques that can be implemented to integrate sustainability into the digital literacy curriculum, providing students with the information and competencies they need to navigate an AI-powered future.

Section 4
AI in Assessment, Vocational Education, and Workforce Development

Chapter 11
Revolutionizing Educational Assessments With AI Technology 227
Kumar Parmar, Marwadi University, India
Damodharan Palaniappan, Marwadi University, India
T. Premavathi, Marwadi University, India
Rituraj Jain, Marwadi University, India

This chapter explores the possibility of using Artificial Intelligence to reform the field of educational assessment, which has been dormant for the last several decades because the traditional approach to learning assessment is laden with several complications. Very often, the conventional approaches in assessment have served the purpose of ascertaining the knowledge and abilities of learners satisfactorily. Still, rarely are they in harmony with mind-perceptiveness in correspondence with an individual's learning styles, cultural factors, or learning rhythm. Drawing from the current AI technologies that make learning assessable, the chapter discusses their application and, therefore, the potential advantages and disadvantages, if any. Finally, it discusses the future opportunities of AI in educational assessment concerning developing trends, risks, and the imperative to use the capability of AI responsibly to create a positive Learning Environment for the students effectively and safely.

Chapter 12
ChatGPT as an Automated Essay Scoring System in Comparison With Human Raters in Malaysia 253
Marwan Abd Jal, Universiti Teknologi Malaysia, Malaysia
Si Na Kew, Universiti Teknologi Malaysia, Malaysia
Ghazali Bunari, Universiti Teknologi Malaysia, Malaysia

This research compares ChatGPT, known as AI chatbot, with human raters to assess its capability as an automated scoring system in grading essays. The objective is to determine whether ChatGPT can effectively evaluate elements such as grammar, coherence, and organisation in essays comparable to human raters. To ensure the evaluation aligns with the Malaysia's education system, this research has utilised written essays from an English university course as a sample. This approach helps the researchers understand how well ChatGPT performs within Malaysian's education context. Data were collected using ChatGPT and human rater. The findings of this study revealed that ChatGPT can be used as an automated scoring system because there is no significant difference between human raters in assessing grammar and organization. However, monitoring from humans is needed as there are significant differences in assessing coherence. It is believed that the findings from this study can help the university and the Ministry of Education to be clear about the ChatGPT as an automated scoring system.

Chapter 13
The Convergence of Technology and Vocational Pedagogy and Artificial Intelligence for Driving Transformation and Creating a Sustainable Workforce 277
Oladiran Stephen Olabiyi, University of Lagos, Nigeria
Caleb Chiidozie Chinedu, Universiti Tun Hussein Onn Malaysia, Malaysia

Integrating Artificial Intelligence (AI) and technology-driven vocational pedagogy in Technical and Vocational Education and Training (TVET) offers transformative potential in preparing students for the modern workforce. AI enhances skill acquisition, making learning more efficient and improving employability. This chapter explores the convergence of AI and vocational pedagogy in shaping workforce development. It defines key concepts, including AI, vocational pedagogy, and TVET, while examining AI's role in enhancing learning, assessment, and workforce readiness. The chapter also discusses the impact of vocational pedagogy on skill development, the integration of technology in TVET, and AI-driven workforce transformation in Nigeria. Challenges faced by TVET educators in adopting AI and its benefits in equipping students with essential competencies are highlighted. The chapter concludes with recommendations for leveraging AI to create a sustainable, industry-relevant vocational education system.

Chapter 14
The Role of Artificial Intelligence Autonomy in Higher Education in India 307
Chirag Khandelwaal, Christ University, India
Pankaj Dhaundiyal, Christ University, India
Abhinav Kataria, Christ University, India

To leverage the benefits of artificial intelligence applications for experiential learning, many higher education institutes have started using artificial intelligence by adopting many artificial intelligence-driven technologies. Some of them are chatbots, generative AI, concepts of virtual tutors, and providing students with various automated assessment tools for their own assessment, which might change the traditional teaching methodology. This chapter examines the role of artificial intelligence autonomy in higher education in India, deep-diving into AI's impact on students' learning outcomes by leveraging AI-driven technologies in education. This research will specifically have five major variables that will be examined and measured. These variables are usage intention, thought autonomy, action autonomy, sensing autonomy, and culture. This study will examine the five main dimensions of AI autonomy: usage intention, thought autonomy, action autonomy, sensing autonomy, and culture.

Compilation of References 329

About the Contributors 375

Index 383

Foreword

Artificial Intelligence (AI) has emerged as one of the most transformative technologies of our time, revolutionizing industries, reshaping economies, and redefining how we live, work, and learn. At the same time, the global community faces an urgent call to embrace sustainable development as a guiding principle for progress. As we stand at the intersection of these two powerful forces—AI and sustainability—an unparalleled opportunity arises to leverage technology to improve education, society, and the environment. This book, *Artificial Intelligence in Sustainable Development Education*, presents a comprehensive exploration of how AI can be harnessed to revolutionize teaching and learning while advancing sustainability goals. It provides a multidimensional perspective on how AI-driven innovations can enhance pedagogy, bridge digital divides, and prepare students for an AI-powered future. The contributors to this volume bring together a wealth of expertise from various academic institutions and industries, offering a rich and diverse set of insights into the transformative potential of AI in education.

Specifically, the book is organized into four key sections, each addressing a crucial aspect of AI-driven sustainable education. The first section, *Foundations of AI in Sustainable Development Education*, examines how AI can reshape pedagogical approaches to sustainability. It explores the ethical implications of AI in education and underscores the importance of cultural inclusivity in AI-enhanced learning environments. These discussions highlight the need for a human-centered approach to AI integration—one that prioritizes equity, accessibility, and ethical considerations.

The second section, *AI-Driven Learning Strategies, and Pedagogical Innovation* delves into the practical applications of AI in revolutionizing education for sustainable development. It examines adaptive learning models, inbound learning methodologies, and virtual learning environments—all demonstrating how AI can enhance engagement, foster critical thinking, and support lifelong learning. These innovations have the potential to break down traditional barriers to education, making learning more accessible and tailored to individual needs.

The third section, *AI Applications in Sustainable Development and Skills Development*, explores how AI can be applied to skill-building and knowledge dissemination in sustainability-related fields. From renewable energy education to predictive analytics in sustainability learning, these chapters provide compelling case studies of how AI can empower students to become active contributors to global sustainability efforts. The emphasis on digital literacy and AI-driven critical thinking skills underscores the need for a future-ready workforce capable of addressing complex environmental and societal challenges.

Finally, the fourth section, *AI in Assessment, Vocational Education, and Workforce Development*, addresses one of the most critical aspects of AI in education—the evaluation and measurement of learning outcomes. Traditional assessment methods often fail to capture the full spectrum of students' abilities and potential. AI-powered assessment tools, automated essay scoring systems, and intelligent feedback mechanisms offer more nuanced and dynamic approaches to evaluating student performance. Additionally, the discussion on AI's role in vocational education highlights its potential to equip learners with industry-relevant skills, thereby fostering a sustainable and adaptive workforce.

What makes this book particularly compelling is its emphasis on interdisciplinary collaboration and real-world applications. The authors do not merely present theoretical frameworks; they offer concrete examples, empirical research, and policy recommendations that can guide educators, policymakers, and institutions in effectively integrating AI into sustainable education. As AI continues to evolve, it is imperative that we adopt a holistic and forward-thinking approach to its implementation—one that balances technological advancements with ethical considerations and social responsibility.

It is with great enthusiasm that I commend the authors and editors of this book for their invaluable contributions to this critical field of study. Their work deepens our understanding of AI's role in sustainable education and inspires us to envision new possibilities for teaching, learning, and global progress. I am confident that this book will serve as a valuable resource for educators, students, and policymakers alike, fostering meaningful discussions and driving impactful change in pursuing a more sustainable and technologically empowered future.

Lai Chee Sern
Malaysia Research Institute for Vocational Education and Training (MyRIVET), Malaysia

Preface

The rapid advancement of Artificial Intelligence (AI) is reshaping nearly every aspect of our lives, from how we work and communicate to how we learn and solve global challenges. As we navigate this transformative era, the intersection between education and sustainable development—stands at a critical juncture. AI holds immense potential to revolutionize the way education for and about sustainability is taught and learned, offering new avenues for problem-solving, innovation, and efficiency. However, alongside its promise, AI also presents ethical and practical challenges that must be carefully examined. How do we harness AI's capabilities to foster a more sustainable and just world? Can AI-driven education truly empower learners with the critical thinking and ethical reasoning needed to address complex global issues such as climate change, resource depletion, and social inequities?

Rethinking the Pedagogy of Sustainable Development in the AI Era dives deep into these pressing questions, offering a multidisciplinary exploration of AI's role in sustainability education. This book brings together perspectives from researchers, educators, and industry practitioners to examine how AI-driven tools and methodologies can enhance sustainability learning while ensuring that human-centered values remain at the core of education. This book analyses AI's influence on teaching strategies, digital literacy, assessment methods, and vocational education for sustainable development through theoretical discussions, case studies, and practical insights.

In today's world, where technological advancements often outpace the ethical and regulatory frameworks that govern them, the intersection of AI and sustainability education is more crucial than ever. Education systems worldwide are grappling with integrating AI into teaching while ensuring it remains a force for good rather than a tool that prioritizes efficiency over meaningful, transformative learning. This book seeks to guide educators, policymakers, and learners in navigating this rapidly evolving landscape, equipping them with the knowledge and strategies needed to use AI as a catalyst for sustainable change.

This book is intended for a diverse audience, including:

- **Educators and Researchers**: Those involved in higher education, technical and vocational education, and sustainability studies who seek to integrate AI into their pedagogical approaches while maintaining ethical and human-centered learning.
- **Policymakers and Institutional Leaders**: Decision-makers shaping educational policies and sustainability initiatives who need evidence-based insights on the role of AI in achieving sustainable development goals (SDGs).
- **Technology and Sustainability Professionals**: Industry practitioners working at the intersection of AI, education, and sustainability who wish to understand the broader implications of AI-driven learning strategies.
- **Students and Lifelong Learners**: Those interested in understanding how AI is transforming the way we learn about and address global sustainability challenges.

By bridging the gap between technology and sustainability education, *Rethinking the Pedagogy of Sustainable Development in the AI Era* aims to inspire a new generation of educators and learners who are not only AI-literate but also critically engaged with the ethical, cultural, and pedagogical implications of this powerful technology. As we move forward, it is imperative that we do not view AI as a mere tool but as a dynamic force that, if harnessed thoughtfully, can drive sustainable progress and reshape the future of learning for the better.

Each chapter presents valuable insights into AI-driven pedagogical innovation, ethical considerations, digital tools, and workforce development strategies. Below is a description of the significance of each chapter:

Section I: Foundations of AI in Sustainable Development Education

Chapter 1: Rethinking the Pedagogy of Sustainable Development in the AI Era: Real-World Applications in Sustainability Education

This chapter establishes the foundation for the book by examining how AI can enhance experiential learning for sustainability education. Learners engage with real-world environmental challenges by integrating AI-driven tools into traditional methodologies, fostering critical thinking and problem-solving. The framework proposed in this chapter is crucial in shaping future AI-driven pedagogies that prioritize sustainability.

Chapter 2: Ethical Implications of AI in Sustainable Development Pedagogy

The ethical considerations of AI integration in education are a pressing concern. This chapter addresses crucial issues such as data privacy, algorithmic bias, digital equity, and inclusivity. The chapter highlights the importance of responsible AI deployment to ensure sustainable and fair learning environments by examining the ethical dilemmas associated with AI-driven education.

Chapter 3: Embracing Cultural Dimensions in AI-Enhanced Sustainability Education: Tailoring Pedagogies for a Global Learner Community

As sustainability education transcends geographical boundaries, this chapter explores the role of cultural dimensions in AI-enhanced learning. Through case studies and empirical research, the chapter emphasizes how AI can personalize learning experiences to cater to diverse cultural backgrounds, ultimately fostering global inclusivity and intercultural understanding in sustainability education.

Section II: AI-Driven Learning Strategies and Pedagogical Innovation

Chapter 4: Revolutionizing Education for Sustainable Development through Adaptive Learning and Artificial Intelligence

Traditional education models often struggle to keep pace with today's rapidly changing sustainability challenges. This chapter introduces AI-powered adaptive learning, demonstrating how personalized learning platforms, real-time feedback, and AI-driven assessments can create dynamic and efficient educational experiences that align with sustainability goals.

Chapter 5: Inbound Learning Active Methodology in Sustainable Development with AI Tools

This chapter presents an innovative approach to sustainability education by exploring active learning methodologies supported by AI. By integrating AI-driven learning models, educators can foster critical thinking, self-directed learning, and engagement in sustainability topics, making this chapter valuable for developing new instructional models.

Chapter 6: Integrating AI into a Virtual Learning Environment to Achieve Sustainability and Circularity

The shift toward virtual learning environments presents new opportunities and challenges in sustainability education. This chapter examines how AI enhances virtual learning experiences, making education more accessible and adaptable to students worldwide. The chapter underscores the role of AI-driven virtual education in fostering circularity, resource efficiency, and lifelong learning.

Section III: AI Applications in Sustainable Development and Skills Development

Chapter 7: AI in Renewable Energy Education: Teaching the Future of Sustainable Power Systems

Education must evolve as the world transitions toward renewable energy to equip students with relevant skills. This chapter explores how AI can enhance renewable energy education through simulations, predictive analytics, and personalized learning, ultimately preparing students for careers in the evolving energy sector.

Chapter 8: Predictive Analytics and AI in Sustainability Education: Bridging Data-Driven Insights with Ethical Learning

AI-driven predictive analytics can personalize sustainability education and enhance decision-making. However, ethical considerations such as algorithmic bias and transparency remain concerns. This chapter discusses how AI can effectively and ethically foster sustainability literacy, providing strategies to balance data-driven insights with ethical responsibility.

Chapter 9: Developing Critical Thinking Skills Through AI-Enhanced Science Education for Sustainability

Science education plays a critical role in sustainability, and this chapter investigates how AI-powered tools can enhance students' critical thinking skills. By leveraging AI for problem-solving and data analysis, students can engage more effectively with sustainability issues such as environmental degradation and climate change.

Chapter 10: Digital Literacy for Sustainability: Preparing Students for the AI-Driven World

In today's AI-driven world, digital literacy is essential for sustainability education. This chapter explores how digital skills, including data analysis and AI ethics, can prepare students to address complex sustainability challenges. It also provides insights into integrating sustainability principles into digital literacy curricula.

Section IV: AI in Assessment, Vocational Education, and Workforce Development

Chapter 11: Revolutionizing Educational Assessments with AI Technology

Traditional assessment methods often fail to capture the complexities of student learning and sustainability education. This chapter explores how AI-driven assessment tools can enhance evaluation accuracy, provide personalized feedback, and support competency-based learning, ultimately leading to fairer and more effective sustainability education assessments.

Chapter 12: ChatGPT as an Automated Essay Scoring System in Comparison with Human Raters in Malaysia

With the increasing use of AI in educational assessment, this chapter examines how ChatGPT compares with human raters in grading essays. By analyzing its effectiveness in assessing grammar, coherence, and organization, the study provides critical insights into the potential and limitations of AI-based evaluation tools in sustainability education.

Chapter 13: The Convergence of Technology and Vocational Pedagogy with Artificial Intelligence for Driving Transformation and Creating a Sustainable Workforce

AI is reshaping vocational education, equipping students with future-ready skills. This chapter explores how AI-driven vocational pedagogy can transform workforce development, focusing on skill acquisition, employability, and industry relevance. The discussion is particularly relevant for TVET institutions aiming to integrate AI into training programs.

Chapter 14: The Role of Artificial Intelligence Autonomy in Higher Education in India

Higher education institutions are increasingly adopting AI-driven tools for experiential learning. This chapter explores AI's autonomy in higher education, focusing on virtual tutors, automated assessments, and AI-driven decision-making. It critically examines how AI autonomy impacts student learning outcomes, academic integrity, and institutional governance.

Integrating artificial intelligence (AI) into sustainability education represents a paradigm shift that challenges conventional teaching and learning approaches while offering unprecedented opportunities for innovation and transformation. Rethinking the Pedagogy of Sustainable Development in the AI Era has brought together diverse perspectives, research findings, and practical applications to explore how AI can enhance sustainability education, making it more accessible, personalized, and impactful.

Through the chapters in this book, contributors have examined the ethical, cultural, and technological implications of AI in sustainability pedagogy. We see how AI-driven adaptive learning, predictive analytics, and virtual environments can revolutionize education by making it more student-centered and data-informed. At the same time, we acknowledge the challenges that arise with AI integration, including ethical concerns, the digital divide, and the need for responsible and equitable deployment of AI technologies.

This book contributes significantly to the ongoing discourse on AI in education by:

- Bridging Sustainability and AI Pedagogy – It presents AI not as a mere tool but as a transformative force that, when thoughtfully integrated, can drive sustainability literacy and equip learners with the skills needed to address complex global challenges.
- Advancing Research and Practice – By offering a balance of theoretical insights and case studies, the book serves as a valuable resource for researchers, educators, and policymakers seeking evidence-based strategies for integrating AI into sustainability education.
- Encouraging Ethical and Inclusive AI Use – The discussions in this book highlight the importance of responsible AI adoption, ensuring that its implementation in education aligns with ethical principles, cultural inclusivity, and global sustainability goals.
- Shaping Future Workforce Development – Focusing on vocational education and AI-driven workforce transformation, the book provides insights into how AI can prepare students for careers in sustainability sectors, fostering a future-ready and environmentally conscious workforce.

By addressing these critical themes, Rethinking the Pedagogy of Sustainable Development in the AI Era not only enriches the academic field but also provides practical guidance for those seeking to harness AI's potential in a meaningful and responsible manner. The insights presented in this book will help shape policies, teaching methodologies, and technological innovations that align with the broader vision of sustainable development.

As we move forward, the challenge remains to balance leveraging AI for efficiency and ensuring that it remains a tool for human empowerment, ethical decision-making, and global equity. This book serves as both a reflection on where we stand and a call to action for reimagining the future of education—one where AI supports, rather than supplants, the core values of sustainability, critical thinking, and lifelong learning.

Section 1
Foundations of AI in Sistainable Development Education

Chapter 1
Rethinking the Pedagogy of Sustainable Development in the AI Era:
Real-World Applications in Sustainability Education

Cynthia Jenny
https://orcid.org/0009-0002-0209-6969
SRM Institute of Science and Technology, India

V. Kiruthiga
https://orcid.org/0000-0002-3570-8987
SRM Institute of Science and Technology, India

ABSTRACT

This paper investigates the transformative potential of integrating artificial intelligence (AI) into experiential learning to advance sustainability education. By enriching traditional educational methodologies, AI enables students to engage with real-world environmental challenges, fostering critical thinking and proactive stewardship. Using a qualitative approach, the study synthesizes literature on experiential learning theories, AI technologies, and sustainability education to propose a framework for integrating AI tools in educational settings.

INTRODUCTION

Over the past few decades, the education sector has undergone a profound transformation, driven by rapid technological advancements and shifting global dynamics. This evolution has expanded education beyond mere knowledge transfer to cultivating practical skills that drive long-term sustainable impact. As education systems adapt to these changes, there is a growing need for sustainable development, requiring a fundamental shift in both knowledge acquisition and its practical application worldwide. Teachers and institutions serve as crucial change agents in this transformation; however, integrating experiential learning with artificial intelligence (AI) remains an underexplored avenue, particularly in

DOI: 10.4018/979-8-3693-9062-7.ch001

sustainability education. The challenge lies in effectively employing AI in educational processes while also providing experiential learning opportunities—two key areas that hold immense potential for enhancing sustainable education.

Experiential learning, grounded in learning through direct experience, prioritizes active engagement, reflection, and hands-on implementation. This approach transcends traditional theory-driven methods and has been widely recognized for fostering enduring values and competencies in students. David Kolb's Experiential Learning Theory provides a structured framework for this approach, emphasizing four essential stages: concrete experiences, reflective observation, abstract conceptualization, and active experimentation. Kolb argues that learning is most impactful when individuals engage in a process that stimulates critical thinking and facilitates the application of newly acquired knowledge. In the context of sustainability, experiential learning serves as a bridge between theoretical understanding and practical application, fostering a sense of responsibility and empowerment in students to take meaningful actions toward sustainable solutions.

Simultaneously, AI has emerged as a transformative force across various industries, including communication, entertainment, healthcare, and finance. Within the education sector, AI-driven tools have been employed to enhance student engagement, personalize learning experiences, and optimize administrative processes. However, the role of AI in sustainability education remains largely unexplored. Given its capacity to analyze vast datasets, model complex scenarios, and create dynamic, adaptive learning environments, AI presents unique opportunities to enrich experiential learning in sustainability contexts. AI-driven solutions can facilitate virtual simulations, interactive feedback, and real-time data analysis, all of which are essential for understanding the intricate and interconnected systems underlying sustainability challenges. Despite its potential, the integration of AI into sustainability education must be carefully designed to align with ethical considerations and educational objectives, ensuring its responsible and effective application.

This study aims to explore the intersection of AI and experiential learning within the framework of sustainable education. Specifically, it seeks to understand how AI-enhanced experiential learning environments can support the development of sustainability-related values, knowledge, and skills among students. The research is guided by three primary objectives. First, it reviews existing literature on experiential learning and AI applications in education to identify synergies that can be leveraged for sustainability education. Second, it examines practical applications of AI-powered experiential learning in sustainability-related contexts, assessing their effectiveness in fostering student engagement and comprehension. Finally, the study evaluates the potential benefits, challenges, and ethical considerations associated with integrating AI into hands-on sustainability education.

The relevance of experiential learning in sustainability education lies in its ability to translate abstract sustainability concepts into concrete, meaningful experiences. Unlike traditional pedagogical approaches that prioritize memorization, experiential learning actively engages students with real-world sustainability challenges, fostering critical thinking, problem-solving skills, and a sense of agency. Examples of experiential learning in sustainability education include fieldwork, environmental stewardship initiatives, community-based projects, and hands-on experimentation. These activities help students connect theoretical knowledge with practical applications, enabling them to critically analyze the social and environmental impacts of their actions.

Moreover, experiential learning emphasizes collaboration and reflection—two essential components in addressing sustainability challenges. Issues such as climate change, resource depletion, and social inequality are inherently complex and require interdisciplinary and cooperative problem-solving approaches. Experiential learning fosters these skills by involving students in group projects, problem-solving exercises, and reflective discussions, all of which are fundamental to developing the systems thinking necessary for tackling sustainability issues.

AI has the potential to further enrich experiential learning in sustainability education by offering tools that simulate real-world scenarios, analyze environmental data, and facilitate collaborative problem-solving. For instance, AI-powered simulations can model the impacts of climate change, allowing students to explore the consequences of different policy decisions in a controlled, virtual setting. AI's ability to process and interpret vast amounts of real-time data from various sources—including environmental sensors, social media, and ecological databases—enables students to engage with live data, deepening their understanding of sustainability challenges. Additionally, AI-powered platforms can foster global collaboration by connecting students from diverse geographical and cultural backgrounds, enabling them to work together on sustainability projects and share insights.

Integrating AI with experiential learning offers a promising approach to sustainability education. AI can enhance experiential learning by providing resources that increase accessibility, engagement, and relevance to sustainability topics. Virtual simulations and augmented reality experiences, for example, can create immersive learning environments where students can explore ecosystems, experiment with sustainable practices, and observe the environmental impact of their actions. These interactive experiences allow students to grasp complex sustainability concepts through direct engagement, rather than passive learning.

Furthermore, AI-driven data analysis tools enable students to interact with real-world sustainability data, fostering critical thinking and problem-solving skills. By analyzing energy consumption, waste management, and carbon emissions data, students can gain insights into sustainability challenges and explore potential solutions. This hands-on engagement with real-world data not only enhances their understanding of sustainability issues but also prepares them for future careers in environmental science, data analysis, and policymaking.

Reflection is a crucial component of experiential learning, and AI can play a significant role in facilitating this process. AI-powered feedback systems can provide students with real-time performance assessments, helping them identify areas for improvement and encouraging deeper reflection on their learning experiences. For example, AI-driven tools can analyze students' contributions to group projects, offering insights into their teamwork skills and areas for growth. This feedback fosters both personal and academic development by promoting self-awareness and continuous learning.

The overarching goal of this study is to examine the potential of integrating AI and experiential learning into sustainability education. By exploring the synergies, practical applications, and ethical considerations of AI-enhanced experiential learning, this research seeks to contribute to the development of innovative, effective, and responsible approaches to sustainability education. In a world of increasingly complex environmental and social challenges, education plays a vital role in equipping the next generation with the skills and mindset necessary to think critically, act responsibly, and collaborate effectively toward a sustainable future.

LITERATURE REVIEW

Experiential Learning and Its Evolution

Experiential Learning Theory (ELT) has long been a foundational educational approach emphasizing experience-driven knowledge acquisition (Kolb, 1984). Influenced by scholars such as Dewey, Piaget, and Lewin, ELT is structured into four cyclical stages: Concrete Experience, Reflective Observation, Abstract Conceptualization, and Active Experimentation. These stages foster deeper comprehension, retention, and real-world application of learning (Beard & Wilson, 2006). Over time, ELT has evolved from a theoretical framework to an applied methodology in diverse disciplines, with its integration into digital and AI-enhanced education marking a significant paradigm shift.

Experiential Learning Applications Across Domains

Kolb's ELT is widely implemented in fields such as business, healthcare, and sustainability education. McCarthy (2016) highlights its role in promoting critical thinking, adaptability, and problem-solving skills, essential in dynamic learning environments. Miettinen (2000) emphasizes the reflective aspect of ELT, which allows students to develop a deeper understanding of complex topics. Beard and Wilson (2006) further argue that experiential learning bridges theory and practice by fostering active knowledge construction.

In sustainability education, ELT has proven particularly effective in cultivating ecological awareness and social responsibility. Anderson (2020) asserts that hands-on sustainability projects help students develop agency in environmental problem-solving. Barth et al. (2007) highlight interdisciplinary approaches, integrating environmental science, economics, and ethics, as essential to fostering sustainability competencies. This aligns with the principles of Education for Sustainable Development (ESD), which advocates for experiential, problem-based learning models to prepare students for real-world sustainability challenges (UNESCO, 2017).

AI in Education: Enhancing Experiential Learning

The integration of artificial intelligence (AI) into education has transformed experiential learning, particularly through immersive and interactive technologies. AI-powered virtual reality (VR) and augmented reality (AR) platforms, such as ClassVR and Google Expeditions, simulate complex real-world scenarios, enhancing engagement and knowledge retention (Dede, 2009; Minocha & Tilling, 2019). AI-driven collaborative learning tools further enable students to connect globally, fostering cross-cultural experiences and shared learning environments (Lim et al., 2021).

Holmes et al. (2019) highlight AI's potential to shift students from passive recipients of information to active participants in their educational journey. Additionally, adaptive learning platforms such as Smart Sparrow and Knewton use AI algorithms to personalize educational experiences, improving retention and engagement (Baker, 2016). Similarly, intelligent tutoring systems (ITS), including Carnegie Learning's MATHia and Pearson's MyLab, provide individualized feedback and guidance, demonstrating positive outcomes in STEM education (VanLehn, 2011; Graesser et al., 2018).

Despite these advancements, concerns persist regarding AI's role in education. Ethical considerations such as data privacy, algorithmic bias, and the over-reliance on technology pose significant challenges (Selwyn, 2019). To address these issues, Williamson and Eynon (2020) advocate for inclusive and ethically responsible AI frameworks in education.

AI-Enhanced Experiential Learning in Sustainability Education

AI-driven experiential learning offers novel approaches to sustainability education. AI-powered VR and AR simulations facilitate interactive learning experiences, allowing students to engage with ecological systems and environmental challenges firsthand (Dede, 2009). Moreover, AI-driven data analytics tools such as IBM's Watson Education and Microsoft's Azure Machine Learning provide real-time insights into student learning patterns, enabling personalized instruction and data-informed decision-making (Siemens & Long, 2011; Peña-Ayala, 2014).

Okada (2025) introduces the CARE-KNOW-DO framework, integrating AI-driven problem-solving techniques into sustainability education. This model enhances students' ability to tackle real-world environmental issues through AI-enhanced experiential learning. Jawaid et al. (2025) further explore the role of AI in redefining experiential learning, particularly in interdisciplinary fields such as environmental science and climate change education.

Additionally, AI applications in sustainability education extend to smart environmental monitoring and data-driven policy simulations. Liu et al. (2024) discuss the role of AI in optimizing ecological management through predictive modeling and intelligent analytics, bridging the gap between theoretical knowledge and practical sustainability solutions.

Addressing Gaps and Future Directions

Despite significant progress, research on AI-enhanced experiential learning in sustainability education remains underdeveloped. Several gaps persist:

1. **Long-Term Impact Assessment:** Limited empirical research examines how AI-enhanced experiential learning influences students' ability to implement sustainable practices in real-world scenarios.
2. **Ethical and Inclusivity Concerns:** AI-driven education raises concerns about data security, digital accessibility, and the potential loss of human-centered learning experiences (Williamson & Eynon, 2020).
3. **Interdisciplinary Integration:** While AI supports experiential learning in specific disciplines, comprehensive frameworks integrating multiple fields remain scarce.

Future research should focus on developing AI-driven experiential learning frameworks that align with sustainability principles while ensuring ethical and inclusive applications. Additionally, longitudinal studies assessing AI's effectiveness in fostering real-world sustainability competencies are necessary.

This review highlights AI's transformative potential in enhancing experiential learning by synthesizing experiential learning theory, AI integration, and sustainability education. However, for AI to effectively support sustainability education, ongoing research and ethical considerations must guide its development and implementation.

AI-Enhanced Experiential Learning Framework

Experiential Learning Theory (ELT) emphasizes active engagement with real-world scenarios to develop critical thinking, adaptability, and problem-solving skills (Kolb, 1984). With the advent of Artificial Intelligence (AI), experiential learning has been significantly enhanced through personalized, collaborative, and immersive learning environments. The AI-enhanced experiential Learning Framework integrates AI-driven tools to create tailored learning pathways, interactive simulations, and real-time data-driven insights that bridge the gap between theoretical knowledge and practical application.

This framework consists of three key components:

1. Immersive AI-Driven Simulations – Enhancing engagement through virtual and adaptive learning environments.
2. AI-powered data Analytics and Personalization – Tailoring learning experiences based on real-time insights.
3. AI-Enabled Collaborative Learning – Facilitating interdisciplinary and globally connected problem-solving.

Each stage leverages AI technologies to create dynamic, responsive, and impactful learning experiences. It prepares students for complex, real-world challenges, particularly in sustainability education, business, and healthcare.

Immersive AI-Driven Simulations

AI-driven simulations and virtual reality (VR) have transformed experiential learning by offering interactive, context-rich, and scalable environments. These simulations provide **safe,** controlled, and cost-effective ways for learners to experiment with real-world situations.

Key Features:

- AI-powered virtual Reality (VR) & Augmented Reality (AR): These tools create interactive environments where learners can explore complex systems that would be otherwise inaccessible.
- Adaptive Learning Scenarios: AI dynamically adjusts challenges based on learner interactions, creating customized and evolving educational experiences.
- Real-Time Behavioral Analytics: AI analyzes learners' decision-making processes to provide instant feedback and insights for improvement.

Application Examples:

a. Environmental Science & Sustainability: VR simulations allow students to explore climate change impacts firsthand. For instance, AI-driven virtual ecosystems simulate rising sea levels and biodiversity shifts, helping students devise data-driven solutions to mitigate environmental damage. *(Dede, 2009;Okada, 2025)*

b. Medical & Healthcare Training: AI-powered clinical simulations enable students to practice diagnosing diseases. These adaptive environments adjust patient symptoms based on the student's responses, improving diagnostic accuracy. *(Graesser et al., 2018)*
c. Crisis Management & Disaster Response: AI-driven role-playing simulations train emergency responders to manage real-time crises, such as wildfires or pandemics, in high-risk, low-stakes environments. *(Holmes et al., 2019)*

AI-Powered Data Analytics and Personalization

Data analytics is crucial for customizing learning experiences to individual needs. AI-driven insights track progress, predict learning roadblocks, and provide personalized feedback to enhance educational outcomes.

Key Features:

- Personalized Learning Pathways: AI curates content based on a learner's performance history, engagement levels, and preferences.
- Intelligent Tutoring Systems (ITS): AI tutors provide real-time support and adaptive guidance, simulating one-on-one mentorship.
- Predictive Analytics: AI anticipates potential challenges students may face, allowing educators to intervene proactively.

Application Examples:

Sustainability Projects: AI recommends relevant case studies and best practices based on a student's research progress. If a student is studying renewable energy, AI suggests data sets on wind and solar energy trends to inform decision-making. *(Siemens & Long, 2011; Peña-Ayala, 2014)*

STEM Education: AI-driven platforms like Pearson's MyLab provide adaptive problem-solving exercises, guiding students through iterative learning to enhance computational skills. *(VanLehn, 2011)*

Workforce Development: AI tracks employee learning behaviors in corporate training programs, adjusting content delivery to maximize retention and skill acquisition. *(Baker, 2016)*

AI-Enabled Collaborative Learning

Collaboration is fundamental to experiential learning. AI facilitates global teamwork, enabling learners to work together across disciplines and geographies. AI-powered platforms enhance communication, automate administrative tasks, and provide real-time decision-making support.

Key Features:

- AI-Powered Teamwork Platforms: Tools like NLP-driven assistants translate languages in real time, breaking down barriers for international collaboration.
- Data-Driven Decision Making: AI provides real-time sustainability data to help learners model and predict future outcomes.

- Generative AI as a Creative Partner: AI suggests innovative solutions, such as generating sustainable urban design prototypes based on input data.

Application Examples:

Interdisciplinary Sustainability Research: AI tools allow environmental scientists, economists, and policymakers to collaboratively analyze carbon emissions, predict climate scenarios, and develop sustainable policies. *(Jawaid et al., 2025)*

AI-Augmented Role-Playing Simulations: Students participate in AI-moderated climate summits, assuming roles as policymakers or activists, while AI ensures a realistic, evidence-based dialogue. *(Okada, 2025)*

Social Impact Projects: AI-driven community sustainability programs help students work with local stakeholders to implement real-world solutions for waste management or renewable energy adoption. *(Anderson, 2020)*

Bridging Theory and Practice:

The Future of AI-Enhanced Experiential Learning

Sustainability education stands at the crossroads of theoretical exploration and practical application. Traditional experiential learning focuses on hands-on engagement, but modern sustainability challenges require scalable, interdisciplinary, and data-driven solutions. AI offers a bridge between theory and practice by:

Enhancing accessibility: AI-driven virtual labs and remote collaboration tools make high-quality experiential learning available globally.

Scaling impact: AI enables real-time monitoring of sustainability projects, measuring progress and suggesting course corrections.

Ensuring ethical AI use: AI must be implemented responsibly, addressing concerns about data security, algorithmic bias, and digital equity. *(Williamson & Eynon, 2020)*

CASE STUDIES

AI tools provide students with real-time data analysis, simulations, and predictive modelling that support deeper engagement with complex sustainability challenges. The ability to apply theoretical knowledge to real-world problems using AI fosters critical thinking and innovation.

1. AI in Action at Stanford University - AI-Driven Sustainable Development Lab

Stanford University's Sustainable Development Lab integrates artificial intelligence into its interdisciplinary curriculum to teach sustainability principles. The program combines cutting-edge AI tools with hands-on experiential learning to address global environmental challenges such as climate change, urbanization, and biodiversity loss.

The lab is structured around a problem-based learning model, where students collaborate on sustainability projects supported by AI technologies. Participants include undergraduate and graduate students from diverse disciplines such as environmental science, computer science, and public policy.

The lab equips students with tools to analyze and interpret vast, complex climate datasets, enabling informed decision-making.

- Implementation: Students use machine learning algorithms to process real-time climate data, including satellite imagery, global weather patterns, and carbon emission trends.
- Example Project: A team developed a machine learning model to predict areas at high risk of deforestation in the Amazon rainforest. By analyzing satellite imagery and historical deforestation patterns, the AI identified vulnerable regions and provided actionable insights to policymakers.

2. University of Oxford's AI-Supported Global Sustainability Initiative

The University of Oxford launched its Global Sustainability Initiative (GSI) with a focus on employing AI technologies to address global environmental challenges. This program brings together academics, students, and practitioners to develop AI-driven solutions for sustainability education and practice.

The initiative is built around a series of workshops, research projects, and fieldwork. Participants leverage AI tools to tackle problems related to renewable energy, biodiversity conservation, and climate resilience. The program emphasizes experiential learning by immersing students in real-world scenarios supported by AI.

The lab emphasizes the importance of engaging with local communities to ensure that sustainability solutions are both practical and impactful.

- Implementation: Students collaborate with community leaders and residents to co-design projects. AI tools provide localized data, such as water usage patterns and agricultural productivity, to guide decision-making.
- Example Project: In collaboration with a rural community in California, students used AI to analyze water consumption patterns. This led to the development of sustainable irrigation techniques, reducing water waste by 20%.

These case studies illustrate the transformative potential of AI in sustainability education. Both programs underscore the importance of interdisciplinary collaboration, ethical AI practices, and community engagement in creating impactful learning experiences and scalable solutions.

Immersive and Interactive Learning Environments

AI-driven technologies, such as virtual reality (VR) and simulations, create immersive environments where students can experiment with scenarios without real-world risks.

- Stanford Example:
  - o Students used VR to simulate urban planning scenarios, allowing them to visualize the impact of sustainable design choices in real-time. This hands-on approach kept students engaged and facilitated better retention of concepts.
- Oxford Example:
  - o AI-powered biodiversity monitoring allowed students to interact with real-world data through drones and computer vision. The tangible outcomes of their work, such as identifying poaching activities, kept them highly motivated.

Impact: Immersive tools transform abstract sustainability challenges into engaging, relatable tasks, boosting student participation and interest.

Collaboration and Teamwork

AI-enhanced projects often require interdisciplinary collaboration, fostering teamwork and communication skills.

Collaboration Platforms: AI-powered tools like real-time data visualization and predictive modeling enhance collaborative efforts. For instance:

- o At Stanford, diverse teams worked together to co-design sustainable urban systems, integrating perspectives from computer science, environmental science, and public policy.
- o Oxford students used AI tools to collectively analyze renewable energy data, combining insights from engineering and environmental economics.

Outcome: Students develop strong interpersonal and collaborative skills, crucial for tackling global sustainability challenges that require coordinated efforts.

Immediate and Adaptive Feedback

One of AI's key strengths is its ability to provide instantaneous and personalized feedback, enabling students to refine their approaches and improve iteratively.

Adaptive Systems:

- o AI systems at Stanford allowed students to receive feedback on their deforestation risk models, highlighting areas for improvement in their data processing techniques.
- o Oxford students used AI analytics to refine their disaster resilience plans based on real-time feedback, ensuring practical applicability.

Outcome: Continuous feedback loops keep students engaged and focused, while also fostering a growth mindset.

Real-World Relevance and Impact

Students are more engaged when their projects have tangible outcomes and real-world applications. AI tools amplify this relevance by enabling impactful, data-driven decisions.

- Stanford Example: The irrigation project reduced water waste by 20%, benefiting local farmers and directly showcasing the value of their efforts.
- Oxford Example: The renewable energy optimization project in rural India provided reliable electricity to underserved communities, creating a lasting impact.

Outcome: Students remain deeply invested in their projects when they see the direct benefits of their work, fostering a sense of purpose and accomplishment.

Teachers' Perspectives on Adapting Sustainable Development Pedagogy in the AI Era

Teachers, as key facilitators of knowledge and skill development, are at the forefront of this transformation and hold diverse perspectives on the implications of AI-driven education. On the one hand, AI offers unprecedented opportunities for personalized learning, data-informed decision-making, and innovative instructional strategies. On the other hand, concerns persist regarding ethical considerations, digital equity, and the potential depersonalization of teaching. From an educational standpoint, teachers recognize the need to balance AI-enhanced instructional methodologies with foundational principles of sustainability, ensuring that technological advancements do not undermine core values such as environmental stewardship, social equity, and economic resilience.

From a pedagogical perspective, AI-driven tools have the potential to enhance students' engagement with sustainability concepts through immersive learning environments, predictive analytics, and real-time feedback mechanisms. Teachers acknowledge that technologies such as virtual reality (VR) and the metaverse can provide experiential learning opportunities that deepen students' understanding of complex sustainability challenges. However, growing concern about the digital divide is growing, particularly in regions with limited access to AI-based resources, which may exacerbate educational inequalities. Furthermore, the reliance on AI in education raises questions about its impact on critical thinking, ethical reasoning, and problem-solving skills, which are fundamental to sustainable development. Educators, therefore, advocate for a pedagogical approach that integrates AI while preserving the humanistic elements of teaching, fostering holistic learning experiences that emphasize ethical decision-making and interdisciplinary problem-solving.

The role of teacher training and professional development is pivotal in equipping educators with the necessary competencies to navigate the intersection of AI and sustainable education effectively. Despite the increasing emphasis on AI in educational discourse, existing teacher preparation programs often lack comprehensive frameworks that address both AI literacy and sustainability pedagogy. Teachers emphasize the need for policy interventions that support AI-integrated sustainability education through structured training, ethical guidelines, and best practices for inclusive implementation. Collaboration among educational institutions, policymakers, and industry stakeholders is essential to developing pedagogical strategies that align technological advancements with the principles of sustainability and equitable learning.

Teachers perceive the integration of AI into sustainability education as a complex yet transformative process that requires careful planning and ethical oversight. While AI presents innovative pathways for enhancing sustainability education, its implementation must be guided by principles of inclusivity, critical inquiry, and responsible technological adoption. As pedagogical frameworks evolve in the AI era, there is a pressing need to ensure that sustainability education remains rooted in ethical considerations, interdisciplinary learning, and equitable access to technological resources.

Challenges and Opportunities in Experiential Learning and AI: Real-World Applications in Sustainability Education

Integrating Artificial Intelligence (AI) with experiential learning offers a transformative approach to sustainability education. AI-driven tools and techniques enable students to engage deeply with real-world challenges, offering dynamic insights and solutions that were previously unattainable. However, the implementation of AI-enhanced experiential learning is not without its challenges. This paper explores the key obstacles and opportunities involved in leveraging AI for real-world applications in sustainability education.

AI technologies require significant computational resources, including high-speed internet, powerful hardware, and access to sophisticated software. Educational institutions in developing regions or rural areas often lack these essential infrastructures.

AI models rely heavily on high-quality, localized datasets to generate meaningful insights. In sustainability education, accessing accurate data related to climate patterns, biodiversity, or urban infrastructure can be difficult due to data privacy regulations or gaps in data collection.

AI applications in sustainability education often raise ethical questions, particularly around bias, transparency, and privacy. For instance, AI-driven monitoring tools for biodiversity may inadvertently breach local privacy laws or cultural norms.

Sustainability education inherently requires interdisciplinary approaches, blending knowledge from environmental science, technology, social sciences, and policy. However, integrating AI into these diverse fields can be challenging due to differing terminologies, methodologies, and priorities.

Experiential learning often involves small, hands-on group activities, which can be resource-intensive and difficult to scale for larger student populations. AI integration can compound this issue due to its high cost and technical requirements.

The integration of AI into sustainability education is still in its early stages, but its potential to revolutionize the field is clear. As technology continues to evolve, new opportunities will emerge for creating even more immersive, personalized, and impactful learning experiences.

Future research should focus on developing best practices for integrating AI into experiential learning, addressing both technical and ethical challenges. Policymakers and educators must also work together to ensure that these innovations are accessible to all students, regardless of their geographical or economic circumstances.

Opportunities in AI-Enhanced Experiential Learning

Personalization of Learning Experiences

One of the most transformative aspects of AI in education is its ability to personalize learning experiences. AI algorithms can analyze individual learning patterns, identify areas where students need additional support, and tailor resources to meet their unique needs. This personalization enhances engagement and accelerates skill development, particularly in complex fields like sustainability.

For instance, an AI-driven platform might recognize that a student struggles with understanding predictive modeling in renewable energy projects but excels in designing energy-efficient systems. The platform could then recommend targeted tutorials or exercises to strengthen the student's weaker areas. By adapting to individual needs, AI ensures that students gain a comprehensive understanding of sustainability concepts, preparing them for real-world applications.

Fostering Real-Time Problem-Solving

AI enables students to engage with real-world challenges in real time, using live datasets and predictive analytics to explore solutions. This immediate feedback loop enhances critical thinking and decision-making skills, which are key competencies for addressing sustainability issues.

For example, students working on urban sustainability projects might use AI tools to simulate the effects of different transportation policies on carbon emissions, refining their strategies based on real-time predictions. This iterative problem-solving process mirrors the complexities of real-world decision-making, preparing students to tackle sustainability challenges with confidence and creativity.

Enhancing Engagement Through Immersive Technologies

AI-powered technologies such as virtual reality (VR) and augmented reality (AR) create immersive learning environments that make abstract sustainability concepts tangible. These tools allow students to visualize and interact with complex systems, fostering a deeper understanding of their interconnections.

For instance, a VR simulation might transport students to a coral reef ecosystem, allowing them to observe the effects of climate change on marine biodiversity. Such experiences not only enhance learning but also inspire a sense of urgency and commitment to sustainability.

Scaling Sustainability Education

AI offers scalable solutions to expand the reach of experiential learning programs, making sustainability education accessible to a larger and more diverse audience. Online platforms, virtual labs, and cloud-based resources enable institutions to deliver high-quality, hands-on learning experiences to students worldwide.

Massive Open Online Courses (MOOCs) powered by AI, for example, can provide interactive modules on topics like sustainable agriculture or climate resilience, reaching thousands of learners across different geographies. By scaling sustainability education, AI ensures that more students are equipped with the skills and knowledge needed to address global challenges.

CONCLUSION

The integration of AI into experiential learning for sustainability education presents both challenges and opportunities. While technological accessibility, data availability, and ethical concerns require careful consideration, the transformative potential of AI cannot be overstated. By personalizing education, fostering real-time problem-solving, and scaling impactful programs, AI empowers students to engage deeply with sustainability challenges and develop innovative solutions.

Educational institutions have a critical role to play in addressing these challenges and harnessing AI's potential to revolutionize sustainability education. By doing so, they can prepare students not only with technical and interdisciplinary skills but also with a sense of responsibility and purpose. As future leaders, these students will be equipped to navigate the complexities of global sustainability challenges and build a more equitable and sustainable future for all.

REFERENCES

Anderson, P. (2020). Experiential Learning in Sustainability Education: Challenges and Innovations. *Sustainability Education Journal, 15*(2), 45–63.

Baker, R. S. (2016). Adaptive Learning Technologies: The Next Generation of Education. *AI & Society, 31*(4), 275–290.

Barth, M., Godemann, J., Rieckmann, M., & Stoltenberg, U. (2007). Developing key competencies for sustainable development in higher education. *International Journal of Sustainability in Higher Education, 8*(4), 416–430. DOI: 10.1108/14676370710823582

Beard, C., & Wilson, J. P. (2006). *Experiential Learning: A Best Practice Handbook for Educators and Trainers*. Kogan Page.

Dede, C. (2009). Immersive interfaces for engagement and learning. *Science, 323*(5910), 66–69. DOI: 10.1126/science.1167311 PMID: 19119219

Graesser, A. C., Conley, M. W., & Olney, A. (2018). Intelligent Tutoring Systems: Past, Present, and Future. *Educational Psychology Review, 30*(1), 109–128.

Holmes, W., Bialik, M., & Fadel, C. (2019). *Artificial Intelligence in Education: Promises and Implications for Teaching and Learning*. Center for Curriculum Redesign.

Jawaid, A., Batool, M., & Arshad, W. (2025). *AI and English Language Learning Outcomes*. Contemporary Journal of Social Sciences, 12(1), 55–71. Retrieved from https://contemporaryjournal.com/index.php/14/article/view/387

Kolb, D. A. (1984). *Experiential Learning: Experience as the Source of Learning and Development*. Prentice Hall.

Lim, C. P., Wang, T., & Tan, S. C. (2021). The Role of AI in Collaborative Learning. *Computers & Education, 168*, 104–118.

Miettinen, R. (2000). The Concept of Experiential Learning and John Dewey's Theory of Reflective Thought and Action. *International Journal of Lifelong Education, 19*(1), 54–72. DOI: 10.1080/026013700293458

Minocha, S., & Tilling, S. (2019). The Use of Augmented Reality in Environmental Education: Opportunities and Challenges. *Journal of Interactive Learning Research, 30*(2), 123–140.

Okada, A. (2025). *CARE-KNOW-DO: Mapping Knowledge in Education and AI Applications*. Springer. Retrieved from https://link.springer.com/chapter/10.1007/978-3-031-54677-8_4

Selwyn, N. (2019). Should Robots Replace Teachers? AI and the Future of Education. *Policy Futures in Education, 17*(1), 10–27.

Siemens, G., & Long, P. (2011). Penetrating the Fog: Analytics in Learning and Education. *EDUCAUSE Review, 46*(5), 30–40.

Williamson, B., & Eynon, R. (2020). AI in Education: Opportunities and Challenges. *Learning, Media and Technology, 45*(3), 251–264.

Chapter 2
Ethical Implications of AI in Sustainable Development Pedagogy

Mohanarajesh Kommineni
https://orcid.org/0009-0002-3897-5949
TEKsystems Global Services LLC, USA

Swathi Chundru
https://orcid.org/0009-0001-3959-4825
Motivity Labs Inc, USA

Praveen Kumar Maroju
https://orcid.org/0009-0007-4000-4400
Clientserver Technology Solutions, USA

P. Selvakumar
https://orcid.org/0000-0002-3650-4548
Nehru institute of Technology, India

ABSTRACT

Educational institutions and policymakers are increasingly incorporating AI into learning environments; addressing the ethical considerations accompanying this technological integration is imperative. Pedagogy lies in its ability to enhance personalized learning experiences, optimize resource management, and foster innovative teaching methods that align with sustainability goals. The deployment of AI technologies aligns with equity, inclusivity, and responsibility principles. One of the primary ethical considerations is the issue of equity and access. AI-powered educational tools have the potential to provide customized learning experiences and resources that cater to individual student needs. However, disparities in access to technology and digital literacy can exacerbate existing educational inequalities. Ensuring the privacy and security of this data is paramount to maintaining trust and safeguarding students' rights.

DOI: 10.4018/979-8-3693-9062-7.ch002

INTRODUCTION TO AI IN SUSTAINABLE DEVELOPMENT PEDAGOGY: ETHICAL CONSIDERATIONS.

Artificial Intelligence (AI) has educational institutions and policymakers increasingly incorporate AI into learning environments, it is imperative to address the ethical considerations that accompany this technological integration. pedagogy lies in its ability to enhance personalized learning experiences, optimize resource management, and foster innovative teaching methods that align with sustainability goals. the deployment of AI technologies aligns with principles of equity, inclusivity, and responsibility. One of the primary ethical considerations is the issue of equity and access. AI-powered educational tools have the potential to provide customized learning experiences and resources that cater to individual student needs. However, disparities in access to technology and digital literacy can exacerbate existing educational inequalities. Ensuring the privacy and security of this data is paramount to maintaining trust and safeguarding students' rights. including transparent data usage policies and consent mechanisms, to protect students from potential misuse or unauthorized access to their information. In the context of education, biased AI algorithms can affect student assessments, learning recommendations, and overall educational outcomes. AI extend to the role of educators and the changing nature of teaching. As AI becomes more integrated into pedagogy, it is vital to redefine the role of educators and ensure that they remain central to the learning process.

Stakeholders, including students, parents, and educators, and how data is handled. Incorporating AI into sustainable development pedagogy also involves considering the long-term implications for sustainability goals. AI has optimizing resource use, reducing waste, and enhancing educational content related to sustainability practices. AI technologies should be aligned with broader sustainability objectives, such as reducing the carbon footprint of AI systems and promoting responsible consumption and production. In conclusion, while AI offers significant opportunities to advance sustainable development pedagogy. Ensuring equity and access, protecting privacy and data security, mitigating bias, maintaining the role of educators, promoting transparency and accountability, and aligning with sustainability goals are all crucial elements in navigating the ethical landscape of AI in education. AI can play a significant role in these areas by enhancing data analysis, optimizing resource management, and creating innovative solutions to complex global challenges. The deployment of AI in achieving SDG 10 (Reduced Inequalities) must be approached with a focus on inclusivity and accessibility. Ethical considerations include ensuring that AI tools are designed and implemented in ways that bridge rather than widen gaps in access and opportunity, particularly in low-income and marginalized communities.AI systems often require extensive data collection and analysis, which can pose risks to individual privacy and security (Ando, H., et al, 2014). Ethical frameworks must ensure that data handling practices are transparent and that individuals' rights are protected.

To align with ethical principles, it is vital to develop and implement AI algorithms that are rigorously tested for bias and are designed to promote fairness and inclusivity. This involves actively addressing any biases in training data and ensuring that AI outputs do not perpetuate discrimination or reinforce stereotypes. Ethical AI practices involve creating transparent systems where decision-making processes are clear, and there are mechanisms for accountability and redress (Braun, V., et al, 2006). To align AI with sustainability goals, it is essential to adopt practices that minimize the environmental footprint of AI technologies, such as using energy-efficient algorithms and promoting responsible disposal of electronic components. However, ethical considerations include ensuring that AI tools enhance rather than replace human interactions and that they are used to support, rather than undermine, the educational mission. Educators and AI developers must work together to ensure that AI applications are designed to complement human teaching and foster. Moreover, the ethical use of AI in achieving SDG 2 (Zero Hunger) involves addressing issues related to food security and agricultural sustainability. AI can enhance agricultural practices through precision farming and resource management, disproportionately benefit large agribusinesses. Ethical AI practices should support equitable access to technology and promote sustainable agricultural practices that benefit all stakeholders(Chai, C.S., et al, 2020).In conclusion, aligning AI with the Sustainable Development Goals requires a comprehensive approach to ethical considerations that encompasses equity, privacy, fairness, transparency, environmental impact, and the responsible use of technology. By addressing these ethical dimensions, stakeholders can ensure that AI contributes positively to global objectives, supports sustainable development, and fosters an inclusive and equitable future.

ETHICAL AI FOR ENVIRONMENTAL SUSTAINABILITY: MITIGATING CLIMATE CHANGE.

AI possesses the potential to drive substantial progress in mitigating climate change, enhancing resource management, and promoting environmental conservation. However, leveraging AI for environmental sustainability must be approached with a strong ethical framework to ensure that these technologies contribute effectively and responsibly to climate goals. opportunities and challenges, demanding careful consideration of ethical implications to maximize positive outcomes while minimizing potential risks (Chai, C.S., et al, 2020).One of the foremost ethical considerations is the environmental impact of AI technologies themselves. While AI can significantly aid in climate change mitigation, the development, deployment, and operation of AI systems can entail considerable energy consumption and contribute to electronic waste. For instance, training large-scale AI models often requires substantial computational resources, which can lead to high carbon emissions if powered by non-renewable energy sources .Moreover, transparency and accountability in AI systems are critical to ensure their ethical use in environmental sustainability. The deployment of AI for climate-related tasks, such as monitoring deforestation or predicting extreme weather events, necessitates transparency in how these technologies operate and the data they use. Ethical AI practices involve making AI systems' methodologies stakeholders, including policymakers, environmental organizations, and the public. Providing clear insights into AI-driven environmental assessments and predictions helps build trust and ensures that AI applications are used responsibly and effectively in climate action strategies.

AI systems trained on historical environmental data may inadvertently reinforce biases or overlook marginalized communities disproportionately affected by climate change. For example, AI models used for resource allocation or disaster response must be designed to consider the needs of vulnerable populations and ensure equitable distribution of aid and resources. Addressing these concerns involves integrating fairness into AI algorithms and ensuring that AI-driven environmental policies and solutions are inclusive and address the needs of all affected communities(Cave, S., et al, 2019).Ethical considerations involve safeguarding this data to prevent misuse and ensuring that data collection practices respect privacy rights. Implementing public trust and support ethical AI practices in environmental sustainability.AI can significantly enhance the precision of climate forecasts and help in devising effective mitigation strategies. However, it is essential to ensure that AI models are validated, rigorously tested, and continuously updated to reflect the latest scientific understanding. Ethical AI practices involve using high-quality data and incorporating interdisciplinary expertise to improve model accuracy and reliability, thereby ensuring that AI-generated insights are dependable and actionable for climate policy and planning(Chiu, T.K., et al, 2020).Furthermore, the ethical deployment of AI in environmental sustainability requires a focus on long-term impacts and sustainability goals. including reducing environmental impact and promoting resilience. This involves considering the lifecycle impacts of AI systems and ensuring that their benefits outweigh any potential harms. Ethical AI practices should support sustainable resource management, conservation efforts, and climate adaptation strategies, aligning with broader environmental and sustainability objectives.

Collaboration and stakeholder engagement are also vital for the ethical use of AI in climate action. Developing effective AI solutions for environmental sustainability requires input from diverse stakeholders. Artificial Intelligence (AI) addressing issues of inequality and injustice, yet its deployment must be guided by ethical considerations to ensure it genuinely benefits marginalized communities and promotes social equity(Chiu, T.K.F., et al, 2016). AI systems can offer powerful tools for analyzing and addressing social inequalities, but if not implemented thoughtfully, they risk perpetuating or even exacerbating existing disparities. For AI technologies to be effectively integrated into efforts to address inequality and injustice, stakeholders—including affected communities—must understand how decisions are made and on what basis. Ethical AI practices involve making algorithms and their decision-making processes transparent, allowing individuals to see how AI-driven conclusions are reached and to challenge them if necessary. This transparency fosters trust and ensures that AI systems are used responsibly and that their impacts on social justice can be scrutinized and understood. This involves not only involving representatives from these communities in the development and implementation of AI systems but also ensuring that AI solutions address their specific needs and challenges (Chiu, T.K.F., et al, 2016). Inclusive AI practices involve engaging in community consultations, conducting impact assessments, and designing systems that are accessible and beneficial to all, rather than perpetuating existing inequalities. Data privacy and protection are also vital ethical concerns when using AI for social sustainability. AI systems often require the collection and analysis of large volumes of personal is conducted with informed consent, and safeguard individuals' privacy. thus, maintaining public trust and protecting individuals' rights. Accountability is another essential ethical principle in the deployment of AI for social sustainability. It is important to establish clear lines of accountability for AI-driven decisions and involve setting up oversight bodies, creating feedback channels, and implementing procedures for addressing grievances related to AI systems.

Furthermore, ethical AI practices must consider the long-term social impacts of these technologies. AI has the potential to drive substantial progress in addressing social inequalities, but it must be deployed with a view toward sustainable and equitable outcomes. This includes evaluating the long-term effects of AI systems on different communities and ensuring that their benefits are distributed fairly. Ethical considerations involve assessing whether AI applications contribute to the overarching goals of social sustainability and whether they support efforts to reduce systemic inequalities and promote social justice. In addition, promoting digital literacy and education is crucial for ensuring that AI technologies contribute positively to social sustainability(Chiu, T.K.F., et al, 2015). This includes providing education on how AI systems work, how to interpret AI-driven decisions, and how to advocate for ethical AI practices. Enhancing digital literacy helps empower individuals to navigate and influence the development and use of AI technologies, contributing to more informed and equitable outcomes. By focusing on mitigating biases, ensuring transparency and inclusivity, protecting data privacy, establishing potential of these technologies in advancing social sustainability and addressing the deep-rooted issues of inequality and injustice that persist in societies worldwide. This involves considering the lifecycle impacts of AI systems and ensuring that their benefits outweigh any potential harms. Ethical AI practices should support sustainable resource management, conservation efforts, and climate adaptation strategies, aligning with broader environmental and sustainability objectives.

ECONOMIC SUSTAINABILITY AND AI: BALANCING GROWTH WITH ETHICAL RESPONSIBILITY.

As the global economy increasingly integrates Artificial Intelligence (AI) into various sectors, balancing economic growth with ethical responsibility becomes a critical challenge. AI promises substantial economic benefits, including enhanced efficiency, innovation, and productivity, which can drive growth across industries. However, these advancements must be managed within a framework of ethical responsibility to ensure that the benefits of AI contribute to long-term economic sustainability and do not exacerbate social inequalities or undermine ethical standards (Chiu, T.K.F., et al, 2017). Economic sustainability with AI involves leveraging the technology to foster innovation and drive productivity while ensuring that growth is inclusive and equitable. AI can optimize processes, reduce operational costs, and create new markets and job opportunities. However, it is essential to manage the transition to AI-driven economies in a way that addresses potential disruptions, such as job displacement and skill gaps. Implementing reskilling and upskilling programs, promoting lifelong learning, and supporting workers in transitioning to new roles are crucial components of ensuring that economic growth is inclusive and sustainable. Another significant ethical consideration is the benefits and power that may arise from AI. economic growth, there is a risk that its benefits could be unevenly distributed, leading to increased economic inequality. Large corporations and technology firms may gain disproportionate advantages, while smaller enterprises and less developed regions may struggle to compete. To address this concern, policies and practices must be implemented to promote fair competition and equitable distribution of AI-related benefits. This includes fostering an environment that supports innovation across various sectors and regions and ensuring that the deployment of AI technologies does not create monopolistic practices or reinforce existing inequalities. This involves optimizing, and promoting responsible disposal and recycling of electronic components. Balancing economic growth with environmental stewardship is essential for ensuring that AI contributes to sustainable development in the long term (Chiu, T.K., et al, 2020). AI systems can influence various economic decisions, such as credit scoring, investment strategies, and pricing models. Ensuring that these decisions are transparent and accountable helps prevent unfair practices and supports ethical economic behavior. Moreover, promoting ethical AI governance and regulation is crucial for balancing economic growth with ethical responsibility. Governments and regulatory bodies play a key role in setting standards and frameworks for the responsible development and deployment of AI. Collaborative efforts between policymakers, industry leaders, and academic experts are essential for developing effective AI governance frameworks that support economic sustainability while addressing ethical concerns.

This includes providing training on ethical AI practices, encouraging open dialogue about ethical issues, and establishing mechanisms for ethical oversight and accountability (Eggleston, J., 2018). In conclusion, balancing economic growth with ethical responsibility in the context of AI requires a multifaceted approach that addresses economic, social, and environmental dimensions. Achieving this balance is crucial for ensuring that AI contributes positively to long-term economic sustainability and supports a fair and just society. The integration of Artificial Intelligence (AI) into education holds significant promise for advancing sustainable development goals, yet it brings with it a range of pedagogical implications that must be carefully considered. AI-powered educational tools can offer tailored learning experiences, enhance accessibility, and optimize educational resources, contributing to a more effective and inclusive educational environment. However, these benefits must be balanced with thoughtful considerations of how AI affects teaching methodologies, learner engagement, and the broader educational landscape. Exploring these pedagogical implications reveals both the potential and the challenges of using AI in education to support sustainable development. This adaptability can support diverse learning needs, allowing educators to address varying paces and styles of learning within a single classroom. By offering personalized feedback and resources, AI can help students progress according to their unique needs and capabilities, potentially leading to more effective learning outcomes (Glatthorn, A.A., et al, 2018). However, this personalization must be implemented carefully to avoid over-reliance on technology and to ensure that it complements, rather than replaces, traditional teaching methods and human interaction.

Accessibility is another crucial aspect of AI-powered education. For example, AI-driven platforms can offer remote learning opportunities, adaptive learning materials, and language translation services, making education more inclusive. Despite these benefits, ensuring equitable access to AI technologies remains a challenge. Socioeconomic disparities, digital divides, and varying levels of digital literacy can impact how effectively these tools are used. Addressing these challenges requires targeted efforts to provide infrastructure, training, and support to underserved communities, ensuring that AI contributes to reducing, rather than exacerbating, educational inequalities. AI's role in education also prompts a re-evaluation of traditional pedagogical roles and methods(Mahadev Madgule, N., et al, 2023). However, there is a risk that reliance on AI for administrative functions might lead to reduced human interaction in the classroom. Maintaining a balance between AI-driven efficientmethods ((the essential human element of education is crucial. Educators must adapt to new roles where they act as facilitators and mentors, guiding students. Educators and institutions must navigate these considerations to build trust and protect students' rights while leveraging AI to enhance learning outcomes.AI tools can provide resources and curricula related to environmental sustainability, social equity, and global citizenship. This integration supports SDG 4 (Quality Education) by equipping students with the knowledge and skills necessary to address global challenges. However, educators must ensure that AI-driven content is accurate, relevant, and aligned with the broader goals of sustainable development. Collaborating with experts in sustainability and curriculum development can help ensure that AI tools effectively support educational objectives related to sustainable development (Margot, K.C., et al, 2019). Ensuring that AI assessments are fair, reliable, and aligned with educational goals is essential. Educators must balance AI-driven assessments with traditional methods to maintain a comprehensive view of student learning and development. In conclusion, AI-powered education offers substantial potential for advancing sustainable development through personalized learning, improved accessibility, and the promotion of relevant skills and knowledge. However, the pedagogical implications of integrating AI into education require careful consideration of issues related to accessibility, the evolving role of educators, data privacy, ethical standards, and the alignment with sustainable development goals.

ETHICAL CONSIDERATIONS IN AI-DRIVEN SUSTAINABLE DEVELOPMENT RESEARCH.

Even exacerbate social and environmental injustices. For example, biased algorithms in environmental monitoring could lead to inaccurate assessments of pollution levels or resource distribution, disproportionately affecting vulnerable communities. To mitigate these risks, researchers must prioritize fairness in AI development by employing techniques for bias detection and correction, using diverse datasets, and regularly auditing AI systems for equitable outcomes (Niemiec, C.P., et al, 2009).Transparency and explainability are critical for ensuring ethical AI practices in sustainable development research. AI models and their decision-making processes should be transparent to enable stakeholders, including policymakers, communities, and researchers, to understand and trust the findings generated. Explainable AI ensures that research outputs are interpretable and actionable, fostering accountability and facilitating informed decision-making. By providing clear explanations of how AI systems arrive at their conclusions, researchers can enhance the credibility of their work and enable stakeholders to assess and challenge AI-driven insights effectively. Equity in the application of AI is essential for addressing the diverse needs of different communities and regions. Sustainable development research often involves tackling global challenges that affect various populations in different ways. AI systems must be designed and implemented to consider these diverse contexts and ensure that benefits are equitably distributed. For instance, AI-driven solutions for climate adaptation should be sensitive to the unique vulnerabilities of different regions and communities, ensuring that interventions do not disproportionately disadvantage already marginalized groups. Ethical AI practices involve engaging with affected communities, incorporating their input into research processes, and ensuring that AI technologies contribute to reducing, rather than reinforcing, existing inequalities.

Accountability in AI-driven sustainable development research involves establishing clear mechanisms for oversight and responsibility (Paramasivam Selvakumar, et al, 2024). Researchers and organizations must be accountable for the ethical use of AI technologies and the impacts of their research findings. This includes setting up governance structures, such as ethics committees or review boards, to oversee AI research activities and address any ethical issues that arise. Additionally, providing channels for feedback and redress enables stakeholders to voice concerns and seek remedies if AI systems produce harmful or unjust outcomes. Accountability ensures that AI research is conducted responsibly and that its benefits are aligned with ethical principles and sustainable development goals. This includes assessing potential risks, unintended consequences, and the overall alignment of AI applications with sustainable development principles. In addition to these considerations, ethical AI research should promote inclusivity and stakeholder engagement. Involving diverse perspectives in the development and application of AI technologies helps ensure that research addresses a wide range of needs and concerns (Paramasivam Selvakumar, et al, 2024). This includes engaging with local communities, experts from various fields, and representatives from marginalized groups. Inclusivity in AI research promotes more comprehensive and equitable solutions and fosters a collaborative approach to addressing global challenges. In conclusion, ethical considerations in AI-driven sustainable development research are fundamental AI), and sustainable development presents a complex landscape where responsible data use is paramount. AI's transformative potential in advancing sustainable development goals relies heavily on the availability and analysis of vast datasets, which can drive insights and innovations across various sectors such as environmental management, healthcare, and resource optimization. However, this reliance on data also brings significant challenges related to privacy and ethical data use. Ensuring that AI applications respect data privacy while contributing to sustainable development requires a comprehensive approach that balances technological advancement with stringent ethical standards.

Data privacy is a critical concern in the context of AI-driven sustainable development because AI systems often process large volumes of personal, sensitive, and potentially identifiable information. This includes data related to environmental conditions, socioeconomic status, health, and more (Patrick, H., et al, 2011). The risk of data breaches, unauthorized access, and misuse of information necessitates robust data protection measures. Moreover, informed consent is a cornerstone of responsible data use in AI. Individuals whose data is being collected and utilized for sustainable development research. Implementing clear consent mechanisms and providing accessible information about data practices are fundamental to maintaining trust and ethical integrity in AI-driven projects. Addressing algorithmic bias is another crucial aspect of ensuring responsible data use in sustainable development. This includes using diverse and representative datasets, conducting regular audits, and implementing fairness-aware algorithms that strive to produce equitable and unbiased results. AI-driven insights and recommendations can influence policy decisions, resource distribution, and community interventions (Piniel, K., et al, 2013). Ensuring that these AI applications are designed to promote social equity and environmental justice is crucial. This involves evaluating the potential impacts of AI solutions on different populations and ensuring that they address the needs of marginalized and underserved communities. Ethical AI practices should focus on inclusivity and fairness, ensuring that technological advancements benefit all stakeholders and do not reinforce existing disparities.

Sustainable development also requires balancing the immediate benefits of AI with long-term considerations. Data privacy and ethical data use are not just about protecting individual information but also about and equitable outcomes over time. This includes assessing the potential environmental impacts of data processing and storage, such as energy consumption and electronic waste. By adopting energy-efficient practices and promoting responsible data management, stakeholders can align AI applications with broader sustainability goals (Ramakrishnan, T., et al, 2022). Accountability and transparency in data handling are vital for maintaining ethical standards in AI-driven sustainable development. Clear mechanisms for oversight and practices adhere to ethical guidelines and regulatory requirements. This includes creating channels for reporting and addressing data privacy concerns, as well as providing stakeholders with visibility into how AI systems use and process data. Transparency fosters trust and ensures that AI technologies are deployed responsibly and in accordance with ethical principles. Furthermore, fostering collaboration between stakeholders is essential for responsible data use in AI applications. Engaging with experts, policymakers, and affected communities can help identify and address potential ethical issues, ensure that data practices align with societal values, and promote shared goals for sustainable development. Collaborative efforts can enhance the effectiveness of AI technologies and support the development of best practices for data privacy and ethical data use (Ryan, R.M., et al, 2000).Training programs and professional development opportunities can help stakeholders build the address ethical challenges and ensure responsible data use in AI-driven sustainable development.. This balanced approach ensures to global sustainability goals and respects the privacy and rights of individuals.

TRANSPARENCY AND EXPLAINABILITY IN AI FOR SUSTAINABLE DEVELOPMENT.

These principles are essential not only for fostering trust and accountability but also for ensuring that AI. By prioritizing transparency and explainability, stakeholders can navigate the complexities of AI while aligning technological advancements with ethical standards and practical outcomes. This principle is crucial in sustainable development because AI systems often inform key decisions related to environmental policies, resource allocation, and social interventions. Ensuring transparency means that the methodologies, data sources, and decision-making processes underlying AI systems are open to scrutiny. This openness enables stakeholders to assess the validity and reliability of AI-driven insights and ensures that these insights are based on sound and unbiased data. For example, when AI is used for environmental monitoring, transparency about the algorithms and data sources helps stakeholders understand how conclusions about pollution levels or climate trends are reached, thereby supporting informed decision-making and fostering accountability. Explainability, on the other hand, refers to the capacity to interpret and communicate the reasoning behind AI system outputs in a manner that is comprehensible to non-experts. In sustainable development, where AI applications can impact various sectors and communities, explainability ensures that stakeholders can grasp how AI-driven recommendations or predictions are derived. This is particularly important in contexts where AI informs policy decisions or public interventions (Sreenivasulu, A., et al, 2022). For instance, if an AI model predicts the impact of a proposed infrastructure project on local ecosystems, explainability helps stakeholders understand how the model arrived at its conclusions, thus enabling more informed debates and decisions about the project's potential effects. Without explainability, AI outputs may be perceived as opaque "black boxes," potentially undermining trust and reducing the effectiveness of AI applications.

AI system used for resource distribution shows patterns of inequity, transparency and explainability can help identify and correct the underlying causes of these biases. Additionally, when AI systems are explainable, it becomes easier to hold organizations accountable for their decisions and actions, as stakeholders can trace and understand the basis of AI-driven outcomes. When stakeholders, including affected communities and the general public, can understand how AI systems work and how decisions are made, they are more likely to support and engage with AI-driven initiatives. For instance, in projects related to climate adaptation or disaster response, transparency about AI's role and explainability of its recommendations can enhance public confidence and encourage collaborative efforts to address environmental challenges. Conversely, a lack of transparency and explainability can lead to skepticism and resistance, potentially hindering the effectiveness of AI in promoting sustainable development. Implementing transparency and explainability requires adopting specific practices and technologies. For example, using explainable AI techniques such as model-agnostic methods, which provide insights into complex models without requiring complete understanding of their internals, can help make AI systems more interpretable. Additionally, developing clear documentation and communication strategies for AI systems ensures that stakeholders have access to relevant information about how AI models operate and make decisions. Engaging with interdisciplinary teams, including ethicists, domain experts, and communication specialists, can further enhance the clarity and effectiveness of AI explainability efforts.AI development, promoting ongoing education and training on ethical AI principles, and encouraging open dialogue about the challenges and limitations of AI. By embedding these values into organizational practices, stakeholders can ensure that AI technologies are developed and applied in ways that support sustainable development objectives while upholding ethical standards. In conclusion, transparency and explainability are fundamental to the responsible use of AI in sustainable development. By making AI systems' processes and decisions clear and understandable, stakeholders can enhance trust, ensure accountability, and address potential biases, thereby supporting effective and equitable outcomes.

Adopting practices that prioritize transparency and explainability not only aligns AI applications with ethical standards but also empowers stakeholders to leverage AI's potential in advancing sustainable development goals. Through these efforts, AI can be harnessed to address pressing global challenges while maintaining a commitment to ethical principles and public trust (Sparks, C., et al, 2016).AI offers transformative potential for addressing global challenges such as poverty, inequality, and environmental degradation, but its deployment must be carefully managed to uphold human rights and avoid exacerbating existing disparities. Social services, law enforcement, or resource allocation could inadvertently reinforce biases against ethnic minorities, low-income communities, or other vulnerable populations. By prioritizing these practices, stakeholders can help prevent AI from perpetuating or worsening human rights violations and ensure that its benefits are distributed equitably. AI into sustainable development efforts, especially when dealing with sensitive information about vulnerable populations. Additionally, ensuring that data collection and use comply with relevant privacy laws and ethical standards is crucial for maintaining trust and protecting human rights. AI deployment in sustainable development. However, the deployment of AI in these areas must be conducted with careful consideration of human rights implications. For example, AI-driven environmental projects should avoid displacing local communities or infringing on their land rights. Ensuring that AI technologies support rather than undermine the rights of indigenous peoples and other vulnerable groups requires engaging with these communities in the planning and implementation of AI projects, respecting their knowledge and perspectives, and ensuring that they benefit from the technological advancements.

Another important aspect is the potential for AI to influence access to essential services such as healthcare, education, and social welfare. AI systems can enhance the delivery and effectiveness of these services, but they must be designed and implemented to ensure equitable access and avoid reinforcing existing inequalities. For example, AI-powered health diagnostics should be accessible to all populations, including those in low-resource settings, and educational AI tools should address diverse learning needs without marginalizing any group. Ensuring that AI applications in these areas are inclusive and equitable helps protect the rights of vulnerable populations and promotes their well-being. The ethical deployment of AI also involves addressing potential harms associated with automation and job displacement. As AI systems are increasingly used to automate tasks and processes, there is a risk that vulnerable workers, particularly in low-income and informal sectors, may face job losses and economic insecurity. To mitigate these risks, it is important to implement policies that support workforce transition and reskilling programs, ensuring that affected individuals have access to new opportunities and are protected from adverse impacts. Integrating AI into sustainable development strategies should include measures to safeguard labor rights and provide support to those impacted by technological changes. Moreover, accountability in AI systems is essential for protecting human rights. Clear mechanisms for oversight and redress should be established to address any adverse effects of AI applications. Finally, fostering a culture of human rights within organizations that develop and deploy AI is crucial. This involves integrating human rights considerations into AI design and implementation processes, promoting awareness of human rights issues among AI practitioners, and engaging with human rights experts to guide ethical practices. Addressing issues related to bias, privacy, equitable access to services, job displacement, and accountability is essential positively to human well-being and do not exacerbate existing inequalities or infringe on fundamental rights.

CULTURAL SENSITIVITY AND AI IN SUSTAINABLE DEVELOPMENT PEDAGOGY.

Sustainable development education aims to prepare individuals and communities to address global challenges while respecting local traditions, values, and needs. As AI becomes increasingly integrated into educational frameworks, it is essential to address the cultural dimensions of AI deployment to maximize its benefits while avoiding potential pitfalls that could undermine cultural integrity or exacerbate inequalities. Cultural sensitivity in AI-driven sustainable development pedagogy involves recognizing and valuing the diverse cultural backgrounds of learners and communities (Sugumaran, K.M., et al, 2024). AI systems and educational content must be designed to respect and integrate local cultural contexts, practices, and languages. For example, AI tools used in environmental education should incorporate local ecological knowledge and traditions to ensure that they resonate with and are relevant to the communities they serve. By integrating indigenous knowledge and culturally specific practices into AI-driven educational materials, stakeholders can foster more meaningful and respectful learning experiences that align with the values and priorities of different cultural groups. Moreover, language and communication are critical aspects of cultural sensitivity in AI applications. AI systems that offer multilingual support can help bridge language barriers and ensure that educational content is accessible to diverse populations. This includes developing AI tools that can translate educational materials into multiple languages and dialects, as well as incorporating cultural nuances and local expressions into AI-generated content. Ensuring that AI systems are linguistically and culturally inclusive enhances their effectiveness and supports equitable access to sustainable development education.

Another key consideration is the potential for AI systems to perpetuate cultural biases if not carefully managed. AI algorithms trained on data from one cultural context may inadvertently introduce biases or fail to accurately reflect the values and needs of other cultures. To mitigate these risks, it is crucial to use diverse and representative datasets that encompass a broad range of cultural perspectives. Cultural sensitivity also involves understanding the impact of AI on local educational practices and institutions. AI technologies should complement rather than disrupt existing pedagogical approaches and cultural traditions. For instance, in regions where traditional teaching methods and community-based learning are prevalent, AI tools should be integrated in ways that enhance and support these practices rather than replace them. Collaborating with local educators and stakeholders to adapt AI technologies to fit culturally specific educational contexts helps preserve cultural practices while leveraging the benefits of AI. In many cultures, there are specific norms and values regarding the collection and use of personal information. AI systems deployed in educational contexts must respect these cultural norms and ensure that data collection practices align with local expectations and legal requirements. Additionally, fostering cultural sensitivity in AI-driven sustainable development pedagogy requires ongoing dialogue and feedback from diverse cultural groups. Continuous engagement with local communities, educators, and cultural experts ensures that AI tools and educational practices remain relevant and respectful of evolving cultural contexts. Establishing mechanisms for feedback and iterative improvement allows for the adaptation of AI technologies to better meet the needs and expectations of different cultural groups (Swanson, D.M., et al, 2016). Providing educators complexities and integrate AI effectively into their teaching practices enhances the overall impact of AI-driven education. This includes offering training on recognizing and addressing biases, understanding cultural differences, and using AI tools in ways that respect and support diverse cultural perspectives.

In summary, integrating cultural sensitivity into AI-driven sustainable development pedagogy is essential for creating inclusive, respectful, and effective educational experiences. By recognizing and valuing cultural diversity, addressing potential biases, and ensuring that AI technologies complement existing practices, stakeholders access to sustainable development education. Ongoing dialogue, community engagement, and professional development are key to navigating the complexities of cultural sensitivity in AI applications, ultimately supporting more meaningful and impactful sustainable development outcomes. AI's capacity to automate tasks across various sectors—from agriculture and manufacturing to services and administration—can lead to significant job displacement. For instance, AI-powered systems in agriculture may automate planting and harvesting processes, reducing the need for manual laborers. Similarly, AI in manufacturing can streamline production lines, potentially leading to reduced demand for assembly line workers. In the context of sustainable development, where AI is increasingly used to manage resources, monitor environmental conditions, and drive policy decisions, it is essential to consider how these technologies will affect employment in both developing and developed economies. To effectively address AI-driven job displacement, it is crucial to implement comprehensive workforce transition strategies. Educational institutions, vocational training centers, and private sector organizations should collaborate to develop training programs that focus on emerging skills in areas such as data analysis, AI management, and green technologies (Tongco, M.D.C., 2017). Another important aspect is the promotion of lifelong learning and adaptability. As the nature of work continues to evolve with AI advancements, for workers to remain competitive. Encouraging individuals to engage in ongoing professional development helps them stay current with technological trends and enhances their ability to adapt to changing job requirements. This can be supported through accessible online learning platforms, government-sponsored training initiatives, and partnerships between educational institutions and industry leaders. In addition to reskilling and lifelong learning, it is important to explore policies that support job creation in sectors that complement AI technologies. For example, as AI systems automate certain tasks, new opportunities may arise in areas such as AI system maintenance, ethical AI governance, and human-AI collaboration. By identifying and promoting growth in these emerging fields, policymakers and industry leaders can help offset the job displacement caused by automation and create pathways for employment in innovative sectors. Social protection measures also play a critical role in addressing the impact of AI-driven job displacement. Governments and organizations should consider implementing safety nets such as unemployment benefits, income support, and job placement services to assist workers who are affected by automation.

These measures provide financial stability and support while individuals transition to new employment opportunities or undergo retraining. Additionally, policies that promote fair wages, job security, and worker rights are essential to ensuring that the benefits of AI are distributed equitably and that displaced workers receive adequate support. Engaging with stakeholders, including workers, employers, and policymakers, is crucial for them. Collaborative efforts can help identify the specific needs of affected communities, gather insights on the impact of AI technologies, and design solutions that are tailored to local contexts. For instance, conducting impact assessments and consultations can provide valuable information on how AI adoption will affect various sectors and regions (Van Haneghan, J.P., et al, 2015). Moreover, integrating AI-driven job displacement considerations into broader sustainable development strategies ensures that economic growth and technological progress do not come at the expense of workers' livelihoods. This involves aligning AI initiatives with goals of social equity, economic inclusion, and sustainable development. By prioritizing these values, stakeholders can ensure that the benefits of AI are harnessed in a way that supports long-term prosperity and resilience for all members of society. In conclusion, addressing AI-driven job displacement in the context of sustainable development requires a comprehensive and proactive approach, implementing social protection measures, and engaging with diverse stakeholders, stakeholders can navigate the challenges of automation and AI while ensuring a just transition for affected workers.

CASE STUDIES: ETHICAL AI IN SUSTAINABLE DEVELOPMENT PEDAGOGY IN PRACTICE.

Case studies of ethical AI in sustainable development how artificial intelligence can be leveraged responsibly to enhance educational outcomes while adhering to ethical principles. These examples illustrate practical implementations of AI that balance technological innovation with respect for human rights, cultural sensitivity, and social equity. By examining real-world applications, educators, policymakers, and technologists can glean lessons on best practices, challenges, and strategies for integrating AI in ways that support sustainable development goals (SDGs).One notable personalized learning environments designed to support students in developing countries. An initiative led by the non-profit organization Khan Academy, in partnership with AI developers, deployed an AI-driven educational platform that adapts content to individual learning paces and styles. This platform utilized performance data and tailor instructional materials to their needs. Ethical considerations were paramount in this project; developers ensured that the AI system was designed to respect data privacy and provided clear consent mechanisms for users. Moreover, the platform incorporated multilingual support and culturally relevant content to address diverse educational contexts. This case demonstrates how AI can enhance educational access and quality while maintaining ethical standards and cultural sensitivity. This system uses AI and environmental data to monitor deforestation, track climate change impacts, and predict natural disasters.

The project emphasized transparency and explainability, with the development team providing detailed documentation on how AI models were trained and how decisions were made. Additionally, the project adhered to ethical guidelines for data use, including stringent measures to protect the privacy of local communities and ensure that their data was used responsibly. By engaging with local stakeholders and integrating their knowledge, UNEP's AI system demonstrated a commitment to ethical practices in environmental sustainability and showcased how AI can be used effectively in global monitoring efforts (Vijayakumar, G., et al, 2024).The AI for Accessibility program by Microsoft is another illustrative case. This initiative focuses on developing AI tools to assist individuals with disabilities, thereby promoting social equity and inclusion. For instance, Microsoft's AI-powered real-time captioning and translation services enhance communication for individuals with hearing impairments, while computer vision technologies aid visually impaired users by describing their surroundings. This case highlights the potential of AI to support human rights and accessibility goals within sustainable development pedagogy. In the realm of sustainable agriculture, the AI-powered platform Agri-Tech offers a practical example of integrating AI into development efforts. The project exemplifies ethical AI use by ensuring that the agricultural data and include inputs from local farmers to make the technology contextually relevant. Additionally, the platform promotes equitable access by making its tools available at low or no cost to smallholder farmers in developing regions, thereby supporting sustainable agricultural practices and economic development.

A final example is the AI-driven health diagnostics initiative by the non-profit organization PathAI, which focuses on improving diagnostic accuracy for diseases such as cancer. PathAI uses to analyze medical images and assist pathologists in identifying disease markers. Ethical considerations in this project include rigorous validation of AI models to ensure diagnostic accuracy and the protection of patient data. The initiative also emphasizes the importance of equitable access to AI-driven diagnostic tools, particularly in underserved areas, to support global health outcomes and address disparities in healthcare access. By prioritizing transparency, cultural sensitivity, and equity, these examples provide a roadmap for integrating AI in ways that and contribute to sustainable development objectives. As AI continues to evolve, these case studies offer valuable lessons for stakeholders seeking to implement AI responsibly and effectively in their own sustainable development initiatives. Integrating Artificial Intelligence (AI) into sustainable development education demands a framework of best practices that ensure ethical implementation while maximizing the technology's potential to advance educational goals. These practices not only guide the effective use of AI but also address critical concerns related to equity, transparency, and cultural sensitivity. Adopting these best practices helps to foster an educational environment where AI contributes positively to sustainable development, respects human rights, and upholds ethical standards. One of the foremost best practices is ensuring that AI tools and educational content are inclusive and equitable.

This involves designing AI systems that accommodate diverse learning needs and contexts. For instance, AI-powered educational platforms should offer multilingual support and adapt to different educational levels and cultural backgrounds. Engaging with educators, students, and community representatives during the design and deployment phases ensures that the AI tools meet the specific needs of various groups and do not reinforce existing inequalities. Equity in access also means making AI educational resources available to underprivileged communities and providing necessary support for those who might be technologically disadvantaged(Wang, Y.Y., et al, 2019).Transparency and explainability are critical for fostering trust and accountability in AI-driven educational systems. Educational institutions and allows users to understand how AI-driven recommendations or assessments are derived, thereby reducing the risk of misunderstandings or misuse. Explainability also involves creating user-friendly interfaces and documentation that demystify AI technology for educators, students, and other stakeholders. Protecting the privacy and security of student data is a fundamental ethical consideration in AI integration. Best practices include implementing robust clear data governance policies helps manage how data is collected, used, and shared, reinforcing trust and safeguarding against potential breaches or misuse. Involving diverse teams in the development of AI tools, including ethicists and cultural experts, can further ensure that the technology operates fairly and inclusively. This involves providing ongoing training and professional development opportunities focused on AI technology, ethical considerations, and pedagogical strategies.

Engaging these groups in the planning, implementation, and evaluation phases helps to align AI tools with community needs and values. Regular feedback loops and participatory approaches ensure that AI systems remain relevant, effective, and respectful of local contexts. This engagement also fosters a sense of ownership and accountability among stakeholders. Developing and adhering to ethical AI guidelines and governance structures is crucial for ensuring responsible AI use. Institutions should establish clear ethical standards and operational procedures for AI integration, including protocols for handling ethical dilemmas and ensuring compliance with legal and ethical norms. Forming interdisciplinary committees that include ethicists, technologists, and educators can help oversee AI projects and address any ethical concerns that arise. Continuous evaluation of AI tools and their effectiveness in educational settings is essential for ensuring their ongoing relevance and impact. Institutions should regularly assess AI systems to measure their educational outcomes, identify areas for improvement, and adapt them based on user feedback and evolving needs. This iterative approach helps to address any issues promptly and ensures that AI tools remain aligned with educational goals and ethical standards. Finally, supporting inclusive innovation in AI development and deployment is crucial for advancing sustainable development education. Promoting inclusive innovation helps ensure that AI tools contribute positively to educational outcomes and support broader goals of sustainability and social equity. In conclusion, integrating AI into sustainable development education requires a careful balance of technological innovation with ethical considerations. By prioritizing inclusivity, transparency, data privacy, fairness, and continuous professional development, and by engaging stakeholders and adhering to ethical guidelines, educational institutions can leverage AI to enhance learning outcomes while upholding the highest standards of responsibility and equity. Implementing these best practices ensures that AI contributes effectively to sustainable development goals, fostering a more just and informed society.

NAVIGATING THE ETHICS OF AI IN SUSTAINABLE DEVELOPMENT PEDAGOGY - A CALL TO ACTION.

As AI technologies are increasingly becoming integral to educational frameworks aimed at achieving sustainability goals, that accompany their integration. This call to action emphasizes the need for a multi-dimensional approach to ensure that in education not only advance learning outcomes but also uphold fundamental ethical principles, promote equity, and respect human rights. Institutions and organizations involved in AI-driven educational initiatives must develop and adopt ethical frameworks that guide. Creating robust ethical guidelines helps align AI technologies with broader objectives of sustainable development and prevents misuse or negative impacts. Transparency involves providing clear information about how AI algorithms function, how data is collected and used, and how decisions are made. Explainability means that users—students, educators, and administrators—can understand and interpret AI-driven outcomes and recommendations. By making AI processes visible and comprehensible, stakeholders can better assess the fairness and accuracy of AI tools, ensuring that they align with educational goals and ethical standards. This includes adopting encryption technologies, anonymizing sensitive information. Engaging with stakeholders to obtain informed consent and provide options for data management empowers and reinforce trust in AI systems. Equity and inclusivity must be prioritized to ensure that AI technologies do not exacerbate existing disparities. Efforts should be made to voices in the development of AI tools, including those from underrepresented and marginalized communities. This inclusive approach helps create culturally sensitive and equitable, supporting a more just and effective educational environment.

Providing training on AI technology, ethical considerations, and pedagogical strategies enables educators to integrate AI in ways that enhance learning outcomes and adhere to ethical standards. Continuous professional development also helps educators stay abreast of emerging technologies and best practices, ensuring that AI applications remain relevant and effective. Engaging with communities and stakeholders is vital for ethical AI integration in sustainable development pedagogy. Collaborative efforts with students, parents, educators, and local organizations help identify needs, gather feedback, and address concerns related to AI technologies. Building partnerships with community members ensures that values and educational priorities, fostering. AI systems and incorporating feedback from users to identify and correct biases. Establishing interdisciplinary teams that include ethicists, technologists, and cultural experts can further enhance the development of fair and unbiased AI tools. By actively addressing bias, stakeholders can ensure that AI systems outcomes. Finally, supporting a culture of ethical reflection within educational institutions promotes ongoing evaluation of AI practices and their impact on students and society. Encouraging critical considerations into the curriculum and fostering an environment of ethical inquiry supports responsible AI use and aligns educational practices with broader goals of sustainability and social justice. In conclusion, navigating the ethics of pedagogy requires a proactive and collaborative approach that prioritizes fairness, transparency, privacy, and inclusivity. By establishing clear ethical guidelines, fostering transparency, protecting data privacy, promoting equity, and engaging with communities, used responsibly and effectively in educational settings.

CONCLUSION

(AI) into sustainable development pedagogy are profound and multifaceted, encompassing considerations of fairness, transparency, privacy, inclusivity, and accountability. As AI technologies increasingly permeate educational frameworks aimed at advancing sustainability goals, it is imperative to navigate these ethical dimensions with deliberate and thoughtful strategies, enhance educational outcomes, and contribute to broader sustainability objectives. However, this potential must be balanced with a commitment to ethical principles that safeguard human rights and promote social equity. One of the central ethical concerns is ensuring that AI systems are fair and equitable. AI tools must be designed to address, rather than exacerbate, existing disparities in education. This involves using diverse datasets to train AI models, continuously auditing these systems for bias, and actively involving marginalized communities in the development process. Transparency and explainability are also crucial in maintaining trust and accountability. Educators, students, and other stakeholders must have clear insights into how AI systems operate and make decisions. Providing accessible explanations of AI algorithms and data usage fosters a greater understanding of how educational outcomes are generated and ensures that AI tools are used appropriately and ethically. Transparency also involves openly communicating the limitations and potential risks associated with AI technologies, allowing for informed decision-making and responsible usage. Additionally, obtaining informed consent from individuals whose data is being used, and offering them control over their information, reinforces trust and aligns with ethical standards. Providing comprehensive training on AI technology, ethical issues, and pedagogical strategies helps educators navigate the complexities of AI integration and ensures that AI applications are used in ways that enhance learning outcomes and adhere to ethical norms. Collaborative efforts that involve students, parents, educators, and community organizations help identify the specific requirements and concerns of different groups. This engagement ensures that AI tools are relevant, culturally sensitive, and responsive to the diverse contexts in which they are deployed. By fostering a participatory approach, stakeholders can build a sense of ownership and accountability in the use of AI technologies. Addressing potential biases in AI systems is crucial for promoting fairness and inclusivity. AI technologies must be continuously monitored and refined to mitigate biases that could affect educational outcomes. This involves using diverse datasets, conducting regular audits, and incorporating feedback from users to identify and address any biases. Ensuring that AI tools are developed with an awareness of and sensitivity to cultural and contextual differences further supports equitable and effective educational practices. By prioritizing fairness, transparency, privacy, inclusivity, and stakeholder engagement, and by addressing biases and fostering ethical reflection, stakeholders. This commitment to ethical principles ensures that AI-driven educational initiatives contribute positively to sustainable development objectives, enhance educational experiences, and support a more just and equitable society.

REFERENCES

Ando, H., Cousins, R., & Young, C. (2014). Achieving saturation in thematic analysis: Development and refinement of a codebook. *Comprehensive Psychology*, *3*, 03.CP.3.4. DOI: 10.2466/03.CP.3.4

Braun, V., & Clarke, V. (2006). Using thematic analysis in psychology. *Qualitative Research in Psychology*, *3*(2), 77–101. DOI: 10.1191/1478088706qp063oa

Cave, S., & Dihal, K. (2019). Hopes and fears for intelligent machines in fiction and reality. *Nature Machine Intelligence*, *1*(2), 74–78. DOI: 10.1038/s42256-019-0020-9

Chai, C. S., Lin, P. Y., Jong, M. S. Y., Dai, Y., Chiu, T. K. F., & Huang, B. Y. (2020) Factors influencing students' behavioral intention to continue artificial intelligence learning. In Proceedings of the International Symposium on Educational Technology, (ISET020), Bangkok, Thailand, 24–27 August.

Chai, C. S., Lin, P. Y., Jong, M. S. Y., Dai, Y., Chiu, T. K. F., & Qin, J. J. (2020). Primary school students' perceptions and behavioral intentions of learning artificial intelligence. *Journal of Educational Technology & Society*.

Chiu, T. K., Jong, M. S. Y., & Mok, I. A. (2020). Does learner expertise matter when designing emotional multimedia for learners of primary school mathematics? *Educational Technology Research and Development*, *68*(5), 2305–2320. DOI: 10.1007/s11423-020-09775-4

Chiu, T. K., & Lim, C. P. (2020). *Strategic Use of Technology for Inclusive Education in Hong Kong: A Content-Level Perspective*. ECNU Rev. Educ.

Chiu, T. K. F., & Churchill, D. (2015). Exploring the characteristics of an optimal design of digital materials for concept learning in mathematics: Multimedia learning and variation theory. *Computers & Education*, *82*, 280–291. DOI: 10.1016/j.compedu.2014.12.001

Chiu, T. K. F., & Churchill, D. (2016). Adoption of mobile devices in teaching: Changes in teacher beliefs, attitudes and anxiety. *Interactive Learning Environments*, *24*(2), 317–327. DOI: 10.1080/10494820.2015.1113709

Chiu, T. K. F., & Churchill, D. (2016). Design of learning objects for concept learning: Effects of multimedia learning principles and an instructional approach. *Interactive Learning Environments*, *24*(6), 1355–1370. DOI: 10.1080/10494820.2015.1006237

Chiu, T. K. F., & Mok, I. A. C. (2017). Learner expertise and mathematics different order thinking skills in multimedia learning. *Computers & Education*, *107*, 147–164. DOI: 10.1016/j.compedu.2017.01.008

Eggleston, J. (2018). *School-Based Curriculum Development in Britain: A Collection of Case Studies*. Routledge. DOI: 10.4324/9780429454622

Glatthorn, A. A., Boschee, F., Whitehead, B. M., & Boschee, B. F. (2018). *Curriculum Leadership: Strategies for Development and Implementation*. SAGE.

Mahadev Madgule, N., Vinayaka, Y., Sonkhaskar, Y. M., Patel, D. R., Karthikeyan, P., & Selvakumar, P. (2023). Mechanical properties and microstructure of activated TIG welded similar joints of Inconel alloys by desirability approaches. *Materials Today: Proceedings*, *77*, 528–533. DOI: 10.1016/j.matpr.2022.12.250

Margot, K. C., & Kettler, T. (2019). Teachers' perception of STEM integration and education: A systematic literature review. *International Journal of STEM Education*, *6*(1), 2. DOI: 10.1186/s40594-018-0151-2

Niemiec, C. P., & Ryan, R. M. (2009). Autonomy, competence, and relatedness in the classroom: Applying self-determination theory to educational practice. *Theory and Research in Education*, *7*(2), 133–144. DOI: 10.1177/1477878509104318

Patrick, H., & Canevello, A. (2011). Methodological overview of a self-determination theory-based computerized intervention to promote leisure-time physical activity. *Psychology of Sport and Exercise*, *12*(1), 13–19. DOI: 10.1016/j.psychsport.2010.04.011 PMID: 21103069

Piniel, K., & Csizér, K. (2013). L2 motivation, anxiety and self-efficacy: The interrelationship of individual variables in the secondary school context. *Studies in Second Language Learning and Teaching*, *3*(4), 523. DOI: 10.14746/ssllt.2013.3.4.5

Ramakrishnan, T., Mohan Gift, M. D., Chitradevi, S., Jegan, R., & Jose, P. S.H.; Nagaraja; Sharma, H.N.R.; Selvakumar, P.; Mekuria Hailegiorgis, S. (2022) Study of Numerous Resins Used in Polymer Matrix Composite Materials. Advances in Materials Science and Engineering, vol. 2022, Article ID 1088926, 8 pages. DOI: 10.1155/2022/1088926

Ryan, R. M., & Deci, E. L. (2000). Self-determination theory and the facilitation of intrinsic motivation, social development, and well-being. *The American Psychologist*, *55*(1), 68–78. DOI: 10.1037/0003-066X.55.1.68 PMID: 11392867

Selvakumar, P. (2024, July 26). Mariappan; Petchiammal; Shunmugam; Sivagami; Samuel Jabez, R.P. (2024) Removal of chemicals from effluent using photobioreactor technology to improve environmental and health impacts. *Zeitschrift für Physikalische Chemie*, *238*(7), 1295–1302. Advance online publication. DOI: 10.1515/zpch-2023-0450

Selvakumar, P. (2025, January 29). Palanisamy; Satheesh Kumar; Cinthaikinian; Selvamurugan; Vigneshkumar; Mariappan; Raja; Palani Kishore, S. (2024) Biosensors and its diverse applications in healthcare systems. *Zeitschrift für Physikalische Chemie*, *239*(1), 37–43. Advance online publication. DOI: 10.1515/zpch-2023-0406

Sparks, C., Dimmock, J., Lonsdale, C., & Jackson, B. (2016). Modeling indicators and outcomes of students' perceived teacher relatedness support in high school physical education. *Psychology of Sport and Exercise*, *26*, 71–82. DOI: 10.1016/j.psychsport.2016.06.004

Sreenivasulu, A., Manimozhi, T., Satheesh Kumar, P., Selvakumar, P., & Singh, P. (2022) The Model of Smart Sensing Device For Sensitive Nanoclusters Modification in Sensing Properties. 2022 2nd International Conference on Advance Computing and Innovative Technologies in Engineering (ICACITE), Greater Noida, India, pp. 1043-1047. DOI: 10.1109/ICACITE53722.2022.9823846

Sugumaran, K. M., Pandiyarajan, V., & Selvakumar, P. (2024) Analysis of Electromyography Signals for Control of Mechanical Prosthesis using Machine Learning Techniques. 2024 2nd International Conference on Intelligent Data Communication Technologies and Internet of Things (IDCIoT), Bengaluru, India, pp. 1059-1067. DOI: 10.1109/IDCIoT59759.2024.10467707

Swanson, D.M.; Pashby, K. (2016) Towards a critical global citizenship? A comparative analysis of GC education discourses in Scotland and Alberta. J. Res. Curric. Instr.

Tongco, M. D. C. (2017). Purposive sampling as a tool for informant selection. *Ethnobotany Research and Applications*.

Van Haneghan, J. P., Pruet, S. A., Neal-Waltman, R., & Harlan, J. M. (2015). Teacher beliefs about motivating and teaching students to carry out engineering design challenges: Some initial data. *Journal of Pre-College Engineering Education Research*, *5*(2). Advance online publication. DOI: 10.7771/2157-9288.1097

Vijayakumar, G., Rajkumar, M., Chandar, N. R., Selvakumar, P., & Duraisamy, R. (2024). Environmentally friendly TDS removal from waste water by electrochemical ion exchange batch-type recirculation (EIR) technique. *Environmental Science. Water Research & Technology*, *10*(4), 826–835. DOI: 10.1039/D3EW00793F

Wang, Y. Y., & Wang, Y. S. (2019). Development and validation of an artificial intelligence anxiety scale: An initial application in predicting motivated learning behavior. *Interactive Learning Environments*.

Chapter 3
Embracing Cultural Dimensions in AI-Enhanced Sustainability Education: Tailoring Pedagogies for a Global Learner Community

Goh Ying Yingsoon
https://orcid.org/0000-0002-6654-2887
MARA University of Technology, Malaysia

Suyan Zhang
https://orcid.org/0009-0003-4518-1650
Shandong Jianzhu University, China

Nurul Ain Chua
https://orcid.org/0000-0003-2915-1577
University Terengganu Malaysia, Malaysia

Yiming Chen
https://orcid.org/0009-0002-8906-2736
Shenzhen University, China

Tie Xiaoyao
Qilu Institute of Technology, China

ABSTRACT

This chapter explores the integration of cultural dimensions in AI-enhanced sustainability education, emphasizing the need to tailor pedagogies for a diverse global learner community. As sustainability challenges transcend geographical boundaries, it is imperative to develop educational approaches that are inclusive and culturally sensitive. The chapter discusses the potential of Artificial Intelligence (AI) in personalizing learning experiences and addressing the unique needs of learners from various cultural backgrounds. By examining case studies and empirical evidence, we demonstrate how AI can be leveraged to adapt sustainability education to different cultural contexts, fostering a deeper understanding and

DOI: 10.4018/979-8-3693-9062-7.ch003

engagement among students. The chapter also highlights the importance of interdisciplinary collaboration and the role of educators in bridging cultural gaps, ultimately contributing to the development of a more sustainable and equitable global society.

INTRODUCTION

A. The growing importance of sustainability education

In an era of climate crises, resource depletion, and environmental injustice, how can education equip future generations with the skills to drive sustainability? AI-enhanced sustainability education is emerging as a transformative approach, integrating personalized learning, real-time analytics, and cultural adaptation to make sustainability education more impactful and inclusive. The goal of sustainability education is to equip learners with the knowledge and tools to address complex sustainability challenges, promoting a lifestyle and professional practices that contribute to a sustainable future (Hider, & Saleem, 2024).

The importance of sustainability education cannot be overstated, given the pressing environmental and social issues facing the world today. As the global population continues to grow, so does the demand for natural resources, leading to environmental degradation, inequality, and the potential for widespread societal disruption. Sustainability education empowers individuals to actively solve real-world challenges. By fostering critical thinking, systems awareness, and ethical responsibility, it equips learners to drive meaningful change. Moreover, sustainability education possesses the capacity to spur innovation, shape policy, and revolutionize societal norms, ultimately leading to a more equitable and prosperous future for all (Abulibdeh, et al, 2024).

B. The role of cultural dimensions in education

Cultural dimensions—such as language, traditions, and social norms—shape how students engage with educational content. For example, an AI-powered sustainability course in China might emphasize community-driven conservation, while in the U.S., it might focus on individual carbon footprints. In the context of education, cultural dimensions play a pivotal role in shaping learners' experiences, engagement, and understanding of the material. Recognizing and respecting these dimensions are essential for creating an inclusive educational environment that acknowledges the diversity of backgrounds and perspectives among students (Abulibdeh, et al, 2024).

To integrate cultural dimensions into sustainable education, educators must adopt a multicultural and interdisciplinary approach that acknowledges and values the diversity of their students. To effectively integrate cultural dimensions into sustainable education, educators must adopt inclusive curriculum design that reflects diverse cultural perspectives, employ culturally responsive teaching methods that resonate with various learning styles, empower student voices to share their cultural insights on sustainability, facilitate cross-cultural collaborations for project-based learning, and engage in continuous professional development to enhance cultural competence and the ability to foster a culturally inclusive and sustainability-focused learning environment (Shwedeh, et al, 2024).

C. The potential of AI in enhancing sustainability education

The potential of Artificial Intelligence (AI) in enhancing sustainability education lies in its ability to personalize learning experiences, adapt to individual student needs, and scale educational resources efficiently. AI can analyze vast amounts of data to understand student behaviors, learning patterns, and knowledge gaps, enabling educators to provide tailored instruction. Additionally, AI technologies such as machine learning, natural language processing, and virtual reality can create immersive learning environments that simulate real-world sustainability challenges, making the educational experience more engaging and impactful (Patil, 2024).

To harness the power of AI in sustainability education, educators and developers can deploy adaptive learning platforms that tailor content to individual needs, intelligent tutoring systems for personalized feedback, data analytics to refine teaching strategies, virtual and augmented reality for immersive learning experiences, and AI for language and cultural adaptation, thereby making education more effective, engaging, and inclusive for a diverse global audience (Edwards-Fapohunda, & Adediji, 2024).

THE NEED FOR CULTURALLY SENSITIVE SUSTAINABILITY EDUCATION

A. Global nature of sustainability challenges

The global nature of sustainability challenges presents a formidable obstacle in the pursuit of culturally sensitive sustainability education. With the world's ecosystems and resources being interconnected, the issues at hand—such as climate change, deforestation, pollution, and loss of biodiversity—are not confined to national boundaries. This interconnectedness necessitates a coordinated response that respects and integrates diverse cultural perspectives, which is inherently challenging. Differences in language, traditions, values, and economic priorities can create barriers to consensus and action. Additionally, the varying levels of development and capacity across countries make it difficult to implement uniform sustainability education programs that cater to the unique needs and contexts of each culture (Eguchi, et al, 2021).

The need for culturally sensitive sustainability education arises from the recognition that solutions to global sustainability challenges must be inclusive and respectful of cultural diversity. By acknowledging and incorporating the knowledge, practices, and worldviews of different cultures, we can foster a sense of ownership and responsibility among all communities. Culturally sensitive education can help bridge gaps in understanding, promote collaboration, and ensure that sustainability initiatives are not only effective but also equitable. Moreover, it empowers local populations by valuing their contributions and encouraging the preservation of traditional ecological wisdom, which often contains valuable insights for sustainable living. In essence, culturally sensitive sustainability education is essential for building a global movement that is both broadly supported and deeply rooted in the diverse experiences of people worldwide (Wu, 2024).

B. Importance of inclusive educational approaches

Inclusive educational approaches are designed to ensure that all students, regardless of their background, ability, or circumstances, have equal opportunities to learn and succeed. This means creating an educational environment that accommodates a wide range of needs, including but not limited to those with disabilities, different learning styles, various cultural backgrounds, and diverse socioeconomic statuses. Inclusive education involves modifying teaching methods, curricula, and school policies to eliminate barriers to learning and to promote a sense of belonging among all students. It also encompasses fostering an atmosphere of respect and empathy, where diversity is celebrated and where every student's voice is heard and valued (Mutambik, 2024).

The Importance of inclusive educational approaches cannot be overstated, as they are crucial for building a fair and equitable society. By embracing inclusivity, educational systems can better prepare students to thrive in a world that is increasingly diverse and interconnected. Inclusive education not only benefits those who might otherwise be marginalized but also enriches the learning experience for all students by exposing them to a variety of perspectives and ways of thinking. This exposure can enhance critical thinking skills, promote social cohesion, and prepare students to be active and responsible citizens. Furthermore, inclusive education can lead to better academic outcomes and increased engagement, as students feel supported and motivated in an environment that recognizes and nurtures their unique talents and challenges (Edeni, et al, 2024).

C. Challenges in addressing diverse cultural backgrounds

Addressing diverse cultural backgrounds in educational settings presents a multifaceted challenge that educators must navigate carefully. Cultural diversity encompasses a wide array of characteristics, including language, religion, customs, traditions, and social norms, each of which can significantly influence a student's learning experience. Challenges arise when educators must balance the need to provide a standardized curriculum with the desire to honor the unique cultural identities of their students. Issues such as language barriers, cultural misunderstandings, and varying levels of prior knowledge can hinder effective communication and engagement. Additionally, the presence of stereotypes and biases, both within the educational system and among students, can create a divided and exclusionary classroom environment (Singh, et al, 2024).

To address the challenges posed by diverse cultural backgrounds, educators must adopt a proactive and multifaceted approach. Firstly, it is essential to create an inclusive classroom culture that values and respects all cultural perspectives. This can be achieved through open discussions about cultural differences, anti-bias training for staff and students, and the integration of multicultural materials into the curriculum. Secondly, educators should use a variety of teaching methods that cater to different learning styles and backgrounds, such as visual, auditory, and kinesthetic techniques, which can help bridge language and cultural gaps. Thirdly, involving parents and the wider community in the educational process can provide valuable insights and support for students from diverse backgrounds. Lastly, ongoing professional development for teachers can enhance their cultural competence, enabling them to better understand and respond to the needs of their diverse student population. By taking these steps, educators can create an environment where all students feel valued and are supported in achieving their full potential (Siham, 2024). Here are three steps to address the challenges of diverse cultural backgrounds in education (refer Table 1).

Table 1. Three steps to address the challenges of diverse cultural backgrounds in education

Number	Step	Elaboration
1	Cultural Competence Training for Educators:	- Conduct comprehensive training sessions for educators to develop cultural competence. This training should include workshops on cultural awareness, sensitivity to cultural differences, and effective cross-cultural communication strategies. By enhancing their understanding of various cultural backgrounds, educators can adapt their teaching methods to be more inclusive and responsive to the needs of all students.
2	Curriculum Adaptation and Inclusion:	- Revise and adapt the curriculum to include diverse cultural perspectives and experiences. This involves incorporating literature, history, and case studies from a wide range of cultures, ensuring that all students can see themselves reflected in the material. Additionally, create opportunities for students to share their own cultural experiences and knowledge, fostering a sense of belonging and respect for diversity within the classroom.
3	Community and Parental Engagement:	- Establish strong partnerships with the community and parents to support students from diverse backgrounds. Organize regular meetings and events to encourage dialogue between educators and families, allowing for the exchange of cultural insights and educational expectations. By involving parents and the community, educators can gain a deeper understanding of students' cultural contexts and create a supportive network that enhances the educational experience for all.

ARTIFICIAL INTELLIGENCE IN PERSONALIZING LEARNING EXPERIENCES

A. AI technologies for adaptive learning

Artificial intelligence (AI) in personalizing learning experiences refers to the use of advanced algorithms and machine learning techniques to tailor educational content and activities to individual learners' needs, preferences, and abilities. This approach leverages AI to analyze a wide range of data, such as students' past performance, learning styles, and engagement levels, to create a customized learning path. By identifying strengths and weaknesses, AI can dynamically adjust the difficulty level of materials, recommend appropriate resources, and provide real-time feedback, thereby enhancing the effectiveness and efficiency of the learning process (Suryanarayana, et al, 2024).

To effectively utilize AI technologies for adaptive learning, educators and instructional designers must first integrate AI systems into the learning management platforms. This involves collecting relevant data on learners, including their interactions with the course materials, assessment results, and self-reported preferences. Once the AI system has accumulated sufficient data, it can be trained to identify patterns and predict learners' needs. Educators can then use the system's recommendations to modify the curriculum, offer personalized learning resources, and provide targeted support. It's essential to regularly monitor and fine-tune the AI algorithms to ensure they continue to meet the evolving needs of the learners, thereby maximizing the potential for personalized and adaptive learning experiences (Yekollu, et al, 2024). Here are three steps to Implement AI technologies for adaptive learning (refer Table 2).

Table 2. Three steps to implement AI technologies for adaptive learning

Number	Step	Elaboration
1	Data Collection and Analysis:	- **Gather Data:** Begin by collecting comprehensive data on learners, including demographic information, prior knowledge, learning preferences, interaction logs, and performance metrics. - **Analyze Patterns:** Utilize AI algorithms to analyze the collected data to identify individual learning patterns, strengths, weaknesses, and engagement levels. - **Establish Baselines:** Set baseline metrics for each learner to serve as a reference point for measuring progress and tailoring the learning experience.
2	Adaptive Learning System Development:	- **Integrate AI Tools:** Incorporate AI tools into the learning management system (LMS) to enable real-time adaptation of the learning content and activities. - **Personalize Content Delivery:** Use the insights gained from data analysis to personalize the delivery of educational content, such as adjusting the difficulty level, sequencing of topics, and type of resources presented to each learner. - **Feedback Mechanisms:** Implement feedback mechanisms that allow the AI system to continuously learn from learner interactions and improve the personalization over time.
3	Continuous Improvement and Evaluation:	- **Monitor Performance:** Regularly monitor learner performance and system effectiveness to ensure that the adaptive learning is having the desired impact. - **Iterative Adjustments:** Make iterative adjustments to the AI algorithms and learning content based on ongoing data analysis and feedback from learners and educators. - **Assess Outcomes:** Conduct formal evaluations to assess the outcomes of the adaptive learning program against educational goals and make strategic improvements as needed.

B. Benefits of personalized learning in sustainability education

Personalized learning in sustainability education offers a range of benefits that enhance both the learning experience and the potential for long-term impact. By tailoring educational content to individual learners' interests, knowledge levels, and learning styles, personalized learning can significantly increase student engagement and motivation. This approach allows learners to explore sustainability topics that are relevant to their own lives and communities, fostering a deeper connection to the subject matter. Additionally, personalized learning can promote a more nuanced understanding of sustainability issues, as learners are able to delve into areas that resonate with them personally, leading to more informed and committed stewards of the environment (Ayeni, et al, 2024).

To effectively implement personalized learning in sustainability education, educators should start by assessing the diverse backgrounds, experiences, and learning preferences of their students. This can be done through surveys, interviews, or initial diagnostic assessments. With this information, educators can design a curriculum that offers a variety of learning pathways, allowing students to choose projects, case studies, and activities that align with their personal interests and goals. Utilizing technology, such as learning management systems equipped with AI, can further support the personalization process by adapting content delivery and providing real-time feedback. Additionally, educators should encourage self-reflection and goal-setting among students, and offer opportunities for hands-on, experiential learning that connects sustainability concepts to practical, real-world applications. Regular feedback and evaluation should be incorporated to ensure that the personalized learning experiences are meeting individual needs and contributing to a comprehensive understanding of sustainability (Kaswan, et al, 2024).

C. Examples of AI-enhanced personalized learning platforms

Knewton is an AI-enhanced personalized learning platform that has made significant strides in the education sector. It uses adaptive learning technology to provide personalized content to students based on their individual learning patterns and performance. Knewton's algorithms analyze how students interact with educational materials and adapt the content in real-time to better meet their needs. For instance, if a student is struggling with a particular concept, Knewton might provide additional resources or alternative explanations to help the student master the material. This level of customization ensures that each student receives an education that is tailored to their unique strengths and challenges (Sandhu, et al, 2024).

Another example is Smart Sparrow, a platform that allows educators to create interactive, adaptive learning experiences. Smart Sparrow's AI technology monitors student engagement and performance, providing insights that inform the adaptive nature of the content. Educators can design courses that automatically adjust the difficulty level and sequence of content based on how well students are grasping the material. For example, if a student demonstrates a strong understanding of a topic, the platform might suggest more advanced content, while a student who is struggling might receive additional practice or review materials. This ensures that all students can progress at their own pace and with appropriate support (Mahmoud, & Sørensen, 2024).

Finally, CogBooks is an AI-driven platform that offers personalized learning experiences by continuously analyzing student responses and adjusting the learning path accordingly. CogBooks' adaptive engine identifies gaps in students' knowledge and tailors the curriculum to address these gaps effectively. The platform uses a mix of text, video, and interactive simulations to cater to different learning styles. For example, if a student is excelling in a subject, CogBooks can challenge them with more complex problems, while simultaneously providing remedial support to a peer who is finding the same subject more difficult. This adaptive approach helps ensure that every student can achieve their full potential, regardless of their starting point (Mao, et al, 2024).

Incorporating real-world applications into the AI discussion significantly bolsters both credibility and engagement. For instance, Knewton employs AI-driven personalized learning paths, enabling the adaptation of sustainability content to cater to diverse learning styles and needs, thereby enhancing educational effectiveness (Zh, 2024). Similarly, Squirrel AI in China provides adaptive tutoring, dynamically adjusting lesson difficulty in response to student progress, ensuring optimal learning experiences in sustainability education (Thinger et al., 2024). Moreover, Google's AI for Climate Action empowers students to analyze environmental data, equipping them with the tools to tackle actual sustainability challenges (Al-Raeei, 2024). These examples not only illustrate the practical utility of AI in education but also underscore its potential to foster a deeper understanding of sustainability issues, demonstrating AI's tangible impact on real-world problems.

CASE STUDIES: AI-DRIVEN SUSTAINABILITY EDUCATION IN VARIOUS CULTURAL CONTEXTS

A. Case Study 1: AI-based learning in a Malaysian context

In Malaysia, an AI-driven sustainability education initiative has been integrated into the national curriculum, leveraging the country's diverse cultural tapestry to enhance learning outcomes. For instance, Malaysian student Aisha, a university student of Non-Chinese learner, reported that AI-powered sustainability lessons helped her understand local conservation challenges in a way traditional textbooks did not. Similarly, another university bumiputera student, Cheah, found that AI-based learning tools enabled interactive environmental simulations, making climate change concepts more tangible. By adapting to the linguistic and ethnic diversity inherent in Malaysian classrooms, the AI system personalizes educational content to cater to the individual learning styles of students, ensuring that topics such as environmental conservation and sustainable development resonate across different cultural backgrounds. This approach not only promotes a deeper understanding of sustainability principles but also fosters a sense of national unity and shared responsibility towards ecological stewardship among Malaysia's multicultural society (Mutambik, 2024).

In Malaysia, the adoption of AI-driven automation in education represents an alternative pathway to sustainable learning experiences, akin to the approach taken in the Kingdom of Saudi Arabia (KSA). By harnessing advanced AI technologies, Malaysian educators are able to create personalized learning environments that adapt to students' needs, thereby optimizing educational resources and reducing the ecological footprint associated with traditional teaching methods. This shift towards AI-assisted education not only aligns with the nation's commitment to sustainable development but also paves the way for a more inclusive and efficient educational system that can cater to a broad range of students, regardless of their socio-economic backgrounds. (Mutambik, 2024).

In Malaysia, Generation Z's engagement with artificial intelligence products has been a focal point for examining the impact on environmental sustainability, offering a cross-cultural comparison with other nations. Malaysian youth, who are digital natives, have readily adopted AI technologies in various aspects of their lives, from education to daily consumption habits. This has led to a notable shift towards more sustainable practices, such as the use of AI for energy management and waste reduction, which contrasts with traditional consumption patterns. However, the impact is not without its challenges, as the Increased use of AI devices also raises concerns about e-waste and energy consumption, highlighting the complex interplay between technological advancement and environmental stewardship in a multicultural society like Malaysia (Al-Sharafi, et al, 2023).

B. Case Study 2: AI-based learning in a China context

In China, the integration of AI-based learning into the educational system has been a strategic move to enhance the quality and accessibility of education, reflecting the nation's commitment to technological innovation and environmental sustainability. Chinese educators have leveraged AI to create personalized learning paths, catering to the individual needs of students in a country with a vast and diverse population. This approach has not only improved educational outcomes but has also contributed to a more resource-efficient system, reducing the need for physical materials and promoting a shift towards digital, eco-friendly learning resources, thereby aligning with China's broader goals for sustainable development (Pinkwart, & Liu, 2020).

In China, artificial intelligence-supported educational technologies have become a cornerstone of modern pedagogy, revolutionizing the way students learn and teachers instruct. These AI-driven tools, ranging from intelligent tutoring systems to adaptive learning platforms, are designed to identify and address individual learning gaps, personalize educational content, and streamline administrative tasks. The widespread adoption of these technologies in Chinese schools and universities not only enhances the efficiency and effectiveness of education but also positions the country at the forefront of educational innovation, aligning with its ambitious goals to foster a highly skilled and competitive workforce in the 21st century (Pinkwart, & Liu, 2020).

In China, the rapid emergence of artificial intelligence in education is transforming the landscape of teaching and learning through cutting-edge technologies, innovative models, and diverse applications. From virtual reality classrooms and intelligent tutoring systems to data analytics for personalized learning, AI is being harnessed to create immersive educational experiences, optimize teaching methods, and improve student outcomes. This integration of AI is not only reshaping traditional educational structures but also driving the development of new educational theories and practices, making China a leader in exploring the potential of AI to enhance and revolutionize the educational process (Koul, et al, 2022).

C. Lessons learned and commonalities across cases

The implementation of AI in education across various cultural contexts, such as Malaysia and China, reveals several key lessons learned and commonalities. Firstly, the success of AI-driven educational initiatives is heavily dependent on the ability to adapt to local cultural, linguistic, and educational norms. In both countries, the integration of AI has been more effective when it respects and enhances the existing educational framework rather than imposing a one-size-fits-all solution. Secondly, the personalization capabilities of AI have proven to be a significant advantage, enabling tailored learning experiences that cater to the diverse needs of students, thereby improving engagement and learning outcomes (Mohamed, 2023).

Moreover, a common challenge identified in both cases is the need for ongoing support and professional development for educators to effectively utilize AI tools. The successful adoption of AI in education often requires a mindset shift and the acquisition of new skills among teachers. Additionally, concerns about data privacy, the digital divide, and the long-term sustainability of AI technologies are universal issues that need to be addressed through policy and practice. Despite these challenges, the cross-case analysis underscores the potential of AI to drive sustainable educational practices and to foster a more inclusive and efficient educational ecosystem when implemented with careful consideration of local contexts and needs (Jia & Tu, 2024). The three key themes are shown in Table 3.

Table 3. Three key themes

Number	Commonality	Elaboration
1	Cultural Relevance	The AI-driven educational technology must be designed to resonate with the cultural, linguistic, and societal norms of the target learning community, ensuring that it is both accessible and engaging for students from diverse backgrounds.
2	Personalization and Adaptability	The technology should offer a high degree of personalization, adapting to individual learning styles, paces, and preferences, while also being flexible enough to accommodate different educational curricula and standards.
3	Sustainability and Scalability	The AI solution should be environmentally sustainable, with a minimal ecological footprint, and capable of scaling effectively to serve a large number of students without compromising on quality or performance.

EMPIRICAL EVIDENCE: ASSESSING THE IMPACT OF AI ON CULTURAL ADAPTATION IN SUSTAINABILITY EDUCATION

A. Methodology and data collection

To assess the impact of AI on cultural adaptation in sustainability education, a mixed-methods approach was employed, combining quantitative and qualitative data collection methods. Quantitative data were gathered through standardized tests, learning analytics, and surveys that measured student performance, engagement levels, and perception of cultural relevance in AI-enhanced educational modules. These metrics were compared across different cultural groups to identify patterns and trends.

Qualitative data were collected through in-depth interviews with educators, students, and stakeholders, as well as through observations in the classroom setting. These methods aimed to capture nuanced insights into the experiences and perceptions of AI's role in cultural adaptation and its effects on sustainability education. Additionally, case studies were developed to provide detailed contextual information on the implementation of AI in various educational environments, allowing for a thorough analysis of the impact on cultural adaptation and sustainability outcomes.

B. Key findings and their implications

The study, which included a total of 200 respondents evenly split between China and Malaysia, found that AI-driven educational tools were effective in engaging students and enhancing their understanding of sustainability education. With 100 students from each country participating, the tools demonstrated their ability to cater to different cultural backgrounds, indicating a promising approach to bridging cultural gaps in educational settings.

The study's findings indicate that AI-driven educational tools in sustainability education have a positive impact on student engagement, understanding, and cultural adaptation. On average, the engagement level was rated at 4.4185 (out of 5), with a standard deviation of 0.9626, while the understanding level was slightly lower at 4.1706 (SD: 0.6251). The cultural adaptation score was the highest among the three metrics, averaging at 4.5363 (SD: 0.3226). Across all metrics, the minimum rating was 1 and the maximum was 5, based on a sample size of 200 students. This suggests that AI tools effectively tailor content to diverse cultural contexts, enhancing the overall educational experience in sustainability (refer table 4).

Table 4. Descriptive statistics of quantitative analysis

Metric	*engagement level*	*understanding level*	*cultural adaptation score*
mean	4.4185	4.1706	4.5363
standard deviation	0.9626	0.6251	0.3226
minimum	1	1	1
maximum	5	5	5
sample size	200	200	200

On engagement level, the Chinese interviewees expressed high levels of engagement with the AI-driven educational tools, finding the content relatable and interesting due to its cultural tailoring. They also noted a significant improvement in their understanding of sustainability concepts, as the AI tools effectively broke down complex ideas into easily digestible parts that resonated with their cultural background. Furthermore, the interviewees appreciated the cultural adaptation of the tools, which showed respect for Chinese traditions and values, thereby enhancing their connection to the material and motivation to learn. The Malaysian interviewees reported a high degree of engagement with the AI educational tools, which effectively integrated elements of Malaysian culture into the sustainability lessons, making the learning process more significant and applicable to their lives. They also praised the culturally sensitive and intuitive nature of the AI-driven content, which illuminated the relevance of sustainability issues within their community and provided a Malaysian-centric approach to addressing these issues. Additionally, the interviewees enjoyed the interactive and fun learning experience, appreciating how local customs and practices were woven into the educational material, creating a more conversational and less didactic learning environment.

On understanding level, the Chinese interviewee found the AI tools to be highly effective in simplifying complex sustainability concepts, making them easily understandable and culturally relevant. The AI-driven education provided clear, society-specific examples and explanations that demystified sustainability topics, allowing the interviewee to grasp their significance within the Chinese context. The interactive nature of the learning experience, coupled with the AI's sensitivity to cultural nuances, significantly enhanced the interviewee's understanding and helped bridge the gap between sustainability principles and personal life in China. The Malaysian interviewee was impressed by the AI educational tools' ability to simplify and contextualize sustainability education, using Malaysian-specific examples to enhance understanding. The AI's customization to the local perspective made sustainability topics more accessible and relevant to daily life, providing a clear picture of their direct impact. This tailored approach not only clarified sustainability concepts but also deepened the interviewee's understanding of how Malaysians can uniquely contribute to a sustainable future.

On cultural adaptation, the Chinese interviewee appreciated how the AI educational tools respected and integrated Chinese culture into the sustainability curriculum, which fostered a sense of connection and motivation to learn. The technology's ability to adapt to the cultural context, rather than presenting generic information, was seen as a refreshing and appreciated approach. The seamless cultural adaptation made the content feel like a natural part of the Chinese cultural narrative, creating a familiar and enlightening learning experience. The Malaysian interviewee emphasized the AI tools' cultural sensitivity and adaptation to Malaysian customs and lifestyle, which significantly enhanced the relevance and applicability of the sustainability lessons. The educational materials went beyond language to deeply understand and respect the Malaysian way of life, seamlessly integrating sustainability into it. This outstanding cultural sensitivity made the sustainability education feel like an intrinsic part of the Malaysian cultural experience, rather than an external imposition (refer Table 5).

Table 5. Interview quotations

	Interview quotation		
	Engagement level	**Understanding level**	**Cultural adaptation**
China interviewee 1	1. "The AI-driven educational tools really captured my attention and kept me engaged throughout the sustainability lessons. I felt like the content was tailored to my cultural perspective, making it more relatable and interesting."	1. "The AI tools really broke down complex sustainability concepts into digestible parts that I could easily understand. It was like having a teacher who knows exactly how to explain things in a way that resonates with my cultural background."	1. "The AI educational tools showed a deep respect for our Chinese culture, incorporating our traditions and values into the sustainability curriculum. This cultural adaptation made me feel more connected to the material and motivated to learn."
China interviewee 2	2. "I was impressed by how the AI technology could adapt the learning materials to reflect our Chinese values and traditions. It made the sustainability concepts easier to understand and remember."	2. "I've always found sustainability topics to be a bit abstract, but the AI-driven education made everything clear. The examples and explanations were so relatable to our Chinese society that I could finally grasp the essence of what sustainability means for us."	2. "It was refreshing to see how the AI technology could adapt to our cultural context. It didn't just present generic information; it really tried to align the sustainability messages with our Chinese heritage, which I appreciated."
China interviewee 3	3. "The interactive nature of the AI tools made the learning experience enjoyable. It was like having a personal tutor who understood my cultural context and helped me connect with the subject matter on a deeper level."	3. "The interactive learning experience with AI really enhanced my understanding. The cultural nuances were not overlooked, and this attention to detail helped me to connect the dots between sustainability and my own life in China."	3. "The cultural adaptation in the AI-driven education was seamless. It felt like the content was a natural extension of our own cultural narrative, making the learning experience both familiar and enlightening."
Malaysia interviewee 1	1. "The AI educational tools were incredibly engaging. They incorporated elements of our Malaysian culture into the sustainability lessons, which made the learning process more meaningful and relevant to us."	1. "The AI educational tools were fantastic in simplifying sustainability education. They used examples from our Malaysian context, which made it so much easier for me to understand the importance and implications of sustainability here."	1. "The AI tools were designed with our Malaysian culture in mind. They reflected our customs and way of life, which made the sustainability lessons much more meaningful and applicable to our reality."

The key findings of the study revealed that AI-driven educational tools significantly enhanced cultural adaptation in sustainability education. Students from diverse cultural backgrounds reported higher levels of engagement and understanding when AI technologies were used to tailor content to their cultural contexts. This suggests that AI can bridge cultural gaps and make sustainability education more relatable and effective. However, the study also highlighted that the success of such tools is contingent upon the careful design and continuous refinement of the AI algorithms to ensure they accurately reflect and respect the cultural nuances of the target audience.

The Implications of these findings are multifaceted. For educators and policymakers, it underscores the importance of investing in AI technologies that are sensitive to cultural diversity, as this can lead to more inclusive and impactful sustainability education. For AI developers, the findings point to the need for ongoing research and collaboration with cultural experts to refine AI systems, ensuring they are not only technologically advanced but also culturally appropriate. This could lead to a paradigm shift in how educational technologies are developed and implemented, with a stronger emphasis on cultural intelligence and adaptability (Romero, 2024).

C. Limitations and future research directions

Despite the significant insights gained, the study faced several limitations. The sample size and geographic scope of the research may not have been representative enough to draw broad, generalizable conclusions about the impact of AI on cultural adaptation in sustainability education across all cultural contexts. Additionally, the reliance on self-reported data and subjective measures of cultural adaptation could introduce bias. The study also did not fully explore the potential long-term effects of AI on educational outcomes and cultural dynamics, which could be critical for understanding the sustained impact of these technologies.

Future research should aim to overcome these limitations by conducting larger-scale, longitudinal studies that include a more diverse range of cultural and educational settings. Researchers should also focus on developing more objective measures of cultural adaptation and the effectiveness of AI in sustainability education. Exploring the ethical implications of AI in education, as well as the potential for AI to exacerbate or mitigate existing educational inequalities, should be a priority. Moreover, investigating the role of AI in fostering intercultural competence and its potential to contribute to broader sustainability goals would provide valuable insights for educators, policymakers, and technology developers (Abulibdeh, et al, 2024).

OVERCOMING CHALLENGES: INTERDISCIPLINARY COLLABORATION AND THE ROLE OF EDUCATORS

A. Importance of interdisciplinary collaboration in AI-enhanced sustainability education

Interdisciplinary collaboration in AI-enhanced sustainability education refers to the integration of knowledge, methods, and expertise from various academic fields to create a more comprehensive and effective educational experience. This approach leverages the strengths of different disciplines, such as environmental science, computer science, social studies, and humanities, to address the multifaceted challenges of sustainability. By combining AI technologies with interdisciplinary insights, educators can design learning experiences that not only impart technical skills but also foster critical thinking, problem-solving, and a holistic understanding of sustainability issues. This collaborative approach ensures that the educational content is rich, diverse, and reflective of the complex nature of sustainable development (Husain, 2023).

To foster interdisciplinary collaboration in AI-enhanced sustainability education, educators must first establish a culture of collaboration within and across academic departments. This can be achieved by creating cross-disciplinary teams that work together to develop curricula, share resources, and co-teach courses. Secondly, educators should design learning activities that require students to engage with multiple perspectives and approaches, encouraging them to apply insights from different disciplines to sustainability problems. Additionally, leveraging AI tools can facilitate collaboration by providing platforms for virtual teamwork, data sharing, and real-time feedback. Educators should also encourage professional development opportunities that focus on interdisciplinary skills and AI proficiency. By doing so, they can equip themselves and their students with the necessary tools to tackle the intricate challenges of sustainability through a collaborative and technologically advanced lens (Zahid, 2024).

B. Strategies for educators to bridge cultural gaps

One strategy for educators to bridge cultural gaps is to intentionally incorporate diverse cultural perspectives into the curriculum. This involves going beyond a one-size-fits-all approach to education and ensuring that the content reflects a variety of cultural backgrounds, histories, and experiences. Educators can achieve this by including case studies, examples, and readings that are relevant to the cultural contexts of their students. By doing so, they create a more inclusive learning environment where students from different cultural backgrounds can see themselves and their traditions represented, fostering a sense of belonging and relevance in the educational process (Hider, & Saleem, 2024).

Another effective strategy is to facilitate cross-cultural dialogues and exchanges within the classroom. Educators can organize group discussions, debates, and projects that encourage students to share their cultural insights and experiences. This not only enriches the learning environment with diverse viewpoints but also helps students to develop empathy and understanding for cultures other than their own. Additionally, educators can establish partnerships with schools or universities in other countries to enable virtual or physical exchanges, allowing students to engage directly with peers from different cultural backgrounds and learn from one another (Dwivedi, et al, 2024).

The third strategy involves leveraging technology to enhance cultural awareness and bridge gaps. Educators can use AI-driven educational tools to tailor content to the cultural backgrounds of their students, as mentioned in the study findings. These tools can provide personalized learning experiences that resonate with individual cultural contexts. Additionally, educators can use multimedia resources such as videos, podcasts, and interactive maps to give students immersive experiences of different cultures. This use of technology not only makes learning more engaging but also helps to demystify and appreciate the cultural diversity that exists within the classroom and beyond (Henriksen, et al, 2024). The steps in implementing the strategies are shown in Table 6.

Table 6. Steps in implementing the strategies

Number	Step	Elaboration
1	Needs Assessment and Curriculum Development	The first step in implementing strategies to bridge cultural gaps is to conduct a thorough needs assessment. Educators should evaluate the current curriculum to identify areas where cultural inclusion is lacking. This involves gathering feedback from students, parents, and other stakeholders to understand the cultural diversity within the classroom. Based on this assessment, educators can then develop or refine the curriculum to include a broader range of cultural perspectives. This may involve selecting new textbooks, creating original teaching materials, or integrating multimedia resources that represent various cultures.
2	Training and Professional Development	Once the curriculum is developed, the next step is to ensure that educators are equipped to teach in a culturally inclusive manner. This requires providing training and professional development focused on cultural competence and the use of technology to enhance cultural awareness. Educators should be trained to recognize and address their own biases, to use culturally responsive teaching methods, and to effectively facilitate cross-cultural dialogues. Professional development can also include workshops on how to use AI and other technologies to create personalized and culturally relevant learning experiences.
3	Implementation and Continuous Evaluation	The final step is the actual implementation of the curriculum and strategies in the classroom, followed by continuous evaluation. Educators should begin to apply the new teaching methods, monitor student engagement and learning outcomes, and gather feedback from students and colleagues. This feedback is crucial for identifying what is working well and what may need adjustment. Regular assessments and reflections can help educators refine their approaches, ensuring that the strategies for bridging cultural gaps are effective and sustainable over time. Additionally, establishing a system for ongoing evaluation can help maintain a commitment to cultural inclusivity and continuous improvement in the educational environment.

C. Professional development for educators in AI and cultural sensitivity

Professional development for educators in AI and cultural sensitivity refers to the ongoing process of learning and growth that educators undergo to enhance their knowledge, skills, and attitudes in the fields of artificial intelligence and cultural sensitivity. This type of development is crucial for educators to effectively integrate AI tools and resources into their teaching practices while ensuring that their approaches are inclusive and respectful of diverse cultural backgrounds. By engaging in professional development in these areas, educators can better prepare their students for an increasingly technology-driven world and foster a learning environment that celebrates and values cultural diversity (Ranson, & Zhang, 2021).

To engage in professional development for educators in AI and cultural sensitivity, several steps can be taken. First, educators should seek out workshops, webinars, and training sessions that focus on AI tools and their applications in education. Additionally, they can participate in online courses or certificate programs that delve into the ethical considerations and social implications of AI. To enhance cultural sensitivity, educators can attend workshops on cultural competence, diversity, and inclusion, as well as engage in self-reflection and peer discussions to challenge their own biases and assumptions. Collaborating with colleagues from diverse backgrounds and participating in cultural exchange programs can also provide valuable insights and perspectives. Finally, educators should continually update their knowledge and skills by staying informed about the latest developments in AI and cultural sensitivity through research, professional networks, and ongoing education (Islam, et al, 2024).

CONTRIBUTIONS TO A SUSTAINABLE AND EQUITABLE GLOBAL SOCIETY

A. Fostering a deeper understanding of sustainability among students

Fostering a deeper understanding of sustainability among students involves equipping them with the knowledge, skills, and attitudes necessary to recognize and address the complex environmental, social, and economic challenges of our time. This process goes beyond the basics of recycling and conservation to include a comprehensive grasp of systems thinking, ecological principles, and the interconnectedness of human activities with the natural world. It aims to empower students to make informed decisions and take responsible actions that promote the well-being of current and future generations, while also considering the justice and equity dimensions of sustainability (Mohamed, 2023).

To foster a deeper understanding of sustainability among students, educators can implement a variety of strategies. Firstly, integrating sustainability themes across the curriculum can ensure that students encounter these concepts repeatedly in different contexts, from science to social studies to literature. Hands-on, experiential learning opportunities, such as school gardens, field trips to local ecosystems, or community service projects, can make sustainability concepts tangible and relevant. Additionally, using project-based learning to address real-world sustainability issues can encourage critical thinking and problem-solving skills. Educators can also model sustainable practices in the classroom and school environment and encourage student leadership in sustainability initiatives. Finally, partnerships with local businesses, non-profits, and government agencies can provide students with insights into career paths related to sustainability and the chance to contribute to real-world sustainability efforts (Sywelem, 2024).

B. Enhancing cross-cultural communication and collaboration

Enhancing cross-cultural communication and collaboration refers to the process of improving the ability of individuals from different cultural backgrounds to effectively exchange information, ideas, and perspectives. It involves developing an awareness and understanding of cultural differences, as well as the skills necessary to work together harmoniously in diverse settings. This process is essential in today's globalized world, where multicultural teams and international partnerships are becoming the norm. By enhancing cross-cultural communication and collaboration, individuals and organizations can leverage diversity to drive innovation, solve complex problems, and build stronger, more inclusive communities (Zmire & Chen, 2024).

To enhance cross-cultural communication and collaboration, several strategies can be employed. First, it is important to promote cultural awareness and empathy through training programs that educate individuals about different cultural norms, values, and communication styles. This can include workshops, simulations, and cultural immersion experiences. Second, organizations should establish clear communication guidelines that accommodate diverse communication preferences and encourage open, respectful dialogue. Encouraging team-building activities that foster mutual respect, and trust can also help break down cultural barriers. Additionally, providing language support and translation services can ensure that all team members can participate fully in discussions. It is also beneficial to create platforms for diverse voices to be heard and to encourage the sharing of personal experiences and perspectives. Finally, leadership plays a crucial role in setting the tone for inclusive behavior and in creating an environment where cross-cultural collaboration is valued and rewarded (Xia, et al, 2024).

C. Developing globally aware and culturally competent citizens

Developing globally aware and culturally competent citizens involves nurturing individuals who have a broad understanding of the world's cultures, economies, and political systems, and who are equipped to engage respectfully and effectively with people from diverse backgrounds. This process aims to cultivate empathy, open-mindedness, and the ability to analyze global issues from multiple perspectives. Globally aware and culturally competent citizens are not only aware of global interconnectedness but are also active participants in creating a more just and inclusive world. They are prepared to address complex challenges, advocate for human rights, and contribute to sustainable development on both local and international levels (Chauhan, et al, 2024).

To develop globally aware and culturally competent citizens, educational institutions, communities, and policymakers must collaborate to implement a multifaceted approach. Educational curricula should include interdisciplinary courses that focus on global issues, world history, and cultural studies, providing students with a comprehensive understanding of different cultures and global challenges. Experiential learning opportunities, such as study abroad programs, service-learning projects, and internships with international organizations, can offer hands-on experiences that deepen cultural understanding. Additionally, promoting language learning and offering language immersion programs can enhance communication skills and cultural empathy. Schools and universities can also foster a diverse and inclusive environment that encourages interaction and dialogue among students from various cultural backgrounds. Community engagement initiatives can connect students with local and global communities, allowing them to apply their knowledge and skills in real-world settings. Finally, continuous reflection and assessment of one's own cultural biases and assumptions are crucial, and this can be facilitated through workshops, mentorship programs, and peer-to-peer discussions focused on cultural competence (Stecyk, & Miciuła, 2024).

CONCLUSION

A. Summary of key points

The key points of this book chapter revolve around the integration of cultural dimensions in AI-enhanced sustainability education. It underscores the necessity of adapting teaching methods to cater to a culturally diverse global student population. The chapter delves into the capabilities of Artificial Intelligence in creating personalized educational experiences that resonate with the individual cultural contexts of learners. Through the analysis of case studies and empirical research, the chapter illustrates AI's potential in tailoring sustainability education, thereby enhancing student comprehension and involvement. Furthermore, the importance of interdisciplinary teamwork and educators' role in narrowing cultural divides are emphasized, with the ultimate goal of fostering a sustainable and equitable global community. To maximize AI's potential in sustainability education: Educators should integrate AI-driven adaptive learning to make sustainability education more personalized and engaging. Policymakers must ensure AI remains ethical, bias-free, and accessible to all students. AI developers should collaborate with cultural experts to ensure AI-driven sustainability lessons respect diverse worldviews.

In summary, the chapter emphasizes the critical need for culturally sensitive and inclusive sustainability education in the face of global challenges. It advocates for the use of AI to customize learning, ensuring that it resonates with the cultural nuances of students worldwide. By showcasing practical examples and the significance of cross-disciplinary collaboration, the chapter underscores the potential for AI to promote a more profound understanding of sustainability and the pivotal role educators play in this transformative process. The overall aim is to equip students with the knowledge and tools necessary to contribute to a more sustainable and equitable world, respectful of the rich tapestry of global cultures.

B. The future of AI-enhanced sustainability education

The future of AI-enhanced sustainability education is a vision of educational systems that leverage the power of Artificial Intelligence to create dynamic, personalized, and culturally attuned learning experiences. This approach will enable students to grasp the complexities of sustainability challenges and to develop the skills necessary to innovate and implement solutions. The future holds the promise of AI technologies that can adapt to the learning styles, cultural backgrounds, and prior knowledge of individual students, thereby making education more effective and inclusive. It also involves the integration of AI in curriculum development, assessment, and the fostering of collaborative learning environments that transcend physical and cultural boundaries (Easouh, et al, 2024

To approach the future of AI-enhanced sustainability education, several strategic steps are essential. Firstly, educators and policymakers must invest in research and development to innovate AI tools specifically designed for educational purposes. This includes creating AI systems that can understand and respect cultural differences. Secondly, teacher training programs must be updated to include proficiency in AI applications and the ethical considerations of using such technologies in the classroom. Curriculum design should be overhauled to integrate AI seamlessly, ensuring that it supports sustainability education goals. Additionally, schools and universities should form partnerships with technology companies and other educational institutions to share resources and best practices. It is also crucial to engage with students and communities to understand their needs and to involve them in the co-creation of AI-enhanced learning experiences. Finally, ongoing evaluation and adaptation of AI-enhanced education programs will be necessary to ensure they remain relevant, effective, and equitable (Kayyali, 2024). While AI personalizes sustainability education, ethical challenges remain. Algorithmic bias can lead to culturally inappropriate content, while data privacy risks raise concerns about student information security. Additionally, AI-driven education must remain accessible to underprivileged communities, preventing the digital divide from widening.

C. Final thoughts on the importance of cultural integration in sustainability education

The importance of cultural integration in sustainability education cannot be overstated; it is the cornerstone of creating a holistic and inclusive approach to teaching and learning. By integrating cultural dimensions, sustainability education becomes more than a transfer of knowledge—it becomes a transformative process that respects and values the diverse experiences and worldviews of students. Cultural integration ensures that the principles of sustainability are not only understood but also felt and lived, fostering a sense of collective responsibility and action. It empowers students to see themselves as part of the solution, recognizing that sustainable practices are deeply rooted in cultural contexts and that diverse perspectives are essential for addressing global challenges (Juarez, et al, 2024).

To achieve cultural integration in sustainability education, a multifaceted and intentional strategy is required. Educators must first acknowledge and celebrate the cultural diversity within their classrooms, creating an environment where all voices are heard and respected. Curriculum development should incorporate a variety of cultural perspectives, with content that reflects the historical and contemporary contributions of different societies to sustainability practices. Teachers can use culturally responsive teaching methods that draw on students' backgrounds and experiences, making learning more relevant and engaging. Additionally, educational institutions should establish partnerships with local communities and cultural organizations to bring in guest speakers, conduct field studies, and participate in community-driven sustainability projects. Professional development for educators should focus on building cultural competence and providing tools for integrating cultural dimensions into their teaching. Finally, assessment strategies should evaluate not only the acquisition of knowledge but also the development of cultural awareness and empathy among students (Wu, 2024).

REFERENCES

Abulibdeh, A., Zaidan, E., & Abulibdeh, R. (2024). Navigating the confluence of artificial intelligence and education for sustainable development in the era of industry 4.0: Challenges, opportunities, and ethical dimensions. *Journal of Cleaner Production*, *437*, 140527. DOI: 10.1016/j.jclepro.2023.140527

Al-Raeei, M. (2024). Artificial intelligence for climate resilience: Advancing sustainable goals in SDGs 11 and 13 and its relationship to pandemics. *Discover Sustainability*, *5*(1), 513. DOI: 10.1007/s43621-024-00775-5

Al-Sharafi, M. A., Al-Emran, M., Arpaci, I., Iahad, N. A., AlQudah, A. A., Iranmanesh, M., & Al-Qaysi, N. (2023). Generation Z use of artificial intelligence products and its impact on environmental sustainability: A cross-cultural comparison. *Computers in Human Behavior*, *143*, 107708. DOI: 10.1016/j.chb.2023.107708

Ayeni, O. O., Al Hamad, N. M., Chisom, O. N., Osawaru, B., & Adewusi, O. E. (2024). AI in education: A review of personalized learning and educational technology. *GSC Advanced Research and Reviews*, *18*(2), 261–271. DOI: 10.30574/gscarr.2024.18.2.0062

Chauhan, D., Bahad, P., & Jain, J. K. (2024). Sustainable AI: Environmental Implications, Challenges, and Opportunities. Explainable AI (XAI) for Sustainable Development, 1-15.

Dwivedi, D. N., Mahanty, G., & nath Dwivedi, V. (2024). Intelligent Conservation: A Comprehensive Study on AI-Enhanced Environmental Monitoring and Preservation. In The Convergence of Self-Sustaining Systems With AI and IoT (pp. 215-226). IGI Global.

Easouh, F. Y. J., Oweis, T. E., & Makahleh, H. A. (2024). A Bibliometric Lens on the Future: How AI continues to transform education institutions. Human Systems Management, (Preprint), 1-20.

Edeni, C. A., Adeleye, O. O., & Adeniyi, I. S. (2024). The role of AI-enhanced tools in overcoming socioeconomic barriers in education: A conceptual analysis. *World Journal of Advanced Research and Reviews*, *21*(3), 944–951. DOI: 10.30574/wjarr.2024.21.3.0780

Edwards-Fapohunda, M. O., & Adediji, M. A. (2024). Sustainable Development of Distance Learning in Continuing Adult Education: The Impact of Artificial Intelligence. *Iconic Research and Engineering Journals*, *8*(1), 113–114.

Eguchi, A., Okada, H., & Muto, Y. (2021). Contextualizing AI education for K-12 students to enhance their learning of AI literacy through culturally responsive approaches. *Kunstliche Intelligenz*, *35*(2), 153–161. DOI: 10.1007/s13218-021-00737-3 PMID: 34376922

Henriksen, D., Mishra, P., & Stern, R. (2024). Creative Learning for Sustainability in a World of AI: Action, Mindset, Values. *Sustainability (Basel)*, *16*(11), 4451. DOI: 10.3390/su16114451

Hider, U., & Saleem, K. (2024). Sustainable Strategies for Education Enhancement: The Role of AI in Curriculum Development.

Husain, N. (2023). Educational Renaissance: Unleashing the Potential of Interdisciplinary AI Integration. *Journal of Environmental Science and Technology*, *2*(1), 159–166.

Islam, A., Ali, R., Singh, G., Islam, B., Islam, A., & Hossain, S. (2024, May). An Evaluation of AI-Enhanced Collaborative Learning Platforms. In 2024 International Conference on Communication, Computer Sciences and Engineering (IC3SE) (pp. 207-211). IEEE.

Jia, X. H., & Tu, J. C. (2024). Towards a New Conceptual Model of AI-Enhanced Learning for College Students: The Roles of Artificial Intelligence Capabilities, General Self-Efficacy, Learning Motivation, and Critical Thinking Awareness. *Systems*, *12*(3), 74. DOI: 10.3390/systems12030074

Juarez, A., Rabago, J., Pliego, L., Salazar, G., & Gonzalez, P. (2024). INTEGRATING AI AND VR IN GLOBAL CLASSROOM: ENHANCING DESIGN COMPETENCIES THROUGH MULTICULTURAL COLLABORATION. In EDULEARN24 Proceedings (pp. 89-97). IATED.

Kaswan, K. S., Dhatterwal, J. S., & Ojha, R. P. (2024). AI in personalized learning. In *Advances in Technological Innovations in Higher Education* (pp. 103–117). CRC Press. DOI: 10.1201/9781003376699-9

Kayyali, M. (2024). Future possibilities and challenges of AI in education. In *Transforming education with generative AI: Prompt engineering and synthetic content creation* (pp. 118–137). IGI Global. DOI: 10.4018/979-8-3693-1351-0.ch006

Koul, R., Wang, T., & Yu, H. (2022). *Artificial Intelligence in Education: Emerging Technologies, Models and Applications* (Cheng, E. C., Ed.). Springer.

Mahmoud, C. F., & Sørensen, J. T. (2024). Artificial Intelligence in Personalized Learning with a Focus on Current Developments and Future Prospects. *Research and Advances in Education*, *3*(8), 25–31. DOI: 10.56397/RAE.2024.08.04

Mao, J., Chen, B., & Liu, J. C. (2024). Generative artificial intelligence in education and its implications for assessment. *TechTrends*, *68*(1), 58–66. DOI: 10.1007/s11528-023-00911-4

Mohamed, A. Z. Z. O. U. A. Z. I. (2023). Fostering sustainable Development Through Artificial Intelligence in Education (ESD): A Comprehensive Evaluation Framework and Key Criteria Analysis.

Mutambik, I. (2024). The Use of AI-Driven Automation to Enhance Student Learning Experiences in the KSA: An Alternative Pathway to Sustainable Education. *Sustainability (Basel)*, *16*(14), 5970. DOI: 10.3390/su16145970

Patil, V. (2024). The Potential of AI in Enhancing Education Access and Quality.

Pinkwart, N., & Liu, S. (Eds.). (2020). *Artificial intelligence supported educational technologies*. Springer. DOI: 10.1007/978-3-030-41099-5

Ranson, H., & Zhang, J. (2021). AI-ASSISTED RESPONSIBLE MANAGEMENT EDUCATION. Principles of Responsible Management Education (PRME) in the Age of Artificial Intelligence (AI): Opportunities, Threats, and the Way Forward, 43.

Romero, M. (2024). Collaborative Design of AI-Enhanced Learning Activities. arXiv preprint arXiv:2407.06660.

Sandhu, R., Channi, H. K., Ghai, D., Cheema, G. S., & Kaur, M. (2024). An Introduction to Generative AI Tools for Education 2030. Integrating Generative AI in Education to Achieve Sustainable Development Goals, 1-28.

Shwedeh, F., Salloum, S. A., Aburayya, A., Fatin, B., Elbadawi, M. A., Al Ghurabli, Z., & Al Dabbagh, T. (2024). AI Adoption and Educational Sustainability in Higher Education in the UAE. In *Artificial Intelligence in Education: The Power and Dangers of ChatGPT in the Classroom* (pp. 201–229). Springer Nature Switzerland.

Siham, E. K. (2024). Tech-Enhanced Ties: AI's Role in Cross-Cultural Peer Education. PROCEEDINGS BOOK, 671.

Singh, E., Vasishta, P., & Singla, A. (2024). AI-enhanced education: Exploring the impact of AI literacy on generation Z's academic performance in Northern India. *Quality Assurance in Education.*

Stecyk, A., & Miciuła, I. (2024). Artificial Intelligence Integrated Energy Education Framework. A Holistic Approach.

Suryanarayana, K. S., Kandi, V. P., Pavani, G., Rao, A. S., Rout, S., & Krishna, T. S. R. (2024). Artificial Intelligence Enhanced Digital Learning for the Sustainability of Education Management System. *The Journal of High Technology Management Research*, *35*(2), 100495. DOI: 10.1016/j.hitech.2024.100495

Sywelem, M. M. G. (2024). Artificial Intelligenc and the Sustainability of Educational Services: An Overview. *WORLD (Oakland, Calif.)*, *10*(1), 8–17.

Thinger, C., Verma, A. S., Thakore, A. K., Purohit, P., Kalyanwat, B., & Sikarwal, P. (2024). AIED-Artificial Intelligence in Education World-Opportunities, Challenges, and Future Research. Challenges, and Future Research (November 14, 2024).

Wu, Y. (2024). Revolutionizing Learning and Teaching: Crafting Personalized, Culturally Responsive Curriculum in the AI Era. *Creative Education*, *15*(8), 1642–1651. DOI: 10.4236/ce.2024.158098

Xia, Y., Shin, S. Y., & Kim, J. C. (2024). Cross-cultural intelligent language learning system (cils): Leveraging ai to facilitate language learning strategies in cross-cultural communication. *Applied Sciences (Basel, Switzerland)*, *14*(13), 5651. DOI: 10.3390/app14135651

Yekollu, R. K., Bhimraj Ghuge, T., Sunil Biradar, S., Haldikar, S. V., & Farook Mohideen Abdul Kader, O. (2024, February). AI-Driven Personalized Learning Paths: Enhancing Education Through Adaptive Systems. In International Conference on Smart Data Intelligence (pp. 507-517). Singapore: Springer Nature Singapore.

Zahid, H. (2024). Educational Renaissance: Unleashing the Potential of Interdisciplinary AI Integration.

Zh, A. M. (2024). ARTIFICIAL INTELLIGENCE IN EDUCATION: POSSIBILITIES FOR PERSONALIZING LEARNING. Экономика и социум, (11-1 (126)), 1317-1323.

Zmire, Z., & Chen, X. (2024). AI's Role in Enhancing Cross Cultural Competence and Leadership through Online Education Programs. In *Proceedings of the International Conference on New Findings in Humanities and Social Sciences* (Vol. 1, No. 1, pp. 1-16). DOI: 10.33422/hsconf.v1i1.268

ADDITIONAL READING

Henriksen, D., Mishra, P., & Stern, R. (2024). Creative Learning for Sustainability in a World of AI: Action, Mindset, Values. *Sustainability (Basel)*, *16*(11), 4451. DOI: 10.3390/su16114451

Hider, U., & Saleem, K. Sustainable Strategies for Education Enhancement: The Role of AI in Curriculum Development.

Mutambik, I. (2024). The Use of AI-Driven Automation to Enhance Student Learning Experiences in the KSA: An Alternative Pathway to Sustainable Education. *Sustainability (Basel)*, *16*(14), 5970. DOI: 10.3390/su16145970

Shwedeh, F., Salloum, S. A., Aburayya, A., Fatin, B., Elbadawi, M. A., Al Ghurabli, Z., & Al Dabbagh, T. (2024). AI Adoption and Educational Sustainability in Higher Education in the UAE. In *Artificial Intelligence in Education: The Power and Dangers of ChatGPT in the Classroom* (pp. 201–229). Springer Nature Switzerland.

Singh, E., Vasishta, P., & Singla, A. (2024). AI-enhanced education: Exploring the impact of AI literacy on generation Z's academic performance in Northern India. *Quality Assurance in Education*.

Suryanarayana, K. S., Kandi, V. P., Pavani, G., Rao, A. S., Rout, S., & Krishna, T. S. R. (2024). Artificial Intelligence Enhanced Digital Learning for the Sustainability of Education Management System. *The Journal of High Technology Management Research*, *35*(2), 100495. DOI: 10.1016/j.hitech.2024.100495

Yang, Y., Sun, W., Sun, D., & Salas-Pilco, S. Z. (2024). Navigating the AI-Enhanced STEM education landscape: A decade of insights, trends, and opportunities. *Research in Science & Technological Education*, •••, 1–25. DOI: 10.1080/02635143.2024.2370764

KEY TERMS AND DEFINITIONS

AI-enhanced education: The integration of artificial intelligence technologies into educational systems to improve learning outcomes, personalization, and efficiency. This includes tools like intelligent tutoring systems, adaptive learning platforms, and automated assessment.

Cultural dimensions: Refers to the various aspects of culture that can be measured and compared across different societies. These dimensions often include values, beliefs, behaviors, and societal norms that influence how individuals and groups interact and perceive the world.

Sustainability: The concept of meeting present needs without compromising the ability of future generations to meet their own needs. In an educational context, sustainability education focuses on fostering knowledge, skills, and attitudes necessary to address environmental, social, and economic challenges.

Global learner community: A diverse group of learners connected through educational platforms, with members from various cultural, geographical, and socioeconomic backgrounds, working together to achieve common educational goals.

Pedagogical adaptation: The process of modifying teaching methods, strategies, and materials to better suit the needs and characteristics of learners, including their cultural backgrounds, learning styles, and prior knowledge.

Cross-cultural learning: A form of education that intentionally incorporates perspectives and content from multiple cultures to promote understanding, empathy, and the ability to work effectively across cultural differences.

Section 2
AI-Driven Learning Strategies and Pedagogical Innovation

Chapter 4
Revolutionizing Education for Sustainable Development Through Adaptive Learning and Artificial Intelligence

Jing Wang
https://orcid.org/0009-0003-6647-9923
Bingtuan Xingxin Vocational and Technical College, China & School of Business and Economics, Universiti Putra Malaysia, Malaysia

ABSTRACT

This chapter explores the impact of adaptive learning and AI for sustainable development education (ESD) and reveals its potential to revolutionize the traditional educational model. In the current global context, which is complicated and constantly changing, traditional educational paradigms appear constrained because they only disseminate information in one direction and do not engage learners sufficiently. Therefore, there is an urgent need to transform ESD using system thinking and sustainable development concepts. The role of AI in adaptive learning, personalized platforms, and data-driven evaluation is explained. AI's ability to provide real-time feedback and its application in educational settings are discussed through various case studies. After that, the incorporation of adaptive learning within ESD is explored, with theoretical underpinnings and useful tactics presented. Finally, the chapter concludes with a series of policy recommendations to guarantee educational fairness and accessibility.

DOI: 10.4018/979-8-3693-9062-7.ch004

SECTION 1: THE CURRENT STATE OF EDUCATION FOR SUSTAINABLE DEVELOPMENT (ESD)

1.1 The Limitations of Current Educational Models

1.1.1 The Unidirectional Transmission of Knowledge

Traditional education follows a one-way knowledge transfer model where teachers lecture, and students passively receive information. This approach fails to address individual learning differences, limiting students' ability to deeply understand and apply knowledge. As societies evolve, education must shift towards a student-centered, inquiry-based model that fosters active participation. With the rapid changes in society, a single way of transferring knowledge can no longer meet the needs of students to adapt to the complex real world. Education needs to shift to a student-centered learning model that encourages students to participate actively in discussion and inquiry.

1.1.2 Insufficient Learner Engagement

Our young students often look like ‘his body is in the classroom, but his mind is far away.’ In our modern education, they have no opportunity to express themselves in the classroom. Their voices are often drowned out in the standardized process, and they rarely have the opportunity to show their spark of thought. When students are disengaged, their creativity suffers. Without opportunities for active participation, they struggle to develop essential skills such as critical thinking and problem-solving. This is particularly problematic in education for sustainable development (ESD), where students need to think innovatively about global challenges.

There's an old Chinese saying: “Education should be like a garden were Let a hundred flowers bloom, and a hundred schools of thought contend”. Education provides a platform for every student to speak out, allowing them to speak freely and be inspired. In such an open and inclusive society, students can learn to ‘let go’, not afraid to make mistakes, not afraid to try, and gradually develop the ability to learn independently and the spirit of teamwork, truly become the ‘protagonist’ in the classroom.

Students' engagement and interest in learning can be enhanced through interactive learning and project-driven methods. According to research, encouraging active student participation is crucial for academic achievement and personal growth. One research in 2024 from Karthika using the CLARA model in ESP (English for Specialized Purposes) classrooms in India has shown that by incorporating interactive and creative projects, student engagement increased significantly, resulting in enhanced learning.

Another study analyzing learner engagement in 2023 showed that cognitive engagement can improve learning outcomes and motivation. In Rahman's test, 67% of students surveyed felt that cognitive engagement had a significant impact on their academic performance (Rahman, 2023).

1.2 The Definition and Necessity of Education for Sustainable Development

1.2.1 The Core Concept of Education for Sustainable Development

The core concept of education for sustainable development (ESD) is to foster students' awareness of sustainability and deepen their understanding of the relationships between ecological, economic and social systems. And help them develop responsible values and behavior patterns in a complex and changing world. This is not "armchair theorizing". Global educational practices are gradually putting this concept into action.

For example, a study conducted in Pakistan observed the teaching practices of 100 teachers, focusing on their attitudes towards integrating the Sustainable Development Goals (SDG) into the curriculum in the classroom. According to Shakir et al. (2024), the findings demonstrated that the majority of educators not only possessed a profound comprehension of the SDG concepts but also exhibited a strong desire to incorporate the SDG principles into their regularly scheduled classes. The term "doers" is used to describe certain educators in the United States. This is due to the fact that they not only impart knowledge to their students in the classroom, but they also take steps to embed sustainable practices within their students' educational experiences.

Another study in a food science course found that problem-based and collaborative learning significantly improved students' critical thinking and problem-solving skills in sustainable food production. According to the results, 75% of the students were able to creatively address the issue of sustainability by developing solutions that focused on real-world problems (Higgins et al., 2024). Aren't we enabling students to 'make a difference' outside the classroom and develop practical solutions using critical thinking?

1.2.2 Critical Needs to Address Complex Challenge

With global challenges such as climate change, social inequality, and resource depletion, traditional education cannot meet the needs of developing talent. Students' ability to innovate and problem-solve. Research shows that interdisciplinary learning is essential for students to develop complex thinking and their ability to problem-solve innovation. Integrating knowledge across multiple disciplines, students can analyze complex problems from different perspectives and propose innovative solutions. For example, in higher education, interdisciplinary learning modules significantly improve students 'critical thinking and innovation skills, especially in issues related to social and environmental issues 75% of students demonstrate excellent problem-solving skills after completing an interdisciplinary program (Tarrete, 2022). In addition, policy research also suggests that combining interdisciplinary education with practice can effectively promote students' innovative thinking and adaptability in the face of complex global challenges (Braunerhjelm & Hepburn, 2023). Therefore, education must be transformed. To foster students' capacity for creativity and problem-solving while assisting them in adjusting to the constantly shifting demands of society. SDE emphasizes Interdisciplinary learning and encourages students to analyze the problem from multiple perspectives Cultivate students' comprehensive thinking skills.

1.2.3 The Importance of System Thinking

The application of systems thinking in sustainability education receives increasing attention because it helps students to go beyond the limitations of a single discipline. Moreover, develop their ability to comprehensively consider economic, social and environmental issues.

Research has shown that systematic thinking can significantly improve students' ability to solve complex problems. For example, a study on applying systems thinking in education found that using project-driven learning methods effectively helps students master the ability to handle interdisciplinary problems and develop more excellent critical thinking and teamwork (Marcos-Sa Sanchez et al., 2022). Moreover, another study emphasized that systems thinking training enables students to understand better the complexity of global sustainability issues and becoming more competitive in their future careers.

SECTION 2: THE ROLE OF ARTIFICIAL INTELLIGENCE IN EDUCATION

2.1 Basic Concepts of Artificial Intelligence

2.1. 1 The link between Artificial Intelligence and adaptive learning

Artificial Intelligence (AI) is gradually reshaping the education system, especially in personalized and adaptive learning. Adaptive learning is a personalized educational approach where AI dynamically adjusts content and teaching strategies based on each learner's progress and needs. This ensures students receive targeted support, enhancing both engagement and learning outcomes. It is an educational model that can dynamically adapt learning content and teaching strategies based on each learner's needs and progress. In this process, AI plays an important role by collecting and analyzing learner behavioral data to Identify learning patterns, knowledge mastery, learning difficulties and blind spots of learners to provide a personalized learning experience. This personalized learning method based on data analysis can significantly improve the learning effect and help students grow and progress in a learning environment suited to their individual needs.

The combination of AI and the education industry currently focuses on three main areas: data collection, data processing and human-computer interaction. In order to gather real-time learner learning data and behavior patterns, artificial intelligence (AI) technology is first and foremost widely utilized in speech recognition, picture recognition, and sensor technology in data acquisition. Secondly, in data processing, AI uses semantic recognition, big data analysis, adaptive algorithms, cognitive computing and affective computing to analyze and process the massive amount of learning data it collects to support personalized teaching decisions. Finally, with the development of augmented reality (AR), virtual reality (VR), robotics and 3D printing, and human-computer interfaces are becoming more intelligent and interactive; this has significantly improved the efficiency of classroom teaching and the sense of experience of learners. Figure 1 shows areas of AI application in education.

Figure 1. Areas of AI Application in Education

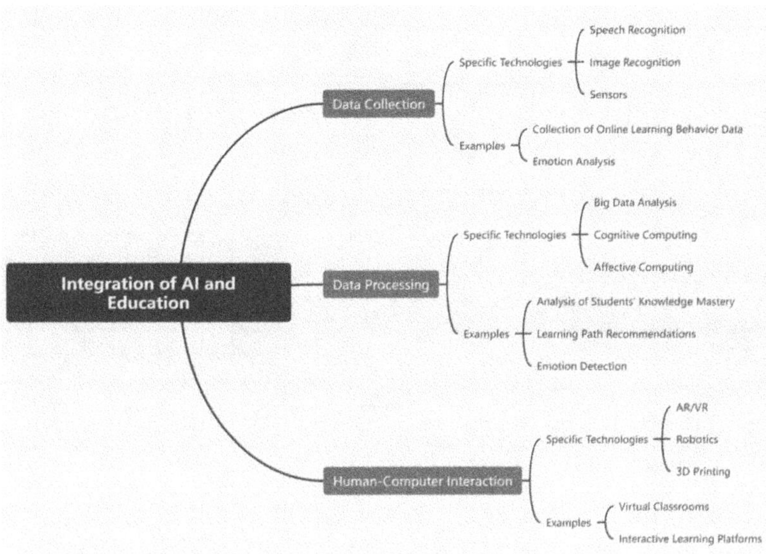

2.1.2 Technical Support and Practical Application of Adaptive Learning

The introduction of AI has extensively promoted the practical application of adaptive learning, especially in the fields of automatic marking of homework, taking photos and searching questions, intelligent evaluation and personalized learning.

(1) Automatic Correction of Homework

The automatic correction of homework is an atypical application of AI in education. With the aid of semantic analysis technology, AI can automatically identify grammatical errors and logical problems in students' homework and provide suggestions for students to correct them. In addition to lessening the workload for educators, this technology produces thorough learning evaluations that assist teachers in comprehending both the individual student differences and the class as a whole. With the continuous maturity of technology, the application of automatic correction of homework will be more extensive, significantly improving teaching efficiency. Figure 2 shows how the AI uses data analysis to grade assignments and generate student reports.

Figure 2. Automatic grading workflow

(2) Taking Photos, Searching Questions and Answering Questions Online

Photo questions are another groundbreaking application of AI in education. Through image recognition technology, students can take photos to upload questions to the platform, and the AI system can give short-term feedback on problem-solving ideas and answers. Such applications have been widely used in primary and secondary schools and extra-curricular guidance to help students enhance their self-learning ability. In addition, with improved recognition accuracy of handwritten questions, the application prospect of photo-searching questions is more comprehensive. This kind of technology provides an efficient and convenient study tool for the student and has promoted study efficiency effectively.

(3) Intelligent Assessment

Intelligent assessment is an important aspect of applying AI technology in education.

Through speech recognition, data analysis, and other technologies, intelligent assessment systems can be used in the learning process to assess student performance in real-time. For example, oral English assessment can use AI technology to provide immediate feedback on students' pronunciation, and pointing out the problem, helping students to practice and improve. In addition, the learning situation analysis system based on big data can identify the weak links in students' knowledge points, help teachers adjust teaching strategies and provide more targeted teaching.

(4) Personalized Learning

Personalized learning is one of the most promising applications of AI in education. Through big data and machine learning technology, personalized learning platforms can describe each student's learning characteristics in detail and provide customized learning paths and content recommendations. Adaptive learning platforms, such as NEWTON, can analyze students' learning data in real-time and dynamically adjust learning resources to ensure that students get the learning experience that best meets their needs. In addition to offering tailored learning recommendations, the Knewton platform is capable of predictive analysis, which involves examining students' learning outcomes and behavior, forecasting their future learning performance, and dynamically modifying the learning path in light of these forecasts.

Table 1 shows the main functions of the personalized learning platform and its impact on students.

Table 1. Functions and impacts of personalized learning platforms

Function	Description	Student Impact
Personalized Recommendation	Dynamically recommends learning resources based on students' learning data and behavior	Provides personalized learning paths, enhancing learning outcomes
Predictive Analytics	Predicts students' future learning performance through data analysis	Helps students identify issues in learning in advance, optimizing learning strategies
Real-time Feedback	Provides real-time feedback on learning outcomes and suggestions based on students' progress	Helps students to adjust their learning methods in time to improve their learning efficiency

2.1.3 Introduction to Machine Learning and Data Analysis

Machine learning, as an essential subfield of artificial intelligence (AI), has been increasing its application in education in recent years. Itscore lies in helping educators identify learning patterns by analyzing students' learning behaviors and performance and then providing personalized teaching feedback. Machine learning not only analyses huge amounts of educational data but also provides real-time personalized support to students based on this data, greatly contributing to the intelligent development of education. In addition, data analytics is essential, particularly when working with extensive educational data. The two together have a lot of promises for pedagogical feedback, individualized learning, and educational management.

Machine learning's core algorithms and applications the combination of the two has shown great potential in areas such as training management, personalized learning and training feedback. Core algorithms and applications of Machine Learning use self-learning algorithms to analyze learners 'behavior patterns, predict learning outcomes, and identify learners' learning outcomes. The following table shows several types of algorithms and their applications in education. Table 2 shows the application process of machine learning and data analysis. And for more deep details, you can refer to Mind Map in Figure 3.

Table 2. The application process of machine learning and data analysis in education

Algorithm Type	Application Scenarios	Example
Decision Tree	Student performance prediction, learning path recommendation	Predicting student performance in exams, recommending personalized learning resources
Support Vector Machine	Classification and regression analysis, binary classification of student performance	Categorizing students into excellent, average, or struggling groups
Random Forest	Combining multiple decision trees for prediction, improving classification accuracy	Analyzing student learning behaviors, identifying key learning patterns
Long Short-Term Memory Network (LSTM)	Time series analysis, real-time learning data prediction, and behavior analysis	Predicting student learning progress and adjusting teaching strategies based on learning progress

Figure 3. The application process of machine learning and data analysis in education

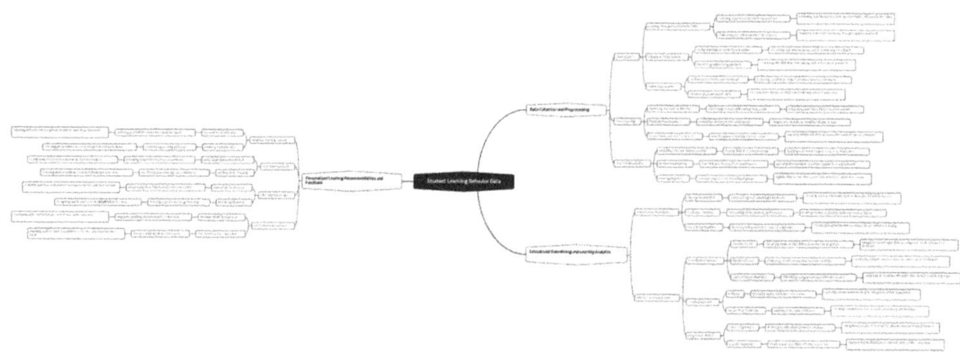

Analyzing patterns, predicting learning outcomes, and identifying knowledge blind spots Identify knowledge blind spots that may occur during the learning process. For example, studies to identify learning patterns and predict learning outcomes use decision trees, support vector machines, and random forests, traditional machine learning techniques have been used extensively.

Clustering and classification techniques allow you to classify learners into different learning groups based on their interests, learning progress and skill level. Each group can then be given a unique learning pathway. This way, education platforms can provide a personalized learning experience for each learner.

Educational data mining (EDM) and learning analytics (LA) are the most common methods used to process educational data. By using these methods, teachers can effectively apply personalized instruction and adaptive learning tactics by gleaning valuable insights from students' behavioral data.

Educational data mining mainly extracts hidden knowledge from large-scale educational data to help administrators and decision-makers better optimize educational management and teaching. These data may be derived from real-time data in online learning systems or traditional educational data accumulated offline. Through data mining technology, education administrators can have a clearer understanding of students 'overall learning situation and make targeted teaching plans.

Learning analysis focuses on the analysis of behavioral data generated during the learning process to support personalized teaching. Learning analysis can create learner models and give teachers immediate feedback through students 'learning behavior, emotional state, and learning results, providing teachers with real-time feedback. For example, by using learning analysis technology, teachers can identify students learning blind spots and emotional changes and adjust the teaching content in time to help students overcome their learning difficulties and improve their learning effects.

Machine learning and data analysis techniques have been widely used in educational systems worldwide. For example, tools such as Microsoft Excel and Access are widely used for statistical description and correlation analysis of data, while commercial software such as IBM's SPSS, MathWorks Matlab, and Wolframs Mathematica provide more advanced data processing capabilities. Open-source software such as R and WEKA can help educators with all the functions of machine learning, including the processing of large-scale data. These tools provide strong technical support for analyzing and mining educational data.

Domestic and foreign studies have demonstrated the effectiveness of machine learning in the field of education. For example, Pena-Ayala (2014) reviewed the research of EDM and screened 240 documents from 2010 to the 2nd quarter of 2013, covering 222 data mining methods and 18 tools. Research shows that the most commonly used data mining methods include classification and cluster analysis, widely used in intelligent teaching systems, learning management systems, and computer-based education. These tools and methods help teachers understand students' learning habits and needs by analyzing students' learning data and providing personalized learning support.

By using the aforementioned research techniques, educators can have a deep understanding of students' learning behavior and develop more targeted teaching strategies through predictive analysis. For example, based on the Online Learning Activity Index (OLAI), researchers have developed an intelligent teaching system that can adjust the teaching content in real-time according to students learning behavior data and improve the teaching effect. This data-driven education approach significantly improves students' learning outcomes.

Despite the promising application prospects of machine learning and data analysis in education, many challenges remain. First, cross-domain cooperation between technicians and educators needs to be further strengthened. Those who understand education may not be technology-savvy, and those who understand technology may need help understanding educational needs. How to combine the technical advantages of machine learning with educational theory is still a problem that needs to be solved in the future. In addition, the large-scale application of machine learning technology in education still needs further technological maturity, especially in constructing personalized learning and real-time feedback systems.

Overall, machine learning and data analysis technologies have great potential for applications in education. By doing a thorough investigation of student learning behavior, educators can obtain more accurate data support, develop personalized teaching plans, and provide real-time learning feedback, thus significantly improving the teaching effect. With the continuous progress of technology, the future education system will be more intelligent and personalized, and the student's learning experience will be greatly optimized.

2.2 The deep combination of artificial intelligence and education

AI has promoted the development of adaptive learning and opened a new education model under the "Internet + education" model. Through more efficient data processing methods and intelligent interactive platforms, AI will form a combined product evolution mode in the field of education and gradually realize the systematic and intelligent teaching process. In the future, the combination of AI and education will be mainly reflected in the three directions of the learner model, teaching model and specific learning field. Table3 shows the details.

Table 3. The combination of AI and education

Learner Model	Teaching Model	Specific Learning Field
Learner models focus on students' individual characteristics, including learning styles, knowledge acquisition, and learning behaviors. Learner models use AI technology to analyze data about a student's learning behavior and create detailed student profiles to help teachers understand each student's needs and provide personalized educational support. For example, AI can analyze a student's learning style, such as whether they are visual or auditory learner and recommend appropriate learning materials and teaching methods based on this analysis.	Instructional modelling focuses on how to optimize teachers' teaching methods to better meet the needs of diverse learners, and AI analyses data from teacher-student interactions to help teachers identify the most effective teaching methods and adapt them to specific situations. For example, AI can adjust the pace and content of a lesson based on classroom feedback to keep all students engaged.	The application of AI to specific areas of learning, such as vocational education and experiential learning, also offers great opportunities. Using AI technology, educational content in these areas can be more precisely tailored. In vocational education, for example, AI can recommend the most appropriate courses and learning resources based on students' vocational orientation and skill level, allowing students to quickly improve their skills. In exam teaching, AI can use big data analytics to identify frequent test moments in exams and provide students with targeted practice and revision suggestions.

With the continuous progress of AI technology, the education industry will usher in more profound changes. AI-powered real-time student learning data analysis, personalized learning route recommendations, and intelligent teacher feedback will greatly increase the effectiveness of instruction and learning outcomes in the educational sector. In the future, the application of AI in education will not only be limited to the current adaptive learning and personalized learning but also cover a more comprehensive range of fields, including emotional computing, intelligent tutoring systems, virtual teachers, etc.

To put it briefly, the full implementation of AI technology in education will result in more intelligent and tailored solutions for the sector, assist students in better adjusting to the pace of learning, enhance the learning experience, lessen the workload for educators, and ultimately realize true educational reform and advancement

2.3 Application Cases of AI in Education

2.3.1 Personalized Learning Platform

The widespread application of artificial intelligence technology in education is reflected in the rise of personalized learning platforms. Squirrel AI is a leading education technology company in China. It analyzes students' learning data in real-time through AI technology adapts the learning material and level of difficulty dynamically based on the requirements and skills of the pupils. This personalized learning approach has significantly improved student performance in general, especially in complex subjects such as mathematics and science. For instance, Chen, a 14-year-old student in Shanghai, struggled with algebra before using Squirrel AI. The platform identified her weak areas in quadratic equations, providing personalized exercises that helped boost her math score by 20% within three months. Such examples highlight AI's potential to offer tailored educational support. The AI-driven learning analysis system can also provide real-time feedback for teachers to help them identify students' learning needs and adjust their teaching strategies promptly. In this way, AI helps teachers optimize their teaching methods and improves students learning efficiency and enthusiasm.

Squirrel AI Also generate personalized learning reports through data-driven learning evaluation. These reports provide teachers and students with comprehensive feedback on their learning situation to help them cope with difficulties and challenges in learning. The interactive learning platform completely demonstrates the potential of artificial intelligence in the field of education by combining gamification, simulation, and other techniques to increase students' participation in learning.

2.3.2 Data-Driven Personalized Learning: The Squirrel AI Show

Squirrel AI is the poster child for data-driven personalized learning. This platform adapts learning material in real-time based on student needs and learning behaviors, letting them learn at their own pace. This personalized approach not only boosts students' performance in challenging subjects but also fosters greater independence and engagement in their learning. The AI algorithms can generate tailored learning resources and pathways that align with each student's unique learning styles and requirements, significantly increasing learning efficiency. Table 4 summarizes the personalized learning features of the Squirrel AI platform and the technological support behind them.

Table 4. Squirrel AI personalized learning features and AI technical support

Feature	Description	AI Technical Support
Student Learning Data Analysis	Analyzing student learning behavior, progress, and knowledge mastery	Data mining, learning analytics algorithms
Personalized Learning Content Recommendation	Adjusting learning content and difficulty based on student needs	Machine learning, deep learning algorithms
Real-time Feedback and Adjustment	Providing feedback and learning suggestions based on student's real-time performance	Real-time data processing, predictive analytics algorithms
Learning Progress Monitoring and Reporting	Generating personalized learning reports to help teachers and students adjust learning strategies	Data analysis, knowledge graph construction

2.3.3 Data-Driven Learning Assessment: The AI Coach

AI has become the secret weapon in the arsenal of data-driven learning assessment. Picture this: AI as a personal tutor that gives instant feedback, keeping a keen eye on student performance and tracking progress like a hawk. It's like having a GPS for the mind, guiding students through the twists and turns of their education journey.

Table 5. Data-driven learning assessment features and applications

Feature	Description	Application Scenario
Real-time Monitoring of Student Learning Progress	Dynamically collects student learning data and tracks progress	Personalized Learning Platforms
Personalized Learning Report Generation	Generates detailed reports by analyzing student learning behavior for teacher reference	Teaching Assessment, Personalized Learning
Automatic Identification of Learning Blind Spots	Automatically identifies difficulties and weak points in learning based on student performance	Adaptive Learning Systems
Teaching Strategy Adjustment Suggestions	Provides suggestions for teachers to adjust teaching methods based on learning data	Data-Driven Teaching Decisions

This data-driven assessment helps teachers better understand student needs and provide personalized learning pathways that ensure students receive the learning support they need most at the right time.

2.3.4 Application of Real-time Feedback Mechanisms in Learning

Real-time feedback mechanisms are an important part of AI in education. This real-time feedback allows students to 'know themselves and their peers' at every critical moment of learning and clearly understand their learning progress and performance. When students encounter 'roadblocks' such as difficulties, the system immediately provides supplementary materials, detailed troubleshooting advice, and even step-by-step guidance to resolve the issue. This immediate support allows students to adjust their learning strategies and find additional resources to help them get the most out of the learning process. Figure 4 shows the workflow of AI providing real-time feedback during the learning process.

Figure 4. AI real-time feedback mechanism workflow

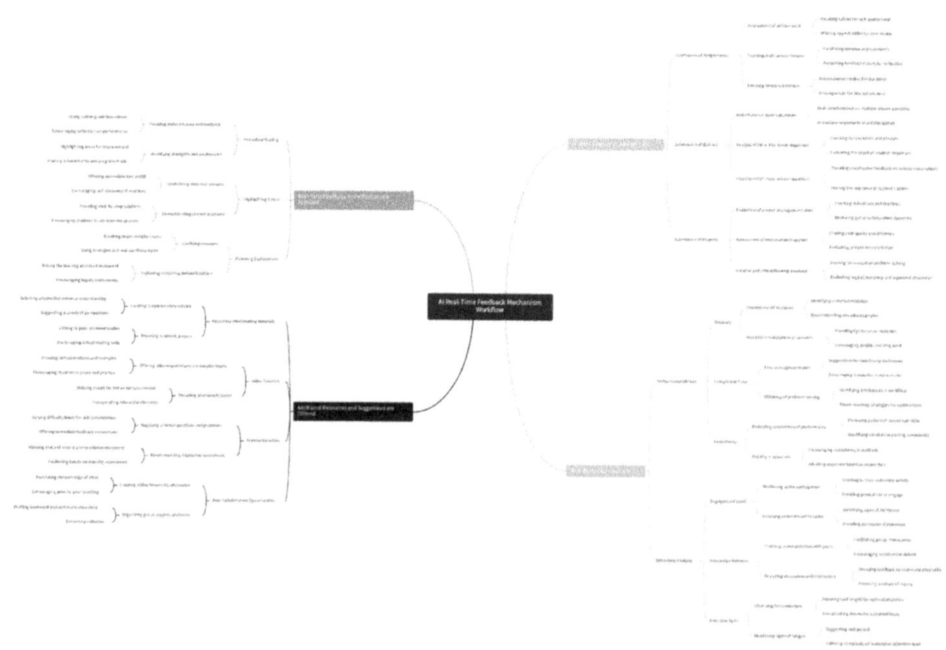

This mechanism not only improves learning efficiency but also boosts students' confidence and creates a positive and enjoyable learning atmosphere. At the same time, teachers can also use feedback data to 'prescribe the right medicine' and adjust their teaching strategies to ensure that each student can truly receive appropriate support.

2.3.5 Representative Products of Artificial Intelligence in Education

In recent years, with the 'ever-changing' development of AI technology, many highly innovative AI products have emerged in the field of education that are truly 'eye-catching'. These products can be divided into different types according to their functions and application scenarios, including intelligent teaching platforms, intelligent evaluation systems, photo search and online Q&A, intelligent speech recognition-assisted teaching, educational robots, game-based teaching platforms, etc. Each type of product shows its own 'unique skills' in the teaching scenario, from intelligent evaluation to timely feedback on learning effectiveness to educational robots supporting classroom interaction, making teaching more personalized and livelier. Figure 5 shows the representative AI products in education.

Figure 5. Analysis of representative AI products in education

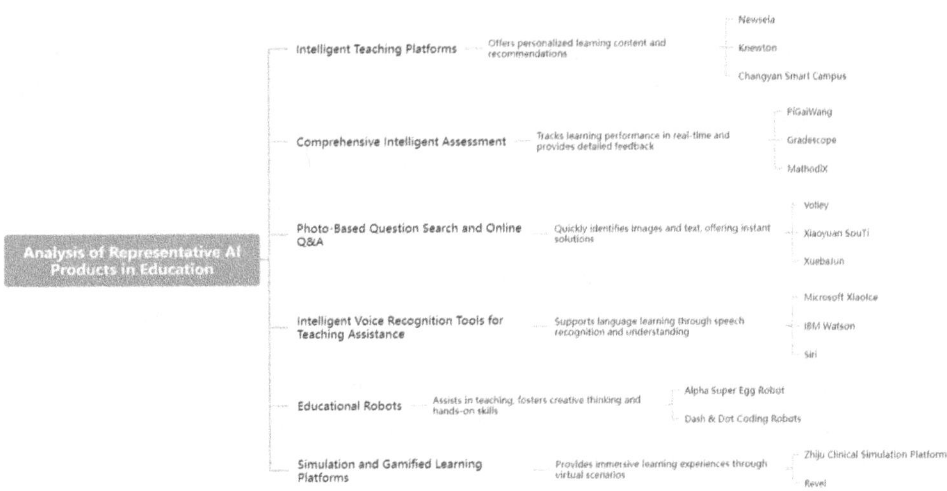

The application of these AI products is like injecting a 'strong drug injection' into the traditional classroom, which not only promotes the process of educational intelligence, but also makes personalized education from an ideal to a reality.AI technology has become a key driving force to promote educational innovation and 'teaching according to materials', opening up new ways to promote the development of education. AI technology has become a key driving force to promote educational innovation and 'teaching according to materials', opening up a new way for education to move with the times.

Each of the AI product demonstrates the broad application of AI technology in education. These products show the extensive application and potential of AI in education, indicating that AI technology is becoming the core power to promote the development of intelligent and individualized education. As technology matures, AI will provide teachers and students with more innovative learning methods and teaching tools.

Conclusion

The application of AI technology in education, especially in personalized learning, data-driven learning assessment and real-time feedback mechanisms, shows great potential. Students can study more efficiently in a customized learning environment with AI, while teachers can offer more precise teaching support based on students' requirements and learning progress. With the further development of technology, AI will bring about more extensive changes in the field of education and promote the intelligent and personalized transformation of the education model.

SECTION 3: INTEGRATING ADAPTIVE LEARNING WITH ESD

3.1 Theoretical Foundations of Adaptive Learning

3.1.1 Learner-Centered and Personalized Education

Adaptive learning emphasizes a learner-centered approach, adjusting instructional content and methods dynamically based on each learner's needs and characteristics. This model not only focuses on the transmission of knowledge but also emphasizes active learner engagement and a personalized learning experience. A learner-centered educational philosophy requires teachers to consider students' backgrounds, interests, and learning styles when designing instruction, providing resources and support that align with individual needs. Personalized education forms the core of adaptive learning, utilizing AI and data analysis to monitor student progress in real-time and adjust teaching strategies accordingly. This personalized learning experience enhances student engagement and equips them with better tools to apply knowledge in complex situations.

Research shows that personalized learning effectively enhances student motivation and academic achievement. This is particularly true in the context of sustainable development education, where students can more deeply explore global issues. Personalized learning relies on high-quality content and intelligent feedback systems, areas in which AI has greatly facilitated development. AI-enabled adaptive learning systems provide dynamic learning paths and precise content recommendations, enabling learners to receive continuous feedback and interaction, thus making learning more efficient.

Table 6. Core functions of adaptive learning systems

Function	Description
Learning Path	Based on knowledge graphs, adjusts paths according to student behavior data to match optimal learning routes
Content Recommendation	Analyzes student learning records to infer skill levels and knowledge gaps, ensuring content matches the student's current level

By integrating learning paths and content recommendations, adaptive learning systems ensure that students learn at their own pace and receive material aligned with their abilities. This learner-centered model improves learning efficiency and promotes independent learning.

3.1.1.1 Personalized Learning Paths and Content Recommendations

Learning paths form a key concept in adaptive learning, analyzing student learning data to create individualized routes based on knowledge graphs. AI and data mining technologies allow systems to continuously refine learning paths, ensuring students receive optimal support based on their abilities and needs. Personalized learning paths use periodic adjustments and feedback to help students master knowledge and address weak areas.

Content recommendation operates similarly to personalized suggestions, using AI to analyze student behavior and recommend resources that match their current learning needs. The system evaluates student ability levels and the difficulty of learning materials through complex algorithms, ensuring that content is appropriately challenging. This approach enhances the relevance of learning materials and ensures students can engage with tasks at the right difficulty level.

Figure 6. Core functions of adaptive learning systems

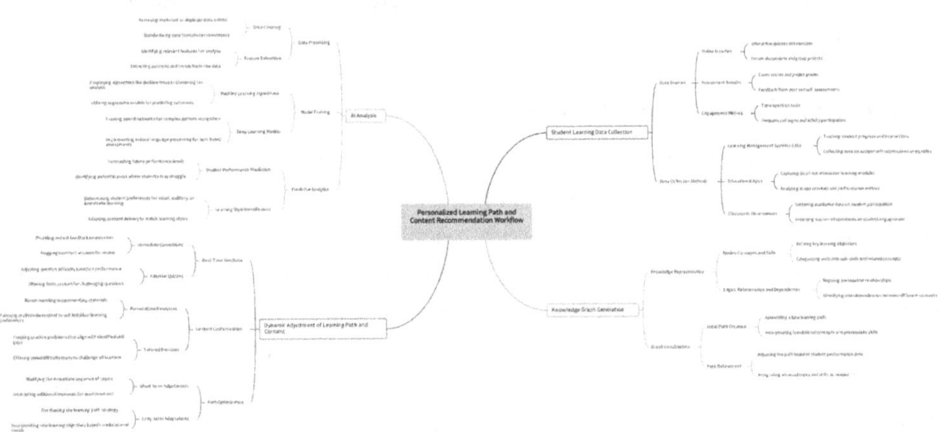

Combining personalized learning paths with content recommendations allows adaptive learning systems to flexibly respond to students' learning needs, continually adjusting and optimizing resource provision. This model significantly improves both learning efficiency and student autonomy.

3.1.1.2 Data-Driven Learning Analytics

The realization of personalized learning depends on data-driven learning analytics. Learning Analytics (LA) involves collecting, measuring, and analyzing learner data to optimize the learning process. Personalized Learning (PL) strategies analyze individual learner needs to apply corresponding teaching methods. Adaptive Learning Systems (ALS) use AI to create learning models suited to each student's cognitive level, addressing the lack of individualized instruction in traditional education.

With the rise of AI and big data technologies, personalized adaptive learning (PL+ALS) has gained widespread use. For instance, learning dashboards—common in adaptive learning systems—visualize student behavior and progress. Platforms like Khan Academy break courses down into hundreds of knowledge points, allowing students to track their progress through dynamic learning graphs. These visual tools not only enhance learning experiences but also help teachers adjust their teaching strategies accordingly.

Table 7. Features of personalized adaptive learning systems

Function	Description
Learning Behavior Data Analysis	Records and analyzes student behavior, generating data-driven progress reports
Dynamic Learning Path Adjustment	Adjusts learning paths in real-time based on learning data, ensuring personalized pacing
Learning Dashboard Visualization	Displays learning progress through data charts, helping students and teachers understand the learning process and adjust strategies as needed

Personalized learning relies on these technologies to help teachers and students make timely adjustments and improve learning outcomes.

3.1.1.3 The Future of Human-Machine Collaboration in Education

AI's application in education not only enhances personalized learning experiences but also promotes new models of collaboration between teachers and machines. In the future, education will increasingly feature collaboration between humans and AI, with machines handling repetitive tasks like grading and assessments, while teachers focus on complex decision-making, instructional design, and providing human support. Through human-machine collaboration, teachers can devote more time to innovative and personalized instruction, while students receive enhanced personalized support during their learning process.

For example, AI systems can analyze student data, generate learning reports, and automatically adjust instructional content. Teachers can then use these reports to further optimize their teaching strategies, ensuring each student receives appropriate support. This model of human-machine collaboration improves both teaching efficiency and student engagement.

Table 8. Applications of human-machine collaboration in education

Task	AI Responsibility	Teacher Responsibility
Assessment and Grading	AI automatically grades assignments and generates reports	Teachers adjust teaching content and strategies based on reports
Personalized Learning Path Design	AI analyzes data and provides personalized learning paths	Teachers offer guidance and human support, fostering comprehensive development
Instructional Design and Innovation	AI assists in standardized tasks, providing real-time feedback	Teachers focus on creative and complex decisions, improving instructional quality

The introduction of a human-AI collaborative education model allows teachers and AI to perform their respective roles, leveraging their strengths to create a more efficient and personalized learning experience.

Conclusion

Adaptive learning is a learner-centered educational model that uses artificial intelligence and big data technologies to deliver personalized learning paths and content. In this model, learners receive customized learning resources and support based on their individual needs and ability levels, significantly improving learning efficiency and motivation. In the future, through human-AI collaboration, AI will continue to enhance personalized learning experiences and provide stronger support for teachers, enabling them to focus on creative and complex teaching tasks, thus driving continuous innovation and development in the education sector.

3.1.2 Enhancing Learning Effectiveness and Engagement

The goal of adaptive learning is to enhance learning effectiveness and student engagement, especially in personalized learning environments, where learners can acquire knowledge more efficiently and at the right level of difficulty through AI technologies, thus avoiding the loss of motivation due to frustration. Holmes et al. (2021) point out that personalized learning environments not only significantly improve students' motivation, but also their academic performance. Through the dynamic adaptation of AI, educators can ensure that each student receives learning materials that match his or her abilities. The system uses real-time feedback to optimize each student's learning experience.

3.1.2.1 Dynamic learning Material Adaptation and Feedback Mechanisms

The core of the Adaptive Learning System lies in its ability to adjust the difficulty dynamically and content of the learning materials through continuous data collection and analysis to ensure that students always learn at the appropriate level. Platforms like Knewton, Squirrel AI, and Duolingo use machine learning algorithms to analyze students' progress and provide customized learning pathways. For example, Knewton adjusts lesson difficulty in real time, ensuring that struggling students receive additional support while advanced learners progress at an accelerated pace. Students' sense of accomplishment is raised and their frustration with learning is successfully decreased by this dynamic adjustment. Educators can access students' learning progress in real time through the system and adjust teaching strategies based on the data to ensure that each student receives personalized Support.

Figure 7. Workflow of adaptive learning system's dynamic adjustments

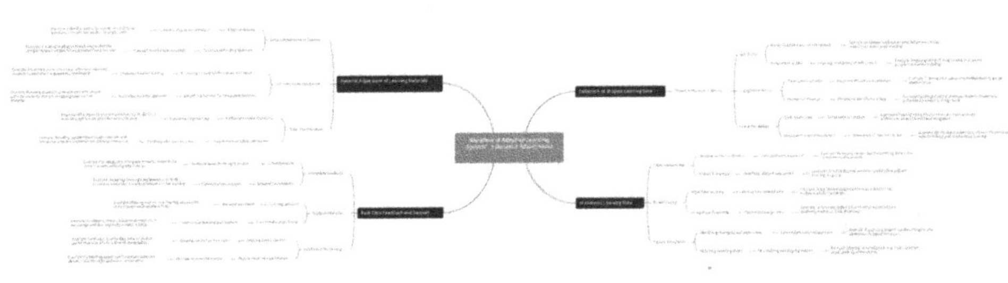

3.1.2.2 Data-Driven Learning Analysis and Intervention

Data-driven learning analysis gives educators a more accurate basis for teaching decisions through big data. Learning analysis technology can help teachers better understand students' learning behavior and needs and integrate multi-source data to predict students' learning performance and provide timely interventions when students face challenges. Especially for "High-risk" learners, learning analysis can identify their learning difficulties in time and improve their academic performance through individualized intervention.

Through the real-time tracking and interaction of students' learning trajectories, learning analysis offers the possibility of self-directed learning. Students can adjust their learning plans based on systematic feedback to optimize learning efficiency. At the same time, teachers can use this data to provide students with targeted learning guidance and support. Ioannou's research shows that learning analysis techniques promote pleasure and empathy in learners through play-based learning design (Ioannou, 2019).

3.1.2.3 optimization of instructional design and personalized feedback

Learning analysis technology also plays a vital role in teaching design. By adopting a data-driven approach, teachers can better evaluate the effectiveness of instructional design and optimize teaching content and activities promptly based on feedback data. To help teachers understand the needs, learning styles, and trajectories of their students and provide effective teaching interventions, learning analysis technology can offer multi-context data. This not only makes instructional design more scientific but also enhances the learning experience for students.

Table 9. Applications of learning analytics in instruction

Function	Description
Real-time Monitoring of Learning Trajectories	Tracks students' learning behavior and progress to help teachers understand learning dynamics
Personalized Feedback and Interventions	Offers personalized feedback and guidance based on student performance to help overcome learning difficulties
Optimizing Instructional Design	Evaluates the effectiveness of instructional strategies and dynamically adjusts to meet student needs

Ferguson points out that data is a powerful catalyst for developing Analytical Learning Technologies. However, due to educational practice's complexity and dynamic nature, learning analysis techniques face many challenges in obtaining multi-source situational data. A fundamental problem is integrating and compatible multi-source heterogeneous data to ensure the accuracy of data analysis results. Although AI technology has made some breakthroughs in enriching students 'behavioral data (such as facial expressions, body language, etc.), effectively integrating and computing these data remains one of the current challenges.

3.1.2.4 Education Big Data Enables Personalized Learning

Since the advent of big data in 2013, innovations in learning technologies and models have led to more complex educational data. Big data in education provides a wealth of data sources and analytical tools for personalized learning design. "Big data is something that can be done on a huge scale, something that cannot be done on a small scale," according to British researcher Mayer-sch önberger (Mayer-sch önberger, 2013). Through big data analysis, educators can better understand the needs of students and conduct accurate teaching interventions.

The application of big educational data not only embodies the optimization of instructional design but also helps students to understand themselves better, plan their learning paths and improve their autonomous learning ability through data-driven learning diagnosis. This data-driven learning analysis model enables educators to identify students 'real needs more accurately and narrow the learning gap through personalized interventions.

Figure 8. Application workflow of educational big data in personalized learning

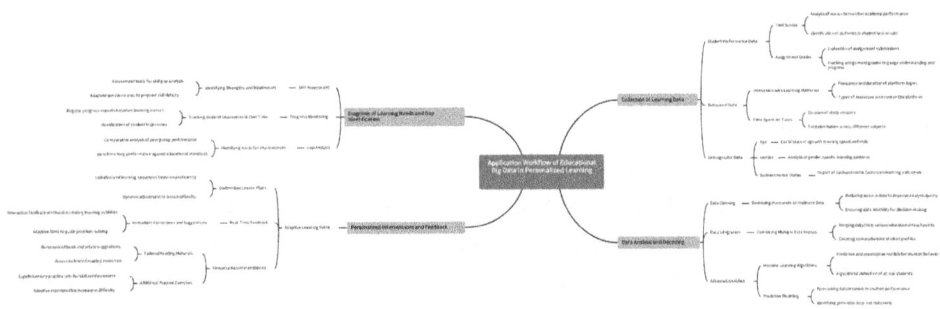

3.1.2.5 Long-Term Benefits and Future Challenges

While data-driven learning analytics have made significant progress in improving learning outcomes and student engagement, there are challenges invalidating their long-term utility. The current learning analysis technology mainly represents the phased benefits of technology in education. How to ensure its effectiveness in the long term is the key problem to be solved in the future. In the future, the key to promoting the development of learning analysis technology will be to obtain diversified and high- quality educational data and follow the scientific data decision-making process.

In addition, the technology of learning analysis faces the challenge of realizing group cooperative learning and multi-source data integration. For example, teaching AI can enrich the dimensions of learning analysis by analyzing behavioral data such as learners' facial expressions and body language, but how to apply this data in group learning is still the focus of current research.

3.1.2.6 data-driven decision-making in the Future of Education

Data-driven learning plays a crucial role in individual learning and promotes transparency and science in educational decision-making. Educators can provide personalized support for students at multiple levels through data empowerment of macro-level educational decision-making, middle-level teaching management, and micro-level learning diagnosis. For example, data-driven educational practices can help learners better understand themselves, develop themselves, and achieve long-term learning goals through self-reflection.

Table 10. Applications of educational big data at different levels

Level	Application Scenario	Impact
Macro-level	Education policy formulation and decision-making	Supports transparency and accountability in decision-making
Meso-level	Teaching management and instructional optimization	Helps teachers improve instructional design and enhances student engagement
Micro-level	Learning diagnostics and personalized interventions	Reduces learning gaps through diagnostics and provides personalized support

The use of big data in education is not limited to classroom instruction. It can also provide a scientific basis for educational policy-making, thus promoting transparency and equity throughout the education system.

Conclusion

Through AI technology and data-driven learning analysis, adaptive learning shows great potential in improving students' learning effectiveness and participation. Real-time feedback, personalized intervention, and data-driven instructional design provide rich support for educators and learners. In the future, AI and big data will continue to drive innovation and development of educational models by further optimizing data collection and analysis techniques and making progress in group learning and long-term validation of benefits. Each of the Eight Immortals crosses the sea and displays his or her own talents.

3.2 Practical Adaptive Learning Strategies

3.2.1 Teaching for Different Learning Styles

Different learners prefer different teaching media and methods, and it is like one old Chinese adage: 'Each of the Eight Immortals demonstrates their unique powers as they cross the sea'. So, teachers need to be flexible and consider the uniqueness of each learner. Effective implementation of adaptive learning necessitates tailoring instruction to align with students' aptitudes. That needs educators considering each learner's uniqueness, especially their learning style. So, teachers need to be flexible and consider the uniqueness of each learner. People who retain information best when presented with visual aids like photos, movies, or diagrams are known as visual learners. For those who learn best by auditory means, the most effective learning tools are audio explanations and group discussions.

hands-on learners prefer to acquire new knowledge through experimentation and practice, as they enjoy the sensation of "It's like being there." Hands-on learners are inclined to acquire new knowledge through experimentation and hands-on manipulation.

In instructional design, teachers should adopt a multifaceted approach and introduce a variety of teaching methods to help learners of different styles find their own learning path. With multimedia content, interactive tools and hands-on activities, the classroom can become a 'thriving' garden that captures students' attention and stimulates their passion for learning. For example, teachers can offer video lectures and diagrams for visual learners, audio materials and discussion sessions for auditory learners, and experiments and simulations for experiential learners to learn 'as if they were there'.

Educational researchers have developed a number of tools to identify different learning styles to better understand learners' needs. One of these is the Memletics Learning Styles Scale, which divides learning styles into seven dimensions: visual, auditory, verbal, logical, social, personal, and kinesthetic. Teachers can analyze learner data or survey feedback to recommend the best learning content and methods for each learner to create a personalized learning experience.

Table 11. Teaching methods for different learning styles

Learning Style	Teaching Method	Application Examples
Visual Learners	Use of videos, images, presentations	Video lectures, chart presentations, visual simulations
Auditory Learners	Audio lectures, discussions, verbal materials	Audio content, language teaching, oral discussions
Kinesthetic Learners	Experiments, simulations, practical activities	Experimental learning, hands-on exercises, simulated practice
Verbal Learners	Concept mastery through reading and writing	Reading materials, writing assignments
Logical Learners	Problem analysis and solving	Logical reasoning activities, math exercises
Social Learners	Group discussions and collaborative learning	Group discussions, collaborative projects
Solitary Learners	Independent and self-directed learning	Independent learning projects, personal learning goals

By analyzing students' behavioral data or questionnaire feedback, teachers can recommend the most appropriate learning material for each student so that each student can acquire knowledge and improve their learning experience like a fish out of water.

3.2.2 Learning Through game and Interactive Design

In recent years, In recent years, game-based learning has become the 'new hotness' in stimulating students' interest in learning and has gradually become an effective means of increasing engagement. The basic idea of learning through play is to integrate play elements into the learning process and promote interest and interaction in learning. The core concept of gamification is to inject 'fun' into the learning process through the use of tasks, challenges, points and instant feedback mechanisms so that students become deeply engaged without even realizing it. Learning through play can increase students' engagement in learning by stimulating their interest in learning through task setting, challenge, integration and feedback mechanisms, and contextual and interactive learning experiences (Zawacki-Richter et al., 2019).

Learning through game not only makes learning more enjoyable, but also promotes deeper learning through interesting and challenging tasks.

3.2.3 Personalized Learning Realization and Feedback

Personalized learning is the 'finishing touch' to adaptive learning, where AI and big data technologies are used to 'personalize' the learning experience for each student to truly meet their individual needs. Personalized learning is based on dynamic analysis of students' learning behaviors, styles and needs, and allows course content to be adapted at any point during the learning process to ensure that each student progresses at their own pace and in their own way.

The model consists of three parts: Learner analytics, service support, and environmental creation. During the Learner Analytics phase, the system gathers and analyzes student learning behaviors to ascertain learning preferences and requirements. Depending on the student's attributes, the system thereafter offers tailored learning resources and assistance, including the formulation of a customized learning trajectory and the suggestion of suitable educational materials. In terms of creating an environment, the system creates a 'fertile soil' for learning, provides timely feedback, and dynamically adjusts the learning path to continuously optimize the student's learning experience.

Based on student performance, the design enables educators to genuinely customize the learning material and modify the educational trajectory for each student in real time. For example, if a student struggles with a particular knowledge point, the system provides additional resources or tips to help the student break through the barrier. At the same time, the system adjusts the difficulty of the content according to the student's learning speed and comprehension ability, ensuring that they are always in an optimal learning state, not too hard, not too easy'. Such personalized learning not only improves learning effectiveness but also greatly enhances student autonomy and motivation, allowing them to feel at ease' in the learning process.

3.2.4 Dynamic and Open Educational Resources

The dynamic openness of educational resources has become an more and more important part of adaptive learning With the 'rapid development' of big data and Internet technology. Dynamic open educational resources means that learning materials can be updated and shared in real time according to learners' needs, and students can obtain learning materials "anytime, anywhere, infinitely" with only one device connected to the Internet. This openness transcends the constraints of time and space, making knowledge dissemination and cross-cultural exchange more widespread.

Table 12. Advantages of dynamic open educational resources

Advantage	Description
Overcoming Time and Space Limits	Learners can access resources through the internet anytime, anywhere
Resource Sharing and Co-creation	Global sharing of educational resources enhances knowledge dissemination and educational opportunities
Rich Learning Choices	Learners can select content based on their needs and interests, increasing flexibility and autonomy

3.2.5 Intelligent and Automatic Teaching Mode

AI technology automatically determines students' learning needs and offers them individualized learning support by evaluating their learning data. This automated teaching intervention reduces teacher workload and ensures every student has timely help.

With the continuous progress of AI technology, the future teaching mode will be more intelligent and automated. Teachers can design the courses with the help of an intelligent teaching platform. Teachers need to follow a few simple steps to make adaptive learning work when implemented. Simultaneously, learning content and difficulty levels can be adjusted in real-time by AI systems that monitor students' progress. This improves the effectiveness of instruction and the quality of the student's education.

3.2.6 Case Studies: Successful Implementation of Adaptive Learning Projects

Simultaneously, AI systems have the potential to monitor students' progress in real-time and adjust the content and difficulty level appropriately. The instruction effectiveness and the student's education quality are both improved by AI systems. These programs not only significantly improve students' academic performance, but also stimulate their critical thinking and problem-solving skills, “hitting the nail on the head”.

University environmental science departments often incorporate adaptive learning platforms. Students learn better using adaptive learning platforms. The platform provides them with personalized learning materials. it also has improved students' comprehension of intricate ecosystems and sustainability concerns to raising course completion rates and overall student happiness.

Figure 9. Implementation process of an adaptive learning project

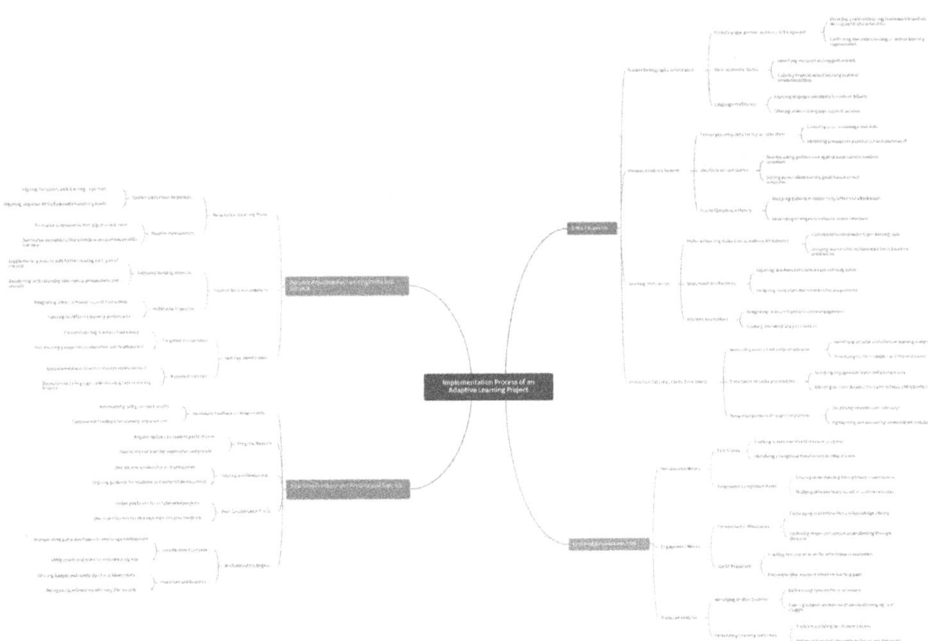

This case shows that adaptive learning platforms can not only optimize the learning process but also help students learn efficiently according to their own needs. Learning may now "shine like a new penny" because to data analytics and artificial intelligence, which allow educators to give pupils individualized assistance.

3.2.7 Implementation Strategies and Outcome Evaluation

Educators need to adopt several key strategies to ensure the success of adaptive learning during its implementation. Collecting and monitoring data is the first critical step.

Second, educators need to build a comprehensive data collection system that allows them to monitor student engagement, assignment completion, test scores, and adaptive learning based on real-time data analytics. Finally, educators can use a learning management system (LMS) to "see" student performance and receive detailed data analytics reports.

Table 13. Steps for implementing adaptive learning strategies

Step	Description
Data Collection and Monitoring	Use LMS to gather student data on assignments, test scores, participation, etc.
Dynamic Adjustment of Content	Regularly adjust teaching methods and content based on data analysis, ensuring personalized learning experiences.
Feedback and Evaluation Mechanism	Periodically assess student outcomes, gather feedback, and optimize teaching strategies to maximize learning results.

Through these steps, teachers can ensure the effectiveness of adaptive learning strategies and provide students with ongoing support and guidance to help them 'go the extra mile' and make real progress in their learning.

3.2.8 Synergies Between Personalized Learning and AI

The purpose of personalized learning is to develop a one-of-a-kind educational strategy for each individual student, taking into account the student's individual interests, talents, and shortcomings. Especially in the context of ESD, where a "one size does not fit all" impact is desired, teachers' ability to modify lesson plans due to the specific requirements of learners is crucial. Students may have varied degrees of difficulty while attempting to make sense of environmental, economic, and social issues and discover answers to these challenges. These components are complicated, and students may confront varying degrees of difficulty.

Section Conclusion

Adaptive learning strategies significantly enhance learning outcomes and student engagement through diverse teaching methods, gamified interactive design, personalized learning feedback and dynamic open educational resources. Teachers can use AI and big data technologies to give students individualized learning experiences, as well as to implement real-time instructional adjustments and automatic intervention. The dynamic and open educational resources, the development of an intelligent teaching platform and the automatic feedback mechanism based on AI have laid the foundation for the innovation of future educational models.

SECTION 4: ETHICAL AND MORAL CONSIDERATIONS

4.1 The Ethical Challenges of Artificial Intelligence in Education

As if opening Pandora's box, the extensive use of AI technology in education has presented us with a new set of moral dilemmas. For example, data protection and educational equity: AI technologies in education use a wealth of student data, from homework to test scores and other information. This data helps create personalized learning experiences, but the shadow of Big Brother grows with every byte processed. More lenient privacy safeguards increase the likelihood of the leak of sensitive student data, which can cause a host of issues, including identity theft .

Privacy is not only about protecting confidentiality, but also about maintaining a level playing field. AI in education must balance innovation with ethical responsibility. One major concern is algorithmic bias, where AI systems may favor certain student demographics based on the data they are trained on. Additionally, AI-based learning requires large datasets, raising concerns about student privacy. To mitigate these risks, educational institutions should implement clear ethical guidelines, transparent AI models, and strict data protection policies. Waiting for state-of-the-art AI tools in schools where even the latest textbooks are hard to come by can be a pipe dream. Students in technologically under-resourced areas could be left far behind, in a David versus Goliath scenario.

4.2. Align AI Applications with Sustainable Development Principles

AI systems must take sustainability principles into account to guarantee that educational AI applications are ethical and promote educational fairness in its development and implementation period. These principles relate not only to technological ethics, but also to social responsibility and educational equity.

4.2.1 Establish an Ethical Framework

One crucial step in guaranteeing the ethics of AI in education is the establishment of a thorough ethical framework. Basic concepts such as algorithmic justice, equality of educational opportunities, privacy and transparency should form the basis of any ethical framework. AI system must function inside a legal framework and adhere to stringent privacy regulations, to make sure that students' privacy is protected.

Additionally, the ideals of transparency and clarity must be incorporated into this framework. In order for educators, students, and parents to have a better understanding of how artificial intelligence operates, the decision-making process for algorithms ought to be open and visible. Because of this openness, not only is confidence established, but it also assists in locating and correcting bias in program algorithms. In order to ensure that the technology is applied in a manner that is both ethical and ecologically responsible, educational and training institutions should conduct periodical evaluations of the artificial intelligence technologies that they will be using.

4.2.2 Ethical Responsibilities of Trainers

When it comes to using AI, educators play a crucial role, and they also are responsible for guiding and protecting children. Zawacki-Richter et al. (2019) argue that educators must be knowledgeable about the capabilities and limitations of AI tools so that these technologies can be used appropriately to provide equitable learning opportunities for students. When using AI technologies, educators should always consider the potential bias of the algorithms and the privacy of students.

Educators need to be involved in assessing and critiquing AI systems to make sure they don't exacerbate current educational inequalities. When considering the use of AI in the classroom, educators need to consider not just the short-term benefits of technology but also its long-term implications. In order for educators to have a substantial influence on the future of society, they must be able to inculcate in students the capacity to think critically and ethically for the greater good. While also being aware of the ethical issues that technology brings. This is necessary when educators want to have a big impact on the future of society.

4.3 Ethical Issues and Future Challenges

The use of artificial intelligence in education has a number of apparent advantages, like the creation of tailored learning paths and intelligent assessment systems. However, if it is not used appropriately, it can lead to an increase in academic misconduct, including cheating on examinations and even plagiarism. In the same way that the proverb "it is better to teach a man to fish than to teach him with a net" is true, what happens when the net breaks? Data breaches are another issue that cannot be overlooked. From student biometrics to data on classroom behavior, today's education institutions are becoming increasingly dependent on artificial intelligence technology. As a result, if this sensitive information is not adequately safeguarded, it might become a target for hackers or even be utilized for illicit purposes.

SECTION 5: FUTURE PERSPECTIVES AND POLICY RECOMMENDATIONS

In anticipation of future developments, it is imperative to formulate progressive policies and recommendations that guarantee the utilization of AI in education enhances learning efficacy and cognitive abilities, while also fostering the integration of educational systems and addressing the challenges of resource scarcity and inequality. Educational institutions can work with technology companies to ensure that technological developments are closely aligned with teaching and learning needs, and government and NGO-funded projects can help under-resourced regions to close the gap with more developed regions. This is an ongoing work that requires the participation and wisdom of us all.

5.1 The Potential of AI in Education

Artificial intelligence (AI) has enormous promise in the classroom, where it may enhance students' ability to retain information and develop their analytical and problem-solving abilities. Additionally, learners are able to participate more actively and creatively in their learning when AI is paired with cutting-edge technologies like AR and VR.

5.1.1 Fostering Critical and Systems Thinking

Promoting students' critical and systems thinking is essential for ESD. AI helps students to analyze and solve complex problems independently by providing personalized learning content and real-time feedback. Students can improve their understanding of complex systems and multi-dimensional problems by interacting with real-world problems in an AI-based learning platform. Learners are more invested in their education and develop better problem-solving skills through interactive learning.

5.1.2 Emerging Technology Trends

Integrating AI with other emerging technologies will further drive educational innovation as technology advances. Imagine doing research in the classroom, but not in a closed lab, but in an infinite digital environment with technological wonders such as Virtual Reality (VR) and Augmented Reality (AR). Students can use these tools to expand their learning beyond the limitations of a traditional classroom, allowing them to avoid space and equipment constraints. This immersion study allows the student to apply their information in a more real-world setting, so improving their practical skills.

Table 14. Potential applications of AI and emerging technologies in education

Technology	Application Scenario	Potential Impact
Virtual Reality (VR)	Virtual experiments, immersive learning environments	Increases student engagement, enhances practical experience
Augmented Reality (AR)	Augmented learning in real-world scenarios	Helps students apply knowledge in real-world contexts
Big Data Analytics	Personalized learning paths, student behavior analysis	Provides precise learning data analysis and decision support

5.2 Challenges and Solutions

Despite the potential of AI in education, its practical implementation faces multiple challenges, especially in integrating technology and education systems, inadequate resources, and educational equity. Among the most troublesome things? Getting this technology to cooperate with our current educational frameworks. You might as well be attempting to force a square peg into a round hole. As if that weren't enough, there is still a long way to go until AI realizes its full potential in schools throughout the world, because to concerns such as unequal access to resources and the never-ending battle for fair educational opportunities. Still, solutions are bubbling up, bit by bit, to bridge these gaps. In order to promote the widespread use of AI, policy makers need to take a number of steps to address these challenges.

CONCLUSION

This chapter examined the possibilities, difficulties, and future policy orientations for AI and adaptive learning in education. The application of AI technology not only increases educational efficiency, but it also offers students with tailored learning support and encourages the development of critical and system thinking skills. However, successful AI application in education faces various challenges, including technological integration, limited resources, and ethical considerations. To this end, policymakers should take proactive measures to promote the widespread use of AI technology through financial support, policy frameworks, and guarantees of educational equity to ensure that all students can benefit from this technological advancement.

Addressing these issues will further revolutionize the education system, and AI technologies will play a greater role in promoting educational equity, enhancing learning outcomes, and addressing global sustainable development challenges. AI-powered adaptive learning has the potential to transform education for sustainable development, making it more personalized, engaging, and effective. To maximize its benefits, educators should integrate AI thoughtfully, ensuring it complements human instruction rather than replacing it. Policymakers must develop ethical guidelines to safeguard student data privacy and ensure equitable access to AI-driven learning tools. Future research should focus on improving AI's ability to assess higher order thinking skills and reducing bias in AI algorithms.

REFERENCES

Braunerhjelm, P., & Hepburn, C. (2023). Climate change, complexity, and policy design. *Oxford Review of Economic Policy*, *39*(4), 667–679. Advance online publication. DOI: 10.1093/oxrep/grad047

Higgins, K., Calvert, A., Thompson, A. S., & Galvin, T. (2024). *Sustainable food systems: Embedding education for sustainable development (ESD) in a food science module*. Open Scholarship of Teaching and Learning., DOI: 10.56230/osotl.77

Holmes, W., Bialik, M., & Fadel, C. (2021). Artificial intelligence in education: Promises and implications for teaching and learning. Center for Curriculum Redesign. https://curriculumredesign.org/wp-content/uploads/AIED-Book-Excerpt-CCR.pdf

Ioannou, A. (2019). A Model of Gameful Design for Learning Using Interactive Tabletops: Enactment and Evaluation in the Socio-emotional Education Classroom [J]. *Educational Technology Research and Development*, *67*(2), 277–302. DOI: 10.1007/s11423-018-9610-1

Marcos-Sánchez, R., Ferrández, D., & Morón, C. (2022). Systems thinking for sustainability education in building and business administration and management degrees. *Sustainability (Basel)*, *14*(19), 11812. DOI: 10.3390/su141911812

Pena-Ayala, A. (2014). Educational Data Mining: A Survey and a Data Min- ing-based Analysis of Recent Works [J]. *Expert Systems with Applications*, *41*(4), 1432–1462. DOI: 10.1016/j.eswa.2013.08.042

Rahman, M. R. (2023). Students' class participation and creative thinking: Basis for class engagement framework. https://doi.org/DOI: 10.54097/hiaad.v3i3.11289

Shakir, F., Naz, A., & Ahmed, S. M. Z. (2024). Exploring teachers' perceptions and practices in education for sustainable development (ESD) in public schools of Karachi. Pakistan. *Journal of the Humanities and Social Sciences*, *12*(1), 902–914. Advance online publication. DOI: 10.52131/pjhss.2024.v12i1.2090

Tarrête, A. (2022). *Navigating difference in inter- & transdisciplinary learning*. https://doi.org/DOI: 10.5463/thesis.14

Chapter 5
Inbound Learning Active Methodology in Sustainable Development With AI Tools

Vitor Lima
https://orcid.org/0009-0007-5765-3079
Instituto Superior de Gestão e Administração de Santarém, Portugal

Ana Filipa Joaquim
https://orcid.org/0000-0002-3419-1242
Instituto Superior de Gestão e Administração de Santarém, Portugal

ABSTRACT

In Portugal, adopting active methodologies has been a growing strategy to engage students and stimulate active participation and autonomy in the educational process. In this context, quality education plays a crucial role in developing sustainable communities, especially with the advancement of AI. AI has the potential to personalize teaching, adapt it to students' individual needs, and facilitate the implementation of methodologies such as Inbound Learning, which focuses on creating relevant and personalized educational experiences. Educational innovation in Portugal seeks to improve the quality of teaching and promote equity and inclusion, ensuring that all students have access to quality educational opportunities. This article presents the IL methodology, which can positively transform teaching-learning. It prepares students to be critical, creative, and adaptable citizens and thus creates the skills and competencies to respond to the challenges of SDG9.

DOI: 10.4018/979-8-3693-9062-7.ch005

INTRODUCTION

According to the *Sustainable Development Report* (Sachs et al., 2023), Portugal's top priorities for implementing the *2030 Agenda* are the Sustainable Development Goals (SDGs) related to Quality Education (SDG 4) and Industry, Innovation and Infrastructure (SDG 9).

SDG 4 aims to ensure inclusive, equitable, quality education and promote lifelong learning for all. In Portugal, this means providing universal access to education from early childhood through higher education, as well as continuing education for adults. It also involves improving teaching quality, teaching training, and aligning curricula with job market needs.

SDG 9 focuses on building resilient infrastructure, promoting inclusive and sustainable industrialization, and fostering innovation. In the national context, this implies investing in physical infrastructure (roads, railways, ports, telecommunications) to drive economic development, and supporting sustainable industries that create jobs and opportunities across society.

These two goals are interrelated: quality education empowers individuals with skills to participate effectively in the economy, fueling innovation and advanced industries, while modern infrastructure improves access to education, creating a virtuous cycle of development. Investments in one sector often benefit the other, highlighting their synergy.

Quality education is essential for sustainable national development. Portugal has universal, compulsory education up to 12th grade (age 18), providing a strong foundation for personal and professional growth (Assembleia da República Portuguesa, 2005). However, achieving *truly* inclusive, high-quality education for all remains challenging. The Portuguese education system still relies heavily on the expository (lecture-based) method, with learning often measured by standardized exams at the end of each cycle (Fernandes, 2007). Over-reliance on this traditional methodology raises concerns: students often become demotivated in class(Almeida & Sartori, 2012; A. R. Lima et al., 2020), critical thinking skills are underdeveloped (Iyer, 2019), and there is minimal integration of Information and Communication Technologies (ICT) to foster digital literacy. The lack of a triad of skills (critical thinking) and tools (ICT) hampers innovation in the business sector.

Given the constant evolution and ubiquity of ICT, it is crucial to incorporate these technologies into the classroom. This requires implementing active learning methodologies in teaching (Rodrigues, 2017). Researchers like Arends (2008) and Bacich & Moran (2018) note that active methodologies make students responsible for their own learning, giving them an active role in the process and refocusing teachers as facilitators. Active learning is not entirely new—educational theorists such as Piaget, Vygotsky, and Freire argued over a century ago that knowledge is constructed through learners' interaction with their environment (Jófili, 2002).

Piaget, for instance, saw the learner as actively constructing knowledge (Becker, 2009). Limiting learning to rote classroom contexts can be counterproductive in the long term, leading to abstract knowledge that students struggle to apply in real life and resulting in demotivation (Almeida & Sartori, 2012).

To address these issues, education must move beyond memorization. Students in the current system often *memorize and reproduce* curricular content mechanically rather than understanding its meaning (Iyer, 2019). Studies show that implementing active methods to develop creative problem-solving and critical thinking is crucial for students to gain skills needed in the workforce(Bacich & Moran, 2018; Postigo et al., 2015; Rumpagaporn, 2007)- Incorporating ICT can foster digital literacy in tandem with critical thinking and problem-solving (Arends, 2008; Bacich & Moran, 2018; Rodrigues, 2017). Notably, this does not require a drastic overhaul of formal curricula, but rather training and sensitizing teachers to use ICT critically in their pedagogy. Rodrigues (2017) points out structural flaws in teachers' digital literacy—Portugal's teaching workforce is *aging,* and the profession faces an "ideological crisis" (OECD, 2018) The need to integrate ICT in secondary education is increasingly urgent ((Joaquim, 2018; Joaquim & Figueiredo, 2024), not only for the reasons above but also because digital competencies are expected of students by the end of compulsory schooling (MEC, 2017).

In vocational training, many organizations endorse active learning, but these methods are still not widely practiced—even among trainers who have appropriate academic qualifications and professional experience. To boost human capital and prevent skills obsolescence in the face of technological change, Portugal passed legislation in 2009 requiring companies to provide employee training (DRE, 2022). Furthermore, the national program Portugal Digital (aligned with the EU's digital strategy) includes an action plan for digital transition, focusing on digital empowerment of people, digital transformation of businesses, and digitalization of the state (Portugal Digital, 2020) As stated in the plan's introduction:

> *(...) [Digital transformation serves] as the country's engine to accelerate progress, leaving no one behind and projecting Portugal into the world. To this end, the Action Plan for the Digital Transition focuses on people's digital empowerment, companies' digital transformation, and the State's digitalization* (Portugal Digital, 2020, p. 4).

Given this context and framework, the aim of this chapter is to present an active teaching and training methodology that incorporates ICT tools, promotes critical thinking and creative problem-solving, and fosters motivation for learning among its participants. In the sections that follow, the authors will discuss the importance of motivation for learning, provide a brief conceptualization of active methodologies, introduce the use of the Learning Management System (LMS), and detail the *Inbound Learning*™ methodology (with its axes and phases) that are proposed. By improving transitions between education and real-world application, this methodology seeks to strengthen human capital development in line with SDG 4 and SDG 9.

MOTIVATION FOR LEARNING

The teaching-learning process is far more complex than simply attending school and listening to teachers in order to pass tests. Teaching requires a foundation of scientific knowledge and pedagogical skills, but learning also requires student (Arends, 2008). Lack of motivation in academic settings is a common complaint among both students and teachers. To understand this phenomenon, a brief historical perspective is useful.

In the 18th century, formal schooling was not seen as crucial for individual development; teaching was often carried out by clergy or laymen without formal pedagogical training. It was only in the 19th century that schooling started to include basic objectives like arithmetic (counting, addition, subtraction) and literacy (reading and writing) (Arends, 2008).

In the 20th century, the "Traditional School" model became predominant, characterized by structured content delivery where the teacher was the primary source of knowledge (Leão, 1999). Opposing this, Jean Piaget's Constructivism (the "Modern School") argued that individuals construct knowledge through interaction with their environment, an approach based on active methods involving the learner and their context (Becker, 2009).

According to Rodrigues and Cabrito (2022) students *only achieve true knowledge if they experience it*, because their motivation often lies outside the classroom. Therefore, teachers should select diverse and engaging methodologies so that students feel school is a welcoming place for learning. This shifts the responsibility of learning more onto the student and recasts the teacher as a facilitator or mediator, rather than a mere content transmitter, while still using expository methods when appropriate (Joaquim, 2018). However, to effectively improve student engagement, it is essential to understand what motivation entails.

For the American Psychological Association (APA), *motivation* is defined as:

> (...) the impetus that gives purpose or direction to behavior and operates in humans at a conscious or unconscious level. Motives are often divided into (a) physiological, primary, or organic motives, such as hunger, thirst, and the need for sleep, and (b) personal, social, or secondary motives, such as affiliation, competition, and individual interests and goals. An important distinction should also be made between internal motivational forces and external factors, such as rewards or punishments, that can encourage or discourage certain behaviors(American Psychological Association, 2022).

In other words, students (and people in general) need a meaningful purpose to engage in learning.

Currently, many students do not perceive such purpose in their school subjects. The authors are not suggesting changing the formal curriculum of subjects; rather, we propose alternative methodological approaches in the teaching-learning process so that motivation and critical thinking are nurtured from the beginning of formal education. Additionally, we aim to highlight the importance of vocational training in developing companies' human capital, linking it to the broader education system.

Portugal's formal curricula need to be taught in step with ICT advancements. Digital technologies are innovating rapidly, and curricula must adapt more quickly to remain relevant. In 2017, the Ministry of Education introduced the *Profile of Students at the End of Compulsory Schooling* (MEC, 2017), which outlines the competencies, attitudes, and knowledge students should acquire by the end of 12th grade. However, reality has lagged behind these goals: there is still a significant digital literacy gap between teachers and students, and many schools lack the technical means to implement all the recommended practices.

According to OECD (2019a, 2019b) digital technologies have gained enormous importance in society and education, but digital skills quickly become obsolete due to constant innovation. Today's students belong to Generation Z (born 1997–2012), a generation raised with the Internet and social networks (Figueiredo & Joaquim, 2023). They spend more time on digital devices than previous generations and prefer on-demand streaming over traditional television (Meola, 2022). In contrast, most teachers are from the Baby Boomer or Generation X cohorts (OECD, 2018). Despite this generational divide, it is critical for teachers to understand students' needs, goals, and social contexts. As Steinmayr et al. (2019) observed, *"Students' motivational beliefs are significantly related to their academic performance"* (p. 3). Teachers should support students' academic goals by incorporating active methodologies when teaching the formal curriculum. While individual teachers cannot change the official curriculum, they can change how learning feels, making school a pleasant, engaging space that connects theory with practice (Joaquim & Figueiredo, 2023).

On the other hand, vocational (professional) training is legally compulsory in Portugal (DRE, 2009). Unfortunately, it is sometimes viewed as a mere obligation, which detracts from its main objective: building human capital. Here too, it is necessary to apply active methodologies that dynamically motivate learners to internalize knowledge. The following sections will briefly conceptualize active methodologies and then present our proposed methodology (*Inbound Learning*™) that addresses motivation in both formal education and vocational training.

ACTIVE METHODOLOGIES: BRIEF CONCEPTUALIZATION

For a long time, traditional teaching methods—such as lectures and demonstrations—were considered sufficient for instructors and students. The primary goal was to transmit knowledge and have students absorb it as immutable truth. However, in the 21st century, with the advent of new technologies, the world can be accessed through a cell phone or laptop screen. The traditional approach is no longer adequate; teachers need to reinvent their classroom practices because student motivation now often lies outside the school environment (Joaquim, 2018).

Rodrigues & Cabrito (2022) noted that criticism of the traditional teaching style has existed for a long time. They cite educational pioneers to illustrate this:

Piaget (1968), with his advocacy for the right to education for all; Freire (1996), with his defense of a democratic and participatory school; and Dewey (1960), who introduced the vision of education as an inherently social process, all critiqued traditional pedagogy (2022, p. 7)

Rather than viewing active methodologies as wholesale replacements for traditional ones, it is important to see them as complementary (Konopka et al., 2015). Certain foundational concepts may still need to be introduced through direct instruction, but active techniques can greatly enhance understanding and application. According to Lopes (2023), the roots of active learning are captured in an old proverb (often attributed to Chinese wisdom and cited by Barbosa and Moura, 2013):

"What I hear, I forget;
What I hear and see, I remember;
What I hear, see, ask or discuss, I begin to understand;
What I hear, see, discuss, and do, I learn by developing knowledge and skills;
What I teach someone, I master" (Barbosa & Moura, 2013, p. 54).

This proverb highlights the difference between passive learning and active learning (Lopes, 2023). In a similar vein, educational theorist William Glasser (as quoted by Faias (2021)) suggested that people generally retain different percentages of knowledge depending on how they engage with it. Approximately:

- *Reading:* 10% retention
- *Writing:* 20% retention
- *Observing:* 50% retention
- *Speaking (and discussing):* 70% retention
- *Practicing (doing):* 80% retention
- *Teaching others:* 90% retention

The first three methods (reading, writing, observing) are relatively passive, whereas the last three (discussing, practicing, teaching) are active forms of learning. This illustrates why active involvement leads to deeper learning.

Active methodologies offer several advantages. For students, they become protagonists of their learning experience, which helps them develop autonomy, critical thinking, problem-solving skills, and confidence (Bonwell & Eison, 1991; Faias, 2021). For teachers, active methods require more careful planning of classroom activities and assessments, which can be challenging but ultimately leads to more meaningful learning outcomes (Arends, 2008; Fernandes, 2007; Leão, 1999). In fact, Arends (2008) argues that active methodologies are among the most demanding yet effective approaches for fostering student learning and motivation, precisely because they place the student at the center of the process.

Educators can choose from a variety of active learning techniques in the classroom. However, using these methodologies is more complex than using traditional lectures. It requires a certain level of media and digital literacy from teachers, and it can make student assessment more challenging. One of the essential tasks, as Arends (2008) points out, is careful planning and alignment with the formal curriculum. Teachers must ensure that the skills and knowledge domains to be assessed are explicitly covered by the active learning activities. When this alignment is achieved, assessments become more effective and less misleading.

Traditional assessment formats often fall short for active and collaborative learning contexts. It can be difficult to evaluate skills and tasks that students develop through real-world, project-based activities using standard tests or exams. Rodrigues and Cabrito (2022) highlight that conventional assessments are not well-suited to measure competencies built via active methods. Therefore, assessment strategies also need to evolve alongside teaching methods.

Researchers Bacich and Moran (2018) and Moran (2015) note that the main benefits of applying active methodologies are the promotion of critical thinking and problem-solving skills. Importantly, active approaches can—and often should—be blended with traditional ones (for example, using brief lectures to introduce concepts before an interactive activity).

A range of teaching methods fall under the umbrella of active methodologies. These include project-based learning, gamification, the flipped classroom, and the use of Learning Management Systems (LMS) as a platform to deliver and manage learning activities. All of these approaches leverage ICT as a critical tool in designing and implementing learning experiences. Despite widespread discussion about the importance of integrating such methods, there remains a gap in actually promoting digital and media literacy in many educational settings.

It is worth noting that while today's students are *born in the digital age*, some argue that they do not inherently know how to use digital tools for deep, critical learning. Bauerlein (2009), for example, controversially described Generation Z as potentially the "most ignorant" generation compared to previous ones. This claim is likely exaggerated, but it underscores a point: being a digital native does not automatically equate to being digitally literate or an effective learner online. Indeed, during the COVID-19 pandemic when education shifted to online platforms, both teachers and students reported that the experience was neither fruitful nor effective for teaching and learning. As evidence, Portugal's results in the 2022 *Program for International Student Assessment* (PISA) showed a decline in learning outcomes compared to other OECD countries (OCDE, 2023). This suggests that simply having technology is not enough—educators and students must know how to use it to facilitate learning.

The shift to e-learning during the pandemic highlighted the urgent need to improve digital competencies in education (OCDE Indicators, 2021).

Rodrigues and Cabrito (2022) echo this, noting that despite the challenges, the development of digital skills in teaching and learning has provided significant experiences with real impacts on education (p. 23). In other words, the crisis accelerated digital learning but also exposed gaps that need addressing.

Consequently, there was a clear need to create a new active learning methodology that addresses all these improvement points in the teaching-learning process. It was understood that integrating ICT into teaching would best be accomplished through a Learning Management System (LMS), a platform where educational resources can be created and made available both synchronously (real-time) and asynchronously, in order to stimulate interest and motivation in learning (P. Oliveira et al., 2016).

The next section will discuss the concept of an LMS and its role in modernizing the educational process.

LEARNING MANAGEMENT SYSTEM (LMS)

The concept of the Learning Management System dates back to 1924, when Sidney Pressey created the first *"teaching machine"* (Petrina, 2004). Pressey's machine, resembling a typewriter with a window for questions and another for answers, allowed students to answer multiple-choice questions and receive immediate feedback. Although primitive by today's standards, it was a revolutionary idea in the 1920s.

Fast forward 100 years, and ICT has transformed the LMS into an extraordinarily powerful methodology with numerous advantages (P. Oliveira et al., 2016).

P. Oliveira et al. (2016) define an LMS as "a virtual environment that aims to simulate face-to-face learning environments using Information Technologies" (p. 160). They reference Lonn and Teasley (2009) to further describe LMSs as *web-based systems that allow teachers and students to share materials, submit and return work, and communicate online* (as cited in P. Oliveira et al., (2016, p. 160). In simpler terms, an LMS is a platform that brings the classroom into the digital space.

It is important to understand how an LMS works and why it supports active methodologies.

An LMS typically provides personalized access to learning content, direct communication between teacher and student, tools for monitoring and managing learning activities, and support for self-paced learning by students. Students are encouraged to engage with materials independently and take initiative in their learning process, while teachers can track progress and provide guidance as needed.

According to Pereira and Lima (2021), *"Digital Transformation is also an ally of innovation in the field of Education"* (p. 102).

As mentioned, integrating technology like an LMS into teaching methodologies is crucial for modern education. The COVID-19 lockdowns in 2020 and 2021 greatly accelerated the adoption of LMS platforms, as schools and universities had to move entirely to virtual instruction almost overnight. Traditional in-person teaching methods were adapted to online formats through LMS tools. This sudden shift also underscored the generational gap in digital literacy: many teachers struggled to effectively use these systems, widening the gap between them and their tech-savvy students (Menezes & Francisco, 2020).

Despite these challenges, an LMS can enable many of the active learning practices discussed earlier. It provides a centralized hub for blended learning, where a teacher can combine videos, reading, quizzes, discussion forums, and real-time webinars into a cohesive learning journey. It also supports analytics to track student engagement and performance, informing the teacher where intervention might be needed. However, an LMS on its own is just a tool; the pedagogy behind its use is what determines its effectiveness. To truly engage students via an LMS, one needs to employ innovative strategies that leverage the platform's capabilities.

With this in mind, the next section introduces Inbound Learning™, an innovative approach that combines the capabilities of an LMS with principles borrowed from the field of marketing, to create a highly personalized and engaging learning experience.

INBOUND LEARNING™

Inbound Learning™ is an educational approach inspired by the principles of Inbound Marketing. Just as modern marketing emphasizes catering to individual customers, Inbound Learning™ focuses on providing a personalized and engaging educational experience tailored to each learner's needs. Education and training should recognize that students have different learning styles, interests, and paces of assimilation. This perspective is reflected in Portugal's *Profile of the Student at the End of Compulsory Schooling* (MEC, 2017) and aligns with the targets of SDG 4 on quality education(ONU Portugal, 2022). The development of the Inbound Learning™ methodology stemmed from a benchmarking process that identified gaps in the education and training sector and sought to fill them by borrowing strategies from the marketing domain. The result is an active learning methodology with a set of defined axes and phases, supported by a digital platform, to enhance learner motivation and provide tools for creative thinking and problem-solving in real-life contexts. In short, incorporating certain marketing techniques into vocational and educational training is seen as an asset to building human capital.

Recognizing the diversity among learners, Inbound Learning™ aims to meet individual needs. V. Lima & Gaspar (2024) describe Inbound Learning™ as creating a *personalized and engaging educational experience* for each student. At its core, this methodology shifts the focus of teaching toward the students (or trainees), delivering content tailored to them and encouraging their active participation in constructing (V. Lima & Gaspar, 2024).

Inbound Learning™ acknowledges that one size does not fit all in education—each learner's journey should be somewhat unique.

Practically, the Inbound Learning™ methodology is built on four key axes (Figure 3), that structure how it is implemented. These axes represent the major components of the approach. Inbound Learning™ also unfolds through a sequence of seven stages or phases (Figure 4) which are interconnected. Below, we outline the four axes first, and then the stages of the Inbound Learning™ process.

Axes of Inbound Learning™ Methodology:

1. Lesson Management: This axis covers the planning and management of lessons using the LMS. It is essentially the architecture of each course or curricular unit. Lesson management involves setting up all the elements of a course on the platform, including lesson summaries, assignments, class schedules, a log of student questions, available quizzes/tests, and assessment activities. In other words, the LMS should allow teachers (facilitators) to organize *everything* related to the course in one place, providing structure and clarity to the learning process. This is the *genesis* of how Inbound Learning™ uses an LMS: by having a centralized system for course content and interactions.
2. Question & Answer Management: This axis involves creating a robust system for questions and answers on the subject matter. In practice, this means using the LMS to host online quizzes, practice exercises, and tests that students can take on their own, receiving immediate feedback. The idea is to give students autonomy to *self-assess* and practice without needing a teacher's constant presence, thus reinforcing learning through repetition and feedback. For Inbound Learning™, a large bank of questions (covering key concepts and skills) is developed for each subject, enabling frequent knowledge checks and practice opportunities. This approach encourages students to take initiative in their learning and helps them identify areas where they need more study.

(These first two axes — lesson management and Q&A management — form a necessary "binomial" for successfully applying Inbound Learning™. They create a structured environment in which active, self-paced learning can occur. It should be noted that implementing these processes involves several stages, which will be described shortly (Figure 4).)

3. Infrastructure (Platform) Adaptation: The third axis pertains to the LMS infrastructure and technological integration required for Inbound Learning™. The LMS platform must be adapted or developed to support the methodology's needs. In this case, a platform called *Virtual First* was created by the agency Crivosoft, Marketing Digital (2023) specifically for this purpose. The platform is designed to include advanced features such as AI integration (for creating student profiles/*personas* and generating personalized questions/challenges) and tools for collaboration. According to Portugal Digital (2020), digital transformation is a key ally in educational innovation. Therefore, the chosen LMS should support forums for idea generation and discussion, co-creation spaces, and gamification elements to promote engagement (V. Lima & Gaspar, 2024). Essentially, the infrastructure axis ensures that the technology (the LMS) has the capabilities to implement the other axes and stages effectively.
4. Content Production: The fourth axis focuses on how learning content is created and delivered. Content production must account for different cognitive styles and stages of learning for each student. In practice, this means producing multiple versions or layers of content: for example, a *simplified version* of materials for beginners or for initial exposure, and a more *in-depth version* with practical examples and complex applications for advanced understanding. By differentiating content complexity, the methodology can accommodate learners at various levels and allow them to progress at their own pace. This axis ensures that all students, regardless of prior knowledge or skill, can engage with the material meaningfully and then delve deeper as they are ready.

These four axes form the foundation of the Inbound Learning™ approach. Together, they ensure that the teaching-learning process is managed, autonomous, technologically supported, and adaptive to student needs.

In the context of Inbound Learning™, gamification is used within the LMS (as part of the infrastructure axis) to make education more engaging, motivating, and effective. Gamified elements such as points, badges, levels, and challenges transform the learning experience into something more akin to a game, which can stimulate students' active participation. For example, the LMS might reward students with experience points for completing tasks or setting up friendly competitions or quests instead of traditional tests. These strategies tap into learners' intrinsic motivation and can lead to deeper and more lasting learning. By incorporating gamification, the platform captivates students' interest and encourages them to persist in learning activities even when they are challenging.

Having described the axes, we now turn to the phases of the Inbound Learning™ process. Inbound Learning™ occurs through several interconnected stages, which together create a continuous learning *journey* for the student. Each stage builds on the previous one and is tailored to maintain student motivation and ensure mastery of content and skills. Below are the stages (phases 1 through 7) of Inbound Learning™:

1. Diagnostic Analysis of the Learner (Phase 1): The starting point is an in-depth analysis of the student's characteristics and preferences. This involves identifying each learner's style of learning (e.g. visual, auditory, kinesthetic), their interests, their strengths, and the areas where they need improvement . To gather this information, diagnostic tests or assessments are administered at the beginning of the learning process. These diagnostics help determine the student's current knowledge level and skills, effectively placing them on a map of the learning journey. Based on the results, the teacher and student collaboratively define individual learning objectives for the student (or trainee). This collaboration ensures that the goals are personalized and meaningful. At this stage, the facilitator

(teacher) often creates a learner persona – a profile that encapsulates the learner's attributes and "pain points" (areas of struggle or concern). Identifying pain points is crucial because it highlights what the student perceives as difficult or what might demotivate them. This entire phase is akin to the marketing practice of segmenting and understanding your customer; here, the "customer" is the student, and their needs drive the next steps. V. Lima & Gaspar (2024) refer to this as *student nurturing*, drawing an analogy to "lead nurturing" in marketing. The idea is to guide the student from the start through the completion of their educational goals by providing personalized support, continuous feedback, adaptation to their needs, and encouragement of intrinsic motivation. In summary, Phase 1 sets a personalized foundation: we know *who* the learner is, *what* they need, and *where* they want to go.

2. Personalized Objective Setting and Human-in-the-Loop Automation (Phase 2): In this phase, the insights from the diagnostic are used to design a tailored learning plan for the student. Concrete objectives are established, targeting the students' weak points and building on their strengths. This planning is a collaborative effort between the facilitator and the student, ensuring buy-in and relevance. At the same time, the methodology leverages technology by introducing a degree of automation into the teaching process. Using the diagnostic data (from Phase 1) combined with analytical capabilities of AI, certain aspects of the learning can be automated (V. Lima & Gaspar, 2024). For instance, the LMS might automatically recommend specific exercises or resources to the student based on their diagnostic profile. However, human oversight remains crucial – a concept known as *"human-in-the-loop."* Even as AI-driven tools provide recommendations and streamline some tasks, a human facilitator is always involved to ensure the learning experience is humane and to intervene where needed. This aligns with Bisen's (2020) notion that systems shouldn't be fully automated in education; the human touch is especially important when adopting AI. Additionally, during this phase, a mentor or tutor is assigned to the student (if not the facilitator themselves), offering mentoring or tutoring sessions on demand. The combination of automation and human guidance in Phase 2 aims to optimize the learning process: routine tasks and basic feedback can be handled by the system, while the facilitator focuses on higher-level guidance and motivation.
3. Contextualized Content Delivery (Phase 3): With objectives in place, the next phase is delivering the content in a way that resonates with the student. Contextualized delivery means presenting the material through channels and formats that the student is comfortable with and interested in. For example, some students may engage better with learning materials delivered via a mobile app or a social media platform, whereas others might prefer the structure of an LMS website. The facilitator (and LMS) will use the channels that are most relevant to the student's daily life to make learning feel less like a separate, formal task and more integrated with their normal activities. Moreover, content is delivered in multiple formats to suit different learning preferences: text documents for those who like to read, videos for visual/auditory learners, podcasts or audio for those who learn by listening, and hands-on interactive simulations or exercises for kinesthetic learners. By diversifying formats, Phase 3 accommodates various learning styles and keeps students engaged. The idea is to meet students *where they are*—both in terms of medium and in terms of starting knowledge. This phase also involves ensuring the content ties back to real-world examples that the student can relate to, making the learning inherently relevant.
4. Active Engagement and Dialogue (Phase 4): In this phase, the focus is on fostering active involvement of students with the content and with others. Learning is not seen as a one-way transmission, but rather as a dialogue. Students are encouraged to take part in group discussions, online forums,

debates, and Q&A sessions about the topics they are studying. For instance, after working through a set of materials, a student might participate in an online discussion board to answer open-ended questions or solve a challenge with peers. This stage leverages the idea that we learn better when we articulate our thoughts and engage in discourse. It corresponds to the higher retention methods (discussion, practice, teaching) mentioned earlier in the context of active learning. The LMS facilitates this through features like discussion threads, chat rooms, or even live webinar sessions. Meanwhile, the facilitator provides continuous feedback (Phase 5 overlaps here) to keep the dialogue productive . By actively exchanging ideas, students deepen their understanding and also learn from each other. This social learning component also helps in developing communication skills and teamwork abilities.

5. Continuous Feedback and Assessment (Phase 5): A cornerstone of Inbound Learning™ is the provision of constant feedback to learners. As students engage with content and activities, the facilitator (and the LMS) continuously monitor their progress. Feedback can take various forms: automated feedback from quizzes, personalized comments on assignments, or analytic reports from the LMS indicating areas of strength and weakness. In this phase, the facilitator gathers information on what is working well for each student and where adjustments are needed. Inbound Learning™ values this ongoing feedback loop because it allows for agile adjustments to the learning plan. For example, if a student is struggling with a particular concept, the system (or facilitator) might suggest a review session or additional practice exercises. Conversely, if a student shows mastery, they might be directed to more challenging tasks. Continuous feedback ensures that the student doesn't veer too far off course; it keeps the learning progression sequential and logical, allowing students to gradually build knowledge and skills (Phase 6 ties in here). Essentially, phase 5 is about making the learning adaptive: using feedback to personalize pacing and content in real time.
6. Sequential Progression and Concept Building (Phase 6): In phase 6, students gradually construct knowledge in a sequential, scaffolded manner. Based on the ongoing feedback and engagement from previous phases, the facilitator ensures that the student moves on to the next topic or skill only when they are ready. The LMS can chart a learner's journey, showing which objectives have been met and which are pending. The curriculum is navigated not just linearly but *logically* – meaning that if a student needs to spend more time reinforcing a foundational concept, they do so before moving forward. This phase is about *consolidation* of learning: concepts introduced earlier are revisited in more complex forms, and disparate topics are connected so that the student can see a coherent big picture. By the end of this phase, the student should have built up a strong understanding of the material in a structured way, with each new concept resting on the firm understanding of previous ones. This careful progression helps prevent gaps in knowledge that could hinder the application of learning in real situations.
7. Real-World Application and Evaluation (Phase 7): The final phase emphasizes applying knowledge in real-world contexts and evaluating learning outcomes in a student-centered way. Active Inbound Learning™ is not complete until students have the opportunity to use what they've learned in practical situations. This could involve case studies, projects, simulations, or any task that mimics real life. For example, a student might complete a capstone project that solves a problem in their community using the skills learned, or a trainee in a vocational program might perform a workplace simulation. Such application cements learning and demonstrates to students the *value* and relevance of their education. In terms of assessment, Inbound Learning™ moves away from solely traditional exams. Instead, evaluation is dynamic and learner-centered, focusing on individual progress and the ability to apply knowledge, not just recall it. Assessments may be portfolio-based, performance-based, or

reflective, and they consider both the knowledge gained and the skills developed (such as problem-solving, collaboration, etc.). Importantly, even in assessment, the methodology looks at learning as ongoing; assessments are also used to provide feedback and set new goals, if needed, rather than just to assign a static grade. This approach aligns with the idea mentioned by Joaquim (2018) and Rodrigues and Cabrito (2022) that *students' motivation often lies outside the classroom* – by making evaluation itself an active, engaging process, students remain motivated and see assessment as part of learning, not the end of it.

The above stages are interconnected and cyclical. Through these phases, Inbound Learning™ allows students to acquire knowledge that aligns with their personal motivations and goals, while still adhering to the formal curriculum standards. Each phase feeds into the next, creating a continuous improvement loop for both the student and the facilitator. The approach ensures that learning is meaningful, personalized, and applied.

To illustrate, Figure 5 in the original text presented a schematic diagram of this methodology. While we cannot show the figure here, the description of the axes and phases serves to outline how the system works. By implementing all these elements, the inherent problems of student and teacher motivation can be addressed. Everyone involved in the process is more engaged: teachers (facilitators) use diverse tools and strategies, and students are active participants in their learning. As a result, formal curriculum content is not just learned for school but internalized and made transversal to daily life and future work (V. Lima & Gaspar, 2024).

It is worth noting how this methodology ties back to the SDGs discussed in the introduction. SDG 4 calls for quality education that is equitable, inclusive, and lifelong. However, vocational training is often a missing piece in discussions of SDG 4. Inbound Learning™ explicitly includes vocational and continuous training in its scope, helping ensure that lifelong education is connected with society's needs (for instance, companies benefiting from better-trained individuals, and individuals continuously updating their skills). SDG 9, which focuses on innovation and infrastructure, can only be fully realized if the workforce is innovative and skilled – which again ties back to education and training. There is frequently criticism in academia about the disconnect between formal education and the real needs of civil society, leading to gaps in skills and literacy. Inbound Learning™ attempts to bridge that gap by interconnecting knowledge transmission with its recipients (the students and the broader community).

Innovation, as Joaquim & Figueiredo (2023) point out, is not limited to creating new products or businesses; it must also occur in the education system. By rethinking teaching tools and methods to encourage creative problem-solving (as Inbound Learning™ does), we foster the type of innovative thinking required for the 21st century. Only through such educational innovations will it be possible to achieve the broader Sustainable Development Goals, especially SDG 4 (Quality Education) and SDG 9 (Industry, Innovation, Infrastructure).

CONCLUSION

Academic studies and reflections on Portugal's education system have highlighted several issues: participants in the teaching-learning process (both students and teachers) often feel unmotivated, content is delivered in an unengaging manner, and the practical applicability of what is taught is not evident in everyday life. In recent years, a younger generation of teachers has attempted to change this paradigm, introducing new methods and technologies. However, the overall teaching workforce is aging, and many educators lack proficiency in ICT tools—a weakness starkly revealed during the COVID-19 lockdowns, when teachers had to suddenly rely on technology for remote teaching.

The 2022 PISA results underscored these challenges: they showed a decline in learning outcomes among Portuguese students compared to other OECD countries and to Portugal's own previous performance (OCDE, 2023) This indicates that Portugal's education system may not be fully meeting its objectives in terms of student learning and skill acquisition. To reverse this trend, it is essential to build bridges between technological innovations and education. In practice, that means integrating new tools and methods into teaching, so that scientific knowledge from the curriculum is coupled with strong ICT skills in students.

Active learning methodologies, as discussed, offer numerous benefits for boosting student motivation and helping students internalize knowledge in a way that they can apply in real life. In this article, we presented a specific method – Inbound Learning™ – which is based on the premises of Inbound Marketing but adapted to the context of national education. Inbound Learning™ is built on four axes and seven phases, which the literature suggests are effective for teaching and learning. A key advantage of this methodology is that it actively involves students in their own learning process and gives them autonomy in choosing certain content and paths. At the same time, it ensures that the formal syllabus of each subject is covered and not neglected.

The goal is for this methodology (and others like it) to be replicated widely and become the norm in Portugal's education and training system, rather than an exception. That said, we acknowledge that achieving such change will be a long journey. On the one hand, many teachers need further training in ICT skills to feel comfortable with these new approaches. On the other hand, changing the deeply ingrained motivational dynamics of students and teachers will not happen overnight; early attempts may face setbacks or limited success, and persistence will be required.

Despite Portugal's relatively good performance on some SDG indicators (Sachs et al., 2023), a closer analysis reveals areas of concern – for example, literacy rates have stagnated. The Portuguese government's *Action Plan for the Digital Transition* (Portugal Digital, 2020) aims to fully digitize society and the economy by 2030, which includes bold steps in digital education and training. This shows a high-level commitment to improving the very areas that Inbound Learning™ targets. While Portugal currently ranks around 18th out of 166 countries in SDG progress (Sachs et al., 2023), there remain significant gaps, particularly in innovation-related goals, that need to be addressed through concerted effort.

One possible critique of the Inbound Learning™ approach is that it might exacerbate inequalities—students from disadvantaged backgrounds or schools with less technology could be left behind if learning relies heavily on ICT. However, ongoing national and international initiatives are rapidly expanding access to digital tools and the internet. Over time, the digital divide is expected to narrow, making the premise of Inbound Learning™ increasingly feasible for all. In fact, ensuring equitable access to the necessary technology and training is part of the broader strategy; without it, the SDG targets cannot be met. Thus, we believe the potential downsides of technology-driven learning are outweighed by the need to modernize education, and with proper support, those downsides can be mitigated.

In conclusion, to achieve the ambitious goals of the SDGs, particularly in quality education and innovation, education systems must innovate from within. Inbound Learning™ represents one such innovation—grounded in research and theory, and oriented towards practical outcomes in student motivation and skill development. By keeping learners engaged, tailoring education to individual needs, and constantly connecting learning to real-world application, we can better prepare students for the challenges of the future and ensure that no one is left behind in the pursuit of sustainable development.

LIMITATIONS AND FUTURE RECOMMENDATIONS

Introducing an innovative methodology like Inbound Learning™ is just a first step. One limitation of this work is the lack of extensive empirical data on the methodology's implementation. As of now, we have primarily theoretical and qualitative support for the approach. More academic research (both quantitative and qualitative) is needed to evaluate its success or failure in real educational contexts. For instance, pilot programs implementing Inbound Learning™ could be analyzed to gather data on student outcomes, engagement levels, and teacher feedback.

The authors recommend establishing a dedicated working group or pilot project to implement Inbound Learning™ in a selection of schools or training centers. This group would oversee the rollout of the methodology, monitor its execution, and collect data. By doing so, any necessary adjustments can be identified and applied in real-time. Such a pilot would also likely uncover "bugs" or issues with the Virtual First platform or any aspect of the process, allowing for investigative troubleshooting and improvement.

Another recommendation is to ensure robust teacher training and support during the adoption of this methodology. Teachers must be comfortable with their role as facilitators and proficient in using the LMS and other ICT tools. Mentorship programs or communities of practice could help teachers share experiences and strategies for active learning.

It is also urgent to address any infrastructural barriers. As noted, integrating ICT (especially AI) into formal curricula is critical to filling the gaps in critical thinking and digital skills. Schools and training institutions will need adequate hardware, software, and internet connectivity for all staff and students. Policymakers should consider investments in these areas as foundational to the success of any modern methodology.

Finally, future research should also look at the long-term effects of approaches like Inbound Learning™. Do students who learn under this system retain knowledge better? Are they more adaptable and skilled in the workplace? Do they become lifelong learners more readily? These are questions that longitudinal studies could answer.

In summary, while Inbound Learning™ holds promise, its effective implementation will require careful planning, resources, and continuous evaluation. The future of education will undoubtedly involve blending traditional wisdom with new technology and methodologies. By doing so thoughtfully, we can hope to achieve a more motivated, skilled, and adaptable generation of learners ready to meet the demands of the 21st century.

REFERENCES

Almeida, T. D. F. S., & Sartori, J. (2012). A relação entre desmotivação e o processo ensino-aprendizagem. Revista Monografias Ambientais, 1870-1886.

American Psychological Association. (2022). *Dictionary of Psychology*. APA Dictionary of Psychology. https://dictionary.apa.org/motivation

Arends, R. (2008). *Aprender a Ensinar*. MacGraw Hill.

Assembleia da República Portuguesa. (2005). *Constituição da República Portuguesa*. https://www.parlamento.pt/Legislacao/Paginas/ConstituicaoRepublicaPortuguesa.aspx

Bacich, L., & Moran, J. (2018). *Metodologias ativas para uma educação inovadora - uma abordagem teórico-prática* (de Oliveira, P. A., Ed.). PENSO EDITORA LTDA.

Barbosa, E., & Moura, D. (2013). Metodologias ativas de aprendizagem na Educação Profissional e Tecnológica. *Boletim Técnico Do Senac*, *39*(2), 48–67. DOI: 10.26849/bts.v39i2.349

Bauerlein, M. (2009). *The Dumbest Generation: How the Digital Age Stupefies Young Americans and Jeopardizes Our Future (Or, Don 't Trust Anyone Under 30)* (1st ed.). TarcherPerigee.

Becker, F. (2009). O que é Construtivismo? *Desenvolvimento e Aprendizagens Sob o Enfoque Da Psicologia II*, 1–8.

Bisen, V. S. (2020). *What is Human in the Loop Machine Learning: Why & How Used in AI?* Medium. https://medium.com/vsinghbisen/what-is-human-in-the-loop-machine-learning-why-how-used-in-ai-60c7b44eb2c0

Bonwell, C. C., & Eison, J. A. (1991). Active Learning: Creating Excitement in the Classroom. 1991 ASHE-ERIC Higher Education Reports. In *ASHE-ERIC Higher Education Report*.

Crivosoft, M. D. L. (2023). *Plataforma Virtual First*. Youtube. https://www.youtube.com/watch?v=h69cEQYxw_s

Digital, P. (2020). Plano de Ação para a Transição Digital de Portugal. In *Economia e Transição Digital*. https://www.portugal.gov.pt/gc22/portugal-digital/plano-de-acao-para-a-transicao-digital-pdf.aspx

DRE. (2009, August 27). *DL n.º 85/2009 - Estabelece o regime da escolaridade obrigatória para as crianças e jovens que se encontram em idade escolar e consagra a universalidade da educação pré-escolar para as crianças a partir dos 5 anos de idade*. Diário Da República n.º 166/2009, Série. *Ide (São Paulo)*.

DRE. (2022). *Código do Trabalho*. Diário Da República n.º 30/2009, Série I de 2009-02-12. https://dre.pt/dre/legislacao-consolidada/lei/2009-34546475

Faias, J. (2021). *Active Methodologies for Learning*. Ukrothe. https://www.ukrothe.eu/en/blog/active-methodologies-learning

Fernandes, D. (2007). A avaliação das aprendizagens no Sistema Educativo Português. *Educação e Pesquisa*, *33*(3), 581–600. DOI: 10.1590/S1517-97022007000300013

Figueiredo, P., & Joaquim, A. F. (2023). The impact of artificial intelligence and intergenerational diversity. In Ince, F. (Ed.), *Leadership Perspectives on Effective Intergenerational Communication and Management* (pp. 72–90). IGI Global., DOI: 10.4018/978-1-6684-6140-2.ch005

Indicators, O. C. D. E. (2021). *Education at a Glance 2020.* OECD Publishing. https://doi.org/https://doi.org/10.1787/69096873-en

Iyer, L. (2019). Critical Thinking and it's Importance in Education. *Cognitive, Psychological and Behavioural Perspectives in Education.* https://www.researchgate.net/publication/339433132_Critical_Thinking_and_it's_Importance_in_Education

Joaquim, A. F. (2018). *O papel do trabalho de projeto no ensino profissional da disciplina de área de integração (Relatório de Prática de Ensino Supervisionada. Mestrado em Ensino de Economia e de Contabilidade)* [Instituto de Educação da Universidade de Lisboa]. http://hdl.handle.net/10451/34940

Joaquim, A. F., & Figueiredo, P. (2023). Entrepreneurship in teaching: The teaching of Economics A with the application of Active Methodologies: Case Study. In Bilodeau, J., & Hughes, L. (Eds.), *Creating Motivational Online Environments for Students.* IGI Global., DOI: 10.4018/978-1-6684-4533-4.ch009

Joaquim, A. F., & Figueiredo, P. (2024). Entrepreneurial Leadership Development in the Digital Age. *European Conference on Management Leadership and Governance, 20*(1), 210–219. DOI: 10.34190/ecmlg.20.1.2942

Jófili, Z. (2002). Piaget, Vygotsky, Freire e a construção do conhecimento na escola. *Educação: Teorias e Práticas, 2*(2), 191–208. https://www.maxwell.vrac.puc-rio.br/7560/7560.PDF

Konopka, C. L., Adaime, M. B., & Mosele, P. H. (2015). Active Teaching and Learning Methodologies: Some Considerations. *Creative Education, 06*(14), 1536–1545. DOI: 10.4236/ce.2015.614154

Leão, D. M. M. (1999). Paradigmas Contemporâneos de Educação: Escola Tradicional e Escola Construtivista. *Cadernos de Pesquisas, 107*(107), 187–206. https://www.scielo.br/j/cp/a/PwJJHWcxknGGMghXdGRXZbB/?format=pdf&lang=pt. DOI: 10.1590/S0100-15741999000200008

Lima, A. R., Cavalcante, A. A., Torquato, C. B., & Vanzella, E. (2020). A correlação entre desmotivação e redução do rendimento escolar: Um estudo da 3ª série do ensino médio no município de Parambu – CE. *Série Educar- Volume 24 – Ensino Fundamental e Médio.* DOI: 10.36229/978-65-86127-39-3.CAP.16

Lima, V., & Gaspar, F. C. (2024). Inbound learning: Revolutionizing educational paradigms. *Brazilian Journal of Business, 6*(2), e69276. DOI: 10.34140/bjbv6n2-010

Lopes, M. A. da S. (2023). *Metodologias ativas vs. passivas: afinal qual a diferença no ensino de Geografia?* (Issue 3) [Mestrado, Universidade do Porto]. https://hdl.handle.net/10216/152679

MEC. (2017). Perfil Dos Alunos À Saída da Escolaridade Obrigatório. *Editorial Do Ministério Da Educação e Ciência*, 1–30. http://www.dge.mec.pt/sites/default/files/Curriculo/Projeto_Autonomia_e_Flexibilidade/perfil_dos_alunos.pdf

Menezes, S. K. de O., & Francisco, D. J. (2020). Educação em tempos de pandemia: Aspectos afetivos e sociais no processo de ensino e aprendizagem. *Revista Brasileira de Informática Na Educação, 28*, 985–1012. DOI: 10.5753/rbie.2020.28.0.985

Meola, A. (2022). *Generation Z: Latest Gen Z News, Research, Facts*. Insider Intelligence | EMarketer. https://www.insiderintelligence.com/insights/generation-z-facts/

Moran, J. (2015). Mudando a educação com metodologias ativas. In: Souza C A, Morales OET (organizadores). *Coleção Mídias Contemporâneas. Convergências Midiáticas, Educação e Cidadania: Aproximações Jovens*, 180. https://www2.eca.usp.br/moran/?p=543

OCDE. (2023). PISA 2022 Results: The State of Learning and Equity in Education. In *Pisa 2022: Vol. I*. OCDE. DOI: 10.31244/9783830998488

OECD. (2018). *Education GPS - Portugal*. Teachers and Teaching Conditions, Lower and Upper Secondary Education. https://gpseducation.oecd.org/CountryProfile?primaryCountry=PRT&treshold=10&topic=TA

OECD. (2019a). PISA 2021 creative thinking framework. *OECD Future of Education and Skills 2030, 53*(9), 1689–1699. https://www.oecd.org/pisa/publications/PISA-2021-creative-thinking-framework.pdf

OECD. (2019b). Skills for 2030. *OECD Future of Education and Skills 2030*, 16. https://www.oecd.org/education/2030-project/teaching-and-learning/learning/skills/Skills_for_2030_concept_note.pdf

Oliveira, P., Cunha, C., & Nakayama, M. (2016). Learning Management Systems (LMS) and e-learning management: An integrative review and research agenda. *Journal of Information Systems and Technology Management, 13*(2), 157–180. DOI: 10.4301/S1807-17752016000200001

Pereira, P., & Lima, V. (2021). INBOUND LEARNING: CONTRIBUTO PARA UMA NOVA METODOLOGIA DE ENSINO Inbound Learning: contribution to a new Learning Methodology Inbound Learning: contribución a una nueva Metodologia de Aprendizaje. In *Rev UI_IPSantarém* (Vol. 9, Issue 4).

Petrina, S. (2004). Sidney Pressey and the Automation of Education, 1924-1934. *Technology and Culture, 45, n.º 2*, 305–330. https://www.jstor.org/stable/40060743

Portugal, O. N. U. (2022). *Objetivos de Desenvolvimento Sustentável*. https://unric.org/pt/objetivos-de-desenvolvimento-sustentavel/

Postigo, G. Z., Foster, C., & Hardy, J. (2015). An Introduction to Critical Thinking and Logic. In *With Good Reason: A Guide to Critical Thinking*. Bridge point Education. DOI: 10.2307/j.ctt1t89436

Rodrigues, A. L. (2017). *A Formação Ativa de Professores com Integração Pedagógica das Tecnologias Digitais* [Instituto de Educação - Universidade de Lisboa]. https://repositorio.ul.pt/handle/10451/28329

Rodrigues, A. L., & Cabrito, B. (2022). *Metodologias de ensino, avaliação e aprendizagem Didática da Economia e Contabilidade* (Coleção Caderno de Mertrado | e-book, Ed.). EDUCA - Associação de Estudos e Publicidade.

Rumpagaporn, M. W. (2007). Students' Critical Thinking Skills, Attitudes To ICT and Perceptions of Ict Classroom Learning Environments Under the ICT Schools Pilot Project in Thailand [University of Adelaide]. In *Development*. https://digital.library.adelaide.edu.au/dspace/bitstream/2440/37896/8/02whole.pdf

Sachs, J. D., Lafortune, G., Fuller, G., & Drumm, E. (2023). *Sustainable Development Report 2023: Implementing the SDG Stimulus Includes the SDG Index and Dashboards*. DOI: 10.25546/102924

Steinmayr, R., Weidinger, A. F., Schwinger, M., & Spinath, B. (2019). The importance of students' motivation for their academic achievement-replicating and extending previous findings. *Frontiers in Psychology, 10*(JULY), 1730. Advance online publication. DOI: 10.3389/fpsyg.2019.01730 PMID: 31417459

Chapter 6

Integrating AI into a Virtual Learning Environment to Achieve Sustainability and Circularity

Anjum Nazir Qureshi
https://orcid.org/0000-0001-8172-5510
Rajiv Gandhi College of Engineering Research and Technology, India

ABSTRACT

The popularity of virtual learning environments has transformed learning and teaching practices. AI is a promising technology extensively used to improve the learning experience for those who opt for virtual or online education. AI has enabled many features in the virtual learning system by which the learners enjoy learning at their own pace. AI will make learning more manageable, but the challenges should be handled carefully to increase its adaptability and acceptability. Learning remotely is easily accessible for enthusiastic learners who believe in upskilling themselves to be compatible with the fast-advancing world. It benefits those who work due to weak financial conditions but still want to complete their education. Virtual education has enabled learning from experts around the world. The virtual learning methods have enhanced global and local collaborations. It will bridge the education gaps for those unable to continue education. This will help to achieve sustainability in education by increasing its affordability and accessibility.

1. INTRODUCTION

The integration of technology has revolutionized the education sector, transforming traditional teaching-learning methods into dynamic, interactive experiences. Virtual Learning Environments (VLEs) and Artificial Intelligence (AI) have played a pivotal role in reshaping education by making learning more accessible, personalized, and engaging. This chapter explores how AI enhances VLEs, the challenges associated with their implementation, and their potential for future educational development. Educators and learners worldwide have started utilizing the technologies for virtual learning and classroom-based learning. Many governments have channeled efforts to develop affordable internet to reach the most re-

DOI: 10.4018/979-8-3693-9062-7.ch006

mote and rural areas through virtual education. It is said that technology has made our lives comfortable. It has brought the world to our fingertips. The same applies to education too. Technologies and virtual learning environments have enabled learning any subject of your choice at your own pace. Though the idea of virtual or online learning started gaining popularity before the coronavirus pandemic, it became widely accepted during the pandemic as schools and colleges were closed worldwide. Educators and learners were forced to adapt to technology-based and virtual learning. The pandemic forced researchers to develop novel techniques to enhance the virtual learning experience through technology.

Traditional classrooms often struggle to provide engaging learning environments and timely evaluations. To address this, schools and educational institutions are increasingly adopting technology-driven solutions. While some educators view gadgets as distractions, integrating technology can significantly enhance learning experiences, making education more interactive and efficient (*Vakaluik et.al., 2021*). The education technology business is expanding with innovations. It makes education accessible for those who cannot attain adequate education facilities. Educators and students have started using social media as a learning tool. Social media sites help people communicate from anywhere and at any time. Moreover, it encourages networking possibilities to connect with other like-minded people. It sometimes helps to search for new job opportunities (*Büyükbaykal, 2015*). Facilities like online classroom calendars allow teachers to display assignments, class schedules, examination schedules, and other related school events. Students use this information to plan for their activities. At the same time, the student response systems allow the teachers to monitor the activities of the students. The teachers can evaluate their performance and provide explanations and guidance if needed (*Biletska et al., 2021*). Projectors, computers, videos, and audio make classroom learning more engaging and entertaining. Students tend to learn better in playful environments. Oral presentations and group participation blended with technology make learning more dynamic and engaging (*Bilotta et.al., 2021*). Digital technologies for the teaching-learning process enable better utilization of resources and expand its impact on the students and the teachers (*Beardsley et.al., 2021*). Virtual learning environments are transforming the way students learn. Moreover, technology is used extensively to make education inexpensive, affordable, and accessible (*Qureshi et al., 2021*).

Laptops, Desktops, mobiles, tablets, and internet connectivity are essential for virtual learning. Chatbots, mobile assistants, mobile applications, intelligent tutoring systems, and automatic grading tools are a few attractive features of virtual learning environments. Artificial Intelligence, the Internet of Things, Virtual Reality, Augmented Reality, and Learning Management systems have opened the doors of virtual learning experiences for everyone. Amongst the numerous benefits of virtual learning and technology usage in education, it is not free from challenges. Some challenges faced while using virtual learning environments are connectivity, interoperability, scalability, security, and privacy. Cost, isolation, social disconnect, distractions, health concerns, and the digital divide can disrupt the flow of the learning experience and decrease the learning outcomes. This chapter will discuss how AI can enhance the virtual learning experience. It will highlight the benefits and challenges of using technologies for virtual learning.

2. VIRTUAL LEARNING ENVIRONMENT

The traditional learning approaches are not free from shortcomings despite several benefits to educators and learners for years. Some of the drawbacks observed in the conventional teaching-learning system that has encouraged education enthusiasts to adopt virtual learning methods are (i) Improper teacher-student ratio (ii) Not addressing the challenges faced by the physically handicapped and medically unfit (iii) Not addressing the issues of students with less attendance resulting into failure of students and increase in dropouts (iv) Teachers are not trained for using digital techniques and technology (v) Unable to reach the students at geographically isolated locations (vi) Unable to understand the perception levels and mindset of the students (vii) Designing course content according to students and making regular changes in it. This chapter will study how virtual learning environments will help to address these challenges and improve the teaching-learning process. It agrees with the words of Swami Vivekananda, who said that if the students cannot reach the school, schools should reach them.

Online platforms and e-learning facilities were a part of the education system in many countries. Globalization of education increased the need to integrate technology to widen its impact for each individual who aspires to learn and find favorable employment opportunities to ensure a good standard of living for the family. Online meeting applications and educational tools were not popular despite their existence. These applications were limited to developed countries and those with higher economic and education standards. Online education, correspondence courses, and teleconferencing facilities existed in the 20th century but these methods lacked flexibility and interactivity. The development of the Internet enhanced the education system by providing dynamic and interactive experiences through a virtual learning environment (VLE). The educators and students are involved in online interactions and learning in the VLE.

The emergence of the pandemic due to the coronavirus and lockdown in 2020 forced everyone to think about the available technologies, make them accessible to everyone, and create awareness among the masses over their usage for conducting classes. Technology emerged as a savior of education during those days (*Javaid et.al.., 2020*). The global crisis made everyone think about an internationally integrated education system. Adaptive learning environments and self-paced learning improve critical thinking and problem-solving skills. These improved skills help students accomplish professional success in the future. Digital tools help educational institutions improve the class atmosphere and design student-centric curricula (*Kosaretsky et.al., 2022*). Some educators do not support using gadgets in class as they cause distractions in their studies. The young generation is, however, tech-savvy and enjoys learning when gadgets and technologies are used in the class. Integrating technology makes children more engaged and interested in the subjects (*Kryukov & Gorin, 2017*). The learners may use digital resources to download the educational content uploaded by their teachers. At the same time, they can upload assignments on the link created by the teachers. This helps teachers monitor the progress of all the students. Teaching and learning become more inspiring and meaningful with technology. Gamification and flipped classroom approaches use digital technologies to optimize learning (*Kumar et.al.., 2022*).

Although VLEs and Learning Management Systems (LMS) are often used interchangeably, they serve distinct purposes. LMS primarily focuses on administrative aspects such as enrollment, tracking, and assessment, whereas VLEs foster interaction, collaboration, and immersive learning experiences. For example, Google Classroom serves as an LMS, while platforms like Moodle and Blackboard function as full-fledged VLEs, enabling real-time discussions, simulations, and personalized learning paths. LMS manages enrolment, tracking, and assessment. It manages the administrative aspects of learning, provides basic collaboration features, allows content delivery, and supports its limited customization. VLE, on the other hand, fosters interaction and collaboration and enhances learning with interactive activities. It offers a more holistic learning environment with extensive customization of the educational content, promoting interaction among the learners (*Meetaverse, 2024*).

2.1 Leveraging VLES

Users can leverage the power of VLEs in the following ways:

2.1.1 Students

Accessibility is an important characteristic of VLE. The students can learn from anywhere and at any time using the internet. All the persons involved can access the right resources and data. The educators use the data to make more informed teaching decisions for the students. The personalized learning approach addresses the different learning needs, interests, and aspirations. The self-paced study options provide a learning plan to the students based on their strengths, skills, and interests. It encourages student autonomy. Students play an active role in designing lessons and projects based on their interests and passions. This helps develop more meaningful and relevant content for students (*Power School, 2023*).

2.1.2 Educational Institutes

Educational institutes enhance the learning environments through digitization and computerization. VLEs are used to offer distance training and augment the learning objectives. It creates a flexible environment using communication tools for academic activities (*Chester et al., 2021*). Furthermore, VLE in universities provides additional benefits like personalized learning, competency-based learning, collaboration, and high-quality products for the learners. It provides favorable opportunities for educators to upskill themselves to deal with the next generation of learners (*Vasylyshyna, 2020*). The VLEs support effective content sharing, standardized evaluations, well-timed feedback, and impressionable quizzes, and ensure improved self-awareness to the students (*Ward et.al, 2018*). VLEs improve the teaching quality and contribute to the generation of self-motivated students with improved competence and knowledge (*Kruk, 2022*). Students enjoy flexible learning environments by using VLEs on phones. Flexible mobile access provides better student engagement and enriched learning environments (*Raftery, 2018*). The interactive learning environments provide opportunities for improving study habits and getting actively involved in learning by clearing concepts despite the internet and device issues (*Dhakal, Sharma, 2016*).

2.1.3 Corporates and Enterprises

Virtual learning initiatives are gaining popularity in modern corporate and enterprise settings. Corporate e-learning systems add to tram achievements in the virtual software teams. They provide personalized knowledge transfer tools for virtual environments, positively impacting organizational success (*Subramaniam., Nakkeeran, 2019*). The e-learning initiatives make learning self-paced and comfortable. The employees upskill themselves according to the requirements of the industry. These initiatives are widely used by the public sector, IT, and business analytics consultancy (*Banerjee, 2022*). Web conferencing software can be used for training in the corporate sector. Virtual training is flexible and cost-effective. The factors that ensure high-quality training in the virtual environment are the learning culture and leadership qualities of the employees and technical as well as financial support by the organization (*Walsh, 2014*). VLE supports better opportunities for informal learning to bridge the gap between industry and academia for the modern workforce (*Jewitt, 2018*). 3D virtual environments in an organization offer better opportunities for leadership development programs to enhance teamwork qualities, their presence, and outcomes among the members working at various geographical locations (*Massey et.al., 2013*).

2.2 Types of VLEs

The VLEs are classified as synchronous, asynchronous, and hybrid, based on the level of interactions among the educators and learners.

2.2.1 Synchronous Virtual Learning

Synchronous virtual learning enables live interaction among the teachers and students during learning activities. It is done in real-time with the teacher delivering lessons and the students participating. All the participants log in according to the schedule. The time slot for a class can either be fixed or varied depending on the type of software used for the learning (*Bello, et.al, 2014*). The students and teachers interact synchronously using audio, video, whiteboards, and chats. The participants can be divided into groups by using breakout rooms. This encourages group activities. The students and teachers interact as they are meeting face to face. The teacher is the moderator who guides and monitors the activities in the virtual class (*Martin & Parker, 2014*). Google Meet, Zoom, and Microsoft Teams are a few popular synchronous virtual learning platforms. These environments reinforce interpersonal connections and student satisfaction.

2.2.2 Asynchronous Virtual Learning

Asynchronous does not occur in real-time or does not happen at the same time or place. The lectures are not delivered in real-time like done in synchronous learning. It consists of prerecorded lectures and assignments with flexible deadlines. It fosters independent learning and allows users to access the materials and complete activities at their own pace. It may also include online discussion forums, exchange of emails among teachers and learners, and course delivery systems to foster communication and instructional materials among many people (*Reiddagnvy, 2022*). Asynchronous learning environments minimize the risks of technical glitches faced during simultaneous synchronous learning systems. Learners have more opportunities to develop their critical thinking capabilities and improve knowledge through online discussion activities. Asynchronous learning provides flexibility for updating the course contents at any time to deliver it quickly to the learners. Direct interaction among learners and educators is missing in these learning platforms. The course contents should be designed carefully to engage the learners and increase participation (*Romero et.al.., 2022*). It is one of the most favorable options for companies who seek opportunities to train their workforce to the in-demand skill sets. Google Classroom and online learning platforms like Udemy are some of the common examples of asynchronous learning.

2.2.3 Blended (Hybrid) Learning

Blended learning merges traditional face-to-face instruction with online educational tools, offering a balanced approach that maximizes engagement and flexibility. Research by Graham et al. (2019) indicates that blended learning improves student retention and critical thinking skills. Universities such as MIT and Harvard have successfully integrated hybrid models, combining in-person lectures with interactive online modules through platforms like edX and Coursera, allowing students to learn at their own pace while still benefiting from classroom discussions. Additionally, the students can learn through discussions with their schoolmates either formally or informally. The students improve their social connections and values by playing and exchanging ideas with others. Furthermore, students use information and communication technologies (ICT) by attending webinars and accessing blogs, digital libraries, and virtual laboratories. The students can be a part of a virtual classroom that allows attending classes at their convenience. The students can access videos and audio of their academic subjects from their teachers and other educational institutions. For example, students watch YouTube videos posted by educators from different areas of the world. Students can watch these videos and learn from them. Blended learning encourages both teaching methods. The teachers and students are comfortable using technology for the teaching-learning process. The flexibility to switch between the two methods makes blended learning more student-centric. Students get wide exposure to the course content. They can communicate with students and teachers worldwide to discuss various topics and subjects (*Dangwal, 2017*).

2.3 Essential Features of VLE

VLE, with the help of digital technologies, will foster collaborative learning environments. It will transform the techniques used by teachers for teaching and by the students for learning and studying. Some of the commonly used VLEs are: i. Online degree, certificate, and diploma courses ii. Recorded videos and lectures iii. Educational Podcasts iv. Webinars v. Live lectures vi. Digital libraries and vii. Interactive Simulations.

The Key features of VLE that should be considered for the selection of an appropriate VLE are:

2.3.1 Flexible and User-Friendly

The educators, teachers, tutors, coaches, students, and participants should be able to access the course material conveniently. They should find the information conveniently without any frustration. The course materials should be accessible from devices including smartphones, laptops, tablets, etc. so that it does not burden the users to buy a specific device, especially for the course. Flexibility and scalability can provide sustainable and successful learning solutions (*Martin 2020*).

2.3.2 Engaging and Interactive Content

The learning methods should be designed based on the learner's interest, knowledge, and skills. VLEs should act as engaging environments to foster opportunities for appropriate learning suitable to a specific individual (*Martin, 2020*). A deeper engagement and participation can be encouraged through video lectures, images, audio recordings, interactive online sessions, quizzes, polls, and discussion forums.

2.3.3 Trust-Based Learning Environments

Trust is one of the key factors that enables communication and relationships among educators and learners. Educational institutions and educators struggle to develop trust among students while using virtual platforms. The social and technical factors likely to influence the student's approach towards trustworthiness should be identified (*Wang, 2014*). Some factors that can affect trust among the students are negative experiences with the tutors or the institutions during prior VLEs, lack of flexibility in accessing the learning material, etc. These challenges can be addressed by displaying the contact details of the tutor or instructor on the dashboard, assertiveness and responsiveness by the tutors to develop a sense of care, disclosing privacy and security policies, and using the security systems or tools.

2.3.4 Timely Analysis of Performance and Attainment

Students should be provided with detailed analytics of their performance, attendance, and tasks accomplished. VLE encourages personalized learning. The results generated after quizzes, polls, and completion of assignments or projects should reach the students as early as possible. Students should receive active feedback so that they feel responsible for their work. It develops interest among the students that their work is being monitored. Otherwise, students may lose interest in the learning due to a lack of personal communication with the educators. On the other hand, educators and educational institutions can use this analysis to make the necessary changes in the course material to provide additional support to the students and cater to their needs.

2.3.5 Inclusivity

VLEs are open to people from all ages and backgrounds. They may have different cultures and speak different languages. Some of them may have disabilities or other health complications. VLEs should be able to engage people from diverse backgrounds by understanding social communication and allowing everyone to join and learn easily. Two persons may have the same area of interest but they cannot pursue the same course due to the differences in the socio-cultural factors. For example, two persons may be interested in pursuing soft skill training. One may be good at English but the other may prefer a regional language. One may have good internet and devices while the other may have poor connectivity and cannot afford the latest devices. In such circumstances, VLE should be able to provide tailored courses to accommodate all types of learners.

2.3.6 Seamless Integration

VLE offers continuity in learning without any time or space limits. It eliminates the gap between places, learning environments, and devices or systems. It is supported by various technologies, such as mobile phones, to support learning in diverse scenarios. The learners should be able to collaborate and interact with their peers in the virtual world. Students can learn efficiently in virtual environments through purposeful interactions among the students and with their faculty. Seamless integration makes learning more interesting and meaningful. It enhances the experience of learning through digital accessibility and inclusivity (*Ossian Nilsson, 2022*). Teachers should be equipped with the latest changes and innovative methods and technology. The administrators on the other hand, should be ready to support the latest innovation and facilitate its usage to exemplify the teaching-learning process.

2.3.7 Support for Professional Development

VLE offers robust support for professional development. It provides good opportunities to utilize the best features of the platform used for online teaching. Manuals, tutorials, live chat with the teachers and peer groups, online support, and mentorship help to solve the technical difficulties, and enhance the learning environment. Moreover, the flexibility to learn at one's own pace helps professionals to have a work-life balance and upskill themselves through advanced courses in their field of interest.

3. OPPORTUNITIES FOR AI IN VLE

AI is an invaluable technology for teachers and students who opt for virtual learning. You can teach and learn foreign languages, mathematics, science, and any subjects you like. However, considering the widespread demand for automation, learners should develop critical and creative thinking skills. The popularity of AI in the education sector is growing due to its capabilities to offer excellent quality education and support personalized learning. The fusion of AI and VLE will enhance the effectiveness of virtual learning and ensure fairness and receptiveness (*You,2024*).

3.1 Personalized Education

AI supports personalized learning by having content tailored exclusively for each learner. It helps learners to learn at their own pace. They have flexibility in changing the speed of learning. They can prioritize the order of learning material and select appropriate technologies. This technique is called an adaptive way of learning. On the other hand, the learning platforms analyze the learners' strengths and weaknesses to offer appropriate content and assignments based on their interests and perception levels. The learners receive individual supervision and personal recommendations. The AI-based learning systems identify the challenges faced by the students while learning. These learning systems adapt to the learners' progress and adjust the educational materials accordingly (*Houtson &Plate, 2024*). The learners receive personalized books, videos, and other related learning materials. Their progress is continuously tracked through practice tests and feedback. The educators gather and analyze the students' performance data to understand each student well, thus developing personalized learning content. Moreover, virtual assistants and chatbots use Natural Language Processing (NLP) to interact with the students. The students can interact to get instant answers to their questions and explanations of queries. This interaction with the virtual assistants and chatbots enables gaining feedback from the students to augment the educational quality (*Willis, 2024*).

3.2 Automation of Tasks

AI enables enhancing the effectiveness of virtual learning by automating tasks. AI-powered systems allow the automatic generation of personalized content, organization of the learning content, and grading of learners based on their performance. The automatic and fast generation of performance reports reduces the burden on educators. They can use these reports to recognize opportunities for the betterment of learners, provide fast evaluation, and encourage discussions. However, the learning platform and the educators should be careful of the ethical implications to avoid compromising or breaching the personalized data of the learners (*Eilermann et.al., 2024*). The educators can devote more time to plan for the syllabus according to the needs of the students and interact with the students based on the generated results and grades. Interaction among the educator and students will support opportunities for easier learning in a comfortable environment. It would help to create an engaging learning platform and improve students' self-esteem and confidence. Live interactions provide support to the learners, and their learning journey becomes interesting.

3.3 Intelligent Scoring Systems and Feedback

Intelligent scoring systems use Machine Learning to improve the efficiency of evaluation. The AI-based scoring systems provide timely scores and feedback to the learners. This scoring system can analyze the learner's performance based on quizzes and essays. It recognizes the strengths and weaknesses of the learners to allow them to focus on their improvement. The informative assessments and feedback are generated by analyzing the learner's performance in real time. Moreover, these intelligent systems can instantly analyze the voluminous data and generate timely responses. Timely feedback generates a sense of belongingness among the learners. They engage with the educators and the educational content and track their progress regularly. Virtual learners use these responses to identify gaps in their knowledge and awareness and plan accordingly to fill the gap by adjusting their learning approaches (*Houtson &Plate, 2024*).

3.4 Development of Real-World Skills

VLE is an excellent medium for those who aspire to acquire new skills at their own pace. However, the competitive world demands regular upgrading of knowledge to survive in the corporate and business sectors. VLE not only supports improving knowledge. It also helps develop many skills that help everyone have a recognized degree and a successful career.

One of the skills is time management. The learners should balance their time to work, learning, and family commitments. They have to meet the deadlines of their course and also their work. At the same time, they have to spend time with family and fulfill their expectations. VLE helps develop your organization skills as you have to manage your class timings, your meetings at the workplace, and assignments. Though most VLE courses offer flexible timings, the learners should develop strategies, to stay organized, acquire new skills, and use them efficiently. Online learners develop proficiency in using digital tools. As classes and all related activities are online, they learn to embrace technology. Eventually, it helps them to use these digital skills in their professional lives and learn other digital tools quickly. VLE is an excellent medium for improving your communication skills. There are educators and learners from diverse backgrounds and you have to communicate with them during your course. This may seem difficult initially but with practice, it removes the hesitation of interacting with new people you come across. Moreover, involving learners from diverse backgrounds, and the various activities that involve group work will improve collaboration and teamwork skills. You develop skills to interact remotely with others which will be helpful as presently many job roles are going remote. It is a common belief that VLE does not promote networking like the offline courses in colleges or universities. You can reach your classmates and teachers through emails and messaging apps. You will have to be in touch with them remotely and it will certainly help to build a network that will benefit your career. A remote learner has to maintain commitment and motivation to continue with the assigned course. The stereotypes exist where people do not value VLE, it is sometimes difficult for the learners to trust online courses and continue with them. Moreover, as you manage to learn, with your work and family responsibilities you have to ignore the tiredness and distractions.

4. CHALLENGES FOR USING AI IN VLE

AI is a prominently discussed term among educators and learners due to its numerous benefits and facilities for self-paced learning. It has several advantages for those interested in learning new things, upgrading skills, or exploring something new. However, integrating AI in VLE has some challenges data privacy, biased information, change in assessment methods, job displacement (*Nguyen, 2023*), over-reliance on AI, lack of trained staff, costs, lack of human interaction, transparency, outdated infrastructure, and integration with existing education system (*Ferrario, 2024*).

4.1 Data Privacy

The AI-based VLE platforms collect the personal data of educators and learners. They also upload their assignments, access the course material, and attend tailored courses. A lot of personal data is collected which raises concerns for data breaches. The educational platforms must ensure that the data is not shared with a third party without the consent of the learners to avoid its misuse.

4.2 Biased Information

AI relies heavily on the data it is trained on, which can sometimes lead to biased outputs and ethical concerns. For instance, AI-powered grading systems have faced criticism for favoring specific writing styles over others, potentially disadvantaging non-native speakers. Additionally, data privacy remains a significant challenge in AI-driven education, as platforms collect vast amounts of student information. To address these concerns, educators and policymakers must establish transparent AI guidelines, ethical data policies, and continuous monitoring to ensure fair and responsible AI use in learning environments. Sometimes, AI systems fail to feed quality and sufficient data. It leads to insufficient and low-quality data, and AI systems may fail to achieve the desired outcomes. Training AI on insufficient data may lead to discrimination of a certain group and weaken fairness and equal opportunities for all. The AI-generated data may sometimes be false and unreliable.

4.3 Change in Assessment Methods

Integrating AI into VLE will be implemented efficiently by changing the conventional assessment methods. The teachers and the instructors can change the assessment methods used to develop a model that suits online learners. It will increase the workload of the teachers. They will have to change the assessment methods. Moreover, helping students to adapt to new learning methods, documenting feedback and assessments, and changing course contents according to the learning capacities will increase the workload.

4.4 Job Displacement

The students rely on virtual assistants, chatbots, intelligent tutors, and social media for immediate responses to their queries. This will reduce the dependency on teachers. Some educational organizations may try to appoint fewer teachers and increase unemployment. The flexibility in virtual learning may attract more learners, and the offline education systems will have to reform themselves to adjust to the requirements of learners.

4.5 Overreliance on AI

The learners will rely completely on AI to complete their assignments and projects. Many free AI tools are available so students can easily complete their tasks. Moreover, teachers depend on AI for suggestions on designing new courses and getting feedback. This will increase dependency on AI tools. The learners and educators will rely on the instant help provided by AI without realizing the importance of critical thinking, creativity, and problem-solving skills.

4.6 Lack of Trained Staff

There is a lack of qualified and trained persons who can handle VLE and AI. The educators, who desire to work in this field should be trained to utilize the features of VLE to benefit the students. These educators may be experts in some subjects but fail to use the technology. They should be curious to adapt to the new teaching-learning techniques, ready to make changes when required and learn to use the technology.

4.7 High Costs

Switching to VLE may decrease the infrastructural requirements. However, integrating AI into the teaching-learning process is not cheap. It will require updated devices that are compatible with the advancing software. The equipment and devices will need regular upgrades to handle the requirements of the latest AI tools. It will increase the initial implementation costs. The fast changes in technology may create the need for new devices in case further upgrades are not possible for the existing ones.

4.8 Transparency

AI depends on the data set given to it and generates results based on it. However, AI may sometimes give wrong results. Some incorrect datasets in AI will cause errors in the results. Transparency of the AI algorithms and educating VLE users on AI will prevent erroneous operations.

4.9 Integration with Existing Education Systems

Though people are adopting VLE, there is a long way to go. People still have biases on accepting VLE and AI. Besides the change in the mindset of the stakeholders, changes in infrastructure, devices, and software need more attention. Moreover, Governments should think of enforcing new policies and regulations to help people accept VLE for their upskilling. There should be changes at the local and global levels to encourage learners to accept VLE.

4.10 Lack of Human Interaction

VLE enables interaction with people from diverse backgrounds and countries. Though it increases your network, many complain about a lack of human interaction and emotional support. AI into VLE can give additional content at your fingertips, but it may fail to get the mental support and warmth from the teachers they receive during offline classrooms. VLE should be developed to provide personalized learning and emotional connections.

5. SUSTAINABILITY AND CIRCULARITY IN EDUCATION

UNESCO defines sustainable education as a learning process based on ideals and principles that determine sustainability. It involves all levels and types of learning that will facilitate quality education and sustainable development of mankind (*Helmers & Ilchmann, 2019*). The three key principles that determine circular economy are eliminating waste, using products for a longer period, and regenerating natural systems (*Ellen MacArthur Foundation, 2014*). A circular education system can be built by increasing the circularity of the learning products. Circular programs, courses, and learning objectives are some approaches that support circularity in education systems (*McGinley & Karlshøj, 2022*).

5.1 Circular Thinking

Circular thinking helps students and teachers use previously learned concepts to develop something new or implement them to benefit society and common people. It fosters capabilities of creative and critical thinking. It is a positive trait for those who like to solve problems and work to reach solutions (*Fiene, 2024*).

The VLE through AI is not limited to personalizing content but encourages the students to present and share knowledge. The AI-based tools are designed specifically to improve learning and accessibility of the pedagogical content. The students learn more, interact more, and achieve more. AI opens up opportunities to create connections between the subjects. Educators can use the feedback and assessments to know where the students are lagging and develop techniques to improve their performance. They can create activities to attain higher learning outcomes (*Misha, 2024*). AI-powered brainstorming tools can be used to enhance creativity. The large amount of data and data analytical capabilities of the neural networks can be utilized to accelerate the brainstorming process. Using AI during brainstorming sessions helps break biases by challenging your assumptions and cultivating inclusive solutions. It helps identify connections by analyzing the available information to create solutions that were missed earlier due to linear and fixed thinking. It generates several ideas quickly so that you can focus on selecting the promising ones (*Pavitra, 2024*).

The brainstorming sessions will be a great step in designing circular programs and courses. Moreover, shared learning through AI platforms encourages interdisciplinary learning. The circular economy involves many concepts like economics, environment, design, etc. With personalized and adaptive learning concepts learners can explore more the interdisciplinary concepts and try to find relations between them. The students have better opportunities to learn about different courses based on their interests. The engaging learning environments, help them learn real-world skills and use these skills to address the environmental and social challenges. As personalized learning environments allow the provision of tailored courses, educational institutions, and educators can design courses in which the product of one course can be fed as an input to the other course. It can be used to bridge the industry-academia gap by having better linkages with the industries so that students prepare themselves to be job-ready after completing the course.

5.2 Circular Courses

Table 1. Levels for having circularity in courses

Level	Approach
Reproduce	Not linear, using the same products every year
Recycle	Constructing new courses every year based on the previous ones
Refurbish	Making changes to the same course annually
Reuse	Reusing previous assignments/activities
Share	Share the work done by students to enable learning by others
Maintain	Maintain and improve the earlier courses

(McGinley & Karlshøj, 2022)

The first level known as reproduce, is linear. It is related to continuously using the same course contents or syllabus year after year. The students and the educators will be involved in learning and teaching the same course without any changes. However, the second and third levels, recycle and refurbish, focus on creating new courses every year and incorporating changes into existing courses. AI algorithms can help design new courses and make changes, by analyzing the feedback and performance of the learners. The data-driven decisions of AI will help in knowing the current trends of courses that the learners and professionals want to pursue for their upskilling and career advancements. Moreover, educational organizations and educators can harness quick analysis and feedback provided by AI to modify the courses to suit the students. For example, in the feedback questionnaire, some questions that can be included are, the difficulty level of the course, suggestions for improving the course, the difficulty level of the quizzes, the quality of the notes and video lectures, etc. should be included. AI tools can analyze the answers received from the learners to know the scope of changes to be made for the next year. Similarly, a survey of the skills required by the industries, fields having more jobs, courses preferred by the students, etc., can help to design new courses to satisfy the learners. AI can interpret the descriptions, align them, and adjust the courses to match the requirements of the learners. The capabilities of AI tools can be used to create a database of the assignments and activities done by the learners for achieving the fourth level known as reuse. The educators can reuse the same techniques to educate the students and encourage effective learning by completing the activities. Moreover, the formation of a database will enable sharing and accessing information on the work done by the other students. They can learn from the available data and try to construct new projects. Social media platforms are one of the best sources to achieve the fifth level known as sharing. Educators can share educational content through social media to increase visibility and ensure availability. The learners can access these contents from anywhere and at any time and derive the benefits of personalized learning. AI can be used to attain the final level by maintaining a record of the assignments, activities, and projects, and its associated feedback. It will help the students to improve their performance. Educators can change the course or teaching techniques to achieve the desired results. This level would play a significant role in making new courses for the learners. It will improve the quality of courses and having a course that fits their needs will retain the enthusiasm. AI into VLE will help create autonomous learners and better courses. These courses can be designed to allow their relation with other courses and can be used by learners from various fields. AI will thus help the formation of courses that can be used by learners from different backgrounds and derive the benefits of virtual learning.

5.3 Circular Learning Objectives

Figure 1. Circular learning objectives

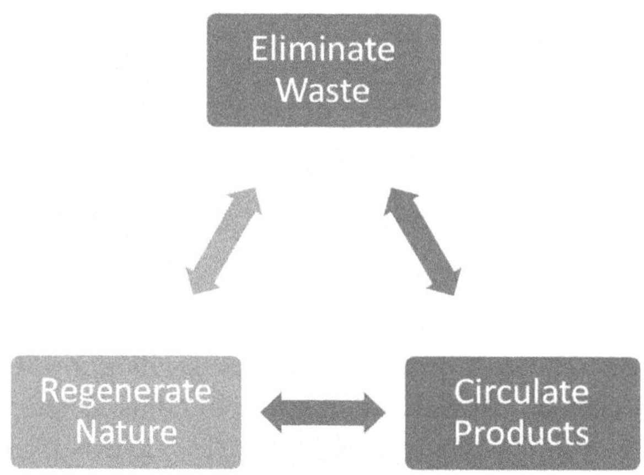

(McGinley & Karlshøj, 2022)

The circular learning objectives try to link the products and inputs from various courses. They focus on supporting the students' professional learning by eliminating wasteful processes to develop a circular education system. This involves three principles: eliminating waste, circulating products, and regenerating natural systems.

Eliminating waste in the virtual education system can be related to the wastage of resources and educational material. Virtual assistants and chatbots, reply to the students' queries as per their requirements. This frees up the educators. They can utilize it to create better courses or new techniques for engaging lectures so that all the students learn well. This reduces the waste of time and effort both for students and educators. Another benefit of using AI in VLE is its ability to create new questions and objectives by studying the existing material. In traditional teaching methods, the students are given an assignment, which they complete and submit to their teachers. These assignments are kept in a place and never used by others. It simply wastes the efforts taken by students as their knowledge and work is not shared with anyone. AI-based virtual learning systems, on the other hand, can store the assignment, and the students can access it from the database. However, teachers can use AI to frame new research questions, based on the earlier assignments so that students can use them as a reference. The students should be supported in answering the research questions and incorporating the changes. Furthermore, AI platforms can support learning and increase interactions among peers. One of the examples is peer evaluation. Teachers can use AI to give different topics to everyone. All the learners submit the assignments. The teachers allow the students to evaluate the assignments of their peers. This allows the students to read the perspectives of others and evaluate them. This process compels them to learn more about the topic before evaluation. Moreover, when educators use AI platforms, they can allow learners to access the assignments submitted by their peers. This will foster learning. However, it will eliminate the waste of time, effort, and knowledge. As the learners can access various content related to their subject, they learn more.

Flipped classrooms are a great source of obtaining circular objectives by ensuring that educational products are used for as long as possible. AI is helpful to educators in preparing engaging and organized lectures to encourage active learning by all. However, due to differences in student's abilities, some may remain disengaged and follow passive learning. Flipping classrooms is an effective approach to encourage active learning. AI tutors can significantly improve the learning experience and make flipped classrooms more interesting. They can adjust the content based on the performance and needs of the students so that they can come well-prepared for the class. Similarly, these AI tutors can help teachers identify the topics where learners may require more guidance and improvement (*Mollick, 2024*). Flipped classrooms support students' learning from diverse perspectives. It helps achieve better student satisfaction and learning outcomes. It emphasizes student-centered learning and encourages more peer interaction. Students learn through online videos, assessments, etc., and then are involved in group discussions or other activities to learn more during class. All these activities help develop critical thinking, problem-solving, and teamwork skills. These skills create employable individuals. Flipped classrooms enable students to learn better, retain what they have learned, and use it for their career growth. Moreover, the teachers can analyze the outputs from students to make changes in the course so that the old contents are only refurbished and not changed completely. This enables the creation of circular courses.

Collaborative learning techniques can be implemented in the VLE for having a regenerative nature and a circular link between the courses. AI technologies can be leveraged to foster group activities among students. Intelligent tutoring systems can be used for personalized guidance, the VLE will allow continuous communication among the learners despite the geographical location and AI-powered tools will enhance learning by providing feedback. The facilities like language processing tools, translation services, and speech-to-text conversions will allow learners from diverse backgrounds to communicate despite the language barriers. Instant feedback allows students to correct mistakes to ensure uninterrupted learning and collaboration. Educators, on the other hand, can use the data-driven approaches of AI to understand the areas that need improvement and bring changes in the teaching methods to create an equitable learning environment (*Frederick, 2024*). These AI characteristics will help the students from different VLE courses learn from each other, comment, and give feedback to each other. They can also design quizzes and activities for others and continue learning.

5.4 Achieving Sustainability

Education is key to achieving sustainable development goals and sustainability. VLE allows learners to continue their education despite their location and profession. It provides an opportunity to learn and grow which would not have been possible for many to balance work and learning. Moreover, the virtualization of courses ensures sustainability in many ways. It reduces the requirements of energy-intensive facilities like lighting, cooling, heating, and ventilation of classrooms. The educators, learners, and others involved in virtual courses meet online. As the learners do not travel to their educational institutes, it helps lower carbon emissions caused by transportation. They do not need vehicles to travel, it saves fuel and reduces pollution. Moreover, online educational content eliminates the need for books, reducing paper usage. The course content, feedback, exams, and assignments are online. It will save a lot of trees and water required to grow trees, thus preserving natural resources. It reduces the costs of printing books, storing, and transporting them. All these factors contribute to lowering the fees of virtual courses and making these courses affordable. Virtual learning promotes interaction with learners from diverse backgrounds who share ideas and solutions for environmental protection. It promotes eco-responsible behaviors and following energy-efficient practices in their daily lives. Embracing online education promotes inclusivity and enhances accessibility. Furthermore, VLE courses can disseminate awareness of environmental protection, climate change, and sustainable practices. It will help them know the significance of preserving the environment and contribute to a greener future.

6. CONCLUSION

The integration of AI in Virtual Learning Environments (VLEs) has revolutionized education by enhancing engagement, personalization, and accessibility. From AI-powered chatbots and intelligent tutoring systems to data-driven analytics, AI offers immense potential to transform how students learn and interact in virtual spaces. However, challenges such as ethical concerns, bias, and technological disparities must be addressed to ensure equitable and responsible AI deployment. Future research should focus on developing more inclusive AI models, refining data privacy regulations, and ensuring that AI-driven education remains accessible to learners worldwide. Personalized learning, feedback, and analysis by AI enhance the teaching-learning process interesting. The educators and the learners both benefit from using AI in virtual learning. The learners acquire real-world skills like time management, networking, collaboration, and digital proficiency. Online platforms and AI promote eco-friendly learning by reducing the energy requirements compared to conventional classroom patterns. VLE promotes greening education and supports circularity and sustainability.

REFERENCES

Василишина, Н. М. (2020). Benefits of digital learning application at universities. Вісник Житомирського Державного Університету Імені Івана Франка. *Педагогічні Науки*, (103), 61–68.

Alina, K. R. U. K. (2022). The benefits of Virtual Learning Environment (VLE) in teaching ESP. АКТУАЛЬНІ ПИТАННЯ ГУМАНІТАРНИХ НАУК, 2022171.

Angela, W. (2014). Virtual Classrooms in the Workplace: an Implementation Study. DOI: 10.21427/D71M8R

Beardsley, M., Albó, L., Aragón, P., & Hernández-Leo, D. (2021). Emergency education effects on teacher abilities and motivation to use digital technologies. *British Journal of Educational Technology, 52*(4), 1455–1477. DOI: 10.1111/bjet.13101

Bed, P. Dhakal., Lekhnath, Sharma. (2016). Virtual Learning Environment (VLE). *The Mathematics Educator*. Advance online publication. DOI: 10.11648/j.edu.20160506.11

Bello, O. W., Ehira, D. N., Ayeni, J. K., Faruk, N., & Balogun, N. A. (2014). Towards the Design of a Synchronous Virtual Learning System [CJICT]. *Covenant Journal of Informatics and Communication Technology*, *2*(2), 59–74.

Biletska, I. O., Paladieva, A. F., Avchinnikova, H. D., & Kazak, Y. Y. (2021). The use of modern technologies by foreign language teachers: Developing digital skills. *Linguistics and Culture Review*, *5*(S2), 16–27. DOI: 10.21744/lingcure.v5nS2.1327

Bilotta, E., Bertacchini, F., Gabriele, L., Giglio, S., Pantano, P. S., & Romita, T. (2021). Industry 4.0 technologies in tourism education: Nurturing students to think with technology. *Journal of Hospitality, Leisure, Sport and Tourism Education*, *29*, 100275. DOI: 10.1016/j.jhlste.2020.100275

Büyükbaykal, C. I. (2015). Communication technologies and education in the information age. *Procedia: Social and Behavioral Sciences*, *174*, 636–640. DOI: 10.1016/j.sbspro.2015.01.594

Cofino, C. L., Atillo, G. N. A., & Velos, S. P. (2021). E-xtension: A virtual learning environment (vle) system for a state university. *International Journal of Computing Sciences Research*, *5*, 663–678.

Eilermann, S., Wehmeier, L., Niggemann, O., & Deuter, A. (2023, July). KIAAA: An AI assistant for teaching programming in the field of automation. In 2023 IEEE 21st International Conference on Industrial Informatics (INDIN) (pp. 1-7). IEEE.

Ellen MacArthur Foundation. (2014). Towards the Circular Economy Vol.3: Accelerating the scale-up across global supply chains. *Ellen MacArthur Foundation*, (January), 1–64. DOI: 10.1162/108819806775545321

Ferrario, M. (2024), The Challenges of Artificial Intelligence In Online Learning, DynDevice, https://www.dyndevice.com/en/news/the-challenges-of-artificial-intelligence-in-online-learning-ELN-1883/

Guillermo, M.-R. (2022). Asynchronous learning: Evaluation of virtual classroom metrics according to the perception of university students. *Indonesian Journal of Electrical Engineering and Computer Science*, *28*(2), 1058–1058. DOI: 10.11591/ijeecs.v28.i2.pp1058-1066

Haoyang, You. (2024). (1) Application of English Online Learning System Based on Artificial Intelligence. DOI: 10.1109/ICICACS60521.2024.10498680

Helmers, E., & Ilchmann, F. (2019). Sustainability Subjects in University Education - Development of a Comprehensive Indicator System and Quantitative Analysis of Degree Programs at German Universities. *European Journal of Sustainable Development Research*, *3*(4), em0092. Advance online publication. DOI: 10.29333/ejosdr/5771

James, Hutson., Daniel, Plate. (2024). (3) Leveraging AI to Personalize and Humanize Online Learning. Advances in mobile and distance learning book series, DOI: 10.4018/979-8-3693-0762-5.ch011

Javaid, M., Haleem, A., Vaishya, R., Bahl, S., Suman, R., & Vaish, A. (2020). Industry 4.0 technologies and their applications in fighting COVID-19 pandemic Diabetes & Metabolic Syndrome. *Clinical Research & Reviews*, *14*(4), 419–422. PMID: 32344370

Jewitt, K. E. (2018). Using virtual reality to enhance informal learning in small and medium enterprises (Doctoral dissertation, University of Glasgow).

Kosaretsky, S., Zair-Bek, S., Kersha, Y., & Zvyagintsev, R. (2022). *General education in Russia during COVID-19: Readiness, policy response, and lessons learned Primary and Secondary Education During covid 19*. Springer.

Kryukov, V., & Gorin, A. (2017). Digital technologies as education innovation at universities. *Australian Educational Computing*, *32*(1), 1–16.

Kumar, A., Agrawal, R., Wankhede, V. A., Sharma, M., & Mulat-Weldemeskel, E. (2022). A framework for assessing social acceptability of industry 4.0 technologies for the development of digital manufacturing. *Technological Forecasting and Social Change*, *174*, 121217.

Lalima, K. L. D., & Lata Dangwal, K. (2017). Blended Learning: An Innovative Approach, Universal. *The Journal of Educational Research*, *5*(1), 129–136. DOI: 10.13189/ujer.2017.050116

Martin, A. (2020). How to optimize online learning in the age of coronavirus (COVID-19): A 5-point guide for educators. *Journal of Chemical Information and Modeling*, *53*(9), 1689–1699.

Martin, F., & Parker, M. A. (2014). Use of Synchronous Virtual Classrooms: Why, Who, and How? *Journal of Online Learning and Teaching*, *10*(2), 192–210.

Massey, A. P., Montoya, M. M., & Wu, P. F. (2013, January). 3D virtual environments and corporate learning: An empirical investigation of benefits. In 2013 46th Hawaii International Conference on System Sciences (pp. 893-902). IEEE.

McGinley, T., & Karlshøj, J. (2022). A Circular Education System for the AEC. In *Proceedings of the 2022 European Conference on Computing in Construction European Council on Computing in Construction*. https://doi.org/DOI: 10.35490/EC3.2022.216

Meetaverse (2024), Virtual Learning Environments Unveiled: A Path to Digitial Education, https://meetaverse.com/blog/virtual-learning-environments/

Misha, A. (2024), How AI Can Foster Creative Thinking in the Classroom and Beyond, EdSurge, https://www.edsurge.com/news/2024-09-18-how-ai-can-foster-creative-thinking-in-the-classroom-and-beyond

Mollick, E. (2024), Using AI Tutors to Flip Your Classroom, Edutopia, https://www.edutopia.org/article/using-ai-tutors-flipped-classroom/

Monica, W. (2018). *Nirase, Fathima, Abubacker*. Effective Utilisation of VLE with Joint Multinational Postgraduate Programme., DOI: 10.1109/NCG.2018.8593057

Nhi Nguyen. (2023), Opportunities and Challenges of AI in Higher Education, Feedback Fruits, https://feedbackfruits.com/blog/opportunities-and-challenges-of-ai-in-higher-education#existing-challenges

Ossiannilsson, E. (2022), Seamless Learning Reflection, In the Book Seamless Learning in Higher Education2, Pressbooks, https://pressbooks.pub/seamlesslearning2/chapter/chapter-8-seamless-learning-reflection/

Pavitra, M. (2024), How to Use AI for Brainstorming (Use Cases and Tools), Click Up, https://clickup.com/blog/how-to-use-ai-for-brainstorming/

Power School. (2023). [Personalized Learning: A Whole Child Approach, https://www.powerschool.com/blog/personalized-learning-crash-course/]. *Future*, *K-12*, •••.

Pratyush, Banerjee. (2022). Corporate E-Learning Initiatives: A New Paradigm for Employee Development. NHRD Network journal, DOI: 10.1177/26314541221088043

Qureshi, M. I., Khan, N., Raza, H., Imran, A., & Ismail, F. (2021). Digital Technologies in Education 4.0. Does it Enhance the Effectiveness of Learning? A Systematic Literature Review. *International Journal of Interactive Mobile Technologies*, *15*(4), 31. DOI: 10.3991/ijim.v15i04.20291

Raftery, D. (2018). Ubiquitous mobile use: Student perspectives on using the VLE on their phone. *Irish Journal of Technology Enhanced Learning*, *3*(2), 47–57.

Reiddagnvy. (2022). Students' perception of Synchronous (virtual chat) or Asynchronous learning (Discussion board). DOI: 10.14293/S2199-1006.1.SOR-.PPSIDGD.v1

Rick Fiene. (2024), Linear and Circular Thinking, https://medium.com/@rickfiene/linear-and-circular-thinking-

Romy Frederick. (2024), AI-Enhanced Collaborative Learning: Fostering Teamwork in the Digital Age, iLeaf Solutions Pvt. Ltd., https://www.ileafsolutions.com/ai-enhanced-collaborative-learning-fostering-teamwork-in-the-digital-age

Subramaniam, R., & Nakkeeran, S. (2019). Impact of corporate e-learning systems in enhancing the team performance in virtual software teams. In Smart Technologies and Innovation for a Sustainable Future: Proceedings of the 1st American University in the Emirates International Research Conference—Dubai, UAE 2017 (pp. 195-204). Springer International Publishing.

Vakaliuk, T. A., Spirin, O. M., Lobanchykova, N. M., Martseva, L. A., Novitska, I. V., & Kontsedailo, V. V. (2021, March). Features of distance learning of cloud technologies for the quarantine organisation's educational process. *Journal of Physics: Conference Series, 1840*(1), 012051. DOI: 10.1088/1742-6596/1840/1/012051

Wang, Y. D. (2014). Building Trust in E-Learning. *Athens Journal of Education*, *1*(1), 9–18.

Willis, V. (2024). The role of artificial intelligence (AI) in personalizing online learning. *Journal of Online and Distance Learning*, *3*(1), 1–13.

Section 3
AI Applications in Sustainable Development and Skills Development

Chapter 7
AI in Renewable Energy Education:
Teaching the Future of Sustainable Power Systems

C. Tamilarasi
https://orcid.org/0009-0003-1026-2127
B.S. Abdur Rahman Crescent Institute of Science and Technology, India

K. Sowmiya
B.S. Abdur Rahman Crescent Institute of Science and Technology, India

G. D. Vignesh
https://orcid.org/0009-0008-8024-3980
St. Joseph's College of Engineering, India

R. L. Jasmine
https://orcid.org/0000-0001-5512-018X
College of Engineering Guindy, Anna University, Chennai, India

P. Nehru
https://orcid.org/0009-0002-5689-2792
B.S. Abdur Rahman Crescent Institute of Science and Technology, India

P. Selvakumar
https://orcid.org/0000-0002-3650-4548
Nehru Institute of Technology, India

ABSTRACT

AI's application in renewable energy education is multifaceted, encompassing areas such as energy management, grid optimization, and predictive maintenance. These simulations enable learners to understand the intricacies of energy systems and develop skills in analyzing data and making informed decisions based on real-time information. In the context of renewable energy education. This implies that students can engage with materials that are specifically designed to address their knowledge gaps and interests, thereby deepening their understanding of complex topics such as solar photovoltaic systems, wind turbine technology, and energy storage solutions. AI-driven platforms can also facilitate interactive learning through virtual labs and simulations, offering students practical experience in designing and testing renewable energy solutions.The integration of AI into renewable energy education also supports the development of critical skills required for the future workforce.

DOI: 10.4018/979-8-3693-9062-7.ch007

INTRODUCTION TO AI IN RENEWABLE ENERGY EDUCATION: PREPARING FOR A SUSTAINABLE FUTURE

AI's application in renewable energy education is multifaceted, encompassing areas such as energy management, grid optimization, and predictive maintenance. These simulations enable learners to understand the intricacies of energy systems and develop skills in analyzing data and making informed decisions based on real-time information.In the context of renewable energy education, this means that students can engage with materials that are specifically designed to address their knowledge gaps and interests, thereby deepening their understanding of complex topics such as solar photovoltaic systems, wind turbine technology, and energy storage solutions. AI-driven platforms can also facilitate interactive learning through virtual labs and simulations, offering students practical experience in designing and testing renewable energy solutions.The integration of AI into renewable energy education also supports the development of critical skills required for the future workforce. AI technologies are increasingly being used in real-world renewable energy applications, such as smart grid management and automated energy systems. By incorporating AI into educational programs, institutions can ensure that students gain proficiency in relevant technologies and are well-prepared for careers in the renewable energy sector.

This includes skills in data analysis, machine learning, and AI system design, which are essential for optimizing energy systems and advancing innovations in renewable energy technologies.In addition to enhancing educational content and skills development, AI plays a crucial role in research and innovation within renewable energy education. AI-driven research tools can analyze vast amounts of data from experiments, simulations, and field studies, accelerating the discovery of new materials, technologies, and methods for harnessing renewable energy. For instance, AI can aid in the design of more efficient solar panels, the optimization of wind turbine placement, and the development of advanced energy storage solutions. By integrating AI into research initiatives, educational institutions can contribute to cutting-edge advancements in renewable energy and provide students with opportunities to engage in groundbreaking research.

AI FUNDAMENTALS FOR RENEWABLE ENERGY STUDENTS: MACHINE LEARNING AND BEYOND

For students pursuing a career in renewable energy, understanding the fundamentals of Artificial Intelligence (AI) and its associated technologies, particularly machine learning, is increasingly crucial (Ahmad, S., et al., 2015). AI's integration into renewable energy systems offers transformative potential by optimizing energy production, improving system efficiency, and advancing innovative solutions to sustainability challenges. Advanced Machine Learning Techniques Beyond basic algorithms, several advanced techniques can significantly enhance renewable energy applications. Understanding these advanced techniques equips students with the tools to tackle more complex challenges in renewable energy systems (Ahmad, T., et al.,2021).Data Considerations and Preprocessing Students should be familiar with these preprocessing techniques to enhance the performance and reliability of their ML models.Future Trends and Innovations The field of AI and machine learning is rapidly evolving, with ongoing research and innovations shaping future applications in renewable energy. Emerging trends such as the use of AI for decentralized energy systems, blockchain integration for energy transactions, and advancements in quantum computing offer new possibilities for enhancing energy efficiency and sustainability (Al-Masri,

R. A., et al.,2019). Staying informed about these trends and innovations allows students to remain at the forefront of the field and contribute to cutting-edge developments in renewable energy. Mastering the fundamentals of AI and machine learning equips renewable energy students with the skills necessary to drive advancements in sustainable energy solutions.

Solar Energy and AI: Optimizing Performance and Predictive Maintenance

The intersection of solar energy and Artificial Intelligence (AI) represents a transformative advancement in optimizing performance and predictive maintenance within photovoltaic systems. As solar power increasingly becomes a cornerstone of sustainable energy solutions, integrating AI technologies offers significant improvements in system efficiency, reliability, and long-term performance. By leveraging AI, stakeholders can enhance the operational capabilities of solar installations, from real-time monitoring to predictive analytics, ensuring that solar energy systems operate at peak efficiency while minimizing downtime and maintenance costs. Enhancing Solar Energy Performance with AI weather conditions, and energy consumption patterns to optimize the alignment and configuration of solar panels (Bansal, M., et al.,2022). This capability enables better planning and management of energy storage systems, load balancing, and grid stability, ultimately improving the reliability and efficiency of solar power integration into the broader energy grid.Predictive Maintenance for Solar Installations Predictive maintenance is a key application of AI in solar energy, focusing on identifying and addressing potential issues before they lead to system failures or reduced performance (Barlas, P., et al.,2015).

AI-driven predictive maintenance systems use data from various sensors installed on solar panels and related equipment to monitor performance and detect anomalies. Machine learning models can analyze this data to identify patterns indicative of wear and tear, degradation, or faults. By predicting when and where maintenance is needed, these systems help prevent unexpected downtimes and extend the lifespan of solar installations.Fault Detection and Diagnostics AI technologies significantly enhance fault detection and diagnostics in solar energy systems. Traditional maintenance approaches often involve periodic inspections or reactive repairs, which can be inefficient and costly. AI-driven systems, however, continuously monitor performance data and use pattern recognition techniques to detect deviations from normal operating conditions. When a potential fault is identified, AI algorithms can diagnose the issue and provide detailed reports on its nature and location (Birol, F. 2022). This proactive approach enables timely interventions and reduces the likelihood of severe system failures, ensuring sustained energy production and operational efficiency. This integration facilitates more efficient use of renewable energy, enhances grid resilience, and supports the transition to decentralized and sustainable energy systems. Environmental and Economic Impact The application of AI in solar energy systems has significant environmental and economic benefits. By optimizing performance and enabling predictive maintenance, AI helps maximize the efficiency of solar installations, leading to higher energy output and reduced operational costs. Additionally, improved system reliability and reduced downtime contribute to a lower environmental impact by ensuring that solar energy can be harnessed consistently and effectively. The economic advantages include reduced maintenance costs, extended equipment lifespan, and increased return on investment for solar energy projects.

Wind Energy and AI: Enhancing Turbine Efficiency and Control

AI-Driven Turbine Efficiency Optimization Machine learning algorithms can process data on wind speeds, turbine vibrations, and power output to optimize turbine settings and performance. For instance, AI can adjust the blade pitch and yaw angles in real-time to maximize energy capture based on changing wind conditions (Cao, K. Y., et al.,2017). This dynamic adjustment ensures that turbines operate at peak efficiency, converting the maximum amount of wind energy into electricity while minimizing energy losses. Advanced Control Systems: AI enables the development of advanced control systems that enhance the operation and coordination of wind turbines within a wind farm. These systems use real-time data to optimize turbine performance and adjust operational parameters to suit prevailing wind conditions. For example, AI algorithms can coordinate the operation of multiple turbines to reduce wake effects and increase overall energy production. By managing the interactions between turbines and optimizing their collective performance, AI helps maximize the efficiency of wind farms and ensures more stable energy output.Real-Time Performance Monitoring Continuous performance monitoring is essential for maintaining the efficiency and safety of wind turbines.

AI-powered systems can process and analyze data from various sensors in real-time, providing operators with valuable insights into turbine performance and health. Advanced analytics tools can detect anomalies, assess the impact of environmental factors, and provide actionable recommendations for improving turbine operations (Castrillón-Mendoza, R., et al.,2020). This real-time monitoring capability enables quick responses to operational issues and ensures that turbines are operating at their best.Fault Detection and Diagnostics AI enhances fault detection and diagnostics by utilizing data-driven approaches to identify and diagnose potential issues. Machine learning models can analyze historical and real-time data to recognize patterns associated with turbine faults. For example, AI can detect irregularities in vibration patterns or changes in power output that may indicate mechanical problems. By pinpointing the nature and location of faults, AI helps reduce the time and cost associated with repairs and minimizes the impact on energy production.Enhancing Turbine Design and Development AI also plays a role in advancing turbine design and development (Chan, Y. T. 2020). By analyzing performance data and simulation results, AI can assist engineers in designing more efficient and reliable turbine components.

AI in Hydrokinetic Energy: Harnessing the Power of Moving Water

The integration of Artificial Intelligence (AI) into hydrokinetic energy systems represents a significant advancement in harnessing the power of moving water for renewable energy production. Hydrokinetic energy, which captures the energy from flowing water bodies such as rivers, tides, and ocean currents, offers a promising alternative to traditional energy sources. AI technologies play a crucial role in optimizing the efficiency, performance, and sustainability of hydrokinetic energy systems, addressing challenges related to system design, operation, and maintenance while unlocking new potentials for clean energy generation.Machine learning models can process historical and real-time data to simulate various scenarios, helping engineers design turbines that are optimized for specific water conditions and ensuring that they are placed in locations with optimal flow rates (Danish, M. S. S., et al., 2020). Real-time performance monitoring ensures that hydrokinetic systems operate at peak efficiency and contributes to the longevity and reliability of the equipment.Predictive Maintenance and Fault Detection AI-driven predictive maintenance uses data from various sensors to predict when and where maintenance will be needed (Danish, M. S. S., et al., 2019). Machine learning models analyze patterns in equipment performance, identifying signs of wear, fatigue, or potential faults before they lead to significant failures. By providing reliable forecasts, AI helps grid operators balance supply and demand, optimize energy storage, and manage the integration of hydrokinetic energy into the broader energy grid.

This forecasting capability ensures that hydrokinetic energy contributes effectively to meeting energy needs and enhances overall grid stability.Environmental Impact Assessment Understanding and mitigating the environmental impact of hydrokinetic energy systems is crucial for sustainable development. AI technologies can assist in assessing the environmental effects of hydrokinetic installations by analyzing data on water quality, aquatic life, and ecosystem changes. AI-driven control systems optimize the performance of hydrokinetic turbines by continuously adjusting their operation to maximize energy capture and ensure stable energy output. This dynamic control enhances the overall efficiency and reliability of hydrokinetic energy systems.Integration with Smart Grid Technologies The integration of AI with smart grid technologies amplifies the benefits of hydrokinetic energy systems. AI-powered smart grids use advanced algorithms to manage and optimize energy distribution, incorporating data from various renewable energy sources, including hydrokinetic systems. Cost Reduction and Economic Benefits The application of AI in hydrokinetic energy systems can lead to significant cost reductions and economic benefits. By optimizing turbine design, enhancing performance, and reducing maintenance costs, AI contributes to lower operational expenses and improved financial returns for hydrokinetic energy projects (Deka, D., et al.,2018). Additionally, increased efficiency and reliability of hydrokinetic systems result in higher energy output and better economic viability, supporting the growth and development of hydrokinetic energy as a competitive renewable energy source.

Geothermal Energy and AI: Exploring New Frontiers in Sustainable Power

The fusion of Artificial Intelligence (AI) with geothermal energy represents a groundbreaking advancement in sustainable power generation, unlocking new possibilities for efficiency, reliability, and innovation within the geothermal sector (Ramakrishnan T., et al.,2022). This synergy not only enhances the effectiveness of geothermal energy but also contributes to its broader adoption as a cornerstone of sustainable energy solutions.Optimizing Drilling and Well Management Drilling and well management are critical components of geothermal energy production. AI technologies enhance these processes by providing real-time data analysis and decision support (Entezari, A., et al.,2023). Additionally, AI can assist in managing geothermal wells by predicting and mitigating potential issues such as scaling or reservoir depletion, ensuring optimal performance and extending the lifespan of geothermal wells. Real-Time Monitoring and System Optimization AI plays a crucial role in the real-time monitoring and optimization of geothermal power plants. This dynamic optimization enhances the overall efficiency and stability of geothermal power plants, ensuring consistent and reliable energy output (Ernst, D., et al.,2004).By identifying early warning signs of wear or malfunction, AI helps operators perform maintenance tasks before issues lead to significant downtime or costly repairs. This proactive approach improves the reliability of geothermal systems, reduces maintenance costs, and extends the lifespan of critical components.Environmental Impact Assessment AI contributes to assessing and mitigating the environmental impact of geothermal energy projects.

By analyzing data on surface and subsurface conditions, AI models can predict the potential environmental effects of geothermal operations, such as changes in land use, water consumption, and emissions. This capability enables developers to design and implement measures that minimize adverse environmental impacts and ensure that geothermal projects are developed in an environmentally responsible manner.

Advanced Simulation and Modeling AI technologies enhance simulation and modeling capabilities for geothermal energy systems. Advanced machine learning algorithms can simulate complex geothermal processes, such as heat transfer and fluid dynamics, to optimize system design and performance. The future of AI in geothermal energy holds exciting possibilities for further innovation and development. Emerging trends include the use of AI for optimizing geothermal energy storage, integrating geothermal systems with other renewable energy sources, and advancing smart grid technologies. Conclusion In conclusion, the integration of AI into geothermal energy systems represents a significant advancement in harnessing the power of Earth's heat for sustainable power generation. By leveraging AI technologies, stakeholders can enhance exploration, optimize drilling and well management, and improve real-time monitoring and system performance.

AI-DRIVEN ENERGY STORAGE SYSTEMS: ENABLING A RENEWABLE ENERGY FUTURE

Artificial Intelligence (AI) is poised to revolutionize energy storage systems, playing a pivotal role in enabling a sustainable renewable energy future. AI enhances the capabilities of energy storage systems, optimizing their efficiency, performance, and integration into the energy grid, thereby facilitating a more reliable and sustainable energy infrastructure (Gabr, A. Z., et al.,2020).This optimization ensures that energy storage systems operate efficiently, maximizing their lifespan and effectiveness. For instance, AI can predict peak demand periods and adjust storage operations accordingly, ensuring that stored energy is available when needed and reducing the need for fossil fuel-based peaking power plants. By predicting maintenance needs and detecting early signs of wear or malfunction, AI helps prevent unexpected downtimes and costly repairs. This proactive approach enhances the reliability of energy storage systems, ensuring consistent performance and extending the lifespan of critical components.

Enhancing Battery Management Systems Battery management systems (BMS) are integral to the functioning of energy storage systems, responsible for monitoring and managing the health and performance of batteries (Sugumaran K. M, D., et al., 2024). AI enhances BMS by providing advanced analytics and control capabilities. Machine learning models can analyze data on battery usage, temperature, and charge levels to optimize charging and discharging processes, prevent overcharging, and improve overall battery health. By optimizing storage operations, improving battery management, and enhancing predictive maintenance, AI helps reduce operational costs and extend the lifespan of storage systems. By optimizing the operation of energy storage systems and integrating them with smart grid technologies, AI contributes to a more resilient and adaptable energy grid. This increased resilience supports the reliable delivery of energy, even in the face of disruptions or fluctuations.Challenges and Considerations cybersecurity measures, and ongoing training for operators and engineers. Furthermore, the lifecycle and environmental impact of storage technologies, such as batteries, must be considered to ensure that AI-driven solutions contribute to overall sustainability (Gladysz, P., et al., 2022).future Directions and Innovations The future of AI in energy storage systems is characterized by ongoing innovation and development. Innovations in AI will also facilitate the development of new storage solutions and enhance the integration of energy storage with other renewable energy technologies. Addressing challenges and embracing future innovations will be essential for maximizing the benefits of AI in energy storage, contributing to a more sustainable and resilient energy infrastructure. Through the continued application of

AI, energy storage systems can achieve new levels of performance and sustainability, driving progress toward a cleaner and more reliable energy future.

Smart Grids and AI: Managing Renewable Energy Distribution and Consumption

Smart grids equipped with AI technologies offer a sophisticated approach to optimizing energy distribution, enhancing grid reliability, and enabling more efficient consumption patterns. This synergy not only supports the integration of renewable energy but also contributes to a more resilient and adaptive energy infrastructure.Real-Time Energy Management AI significantly enhances the real-time management of energy distribution within smart grids. For example, during periods of high renewable energy generation, AI systems can prioritize the distribution of renewable power, reducing reliance on fossil fuel-based sources and ensuring that energy is used efficiently.Demand Response Optimization Effective demand response is crucial for balancing supply and demand within the grid. AI-driven smart grids use real-time data to optimize demand response strategies, adjusting energy consumption patterns in response to supply conditions (Hettiarachchi, H., et al., 2019).Grid Stability and Reliability Maintaining grid stability and reliability is a primary concern for grid operators. AI contributes to grid stability by providing advanced predictive analytics and control capabilities. Machine learning models can forecast potential issues such as equipment failures, voltage fluctuations, or outages based on historical and real-time data. AI systems can then trigger preventive measures or automated responses to address these issues before they impact grid stability.

This proactive approach enhances the reliability of the grid and reduces the likelihood of disruptions. Integration of Distributed Energy Resources (DERs) AI algorithms analyze data from DERs to manage their output, storage, and interaction with the grid (Vijayakumar G, et al., 2024). This coordination ensures that DERs contribute effectively to grid stability and energy supply, supporting the overall integration of renewable energy sources.Energy Storage Optimization Machine learning models can predict periods of high or low energy generation and adjust storage operations accordingly. This optimization ensures that energy storage systems are used efficiently, maximizing their contribution to grid stability and reducing the need for fossil fuel-based backup power.Advanced Fault Detection and Diagnosis AI-driven smart grids improve fault detection and diagnosis by analyzing data from grid sensors and infrastructure. Machine learning algorithms can identify anomalies and predict potential faults, such as equipment malfunctions or network disturbances, based on historical and real-time data (Hines, A., et al.,2019). This capability enables rapid response to issues, minimizing downtime and reducing the impact on energy supply. By addressing faults proactively, AI enhances the resilience and reliability of the grid.Consumer Engagement and Energy Efficiency AI enhances consumer engagement by providing personalized insights and recommendations for energy usage. Smart grid systems can analyze individual consumption patterns and offer tailored suggestions for improving energy efficiency, such as adjusting heating and cooling settings or shifting energy use to times of lower demand. Emerging trends include the development of more sophisticated AI algorithms for energy management, the integration of AI with blockchain technology for secure transactions and decentralized energy trading, and the exploration of AI applications for optimizing grid resilience in the face of extreme weather events. Continued research and development in AI technologies will drive improvements in smart grid systems, supporting the transition to a more sustainable and resilient energy future. Addressing challenges and embracing future innovations will be essential for maximizing the benefits of AI in smart grids, contributing to a cleaner, more resilient, and economically viable energy future. Through the continued application of AI, smart grids can achieve new levels of performance and sustainability, driving progress toward a more sustainable and reliable energy landscape.

AI IN RENEWABLE ENERGY POLICY AND ECONOMICS: INFORMING DECISION-MAKING

The integration of Artificial Intelligence (AI) into renewable energy policy and economics represents a profound shift in how energy strategies are developed, analyzed, and implemented. As the global energy landscape evolves towards increased reliance on renewable sources such as solar, wind, and hydro, policymakers and economists face the challenge of designing effective, data-driven strategies that balance economic growth, environmental sustainability, and energy security(Paramasivam Selvakumar, et al.,2024). AI offers advanced tools and methodologies to enhance decision-making processes, providing valuable insights into policy impacts, economic implications, and market dynamics within the renewable energy sector.Data-Driven Policy Formulation AI significantly enhances the formulation of renewable energy policies by providing comprehensive data analysis and predictive modeling. For example, AI can model the potential impacts of different policy scenarios, such as subsidies, tax incentives, or regulatory changes, on renewable energy adoption rates and market behavior (Inoue, N., et al.,2019). This data-driven approach helps policymakers create evidence-based policies that are more likely to achieve desired outcomes.Economic Impact Analysis AI plays a crucial role in assessing the economic impacts of renewable energy policies and projects. By analyzing economic data, including investment flows, job creation, and industry growth, AI models can predict the broader economic effects of renewable energy initiatives. For instance, AI can estimate the economic benefits of transitioning to renewable energy, such as reduced energy costs, improved energy security, and the creation of green jobs.

This analysis supports policymakers in making informed decisions about resource allocation and investment priorities, ensuring that renewable energy policies contribute positively to economic development.Market Forecasting and Trend Analysis AI enhances market forecasting and trend analysis within the renewable energy sector by processing complex datasets and identifying emerging trends. Machine learning models can analyze data on energy prices, technology advancements, and market demand to provide accurate forecasts of future market conditions. These forecasts help stakeholders, including investors and policymakers, anticipate market shifts and make strategic decisions. For example, AI can predict price trends for renewable energy technologies, enabling investors to make informed decisions about where to allocate capital.Optimizing Incentive Structures AI can optimize incentive structures for renewable energy projects by analyzing the effectiveness of various incentive mechanisms, such as feed-in tariffs, tax credits, and grant programs. By evaluating historical data on incentive performance and project outcomes, AI models can identify which incentive structures are most effective in promoting renewable energy adoption (Jafari, H., et al.,2022). This optimization helps policymakers design more efficient and targeted incentives that maximize the impact of public funding and support the growth of renewable energy markets.

Risk Assessment and Management The integration of AI into renewable energy policy and economics enhances risk assessment and management by providing advanced predictive analytics. AI models can analyze data related to technological risks, financial uncertainties, and market volatility to identify potential risks associated with renewable energy projects. For instance, AI can forecast potential supply chain disruptions or fluctuations in energy prices that could impact project viability. This risk assessment helps policymakers and investors develop strategies to mitigate risks and ensure the stability of renewable energy investments.Enhancing Stakeholder Engagement AI facilitates stakeholder engagement by providing tools for analyzing public sentiment and feedback related to renewable energy policies. Natural language processing (NLP) algorithms can analyze social media posts, public comments, and other forms of feedback to gauge public opinion on renewable energy initiatives. This analysis helps policymakers understand stakeholder concerns, preferences, and priorities, leading to more inclusive and responsive policy development. For instance, AI can analyze successful renewable energy policies from various countries and provide recommendations for adapting these policies to different contexts. Continued research and development in AI technologies will drive advancements in renewable energy policy and economics, supporting the transition to a more sustainable and equitable energy future.Conclusion In conclusion, AI is transforming renewable energy policy and economics by providing advanced tools for data analysis, forecasting, and decision-making. By enhancing policy formulation, economic impact analysis, and market forecasting, AI supports the development of effective and evidence-based renewable energy strategies.

TEACHING AI IN RENEWABLE ENERGY: CURRICULUM DEVELOPMENT AND PEDAGOGY

The integration of AI into renewable energy systems is transforming how energy is generated, managed, and optimized, creating a demand for skilled individuals who understand both the technical and practical applications of AI in this sector (Selvakumar, P.,2023). Developing a curriculum and pedagogy that effectively incorporates AI into renewable energy education involves several key considerations, including the identification of core competencies, the design of instructional materials, and the implementation of innovative teaching methods.Defining Core Competencies and Learning Outcomes Core competencies might include machine learning algorithms, data analytics, predictive modeling, and optimization techniques, alongside a deep understanding of renewable energy technologies such as solar, wind, hydro, and geothermal(Jiang, Y., et al.,2022). Learning outcomes should ensure that students can effectively apply AI techniques to real-world problems, such as optimizing energy production, improving grid management, and enhancing system reliability.Integrating AI and Renewable Energy Concepts For example, students might explore how AI can optimize solar panel placement using spatial analysis, predict wind turbine performance based on historical data, or improve energy storage management through predictive algorithms. These experiences not only enhance students' technical skills but also develop their problem-solving abilities and understanding of industry-specific challenges.Utilizing Industry Partnerships and Real-World Data (Kalton, G., et al.,2003) Industry partners can offer valuable data sets for analysis, provide mentorship, and contribute to the design of relevant case studies and projects. Access to real-world data ensures that students work with authentic scenarios and develop skills that are directly applicable to the workforce.

Incorporating Emerging Technologies and Tools The rapid advancement of AI technologies necessitates the inclusion of emerging tools and techniques in the curriculum. This might involve teaching students to use cutting-edge AI platforms and software, such as TensorFlow, PyTorch, or IBM Watson, and incorporatig new methodologies such as deep learning or reinforcement learning..Promoting Interdisciplinary Learning AI in renewable energy is inherently interdisciplinary, requiring knowledge from fields such as computer science, engineering, environmental science, and economics. Encouraging interdisciplinary learning helps students gain a broader perspective and understand the interconnected nature of these fields. For example, integrating environmental science principles with AI algorithms can help students develop models for predicting the environmental impact of renewable energy projects. Interdisciplinary collaboration also fosters creativity and innovation, as students draw on diverse knowledge and expertise.Emphasizing Ethical and Societal Implications As AI technologies become more prevalent, understanding their ethical and societal implications is crucial.

The curriculum should address topics such as data privacy, algorithmic bias, and the potential impacts of AI on employment and social equity. Implementing Innovative Teaching Methods Innovative teaching methods, such as flipped classrooms, online simulations, and interactive workshops, can enhance the learning experience. Flipped classrooms, where students review theoretical content at home and engage in practical activities during class, allow for more hands-on and collaborative learning. Online simulations and virtual labs provide opportunities for students to experiment with AI algorithms and renewable energy systems in a controlled environment. Interactive workshops and guest lectures from industry experts offer additional insights and real-world perspectives.Assessing and Iterating the Curriculum Regular assessment and iteration of the curriculum are essential to ensure its effectiveness and relevance. Feedback from students, industry partners, and educators can provide valuable insights into the strengths and areas for improvement in the curriculum. Conclusion In conclusion, teaching AI in renewable energy requires a thoughtfully developed curriculum and innovative pedagogy that integrate AI concepts with practical applications in the energy sector. By defining core competencies, incorporating hands-on projects, utilizing real-world data, and addressing ethical considerations, educators can prepare students to effectively apply AI in renewable energy contexts. Continuous assessment, interdisciplinary learning, and the incorporation of emerging technologies ensure that the curriculum remains relevant and impactful.

Case Studies: AI in Renewable Energy Education - Success Stories and Lessons Learned

Case studies of AI in renewable energy education reveal a wealth of success stories and valuable lessons that underscore the transformative potential of integrating artificial intelligence into educational programs (Karagiannopoulos, S., et al.,2019). The key lesson learned from this case study is the importance of integrating real-world data and industry partnerships into the curriculum to provide students with hands-on experience and relevant skills (Lesage-Landry, A., et al.,2018).Stanford University - AI-Driven Wind Turbine Performance Analysis Stanford University's curriculum in renewable energy incorporates AI to enhance the efficiency and performance of wind turbines. Through collaborative projects with wind energy companies, students use machine learning algorithms to analyze turbine performance data and predict maintenance needs. This approach has led to significant improvements in turbine reliability and reduced downtime. The case study highlights the benefits of industry collaboration and the use of real-time data for practical learning experiences. Key lessons include the value of industry partnerships in providing students with authentic project opportunities and the need for advanced data analysis tools to support AI-driven research.Delft University of Technology - Smart Grids and AI Delft University of Technology in the Netherlands offers a specialized program that focuses on smart grids and the role of AI in managing renewable energy distribution. Students work on projects that involve designing and implementing AI algorithms for optimizing grid operations, integrating distributed energy resources, and improving grid stability. The success of this program is reflected in its ability to produce graduates with expertise in both AI and smart grid technologies(Li, J. H., et al.,2022). Lessons learned from this case study emphasize the importance of interdisciplinary learning and the need for curricula that address emerging technologies and their applications in energy systems.

The program's success is evident in the advancements made in energy storage technologies and the practical skills students gain in AI and data analysis. The key lesson from this case study is the value of focusing on specific areas within renewable energy, such as energy storage, to provide students with targeted knowledge and skills.Technical University of Munich - AI and Geothermal Energy The Technical University of Munich incorporates AI into its geothermal energy curriculum, focusing on optimizing geothermal resource management and predicting geothermal reservoir behavior. Students use AI algorithms to analyze geological data and model geothermal energy production. This approach has led to improved resource management and more accurate predictions of geothermal output. The case study highlights the importance of specialized AI applications in niche areas of renewable energy and the need for curricula that address the unique challenges of different energy technologies. Students work on projects that involve designing and implementing AI algorithms for optimizing grid operations, integrating distributed energy resources, and improving grid stability. University of Tokyo - AI and Wind Farm Optimization The University of Tokyo has developed a program that focuses on using AI to optimize wind farm operations. Students work on projects that involve analyzing wind farm data, predicting wind patterns, and improving turbine performance using machine learning algorithms. The success of this program is reflected in the improved efficiency and performance of wind farms. Lessons learned from this case study emphasize the need for practical, project-based learning and the importance of addressing specific challenges within renewable energy technologies.University of New South Wales - AI for Energy Efficiency in Buildings The University of New South Wales offers a course that explores the application of AI in improving energy efficiency in buildings. Students use machine learning algorithms to analyze building energy usage data and develop models to optimize heating, ventilation, and air conditioning (HVAC) systems.

The success of this program is demonstrated by the improved energy efficiency and cost savings achieved in building management. The key lesson from this case study is the value of applying AI to energy efficiency solutions and the importance of integrating real-world data into the curriculum.University of Cape Town - AI in Renewable Energy Education for Developing Regions The University of Cape Town has developed a curriculum focused on using AI to address renewable energy challenges in developing regions. Students work on projects that involve designing AI-driven solutions for energy access, off-grid systems, and renewable energy integration in underserved communities (Majeed, A.,et al.,2022). The success of this program is evident in the innovative solutions developed and the impact on local communities. Lessons learned from this case study include the importance of addressing the unique needs of developing regions and the value of designing curricula that promote sustainable development and equitable access to energy.Conclusion In conclusion, case studies of AI in renewable energy education highlight the significant impact that integrating AI can have on learning outcomes and industry preparedness. By examining successful implementations and lessons learned, educators can gain valuable insights into effective curriculum development, innovative teaching methods, and the importance of real-world applications.

AI-DRIVEN RENEWABLE ENERGY RESEARCH: ADVANCING THE STATE OF THE ART

AI-driven research is enhancing energy forecasting capabilities by developing advanced predictive models that analyze a wide range of data, including weather patterns, historical energy production, and market conditions (Middleton, P. 2018). These models can provide highly accurate forecasts of energy availability and demand, enabling better planning and decision-making for energy operators and policymakers. Improved forecasting helps to minimize the impact of variability and intermittency in renewable energy sources, leading to more reliable and efficient energy systems.Facilitating Renewable Energy Policy Development AI is also playing a role in shaping renewable energy policies by providing data-driven insights into policy impacts and effectiveness. Research in this area includes the development of AI models that simulate the effects of different policy scenarios on energy markets, economic outcomes, and environmental impacts. These models help policymakers evaluate the potential benefits and drawbacks of various policy measures, such as subsidies, tax incentives, and regulatory changes. By incorporating AI into policy analysis, researchers can provide more accurate and actionable recommendations for promoting the adoption of renewable energy and achieving sustainability goals.Promoting Sustainable Energy Practices AI-driven research is advancing sustainable energy practices by identifying opportunities for improving energy efficiency and reducing environmental impact (Neshat, N.,et al.,2014). This research contributes to the broader goal of promoting sustainable energy practices and reducing the carbon footprint of energy systems.Addressing Challenges and Uncertainties Despite the advancements, AI-driven research in renewable energy faces several challenges and uncertainties. These include the need for high-quality data, the potential for algorithmic bias, and the complexity of integrating AI models into existing systems. Researchers are working to address these challenges by developing robust data collection methods, ensuring transparency in AI algorithms, and creating standards for integrating AI solutions into energy systems. Ongoing research aims to enhance the reliability and effectiveness of AI-driven approaches, ensuring that they contribute positively to the development of renewable energy technologies.Encouraging Collaboration and Innovation The advancement of AI in renewable energy research is also driven by collaboration and innovation across various sectors.

ETHICS AND SUSTAINABILITY IN AI-DRIVEN RENEWABLE ENERGY EDUCATION

Ethics and sustainability are pivotal considerations in AI-driven renewable energy education, influencing how the next generation of professionals approaches the intersection of technology, environmental stewardship, and social responsibility. As artificial intelligence increasingly integrates into renewable energy systems, ensuring that educational programs address ethical implications and promote sustainable practices is essential for shaping a responsible and innovative workforce (Omitaomu, O., et al.,2021). This approach encompasses several key dimensions: ethical design and deployment of AI technologies, environmental impact assessment, social equity, and long-term sustainability goals.Educators should include discussions on the energy consumption associated with AI and the importance of developing energy-efficient algorithms and systems. For instance, research into more efficient machine learning techniques, such as those requiring less computational power, aligns with the broader goals of sustainability. By addressing these issues, educational programs can guide students in making informed decisions that minimize the environmental footprint of AI technologies.Promoting Social Equity AI-driven renewable energy education must also address social equity considerations (Pandey, N., et al.,2022). Renewable energy technologies have the potential to democratize energy access, but without careful planning, they could also widen existing disparities. Students should be trained to consider the social dimensions of renewable energy projects, including how to ensure that AI solutions are inclusive and beneficial for all segments of society. This includes understanding how different communities might be impacted by energy transitions and ensuring that AI-driven solutions do not disproportionately disadvantage vulnerable populations. Educators can incorporate case studies and project-based learning that emphasize the importance of social equity in the deployment of renewable energy technologies.Long-Term Sustainability Goals Incorporating long-term sustainability goals into AI-driven renewable energy education involves aligning educational objectives with global sustainability frameworks and targets, such as the United Nations Sustainable Development Goals (SDGs).

Ethical Data Management Data plays a central role in AI-driven renewable energy systems, making ethical data management a critical area of focus. Educational programs should cover best practices for data collection, storage, and use, ensuring that students understand issues related to data privacy, consent, and security. For example, when using data to train AI models for renewable energy forecasting, it is important to handle sensitive information responsibly and ensure that data collection practices comply with ethical and legal standards. Teaching students about the ethical implications of data use prepares them to navigate complex issues related to data governance and enhances their ability to develop AI solutions that respect user rights and privacy.Collaboration and Multidisciplinary Approaches Addressing ethics and sustainability in AI-driven renewable energy education requires a collaborative and multidisciplinary approach. Students should be encouraged to work with experts from various fields, including environmental science, engineering, policy, and social sciences, to develop holistic solutions that balance technological innovation with ethical considerations. Collaborative projects and interdisciplinary coursework help students understand the multifaceted nature of sustainability challenges and promote innovative solutions that integrate diverse perspectives and expertise. By examining successful projects and identifying potential pitfalls, students can learn from real-world experiences and develop a nuanced understanding of how to apply ethical principles in practice. For example, case studies on AI-driven energy management systems that have successfully addressed social equity issues or minimized environmental impacts can serve as valuable learning tools.Ethical Decision-Making Frameworks Educators should introduce students to ethical decision-making frameworks and tools that can guide their work in AI-driven renewable energy projects(Rajendran, D. P. D., et al., 2021). These frameworks help students evaluate the potential ethical implications of their decisions and consider various perspectives when developing and implementing AI solutions.

WORKFORCE DEVELOPMENT: PREPARING STUDENTS FOR AI-DRIVEN RENEWABLE ENERGY CAREERS

Workforce development in the context of AI-driven renewable energy careers is crucial as the sector evolves to address global sustainability challenges and technological advancements. As AI technologies increasingly permeate renewable energy systems, educational institutions and training programs must equip students with the skills and knowledge necessary to thrive in this dynamic field(Tarmanini, C., et al.,2022). This preparation involves a multifaceted approach that integrates technical proficiency, interdisciplinary knowledge, and practical experience to ensure that graduates are well-prepared for the future workforce.Technical Proficiency and AI Skills Central to preparing students for AI-driven renewable energy careers is the development of technical proficiency in both AI technologies and renewable energy systems. Students must gain a solid foundation in machine learning, data science, and AI algorithms, as well as an understanding of their application within the context of renewable energy technologies such as solar, wind, hydro, and geothermal. Educational programs should offer specialized courses and hands-on training in these areas, including programming, statistical analysis, and algorithm development (Sabory, N. R., et al., 2021). This technical expertise enables students to design and implement AI solutions that optimize energy production, enhance system efficiency, and manage renewable energy resources effectively.Practical Experience and Industry Collaboration Providing students with practical experience through internships, co-op programs, and industry partnerships is critical for workforce development.

Additionally, project-based learning, where students work on real-world AI and renewable energy projects, helps them develop problem-solving skills and a portfolio of work that demonstrates their capabilities to potential employers. Educational programs should incorporate training in these areas to prepare students for collaborative work environments and effective interaction with stakeholders. Workshops, seminars, and extracurricular activities can help students develop these skills, enhancing their ability to present complex technical concepts, lead projects, and work effectively in diverse teams. Professional development opportunities, including mentorship programs and career counseling, can also support students in navigating their career paths and achieving their professional goals.This includes exposure to emerging technologies, such as advanced AI techniques and next-generation renewable energy systems, and the encouragement of creative problem-solving approaches (Tebenkov, E.,et al.,2021). By promoting an innovative mindset and adaptability, educational institutions can prepare students to tackle new challenges and contribute to the ongoing development of AI-driven renewable energy solutions. Incorporating ethics into the curriculum ensures that students are prepared to develop AI solutions that align with sustainability goals and adhere to responsible practices. This focus on ethics and sustainability helps students become conscientious professionals who contribute positively to the field and address the broader societal and environmental impacts of their work.Industry Trends and Future Directions Keeping students informed about industry trends and future directions in AI and renewable energy is vital for workforce readiness. Educational programs should integrate up-to-date information on industry developments, technological advancements, and market dynamics. This includes providing insights into emerging applications of AI in renewable energy, such as energy storage optimization, smart grids, and decentralized energy systems. By understanding current and future industry trends, students can better align their skills and knowledge with the needs of the job market and position themselves for success in their careers..

THE FUTURE OF AI IN RENEWABLE ENERGY EDUCATION - EMPOWERING A SUSTAINABLE TOMORROW

This vision of the future encompasses several critical areas: advanced curriculum development, cutting-edge research opportunities, industry-academic partnerships, and a focus on global sustainability goals.Advanced Curriculum Development To prepare students for the future of AI in renewable energy, educational institutions must develop and implement advanced curricula that integrate AI technologies with renewable energy principles (Valle-Cruz, D., et al.,2020). This includes introducing courses that cover the latest developments in machine learning, data analytics, and AI applications specific to renewable energy systems such as solar, wind, and hydroelectric power. Cutting-Edge Research Opportunities The future of AI in renewable energy education will be significantly shaped by research opportunities that push the boundaries of technology and innovation. Students and researchers will need access to state-of-the-art facilities, data sets, and computational resources to explore novel AI algorithms and their applications in energy systems (Wei, C. C., et al.,2022).Industry-Academic Partnerships Strong partnerships between educational institutions and industry stakeholders are essential for bridging the gap between theoretical knowledge and practical application. By collaborating with renewable energy companies, technology providers, and policy-makers, educational programs can align their curricula with current industry needs and emerging trends. These partnerships can facilitate internships, co-op programs, and collaborative research projects that provide students with valuable hands-on experience and industry insights. Furthermore, industry experts can contribute to curriculum development, ensuring that educational content remains relevant and responsive to technological advancements and market demands.Focus on Global Sustainability Goals Educational programs should emphasize the role of AI in achieving targets related to clean energy, climate action, and sustainable communities (Yang, Y. Y., et al.,2013). This involves teaching students how to design and implement AI solutions that contribute to reducing carbon emissions, increasing energy efficiency, and promoting equitable access to renewable energy resources.

Accessibility and Inclusivity Ensuring that AI-driven renewable energy education is accessible and inclusive is critical for building a diverse and equitable workforce. Educational institutions should develop strategies to reach underrepresented groups and provide opportunities for all students to engage with AI and renewable energy technologies. This includes offering scholarships, creating mentorship programs, and providing resources to support diverse learners. By fostering an inclusive educational environment, institutions can attract a wide range of talent and perspectives, enriching the field and promoting innovation.Preparing for a Dynamic Job Marke The renewmable energy sector is rapidly evolving, and students must be prepared for a dynamic job market. Educational programs should include career development resources, such as job placement services, networking opportunities, and industry certifications, to help students transition smoothly into the workforce. Additionally, institutions should provide guidance on emerging career paths and the skills required for various roles within the AI and renewable energy sectors. By equipping students with the tools and knowledge to navigate their careers, institutions can help ensure their success in a competitive job market.Lifelong Learning and Professional Development Given the rapid pace of technological advancement, lifelong learning and professional development will be essential for staying current in AI-driven renewable energy careers (Zeng, L. T., et al.,2022). Educational institutions should promote a culture of continuous learning by offering advanced courses, certifications, and training programs for graduates and professionals. By supporting ongoing education and skill development, institutions can help individuals adapt to new technologies and remain at the forefront of the field throughout their careers.Conclusion The future of AI in renewable energy education is poised to shape a sustainable tomorrow by preparing students with the knowledge, skills, and experiences necessary to drive innovation and address global energy challenges. Through advanced curricula, cutting-edge research, industry partnerships, and a focus on sustainability, educational programs can empower the next generation of professionals to make meaningful contributions to the renewable energy sector.

CONCLUSION

AI offers unparalleled opportunities to enhance educational methodologies by providing adaptive learning environments, facilitating real-time data analysis, and simulating complex energy systems to foster deeper understanding. Through AI-driven platforms, students can engage with interactive models, predictive analytics, and scenario-based learning, which can significantly bolster their ability to innovate and implement cutting-edge solutions in renewable energy.Furthermore, AI's role extends beyond the classroom, influencing research and practical applications in the field of sustainable power systems. By harnessing AI, educational institutions can collaborate with industry leaders to develop curricula that are not only aligned with current technological advancements but also anticipate future trends and needs. This synergy between education and industry ensures that graduates are well-prepared to tackle emerging challenges and leverage new opportunities in renewable energy technologies. The data-driven insights provided by AI also enable educators to tailor programs to address specific learning needs and track progress in ways that were previously unimaginable.The future of renewable energy relies on innovative solutions and a well-informed, skilled workforce capable of driving progress. AI-enhanced education represents a significant step toward achieving these goals, providing students with the knowledge and skills required to lead in the development of sustainable energy systems. As we move forward, continued investment in AI technologies and educational frameworks will be essential to harnessing the full potential of this transformative tool. By prioritizing AI in renewable energy education, we not only advance the field of sustainable power but also contribute to a more resilient and sustainable future for all.

REFERENCES

Ahmad, S., Tahar, R. M., Muhammad-Sukki, F., Munir, A. B., & Rahim, R. A. (2015). Role of feed-in tariff policy in promoting solar photovoltaic investments in Malaysia: A system dynamics approach. *Energy*, *84*, 808–815. DOI: 10.1016/j.energy.2015.03.047

Ahmad, T., Zhang, D. D., & Huang, C. (2021). Methodological framework for short-and medium-term energy, solar and wind power forecasting with stochastic-based machine learning approach to monetary and energy policy applications. *Energy*, *231*, 120911. DOI: 10.1016/j.energy.2021.120911

Al-Masri, R. A., Chenoweth, J., & Murphy, R. J. (2019). Exploring the status quo of water-energy nexus policies and governance in Jordan. *Environmental Science & Policy*, *100*, 192–204. DOI: 10.1016/j.envsci.2019.06.012

Bansal, M., Goyal, A., & Choudhary, A. (2022). A comparative analysis of k-nearest neighbor, genetic, support vector machine, decision tree, and long short term memory algorithms in machine learning. Decision Analytics Journal, 3, Article 100071.

Barlas, P., Lanning, I., & Heavey, C. (2015). A survey of open source data science tools. *International Journal of Intelligent Computing and Cybernetics*, *8*(3), 232–261. DOI: 10.1108/IJICC-07-2014-0031

Birol, F. (2022). *World Energy Outlook 2022 (Technical)*. International Energy Agency., Available at https://iea.blob.core.windows.net/assets/830fe099-5530-48f2-a7c1-11f35d510983/WorldEnergyOutlook2022.pdf

Cao, K. Y., Xu, X. P., Wu, Q., & Zhang, Q. P. (2017). Optimal production and carbon emission reduction level under cap-and-trade and low carbon subsidy policies. *Journal of Cleaner Production*, *167*, 505–513. DOI: 10.1016/j.jclepro.2017.07.251

Castrillón-Mendoza, R., Rey-Hernández, J. M., & Rey-Martínez, F. J. (2020). Industrial decarbonization by a new energy-baseline methodology. Case study. *Sustainability (Basel)*, *12*(5), 1960. DOI: 10.3390/su12051960

Chan, Y. T. (2020). On the impacts of anticipated carbon policies: A dynamic stochastic general equilibrium model approach. *Journal of Cleaner Production*, *256*, 120342. DOI: 10.1016/j.jclepro.2020.120342

Danish, M. S. S., Elsayed, M. E. L., Ahmadi, M., Senjyu, T., Karimy, H., & Zaheb, H. (2020). A strategic-integrated approach for sustainable energy deployment. *Energy Reports*, *6*, 40–44. DOI: 10.1016/j.egyr.2019.11.039

Danish, M. S. S., Senjyu, T., Funabashia, T., Ahmadi, M., Ibrahimi, A. M., Ohta, R., & Sediqi, M. M. (2019). A sustainable microgrid: A sustainability and management-oriented approach. *Energy Procedia*, *159*, 160–167. DOI: 10.1016/j.egypro.2018.12.045

Deka, D., Backhaus, S., & Chertkov, M. (2018). Structure learning in power distribution networks. *IEEE Transactions on Control of Network Systems*, *5*(3), 1061–1074. DOI: 10.1109/TCNS.2017.2673546

Entezari, A., Aslani, A., Zahedi, R., & Noorollahi, Y. (2023). Artificial intelligence and machine learning in energy systems: A bibliographic perspective. Energy Strategy Reviews, 45, Article 101017.

Ernst, D., Glavic, M., & Wehenkel, L. (2004). Power systems stability control: Reinforcement learning framework. *IEEE Transactions on Power Systems*, *19*(1), 427–435. DOI: 10.1109/TPWRS.2003.821457

Gabr, A. Z., Helal, A., & Abbasy, N. (2020). Economic evaluation of rooftop grid-connected photovoltaic systems for residential building in Egypt. *International Transactions on Electrical Energy Systems*, *30*(6), e12379. DOI: 10.1002/2050-7038.12379

Gladysz, P., Strojny, M., Bartela, Ł., Hacaga, M., & Froehlich, T. (2022). Merging climate action with energy security through CCS-a multi-disciplinary framework for assessment. *Energies*, *16*(1), 35. DOI: 10.3390/en16010035

Hettiarachchi, H., & Kshourad, C. (2019). Promoting waste-to-energy: Nexus thinking, policy instruments, and implications for the environment. In Kumar, S., Kumar, R., & Pandey, A. (Eds.), *Current developments in biotechnology and bioengineering* (pp. 163–184). Elsevier. DOI: 10.1016/B978-0-444-64083-3.00009-9

Hines, A., Schutte, J., & Romero, M. (2019). Transition scenarios via backcasting. *Journal of Futures Studies*, *24*, 1–14.

Inoue, N., & Matsumoto, S. (2019). An examination of losses in energy savings after the Japanese Top Runner Program? *Energy Policy*, *124*, 312–319. DOI: 10.1016/j.enpol.2018.09.040

Jafari, H., Safarzadeh, S., & Azad-Farsani, E. (2022). Effects of governmental policies on energy-efficiency improvement of hydrogen fuel cell cars: A game-theoretic approach. *Energy*, *254*, 124394. DOI: 10.1016/j.energy.2022.124394

Jiang, Y., & Zhao, C. H. (2022). Attention classification-and-segmentation network for micro-crack anomaly detection of photovoltaic module cells. *Solar Energy*, *238*, 291–304. DOI: 10.1016/j.solener.2022.04.012

Kalton, G., & Flores-Cervantes, I. (2003). Weighting methods. *Journal of Official Statistics*, *19*, 81–97.

Karagiannopoulos, S., Aristidou, P., & Hug, G. (2019). Data-driven local control design for active distribution grids using off-line optimal power flow and machine learning techniques. *IEEE Transactions on Smart Grid*, *10*(6), 6461–6471. DOI: 10.1109/TSG.2019.2905348

Lesage-Landry, A., & Taylor, J. A. (2018). Setpoint tracking with partially observed loads. *IEEE Transactions on Power Systems*, *33*(5), 5615–5627. DOI: 10.1109/TPWRS.2018.2804353

Li, J. H., & Xu, G. C. (2022). Circular economy towards zero waste and decarbonization. Circular Economy, 1, Article 100002.

Majeed, A., Ahmad, M., Rasheed, M. F., Khan, M. K., Popp, J., & Oláh, J. (2022). The dynamic impact of financial globalization, environmental innovations and energy productivity on renewable energy consumption: Evidence from advanced panel techniques. *Frontiers in Environmental Science*, *10*, 10. DOI: 10.3389/fenvs.2022.894857

Middleton, P. (2018). Sustainable living education: Techniques to help advance the renewable energy transformation. *Solar Energy*, *174*, 1016–1018. DOI: 10.1016/j.solener.2018.08.009

Neshat, N., Amin-Naseri, M., & Danesh, F. (2014). Energy models: Methods and characteristics. *Journal of Energy in Southern Africa*, *25*(4), 101–111. DOI: 10.17159/2413-3051/2014/v25i4a2243

Omitaomu, O., & Niu, H. R. (2021). Artificial intelligence techniques in smart grid: A survey. *Smart Cities*, *4*(2), 548–568. DOI: 10.3390/smartcities4020029

Pandey, N., de Coninck, H., & Sagar, A. (2022). Beyond technology transfer: Innovation cooperation to advance sustainable development in developing countries. *Wiley Interdisciplinary Reviews. Energy and Environment*, *11*(2), e422. DOI: 10.1002/wene.422

Rajendran, D. P. D., & Sundarraj, R. (2021). Using topic models with browsing history in hybrid collaborative filtering recommender system: Experiments with user ratings. *International Journal of Information Management Data Insights*, *1*(2), 100027. DOI: 10.1016/j.jjimei.2021.100027

Ramakrishnan, T., Mohan Gift, M. D., Chitradevi, S., Jegan, R., Hency Jose, P. S., Nagaraja, H. N., & Hailegiorgis, S. M. (2022). Study of numerous resins used in polymer matrix composite materials. *Advances in Materials Science and Engineering*, *2022*(1), 1088926.

Sabory, N. R., Senjyu, T., Momand, A. H., Waqfi, H., Saboor, N., Mobarez, R., & Razeqi, F. (2021). LEED scores of residential buildings in poor cities: Kabul city case. *Sustainability (Basel)*, *13*(12), 6959. DOI: 10.3390/su13126959

Selvakumar, P. (2023). Biomedical applications of polymers in biosensors, cancer vaccines and drug delivery systems. *Biopolimery i Kletka*, *39*(4), 245–256. DOI: 10.7124/bc.000AA0

Selvakumar, P., Mariappan, P., Shunmugam, S., Paul, R., & Jabez, S. (2024). Removal of chemicals from effluent using photobioreactor technology to improve environmental and health impacts. *Zeitschrift für Physikalische Chemie*, *2024*(7), 1295–1302. Advance online publication. DOI: 10.1515/zpch-2023-0450

Kanipriya, M., Sugumaran, D., Pandiyarajan, V., Yogananda, B. S., Selvakumar, P., & Mohan, S. (2024, January). Analysis of Electromyography Signals for Control of Mechanical Prosthesis using Machine Learning Techniques. In 2024 2nd International Conference on Intelligent Data Communication Technologies and Internet of Things (IDCIoT) (pp. 1059-1067). IEEE.

Tarmanini, C., Sarma, N., Gezegin, C., & Ozgonenel, O. (2022). Short term load forecasting based on ARIMA and ANN approaches. *Energy Reports*, *9*, 550–557. DOI: 10.1016/j.egyr.2023.01.060

Tebenkov, E., & Prokhorov, I. (2021). Machine learning algorithms for teaching AI chat bots. *Procedia Computer Science*, *190*, 735–744. DOI: 10.1016/j.procs.2021.06.086

Valle-Cruz, D., Criado, J. I., Sandoval-Almazán, R., & Ruvalcaba-Gomez, E. A. (2020). Assessing the public policy-cycle framework in the age of artificial intelligen From agenda-setting to policy evaluation. *Government Information Quarterly*, *37*(4), 101509. DOI: 10.1016/j.giq.2020.101509

Vijayakumar, G., Rajkumar, M., Rajiv Chandar, N., Selvakumar, P., & Duraisamy, R. (2024). Environmentally friendly TDS removal from waste water by electrochemical ion exchange batch-type recirculation (EIR) technique. *Environmental Science. Water Research & Technology*, *10*(4), 826–835. DOI: 10.1039/D3EW00793F

Wei, C. C., Zhang, C. G., Vardar, O., Watson, J., & Canbulat, I. (2022). Quantitative assessment of energy changes in underground coal excavations using numerical approach. *Geohazard Mechanics*, *1*(1), 58–68. DOI: 10.1016/j.ghm.2022.11.003

Yang, Y. Y., Sun, X. L., Zhu, X. Q., & Xie, Y. J. (2013). Scenario simulation and policy analysis on energy development in Qinghai Province. *Procedia Computer Science*, *17*, 720–728. DOI: 10.1016/j.procs.2013.05.093

Zeng, L. T., Qiu, D. W., & Sun, M. Y. (2022). Resilience enhancement of multi-agent reinforcement learning-based demand response against adversarial attacks. *Applied Energy*, *324*, 119688. DOI: 10.1016/j.apenergy.2022.119688

Chapter 8
Predictive Analytics and AI in Sustainability Education: Bridging Data-Driven Insights With Ethical Learning

Soumya Sankar Ghosh
https://orcid.org/0000-0002-4469-4070
VIT Bhopal University, India

ABSTRACT

This study explores how predictive analytics and Artificial Intelligence (AI) can revolutionize sustainability education by fostering personalized learning, ethical reasoning, and inclusivity. Statistical modeling demonstrated significant improvements in sustainability literacy across diverse cohorts, with the greatest gains observed among underperforming students. However, challenges such as algorithmic transparency, bias, and access disparities highlight the need for ethical AI design and infrastructural investments. Combining personalized AI-driven tools with human oversight emerged as essential for meaningful engagement and equity. Recommendations include developing ethical AI systems, fostering digital inclusion, and promoting interdisciplinary research to scale AI-driven sustainability education effectively.

1. INTRODUCTION

In 2022, a premier Indian university piloted an AI-driven sustainability education program aimed at helping students make data-informed decisions about energy consumption. Students used predictive models to simulate real-world sustainability challenges, such as optimizing energy efficiency in Indian urban and rural settings. Over the semester, their engagement with AI-based tools significantly enhanced their understanding of sustainability metrics, ethical decision-making, and long-term environmental planning. This real-world example illustrates the growing intersection of artificial intelligence (AI) and sustainability education, highlighting how technology can revolutionize learning experiences while fostering ethical responsibility. This chapter explores the role of predictive analytics and AI in sustain-

DOI: 10.4018/979-8-3693-9062-7.ch008

ability education, examining how data-driven insights can be effectively integrated into ethical learning frameworks.

The role of education in advancing sustainability has never been more critical than in today's world, where global challenges such as climate change, resource depletion, and environmental degradation demand urgent solutions. Sustainability education, framed by the United Nations Sustainable Development Goals (SDGs), emphasizes knowledge dissemination and cultivating critical thinking, ethical decision-making, and action-oriented behaviors. It is an educational paradigm that encourages learners to become responsible global citizens who understand the complexities of sustainability and act to resolve them (UNESCO, 2020). However, traditional educational methods often fail to deliver personalized, data-driven learning experiences to prepare learners for these challenges. This is where emerging technologies such as Artificial Intelligence (AI) and predictive analytics come into play, offering unprecedented opportunities to enhance sustainability education by aligning pedagogical strategies with actionable insights.

Predictive analytics, a subset of data analysis, involves using statistical models and machine learning techniques to forecast future outcomes based on historical and real-time data. In education, predictive analytics can help identify trends in student performance, forecast learning pathways, and customize teaching interventions to meet the specific needs of learners (Siemens & Baker, 2012). When applied to sustainability education, predictive models can assess how various pedagogical approaches influence sustainability literacy and ethical decision-making. This provides educators with empirical insights that can help optimize curriculum design and teaching methodologies, ensuring that learning outcomes are not only achieved but are also aligned with sustainability goals. Simultaneously, AI is transforming education by automating administrative tasks, personalizing learning, and improving access to resources. AI-driven tools like intelligent tutoring systems, natural language processing models, and adaptive learning environments can help tailor content delivery to individual student needs, making learning both effective and inclusive (Saija et al., 2024). In sustainability education, AI enables the creation of dynamic, context-specific learning modules that are continuously updated based on real-time data and learner feedback. For instance, machine learning algorithms can assess students' understanding of sustainability concepts and predict their readiness to apply these concepts in practical scenarios, thereby bridging the gap between knowledge and action.

Despite the transformative potential of AI and predictive analytics, their integration into sustainability education is not without challenges. One of the most significant concerns is the ethical dimension of technology-driven learning. Ethical learning, which emphasizes values such as fairness, equity, and social responsibility, must be carefully balanced with data-centric approaches. AI systems, while powerful, can perpetuate biases present in data or algorithms, leading to inequitable outcomes (Borenstein & Howard, 2021). For instance, predictive models that rely on incomplete or biased datasets may reinforce disparities rather than mitigate them, particularly in resource-constrained educational contexts. Therefore, sustainability education must prioritize ethical considerations alongside technological advancements to ensure that AI-driven learning environments are equitable, inclusive, and aligned with the broader goals of sustainability. The growing need to align predictive analytics and AI with ethical learning underscores the importance of data-driven decision-making in sustainability education. By leveraging statistical modeling techniques such as regression analysis, clustering, and machine learning algorithms, educators can gain deep insights into the factors influencing sustainability literacy and behavior. Statistical models allow for the identification of correlations, patterns, and causal relationships that might otherwise remain hidden. For example, regression models can quantify the impact of specific learning interventions on student engagement and performance, while clustering techniques can segment learners into groups based on their learning patterns and ethical behaviors. These insights can inform targeted interventions, ensuring that educational strategies are both effective and contextually relevant.

Furthermore, predictive analytics provides a robust foundation for personalized learning pathways, which are essential in sustainability education. Personalized learning tailors educational content, pace, and delivery methods to individual learner needs, fostering greater engagement and improved outcomes (Pane et al., 2015). In the context of sustainability, predictive models can identify students who may require additional support in understanding complex sustainability concepts or applying ethical decision-making frameworks. Students who struggle with grasping the interconnectedness of environmental, social, and economic systems can be provided with customized learning modules that address their specific challenges. By combining AI-driven personalization with predictive insights, educators can ensure that all learners, regardless of their background or abilities, achieve a comprehensive understanding of sustainability. The ethical dimension of AI in education cannot be overstated, particularly when it comes to ensuring fairness, transparency, and inclusivity. Ethical learning requires educators and policymakers to critically evaluate how predictive models and AI tools are designed, implemented, and monitored. Questions such as "Who decides what data is collected?", "How are biases in AI algorithms mitigated?", and "What safeguards are in place to protect student privacy?" must be addressed to ensure that technology-driven learning aligns with ethical principles (Floridi & Cowls, 2022). Additionally, educators must emphasize the importance of ethical reasoning as part of the curriculum, enabling students to critically engage with AI systems and understand their societal implications.

This chapter, in this regard, aims to explore the integration of predictive analytics and AI in sustainability education, focusing on how data-driven insights can be effectively bridged with ethical learning frameworks. The research objectives are twofold:

(1) To analyze the role of predictive analytics and statistical modeling in enhancing sustainability education outcomes.
(2) To examine the ethical considerations associated with AI-driven learning environments.

By addressing these objectives, this chapter seeks to provide a comprehensive understanding of how technology can be harnessed to advance sustainability education while upholding the principles of equity, inclusivity, and ethical responsibility.

To attain the answers to these questions the chapter is organized as follows: Section 2 provides a theoretical framework that discusses the concepts of sustainability education, predictive analytics, and ethical learning. It situates these ideas within the broader context of AI-driven educational transformation. Section 3 outlines the methodology, including data collection, statistical modeling techniques, and analytical frameworks used to explore the research questions. Section 4 presents the results of statistical modeling, including regression analysis, predictive modeling, and clustering outcomes, highlighting key trends and insights. Section 5 discusses the implications of the findings, focusing on the ethical dimensions of AI and the practical applications of predictive analytics in sustainability education. Finally, through Sections 6 and 7, the chapter concludes by summarizing the key insights and offering recommendations for future research and practice.

2. THEORETICAL FRAMEWORK

Sustainability education occupies a critical space in the discourse surrounding global efforts to address climate change, social inequality, and economic instability. Despite its importance, existing educational paradigms often fall short of nurturing a holistic understanding of sustainability that emphasizes ethical reasoning and actionable competencies. To bridge this gap, researchers and educators are increasingly turning to technological innovations such as predictive analytics and Artificial Intelligence (AI). These tools hold immense potential to transform sustainability education by enabling personalized learning experiences, data-driven decision-making, and the integration of ethical learning frameworks. However, this intersection of sustainability education, predictive analytics, and AI presents unique challenges and opportunities that require a deeper theoretical exploration. The foundation of sustainability education lies in its ability to adopt critical thinking, problem-solving, and ethical decision-making skills among learners. It aims to empower individuals to navigate complex interconnections between environmental, social, and economic systems while contributing to sustainable development goals (Sterling, 2013). However, traditional educational methods often lack the flexibility to address the diverse needs of learners or to adapt to the rapidly evolving nature of sustainability challenges (Shephard, 2015). This rigidity has resulted in a disconnect between theoretical knowledge and practical application, limiting the impact of sustainability education on real-world outcomes (Tilbury, 2011).

2.1 AI in Education: Transforming Learning Paradigms

Predictive analytics, a branch of data analytics that uses historical and real-time data to forecast future outcomes, has emerged as a transformative tool in education. It enables educators to identify at-risk learners, optimize resource allocation, and personalize teaching strategies based on predictive insights (Siemens & Baker, 2012). For example, regression analysis and machine learning models can reveal correlations between student behaviors and academic outcomes, providing actionable insights that inform curriculum design (Baker et al., 2016). Despite its success in general education, predictive analytics remains underutilized in sustainability education, particularly in assessing non-academic outcomes such as sustainability literacy and ethical competencies (Shah, 2023; Hutson & Ceballos., 2023). This gap highlights the need for tailored predictive models that address the unique dimensions of sustainability education. AI complements predictive analytics by enabling dynamic, adaptive learning environments that cater to individual learner profiles. Tools such as intelligent tutoring systems, natural language processing models, and adaptive learning platforms have revolutionized education by automating administrative tasks and enhancing learner engagement (Fadel et al., 2019). In sustainability education, AI can facilitate personalized learning pathways that address the diverse needs of learners, ensuring that educational interventions are both effective and equitable (Anderson et al., 2018). However, the integration of AI into sustainability education is not without challenges. Ethical concerns related to algorithmic bias, data privacy, and transparency remain significant barriers to adoption (Cath, 2018).

2.2 Ethical Considerations in AI-Driven Learning

The ethical dimension of sustainability education is particularly significant, as it emphasizes values such as equity, responsibility, and future-oriented thinking. These values align closely with the principles of ethical AI, which advocate for fairness, accountability, and inclusivity in AI-driven systems (Porayska-

Pomsta et al., 2023). However, existing research often treats ethical learning and AI as separate domains, overlooking their potential integration into sustainability education. While AI-driven tools can enhance learning outcomes, they may inadvertently reinforce existing inequities if not carefully designed and monitored (Tagliagambe, 2023). This underscores the need for interdisciplinary research that bridges the gap between technology and ethical learning frameworks.

One of the critical research gaps in this domain is the lack of robust frameworks for integrating predictive analytics and AI into sustainability education. While these technologies have been extensively studied in other educational contexts, their application to sustainability education remains limited (Samaranayake, 2024). Existing studies have primarily focused on technical aspects, such as model accuracy and algorithm performance, neglecting the broader pedagogical and ethical implications (Cath, 2018). This narrow focus fails to capture the complexity of sustainability education, which requires a holistic approach that considers both quantitative and qualitative dimensions. Another significant challenge is the measurement of learning outcomes in sustainability education. Unlike traditional academic metrics, sustainability competencies are inherently multidimensional, encompassing cognitive, behavioral, and ethical aspects (Tilbury, 2011). For example, while it is relatively straightforward to assess knowledge acquisition through standardized tests, measuring ethical reasoning or sustainability literacy requires more nuanced methods (Shephard, 2015). This limitation calls for innovative assessment frameworks that combine predictive analytics with qualitative approaches, such as case studies and ethnographic research (Tagliagambe, 2023).

2.3 Challenges in Implementation: Bridging the Gap Between Technology and Ethics

AI-driven personalization offers a promising avenue for addressing these challenges by tailoring educational content, pace, and delivery methods to individual learner needs. Natural language processing algorithms can analyze student responses to identify gaps in understanding and suggest targeted interventions (Fadel et al., 2019). Similarly, adaptive learning platforms can adjust the difficulty level of sustainability modules based on real-time learner feedback, ensuring that educational content remains both challenging and accessible (Anderson et al., 2018). However, the effectiveness of these tools depends on the availability of high-quality, representative data. Studies have shown that biased or incomplete datasets can lead to inaccurate predictions, disproportionately affecting marginalized learners (Peters et al., 2020). This highlights the importance of developing inclusive data collection frameworks that prioritize equity and diversity. The integration of ethical learning into AI-driven education presents unique opportunities to enhance the impact of sustainability education. AI algorithms can be programmed to incorporate ethical principles, such as fairness and transparency, into their decision-making processes (Porayska-Pomsta et al., 2023). This ensures that predictive models not only optimize learning outcomes but also align with the values of sustainability education (Samaranayake, 2024). Moreover, embedding ethical considerations into AI systems can help address potential risks, such as algorithmic bias and data misuse, thereby fostering trust among learners and educators (Cath, 2018).

Despite these advancements, there is a need for more interdisciplinary research that bridges the gap between technology and pedagogy. While AI and predictive analytics have been widely adopted in STEM education, their application to sustainability education remains underexplored (Siemens & Baker, 2012). This gap is particularly evident in the context of ethical learning, where existing studies have focused primarily on theoretical discussions rather than practical implementations (Tagliagambe, 2023).

By integrating insights from education, technology, and ethics, researchers can develop holistic frameworks that address the unique challenges of sustainability education. Another area that requires further exploration is the scalability of AI-driven sustainability education. While pilot studies and small-scale implementations have demonstrated promising results, scaling these initiatives to broader educational contexts presents significant logistical and ethical challenges (Anderson et al., 2018). The deployment of AI tools in resource-constrained settings may exacerbate existing inequalities, particularly if access to technology is unevenly distributed (Shah, 2023; Hutson & Ceballos., 2023). This underscores the importance of developing scalable, cost-effective solutions that prioritize inclusivity and equity.

Thus, the integration of predictive analytics and AI into sustainability education represents a significant opportunity to enhance learning outcomes, personalize educational experiences, and foster ethical reasoning. However, this potential can only be realized by addressing this section's critical research gaps and challenges. Researchers and educators can create a transformative approach to sustainability education that bridges data-driven insights with ethical learning by developing inclusive data collection frameworks, interdisciplinary research collaborations, and robust ethical guidelines. This theoretical framework sets the stage for the subsequent exploration of methodological approaches, which will delve into the specific tools, techniques, and frameworks used to implement predictive analytics and AI in sustainability education.

3. METHODOLOGY

This study investigates the integration of predictive analytics and Artificial Intelligence (AI) into sustainability education, emphasizing their role in fostering sustainability literacy and ethical learning. The research methodology has been meticulously designed to ensure a comprehensive topic analysis, employing a mixed-methods approach that combines quantitative and qualitative techniques. By capturing measurable outcomes alongside subjective insights, the methodology aligns with the study's objectives to bridge data-driven innovations with pedagogical and ethical considerations. The research spans one year, conducted from December 2023 to November 2024, in three geographically and socio-economically diverse educational institutions located in India: a metropolitan private university in New Delhi, a rural government college in Madhya Pradesh, and a community-based learning center in Tamil Nadu. These settings were chosen to represent the diverse contexts of sustainability education in India, ensuring that the findings are contextually rich and broadly applicable. The research design is rooted in a longitudinal mixed-methods framework. A longitudinal approach allows for tracking changes in sustainability literacy and ethical competencies over time, providing insights into both immediate and sustained impacts of AI-driven educational interventions. This is critical given the evolving nature of sustainability challenges and the dynamic interplay between learning experiences and ethical reasoning. The mixed-methods design integrates quantitative statistical modeling with qualitative thematic analysis, ensuring a robust examination of the research questions. Quantitative methods focus on identifying trends and correlations using statistical tools such as regression analysis and clustering, while qualitative methods provide depth by exploring the lived experiences and perceptions of participants.

The mixed-methods approach, as follows in this work, is particularly valuable in sustainability education research as it allows for a more comprehensive understanding of both quantitative trends and qualitative experiences. By integrating statistical modeling (e.g., regression analysis, clustering) with thematic analysis of student interactions and perceptions, this study captures not only measurable learning outcomes but also the ethical and cognitive dimensions of AI-driven learning. The combination of structured assessments and open-ended narratives provides a balanced perspective, ensuring that the findings are both data-driven and contextually rich. The study involves a carefully selected group of participants to ensure diversity and inclusivity. The primary participants are 300 students aged 16 to 22, drawn from secondary and tertiary education levels across the three study sites. These students are actively engaged in sustainability-focused curricula, including courses on environmental science, social justice, and global citizenship. Stratified random sampling ensures that the student cohort represents various socio-economic backgrounds, genders, and geographic regions. Additionally, 50 educators, including teachers, curriculum designers, and school administrators, participated in the study, offering insights into the pedagogical strategies and challenges associated with integrating AI-driven tools into sustainability education. To capture the broader systemic and technological dimensions, 20 policymakers and AI technologists are also included.

Qualitative data are collected through semi-structured interviews and focus group discussions, which provide nuanced insights into the experiences and perceptions of participants. Educators are interviewed to explore their views on the effectiveness and limitations of AI-driven tools in sustainability education. Similarly, focus group discussions with students are conducted to understand their learning experiences, challenges, and expectations regarding personalized and technology-enhanced education. These qualitative methods are essential for capturing the subjective dimensions of learning that cannot be quantified, such as students' motivation, ethical reflections, and sense of empowerment. The study also incorporates data from the AI-driven tools themselves. System-generated logs and analytics are analyzed to assess how students interact with adaptive learning platforms and intelligent tutoring systems. These tools, equipped with natural language processing capabilities, personalize learning pathways based on real-time performance data. For example, a student struggling with sustainability ethics might receive additional resources or exercises tailored to their specific needs, while high-performing students are challenged with more complex tasks. By analyzing these interaction logs, the study evaluates the effectiveness of AI algorithms in adapting to diverse learning profiles and enhancing educational outcomes.

Data analysis employs a combination of statistical and qualitative methods to ensure a holistic interpretation of the findings. Statistical techniques, such as multiple regression analysis, are used to identify the factors influencing student performance and sustainability literacy. Regression models explore the relationship between prior knowledge, engagement levels, and post-intervention test scores, providing empirical evidence of the impact of AI-driven tools. Clustering techniques, such as K-means, segment students into distinct groups based on their learning behaviors and ethical decision-making patterns. These clusters are then analyzed to design targeted interventions, ensuring that the educational strategies are tailored to the unique needs of different learner cohorts. Qualitative data are analyzed using thematic analysis, a method well-suited to identifying recurring patterns and themes within textual data. Interview transcripts and focus group recordings are coded to uncover themes related to the perceived benefits and limitations of AI in sustainability education, the ethical implications of predictive analytics, and the broader socio-cultural context of learning. The integration of these quantitative and qualitative findings provides a nuanced understanding of the research questions, ensuring that the study captures both measurable outcomes and subjective experiences. The chosen time frame of December 2023 to November 2024 allows for a comprehensive examination of both short-term and long-term impacts of the interventions. The study is structured into three phases: baseline data collection during the first three months, implementation of AI-driven tools and predictive analytics over the subsequent six months, and post-intervention assessments and qualitative interviews during the final three months. This phased approach ensures that the research captures the dynamic and iterative nature of learning, providing insights into how students' sustainability literacy and ethical reasoning evolve over time.

The study's methodology also places significant emphasis on ethical considerations, aligning with the principles of responsible research and AI ethics. All participants provide informed consent, and stringent measures are taken to protect their privacy and data security. Student performance data are anonymized before analysis, and access to sensitive information is restricted to authorized researchers. The ethical implications of AI-driven learning tools are also critically examined, particularly in terms of algorithmic bias and data privacy. By addressing these ethical dimensions, the study ensures that its findings contribute not only to academic knowledge but also to the responsible and equitable implementation of AI in education.

This work combines a mixed-methods research design, a diverse participant base, and a rigorous data collection and analysis framework to explore the integration of predictive analytics and AI in sustainability education. By focusing on both quantitative and qualitative dimensions, the study ensures a comprehensive understanding of the research questions. Furthermore, the emphasis on ethical considerations and longitudinal analysis highlights the study's commitment to responsible and impactful research. This methodology lays the groundwork for the subsequent section, which delves into the results and analysis, presenting the key findings and their implications for sustainability education.

4. RESULTS AND ANALYSIS

The results of this study provide a comprehensive understanding of the integration of predictive analytics and Artificial Intelligence (AI) in sustainability education. The findings highlight how these technologies influence sustainability literacy, ethical competencies, and personalized learning outcomes across diverse educational settings. The study began with baseline assessments to evaluate the initial levels of sustainability literacy and ethical reasoning among the participants. These assessments revealed significant variability across cohorts, highlighting disparities in prior exposure to sustainability concepts. Consider the following:

Table 1. Comparative analysis of pre- and post-intervention scores by Cohort

Cohort	Pre-Intervention Mean (SD)	Post-Intervention Mean (SD)	Mean Difference	t-Statistic	p-Value
Metropolitan	60.2 (12.8)	82.1 (10.5)	21.9	9.74	<0.001
Rural	48.7 (15.3)	75.3 (12.7)	26.6	11.12	<0.001
Community-Based	50.4 (14.2)	74.2 (11.8)	23.8	10.15	<0.001

The baseline results, in Table 1, revealed substantial variability across cohorts, with metropolitan students outperforming their rural and community-based peers. The mean pre-intervention test score for metropolitan students was significantly higher (60.2) compared to rural (48.7) and community-based (50.4) cohorts. This disparity underscores the unequal starting points of students, influenced by factors such as access to resources, prior exposure to sustainability concepts, and educational infrastructure. The standard deviations also highlighted a wider range of abilities among rural and community-based students, pointing to the need for tailored interventions. This observation set the stage for evaluating how AI-driven tools and predictive analytics could address these disparities. The baseline data provided a critical reference point for measuring the effectiveness of the interventions, as analyzed in the subsequent regression analysis. The differences in baseline scores across cohorts also underscore disparities in prior exposure to sustainability concepts, with metropolitan students starting with higher mean scores.

To assess the impact of predictive analytics, a regression analysis was conducted to identify key predictors of post-intervention test scores. Engagement metrics, personalized AI-driven modules, and participation in ethical learning activities emerged as significant contributors to improved performance.

Table 2. Multiple regression analysis of post-intervention test scores

Predictor Variable	Coefficient (β)	Standard Error	t-Statistic	p-Value	Variance Inflation Factor (VIF)
Engagement Metrics	0.47	0.07	6.71	<0.001	1.12
Personalized AI Modules	0.34	0.08	4.25	<0.001	1.18
Ethical Learning Activities	0.26	0.06	4.33	<0.001	1.09
Socio-Economic Status (SES)	0.21	0.05	4.2	<0.001	1.15

Table 2 presents the coefficients, standard errors, and significance levels for variables such as engagement metrics, participation in personalized AI modules, and ethical learning activities. The analysis identified engagement metrics as the strongest predictor ($\beta = 0.47$, $p < 0.001$) of improved test scores. This finding aligns with existing literature that emphasizes the importance of active participation in learning outcomes. Personalized AI modules also emerged as a significant contributor ($\beta = 0.34$, $p < 0.001$), demonstrating the effectiveness of adaptive learning systems in meeting individual learner needs. Ethical learning activities, while having a smaller effect size ($\beta = 0.26$), were statistically significant ($p < 0.001$), highlighting their role in fostering moral reasoning alongside academic improvement. The inclusion of socio-economic status (SES) as a predictor added an equity dimension to the analysis. While SES had a smaller coefficient ($\beta = 0.21$), its significance ($p < 0.001$) underscores the interplay between socio-economic factors and educational outcomes. These results provided a foundation for exploring how different groups of students responded to AI interventions, as further analyzed through clustering.

K-means clustering was employed to segment students based on their learning behaviors, engagement levels, and test score improvements. The following table categorizes students into three clusters: High Achievers, Moderate Achievers, and Low Achievers. Consider the Table 3 for better understanding:

Table 3. Characteristics of student clusters

Cluster	Percentage	Engagement Level	Average Pre-Test Score	Average Post-Test Score	Improvement (%)
High Achievers	30%	High	72.1	90.5	25.5
Moderate Achievers	50%	Moderate	54.2	79.6	46.8
Low Achievers	20%	Low	41.7	65.4	56.8

Using K-means clustering, students were grouped into three distinct profiles based on their learning behaviors, engagement levels, and test score improvements. Table 3 outlines the characteristics of each cluster, including the percentage of students, pre- and post-test scores, and the magnitude of improvement. Cluster 1, labeled "High Achievers," included students who consistently demonstrated strong engagement and academic performance. These students benefited from the fine-tuning of their learning experiences through AI tools, which pushed them to achieve even higher scores. Cluster 2, "Moderate Achievers," represented the largest group and showed substantial improvements, highlighting the effectiveness of AI in supporting learners who required consistent but moderate assistance. Cluster 3, "Low Achievers," exhibited the greatest percentage improvement despite starting with the lowest baseline scores. This finding underscored the potential of AI-driven personalization to uplift students who face significant learning challenges. The clustering results aligned with the predictors identified in the regression analysis. Engagement metrics were a distinguishing factor between the clusters, reinforcing the importance of active participation in achieving learning gains. The success of low achievers also pointed to the role of targeted interventions, which were guided by the high predictive accuracy of AI algorithms discussed next.

To ensure the reliability of AI-driven tools, their predictive accuracy was evaluated using three algorithms: Random Forest, Support Vector Machine (SVM), and Logistic Regression. Table 4 presents the precision, recall, F1-score, accuracy, and Area Under the Curve (AUC) for each algorithm.

Table 4. Predictive accuracy of AI algorithms

Algorithm	Precision	Recall	F1-Score	Accuracy	Area Under Curve (AUC)
Random Forest	0.88	0.86	0.87	87.50%	0.91
Support Vector Machine (SVM)	0.84	0.82	0.83	84.20%	0.89
Logistic Regression	0.8	0.78	0.79	79.60%	0.85

The Random Forest algorithm outperformed the others, achieving the highest accuracy (87.5%) and AUC (0.91). This made it the most reliable model for forecasting student performance and personalizing learning pathways. The superior performance of Random Forest can be attributed to its ability to handle complex, non-linear relationships in the data, making it well-suited for the diverse learning profiles observed in the clustering analysis. The high predictive accuracy of these algorithms validated their use in tailoring educational strategies. For instance, the algorithms' ability to identify at-risk students early allowed for timely interventions, which were particularly impactful for Cluster 3 learners. These results also informed the thematic insights derived from qualitative data, which explored participants' experiences with AI recommendations.

The qualitative data, gathered through interviews and focus group discussions, provided a deeper understanding of how students and educators perceived AI-driven tools. Three major themes emerged from the analysis, as summarized in Table 5, personalized learning, ethical challenges, and equity in access.

Table 5. Thematic insights from qualitative analysis

Theme	Description	Representative Quote	Observed Challenges	Suggested Improvements
Personalized Learning	Enhanced engagement through tailored content	"The AI modules knew exactly where I needed help."	Over-reliance on AI for learning pathways	Blend AI recommendations with human feedback
Ethical Challenges in AI Decisions	Concerns about fairness and transparency	"Sometimes I wasn't sure why the AI recommended certain actions."	Lack of explainability in AI recommendations	Develop more transparent AI systems
Equity in Access	Addressing digital divide issues	"In rural areas, access to reliable internet is still a challenge."	Limited infrastructure in rural settings	Invest in digital infrastructure
Motivation and Learner Autonomy	Increased ownership of learning	"I felt more in control of my studies because I could track my progress."	Risk of reduced motivation in low achievers	Combine self-tracking tools with mentorship
Collaboration and Peer Learning	Facilitated group discussions on sustainability topics	"The AI encouraged us to share ideas and solve problems together."	Unequal participation in group tasks	Integrate AI tools that foster balanced collaboration

The theme of personalized learning emerged as one of the most frequently discussed aspects of AI-driven interventions. Participants noted how the AI modules adapted content and pace to their specific needs, particularly benefiting those in the Low Achievers cluster. For instance, a rural student shared, "Before, I would struggle with new concepts, but the extra exercises provided by the AI helped me a lot." This individualized support enhanced engagement and retention, as also reflected in the improved test scores in Clusters 2 and 3 (see Table 3). However, some participants expressed concerns about over-reliance on AI, fearing that students might lose the ability to self-direct their learning. These observations highlight the need to balance AI recommendations with human feedback, ensuring that learners retain agency over their educational journeys.

A significant number of students and educators raised concerns about the ethical implications of AI-driven recommendations. Participants often questioned the transparency of AI algorithms, as illustrated by a student's comment: "I couldn't understand why the AI told me to focus on certain topics when I felt confident in them." This lack of explainability led to frustration and skepticism among some users. These ethical challenges align with the findings in Table 4, where the predictive accuracy of algorithms was evaluated. While the Random Forest algorithm performed well, its complexity made it less interpretable for end users. Addressing this challenge requires the development of explainable AI systems that clearly communicate the rationale behind their recommendations. Additionally, workshops or tutorials could help users better understand how AI systems function.

Equity in access was a recurring theme, particularly among rural and community-based participants. Limited digital infrastructure often hindered the seamless use of AI tools. One rural student noted, "It was hard to complete the tasks because of frequent power cuts and poor internet." This challenge disproportionately affected Cluster 3 learners, who already faced significant educational barriers (see Table 3). To address this issue, educators and policymakers suggested investing in digital infrastructure and providing offline learning options. For instance, downloadable AI modules or printed materials could ensure continuity in learning for students in resource-constrained settings. The demographic analysis in Table 6 further supports this finding, showing that rural students made significant gains despite these challenges.

AI-driven tools were found to increase learner autonomy, with participants reporting greater ownership of their educational progress. A student from the Moderate Achievers cluster commented, "The dashboard showing my progress made me want to improve each week." This sense of control motivated students to engage more actively with the content, aligning with the engagement metrics identified as a key predictor in Table 2. However, low achievers sometimes struggled to maintain motivation when progress was slow. This observation highlights the importance of combining AI tools with mentorship or peer support, ensuring that students receive encouragement and guidance alongside automated feedback.

While most discussions focused on individualized learning, some participants highlighted how AI tools fostered collaboration. For example, group tasks and AI-facilitated discussions encouraged students to exchange ideas on sustainability topics. An educator shared, "The AI suggested group challenges that brought out creative solutions from students." However, unequal participation in group activities was noted as a challenge, with some students dominating discussions while others remained passive. To address this, educators suggested integrating AI tools that monitor and encourage balanced participation, ensuring that all voices are heard. This theme connects to the clustering analysis (Table 3), where High Achievers often took on leadership roles in group settings.

The expanded thematic insights in Table 5 build on and contextualize the quantitative findings presented in previous tables. For instance, the concerns about algorithmic transparency raised in the ethical challenges theme are directly tied to the predictive accuracy and interpretability issues discussed in Table 4. Similarly, the equity in access theme complements the demographic disparities analyzed in Table 6, providing a qualitative perspective on the structural barriers faced by rural and low-SES students. By integrating these qualitative insights with the statistical trends, the study underscores the importance of a holistic approach to AI-driven sustainability education. The findings highlight not only the strengths of predictive analytics and AI but also the challenges and ethical considerations that must be addressed to maximize their impact.

Table 6. Improvements in sustainability literacy by demographics

Demographic Variable	Group	Pre-Test Mean	Post-Test Mean	Improvement (%)	p-Value
Gender	Male	54.2	78.4	44.7	<0.001
	Female	51.7	79.6	54	<0.001
SES	Low	48.1	73.3	52.4	<0.001
	High	58.9	82.7	40.4	<0.001

Table 6 highlights the mean score changes by gender, socio-economic status (SES), and geographic location. Female students showed greater improvements compared to their male counterparts, suggesting that AI-driven tools effectively addressed gender-based disparities. Similarly, students from low SES backgrounds exhibited significant gains, aligning with the study's goal of promoting inclusivity in sustainability education. These results reinforced the clustering analysis, where low achievers (often from underserved demographics) benefited most from personalized interventions. The demographic analysis also underscored the interplay between technology and access. While rural students demonstrated substantial improvements, their challenges with digital infrastructure pointed to the need for systemic support to maximize the impact of AI-driven tools. This finding connects back to the equity concerns raised in the qualitative analysis, emphasizing the importance of addressing structural barriers alongside implementing technological solutions.

The statistical analyses and qualitative findings form a cohesive narrative that highlights the multi-dimensional impact of predictive analytics and AI in sustainability education. The baseline assessments in Table 1 established the need for personalized interventions, which were subsequently validated through the regression analysis in Table 2. The clustering analysis in Table 3 provided a nuanced understanding of learner diversity, further supported by the predictive accuracy results in Table 4. The thematic insights in Table 5 added depth to the statistical trends, while the demographic analysis in Table 6 emphasized the equity implications of these interventions. Together, these findings demonstrate that AI-driven tools, when combined with predictive analytics and ethical learning frameworks, have the potential to transform sustainability education. By addressing disparities, personalizing learning, and fostering ethical reasoning, these technologies can pave the way for a more inclusive and effective educational paradigm.

5. DISCUSSION

The results of this study demonstrate the significant potential of predictive analytics and Artificial Intelligence (AI) in enhancing sustainability education by providing tailored learning experiences, fostering ethical reasoning, and bridging educational disparities. The findings indicate that these tools can address many challenges inherent in traditional educational systems, including the rigidity of standardized instruction, unequal access to resources, and the difficulty of fostering engagement in complex subjects like sustainability. However, as transformative as these technologies may be, their implementation brings with it a series of ethical, logistical, and practical considerations that need careful attention. This section discusses these aspects in a continuous narrative, building on the results presented earlier and situating them within the broader educational and societal context.

The evidence presented in this study underscores the importance of personalized learning in addressing individual needs and promoting academic success. Students in the Low Achievers cluster showed significant improvements in sustainability literacy, illustrating the ability of AI-driven tools to provide targeted support to those who face the greatest challenges. By dynamically adapting content to meet the unique needs of each learner, these tools create opportunities for students to engage with material at their own pace, overcoming the limitations of one-size-fits-all approaches. This individualized attention is particularly relevant in sustainability education, where students often start with vastly different levels of prior knowledge and interest. The role of personalization is further amplified when viewed alongside the challenges of fostering meaningful engagement in topics that require critical thinking, interdisciplinary knowledge, and an understanding of global systems. While the effectiveness of AI in tailoring educational pathways is evident, the issue of over-reliance on these tools raises concerns. Automated systems, no matter how sophisticated, cannot replicate the nuanced guidance provided by educators or the value of human interactions in the learning process. Students who rely solely on AI recommendations risk losing opportunities to develop critical thinking, self-regulation, and metacognitive skills, which are essential for navigating complex sustainability issues. This limitation highlights the importance of integrating AI tools into a broader pedagogical framework where human oversight remains central. Educators play a vital role in contextualizing AI-driven insights and providing the mentorship and guidance necessary to cultivate well-rounded learners.

The equity implications of AI interventions form another critical dimension of the discussion. The baseline assessments revealed disparities in sustainability literacy across different socio-economic and geographic groups, particularly between metropolitan and rural students. While AI tools successfully narrow these gaps, the persistent challenge of unequal access to technology limits their potential impact. Rural and underserved communities often lack the infrastructure needed to support digital learning, such as reliable internet connectivity and access to devices. These systemic barriers create an uneven playing field, where the benefits of AI-driven education are not equally distributed. Addressing these disparities requires concerted efforts at multiple levels. Investments in digital infrastructure are essential to ensure that all students, regardless of their location or socio-economic background, can access the tools and resources needed for effective learning. Offline-compatible AI tools and localized content can also play a crucial role in mitigating the challenges posed by infrastructure deficits. These innovations would enable learners in remote areas to benefit from adaptive learning technologies, even in the absence of continuous internet connectivity. However, such measures must be coupled with broader policy initiatives that prioritize equity in education and address the root causes of digital exclusion.

The ethical dimensions of AI in education emerged as a recurring theme in this study. The lack of transparency in AI algorithms was a source of concern for many participants, who expressed discomfort with recommendations they could not fully understand. Algorithmic opacity can undermine trust in AI systems, particularly when students and educators are unable to discern the rationale behind specific decisions. This challenge is compounded by the potential for bias in AI algorithms, which, if left unaddressed, can perpetuate existing inequalities. Ensuring that AI systems are designed and implemented with fairness and inclusivity in mind is therefore a critical priority. To build trust in AI-driven education, developers must prioritize the creation of explainable AI systems. These systems should be capable of clearly articulating the logic and data underpinning their recommendations, empowering users to make informed decisions. In parallel, educators and students must be equipped with the knowledge and skills needed to critically engage with AI tools, fostering a culture of transparency and accountability. Ethical frameworks for AI in education should also be established, emphasizing the principles of fairness, inclusivity, and user agency. By embedding these values into the design and deployment of AI systems, stakeholders can ensure that technological advancements align with the broader goals of sustainability education.

Another dimension of the discussion concerns the role of collaboration and social learning in sustainability education. AI tools were found to facilitate group discussions and collaborative problem-solving, enabling students to share ideas and develop collective solutions to sustainability challenges. These interactions are vital in cultivating the skills needed to address the interconnected nature of global issues, from climate change to social justice. However, the unequal participation observed in group activities highlights a challenge that needs to be addressed. While some students thrive in collaborative settings, others may struggle to find their voice or engage meaningfully in discussions. AI systems can play a role in mitigating these disparities by monitoring group dynamics and encouraging balanced contributions. For example, adaptive tools can prompt quieter students to participate, ensuring that all voices are heard and valued. The role of educators in facilitating collaboration remains indispensable. While AI tools can support group activities, they cannot replace the nuanced understanding and interpersonal skills that educators bring to managing group dynamics. Educators must actively foster an inclusive environment where all students feel empowered to contribute, ensuring that collaborative learning becomes a source of mutual growth and discovery.

The integration of predictive analytics and AI into sustainability education also raises important questions about the long-term impact of these tools on learners' values and behaviors. While the study demonstrated significant short-term gains in sustainability literacy and ethical reasoning, the durability of these outcomes remains an open question. Longitudinal research is needed to explore how AI-driven interventions influence learners over time, particularly in terms of their ability to apply sustainability principles in real-world contexts. Understanding the lasting effects of AI-driven education will provide valuable insights into its transformative potential and its role in shaping future generations. Scalability is another critical consideration. While this study showed promising results in specific educational settings, scaling AI-driven interventions to diverse contexts presents significant challenges. Cultural, linguistic, and socio-economic differences can affect how learners interact with AI tools and respond to their recommendations. To address this, future research should explore how AI systems can be adapted to meet the unique needs of different populations. This includes developing culturally sensitive content, incorporating local knowledge into sustainability curricula, and ensuring that AI tools are accessible and relevant across diverse settings.

Interdisciplinary collaboration will be essential in addressing these challenges. The intersection of education, technology, and ethics offers a fertile ground for innovation, where researchers, educators, and technologists can work together to develop holistic models for sustainability education. This collaboration should extend beyond academia to include policymakers, industry leaders, and community organizations, creating a shared vision for the future of education in a rapidly changing world. The implications of this study extend to policy as well. Policymakers must recognize the transformative potential of AI in education while addressing the systemic barriers that limit its effectiveness. This includes establishing regulatory frameworks that ensure the ethical use of AI, promoting investments in digital infrastructure, and supporting capacity-building initiatives for educators. By taking a proactive approach, policymakers can create an enabling environment where AI-driven tools enhance the quality and equity of education. Educators, too, have a critical role to play in shaping the future of AI in sustainability education. Beyond adopting new technologies, educators must reimagine their pedagogical approaches to integrate AI-driven insights with human-centric practices. This involves designing learning experiences that encourage critical thinking, ethical reasoning, and collaborative problem-solving, ensuring that students are prepared to tackle the complexities of sustainability challenges.

Hence, the findings of this study highlight both the opportunities and challenges of integrating predictive analytics and AI into sustainability education. While these technologies offer powerful tools for enhancing learning outcomes, their implementation must be guided by principles of equity, transparency, and ethical responsibility. A balanced approach that combines technological innovation with systemic investments, human oversight, and interdisciplinary collaboration is essential. By addressing these dimensions, stakeholders can harness the full potential of AI to transform sustainability education, empowering learners to become active, informed, and responsible global citizens. This discussion underscores the need for continued exploration and dialogue to ensure that the integration of AI in education aligns with the broader goals of building a sustainable and equitable future.

6. CONCLUSION AND RECOMMENDATIONS

The integration of predictive analytics and AI into sustainability education represents a pivotal shift in the way we approach teaching and learning in the 21st century. This study has demonstrated the transformative potential of these technologies, highlighting their ability to personalize learning, foster ethical reasoning, and address educational inequities. At the same time, it has underscored the complexities and challenges associated with their implementation, emphasizing the need for a balanced and thoughtful approach. This final section synthesizes the key insights from the study, outlines practical recommendations for stakeholders, and identifies avenues for future research. The findings have established that predictive analytics and AI-driven tools can significantly enhance sustainability literacy across diverse learner profiles. By dynamically adapting content to individual needs, these technologies empower students to engage with complex sustainability issues at their own pace, thereby overcoming the limitations of traditional instructional methods. The clustering analysis revealed that students who were initially struggling showed the greatest improvements, indicating that AI interventions can serve as a powerful equalizer in education. However, the study also highlighted persistent disparities in access to digital infrastructure and technology, which continue to limit the reach and impact of these innovations.

The ethical dimensions of AI in education emerged as a central theme, with participants raising concerns about transparency, fairness, and inclusivity. While the high predictive accuracy of AI algorithms demonstrated their technical robustness, the lack of explainability in some systems created skepticism and highlighted the importance of designing user-friendly, ethical AI tools. This underscores the need for ethical frameworks and guidelines that prioritize accountability, user agency, and equity in the deployment of AI systems in education. Based on these findings, the following recommendations are proposed for educators, policymakers, technologists, and researchers:

1. Prioritize Infrastructure Development and Accessibility

To ensure that all learners benefit from AI-driven education, investments in digital infrastructure are essential. Governments and educational institutions should work together to expand internet access, provide affordable digital devices, and develop offline-compatible AI tools for regions with limited connectivity. These measures will help bridge the digital divide and promote equitable access to quality education.

2. Develop Ethical and Transparent AI Systems

AI developers must prioritize the creation of systems that are explainable, inclusive, and fair. Training datasets should be representative of diverse populations to minimize bias, and algorithms should be designed to provide clear, understandable recommendations. Policymakers should establish ethical standards and regulatory frameworks to ensure that AI systems align with the principles of sustainability education.

3. Empower Educators Through Professional Development

Educators play a critical role in integrating AI into the classroom. Professional development programs should equip them with the skills and knowledge needed to use AI tools effectively, address ethical challenges, and design pedagogical strategies that complement technology-driven learning. Training should also emphasize data literacy, enabling educators to interpret and apply AI-generated insights in meaningful ways.

4. Foster Learner Autonomy and Critical Thinking

While AI tools excel at personalizing learning, they must be used in ways that encourage, rather than diminish, learner autonomy. Educators should design activities that challenge students to critically engage with AI-generated recommendations, reflect on their learning processes, and develop independent problem-solving skills. This balance between automation and agency is essential for preparing students to navigate complex sustainability challenges.

5. Promote Collaboration and Interdisciplinary Approaches

Sustainability education requires the integration of diverse perspectives and expertise. Educators and technologists should collaborate to design AI systems that foster group learning, encourage balanced participation, and support collaborative problem-solving. Interdisciplinary research that bridges education, technology, and ethics will be critical in developing holistic models for AI-driven sustainability education.

6. Evaluate Long-Term Impacts and Scalability

Future research should focus on the long-term impacts of AI-driven interventions on learners' sustainability literacy, ethical reasoning, and real-world behaviors. Longitudinal studies will provide insights into the durability of these outcomes and inform strategies for scaling AI tools to diverse educational contexts. Research should also explore how emerging technologies, such as generative AI and augmented reality, can further enhance sustainability education.

As we move forward, it is imperative to adopt a holistic approach that integrates technological innovation with systemic investments, ethical considerations, and human-centered practices. Predictive analytics and AI have the potential to revolutionize sustainability education, but their success depends on our ability to harness these tools responsibly and equitably. By working together, educators, policymakers, technologists, and researchers can create an educational paradigm that prepares learners to address the pressing challenges of sustainability while fostering values of inclusivity, responsibility, and global citizenship. This study contributes to the growing body of knowledge on AI in education, offering valuable insights into its application in the context of sustainability. While it has addressed key questions, it has also raised important issues that require further exploration. The journey toward integrating AI into education is still unfolding, and continued innovation, collaboration, and reflection will be essential in shaping its future. In aligning technology with the goals of sustainability education, we take a step closer to empowering the next generation to lead the way toward a more equitable and sustainable world.

7. FUTURE DIRECTIONS IN AI AND SUSTAINABILITY EDUCATION

Building on the findings and discussions presented in this study, it is essential to consider the trajectory of AI-driven sustainability education and how it can continue to evolve in alignment with technological advancements, ethical considerations, and equitable learning opportunities. While AI has already begun transforming sustainability education, its long-term impact depends on continuous innovation, interdisciplinary collaboration, and responsible implementation. Future efforts must address the challenges identified in this research while harnessing AI's full potential to enhance learning, foster critical thinking, and improve decision-making in sustainability education. As AI and predictive analytics mature, their application in sustainability education will expand beyond personalization to include predictive learning interventions. These systems will use real-time data to forecast student needs and provide targeted support, enhancing learning outcomes. Moreover, AI-driven sustainability simulations will enable students to explore complex environmental challenges in a controlled, data-driven setting, reinforcing theoretical knowledge with experiential learning. The growing role of AI in decision-making will also necessitate the integration of AI ethics education to equip learners with the skills to critically evaluate algorithmic biases and ethical dilemmas in AI-driven sustainability initiatives.

Collaboration among educators, researchers, policymakers, and technology developers will be key to maximizing AI's benefits in sustainability education. AI-powered platforms will facilitate global knowledge-sharing, enabling educators to co-develop curricula, share best practices, and work together on sustainability challenges. This interconnected approach will create a more inclusive and adaptive learning environment, ensuring that AI-driven sustainability education remains relevant and impactful across diverse educational settings. The integration of AI into sustainability education represents a pivotal shift in the way learning is structured and delivered. This study has demonstrated the transformative potential of AI-driven tools, highlighting their ability to enhance personalized learning, foster ethical reasoning, and address disparities in access to quality education. However, as these technologies evolve, it is crucial to ensure their ethical and equitable application.

To fully realize the benefits of AI-driven sustainability education, stakeholders must collaborate in creating policies and infrastructures that support equitable access to AI-enhanced learning. Investing in research to develop transparent, fair, and explainable AI models will be critical in mitigating biases and ensuring inclusivity in sustainability education. Additionally, efforts must be made to scale AI-driven sustainability solutions across diverse educational settings, ensuring that students from all backgrounds benefit from these technological advancements. Future research should focus on evaluating the long-term impacts of AI-driven sustainability education, examining how students apply sustainability concepts beyond the classroom. Understanding the scalability and adaptability of AI solutions in different educational contexts will provide valuable insights into best practices for their implementation.

REFERENCES

Anderson, J., Rainie, L., & Luchsinger, A. (2018). Artificial intelligence and the future of humans. *Pew Research Center, 10*(12).

Baker, R. S., Martin, T., & Rossi, L. M. (2016). Educational data mining and learning analytics. *The Wiley handbook of cognition and assessment: Frameworks, methodologies, and applications*, 379-396.

Borenstein, J., & Howard, A. (2021). Emerging challenges in AI and the need for AI ethics education. *AI and Ethics, 1*(1), 61–65. DOI: 10.1007/s43681-020-00002-7 PMID: 38624388

Cath, C. (2018). Governing artificial intelligence: Ethical, legal and technical opportunities and challenges. *Philosophical Transactions. Series A, Mathematical, Physical, and Engineering Sciences, 376*(2133), 20180080. DOI: 10.1098/rsta.2018.0080 PMID: 30322996

Fadel, C., Holmes, W., & Bialik, M. (2019). *Artificial intelligence in education: Promises and implications for teaching and learning*. Centre for Curriculum Redesign.

Floridi, L., & Cowls, J. (2022). A unified framework of five principles for AI in society. *Machine learning and the city: Applications in architecture and urban design*, 535-545.

Hutson, J., & Ceballos, J. (2023). Rethinking education in the age of AI: The importance of developing durable skills in the Industry 4.0. *Journal of Information Economics, 1*(2), 26–35. DOI: 10.58567/jie01020002

Pane, J. F., Steiner, E. D., Baird, M. D., & Hamilton, L. S. (2015). *Continued progress: Promising evidence on personalized learning*. RAND Corporation. DOI: 10.7249/RR1365

Porayska-Pomsta, K., Holmes, W., & Nemorin, S. (2023). The ethics of AI in education. In *Handbook of Artificial Intelligence in Education* (pp. 571–604). Edward Elgar Publishing. DOI: 10.4337/9781800375413.00038

Sajja, R., Sermet, Y., Cikmaz, M., Cwiertny, D., & Demir, I. (2024). Artificial intelligence-enabled intelligent assistant for personalized and adaptive learning in higher education. *Information (Basel), 15*(10), 596. DOI: 10.3390/info15100596

Samaranayake, P. N. (2024). Navigating The Moral Prospect: Ethical Consideration in The Digital Age. *Journal of Ethics and Emerging Technologies, 34*(1), 1–13. DOI: 10.55613/jeet.v34i1.144

Shah, P. (2023). *AI and the Future of Education: Teaching in the Age of Artificial Intelligence*. John Wiley & Sons.

Shephard, K. (2015). *Higher education for sustainable development*. Springer. DOI: 10.1057/9781137548412

Siemens, G., & Baker, R. S. (2012). Learning analytics and educational data mining: Towards communication and collaboration. *Proceedings of the 2nd International Conference on Learning Analytics and Knowledge*, 252–254. DOI: 10.1145/2330601.2330661

Sterling, S. (2013). Learning for resilience, or the resilient learner? Towards a necessary reconciliation in a paradigm of sustainable education. In *Resilience in social-ecological systems* (pp. 45–62). Routledge.

Tagliagambe, S. (2023). Phenomenology and the Digital World: Problems and Perspectives. *Foundations of Science*, *28*(4), 1157–1174. DOI: 10.1007/s10699-022-09863-z

Tilbury, D. (2011). *Education for sustainable development: An expert review of processes and learning*. UNESCO.

UNESCO. (2020). *Education for sustainable development: A roadmap*. United Nations Educational, Scientific and Cultural Organization.

Chapter 9
Developing Critical Thinking Skills Through AI-Enhanced Science Education for Sustainability

Nofouz Mafarja
https://orcid.org/0000-0001-7367-3431
Universiti Malay, Malaysia

Hutkemri Zulnaidi
https://orcid.org/0000-0002-7799-1223
Universiti Malay, Malaysia

Mimi Mohaffyza Mohamad
https://orcid.org/0000-0001-5916-7444
Universiti Tun Hussein Onn Malaysia, Malaysia

ABSTRACT

In an era where artificial intelligence (AI) is rapidly transforming every aspect of our lives, the education sector must adapt to equip students with the skills needed to address complex global challenges, particularly in sustainable development. This chapter, titled "Developing Critical Thinking Skills Through AI-Enhanced Science Education for Sustainability," will explore how AI can be integrated into science education to foster critical thinking and problem-solving skills, essential for addressing issues like environmental degradation, renewable energy, and climate change education. This chapter aligns with the overall theme of the book, "Rethinking the Pedagogy of Sustainable Development in the AI Era," by addressing the critical role that AI can play in reshaping science education to better prepare students for the complexities of sustainable development. It highlights the potential of AI to not only enhance educational outcomes but also to empower the next generation of learners to contribute meaningfully to global sustainability efforts.

DOI: 10.4018/979-8-3693-9062-7.ch009

1. INTRODUCTION TO AI IN SUSTAINABILITY AND SCIENCE EDUCATION

The integration of Artificial Intelligence (AI) in science education is reshaping traditional teaching and learning processes, showing strong potential to enhance educational outcomes. AI-driven tools, including intelligent tutoring systems, adaptive learning platforms, and automated assessments, support a personalized learning approach, which can improve student engagement and understanding of complex scientific concepts. As Roll and Wylie (2016) note, AI systems adapt to individual learning needs by providing tailored feedback and scaffolding, which enhances comprehension by aligning resources with students' levels. These adaptive capabilities empower educators to analyze large datasets for identifying learning patterns, thus allowing them to design more effective instructional strategies (Zawacki-Richter et al., 2019).

The role of AI in science education is particularly significant for sustainability education, where complex topics like climate change and resource management require innovative approaches. Sustainability education emphasizes critical thinking and problem-solving as essential competencies for addressing real-world challenges. According to UNESCO (2017), education for sustainable development (ESD) should equip learners with the skills to analyze environmental, social, and economic issues and to devise solutions that balance these demands. By promoting these skills, students are better prepared to navigate sustainability challenges and contribute meaningfully to their communities (Biasutti & Frate, 2017).

AI tools enhance sustainability education by immersing students in real-world scenarios, such as through AI-powered simulations that model human impacts on ecosystems. Students can experiment with various environmental actions and observe the outcomes, deepening their understanding and encouraging critical thinking. Additionally, AI-based project-based learning (PBL) provides access to real-time data on issues like energy consumption or carbon emissions, allowing students to work on data-driven projects that mirror real sustainability challenges (Wiek et al., 2011). This data-focused approach not only helps students develop analytical skills but also fosters active learning through engagement with current environmental concerns.

Research indicates that AI-driven platforms contribute to improved assessment outcomes for students, especially for those performing below grade level, with a reported 23% improvement in scores (Bezzina & Dingli, 2024). These tools support personalized learning by adapting to various learning styles and paces, enhancing motivation through gamified features and immediate feedback mechanisms. Such platforms encourage critical thinking and problem-solving, essential for science education's increasingly interactive nature (Selvam, 2024).

Additionally, AI competitions allow students to create community-focused AI prototypes, increasing AI literacy and confidence, especially in underserved communities. Using real-world issues, like security concerns, in interactive games makes complex AI concepts more accessible and engaging (Sintov et al., 2017). These immersive methods demonstrate the potential of AI in enhancing problem-solving skills and fostering engagement with science topics.

However, there are challenges to consider. Data privacy, algorithmic bias, and the need for technical infrastructure can impact equitable access to AI-based learning, especially for marginalized groups (Eden et al., 2024). While AI simulations and immersive technologies, such as virtual reality (VR) and augmented reality (AR), offer innovative educational experiences, they should complement traditional teaching methods rather than replace them entirely. Balancing AI with conventional approaches can ensure that interpersonal and critical thinking skills remain central in education.

2. LEVERAGING AI FOR REAL-WORLD PROBLEM IN SUSTAINABLE DEVELOPMENT

The concept of sustainable development, defined as meeting the needs of the present without compromising the ability of future generations to meet their own needs, is a cornerstone of global efforts to address environmental, social, and economic challenges. Since the United Nations introduced the Sustainable Development Goals (SDGs) in 2015, there has been a growing need for innovative approaches to achieve these ambitious targets by 2030. Among these approaches, artificial intelligence (AI) is emerging as a transformative tool capable of tackling complex problems in sustainable development across multiple domains, including agriculture, energy, healthcare, and climate action (Vinuesa et al., 2020).

However, AI in sustainable development faces challenges, including ethical concerns, the digital divide, and regulatory needs. Issues like model bias and data access disparities must be addressed to ensure equitable AI deployment. Despite these challenges, AI's potential for fostering cross-sector collaboration and innovation promises accelerated progress toward the SDGs, including responsible consumption, climate action, and more sustainable resource management.

2.1. AI Tools for Simulation and Modeling: Exploring AI-Driven Technologies for Real-World Scenarios in Sustainability

Artificial Intelligence (AI) technologies have become powerful tools for simulating and modeling real-world scenarios, especially in fields like sustainability where understanding complex environmental systems is essential. AI-driven simulations allow students, researchers, and policymakers to engage with dynamic systems, predict outcomes, and explore the impacts of various sustainability interventions. These tools are essential in education and research as they enhance problem-solving skills, promote critical thinking, and offer insights into potential long-term consequences of decisions.

2.2 AI Technologies for Simulation and Modeling

2.2.1 Machine Learning-Based Simulations

Machine learning (ML) is widely used in simulations that require pattern recognition and predictive analytics. In environmental science, for instance, ML algorithms can simulate climate change models by analyzing historical climate data and predicting future trends based on various interventions. These models allow users to explore the potential effects of carbon reduction policies, renewable energy adoption, and reforestation efforts on global temperature rise (Rolnick et al., 2019). By incorporating real-world data, ML-based simulations provide accurate and adaptive models for complex systems that continuously evolve.

1. Agent-Based Modeling (ABM)

Agent-Based Modeling (ABM) is a powerful AI tool that simulates interactions between individual agents within a system. These agents could represent people, animals, vehicles, or even policies, each with their own behaviors and decision-making rules. ABM is highly applicable in sustainability education because it helps simulate scenarios where human behavior impacts environmental outcomes. For example, ABM can be used to model the effects of urban development on ecosystems or to explore how individual actions, like reducing energy consumption, collectively influence environmental sustainability (Macal & North, 2010).

2. Neural Networks for Environmental Prediction

Neural networks, a subset of AI technologies inspired by the human brain, are used for complex environmental modeling, including simulations of ecosystems and climate systems. Convolutional neural networks (CNNs) and recurrent neural networks (RNNs) can process large amounts of spatial and temporal data, making them ideal for weather forecasting, pollution tracking, and water resource management. These AI models predict outcomes by learning from past events, offering valuable insights into the potential future impacts of various sustainability interventions (Badr et al., 2020).

3. Digital Twins

A digital twin is a virtual replica of a physical system or environment that is continuously updated with real-time data. AI technologies underpin digital twins by integrating data from IoT (Internet of Things) devices, sensors, and historical records to create accurate simulations of real-world systems. In sustainable development, digital twins can be used to simulate entire cities, allowing students and researchers to predict the outcomes of smart city interventions like green infrastructure, energy optimization, or waste management (Tao et al., 2018). These simulations enable real-time decision-making and scenario testing, which is crucial for understanding the immediate and long-term effects of sustainability policies.

4. Reinforcement Learning for Dynamic Systems

Reinforcement learning (RL) is an AI technique that uses trial and error to optimize decision-making in dynamic environments. RL is particularly useful for simulating real-world systems where decisions have consequences over time, such as managing water resources, balancing energy grids, or controlling deforestation rates. By simulating sustainability interventions in complex, changing environments, RL allows users to identify optimal strategies for long-term sustainability outcomes. For instance, RL-based models could simulate the allocation of water resources under different climate change scenarios, helping policymakers design effective water conservation strategies (Silver et al., 2017).

5. AI-Enhanced Geographic Information Systems (GIS)

Geographic Information Systems (GIS) enhanced with AI can simulate environmental changes over time, integrating spatial data with machine learning for more sophisticated modeling of real-world scenarios. AI-enhanced GIS allows students and researchers to simulate the effects of deforestation, urbanization, or rising sea levels on ecosystems. These simulations offer a visual and data-driven way to engage with sustainability challenges and explore the outcomes of various interventions in land management, conservation, and biodiversity protection (Yuan et al., 2018).

2.3 Educational and Research Implications

In sustainability education, AI-driven simulation tools help students visualize the complex and interconnected nature of environmental systems. These tools not only facilitate understanding but also promote active learning, where students can test their own sustainability interventions and analyze the outcomes. AI simulations are also instrumental in research, enabling experts to experiment with policies and interventions without real-world consequences, ultimately contributing to better decision-making and policy design. By leveraging AI technologies like machine learning, neural networks, and digital twins, educators can bring real-world environmental challenges into the classroom, enabling learners to engage deeply with sustainability issues and practice solving complex problems. Moreover, these tools offer insights into long-term trends and enable policymakers to develop more effective sustainability strategies that are based on predictive and adaptive models.

2.4 Examples of AI Tools That Support Students in Modeling and Solving Complex Environmental Problems

Artificial Intelligence (AI) tools are increasingly being integrated into education, enabling students to engage with complex environmental problems through simulation, prediction, and optimization techniques. These tools provide students with interactive platforms where they can model environmental systems, predict the impacts of interventions, and develop solutions to sustainability challenges. Below are examples of AI tools that support students in tackling complex environmental issues:

1. ClimateAI

ClimateAI is a platform that uses machine learning algorithms to help users, including students, analyze climate risk and make predictions about future environmental changes. Through ClimateAI, students can model scenarios related to agriculture, water resource management, and disaster risk reduction, allowing them to experiment with different strategies for climate adaptation (ClimateAI, 2021).

Educational Impact: Students use ClimateAI to analyze large datasets, including historical weather data and crop yield information, and predict how climate change might affect specific regions. The tool fosters critical thinking by allowing students to test interventions like crop rotation or water-saving technologies and observe their potential impact on food security and environmental sustainability.

Example: In classroom projects, students can use ClimateAI to explore the effects of climate change on agriculture in different regions, analyzing how temperature shifts and precipitation changes affect crop productivity.

2. Earth Engine by Google

Google Earth Engine is a powerful cloud-based platform for planetary-scale environmental data analysis. It provides access to satellite imagery and geospatial datasets, enabling students to visualize and model environmental changes such as deforestation, water resource management, and biodiversity loss. With its machine learning capabilities, students can develop models that predict environmental trends and evaluate the effectiveness of conservation efforts (Gorelick et al., 2017).

Educational Impact: Students can use Earth Engine to map changes in land use over time, predict the impact of human activity on ecosystems, and model the effects of climate change on various environmental variables. This enables students to gain hands-on experience with real-world environmental data and apply AI-driven modeling techniques to solve pressing global challenges.

Example: In a project on deforestation, students can use satellite data to monitor forest loss over time, apply machine learning to predict future deforestation hotspots, and model the effects of reforestation efforts on local biodiversity.

3. DeepMind's AI for Climate Prediction

DeepMind has developed AI models that improve weather forecasting and climate predictions. These models leverage neural networks to predict precipitation, temperature variations, and extreme weather events with greater accuracy than traditional models. By integrating these AI models into educational programs, students can use AI to explore complex climate systems and predict environmental outcomes with high precision (DeepMind, 2021).

Educational Impact: Students can use AI models from DeepMind to understand the intricate interactions between atmospheric elements and predict the occurrence of extreme weather events like hurricanes, floods, and droughts. This helps students develop skills in climate modeling and disaster preparedness.

Example: In a class focused on environmental risk management, students can simulate how AI predictions of future storms influence urban planning and emergency response strategies.

4. SimEarth: The Living Planet

SimEarth is an educational simulation game that allows students to model and manage planetary ecosystems. The AI-driven simulation presents students with the challenge of balancing environmental, economic, and social systems to maintain a sustainable planet. Students can experiment with variables like carbon emissions, land use, and resource extraction, observing how these changes affect the Earth's ecosystem (Wright, 1990).

Educational Impact: Through SimEarth, students learn the consequences of human activities on the planet, including climate change, species extinction, and environmental degradation. The platform encourages students to think critically about the trade-offs involved in environmental management and to design interventions that promote sustainability.

Example: Students in environmental science courses use SimEarth to simulate the long-term impact of deforestation on biodiversity, experimenting with different conservation strategies to balance ecosystem health and economic growth.

5. En-ROADS Climate Solutions Simulator

En-ROADS, developed by Climate Interactive and MIT Sloan, is a user-friendly simulation tool that allows students to explore the impact of various climate policies on global temperature. The tool enables users to manipulate different policy levers, such as renewable energy adoption, carbon taxes, reforestation, and energy efficiency improvements, and observe their effects on climate outcomes (Climate Interactive, 2020).

Educational Impact: En-ROADS helps students understand the complexity of climate change mitigation, providing a comprehensive view of how economic and political decisions influence global environmental outcomes. By adjusting various parameters, students can visualize the long-term impact of policy decisions on CO2 emissions, temperature rise, and energy use.

Example: In a classroom setting, students use En-ROADS to explore how a combination of renewable energy investments, carbon pricing, and reforestation could limit global warming to below 2°C, comparing their strategies with real-world policy initiatives.

2.5 Integrating AI into Science Curricula to Address Sustainability Challenges

The integration of Artificial Intelligence (AI) into science education presents an opportunity to enhance students' ability to tackle real-world sustainability challenges. By incorporating AI tools into curricula, students can engage with complex environmental problems, explore data-driven solutions, and develop skills in predictive modeling and systems thinking. This approach not only helps students understand global issues like climate change, biodiversity loss, and resource depletion, but also prepares them to use cutting-edge technologies in addressing these challenges.

1. Enhancing Systems Thinking and Problem-Solving Skills

AI-driven tools like simulations and modeling platforms provide students with a hands-on, immersive experience in understanding how interconnected environmental systems work. Integrating these tools into science curricula fosters systems thinking—an essential skill for addressing sustainability issues, which often involve complex interactions between natural and human systems (Capra, 2005; Miller & Madsen, 2015).

Example: Students learning about ecosystems can use AI tools such as Google Earth Engine to model deforestation's impact on biodiversity and climate, providing a clear visualization of the consequences of land-use changes over time. By seeing how these systems interact, students can develop holistic approaches to sustainability challenges, understanding the importance of balancing environmental, economic, and social factors.

AI tools can also support problem-based learning, where students are presented with real-world environmental problems and must apply AI to develop solutions. For instance, in a unit on water management, students might use AI algorithms to predict water availability under different climate scenarios, helping them devise strategies for efficient water use in drought-prone regions.

2. Promoting Data Literacy and Critical Analysis

AI allows students to access and analyze vast amounts of environmental data, promoting data literacy and critical thinking (Berland & Wilensky, 2016). By integrating AI into science curricula, educators can teach students how to interpret complex datasets, recognize patterns, and make evidence-based decisions.

Example: In a climate change module, students might use machine learning algorithms in platforms like ClimateAI to predict the future impact of rising temperatures on agricultural yields. They would analyze historical weather data, crop patterns, and other variables, learning to differentiate between short-term fluctuations and long-term trends. This process enhances their ability to critically analyze scientific data and draw meaningful conclusions (Sarkar & Gilman, 2018).

Furthermore, AI-based simulations can be used to evaluate the potential effectiveness of sustainability interventions. For instance, students can model carbon emission reduction strategies in an AI platform like En-ROADS, testing policies like carbon taxes, renewable energy investments, or afforestation programs. This exercise promotes critical evaluation of solutions, teaching students the importance of feasibility, scalability, and long-term outcomes in addressing sustainability challenges.

3. Encouraging Collaboration and Interdisciplinary Learning

Sustainability challenges often span multiple scientific disciplines, and AI can facilitate interdisciplinary learning by enabling collaboration across different fields. Integrating AI into the science curriculum encourages students to combine knowledge from areas such as biology, physics, earth science, and computer science to solve complex problems.

Example: In a project on urban sustainability, students from different science disciplines might collaborate to use AI tools to model energy use, transportation patterns, and pollution levels in a city. By working together, they can understand how urban planning, environmental science, and technology intersect to influence sustainability outcomes (Gray & Kneale, 2014).

AI-driven projects also encourage collaboration between students, fostering teamwork and communication skills. For example, in a group project on renewable energy, students could use AI-powered energy models to simulate the impact of wind and solar energy integration on the electricity grid. Different team members can focus on specific components of the system—like energy storage, grid stability, or economic viability—promoting both collaboration and a deeper understanding of the problem (De Jong & Van Joolingen, 2019).

4. Empowering Students as Future Innovators

Integrating AI into science education empowers students to become innovators and problem-solvers for the future. By working with AI tools, students gain the technical expertise necessary to develop sustainable solutions in fields such as environmental management, agriculture, and urban planning.

Example: A high school science course might include a unit where students design AI-driven solutions for improving local air quality. Using machine learning models, students could analyze data on pollution sources and simulate the effects of different mitigation strategies, such as traffic management or industrial emission regulations. This type of project encourages creativity and innovation, as students experiment with various approaches to solve real-world problems (Silva & Salinas, 2020).

Additionally, AI can introduce students to advanced technologies like predictive analytics, machine learning, and robotics, which are becoming critical tools in sustainability efforts. By mastering these technologies early, students are better equipped to contribute to fields like renewable energy, sustainable agriculture, and climate science in their future careers (Bower & Stavenhagen, 2021)

5. Improving Engagement with Real-World Problems

One of the key advantages of AI integration in science education is its ability to make abstract sustainability challenges more tangible and relatable. AI simulations allow students to visualize real-world scenarios and experiment with the outcomes of different environmental decisions in a controlled, risk-free environment (Hmelo-Silver & Azevedo, 2017).

Example: In an environmental science class, students could use AI to simulate the impact of different agricultural practices on soil health and crop yields. By experimenting with factors such as irrigation techniques, fertilizer use, and crop rotation, students gain a deeper understanding of the trade-offs involved in sustainable farming. This hands-on, interactive learning experience increases engagement and helps students see the real-world relevance of their studies (Green & Petty, 2019).

Moreover, by working with AI tools that are used by professionals in fields like environmental management, students gain a sense of agency and responsibility. They can see how their learning connects to broader societal efforts to combat climate change, conserve natural resources, and promote sustainability.

6. Challenges and Considerations for Integration

While the integration of AI into science curricula offers significant benefits, there are challenges to consider. Teachers must have access to AI tools and training to effectively implement these technologies in the classroom. Additionally, schools need adequate resources and infrastructure, such as access to computers and reliable internet, to support the use of AI platforms (Moller & Herrick, 2020).

Moreover, ethical considerations should be addressed when teaching AI. Students need to understand the potential biases in AI algorithms, the importance of data privacy, and the broader societal implications of AI in solving sustainability challenges. Educators should incorporate discussions on the responsible use of AI to ensure that students are aware of both the potential and limitations of these technologies (Binns & Gallo, 2021).

Integrating AI into science curricula offers a powerful way to enhance students' ability to address sustainability challenges. AI tools foster systems thinking, data literacy, collaboration, and innovation, providing students with the skills they need to tackle complex environmental problems. By engaging with real-world issues through AI-driven simulations and data analysis, students can develop critical thinking and problem-solving skills that will prepare them to contribute to a sustainable future.

3. FOSTERING CRITICAL THINKING THROUGH DATA ANALYSIS AND AI-GENERATED INSIGHTS

In an era marked by rapid technological advancements, the integration of data analysis and AI-generated insights into education has emerged as a critical tool for fostering critical thinking skills. Critical thinking, defined as the ability to analyze, evaluate, and synthesize information in a reasoned and reflective manner, is essential for students to navigate the complexities of the modern world. As societies become increasingly data-driven, educators are leveraging these technologies to help students develop not only the technical skills necessary for data analysis but also the cognitive skills required for higher-order thinking.

Data analysis provides a foundation for critical thinking by encouraging students to engage with real-world problems in a structured and analytical way. Through the process of collecting, cleaning, and interpreting data, students are prompted to question assumptions, identify patterns, and make evidence-based decisions. For example, studies have shown that engaging students in data-driven projects, such as analyzing social trends or environmental data, significantly enhances their ability to apply logic and reason to complex issues (Kuhn, 2020).

Moreover, data analysis fosters a deep understanding of the need for precision and accuracy in problem-solving. Students learn to assess the reliability of data sources, recognize biases, and account for variability, all of which are essential components of critical thinking (Facione, 2015). This process teaches students not only how to manipulate data but also how to approach problems with a critical and reflective mindset.

The advent of AI and machine learning has added a new dimension to the cultivation of critical thinking in education. AI-generated insights can reveal patterns and correlations within datasets that might be overlooked by human analysis. By working with AI tools, students are exposed to complex data interpretations, which challenge them to think critically about the validity and implications of the results.

For instance, in fields such as predictive modeling, AI can forecast trends based on vast amounts of data, offering students a platform to question the reasoning behind the predictions and evaluate their accuracy. This engagement with AI tools enhances students' capacity for deductive reasoning and decision-making, particularly when assessing the implications of AI-generated findings (Rosenberg & Holm, 2021).

AI can also simulate various scenarios, allowing students to explore hypothetical situations and evaluate the potential outcomes of different choices. Such simulations are particularly useful in STEM education, where students must analyze how changes in variables can affect system behavior (Santos & Castro, 2019). Through this process, students sharpen their ability to think critically about cause-and-effect relationships, deepening their understanding of the scientific method and problem-solving techniques.

Integrating data analysis and AI-generated insights into the classroom is reshaping educational practices to emphasize critical thinking as a key competency. Educators are increasingly using AI-based platforms that provide personalized feedback, guiding students in identifying errors in their reasoning and suggesting alternative approaches. This formative feedback is invaluable in cultivating a mindset geared towards continuous improvement and reflective thinking (Goh & Sanders, 2019).

Moreover, AI-driven tools enable adaptive learning environments where students can work at their own pace and receive real-time feedback on their progress. This adaptive approach allows students to take ownership of their learning, fostering a sense of agency that is crucial for critical thinking development (Pane et al., 2017).

In conclusion, the integration of data analysis and AI-generated insights into education represents a transformative approach to fostering critical thinking. By engaging students with these advanced technologies, educators can equip them with the skills necessary to thrive in a world increasingly shaped by data and AI-driven decision-making.

3.1 Techniques for using AI to analyze large datasets in science education

The increasing integration of artificial intelligence (AI) into science education has revolutionized how educators and students approach data analysis, particularly in the context of large datasets. AI-powered techniques enable educators to process, analyze, and interpret complex data more efficiently, fostering deeper insights into learning processes and outcomes.

One key technique is **machine learning (ML)**, which utilizes algorithms to identify patterns and trends in vast datasets. For example, ML models can be trained on educational data to predict student performance, identify at-risk learners, and personalize learning experiences based on real-time analysis of their interactions with digital platforms (Baker & Siemens, 2014). These techniques are particularly useful in assessing science competencies where large datasets are generated from lab simulations, student responses, or environmental sensors (Zawacki-Richter et al., 2019).

Natural language processing (NLP) is another AI technique gaining traction in science education. NLP allows for the automated analysis of large volumes of written student responses, providing insights into conceptual understanding, misconceptions, and scientific argumentation skills (Rebedea et al., 2020). In addition, NLP can assist in evaluating students' engagement with scientific texts, contributing to improved instructional strategies tailored to individual learners' needs.

AI-driven **data mining techniques** such as clustering and classification are also widely used to analyze student interactions with virtual labs and simulations in science education. These techniques enable the identification of different learning behaviors and styles, which can inform personalized feedback and adaptive learning pathways (Romero & Ventura, 2020). By analyzing large datasets collected from virtual experiments, educators can optimize curriculum design and better align instructional strategies with student learning patterns.

Additionally, **deep learning algorithms** have been instrumental in analyzing complex scientific data in education. For instance, deep neural networks can process data from remote laboratories, citizen science projects, and online platforms, extracting meaningful patterns that would be challenging to discern through traditional methods (Chassignol et al., 2018). Such applications allow students and educators to engage with large-scale datasets, fostering a more data-centric approach to scientific inquiry.

Furthermore, **AI-powered visualization tools** enable educators to represent complex datasets in a more accessible manner. Visual analytics can break down vast amounts of scientific data into dynamic, interactive formats that promote better understanding and engagement for students. These tools are particularly useful for subjects like physics, biology, and environmental science, where large datasets are often the norm (Lee & Wilkerson, 2018).

In summary, AI techniques like machine learning, natural language processing, data mining, deep learning, and AI-based visualizations are transforming how large datasets are analyzed in science education. These advancements not only enhance educators' ability to assess and improve learning outcomes but also provide students with the skills needed to navigate data-intensive scientific disciplines.

3.2 AI-Generated Insights in Fostering Critical Thinking and Evidence-Based Learning

Artificial intelligence (AI) has gained prominence as a tool for enhancing educational experiences by transforming how students approach learning tasks, particularly in cultivating critical thinking and problem-solving skills. AI-generated insights, which stem from complex data analysis, can prompt students to question assumptions, recognize patterns, and develop evidence-based conclusions.

Questioning Assumptions

AI can provide insights that challenge conventional wisdom or preconceived notions held by students. For instance, when students interact with AI-driven learning platforms, they are exposed to alternative perspectives and unexpected patterns in data, which encourages them to reconsider their initial assumptions. According to Kose et al. (2023), AI tools can simulate different scenarios and outcomes, leading students to ask critical questions about why certain predictions or trends differ from their expectations.

This dynamic interaction fosters an environment where students critically evaluate their own beliefs and refine their understanding based on data.

Recognizing Patterns

AI is adept at identifying trends and patterns within vast datasets, a task that is often beyond human capacity due to the volume and complexity of the information. By presenting these patterns to students, AI can help them discern underlying structures and relationships that may not be immediately visible. For example, students analyzing climate data with AI tools can identify trends in temperature changes and carbon emissions, leading to a deeper understanding of environmental patterns (Selman et al., 2021). This capability not only enhances their ability to process large amounts of information but also improves pattern recognition, which is a key aspect of critical thinking.

Developing Evidence-Based Conclusions

One of the most valuable contributions of AI in education is its role in helping students develop evidence-based conclusions. AI-generated insights are typically grounded in extensive data, making them an excellent resource for students to validate their claims with empirical evidence. In a study by Schank et al. (2022), students who used AI tools to analyze historical and scientific data were more likely to base their conclusions on verifiable facts, as the AI system guided them toward relevant data sources and analyses. This process reinforces the importance of evidence-based reasoning, a core element of scientific inquiry and critical thinking. By prompting students to question assumptions, recognize patterns, and form evidence-based conclusions, AI-generated insights contribute to the development of essential 21st-century skills. Educators can leverage AI-driven tools to create learning environments where students actively engage with information, think critically, and make informed decisions. This approach not only enhances students' cognitive abilities but also prepares them for complex problem-solving in various academic and real-world contexts.

3.3 Strategies for Encouraging Students to Critically Evaluate AI Outputs

In an era where artificial intelligence (AI) increasingly influences scientific inquiry and decision-making, it is vital to equip students with the skills to critically evaluate AI-generated outputs. Encouraging students to assess AI models fosters a deeper understanding of scientific processes, from hypothesis formulation to data analysis, while instilling ethical considerations about AI's role in society.

1. Integrating AI Literacy into STEM Education to promote critical evaluation, students must first understand how AI systems function. Incorporating AI literacy in STEM curricula can demystify AI's capabilities and limitations. AI literacy involves teaching students the basics of machine learning, algorithmic processes, and data biases. When students comprehend the inner workings of AI, they can question outputs critically rather than accepting them at face value. Research shows that AI literacy positively impacts students' ability to interrogate AI-generated data, promoting independent analysis and evaluation of results (Long & Magerko, 2020).

2. Encouraging Scientific Methodology in AI Analysis Another strategy to develop critical thinking in AI contexts is aligning AI evaluation with the scientific method. Students should be encouraged to approach AI outputs with the same skepticism applied to traditional experimental data. This involves verifying results, considering alternative explanations, and understanding potential biases within AI datasets and algorithms. By comparing AI-derived insights to established scientific principles, students can better assess the reliability of the outputs (Wing, 2020).
3. Ethical Considerations in AI Systems Fostering critical thinking about AI also requires addressing the ethical implications of AI use. Students need to evaluate the consequences of AI decisions, particularly in sensitive areas such as healthcare, climate modeling, and criminal justice. Incorporating case studies that focus on algorithmic bias, privacy concerns, and the societal impact of AI systems helps students consider the broader implications of AI technology. Engaging students in discussions on fairness, accountability, and transparency in AI processes ensures they are not only critical evaluators of the technology but also mindful of its ethical dimensions (Bynum & Rogerson, 2022).
4. Project-Based Learning and Collaborative Evaluation Hands-on, project-based learning (PBL) can be an effective way to encourage students to critically evaluate AI outputs. In PBL settings, students can collaborate on real-world problems, analyzing AI-generated solutions, identifying limitations, and proposing improvements. This active learning approach supports deeper engagement with AI's potential and limitations while fostering teamwork and communication skills critical to scientific discourse (Barak & Assal, 2018). Through peer collaboration, students challenge each other's assumptions, leading to richer, more critical discussions.

Empowering students to critically assess AI outputs is essential for developing their scientific reasoning and ethical awareness in a technology-driven world. By integrating AI literacy, aligning evaluation with scientific principles, addressing ethical considerations, and engaging in collaborative learning, educators can cultivate a generation of scientifically literate individuals capable of responsibly navigating the complexities of AI.

3.4 A model of critical thinking in environmental and sustainability education

Inspired by Davies' (2015) paradigm for critical thinking in higher education, Figure 1 presents a critical thinking model for environmental and sustainability education. In order to show how critical thinking within ESE may be understood, especially in terms of the relationship between thinking and action, this model modifies Davis's categorization.

This model illustrates how the four conceptualizations of critical thinking—logic-analytical, criticality, critical pedagogy, and critical openness—relate to one another. The conceptualizations are arranged in a reverse pyramid, where the narrowest conceptualization of critical thinking is represented by the logic-analytical concept, and the broadest by critical openness. Each conceptualization offers a distinct perspective on the action element within critical thinking, and the brackets indicate which aspects are shared by the various conceptualizations. The component of action is described inside the reversed pyramid, and the term "conscious dialogue as action" runs diagonally lengthwise, amplifying dialogue as a form of action. As a result, dialogue is applicable to all conceptualizations, embracing both indirect and direct forms, as previously elaborated. An arrow pointing to two distinct critical thinking focal points is located to the left of the inverted pyramid; a bidirectional arrow suggests two continuums. Initially, it indicates a range from an individual's own cognitive processes to external social factors. Second, critical action is located in the midst of the continuum that moves from critical cognition to critical being. To differentiate between the limited conceptualization of the CT movement and the more expansive ideas that encompass critical doing and critical being, the term "critical cognition" is used in place of "critical thinking." This distinction is meant to make it clear that critical cognition, critical action, and critical being are all included within the general phrase of "critical thinking."

The model depicts the distinctions between diverse teaching approaches and ESE pedagogies. In this model, ESE pedagogies are mostly associated with the outside parts of critical thinking rather than the interior aspects inherent in the CT-movement, and the pluralistic approach is positioned somewhere in the center as criticality. Depending on the location of the ESE positions, critical thinking as cognition may not be a desirable goal in ESE; rather critical doing or critical being would be more appropriate.

Critical thinking is not to be viewed as a stand-alone activity in ESE, but rather as an integral part of action. As a result, critical thinking and critical action are crucial. Although the inner parts of critical thinking as cognition are not highlighted in ESE perspectives, they are vital for self-development, which is particularly emphasised in dark pedagogy. Furthermore, the ego, which entails cognitive characteristics, must play a role in relation to the non-human world and activities including fighting or rebellion, as demanded by wild and pyro pedagogies.

In ESE, multiple conceptualizations of critical thinking might thus serve a variety of equally essential educational goals. We claim that several conceptualisations of critical thinking are required in ESE, ranging from wide to narrow. The various critical thinking positions differ, yet they can also be complementary. In an environmental and sustainability context, thinking alone will not develop or sustain the world, as both demand some form of action. However, simply thinking will help you make better decisions. Critical ESE requires action in order to change the planet's current quo. However, not every scenario, location, and time during the school week can be action-packed. Some tasks require only cognitive thinking, speech, and exploration. As a result, we suggest that diverse conceptualisations of critical thinking are appropriate for different purposes, and that one should not exclude the others. To critically assess and modify the existing quo, diverse educational possibilities must be explored in order to broaden educational practices. The contradictions between the conceptualisations can be exploited to advance critical ESE and how critical thinking is perceived and applied.

The paradigm is not intended to be interpreted as a developmental sequence, with skills leading to openness being a straight path to acquiring critical thinking. Rather, the model is intended to represent a range of critical thinking viewpoints, providing a tool that can help academics empirically discern ESE positions and translate them into a reflection tool for practitioners. Recognizing the model's limits, it is vital to stress that we do not intend to include all aspects of critical thinking. For example, the paradigm does not emphasize emotional, affective, or, say, postcolonial or feminist viewpoints as components of critical thought. Constructs from wild and dark pedagogies, which lay a strong focus on the beyond-human world, are likewise excluded. The model's focus was purposefully chosen to emphasize the links between critical thinking and action in formal education in Nordic countries.

Figure 1. A Model of critical thinking in environmental and sustainability education

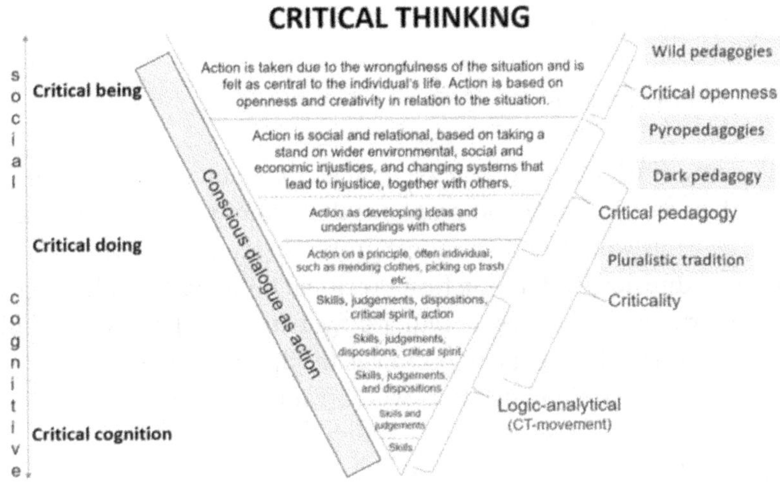

3.5 Pedagogical Strategies for Enhancing Critical Thinking

Critical thinking is an essential skill in modern education, particularly in fostering students' ability to analyze, evaluate, and create new knowledge. As education shifts towards more learner-centered approaches, the role of pedagogical strategies in enhancing critical thinking becomes crucial. Pedagogical strategies refer to the diverse teaching methods that are specifically designed to engage students in higher-order thinking, problem-solving, and decision-making (Brookfield, 2012). These strategies focus on developing students' ability to think critically across different contexts, thereby enabling them to apply their reasoning skills to both academic and real-world situations.

Active Learning Strategies

Active learning, a student-centered instructional method, is one of the most effective pedagogical approaches for promoting critical thinking. It involves students engaging directly with the material through activities such as discussions, problem-solving, group work, and case studies (Bonwell & Eison, 1991). These methods encourage students to analyze information rather than passively receive it, facilitating a deeper understanding of concepts. Research indicates that active learning significantly improves students' critical thinking abilities by requiring them to continuously question and reflect upon their learning experiences (Prince, 2004).

Socratic Questioning

Socratic questioning, an ancient pedagogical technique, is widely used to cultivate critical thinking by fostering an inquisitive mindset. It involves posing deep, thought-provoking questions that challenge students to scrutinize their assumptions, explore alternative viewpoints, and consider the implications of their ideas. According to Paul and Elder (2007), this method encourages learners to engage in a dialogical process, pushing them to clarify their thoughts and develop well-reasoned arguments. By systematically questioning students' responses, educators can help them refine their reasoning and cultivate an open-minded approach to problem-solving.

Problem-Based Learning (PBL)

Problem-based learning (PBL) is another pedagogical approach that enhances critical thinking by presenting students with complex, real-world problems that require investigation and solution (Hmelo-Silver, 2004). In PBL, students work in collaborative groups to identify what they need to learn to solve a given problem. This self-directed exploration fosters critical thinking as students must apply analytical and evaluative skills to formulate hypotheses, gather information, and propose solutions. Studies have shown that PBL encourages deep learning and promotes the application of knowledge in new and unfamiliar contexts, reinforcing critical thinking (Barrows & Tamblyn, 1980).

Inquiry-Based Learning

Inquiry-based learning involves students generating questions, conducting research, and synthesizing information to develop conclusions. It encourages exploration and investigation, allowing students to take ownership of their learning (Kuhn, 2010). In the process, students engage in critical thinking as they evaluate sources of information, assess the validity of evidence, and draw logical inferences. According to Pedaste et al. (2015), inquiry-based learning helps students develop critical thinking by encouraging them to become active participants in the learning process rather than passive recipients of information.

Reflective Practice

Reflective practice is a critical component of developing critical thinking skills in students. It involves encouraging students to reflect on their learning experiences, thoughts, and actions to gain insights and make improvements (Schön, 1983). Teachers can facilitate reflection through journaling, peer feedback, or self-assessment activities. According to Moon (1999), reflective practice helps learners to make connections between theory and practice, assess the outcomes of their decisions, and revise their strategies based on their reflections, ultimately fostering critical thinking.

Collaborative Learning

Collaborative learning, which involves students working together to achieve a common goal, also supports the development of critical thinking. Group discussions, debates, and team projects allow students to exchange ideas, challenge each other's perspectives, and constructively critique arguments. Gokhale (1995) found that collaborative learning promotes critical thinking by encouraging students to consider different viewpoints, defend their ideas, and synthesize diverse perspectives. When learners are required to explain their reasoning to peers, they are more likely to engage in deeper cognitive processing, which is key to developing critical thinking skills.

The integration of pedagogical strategies such as active learning, Socratic questioning, problem-based learning, inquiry-based learning, reflective practice, and collaborative learning can significantly enhance critical thinking skills in students. These methods promote deep engagement with content, encourage exploration, and facilitate the development of reasoning abilities. By implementing such strategies, educators can prepare students to critically analyze information, solve problems creatively, and make informed decisions in both academic and real-life situations.

4. CONCLUSION AND FUTURE DIRECTIONS

This chapter highlights the transformative potential of AI in developing critical thinking and problem-solving skills in science education for sustainability. By integrating AI tools such as machine learning, predictive modeling, and data analytics into science curricula, students are empowered to address real-world sustainability challenges. The chapter explores how AI enhances personalized learning, promotes data-driven inquiry, and fosters systems thinking. Through case studies, the chapter provides insights into successful implementations of AI-driven education in fields like environmental science, renewable energy, and climate change education. Key insights from the chapter include the role of AI in personalizing learning experiences, fostering systems thinking, and enabling students to tackle real-world sustainability challenges with data-driven approaches. By providing tools for real-time data analysis, AI promotes a deeper engagement with complex environmental and social issues such as climate change, renewable energy, and resource management. AI also enhances collaborative learning by enabling interdisciplinary teamwork and providing access to advanced tools previously reserved for professional settings.

Through the case studies highlighted, it is evident that AI-based learning encourages students to think critically, evaluate diverse data sources, and apply their knowledge in practical, real-world scenarios. These skills are essential for developing innovative solutions to the complex sustainability issues that our world faces.

4.1 Future Potential of AI in Enhancing Critical Thinking Skills in Science Education

As AI technologies continue to evolve, their potential to enhance critical thinking in science education will expand significantly. AI-driven simulations, virtual labs, and immersive technologies such as augmented reality (AR) and virtual reality (VR) can provide students with more engaging, real-world learning experiences. Additionally, AI can facilitate interdisciplinary learning, enabling students to integrate knowledge from various scientific fields. As AI tools become more accessible, they will democratize science education, allowing students from diverse backgrounds to tackle complex global sustainability issues.

The future of AI in science education holds vast potential, especially in enhancing students' ability to think critically and solve problems. Some promising directions include:

AI-Driven Immersive Learning: The integration of AI with virtual reality (VR) and augmented reality (AR) will provide students with highly immersive learning experiences, enabling them to engage in complex scientific simulations that mirror real-world scenarios. For example, students could use VR to explore ecosystems, model the impact of human activities on biodiversity, or simulate sustainable urban planning. This will foster critical thinking by allowing students to experiment, analyze outcomes, and refine their problem-solving strategies.

Adaptive Learning Systems: AI's ability to adapt learning materials in real-time based on student performance and engagement can further enhance critical thinking. As AI tools become more sophisticated, they will be able to guide students through increasingly complex tasks, offering customized feedback that encourages deeper reflection and analysis. This will lead to a more personalized learning experience, helping students not only to grasp scientific concepts but to apply them in a variety of contexts.

Interdisciplinary Learning and AI-Enhanced Collaboration: AI's role in fostering interdisciplinary collaboration will continue to grow. Students from different fields can use AI tools to tackle shared sustainability challenges, integrating perspectives from biology, physics, earth science, and computer science. AI-powered collaborative platforms will enable them to work together, share data, and co-create solutions to global issues such as climate change and resource scarcity.

AI-Enhanced Predictive Modeling and Scenario Analysis: As AI tools evolve, they will play an even more critical role in developing students' abilities to think ahead and evaluate potential future scenarios. Predictive models for energy consumption, climate change mitigation, or urban sustainability will become more accessible, allowing students to engage with real-time data and generate forward-looking solutions.

AI for Ethical Decision-Making: The future of AI-enhanced education will increasingly focus on ethical considerations. Students will not only need to engage with technical skills but also critically evaluate the ethical implications of AI-driven decisions, such as biases in data sets, privacy concerns, and the broader societal impact of their solutions. AI could be used to simulate ethical dilemmas and decision-making processes in complex sustainability scenarios, helping students to navigate these challenging issues.

4.2 Recommendations for Educators and Policymakers

To fully realize the potential of AI in promoting critical thinking and problem-solving in science education, educators and policymakers must take proactive steps to integrate these technologies into learning environments effectively. The following recommendations outline a roadmap for incorporating AI into science education to support sustainable development:

1. Curriculum Design with AI Integration:
    - Educators should design curricula that incorporate AI tools as part of project-based and inquiry-driven learning models. AI should not be viewed as an add-on but rather as an integral part of the learning experience, enabling students to analyze data, simulate real-world problems, and explore sustainability solutions. AI-powered platforms like Google Earth Engine and ClimateAI could be embedded into lessons on environmental science, renewable energy, and urban planning.
    - Real-world, data-driven case studies should be integrated into curricula, allowing students to tackle sustainability challenges while honing their critical thinking and problem-solving skills through AI-enhanced simulations and analytics.
2. Professional Development and Teacher Training:
    - Continuous professional development is essential to ensure teachers have the technical skills to integrate AI into their teaching. Training programs should focus not only on the technical aspects of AI but also on how to use these tools to foster inquiry-based learning, collaboration, and ethical decision-making. Teachers should be equipped to guide students in inter-

preting AI-generated insights, ensuring that students develop the necessary critical thinking skills to evaluate data outputs critically.
    - AI training should include ethical considerations, helping educators teach students about algorithmic biases, data privacy, and the societal implications of AI, particularly in the context of sustainable development.
3. Develop AI Literacy for Students:
    - AI literacy should be prioritized as a key component of science education. Students must understand how AI tool's function, including their limitations and potential biases. By incorporating AI literacy into the curriculum, educators can help students become discerning users of AI technologies who can question and critique the data and outputs they encounter. This is crucial for developing informed and responsible global citizens capable of using AI for good.
    - AI literacy should also include the ethical dimensions of AI, preparing students to navigate complex issues such as the impact of AI on labor markets, privacy, and equity.
4. Support Collaboration and Interdisciplinary Learning:
    - Schools and educational institutions should encourage interdisciplinary collaborations that bring together students from different fields to solve complex sustainability problems using AI tools. For example, AI-powered projects can bring together students from environmental science, engineering, economics, and policy studies to tackle challenges such as energy management or climate adaptation.
    - Collaborative learning platforms that enable shared problem-solving through AI-enhanced tools should be a focus. AI-powered chatbots, for example, can assist students in breaking down problems and guiding discussions, fostering deeper engagement with content.
5. Investment in AI Infrastructure and Access:
    - Governments and educational institutions must invest in AI infrastructure to ensure equitable access to AI tools and resources. Access to reliable internet, AI-powered educational platforms, and digital resources should be a priority, particularly for underserved communities. AI can help bridge educational gaps, but only if access is universal.
    - Policymakers should also work to establish ethical guidelines and frameworks that promote the responsible use of AI in education, addressing concerns around data privacy, transparency, and accountability.
6. Integration of AI for Sustainable Development Education:
    - AI should be leveraged to promote education for sustainable development (ESD) by using AI tools to help students engage with global sustainability goals, such as climate action, responsible consumption, and biodiversity conservation. By integrating AI into sustainability education, students can work on real-world problems like deforestation, energy efficiency, or sustainable agriculture, gaining hands-on experience with AI-powered solutions.
    - AI tools that support real-time data analysis and scenario modeling should be utilized to allow students to visualize the outcomes of various sustainability policies and interventions, encouraging them to develop data-driven, evidence-based approaches to problem-solving.

REFERENCES

Badr, H. S., Zaitchik, B. F., & Guikema, S. D. (2020). Machine learning for precipitation and streamflow forecasting in the western United States. *Environmental Modelling & Software*, *126*, 104660.

Baker, R. S., & Siemens, G. (2014). *Educational data mining and learning analytics*. Cambridge Handbook of the Learning Sciences, 253-272.

Barak, M., & Assal, M. (2018). Robotics and STEM learning: Students' achievements in assignments according to the P3 Task Taxonomy—practice, problem solving, and projects. *International Journal of Technology and Design Education*, *28*(1), 121–144. DOI: 10.1007/s10798-016-9385-9

Barrows, H. S., & Tamblyn, R. M. (1980). *Problem-based learning: An approach to medical education*. Springer Publishing Company.

Berland, M., & Wilensky, U. (2016). Integrating AI and data science tools into classroom settings: A means of enhancing critical analysis and environmental awareness. *Learning, Media and Technology*, *41*(3), 370–389.

Bezzina, S., & Dingli, A. (2024). The transformative potential of Artificial Intelligence for Education. *Networked Learning Conference, 14*(1). https://doi.org/DOI: 10.54337/nlc.v14i1.8077

Biasutti, M., & Frate, S. (2017). A conceptual framework for the sustainability of education for sustainable development. *Journal of Cleaner Production*, *168*, 144–152.

Binns, R., & Gallo, G. (2021). Addressing biases and ethics in AI education: A framework for responsible integration. *Journal of Technology and Society*, *19*(2), 123–139.

Bonwell, C. C., & Eison, J. A. (1991). ASHE-ERIC Higher Education Report: Vol. 1. *Active learning: Creating excitement in the classroom*. The George Washington University.

Bower, M., & Stavenhagen, C. (2021). Empowering students to innovate: AI-driven problem-solving in sustainability education. *Journal of Computer Assisted Learning*, *37*(1), 43–55.

Brookfield, S. D. (2012). *Teaching for critical thinking: Tools and techniques to help students question their assumptions*. John Wiley & Sons.

Bynum, T., & Rogerson, S. (2022). *Computer Ethics and Professional Responsibility*. John Wiley & Sons.

Capra, F. (2005). *Systems thinking as a framework for sustainability education*. Center for Ecoliteracy.

Chassignol, M., Khoroshavin, A., Klimova, A., & Bilyatdinova, A. (2018). Artificial Intelligence trends in education: A narrative overview. *Procedia Computer Science*, *136*, 16–24. DOI: 10.1016/j.procs.2018.08.233

Climate, A. I. (2021). *Climate Risk Analytics for a Resilient Future*. ClimateAI. Retrieved from https://climate.ai

Climate Interactive. (2020). *En-ROADS: Climate Solutions Simulator*. Climate Interactive. Retrieved from https://www.climateinteractive.org/tools/en-roads

Davies, M. (2015). A Model of Critical Thinking in Higher Education. In Paulsen, M. B. (Ed.), *Higher Education: Handbook of Theory and Research* (pp. 41–82). Springer. DOI: 10.1007/978-3-319-12835-1_2

De Jong, T., & Van Joolingen, W. R. (2019). AI tools as interdisciplinary bridges in education: From biology to earth sciences. *Educational Research Review*, *29*, 100309.

DeepMind. (2021). Deep Learning for Precipitation Nowcasting. *Nature*, *597*, 672–677.

Eden, C. A., Adeleye, O. O., & Adeniyi, I. S. (2024). A review of AI-driven pedagogical strategies for equitable access to science education. *Magna Scientia Advanced Research and Reviews, 10*(2), 044-054.

Facione, P. A. (2015). *Critical Thinking: What It Is and Why It Counts*. Insight Assessment.

Goh, A., & Sanders, D. (2019). Using AI to Improve Student Learning: A Critical Look at AI-Driven Feedback Systems. *Journal of Educational Technology*.

Gokhale, A. A. (1995). Collaborative learning enhances critical thinking. *Journal of Technology Education*, *7*(1), 22–30. DOI: 10.21061/jte.v7i1.a.2

Gorelick, N., Hancher, M., Dixon, M., Ilyushchenko, S., Thau, D., & Moore, R. (2017). Google Earth Engine: Planetary-scale geospatial analysis for everyone. *Remote Sensing of Environment*, *202*, 18–27. DOI: 10.1016/j.rse.2017.06.031

Gray, L., & Kneale, P. (2014). Interdisciplinary learning through AI: Engaging students in environmental science projects. *Journal of Science Education and Technology*, *23*(5), 715–728.

Green, R., & Petty, T. (2019). Student engagement through AI simulations in environmental science courses. *The Journal of Environmental Education*, *50*(3), 237–249.

Hmelo-Silver, C. E. (2004). Problem-based learning: What and how do students learn? *Educational Psychology Review*, *16*(3), 235–266. DOI: 10.1023/B:EDPR.0000034022.16470.f3

Hmelo-Silver, C. E., & Azevedo, R. (2017). Using AI to simulate real-world problem-solving in sustainability education. *Cognitive Science and Education*, *42*(2), 230–245.

Kuhn, D. (2010). *Education for thinking*. Harvard University Press.

Kuhn, D. (2020). *Education for Thinking*. Harvard University Press.

Lee, V. R., & Wilkerson, M. H. (2018). Data use by middle and secondary students in the digital age: A status report and future prospects. *British Journal of Educational Technology*, *49*(5), 848–863.

Long, D., & Magerko, B. (2020). What is AI literacy? Competencies and design considerations. *Proceedings of the 2020 CHI Conference on Human Factors in Computing Systems*, 1-16. DOI: 10.1145/3313831.3376727

Macal, C. M., & North, M. J. (2010). Tutorial on agent-based modelling and simulation. *Journal of Simulation*, *4*(3), 151–162. DOI: 10.1057/jos.2010.3

Miller, E., & Madsen, L. (2015). Educating the 21st-century global citizen: How AI simulations develop systems thinking and environmental literacy. *The Journal of Environmental Education*, *46*(2), 95–111.

Moller, S. J., & Herrick, T. (2020). Overcoming barriers to AI integration in K-12 science education. *International Journal of Education Technology*, *38*(4), 569–585.

Moon, J. A. (1999). *Reflection in learning and professional development: Theory and practice*. Kogan Page.

Pane, J. F., Griffin, B. A., McCaffrey, D. F., & Karam, R. (2017). *Effectiveness of Cognitive Tutor Algebra I at Scale*. RAND Corporation.

Paul, R., & Elder, L. (2007). *The miniature guide to critical thinking: Concepts and tools*. Foundation for Critical Thinking.

Pedaste, M., Mäeots, M., Siiman, L. A., de Jong, T., van Riesen, S. A., Kamp, E. T., Manoli, C. C., Zacharia, Z. C., & Tsourlidaki, E. (2015). Phases of inquiry-based learning: Definitions and the inquiry cycle. *Educational Research Review*, *14*, 47–61. DOI: 10.1016/j.edurev.2015.02.003

Prince, M. (2004). Does active learning work? A review of the research. *Journal of Engineering Education*, *93*(3), 223–231. DOI: 10.1002/j.2168-9830.2004.tb00809.x

Rebedea, T., Dascalu, M., Trausan-Matu, S., & Crossley, S. A. (2020). Exploring students' argumentative discourse through natural language processing: Implications for science education. *International Journal of Artificial Intelligence in Education*, *30*(1), 1–27.

Roll, I., & Wylie, R. (2016). Evolution and revolution in artificial intelligence in education. *International Journal of Artificial Intelligence in Education*, *26*(2), 582–599. DOI: 10.1007/s40593-016-0110-3

Rolnick, D., Donti, P., & Kaack, L. (2019). Tackling climate change with machine learning. *Nature Machine Intelligence*, *1*(3), 144–153. arXiv1906.05433 PMID: 31161156

Romero, C., & Ventura, S. (2020). Educational data mining and learning analytics: An updated survey. *Wiley Interdisciplinary Reviews. Data Mining and Knowledge Discovery*, *10*(3), e1355. DOI: 10.1002/widm.1355

Rosenberg, A., & Holm, S. (2021). AI and Critical Thinking in Education: Opportunities and Challenges. *Learning, Media and Technology*, *46*(3), 271–284.

Santos, P., & Castro, F. (2019). Simulation-Based Learning and AI Applications in STEM Education. *Computers in Human Behavior*.

Sarkar, D., & Gilman, M. (2018). AI in climate education: Using machine learning to teach about environmental impacts. *International Journal of Climate Education*, *12*(1), 30–45.

Schön, D. A. (1983). *The reflective practitioner: How professionals think in action*. Basic Books.

Selvam, A. A. A. (2024). Exploring the Impact of Artificial Intelligence on Transforming Physics, Chemistry, and Biology Education. *Science Education*, *2*. Advance online publication. DOI: 10.21428/a70c814c.747297aa

Silva, J. M., & Salinas, A. (2020). The role of AI in fostering innovation in sustainability education. *Sustainability in Higher Education*, *15*(3), 189–205.

Silver, D., Schrittwieser, J., Simonyan, K., Antonoglou, I., Huang, A., Guez, A., Hubert, T., Baker, L., Lai, M., Bolton, A., Chen, Y., Lillicrap, T., Hui, F., Sifre, L., van den Driessche, G., Graepel, T., & Hassabis, D. (2017). Mastering the game of Go without human knowledge. *Nature*, *550*(7676), 354–359. DOI: 10.1038/nature24270 PMID: 29052630

Sintov, N., Kar, D., Nguyen, T., Fang, F., Hoffman, K., Lyet, A., & Tambe, M. (2017). Keeping it Real: Using Real-World Problems to Teach AI to Diverse Audiences. *AI Magazine*, *38*(2), 35–47. DOI: 10.1609/aimag.v38i2.2733

Tao, F., Zhang, H., Liu, A., & Nee, A. Y. C. (2018). Digital twin in industry: State-of-the-art. *IEEE Transactions on Industrial Informatics*, *15*(4), 2405–2415. DOI: 10.1109/TII.2018.2873186

UNESCO. (2017). *Education for sustainable development goals: Learning objectives*. United Nations Educational, Scientific and Cultural Organization.

Vinuesa, R., Azizpour, H., Leite, I., Balaam, M., Dignum, V., Domisch, S., & Nerini, F. F. (2020). The role of artificial intelligence in achieving the Sustainable Development Goals. *Nature Communications*, *11*(1), 1–10. DOI: 10.1038/s41467-019-14108-y PMID: 31932590

Wiek, A., Withycombe, L., & Redman, C. L. (2011). Key competencies in sustainability: A reference framework for academic program development. *Sustainability Science*, *6*(2), 203–218. DOI: 10.1007/s11625-011-0132-6

Wing, J. M. (2020). The data life cycle as an organizing principle for big data research. *Harvard Data Science Review*, *2*(2).

Wright, W. (1990). *SimEarth: The Living Planet*. Maxis Software.

Yuan, F., Shen, Z., Wei, X., Sun, C., & Li, M. (2018). Machine learning approaches for geospatial big data analysis: A review. *Big Earth Data*, *2*(3), 276–296.

Zawacki-Richter, O., Marín, V. I., Bond, M., & Gouverneur, F. (2019). Systematic review of research on artificial intelligence applications in higher education – where are the educators? *International Journal of Educational Technology in Higher Education*, *16*(1), 1–27. DOI: 10.1186/s41239-019-0171-0

Chapter 10
Digital Literacy for Sustainability:
Preparing Students for the AI-Driven World

Mustafa Kayyali
https://orcid.org/0000-0003-3300-262X
HE Higher Education Ranking, Syria

ABSTRACT

As the world faces more complex sustainability concerns, the role of digital literacy in influencing students' abilities to contribute to a sustainable future has never been more vital. The rapid breakthroughs in Artificial Intelligence (AI) have created opportunities and difficulties in education, requiring the integration of digital literacy with sustainability education. This article investigates the convergence of digital literacy and sustainability, claiming that preparing students for an AI-driven society is vital for equipping them with the skills necessary to address global concerns. It studies how digital literacy may be harnessed to achieve sustainable development, including the ability to use digital tools, analyze data, and engage critically with technology. The study also explores the pedagogical techniques that can be implemented to integrate sustainability into the digital literacy curriculum, providing students with the information and competencies they need to navigate an AI-powered future.

INTRODUCTION

In the rapidly expanding landscape of the 21st century, few topics have caught the interest of educators, policymakers, and global leaders as much as sustainability and the role of technology in crafting a sustainable future. As we face enormous issues such as climate change, resource depletion, and social injustice, the need for education that educates future generations to handle this complexity has grown more critical than ever. In this setting, digital literacy emerges as a vital competency for preparing students with the skills and knowledge essential to interact with these global concerns. As technology continues to evolve at an exponential rate, particularly with the rise of artificial intelligence (AI), digital literacy has shifted from a supplementary ability to a core prerequisite for success in the modern world. At the heart of this conversation is the important convergence between digital literacy and sustainability. Digital literacy, broadly defined as the capacity to effectively and critically use digital tools and platforms,

DOI: 10.4018/979-8-3693-9062-7.ch010

is no longer restricted to fundamental computer abilities (McDougall et al, 2018). It has developed to cover competencies like as data analysis, ethical decision-making in a digital context, and a grasp of the societal consequences of technology. As the digital age evolves, the necessity for informed, digitally literate people capable of solving sustainability concerns becomes increasingly obvious. Sustainability, as defined by the United Nations 2030 Agenda for Sustainable Development, refers to addressing the requirements of the present without sacrificing the ability of future generations to meet their own needs. Achieving sustainability needs systemic improvements across several sectors, including energy, agriculture, urban development, and education (Lim et al, 2018). Digital technologies, particularly AI, can drive breakthroughs in many industries, giving solutions that can reduce environmental impacts, maximize resource use, and address complex societal challenges. However, new technologies also bring concerns, such as perpetuating inequities or aggravating environmental damage if not handled wisely. This dual nature of technology underlines the significance of integrating sustainability education with digital literacy to guarantee that future generations not only have the ability to utilize technological breakthroughs but also comprehend their ethical, social, and environmental outcomes.

As the globe becomes increasingly interconnected through digital platforms, it is obvious that digital literacy plays a crucial role in molding students' abilities to actively participate in and contribute to global efforts toward sustainable development (Gustian et al, 2024). However, traditional forms of education have frequently regarded sustainability and digital literacy as different areas, leaving a gap in the preparedness of students to think critically and holistically about both. In an era where technology innovations are inextricably connected with the destiny of our planet, this division is no longer viable. Instead, there is an urgent need to integrate digital literacy and sustainability education into a seamless framework that empowers students to use technology not only for personal or commercial gain but also for the general good of society and the environment. This chapter intends to analyze the increasing relationship between digital literacy and sustainability in the context of higher education. It believes that the convergence of these two domains is vital for training students to flourish in an AI-driven society that is increasingly shaped by global concerns. By studying the role of digital literacy as a tool for sustainability, this article will define the critical competences required for students to become educated and responsible global citizens. Furthermore, it will address pedagogical approaches that can be employed to teach digital literacy in the context of sustainability, highlighting the necessity for a multidisciplinary, collaborative approach to education. Finally, the chapter will cover the problems connected with implementing such an integrated curriculum and analyze the prospects and innovations developing in this field.

THE ROLE OF ARTIFICIAL INTELLIGENCE IN SHAPING SUSTAINABLE DEVELOPMENT

As the globe grapples with challenges like climate change, environmental degradation, and resource shortages, the need for innovative solutions to advance sustainable development has become increasingly critical (Mehta et al, 2023). Traditional approaches to sustainability have made achievements in many areas, but the rapid expansion of technology, particularly artificial intelligence (AI), offers new potential to expedite progress. AI's potential to influence sustainability is enormous and varied, stretching across industries, sectors, and disciplines (Nishant et al, 2020). By leveraging the potential of AI, we cannot only address the pressing demands of today but to help design a more sustainable and equitable future. At its foundation, sustainable development is about balancing economic, social, and environmental concerns to guarantee that the demands of the present are satisfied without sacrificing the ability of future generations to meet their own needs. Achieving this balance demands innovation, insight, and, perhaps more than ever before, the integration of cutting-edge technologies. AI, with its power to handle enormous quantities of data, spot trends, and build predictive models, plays a critical role in defining how we approach sustainability. From maximizing resource use to improving sustainable energy technologies, AI is bringing fresh answers that were long thought to be beyond human reach. One of the most significant ways AI contributes to sustainable development is by enhancing efficiency in many industries. In the energy sector, for example, AI is transforming how energy is produced, distributed, and consumed (Ahmad et al, 2021). Machine learning algorithms can assess energy usage trends, enabling utilities to estimate demand more accurately and optimize energy distribution (Ahmad, et al, 2022). This leads to less energy waste and a more efficient use of resources. AI can help speed the development of renewable energy technologies, such as solar and wind power, by giving more exact data for better energy storage and grid integration. These innovations assist directly in reducing carbon emissions and diminishing the environmental footprint of energy generation.

In agriculture, AI is enabling more sustainable farming practices through precision agriculture (SS et al, 2024). By assessing soil conditions, weather patterns, and crop health, AI-powered technologies help farmers make better decisions regarding irrigation, fertilization, and pest control. This not only enhances agricultural yields but also eliminates the need for artificial fertilizers and pesticides, which can be damaging to the environment. AI is also helping to optimize water usage in areas confronting water scarcity, further boosting sustainability. The integration of AI in agriculture is thereby supporting food security while lowering the ecological impact of farming techniques. AI's involvement in sustainable development is also crucial in urban planning and the development of smart cities. As the global population expands and urbanization accelerates, cities face rising constraints related to waste management, transportation, and infrastructure. AI is being used to develop smarter cities that optimize the use of resources, minimize pollution, and enhance the quality of life for citizens (Al-Raeei, 2024). For instance, AI-powered devices can help monitor air quality, assess traffic patterns, and improve waste collection schedules. This real-time data enables more responsive and efficient urban management, contributing to more sustainable urban environments. Additionally, AI-driven solutions are contributing to the creation of green infrastructure, such as energy-efficient buildings and sustainable transportation systems, which are vital for decreasing the environmental effects of urban areas.

Another significant area where AI is having a profound impact on sustainability is in climate change mitigation and adaptation (Kaack et al, 2022). AI is being utilized to construct prediction models that can forecast climate-related occurrences, such as extreme weather, heatwaves, and floods. These models assist governments, organizations, and communities prepare for future disasters by offering early warnings and facilitating better decision-making. AI is playing a role in carbon capture systems by optimizing the processes involved in capturing and storing carbon dioxide (Priya et al, 2023). By enhancing the effectiveness of these technologies, AI could considerably contribute to reducing greenhouse gas emissions and alleviating the consequences of climate change. The relevance of AI in sustainable development extends beyond environmental concerns (Nishant et al, 2020). In the field of social sustainability, AI is being utilized to address challenges linked to inequality, poverty, and education. In the healthcare industry, AI-driven solutions are boosting access to medical care, particularly in impoverished locations. AI tools are being utilized for diagnostics, enabling more accurate and faster diagnosis of diseases, which can lead to better health outcomes (Ahmed et al, 2020). Additionally, AI-powered telemedicine platforms are boosting access to healthcare services, bridging the gap for individuals who live in distant or resource-limited places.

In education, AI is helping to develop more tailored learning experiences (Tapalova & Zhiyenbayeva, 2022). By assessing data on individuals' learning styles, skills, and shortcomings, AI can personalize educational content to match the particular needs of each student. This strategy not only increases learning outcomes but also ensures that education is more inclusive and accessible to all. By making education more effective and equitable, AI helps societal sustainability by giving possibilities for personal and professional advancement across diverse groups. While the benefits of AI in promoting sustainability are clear, there are also obstacles and ethical considerations that must be addressed (Cath, 2018). One of the key issues is the environmental impact of AI itself (Van Wynsberghe, 2021). AI systems, particularly those that rely on large-scale data processing, can be energy-intensive. The computer resources required to train AI models, especially in deep learning, consume considerable quantities of energy, which can contribute to the carbon footprint of AI (Alzoubi & Mishra, 2024). The technology is improving rapidly, and there are continuing efforts to make AI more energy-efficient. Researchers are designing algorithms that require less data and computational power, as well as studying ways to harness renewable energy sources to run AI systems. These efforts are needed to ensure that the advantages of AI do not come at the cost of increased environmental degradation.

Another problem is ensuring that AI systems are developed and deployed in ways that are ethical and inclusive (Yellu et al, 2021). As AI becomes more integrated into decision-making processes, there is a risk that technology could aggravate existing disparities or reinforce biases. For example, AI algorithms educated on biased data may yield outputs that disproportionately disfavor particular groups of individuals. To address these concerns, AI systems must be created with justice, transparency, and accountability in mind. This requires not only employing varied and representative data but also ensuring that AI developers and users are held accountable for the impact of their technologies. Additionally, there is a need for regulation and control to ensure that AI is deployed in ways that correspond with the values of sustainability and social justice.

Despite these challenges, the potential for AI to build a sustainable future is great. The technology's ability to analyze complicated data, automate processes, and predict results puts it as a vital enabler of sustainable development. As AI continues to evolve, its incorporation into sustainable practices will undoubtedly deepen, leading to more innovative and beneficial solutions. From reducing carbon footprints to promoting social fairness, AI has the power to create disruptive change across sectors and businesses. However, to fully achieve its potential, we must guarantee that AI is developed and utilized ethically, with careful consideration of its environmental, social, and ethical outcomes. By doing so, we can harness the power of AI to create a more sustainable and equitable society for future generations.

DIGITAL LITERACY AS A KEY COMPETENCY FOR SUSTAINABLE FUTURES

In today's fast-paced world, digital literacy has emerged as a vital ability for managing the intricacies of modern life (Anurogo et al, 2023). With the rapid evolution of technology and the widespread use of digital tools, being digitally literate has become more than just a fundamental necessity—it is a cornerstone of sustainable development and a crucial driver for a sustainable future. The ability to utilize, comprehend, and critically engage with digital technologies is vital for individuals, companies, and communities to prosper in an increasingly digital environment. Digital literacy refers to the skills, knowledge, and attitudes necessary to effectively and ethically navigate the digital domain. It involves the ability to use technology to acquire, assess, and produce information, as well as the capacity to apply digital tools in a way that promotes personal, professional, and social goals. In the context of sustainability, digital literacy enables individuals to participate in global conversations, make informed decisions, and contribute to the creation of solutions for pressing environmental, social, and economic concerns (Chetty et al, 2018). As the globe faces unprecedented environmental degradation, resource depletion, and social inequality, digital literacy can empower individuals to actively engage in sustainable activities, both at a personal and societal level.

One of the primary reasons that digital literacy is a critical component of sustainable futures is its role in fostering informed decision-making. As the globe grows more interconnected through digital technology, humans are continually assaulted with information—much of it relevant to sustainability. From climate change research to news on biodiversity, from sustainable consumption practices to social movements calling for justice, the abundance of information can be overwhelming. To make informed choices about how to live more sustainably, people need the ability to critically examine this information, assess its authenticity, and make decisions based on facts rather than disinformation or confusion. Digital literacy equips individuals with these talents, enabling them to discern fact from fiction and make responsible, educated choices about anything from energy use to buying habits. Digital literacy allows individuals to actively contribute to sustainability by engaging with digital platforms, tools, and communities that support sustainable practices. Social media, for example, has a crucial role in raising awareness about climate change, environmental degradation, and other sustainability issues (Dwivedi et al, 2022). Digital literacy enables people to learn how to use these platforms successfully, whether it's by participating in global debates, organizing campaigns, or distributing educational content that supports sustainability. Furthermore, digital literacy permits people to join in discussions regarding policy reforms, technical advances, and cultural upheavals that have the potential to support sustainability on a larger scale.

The value of digital literacy in encouraging creativity cannot be emphasized (Bereczki, E. O., & Kárpáti, 2021). As technology progresses, new solutions to environmental and societal concerns are being developed at a rapid speed. From renewable energy technologies to AI-driven systems for managing natural resources, the landscape of sustainability is increasingly determined by technological advances (Fan et al, 2023). Whether it's using data analytics to detect wasteful practices in manufacturing or leveraging machine learning algorithms to optimize energy consumption, digital literacy enables individuals to participate in these breakthroughs and contribute to their growth.

In the context of education, digital literacy is crucial in educating students about the problems and opportunities of the future (Falloon, 2020). As the demand for sustainable practices develops, educational institutions must educate students with the skills they need to flourish in an AI-driven society. By incorporating digital literacy into curricula across all disciplines, students obtain the knowledge and skills necessary to address sustainability concerns utilizing technology. This goes beyond merely teaching students how to utilize digital tools—it requires creating a profound awareness of how technology can be harnessed to promote beneficial social and environmental change. Whether students are studying business, science, engineering, or the arts, digital literacy gives them the tools to think critically about how they may utilize technology to create sustainability in their respective disciplines. For instance, students studying business management must comprehend how digital technologies are reshaping businesses and generating new chances for sustainable practices. From the use of blockchain for transparent supply chains to AI for forecasting environmental impacts, digital literacy helps students recognize the potential for technology to alter sectors in sustainable ways. Similarly, people studying environmental science must be able to use digital technologies to collect and evaluate data, simulate environmental situations, and model the impact of different policy choices (Sun & Scanlon, 2019). By educating students with these abilities, educational institutions educate them to be active agents of change in the fight for sustainability.

Beyond the classroom, digital literacy is crucial for individuals to engage in the rising digital economy (Buckingham, 2020). As more and more businesses become digitized, the demand for digital skills is growing. Workers must be adept in digital technologies and platforms to remain competitive in the employment market. This involves not just technical abilities such as coding and data analysis but also the capacity to understand how these technologies may be used to enhance sustainability. By prioritizing digital literacy, individuals may ensure they are equipped for the digital economy and ready to contribute to sustainability in the workplace (Chetty et al, 2018). Digital literacy also plays a crucial role in addressing social sustainability. The digital divide remains a considerable barrier in many regions of the world, with unequal access to technology and internet connectivity limiting prospects for many individuals. This disparity exacerbates existing inequities, making it more difficult for underprivileged communities to engage in global talks about sustainability, access resources, or profit from technological breakthroughs. Promoting digital literacy helps bridge this barrier, providing individuals from all backgrounds with the tools they need to participate fully in the digital world. In this view, digital literacy is not only about preparing folks for a sustainable future—it is about ensuring that the future is inclusive and accessible to all. The convergence of digital literacy and sustainability also raises considerations regarding the ethical implications of technology use. As digital tools become more incorporated into sustainability efforts, there are growing worries about issues such as privacy, data security, and algorithmic bias. For example, while AI-powered systems can be used to optimize energy use and eliminate waste, they also raise problems about the ownership of data, the transparency of algorithms, and the possibility of technical discrimination. Digital literacy comprises not simply the ability to utilize technology, but also the capability to critically examine its ethical consequences and make responsible judgments. This is especially essential in the context of sustainability, where the stakes are high, and the repercussions of unethical technology use could have far-reaching impacts on the environment and society.

As we move into the future, the importance of digital literacy in designing sustainable futures becomes even more crucial. With developing technologies such as blockchain, machine learning, and the Internet of Things, the potential for digital solutions to address sustainability concerns is higher than ever before. However, to fully achieve this potential, individuals must be educated with the digital literacy skills necessary to engage with these technologies and use them in ways that promote sustainability. This means that digital literacy must be promoted in education systems, businesses, and communities, ensuring that everyone, regardless of their background or location, has the chance to participate in and contribute to the sustainable development agenda. Digital literacy is not only a tool for personal advancement—it is a critical capability for negotiating the challenges of sustainability in the modern world. By educating individuals with the information, skills, and attitudes essential to utilizing technology ethically and creatively, digital literacy plays a key role in crafting a sustainable future. As the digital landscape continues to evolve, we must continue to prioritize the development of digital literacy as a core component of sustainable development efforts. Through education, innovation, and ethical technology use, we can ensure that digital literacy becomes a potent force for good in creating a more sustainable and fair world for future generations.

PREPARING STUDENTS FOR AN AI-DRIVEN WORLD: PEDAGOGICAL APPROACHES

As we stand on the verge of a new era defined by artificial intelligence (AI), it has become increasingly evident that the future workforce must be equipped with skills and knowledge to flourish in an AI-driven environment. The rapid emergence of AI technology has already altered industries, economies, and society. From automated industrial processes to personalized learning algorithms, AI is transforming the entire fabric of how we work, live, and learn. In this context, educating students for an AI-driven society is not only about familiarizing them with the technology itself but also integrating a deep awareness of its consequences and cultivating abilities that will help them navigate and create the future.

For educators, the issue arises: how can we educate students in a society where AI plays such a key role?

The answer lies in adopting new educational techniques that are not only aligned with the capabilities of AI but also focused on the crucial human skills that will complement and enhance the usage of this technology. The goal is to create learners who are not only consumers of technology but also knowledgeable, creative, and ethical users, able to adapt and innovate in an ever-evolving technological context. One of the most fundamental transformations needed in education is shifting away from traditional, content-focused training toward a more skills-based, competency-driven approach. In an AI-driven world, the capacity to think critically, solve complex problems, cooperate across disciplines, and apply knowledge in dynamic circumstances is paramount (Sanabria Zepeda, 2024). These talents are not simply "nice-to-have" in the current workforce—they are crucial for success in an AI-enhanced environment (Kruse et al, 2019). A crucial educational strategy for building these competences is the integration of active learning practices, which position students at the center of the learning process, making them active participants rather than passive users of information.

Active learning strategies, such as problem-based learning (PBL), case-based learning, and collaborative group projects, are particularly useful in promoting critical thinking and problem-solving skills (Akbaş, 2024). In PBL, students engage in real-world problems that often need transdisciplinary knowledge and creativity, helping them learn both the technical abilities needed to work with AI and the broader cognitive skills essential to negotiate complicated, open-ended tasks. For example, students might be challenged with building a sustainable business plan for a corporation employing AI technology to optimize resource consumption. Such initiatives not only educate them on the technical uses of AI but also encourage them to think strategically, morally, and creatively about how technology might be utilized to address global concerns. Another significant pedagogical method is inquiry-based learning, which encourages students to ask questions, examine other views, and engage in independent study. This approach matches closely with how AI is deployed in the actual world—often in sophisticated, context-dependent ways. By encouraging a mentality of inquiry and curiosity, educators may help students develop the flexibility and adaptability required to flourish in an environment where AI is always evolving and changing. In this paradigm, students are encouraged to study how AI works, its limitations, and its potential for promoting beneficial social and environmental change, while also contemplating its ethical implications.

In addition to active learning and inquiry-based techniques, there is a rising acknowledgment of the value of interdisciplinary learning. The advent of AI has blurred the borders across fields such as computer science, business, healthcare, and the social sciences (El-Swaify, 2022). To prepare students for a world where AI is incorporated into practically every industry, education must embrace a multidisciplinary curriculum that enables students to draw on knowledge from many areas. By integrating technological expertise with a comprehension of human behavior, societal implications, and ethical considerations, students can become well-rounded thinkers who are capable of using AI in meaningful ways. For instance, a student researching AI might also take classes in sociology or environmental science to understand the societal outcomes of their work and discover how AI might be utilized to address environmental concerns. Equally essential is the integration of ethical considerations into the AI curriculum. As AI technologies continue to improve, they create complicated ethical problems that demand careful thought and attention (Helbing, 2019). Issues such as algorithmic prejudice, privacy concerns, and the influence of automation on employment are just a few of the challenges that must be addressed. Therefore, students must be not only taught how to utilize AI but also how to examine the ethical, legal, and societal outcomes of its use. This could include talks on the ethical problems faced by AI, case studies analyzing the unintended consequences of AI deployment, and chances for students to engage in debates on the duties of AI inventors and users. By integrating ethics into the AI curriculum, we can ensure that students develop a strong sense of responsibility and understanding of the potential hazards and rewards of AI. In a fast-changing environment, it is also crucial to emphasize the development of lifelong learning skills. AI is advancing at a pace that makes it challenging for even the most skilled people to keep up with every breakthrough (Dwivedi et al, 2021). As a result, students must be taught how to learn autonomously, using digital tools and resources to continue their education throughout their careers. This can include developing metacognitive skills that allow students to reflect on their learning process, create goals, and monitor their progress. Digital literacy, as a core ability, plays a crucial role in supporting this self-directed learning, enabling students to access information, learn new skills, and keep up to date with the newest AI breakthroughs.

The importance of AI itself in advancing education cannot be disregarded (Pedro et al, 2019). AI-powered educational technologies, such as adaptive learning systems, intelligent tutoring systems, and personalized learning platforms, have the potential to transform the way students engage with learning content. These technologies can deliver individualized learning experiences that respond to specific student needs, letting students grow at their speed and ensuring that they have the assistance they need to succeed. For example, AI can be used to identify students who are struggling with particular ideas and offer them more resources or tasks. AI can also be used to monitor student performance and provide educators with data-driven ideas on how to enhance teaching methods and curricular design. In this sense, AI can both enhance the learning experience and make the educational process more efficient and successful. The idea of a "flipped classroom" is another instructional strategy that can be advanced by AI. In a flipped classroom, students engage with educational information outside of class, commonly through videos, online modules, or interactive learning platforms (Wang & Zhu, 2019). This permits in-class time to be used for more engaging, hands-on activities, such as debates, problem-solving, and collaborative projects. AI can enhance flipped learning by delivering individualized learning experiences, enabling students to review content at their leisure, and giving professors insights into which students need more help or are ready for more advanced material.

One of the most crucial components of preparing students for an AI-driven environment is encouraging a growth mentality (Mutambik, 2024). In a world where technology is continuously advancing, students must learn to embrace change and perceive problems as opportunities for growth. This mindset, which emphasizes the significance of endurance, resilience, and adaptability, is important for navigating a future shaped by AI. By creating a growth mindset in students, educators may help them build the confidence and motivation to continuously learn and adapt when new technologies and opportunities arise (Reinhardt & Elwood, 2019). Educating students in an AI-driven world demands a diverse teaching approach that mixes technical skills with critical thinking, creativity, and ethical awareness. By concentrating on active learning, inquiry-based education, multidisciplinary curricula, and lifelong learning, educators may equip students with the competencies they need to flourish in an AI-enhanced society. Additionally, by promoting a growth mentality and emphasizing the ethical use of AI, we can ensure that students not only understand the power of AI but also approach it with the care and responsibility necessary to design a better, more sustainable future. In doing so, we will train the next generation of leaders, thinkers, and innovators to negotiate the complexity of an AI-driven world and leverage technology to achieve positive change for society and the world.

INTEGRATING SUSTAINABILITY INTO DIGITAL LITERACY CURRICULUM

In today's fast-expanding world, the convergence of technology and sustainability has become increasingly significant (Heidari et al, 2023). As digital tools and technology continue to infiltrate all sectors of life, it is vital to guarantee that the younger generation is prepared not only with technological competency but also with the capacity to manage the intricacies of sustainability. This is where the concept of integrating sustainability into the digital literacy curriculum comes into play.

Digital literacy has long been acknowledged as a vital ability for the modern world, with students expected to use technology successfully to solve problems, communicate, and collaborate (Falloon, 2020). However, as the impact of human actions on the earth becomes more visible, it has become evident that digital literacy must evolve to incorporate a significant focus on sustainability. The challenge is not only whether students can use technology, but how they can use it to enhance environmental, social, and economic well-being. This shift calls for a new concept of digital literacy that goes beyond traditional technical skills and integrates critical thinking about the environmental and societal effects of digital technology. One of the key purposes of integrating sustainability into the digital literacy curriculum is to promote an understanding of the relationship between technology and the environment. Technology, in various ways, has contributed to environmental degradation—whether through the exploitation of natural resources, energy consumption, or the development of electronic waste (Rene et al, 2021). Yet, technology also holds immense promise as a tool for solving some of the world's most critical environmental concerns, from renewable energy technologies to data-driven solutions for climate change. To enable students to properly engage with this dual nature of technology, digital literacy education must involve a deeper exploration of the environmental implications of digital tools, platforms, and systems.

The first step in integrating sustainability into the digital literacy curriculum is to enhance awareness of the environmental imprint of digital technology. Students should be taught about the resource-intensive nature of many technological processes, such as the mining of rare earth metals for electronics, the energy consumption of data centers, and the pollution caused by discarded devices. This understanding can help students comprehend that the digital world is not as "ethereal" as it might appear and that behind every device, software, and service, there are concrete resources and environmental consequences (Shapiro, 2018). Through lessons and discussions that address these concerns, students can begin to think critically about how the technology they use and build might contribute to environmental degradation and how they might advocate for more sustainable practices. Incorporating sustainability into digital literacy also involves educating students on how to analyze and use technology in ways that minimize negative environmental implications. This includes studying methods like sustainable design, energy efficiency, and the reduction of technological waste. Students can study "green" technologies, such as energy-efficient data centers, renewable energy-powered gadgets, and the principles of circular economy design, where items are built to be reused, mended, and repurposed rather than wasted. As part of their curriculum, students can be encouraged to research and create projects that explore sustainable technology practices, whether it's designing a more energy-efficient app, proposing a recycling initiative for electronic waste, or creating an algorithm that optimizes energy use in a digital environment.

Another component of integrating sustainability into the digital literacy curriculum is teaching social responsibility in the digital age (Herden et al, 2021). The impact of technology on sustainability is not confined to the environment—it also has significant social implications. Digital literacy should not only focus on the skills necessary to use technology but also on the ethical and social outcomes of its use. Students should grasp how technology may either worsen or alleviate social inequities, and they should be prepared with the means to advocate for social justice in the digital domain. This involves studying the role of AI in decision-making, the digital gap, access to technology, and challenges such as online privacy and monitoring. Educators should educate students to focus on the social outcomes of digital habits and examine how they may utilize their talents to address challenges such as access to information, education, and healthcare in marginalized places. The incorporation of sustainability into digital literacy also requires a critical analysis of the corporate models that drive the technology industry (Brenner, 2018). Many tech companies prioritize profit over sustainability, sometimes underestimating the environmental and social implications of their operations. By researching case studies of organizations that have made strides in incorporating sustainability into their business models, students can obtain insights into how they might innovate for positive change within the digital economy. For instance, organizations that commit to decreasing carbon footprints, employing renewable energy, or establishing fair labor standards offer useful examples of how the digital world might become more aligned with sustainable development goals. By analyzing these examples, students can construct a framework for ethical decision-making that informs their usage and creation of technology. Sustainability in digital literacy is not only about the individual's use of technology; it's also about the structural adjustments required to make the entire technical landscape more sustainable (Radesky & Hiniker, 2022). For this reason, digital literacy education must inspire students to think about the wider picture—how industries, governments, and communities can work together to achieve a sustainable digital future. This involves teaching students about legislation, regulation, and lobbying in the context of digital sustainability.

How can students affect the creation of laws and policies that control technology and its environmental impact? What role can they play in pressing for legislation that supports sustainability in the tech industry?

Students should be encouraged to think about how they may participate in public discourse and activism connected to digital sustainability and how they can utilize their digital literacy abilities to advocate for change (Gleason & Von Gillern, 2018). Practical uses of digital literacy in sustainability could also include programs that allow students to directly engage with sustainability concerns using technology (Buchanan et al, 2018). For example, students could build a website or app that promotes sustainable behaviors within their community, such as an app that helps individuals measure their carbon footprint or a website that connects users with local recycling programs. They might also work on data-driven initiatives that employ technology to solve environmental challenges, such as constructing a model to predict the impact of climate change on local ecosystems or designing a system to track and cut energy consumption in a given industry. These projects offer students the opportunity to apply their digital abilities in ways that directly contribute to sustainability goals and reinforce the idea that technology can be a powerful weapon for change.

Importantly, integrating sustainability into the digital literacy curriculum also involves cultivating a sense of empowerment (Martínez-Bravo et al, 2022). Students need to believe that they have the power to make a difference and that their efforts, whether as individuals or as part of a broader community, matter. By nurturing this sense of agency, educators may inspire students to think creatively and take responsibility for the future they are working to construct. This can be achieved through hands-on projects, immersive learning opportunities, and real-world implementations of sustainability principles in the context of digital technology. Integrating sustainability into the digital literacy curriculum is vital for training students to prosper in an AI-driven society while being cognizant of the environmental, social, and economic repercussions of the technology they use and build. By stressing the interdependence of technology and sustainability, digital literacy may be converted from a strictly technical competence into a full framework for ethical, responsible, and inventive behavior. As we move forward, it will be vital to ensure that students are not just adept at using digital tools but are also equipped to make informed, sustainable decisions that contribute to a more equitable and sustainable future for all.

CHALLENGES IN TEACHING DIGITAL LITERACY FOR SUSTAINABILITY

In recent years, the importance of education in promoting a sustainable future has attracted increasing emphasis (Kayyali, 2025). One of the primary areas of concentration is training students with digital literacy, not only to prepare them for an increasingly digital world but also to help them comprehend the confluence between technology and sustainability. While the inclusion of sustainability into digital literacy curricula is a critical and required step forward, it is not without its problems. Educators encounter a variety of hurdles in teaching digital literacy for sustainability, ranging from the complexity of the curriculum to the opposition to change within educational systems and even the limited resources available to support such revolutionary teaching techniques (Collins & Halverson, 2018). To address these problems and proceed toward genuine development, it is vital to examine the difficulties that come with this attempt.

One of the primary obstacles in teaching digital literacy for sustainability is the intrinsic complexity of sustainability itself. Sustainability is a multidimensional notion that incorporates environmental, economic, and social components, sometimes involving complicated systems that are interrelated (Clayton & Radcliffe, 2018). It is challenging to encompass the whole spectrum of sustainability in a curriculum, especially in a way that combines seamlessly with digital literacy. Teaching students how to utilize technology for sustainability is not just about training them how to use certain tools, but also about encouraging a comprehensive awareness of how digital technology intersects with and can influence sustainable development goals. This difficulty is worsened by the ever-evolving nature of both digital literacy and sustainability. Digital tools, platforms, and technologies are continually changing, and educators are expected to stay up with the latest trends and advances (Haleem et al, 2022). As technology continues to advance at a quick pace, it can be challenging to ensure that students are acquiring the most up-to-date and relevant knowledge and skills. For example, new digital technologies designed to assist in monitoring and minimizing carbon footprints or track sustainability goals can arise faster than educators can incorporate them into their teaching. Similarly, sustainability concerns themselves are developing, and what was perceived as a critical issue five years ago may not be as pressing now, forcing educators to constantly adjust their teaching materials and methodologies to remain relevant.

Another problem is the varied spectrum of students that educators must teach (Westwood, 2018). Students come from varying origins, have different levels of prior knowledge about sustainability, and possess differing levels of familiarity and comfort with technology. Some students may already be highly engaged with sustainability and may have a good basis in digital literacy, while others may fail to understand the essential principles of either. Designing a curriculum that caters to these various requirements is a tricky balancing act. There is the possibility that some students would be overwhelmed by the complexity of both sustainability issues and the technologies involved, while others might not find the curriculum rigorous enough. This difference might result in students disengaging from the curriculum or failing to properly appreciate the linkage of sustainability and digital literacy (Aldhafeeri & Alotaibi, 2022). Even for educators who are well-versed in both technology and sustainability, teaching digital literacy for sustainability demands them to break away from traditional teaching approaches and embrace innovative pedagogical strategies. The incorporation of sustainability into digital literacy entails not just teaching technical abilities but also developing critical thinking, problem-solving, and ethical decision-making. This is not an easy endeavor, especially since traditional teaching approaches focus heavily on conveying factual content and measuring students' capacity to recall information. Encouraging students to think critically about the impact of technology on society and the environment requires educators to create an open, interactive learning environment, where students can engage in debates, explore case studies, and work on projects that allow them to make connections between digital tools and sustainability goals. The shift from a knowledge-based to a more skills- and inquiry-based approach may be a difficult transition for both educators and students, particularly when education systems are structured around inflexible standards and exams that value the memorizing of facts over practical abilities.

The resources needed to properly teach digital literacy for sustainability are another big obstacle (Radovanović, 2020). While there has been substantial investment in technology in education, many colleges and institutions still lack the infrastructure and resources required to fully execute a curriculum that integrates sustainability with digital literacy. Access to technology is typically inconsistent, both within and between countries, and even inside institutions. In some places, students may not have dependable access to computers or the internet, let alone the latest software tools that could enhance their learning about sustainability. In such situations, teaching digital literacy for sustainability becomes a demanding undertaking. Even when the technology is accessible, instructors may not have the training or support needed to use these tools effectively in a sustainable setting. In certain circumstances, educators themselves may not be entirely digitally literate or may not possess the requisite skills to combine technology with sustainability in a meaningful way (Monteiro & Leite, 2021). There is also the problem of designing a cohesive and complete curriculum for teaching digital literacy for sustainability. While there are numerous resources and programs available that focus on either digital literacy or sustainability, few seek to merge these two areas into a cohesive curriculum. Educators may find themselves stitching together different resources, tools, and materials from multiple sources, which can result in a fragmented and disjointed learning experience for students (Spillane et al, 2022). Without a clear and well-organized framework that integrates digital literacy with sustainability, students may fail to recognize the connections between the two subjects, resulting in confusion and lack of interest.

Sustainability education typically comes with a degree of urgency, as climate change and environmental degradation continue to develop at alarming rates (Sonetti et al, 2019). This sense of urgency can put pressure on educators to offer knowledge quickly and effectively, which may not always be realistic given the complexities of both sustainability and technology. Faculty members could feel overwhelmed by the need to stay on top of fast-emerging concerns and technologies, leaving little opportunity to discuss the deeper, more philosophical questions regarding the relationship between technology and sustainability. This lack of time and space to critically reflect on the long-term outcomes of digital technology for the environment and society is a serious impediment to cultivating the kind of deliberate, meaningful engagement with sustainability that students need.

Another key difficulty is the lack of congruence between educational policy and sustainability goals (Repo et al, 2018). While many educational institutions increasingly understand the need for sustainability, the integration of sustainability into curricula generally happens in a piecemeal approach, with little coordination or guidance. Digital literacy is typically taught as a single subject, while sustainability might be introduced in independent courses or as part of multidisciplinary initiatives. This lack of integration implies that students may not completely comprehend how digital literacy ties with broader sustainability objectives, and they may struggle to apply their knowledge in real-world circumstances. Aligning curricula with global sustainability frameworks, such as the United Nations Sustainable Development Goals (SDGs), would help to guarantee that students can see the importance of their digital literacy abilities in addressing complex global concerns (Lemarchand et al, 2022).

In addition, there is the difficulty of addressing the ethical implications of both digital technology and sustainability. Many digital technologies, such as artificial intelligence, data analytics, and blockchain, have the potential to greatly improve sustainability, but they also create a variety of ethical problems. How can we ensure that digital technologies are used in ways that are equal, just, and sustainable? How can we limit the possible negative effects of technology such as e-waste, monitoring, or digital exclusion?

Teaching students to think critically about the ethical implications of technology, particularly in the context of sustainability, is a vital facet of digital literacy. It demands educators to go beyond technical skills and create deeper talks about accountability, justice, and the role of technology in influencing the future of the world (Schleicher, 2018). While teaching digital literacy for sustainability holds great promise, it is accompanied by several substantial hurdles. From the complexity of sustainability itself to the absence of resources, infrastructure, and alignment within educational systems, the task of training students to navigate the digital world ethically and sustainably is not an easy one. However, these obstacles are not insurmountable. By tackling these concerns through new instructional practices, collaboration, and increased investment in resources, educators may make gains toward ensuring that students are not just adept in digital technologies but also ready to utilize them responsibly and sustainably.

CASE STUDIES: EFFECTIVE EDUCATIONAL MODELS IN AI-DRIVEN SUSTAINABILITY

The integration of Artificial Intelligence (AI) into education has opened up new possibilities for teaching and learning in many disciplines, including sustainability (Pedro et al, 2019). With the increased emphasis on educating future generations for an AI-driven world, many educational institutions are beginning to embrace AI as a tool not just for strengthening teaching techniques but also for supporting sustainable growth. However, the use of AI in sustainability education is still a young topic, and understanding how it is being applied successfully involves looking at real-world examples where AI is actively being utilized to promote sustainability in education.

One example of a forward-thinking university is the University of California, Berkeley, which has created a unique AI-driven sustainability program that blends advanced data analytics with environmental research (Islam et al, 2025). The program combines AI techniques to analyze complicated environmental data, enabling students to spot trends, predict future difficulties, and explore sustainable solutions. Through the use of machine learning algorithms, students gain insights into how ecosystems function, how to manage carbon emissions, and how to optimize energy use. The curriculum employs AI not just as a tool for analysis but as an enabler of sustainable thinking (Southworth et al, 2023). Students are urged to think critically about how AI may assist address real-world concerns, such as climate change, resource depletion, and biodiversity loss. By exposing students to the actual uses of AI in sustainability, UC Berkeley is producing a generation of environmentally conscious graduates who are equipped with both the technical abilities and ethical mentality to make meaningful contributions to sustainability efforts.

Another example is the University of Melbourne's interdisciplinary approach to AI and sustainability in its environmental sciences curriculum (Pattison et al, 2023). This model focuses on how AI may be used to forecast environmental patterns, improve agricultural practices, and reduce waste in industrial processes. By combining AI training with sustainable habits, students are given the tools to make data-driven decisions that can drastically lower their carbon impact (Obracht-Prondzyńska et al, 2022). For instance, students are taught how to apply AI to improve water usage in agriculture or predict the energy consumption trends in industrial processes. This hands-on approach not only increases students' understanding of AI but also emphasizes its potential to promote systemic change in the way enterprises and societies address sustainability concerns. This educational model highlights the importance of interdisciplinary learning, where students from varied professions, such as engineering, economics, and environmental science, collaborate to address real-world sustainability problems using AI.

In addition to traditional colleges, there are now new AI-driven sustainability projects in online education. One notable example is the "AI for Earth" program from Microsoft, which partners with universities, non-profit groups, and researchers to develop AI solutions that support environmental sustainability (Nost & Colven, 2022). The initiative focuses on many challenges, such as climate change, agriculture, and biodiversity protection, and provides online courses and tools for educators and students to investigate the interface of AI and sustainability. Through these online platforms, students can access knowledge and resources to interact with sustainability concerns in a global context. They learn how to apply AI to real-world settings, from analyzing satellite data to monitor deforestation to applying AI models to anticipate the implications of climate change on coastal ecosystems. By democratizing access to AI education, the "AI for Earth" initiative is allowing students around the world to become changemakers in sustainability, regardless of their physical location. Another noteworthy example comes from Singapore, where the National University of Singapore (NUS) has established an AI-powered platform for sustainability education (Foong et al, 2024). The platform employs AI to create tailored learning experiences for students, helping them understand complicated sustainability ideas by adjusting the content to individual learning preferences and paces. This technology enables students to connect more deeply with the topic, as it delivers data visualizations, simulations, and predictive models tailored to their particular needs. The AI-powered application also integrates real-time environmental data, allowing students to monitor and respond to sustainability concerns as they arise. This approach emphasizes active learning and critical thinking, enabling students to not only grasp theoretical sustainability principles but also apply them to real-world challenges. By employing AI to create tailored learning journeys, NUS is cultivating a generation of sustainability experts who are competent at using digital technologies to effect meaningful change.

In the business world, corporations such as Google and IBM are cooperating with universities to establish AI-driven sustainability education programs that bridge the gap between academic learning and industry needs (Wang, 2023). These collaborations provide students with the opportunity to collaborate on AI-powered sustainability projects that have real-world implications. For example, IBM's "Green Horizons" initiative employs AI to increase energy efficiency in cities by evaluating data from sensors embedded throughout urban infrastructure (Alzoubi & Mishra, 2024). Students from partner colleges are given the option to work on AI models that anticipate energy consumption trends, identify areas of waste, and offer methods to lessen the environmental effects of cities. This not only gives students hands-on experience in applying AI for sustainability but also guarantees that they are prepared to address the growing need for AI capabilities in companies focused on environmental impact.

Similarly, in Europe, the University of Amsterdam has built an AI-driven sustainability lab that allows students to experiment with cutting-edge technology to solve sustainability concerns (Mesquita & de-Lima-Santos, 2024). The lab is meant as a collaborative place where students from varied academic backgrounds come together to work on AI projects that address issues such as renewable energy optimization, trash management, and climate change mitigation. The lab is equipped with a wide array of AI tools and technologies, including machine learning algorithms, predictive modeling software, and environmental sensors, which students can utilize to generate new solutions to sustainability concerns. This hands-on, collaborative approach not only develops students' technical skills but also fosters a culture of teamwork and creativity, crucial for addressing the complex sustainability concerns of the future.

These case studies all have numerous common threads that can serve as significant lessons for educational institutions looking to integrate AI into sustainability education. One significant message is the need for interdisciplinary teamwork. Whether through partnerships between universities and businesses or by bringing together students from multiple academic disciplines, the most successful educational models for AI-driven sustainability are those that stress the mixing of knowledge and experience across domains. Sustainability concerns are inherently complicated and demand a varied solution, which is why having a diverse collection of ideas is vital (Buhl et al, 2019). The case studies demonstrate how interdisciplinary teams are more likely to produce innovative, holistic solutions to sustainability problems, and this collaborative approach should be cultivated in educational environments.

Another crucial conclusion is the need for real-world, hands-on learning experiences (Luse & Rursch, 2021). In each of these case studies, students are not merely taught theoretical principles but are actively involved in initiatives that have practical, real-world implications. By engaging with real-time data, simulations, and AI models, students develop the skills they need to apply AI to sustainability concerns in meaningful ways. This practical exposure is vital for building the technical competence and critical thinking abilities that are required to handle the sustainability concerns of the future. In an increasingly complicated and data-driven world, students must learn how to handle the difficulties and opportunities that AI brings in the context of sustainability. The case stories underline the significance of individualized, adaptive learning. AI may be exploited to build tailored learning experiences that adapt to students' specific strengths and shortcomings. By adapting the educational content to the needs of each student, AI can assist ensure that all learners, regardless of their background or past knowledge, have the opportunity to succeed. Personalized learning can also assist create a deeper comprehension of the material, as students can engage with the content at their own pace and in a way that suits their learning style.

Lastly, these case studies demonstrate the need to promote ethical issues in AI-driven sustainability teaching. As students learn how to use AI for sustainability, they must also be trained to understand the ethical implications of their work. How can AI be utilized responsibly to enhance sustainability without escalating inequality or environmental degradation? These are questions that need to be addressed in an AI-driven sustainability curriculum. The most successful programs integrate ethical considerations into the learning process, encouraging students to think critically about how their technical discoveries may be used for the greater benefit. The case studies provided here offer significant insights into the effective integration of AI in sustainability education. By providing students with the tools, information, and experiences they need to comprehend and use AI in a sustainability context, these educational models are training the next generation of leaders to confront the world's most serious environmental concerns. The lessons gleaned from these case studies—interdisciplinary collaboration, hands-on learning, tailored education, and ethical considerations—can serve as a guide for universities wishing to create their AI-driven sustainability initiatives. As AI continues to grow, the role of education in building a sustainable future will become ever more vital, and these creative models will help ensure that students are equipped to handle the challenges ahead.

FUTURE DIRECTIONS: ADVANCING DIGITAL LITERACY FOR SUSTAINABILITY IN HIGHER EDUCATION

As the world continues to address the complex challenges of climate change, resource depletion, and socioeconomic inequities, the role of higher education in molding the future becomes increasingly essential. Institutions of higher education are ideally positioned to equip the next generation with the skills, knowledge, and values necessary to promote sustainable development. In this setting, digital literacy is developing as a core competency for students, not merely as a tool for personal or professional success but as a critical enabler of sustainability.

At the heart of the future of digital literacy for sustainability lies the integration of sustainability-focused content into all elements of digital education (Binagwaho et al, 2022). Traditionally, digital literacy has been considered as a set of technical skills—understanding how to operate software, handle data, or apply online platforms. As the world progressively advances toward a digital and AI-driven economy, it is becoming evident that digital literacy must expand to incorporate a deeper grasp of how technology may be leveraged to address environmental and social concerns. Future digital literacy programs in higher education must go beyond basic technological abilities to embrace a critical knowledge of the role of technology in constructing sustainable futures. This means that digital literacy needs to be understood as an interdisciplinary ability, one that relies upon subjects as diverse as environmental science, ethics, data science, and social justice, preparing students to think critically about the outcomes of their technology choices.

One of the most intriguing developments in this field is the potential for colleges to build digital literacy programs that are deliberately tailored to handle sustainability challenges (Abulibdeh et al, 2024). Higher education institutions can offer specialized programs that educate students with the technical skills needed to deal with emerging technologies—such as AI, blockchain, and big data—while also educating them on how these tools might be used to sustainability concerns. For example, programs focused on smart cities, renewable energy, and sustainable agriculture could mix courses on digital technologies like geographic information systems (GIS), data analytics, and IoT sensors with sustainability-oriented modules (Talebkhah et al, 2023). In this approach, digital literacy becomes not only a means of technological fluency but also an active driver of sustainable innovation. The purpose is not merely to equip students to enter the workforce but to enable them to be agents of change who can utilize technology for the greater good.

As the pace of technological innovation accelerates, so too does the necessity for higher education institutions to adjust their courses to keep pace with emerging trends. The future of digital literacy for sustainability will likely feature a dynamic and flexible curriculum that changes alongside the technology and sustainability concerns of the day. This may require colleges to take a more modular, project-based approach to teaching, where students are entrusted with solving real-world sustainability problems using the latest technologies. For instance, a student might work on a project that uses AI to predict and minimize the environmental impact of a large-scale industrial operation or employ blockchain technology to establish a more transparent and sustainable supply chain. The essential to these projects is that they are not merely intellectual exercises but meaningful contributions to tackling the pressing ecological concerns facing the planet.

Collaboration between academics, industry, and government will also play a crucial role in developing digital literacy for sustainability in higher education (Khan et al, 2022). As sustainability concerns become more complicated, there is an increasing demand for multi-stakeholder solutions that use the knowledge of multiple sectors (Nonet et al, 2022). Universities are already beginning to develop partnerships with corporations, non-profits, and governments to tackle sustainability concerns, and these collaborations can help shape the future of digital literacy programs. For example, partnerships between universities and technology businesses might provide students with access to cutting-edge tools and platforms for learning about sustainability, while also helping these companies build the next generation of sustainable innovations. In response, universities can provide these corporations with a pipeline of smart students who are not just technologically adept but also well-versed in the ethical, environmental, and social components of sustainability. These collaborations will likely be crucial in building a feedback loop that ensures that digital literacy for sustainability remains relevant and impactful.

One problem that many colleges will encounter in promoting digital literacy for sustainability is the need to guarantee that these programs are accessible to all students, regardless of their background or past familiarity with technology (Alenezi, 2023). As digital literacy becomes a crucial aspect of a sustainable future, there is a risk that students who lack access to technology or the basic abilities to engage with it may be left behind. To solve this, institutions must be proactive in establishing initiatives to cross the digital gap. This could involve offering basic digital literacy classes for students from underrepresented backgrounds, providing subsidized access to the latest technology, or enabling remote learning options that allow students in low-resource areas to access high-quality digital education. Colleges must make sure that their sustainability-focused digital literacy programs are inclusive and reflect the complexity of global sustainability concerns. Sustainability is a global issue that affects people and communities in different ways, and digital literacy programs must take this into account to ensure that all students have the skills they need to make a significant difference. The role of ethics in digital literacy for sustainability will also be increasingly significant as higher education institutions expand their courses in this area (Anthonysamy et al, 2020). With the expanding influence of AI and other emerging technologies, there is an urgent need to address the ethical implications of these technologies. How can we ensure that AI is used to address environmental concerns without worsening social inequalities? What role does data privacy play when dealing with sensitive environmental information? These are the kinds of issues that will need to be introduced into digital literacy programs in the future. Teaching students not only how to use technology but also how to use it responsibly is vital to ensuring that digital literacy for sustainability leads to beneficial, long-term effects for both people and the earth.

In terms of teaching approaches, the future will undoubtedly witness a larger emphasis on experiential learning (Burch et al, 2019). This strategy has been demonstrated to be particularly effective in creating deep comprehension and engagement. By immersing students in real-world sustainability challenges and having them apply their digital literacy abilities to address problems, colleges can ensure that students are not just passively collecting knowledge but actively interacting with the topic. In the future, we may expect to see more digital literacy programs that combine simulations, data-driven decision-making tools, and even virtual or augmented reality settings that allow students to interact with complicated sustainability scenarios. These immersive learning experiences will help students build a better sense of agency and responsibility, empowering them to take action and contribute to sustainability solutions in their communities. In addition to strengthening teaching and learning methods, universities will also need to engage in faculty development to ensure that educators are qualified to teach digital literacy for sustainability. As the landscape of technology and sustainability continues to grow, faculty members must stay current with the latest tools and pedagogical practices. This will involve continuing professional growth, engagement with other experts, and a dedication to lifetime learning. To effectively teach digital literacy for sustainability, instructors must be comfortable negotiating the center of technology, sustainability, and ethics, and they must be able to transfer these abilities to their students in a way that is relevant, engaging, and impactful.

The future of digital literacy for sustainability will be molded by the growing understanding of sustainability as a worldwide and transdisciplinary issue (Bibri, 2019). Digital tools and technology will continue to play a crucial role in addressing environmental and social concerns, and higher education must be at the forefront of ensuring that the next generation of students can navigate this new world. By integrating sustainability-focused content into digital literacy programs, facilitating collaboration between many sectors, and emphasizing ethical and inclusive behaviors, colleges may help design a future where technology is a stimulant for positive change. Developing digital literacy for sustainability in higher education is not only about teaching students how to use technology—it is about empowering them to use technology to create a more sustainable society. As we look to the future, the role of higher education in creating sustainable development has never been more crucial. By rethinking digital literacy as a multidimensional, interdisciplinary talent that is directly tied to sustainability, colleges can help educate students about the challenges and opportunities of an AI-driven society. Through innovative teaching, cooperation, and an emphasis on ethics and inclusivity, higher education can be a driving force in improving sustainability and creating a more equitable and resilient global society.

CONCLUSION

The convergence of digital literacy and sustainability presents a great opportunity to revolutionize education and prepare students for the complexity of an AI-driven society. As global concerns such as climate change, social injustice, and resource depletion deepen, the need for a technologically literate and sustainability-conscious generation has never been more critical. In this context, digital literacy is no longer just about being proficient with computers or software tools; it encompasses a broad range of skills that enable individuals to engage meaningfully with technology, critically assess its implications, and leverage it for the greater good of society and the environment.

Throughout this chapter, we have explored the evolving nature of digital literacy and its critical role in addressing sustainability concerns. As technology, particularly artificial intelligence, continues to alter businesses, economies, and societies, it is evident that students must acquire not only technical abilities but also a thorough awareness of the ethical, social, and environmental outcomes of their technological engagement. Digital literacy, when combined with a firm grounding in sustainability concepts, can equip students to think holistically, make informed decisions, and take innovative steps to address the pressing concerns of our time. AI, in particular, has the potential to be a transformative force in the pursuit of sustainability. From managing energy usage to pushing developments in clean technologies and sustainable agriculture, AI offers solutions that can help reduce environmental damage, enhance resource efficiency, and build more egalitarian societies. However, these benefits are not guaranteed. The uncritical or irresponsible use of AI could worsen current problems, such as increased inequality or environmental destruction. This highlights the necessity of preparing students with the tools and frameworks to manage these challenges, ensuring that they are prepared not only to utilize AI but also to guide its growth in ways that promote sustainability.

The integration of digital literacy and sustainability education is not only a solution to present concerns; it is an investment in the future. As AI technologies become increasingly ingrained in everyday life, the ability to understand, analyze, and contribute to these technologies will be a defining characteristic of an informed and empowered populace. Students who are digitally literate and sustainability-focused will be better ready to engage in the creation and implementation of policies and solutions that address global concerns. They will be the ones pushing innovation in domains like green technologies, renewable energy, sustainable urban planning, and circular economies—fields that are vital to reaching the United Nations' Sustainable Development Goals (SDGs). Accomplishing this convergence of digital literacy with sustainability demands a paradigm shift in education. Traditional educational paradigms have frequently addressed these two domains independently, with digital literacy taught as a technical skill and sustainability as a set of principles or aims. This approach is no longer sufficient in a world where technology and sustainability are inextricably interwoven. To prepare students for the future, education must embrace a more integrated approach, one that not only teaches them the technical skills they need but also encourages a mindset of critical inquiry, ethical awareness, and long-term thinking. This approach must be multidisciplinary, relying on information from domains such as environmental science, economics, ethics, and technology, and fostering collaboration between students, educators, and experts from varied backgrounds. The pedagogical solutions necessary to integrate digital literacy with sustainability education are as varied as the difficulties they seek to address. Professors must move beyond merely delivering knowledge to involve students in problem-solving, critical thinking, and collaborative learning. They must develop learning settings that inspire students to question assumptions, study the social and environmental outcomes of technology, and actively engage in projects that tackle real-world sustainability issues. By doing so, educators may help students build the abilities needed to become leaders in the digital, AI-driven world while ensuring that sustainability remains at the center of their work.

In addition to curricular improvements, the larger educational ecosystem must also adapt to enable this integrated approach. Institutions must invest in the resources, tools, and professional development essential to provide educators with the skills and knowledge to teach digital literacy in a sustainability context. They must also establish relationships with industry, governments, and civil society organizations to ensure that students are exposed to the newest technologies and have the opportunity to apply their learning in real-world contexts. Despite the potential, the journey toward incorporating digital literacy and sustainability into education is not without its hurdles. There are major challenges to overcome, including a lack of clarity on what digital literacy and sustainability education should involve, inadequate resources for colleges and universities, and reluctance to change within existing educational organizations. However, these challenges also create an opportunity for creativity and collaboration. By confronting these hurdles head-on, educators, policymakers, and stakeholders can establish a more dynamic and forward-thinking educational system that prepares students not only for the technology needs of the future but also for the ethical and environmental imperatives that come with it.

As we go more into the AI-driven world, the significance of preparing students for a sustainable future cannot be stressed. The world's most critical challenges—climate change, resource depletion, social injustice—are all connected with the rise of technology. Thus, teaching students to use technology for sustainability is not only a matter of giving technical skills; it is about fostering a feeling of responsibility, inventiveness, and resilience. By fostering a generation that is digitally literate, sustainability-minded, and competent in navigating the intricacies of the AI-driven world, we can ensure that technology becomes a force for positive change rather than an instrument of further divide and destruction. The integration of digital literacy and sustainability education is vital for equipping students to flourish in an AI-driven society that needs both innovation and responsibility. By preparing students with the information, skills, and mindset to engage with technology in ways that promote sustainability, we can enable them to face the global challenges of the future and contribute to a more equitable, resilient, and sustainable society. The future belongs to those who can harness the power of technology to construct a better, more sustainable tomorrow—and education has a crucial role to play in defining this future.

REFERENCES

Abulibdeh, A., Zaidan, E., & Abulibdeh, R. (2024). Navigating the confluence of artificial intelligence and education for sustainable development in the era of industry 4.0: Challenges, opportunities, and ethical dimensions. *Journal of Cleaner Production*, *437*, 140527. DOI: 10.1016/j.jclepro.2023.140527

Ahmad, T., Madonski, R., Zhang, D., Huang, C., & Mujeeb, A. (2022). Data-driven probabilistic machine learning in sustainable smart energy/smart energy systems: Key developments, challenges, and future research opportunities in the context of smart grid paradigm. *Renewable & Sustainable Energy Reviews*, *160*, 112128. DOI: 10.1016/j.rser.2022.112128

Ahmad, T., Zhang, D., Huang, C., Zhang, H., Dai, N., Song, Y., & Chen, H. (2021). Artificial intelligence in sustainable energy industry: Status Quo, challenges and opportunities. *Journal of Cleaner Production*, *289*, 125834. DOI: 10.1016/j.jclepro.2021.125834

Ahmed, Z., Mohamed, K., Zeeshan, S., & Dong, X. (2020). Artificial intelligence with multi-functional machine learning platform development for better healthcare and precision medicine. *Database : The Journal of Biological Databases and Curation*, *2020*, baaa010. DOI: 10.1093/database/baaa010 PMID: 32185396

Akbaş, M. (2024). EXPLORING ACTIVE LEARNING METHODS FOR EFFECTIVE NURSING EDUCATION. *International Journal of Pedagogics*, *4*(12), 8–13.

Al-Raeei, M. (2024). The smart future for sustainable development: Artificial intelligence solutions for sustainable urbanization. *Sustainable Development*.

Aldhafeeri, F. M., & Alotaibi, A. A. (2022). Effectiveness of digital education shifting model on high school students' engagement. *Education and Information Technologies*, *27*(5), 6869–6891. DOI: 10.1007/s10639-021-10879-4 PMID: 35103044

Alenezi, M., Wardat, S., & Akour, M. (2023). The need of integrating digital education in higher education: Challenges and opportunities. *Sustainability (Basel)*, *15*(6), 4782. DOI: 10.3390/su15064782

Alzoubi, Y. I., & Mishra, A. (2024). Green artificial intelligence initiatives: Potentials and challenges. *Journal of Cleaner Production*, *468*, 143090. DOI: 10.1016/j.jclepro.2024.143090

Anthonysamy, L., Koo, A. C., & Hew, S. H. (2020). Self-regulated learning strategies in higher education: Fostering digital literacy for sustainable lifelong learning. *Education and Information Technologies*, *25*(4), 2393–2414. DOI: 10.1007/s10639-020-10201-8

Anurogo, D., La Ramba, H., Putri, N. D., & Putri, U. M. P. (2023). Digital Literacy 5.0 to enhance multicultural education. *Multicultural Islamic Education Review*, *1*(2), 109–179. DOI: 10.23917/mier.v1i2.3414

Bereczki, E. O., & Kárpáti, A. (2021). Technology-enhanced creativity: A multiple case study of digital technology-integration expert teachers' beliefs and practices. *Thinking Skills and Creativity*, *39*, 100791. DOI: 10.1016/j.tsc.2021.100791

Bibri, S. E. (2019). On the sustainability of smart and smarter cities in the era of big data: An interdisciplinary and transdisciplinary literature review. *Journal of Big Data*, *6*(1), 25. DOI: 10.1186/s40537-019-0182-7

Binagwaho, A., Bonciani Nader, H., Brown Burkins, M., Davies, A., Hessen, D. O., Mbow, C., & Tong, S. (2022). *Knowledge-driven actions: transforming higher education for global sustainability: independent expert group on the universities and the 2030 agenda*. UNESCO Publishing.

Brenner, B. (2018). Transformative sustainable business models in the light of the digital imperative—A global business economics perspective. *Sustainability (Basel)*, *10*(12), 4428. DOI: 10.3390/su10124428

Buchanan, J., Pressick-Kilborn, K., & Maher, D. (2018). Promoting environmental education for primary school-aged students using digital technologies. *Eurasia Journal of Mathematics, Science and Technology Education*, *15*(2), em1661.

Buckingham, D. (2020). Epilogue: Rethinking digital literacy: Media education in the age of digital capitalism. *Digital Education Review*, (37), 230–239. DOI: 10.1344/der.2020.37.230-239

Buhl, A., Schmidt-Keilich, M., Muster, V., Blazejewski, S., Schrader, U., Harrach, C., Schäfer, M., & Süßbauer, E. (2019). Design thinking for sustainability: Why and how design thinking can foster sustainability-oriented innovation development. *Journal of Cleaner Production*, *231*, 1248–1257. DOI: 10.1016/j.jclepro.2019.05.259

Burch, G. F., Giambatista, R., Batchelor, J. H., Burch, J. J., Hoover, J. D., & Heller, N. A. (2019). A meta-analysis of the relationship between experiential learning and learning outcomes. *Decision Sciences Journal of Innovative Education*, *17*(3), 239–273. DOI: 10.1111/dsji.12188

Cath, C. (2018). Governing artificial intelligence: Ethical, legal and technical opportunities and challenges. *Philosophical Transactions. Series A, Mathematical, Physical, and Engineering Sciences*, *376*(2133), 20180080. DOI: 10.1098/rsta.2018.0080 PMID: 30322996

Chetty, K., Qigui, L., Gcora, N., Josie, J., Wenwei, L., & Fang, C. (2018). Bridging the digital divide: Measuring digital literacy. *Economics*, *12*(1), 20180023. DOI: 10.5018/economics-ejournal.ja.2018-23

Clayton, T., & Radcliffe, N. (2018). *Sustainability: a systems approach*. Routledge. DOI: 10.4324/9781315070711

Collins, A., & Halverson, R. (2018). *Rethinking education in the age of technology: The digital revolution and schooling in America*. Teachers College Press.

Dwivedi, Y. K., Hughes, L., Ismagilova, E., Aarts, G., Coombs, C., Crick, T., Duan, Y., Dwivedi, R., Edwards, J., Eirug, A., Galanos, V., Ilavarasan, P. V., Janssen, M., Jones, P., Kar, A. K., Kizgin, H., Kronemann, B., Lal, B., Lucini, B., & Williams, M. D. (2021). Artificial Intelligence (AI): Multidisciplinary perspectives on emerging challenges, opportunities, and agenda for research, practice and policy. *International Journal of Information Management*, *57*, 101994. DOI: 10.1016/j.ijinfomgt.2019.08.002

Dwivedi, Y. K., Hughes, L., Kar, A. K., Baabdullah, A. M., Grover, P., Abbas, R., Andreini, D., Abumoghli, I., Barlette, Y., Bunker, D., Chandra Kruse, L., Constantiou, I., Davison, R. M., De', R., Dubey, R., Fenby-Taylor, H., Gupta, B., He, W., Kodama, M., & Wade, M. (2022). Climate change and COP26: Are digital technologies and information management part of the problem or the solution? An editorial reflection and call to action. *International Journal of Information Management*, *63*, 102456. DOI: 10.1016/j.ijinfomgt.2021.102456

El-Swaify, M. A. (2022). The global nexus: Bridging science, technology, and business in the international landscape. International Multidisciplinary Journal of Science. *Technology & Business*, *1*(01), 22–28.

Falloon, G. (2020). From digital literacy to digital competence: The teacher digital competency (TDC) framework. *Educational Technology Research and Development*, *68*(5), 2449–2472. DOI: 10.1007/s11423-020-09767-4

Fan, Z., Yan, Z., & Wen, S. (2023). Deep learning and artificial intelligence in sustainability: A review of SDGs, renewable energy, and environmental health. *Sustainability (Basel)*, *15*(18), 13493. DOI: 10.3390/su151813493

Foong, Y. P., Pidani, R., Sithira Vadivel, V., & Dongyue, Y. (2024). Singapore smart nation: journey into a new digital landscape for higher education. In *Emerging Technologies in Business: Innovation Strategies for Competitive Advantage* (pp. 281–304). Springer Nature Singapore. DOI: 10.1007/978-981-97-2211-2_13

Gleason, B., & Von Gillern, S. (2018). Digital citizenship with social media: Participatory practices of teaching and learning in secondary education. *Journal of Educational Technology & Society*, *21*(1), 200–212.

Gustian, D., Marzuki, M., Nukman, N., Purnama, Y., & Abdurrahman, D. (2024). Synergies In Education: Integrating Character, Literacy, And Technology For Enhanced Outcomes: Current Perspectives From Global Education Experts. *International Journal Of Teaching And Learning*, *2*(2), 498–512.

. Haleem, A., Javaid, M., Qadri, M. A., & Suman, R. (2022). Understanding the role of digital technologies in education: A review. Sustainable operations and computers, 3, 275-285.

Heidari, A., Navimipour, N. J., Jamali, M. A. J., & Akbarpour, S. (2023). A green, secure, and deep intelligent method for dynamic IoT-edge-cloud offloading scenarios. *Sustainable Computing : Informatics and Systems*, *38*, 100859. DOI: 10.1016/j.suscom.2023.100859

Helbing, D. (2019). *Societal, economic, ethical and legal challenges of the digital revolution: from big data to deep learning, artificial intelligence, and manipulative technologies.* Springer International Publishing.

Herden, C. J., Alliu, E., Cakici, A., Cormier, T., Deguelle, C., Gambhir, S., . . . Edinger-Schons, L. M. (2021, March). "Corporate Digital Responsibility" New corporate responsibilities in the digital age. In Sustainability Management Foruml NachhaltigkeitsManagementForum (Vol. 29, No. 1, pp. 13-29). Berlin/Heidelberg: Springer Berlin Heidelberg.

Islam, M. E., Polas, M. R. H., & Rahman, M. M. (2025). Sustainability and AI in Transnational Higher Education. In Bridging Global Divides for Transnational Higher Education in the AI Era (pp. 379-400). IGI Global Scientific Publishing.

Kaack, L. H., Donti, P. L., Strubell, E., Kamiya, G., Creutzig, F., & Rolnick, D. (2022). Aligning artificial intelligence with climate change mitigation. *Nature Climate Change*, *12*(6), 518–527. DOI: 10.1038/s41558-022-01377-7

Kayyali, M. (2025). The Future of AI in Education: Predictions and Emerging Trends. Next-Generation AI Methodologies in Education, 367-406.

Khan, N., Sarwar, A., Chen, T. B., & Khan, S. (2022). Connecting digital literacy in higher education to the 21st century workforce. *Knowledge Management & E-Learning*, *14*(1), 46–61.

. Kruse, L., Wunderlich, N., & Beck, R. (2019). Artificial intelligence for the financial services industry: What challenges organizations to succeed.

Lemarchand, P., McKeever, M., MacMahon, C., & Owende, P. (2022). A computational approach to evaluating curricular alignment to the united nations sustainable development goals. *Frontiers in Sustainability*, *3*, 909676. DOI: 10.3389/frsus.2022.909676

Lim, M. M., Jørgensen, P. S., & Wyborn, C. A. (2018). Reframing the sustainable development goals to achieve sustainable development in the Anthropocene—A systems approach. *Ecology and Society*, *23*(3), art22. DOI: 10.5751/ES-10182-230322

Luse, A., & Rursch, J. (2021). Using a virtual lab network testbed to facilitate real-world hands-on learning in a networking course. *British Journal of Educational Technology*, *52*(3), 1244–1261. DOI: 10.1111/bjet.13070

Martínez-Bravo, M. C., Sádaba Chalezquer, C., & Serrano-Puche, J. (2022). Dimensions of digital literacy in the 21st century competency frameworks. *Sustainability (Basel)*, *14*(3), 1867. DOI: 10.3390/su14031867

McDougall, J., Readman, M., & Wilkinson, P. (2018). The uses of (digital) literacy. *Learning, Media and Technology*, *43*(3), 263–279. DOI: 10.1080/17439884.2018.1462206

Mehta, A., Shah, T., & Thomas, R. J. (2023). Strategies to address environmental degradation in developing nations: A multifaceted approach. *Journal of Intelligent Connectivity and Emerging Technologies*, *8*(2), 17–34.

Mesquita, L., & de-Lima-Santos, M. F. (2024). Google news initiative innovation challenge in Latin America: Business models between path dependence and power relations. *Journal of Media Business Studies*, •••, 1–26. DOI: 10.1080/16522354.2024.2402630

. Monteiro, A., & Leite, C. (2021). Digital literacies in higher education: Skills, uses, opportunities and obstacles to digital transformation. Revista de Educación a Distancia (RED), 21(65).

Mutambik, I. (2024). The use of AI-driven automation to enhance student learning experiences in the KSA: An alternative pathway to sustainable education. *Sustainability (Basel)*, *16*(14), 5970. DOI: 10.3390/su16145970

Nishant, R., Kennedy, M., & Corbett, J. (2020). Artificial intelligence for sustainability: Challenges, opportunities, and a research agenda. *International Journal of Information Management*, *53*, 102104. DOI: 10.1016/j.ijinfomgt.2020.102104

Nonet, G. A. H., Gössling, T., Van Tulder, R., & Bryson, J. M. (2022). Multi-stakeholder engagement for the sustainable development goals: Introduction to the special issue. *Journal of Business Ethics*, *180*(4), 945–957. DOI: 10.1007/s10551-022-05192-0 PMID: 36065323

Nost, E., & Colven, E. (2022). Earth for AI: A political ecology of data-driven climate initiatives. *Geoforum*, *130*, 23–34. DOI: 10.1016/j.geoforum.2022.01.016

Obracht-Prondzyńska, H., Duda, E., Anacka, H., & Kowal, J. (2022). Greencoin as an AI-based solution shaping climate awareness. *International Journal of Environmental Research and Public Health*, *19*(18), 11183. DOI: 10.3390/ijerph191811183 PMID: 36141452

Pattison, P., Bridgeman, A., Bulmer, A., McCallum, P., & Miles, R. (2023). Renewing the Sydney undergraduate curriculum. *Higher Education*, *86*(6), 1489–1506. DOI: 10.1007/s10734-022-00982-x PMID: 36536882

. Pedro, F., Subosa, M., Rivas, A., & Valverde, P. (2019). Artificial intelligence in education: Challenges and opportunities for sustainable development.

Priya, A. K., Devarajan, B., Alagumalai, A., & Song, H. (2023). Artificial intelligence enabled carbon capture: A review. *The Science of the Total Environment*, *886*, 163913. DOI: 10.1016/j.scitotenv.2023.163913 PMID: 37150463

Radesky, J., & Hiniker, A. (2022). From moral panic to systemic change: Making child-centered design the default. *International Journal of Child-Computer Interaction*, *31*, 100351. DOI: 10.1016/j.ijcci.2021.100351 PMID: 35340408

Radovanović, D., Holst, C., Belur, S. B., Srivastava, R., Houngbonon, G. V., Le Quentrec, E., Miliza, J., Winkler, A. S., & Noll, J. (2020). Digital literacy key performance indicators for sustainable development. *Social Inclusion (Lisboa)*, *8*(2), 151–167. DOI: 10.17645/si.v8i2.2587

Reinhardt, K. S., & Elwood, S. (2019). Promising practices in online training and support: Microlearning and personal learning environments to promote a growth mindset in learners. In *Handbook of research on virtual training and mentoring of online instructors* (pp. 298–310). IGI Global. DOI: 10.4018/978-1-5225-6322-8.ch013

Rene, E. R., Sethurajan, M., Ponnusamy, V. K., Kumar, G., Dung, T. N. B., Brindhadevi, K., & Pugazhendhi, A. (2021). Electronic waste generation, recycling and resource recovery: Technological perspectives and trends. *Journal of Hazardous Materials*, *416*, 125664. DOI: 10.1016/j.jhazmat.2021.125664 PMID: 33838506

Repo, P., Anttonen, M., & Mykk, Ã. (2018). Lack of congruence between European citizen perspectives and policies on circular economy. *European Journal of Sustainable Development*, *7*(1), 249–249. DOI: 10.14207/ejsd.2018.v7n1p249

Sanabria Zepeda, J. C., Olivo Montaño, P. G., Artemova, I., & Argüelles Cruz, A. J. (2024). Prospective narratives on global issues: An AI-based pedagogical model for assessing complex thinking. JOTSE. *Journal of Technology and Science Education*, *14*(1), 184–199. DOI: 10.3926/jotse.2445

Schleicher, A. (2018). Educating learners for their future, not our past. *ECNU Review of Education*, *1*(1), 58–75. DOI: 10.30926/ecnuroe2018010104

Shapiro, J. (2018). Digital Play for Global Citizens: A Guide from the Joan Ganz Cooney Center at Sesame Workshop. In Joan Ganz Cooney Center at Sesame Workshop. Joan Ganz Cooney Center at Sesame Workshop. 1900 Broadway, New York, NY 10023.

Sonetti, G., Brown, M., & Naboni, E. (2019). About the triggering of UN sustainable development goals and regenerative sustainability in higher education. *Sustainability (Basel)*, *11*(1), 254. DOI: 10.3390/su11010254

Southworth, J., Migliaccio, K., Glover, J., Reed, D., McCarty, C., Brendemuhl, J., & Thomas, A. (2023). Developing a model for AI Across the curriculum: Transforming the higher education landscape via innovation in AI literacy. *Computers and Education: Artificial Intelligence*, *4*, 100127. DOI: 10.1016/j.caeai.2023.100127

Spillane, J. P., Blaushild, N. L., Neumerski, C. M., Seelig, J. L., & Peurach, D. J. (2022). Striving for coherence, struggling with incoherence: A comparative study of six educational systems organizing for instruction. *Educational Evaluation and Policy Analysis*, *44*(4), 567–592. DOI: 10.3102/01623737221093382

SS, V. C., Hareendran, A., & Albaaji, G. F. (2024). Precision farming for sustainability: An agricultural intelligence model. Computers and Electronics in Agriculture, 226, 109386.

Sun, A. Y., & Scanlon, B. R. (2019). How can Big Data and machine learning benefit environment and water management: A survey of methods, applications, and future directions. *Environmental Research Letters*, *14*(7), 073001. DOI: 10.1088/1748-9326/ab1b7d

Talebkhah, M., Sali, A., Gordan, M., Hashim, S. J., & Rokhani, F. Z. (2023). Comprehensive review on development of smart cities using industry 4.0 technologies. *IEEE Access : Practical Innovations, Open Solutions*, *11*, 91981–92030. DOI: 10.1109/ACCESS.2023.3302262

Tapalova, O., & Zhiyenbayeva, N. (2022). Artificial intelligence in education: AIEd for personalised learning pathways. *Electronic Journal of e-Learning*, *20*(5), 639–653. DOI: 10.34190/ejel.20.5.2597

Van Wynsberghe, A. (2021). Sustainable AI: AI for sustainability and the sustainability of AI. *AI and Ethics*, *1*(3), 213–218. DOI: 10.1007/s43681-021-00043-6

Wang, K., & Zhu, C. (2019). MOOC-based flipped learning in higher education: Students' participation, experience and learning performance. *International Journal of Educational Technology in Higher Education*, *16*(1), 1–18. DOI: 10.1186/s41239-019-0163-0

Wang, Y. (2023). Synergy in Silicon: The Evolution and Potential of Academia-Industry Collaboration in AI and Software Engineering. *Authorea Preprints*.

Westwood, P. (2018). *Inclusive and adaptive teaching: Meeting the challenge of diversity in the classroom*. Routledge. DOI: 10.4324/9781351061261

Yellu, R. R., Maruthi, S., Dodda, S. B., Thuniki, P., & Reddy, S. R. B. (2021). AI Ethics-Challenges and Considerations: Examining ethical challenges and considerations in the development and deployment of artificial intelligence systems. *African Journal of Artificial Intelligence and Sustainable Development*, *1*(1), 9–16.

KEY TERMS AND DEFINTIONS

Digital Literacy: The ability to effectively and critically use digital tools and platforms, including skills such as data analysis, ethical decision-making in a digital context, and understanding the societal impact of technology.

Sustainability: The practice of meeting present needs without compromising the ability of future generations to meet their own, encompassing environmental, economic, and social dimensions as defined by the United Nations Sustainable Development Goals.

Artificial Intelligence (AI) in Education: The use of AI-driven technologies to enhance learning, personalize instruction, and improve student engagement while addressing ethical concerns such as bias, privacy, and accessibility.

Sustainable Development: A holistic approach to growth that balances economic progress, environmental protection, and social inclusion to ensure long-term global stability.

Digital Citizenship: The responsible use of digital technologies, emphasizing ethical behavior, critical thinking, and active participation in online communities while addressing misinformation and privacy concerns.

Ethical AI: The development and application of artificial intelligence technologies in ways that are transparent, fair, and accountable, ensuring they do not perpetuate bias or harm vulnerable populations.

Interdisciplinary Education: A teaching approach that integrates knowledge and methods from multiple disciplines, encouraging students to apply digital literacy to real-world sustainability challenges.

Smart Technologies for Sustainability: The use of AI, big data, and IoT (Internet of Things) to optimize resource use, reduce environmental impact, and promote efficiency in sectors such as energy, agriculture, and urban planning.

Digital Divide: The gap between individuals or communities with access to digital technologies and those without, which affects educational opportunities, economic growth, and social equity.

Section 4

AI in Assessment, Vocational Education, and Workforce Development

Chapter 11
Revolutionizing Educational Assessments With AI Technology

Kumar Parmar
https://orcid.org/0000-0002-2502-5680
Marwadi University, India

Damodharan Palaniappan
https://orcid.org/0009-0003-0721-3068
Marwadi University, India

T. Premavathi
https://orcid.org/0009-0003-0172-2021
Marwadi University, India

Rituraj Jain
https://orcid.org/0000-0002-5532-1245
Marwadi University, India

ABSTRACT

This chapter explores the possibility of using Artificial Intelligence to reform the field of educational assessment, which has been dormant for the last several decades because the traditional approach to learning assessment is laden with several complications. Very often, the conventional approaches in assessment have served the purpose of ascertaining the knowledge and abilities of learners satisfactorily. Still, rarely are they in harmony with mind-perceptiveness in correspondence with an individual's learning styles, cultural factors, or learning rhythm. Drawing from the current AI technologies that make learning assessable, the chapter discusses their application and, therefore, the potential advantages and disadvantages, if any. Finally, it discusses the future opportunities of AI in educational assessment concerning developing trends, risks, and the imperative to use the capability of AI responsibly to create a positive Learning Environment for the students effectively and safely.

DOI: 10.4018/979-8-3693-9062-7.ch011

1. INTRODUCTION

Technology has changed many fields and the education sector has not been exempted from it especially with the use of Artificial intelligence (AI). One of the most vulnerable spheres caused by the AI is educational assessments which are under changes. Standard formative and summative assessments, which have been chastised for being traditional and generic, time consuming, and bias are being reconsidered by virtue of the capabilities of AI. This chapter looks at how artificial intelligence is disrupting traditional assessments in education, by coming up with improved methods that boost precision, individuality, and speed (Swiecki et al., 2022, Gao et al., 2024). Standardized assessments, including tests, have been valuable in determining the learning achievements of learners but are challenged in diverse learning contexts. Unfortunately, such tests deny the principles of learning style, cultural background, and rate of learning that is correct for every learner. Furthermore, the nit and grainy evaluative nature of carrying out grading particularly in quality assessment may result in inconsistency and biasness in the assessments done (Kim & Zabelina, 2015) as further supported by Gernsbacher et al., 2020).

AI offers innovative, effective and flexible forms of assessments which eradicate these drawbacks. Computer-adaptive tests allow the difficulty level of the questions posed to students to be changed automatically in real-time based on the students' performance. AI also assists in automated scoring leading to increased efficiency as well as helpful for educators as they do not have to spend much time on grading (Steiss et al., 2024; Scarfe et al., 2024). In addition, AI useful in revealing cheating and submits useful data to the assembly through data analysis enhancing decision making as well as the overall perfection of educational delivery.

1.1 Overview of Traditional Assessment Methods

Pre-service teachers' formative assessments have in the past involved the use of paper and pencil tests, written assignments and assessments based on student's performance. Various types of tests and achievement and aptitude tests such as college or university entrance exams for example the SAT or ACT are typical. These tests should give a fair assessment of the learners' knowledge and skills to make comparisons with other schools and regions (Ludwikowska, 2022). Paper tests to include multiple choice, short answer and substantive question can determine whether a student has understood certain areas of knowledge or not. By contrast, the performance-assessment tests allow students to show what they have learned through action – projects or presentations; it also provides a more holistic way to assess learning (Murphy et al., 2023). Soucy illustrates in figure 1 that there are several different major categories of assessments and classification tests. Diagnostic (Pre-Assessment) analyses learners' ability and deficiency before learning. Formative Assessment is used to check progress as well as the learning process during the implementation of knowledge and understanding. Summative Assessment focuses on the accomplishment of learning objectives at a specific point of time of the teaching learning process. In addition to the confirmative form of assessment, which takes place a year after teaching for the purpose of evaluating the effectiveness of the strategies used. Norm-Referenced Assessment use fellow students' performance to base their performance and Criterion-Referenced Assessment measures students' performance against established proficiency levels. Ipsative Assessment is like the Magna Tests and its primary goal is the comparison of the current level of performance to that of in the past since its objective is the improvement of the subject. Traditional assessments are, however, criticized for being universal and for having inherent bias (Sun et al., 2023). Such limitations call for improved techniques in assessments for learning, and AI fundamental to increasing this improvement.

Figure 1. Types of assessment in traditional education system

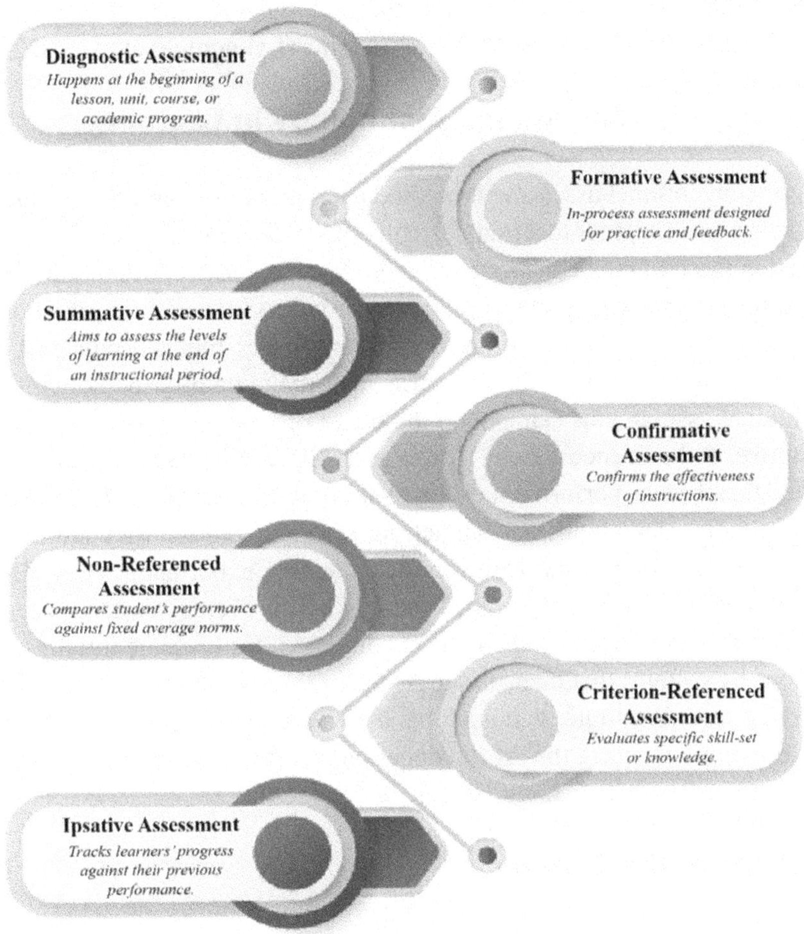

(Joshi, 2020)

1.2 The Need for Transformation in Educational Assessments

The conventional forms of assessment like tests, paper and pen assessment, performance tests are areas that have brought about the realization that there is need to transform tests. Even though these methods can be designed to yield an equal measure of learning for each of the students, the actual potential and learning styles of most students are not easily quantifiable. Standardized test is a very limited method Villeval which only aims at drilling students and assessment of their knowledge through multiple-choice questions and does not allow for demonstrating critical thinking skills, creativity and problem-solving necessary in 21st century job markets. Also, they lack differentiation for learning modality, culture and individual learning progress, which puts many learners out of favors (Abdamia et al., 2023; AL-Roomy,

2023; Millikin, 2023). On the same note, even though written examinations facilitate deeper exploration of the subject, problems like subjectivity and bias surface due to the examinee's marks. Some of the traditional assessment methods are not effective since they do not provide individual feedback based on a specific student's strengths and weaknesses. It, therefore, becomes necessary to incorporate user-friendly technologies that yield more sensitive and broader assessments of the learning systems among the students (Challis, 2005). This shift's purpose is to build realistic, fair assessment practices that are more productive and useful for instructors and their students (Langenfeld et al., 2022).

1.3 Adoption of Artificial Intelligence Technology in Learning

The limitations of conventional assessment methods, which fail to capture the complexities of individual learning, have opened the door to a transformative force in education: Artificial intelligence (AI) Creativity: Imagination is a complex construct and a fundamental aspect of human endeavours that can be defined as 'the ability to create new ideas, products, or works by using the mind or other mental facilities. This removes many of the shortcomings of traditional assessments because AI can work through an enormous amount of data, recognize data patterns, and make data-based conclusions. That is why using AI, the educational assessments can extend the usage of tests and assessments and become more individualized, adaptive, and evidence-based (Hooda et al., 2022; Swiecki et al., 2022). AI technologies work in real-time and then breaks performance data of students into strengths and areas of improvement for individual student paths. This helps in channelling resources where they are needed most, therefore helping to offer a more efficient and well-rounded teaching experience. They also offer formative evaluation that allows the students to keep record and make improvement where necessary. Apart from the assessments, there are other applications of AI in education, for instance intelligent tutoring system where teaching is done by systems that incorporate AI features, automated grading systems and adaptive learning which is a new teaching strategy that adopts the use of learning theories to deliver customized services. Nevertheless, implementing the AI in education should consider ethical issues, data privacy, the changes in educators' roles (Ma & Jiang, 2023).

1.4 Scope and Aims of the Chapter

This chapter examines the role of Artificial Intelligence in shedding new light to the future of assessment in education. It also discusses how AI can overcome these shortcomings by developing better and effective way of assessing the effectiveness of learning through development of more personalized, flexible and analytic assessments. Details about artificial intelligence technologies used in assessment, benefits and risks of AI-based assessments, and the changing role of tutor in an expert system will be demonstrated in the chapter. Moreover, it will include actual scenarios of implementation of AI, the issues of ethical considerations in applying AI in educational assessment and the factors that define the tendencies of applying AI in future.

2. UNDERSTANDING THE CONCEPT OF AI IN EDUCATIONAL SETTING

AI is transforming education sector by providing individualized learning process, using it automation processes, and analytics. NALM systems incorporate intelligent techniques in modification of content to meet student needs and intelligent tutoring systems which are available on 24/7. Smart systems can write letter reports, and grading and provide feedback for papers in the meantime allowing teachers more time for meaningful engagement. Still, we are aware of the limitation that use of AI introduces into education including data privacy risks, algorithmic bias and overemphasize on the use of technology. Opponents of AI also say that the technology reduces human control in the teaching process and contributes to the widening gap of students' ability to attain quality learning (Kamalov et al., 2023). Nevertheless, the prospects for leveraging of AI to improve learners' performance are great. It can early identify those students who may be in danger or academic failure, tailor instruction for learning and also name students for job market marked by continual growth of artificial intelligence. It can be expected that with the development of AI more and more it will be used in education which will constantly fuel the debate regarding the ethical usage of AI in the spheres of teaching and learning (Ayala-Pazmiño, 2023).

2.1 What is Artificial Intelligence?

Artificial Intelligence (AI) refers to the ability of creating systems and machines that can perform a range of tasks that are said to be intelligent in human beings and this includes learning, reasoning and self-correction among others (Rupali & Amit, 2017). These systems are essentially data analysis systems that take large amounts of data, perform logic on the findings as well as recognize trends that are likely to occur based on the available information. The term Artificial Intelligence includes a variety of methods and paradigms which is illustrated in figure 2.

Such techniques include Machine Learning; this is a class of algorithms which gives the abilities of learning to the computers without being programmed. This comprises of supervised, unsupervised, and reinforcement learning techniques (Sze et al., 2017). There are different subgroups of machine learning, and one of the most popular and powerful is called deep learning – the artificial neural networks with more than one layer used for analysis to highlight more and more complicated characteristics. Another one is Natural Language Processing (NLP), which enables the computer and machine to understand, analyze, and even create human language that is vital in developing applications such as chatbots, text summarization and language translation among others.

Figure 2. The era of artificial intelligence

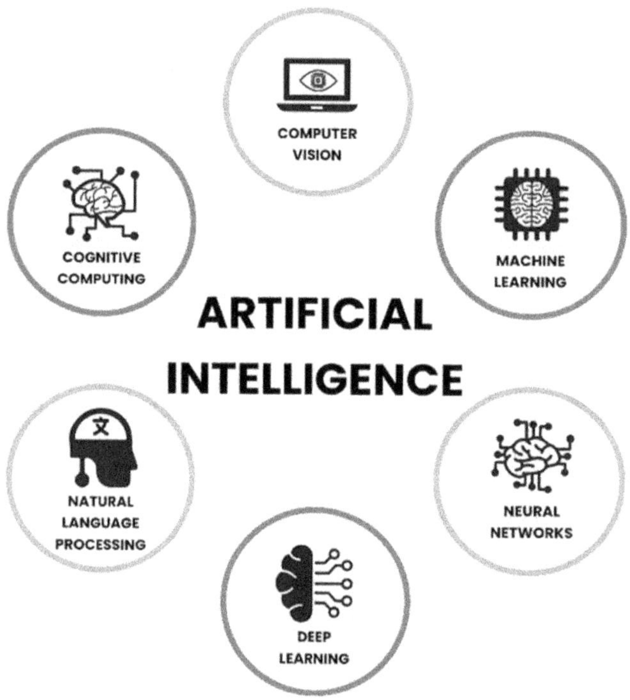

(Matos, 2023)

2.2 The Role of AI in Modern Education

This paper aims at establishing how Artificial Intelligence is transforming education by solving some of the problems which have for instance persisted for years while at the same time improving the way students and teachers learn. It can be noted from the figure 3 that AI has several roles in the current system of education (Zhai et al., 2021). AI is perhaps most useful in individualised learning. Cognitive learning variables entail identifying student learning style, preferred mode, and learning progress and AL decides on learning modalities that suit students to help them progress through parts that are easy for them and drill parts that require more time on the practice. This in addition to artificial intelligence upgrading Intelligent Tutoring Systems whereby students receive instructions and feedback in a same manner as they would with a human instructor whenever they face challenges while learning. The adaptive learning platforms apply artificial intelligence when presenting content and their difficulty level depends with the performance of the students to ensure that students continue studying comfortably and not struggle. In addition, it has a function of the predictor, which will allow focusing on students at risk of poor academic performance to provide them intervention at the right time (Brdesee et al., 2022; Zheng et al., 2024). It also improves the principles of students with disabilities and independent learning software, such as text-to-speech and speech-to-text, and language translation devices to those students who come from different parts of the world (Kamalov et al., 2023; Liu, 2023).

Figure 3. The role of AI in modern education

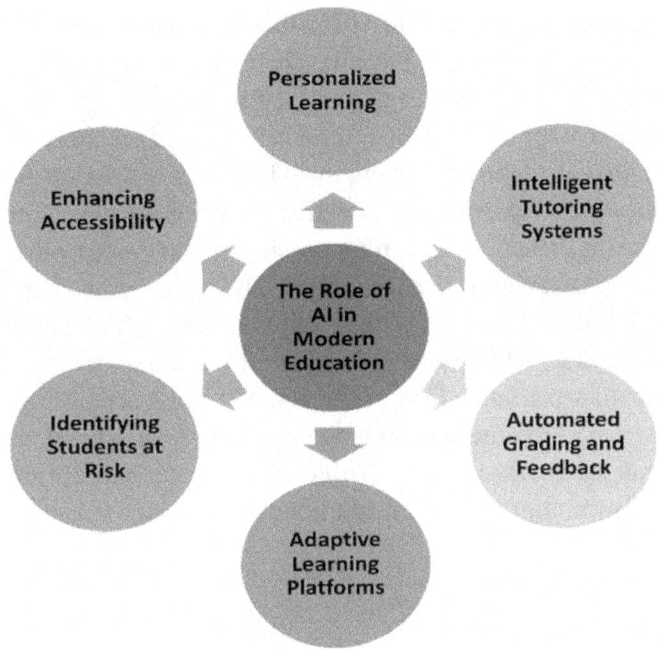

2.3 Key AI Technologies Used in Assessments

Technology is making a significant impact on the practices of educational assessment by moving from norm referenced to criterion referenced type of assessment. Some of them include automated grading systems where machine learning algorithms are used in grading objective test items such as multiple choice, true/false, fill in the blank and some aspect of the subjectivity tests such as grammar and spelling of written answers (Agrawal & Reed, 2022). The adaptive learning platforms rely on artificial intelligence to deliver lessons and quizzes in a way that is challenging enough to the students while avoiding overstressing the poor performing students. NLP technology has found a way of allowing computers to read and analyze human language and thus, computerizing essay grading and the style, grammatical and argumentation feedbacks. Furthermore, computer vision technologies examine students' works in different forms including handwritten assignment, visual graphics, lab experiments and others in ways that provide more informative and accurate evaluation of learning and achievements done by students (Méndez-Ortega et al., 2021). Through performance data analysis by AI, the solution of predictive analytics is to predict the student's future performance since educator interjection is possible during patterns recognition (How, 2019).

2.4 Benefits of AI-Driven Assessments

The following are some of the benefits accrued from the assessments being performed by AI as pointed out in figure 4 below: Another advantage that can be derived from personalization is that machine can offer assessments which can be developed in accordance to the student's needs and learning process. This results in better assessment for the level of comprehension and feedback that is more specific to the matter. Another benefit is that of adaptivity, where the AI-based assessments provide adjustments in the levels of difficulties in questions depending on students' performance hence, improving on engagement levels and efficiency. There is efficiency too in processing student assessment and feedback since the system can go a long way in relieving the teachers from the pressure and time that may be consumed in the process of grading while they can spend their time on better functionality like mentoring. Moreover, the AI- based evaluation avoid biases and subjectivity as compared to manual assessments thus providing accurate and evaluated results. One of the benefits of incorporating AI is that it makes continual checking of learners' performance possible as opposed to occasional, and stressful testing. Last but not the least, actionable insights are made possible with data analytics in student performance while enabling educators receive meaningful recommendations that enhance teaching and learning techniques (Kamalov & Gurrib, 2023).

Figure 4. Benefits of AI-driven assessments

3. THE EVOLUTION OF ASSESSMENT PRACTICES

Over the course of years, the traditional form of giving assessments that includes only multiple-choice tests and other paper-based tests have shifted to forms that that can vary in format and can be more effective in capturing students' learning abilities and progress. In the first validation studies, researchers often adopted a narrow focus on special knowledge stored in memory and testing and, sometimes, learning impairments were not taken into consideration. Due to the realization that there is the need for more thoroughly and timed evaluations, the TAE process today includes formal assessments, foundational assessments, other project assessments, and digital assessments. In the present day, artificial intelligence elevated assessments to the next level through making it possible to develop adaptive test and automatic grading that increases the accuracy in testing, efficiency, and inclusiveness in delivering consistent determining performance of student. This constant evolution is because of the dynamism in the requirement and emphasis of modern education.

3.1 Brief History of Educational Assessments

Like most features of our society and education, the history of assessments reflects the society and teaching practices. At first, the examinations were completely unsophisticated, and included observation only and oral check-ups. When education structures evolved and became more structured so did the process of assessments (Glaser & Silver, 1994). Standardized testing became popular in the early part of the 20th century as a means of trying to get at the achievement of large numbers of students in a systematic and organized manner. These were usually in form of multiple choice, and their purpose was meant to standardize the assessment of the desired knowledge and skills (Nettles, 2019). However, in the mid of the twentieth century formative assessments came into light emphasizing on the kind of assessments that are used to track student's progress and to inform the instruction. This led towards moving the focus to improvement of teaching and learning from concentrating on the mere measurement of accomplishment. Thus, with certain evaluation problems being identified during the 20th century, such forms of assessment as performance-based assessments, portfolios, and authentic assessments appeared towards the end of the century.

3.2 The Limitations of Conventional Assessment Methods

The conventional forms of assessment as mentioned above are quite popular and have their shortcomings as highlighted below. Several questions include understanding of concepts; these tests are also known to reinforce memory rather than the ability to reason, solve problems, or think creatively (Mohammed-Marzouk 2012). Furthermore, these traditional approaches tend to be uniform and homogenous and do not consider the learning differences, rates and requirements of the learners (Swiecki et al., 2022). Traditional assessments also give infrequent and delayed feedback in most cases in form of scores that may not help students learn as they are slow and sometimes not very specific (Ira & Assessment, 1995). However, these methods seem to fail in testing skills and competencies such as teamwork, other interpersonal skills and problem-solving skills that are very much important in the contemporary workplace. Last but not the least, the grading of the subjective assessments including the essays can also be off the mark due to probability of biasness from the side of the teacher.

3.3 The Shift Toward Digital and Automated Assessments

Technological advancement has highly affected the assessment methods, where most of them have gone digital and automated (Langenfeld et al., 2022). Such a shift has been realised following the occurrence of several fundamental changes that include the following. Engaging and creatively constructed assessments are possible due to the existing advanced computing therefore accommodation, enhanced software, and the reason of having access to the internet. Also, the need for efficiency has been an important factor which e-assessments enhance by eliminating time-consuming processes like grading, data processing and report writing compared to paper based assessments. This shift has also been brought by the demand of personalized learning where with the use of digital assessments, learning can be customized to fit a particular student and more feedback is provided. In addition, the availability also stands as another strength as digital assessments can get in touch with more students including the learners with learning disabilities or difficulties and those learners in rural areas through online platforms and mobile applications. Finally, it has continual assessment capabilities which do not only allow for more frequent and regular formative assessments but also eliminates substantial paper-pencil based high stakes tests.

3.4 The Emergence of AI in Educational Evaluations

Considering the opportunities created by the development and implementation of digital assessment, AI can become the basis for significant improvements in educational evaluations and correction of many shortcomings currently existing in traditional forms of assessment. Thus, AI provides several main benefits to the assessment field. The first advantage is that of personalisation: through vast datasets concerning students, AI algorithms can devise rather specific learning profiles and, therefore, deliver personalized assessments and individual feedback can be provided. Also, self-assessing through AI-assisted assessments offers feedback immediately, allowing a student to notice his or her weaknesses and change the pattern of learning instantly (Shaik et al., 2022).

4. AI-POWERED ASSESSMENT TOOLS

The use of Artificial Intelligence in designing assessments for learning has seen the development of several effective tools with a lot of potential for changing the modes of assessing the performance of learners. With these tools, one can have a variety of purposes, but ranging from automating the time-consuming process of grading assignments to adapting the learning process to the individual learner. Here's a closer examination of some of the most prominent AI-powered assessment tools:

4.1 Automated Grading Systems

Automated grading systems employ the use of artificial intelligence especially the machine learning technology to analyze and grade the written responses of students to objective items such as multiple choice, true/false and fill in blanks. The established systems are trained with voluminous data sets of prior graded responses which facilitate identification of the right methods of grading or correct answers hence enhancing the speed and accuracy of grading novel responses (Erickson et al., 2020). It is common to identifying increased efficiency as one of the key advantages of automated grading system because they can take a lot of time of educators. This enables teachers to dedicate their time and efforts to more effective processes like offering comments, creating an interesting lesson plan, or attend to the needs of different learners (Marcelo et al., 2021). Moreover, it eliminates the possibilities of bias and unfair grading as it will always grade all students according to a set of already designed rules. Another advantage of feedback is that it is immediate which enables the students to find their error statuses and work independent of the teacher. Further, these systems provide knowledge on overall class performance as well as individual's performance that can greatly assist the educators in making informed instructional decisions.

4.2 Adaptive Learning Platforms

Educational technologies which incorporate adaptive learning come as one of the biggest steps forward when it comes to personalised teaching and learning with the help of artificial intelligence. They observe one's learning progress and modify the level of the following content depending on the performance of the student. First, learners sit for sample assessments to determine their existing competencies and knowledge level. The platform then develops a plan, providing material and tasks that would be most suitable for the child paralleling the areas that need most work. Highlighting the benefits of the platform, it can be mentioned that it helps students work with the material and make the required changes to the difficulty level during the learning process. The students who are proficient in the tasks are provided with other more complex materials while the slow learners are given extra practice and assistance. It also is important to pinpoint the advantages of the usage of the adaptive learning platforms. It provides a learning style that makes it easier to comprehend, interested and to be able to remember what has been learnt. It was designed in such a way that students can learn step by step while they are also reinforced in their understanding of previous lessons on the topic before they proceed to the next level. This enhances growth of the pupils since it does not frustrate the learners as is the case with other linear conventional methods.

4.3 AI-Driven Quiz and Test Generators

Systems that generate quizzes and tests using advanced Artificial Intelligence techniques are reshaping the generation and the delivery of tests and quizzes in teaching and learning. These tools help free the educators' time in terms of creating the assessments, not to mention making the assessments of higher quality, relevant and more engaging for the students – all through the help of artificial intelligence. How AI-Driven Quiz and Test Generators Work: These systems start with text documents created by educators including but not limited to chapter excerpts from text books, lecture notes and web resources. The processes of AI involve meaning- making by extracting important concepts and words from texts as well as relations among them. From this analysis the AI creates a myriad of assessment questions, multiple choice, true/false, match the columns, complete the following, and short answer questions. Hence the four types of questions are geared towards testing diverse facets of students' comprehension ranging from depth of knowledge to problem-solving abilities. Nevertheless, tutors defend the right to make the final decision about students' performance's evaluation. It allows them to choose the kind of questions they desire, the level of difficulty of the questions, editing and modifying questions and even including their own set of questions.

4.5 Examples of AI Tools in Real Educational Settings

The use of AI technology has bright prospects for application and indeed, it is already penetrating educational environments, bringing considerable changes into the learning-teaching process. A good example is Duolingo, which is a language learning application available for download, it incorporates the use of artificial intelligence in delivering lesson plans, monitoring the learners' progress and modifying the strategies used according to the learning preferences of the learners as noted by Hacker and Carnegie in 2012. Another typical example is Khan academy which is a non-for-profit venture that offer abundant lessons and practice activities online. Some of the applications of AI in Khan Academy include recommendation and feedbacks given to the student (Murphy et al., 2023). Also, Grammarly helps as an AI writing tool that assists students to improve on their language errors and writing and style by correcting it and offering feedbacks instantly (Ghufron and Rosyida, 2018). For instance, Google Classroom, which is one of the LMSs currently used at a large scale, has integrated several AI functions for automatic checking of assignments, plagiarism identification, and even for recommendations of students' learning (Phuoc et al. 2021). Lastly, Coursera, which is an online learning platform that partners with universities and organizations leveraging AI to very learner's experience and provide them with smart outcome assessments (Littenberg-Tobias & Reich, 2020). These examples show how AI is transforming education and enhance learning processes and student's achievements. The functionalities, advantages and challenges of the main AI-powered assessment tools are described in Table 1 below.

Table 1. AI-powered assessment tools - functionalities, advantages and challenges

Tool	How It Works	Benefits	Challenges
Automated Grading Systems	Uses AI to evaluate objective assessments (multiple choice, true/false, fill-in-the-blank) by learning patterns from graded responses.	- Increased efficiency - Objective and consistent evaluation - Immediate feedback - Data-driven insights for targeted interventions	- Limited scope (difficulty with subjective, complex responses) - Over-reliance on keywords - Ethical considerations (bias in training data)
Adaptive Learning Platforms	Tracks student performance and adjusts the difficulty of content in real-time, providing personalized learning paths based on diagnostic assessments.	- Personalized learning experience - Mastery-based progression - Data-driven insights for educators	- High cost and implementation requirements - Data privacy and security concerns - Need for teacher training and support
AI-Driven Quiz and Test Generators	Analyzes learning materials and automatically generates questions in various formats (MCQs, true/false, matching, etc.), with customization options for educators.	- Time savings for educators - Alignment with learning objectives - Increased question variety and quality - Reduced bias in assessment design	- Over-reliance on keywords - Struggles with creativity and higher-order thinking questions - Ethical considerations in question design
Intelligent Tutoring Systems (ITS)	Acts as virtual tutors with expert models, student models, and tutoring models that provide personalized, interactive instruction and real-time feedback.	- Personalized instruction - Targeted support - Adapts to student learning pace	- Complex setup - High development cost - Requires accurate modeling of student learning processes
Real-World AI Tools	- Duolingo: Personalized language lessons with AI - Khan Academy: AI-based recommendations and feedback - Grammarly: Real-time writing assistance - Google Classroom: AI for grading and learning recommendations - Coursera: Adaptive assessments and personalized learning	- Personalized learning experiences - Immediate feedback - Scalability and accessibility for a wide range of learners	- Data privacy and security - Potential for over-dependence on AI for instructional design and evaluation

5. PERSONALIZATION AND ADAPTIVITY IN AI ASSESSMENTS

Current teaching techniques do not always allow teachers to bring in innovative approaches that will fit all students. To solve this problem, the concept of personalized learning, which entails flexibility in designing instructional lessons depending on students' learning capabilities and inclinations, has been developed. This is where AI is rapidly finding its application especially due to the flexibility that is offered by the system in the general application of the approach, especially in the flexible assessments for students. Using of several crucial strategies, AI-powered personalized learning assessment aim at enhancing the learning process as discussed below. Another traditional technique is adaptive testing, which apply changes to the test questions depending on the reactions of the student. For example, if the student responds correctly, the system offers more difficult questions; conversely, the system offers less difficult questions or helps the student if he or she is having difficulties. This makes some assessments impossibly difficult while others too easy thus ensuring that every student's potential is fully exploited. A potentially useful other strategy is selection of questions to address on a per-individual basis. AI goes through a large population of assessment items to select those that should be useful to the learner's past learning experiences, current knowledge, and future learning plans. It enables member teachers to be able to concentrate on teaching of content that is most relevant to the student, thus enabling a more comprehensive study.

Furthermore, some of the AI-based assessment delivery systems take into consideration learning style to format the questions in a way that they are more engaging and easier to comprehend due to the learning style of the candidate. However, real-time feedback and hints are also considered the critical factors to achieve the intended performance. It gives an instant quantitative and qualitative feedback to the answers given by the students and the areas where they are more confused, which in return helps an effective and personalized hint to the students and explanation which leads them to the whole-some understanding of the correct answer, and thus develop deeper thinking. Some of the universities and organizations have already used application of artificial solution in personalized learning paths. For example, Khan Academy, a non-profit organization, takes advantage of artificial intelligence in course delivery to espouse performance data to recommend the lessons and exercises to students depending on their level of understanding thus enhancing personalized learning (Murphy et al., 2023). Hacker & Carnegie (2012 cited in Duolingo) explained that Duolingo, which is a language learning application for mobile devices also self-adapts the lessons to the users' pace and learning style. Another example is Carnegie Learning – this company specializes in tutoring software based on artificial intelligence that adjusts to the student's rate and ways of learning to help him grasp the matter as effectively as possible, together with instant feedback (Ritter et al., 2007).

6. REAL-TIME FEEDBACK AND CONTINUOUS ASSESSMENT

Technological application in real-time feedback will revolutionize education since it provides instant feedback on performance by the students. As it is clear, traditional assessment practices are characterized by delayed feedback, which is counterproductive. As opposed to this conventional style of learning, the use of AI driven tools can ensure that a student receives prompt feedback and can thus understand his/her proficiency as well as his/her disadvantages. It also allows students to correct misconceptions as soon as possible to guarantee better education outcomes and a more suitable learning experience for the students

(Kerimbayev et al., 2023). The importance of feedback cannot be overemphasized especially where it is given as and when due. When feedback is timely, the students can easily identify what they are good at and what is difficult for them to understand so that they can change their learning approaches, ask the teacher for clarification on concepts or content that was taught in class and cement their understanding (Chen et al., 2006). On the other hand, that such feedback is not immediate in most cases can have an unpleasant effect of reinforcing misconceptions among learners as they may get frustrated and discouraged in the process. Feedback is also useful to remind the students on what is expected of them within a certain period, keep the students motivated and gain further knowledge about the topic of concern.

Instant feedback is facilitated by the AI as a central component of the provision of personalized experience. Machine learning algorithms for assessment can identify answers or errors, and suggest corrective actions that should be taken instantly. This kind of feedback enables learners correct their mistakes when the subject content is fresh and is more effective than providing feedback weeks after the tests have been written. AI allows students to first come up with different solutions and receive feedback almost instantly; students understand that making mistakes is part of growing or developing the 'growth mindset' (Wong, 2023). Also, AI algorithms deal with large data and assess the performance patterns and trends of the students, which helps the educators to give appropriate feedback and recommendations for improvement in resources or help in terms of learning impairments. It is also helping to move away from the use of simplistic assessment as end of topic, end of unit, end of term tests. Formative assessment is one that is done from time to time during the learning process to check the progress of the learners while summative assessment is done at the end of the learning process to measure the achievements of the learners. The use of AI enables the monitoring of the progress made by students at every stage in real-time, hence giving insights on the learning factor and areas that the students may require assistance in. Knowledge from such data enables instructors to provide individualized assistance and set the learning and teaching rate according to the students' rate and capacity (Mohammad et al., 2023; Choi et al., 2024; Chow et al., 2024).

Some examples include the following which give illustration of real time feedback using artificial intelligence. Applying artificial intelligence in the Carnegie Learning's MATHia, students' progress in mathematics is supervised and they are provided with immediate feedback and personalised instruction, which leads to higher rates of achievement and self-esteem (Ritter et al., 2007; Walker et al., 2009). For instance, in a language learning application such as Duolingo, artificial intelligence is used to give feedback in exercises immediately and speed up how fast one can learn a new language as well as enhance the retention levels of the students (Ahn, 2012; Loewen et al., 2019). To handle numerous papers of students, EdX incorporates an intelligent essay grader that gives feedbacks in large number as well as refines the writing skills of the learners instantly (Reilly et al., 2014; Klobucar et al., 2013). Pearson's REVEL program delivers feedback on quizzes and assignments instantaneously increasing the knowledge of students and passiveness (Revel, 2023; Pearson Results Team, 2023). Feedback Fruits' peer review tool relies on the AI in giving constructive feedback to peers which in turn leads to better feedback and productivity (Nguyen, 2022; Collett, 2023). The cases explain how the use of intelligent real-time feedbacking can revolutionise the learning process by offering timely, customised and actionable feedback forwards more productive and interesting learning encounter.

7. OVERCOMING CHALLENGES IN AI-DRIVEN ASSESSMENTS

From the current analysis, handling of challenges is very important to achieve the goals of implementation of artificial intelligence assessments in the education sector. It is also an area of significant concern, because AI algorithms often reiterate the bias and then prejudiced found in the training data set means poor fairness. To mitigate this, it is imperative to use various datasets and perform self- audits now and then to enhance fairness. Further, data privacy also raises important considerations with matters like security to ensure the integrity of student data, which requires certain measures such as encryption and meeting regulatory requirements. The inclusion of AI tools can sometimes pose challenges in integration, this is because there must be compliance to education standards for better integration, and providing enough training to educators can also solve the problem. It means that accuracy and reliability are paramount for proper AI evaluations and therefore, it is required to modify algorithms respectively and implement strict people supervision on a regular basis. The above challenges can however be mitigated if AI assessments are implemented in education and this will lead to improvement of students' experience, equity, security and accuracy.

7.1 Ethical Considerations and Privacy and Data Security in AI

Algorithmic bias is one of the significant factors of worry in hiring AI to serve in the education system. For example, while becoming increasingly sophisticated using large sets of data, AI systems may also 'learn' biases and discriminations present in data samples if the sets are not mainstream (Chen, 2023). For instance, an assessment tool developed by an artificial neural network Looking primarily at data from affluent school may end up disadvantage students from less privileged schools. The best way to approach and correct it is to use correct samples of datasets, intensify the process of detecting and correcting the bias, and explain the process of AI in the best possible ways. It is important to strive to be fair and equal in our selection process not only by overcoming the problems of the algorithms but also for the learning styles of all children. This includes assistance to learners with special needs, special attention to, learners with Limited English Proficiency LEP, and learners from diverse economic background. To promote equity some approaches, include; adopting UDL when developing assessments, use of accommodations such as Text to speech and or other input methods for learners with disability and or design culturally sensitive formative and summative assessments without prejudice.

Another observation to the incorporation of AI tools is that it calls for adjustment or adaptation on both the side of the teacher and the students. Teachers require training on how to incorporate the tools into their practice and how to make sense of them as a part of teaching. While working with AI driven assessments, the students themselves need to be trained to understand what the tool is telling them and how to work with it. Teachers and students must both adopt a growth mindset for utilizing the AI devices because the technology employed is there to facilitate learning and not to override the human brain's capability to make decisions. Other concerns relate to privacy and data protection as AI-based evaluations imply the collection of significant amounts of student data, including personal and academic information. It is needed to adhere to data minimization, anonymize or de-identify data and use proper security measures about data storage and transfers. The information about learners should be protected to the required standards as required by the privacy laws including the FERPA for the U. S and the GDPR for the European region.

7.2 Case Studies: Addressing Challenges in AI Integration

Case Study 1: bias mitigation in IBM's Watson Tutor (Afzal et al., 2019; Afzal et al., 2018).

The journey of IBM's Watson Tutor, an AI-based tool used in education, it started with problems of biases in the feedback given and the suggestions provided. Biased performance was also realized in early forms of the system with the minority students being most affected. To tackle this, IBM enlarged the variability of the training data sets, as well as availed fairness algorithms to identify biased patterns and rectify them. Bias checks were also set up recurring, so that the best practices of AI's fairness could be maintained regularly. Such measures enhanced the fairness of the feedback a great deal in a way that all the students in the class will receive more credible support.

Case Study 2: Data Privacy in Classcraft's AI-Powered Assessment Tools (Huang, 2023)

Classcraft integrated technologies in form of artificial intelligence assessment to improve learners' morale and monitor performance. One vital challenge that was discussed was how the data of students that would be collected would be protected. Classcraft overcome this challenge by putting great measure in encryption; storage of the data; and compliance with General Data Protection Regulation. They also had well-stipulated policies on usage of data and ensured that consumers especially students and parents gave their informed consent. These steps-maintained trust and adherence creating favourable ground for Classcraft to apply the AI technology in learning without compromising on security.

Case Study 3: Integration Challenges in DreamBox Learning (Renz & Hilbig, 2020)

DreamBox Learning was to suppose its adaptive math program with school systems but it faced challenge in integration of its Math system into Learning Management Systems (LMS) and other educational technologies. To counter this, DreamBox has ensured the creation of integration tools that are flexible as well as ensuring that teachers were trained abundantly with technical support while implementing the integration tools. This approach helped avoid the resistance when utilizing DreamBox's AI tools to make learning process better and achieve better results in mathematics among students.

Case Study 4: Accuracy and Reliability in Turnitin's AI-Based Plagiarism Detection (Liang et al., 2023)

As part of efforts to improve on academic integrity, Turnitin incorporated an Artificial Intelligence plagiarism detection tool. Hence, it was important to achieve high reliability of this system in terms of accuracy. Turnitin has been able to do this by enhancing algorithms constantly, testing and approving the effectiveness of Turnitin and again including feedback from users to improve the amount of accuracy. The involvement of human in the decision-making process was applied for checking the cases with high coefficients, which were found by AI. These efforts were achieved with improvements in the efficiency of a plagiarism detection system to lower false positives/negatives and maintaining the academic honesty.

Case Study 5: Adaptability in Khan Academy's AI Tools (Academy, 2023)

Khan Academy used artificial intelligence to deliver content, the company was facing a problem how to adapt it to the different learning approaches and different academic level. They responded to this challenge by using algorithms that were learned adaptively and determined content difficulty according to the performance of the students and feedback loops to refine adaptability. Engagement in developmental activities using AI tools enabled the students to better prepare and allowed the tools to meet a variety of learning needs more appropriately and efficiently in contributing to the betterment of the educational dispensation ranging from the basic level to other higher levels. The following list encapsulates the findings of the case studies as elaborated below in Table 2.

Table 2. Challenges, solutions, and outcomes of AI integration in educational tools

Case Study	Background	Challenge	Solution	Outcome
Bias Mitigation in IBM's Watson Tutor	IBM's Watson Tutor, an AI educational tool, faced bias in feedback.	Biased performance in recommendations, especially affecting students from diverse backgrounds.	Enhanced diversity in training datasets, implemented fairness algorithms, and conducted regular bias audits.	Improved equity in feedback, ensuring unbiased and accurate support for all students.
Data Privacy in Classcraft's AI-Powered Assessment Tools	Classcraft developed AI tools to enhance engagement and performance monitoring.	Ensuring privacy and security of student data.	Implemented encryption protocols, secure storage, GDPR compliance, and obtained explicit consent from students and parents.	Privacy measures-maintained trust, enabling safe and effective use of AI for student learning.
Integration Challenges in DreamBox Learning	DreamBox, an adaptive math program, aimed to integrate AI-driven assessments with school systems.	Schools struggled to integrate DreamBox with LMS and other technologies.	Developed flexible integration tools, provided educator training, and technical support.	Successful integration enhanced educational experiences and improved student math outcomes.
Accuracy and Reliability in Turnitin's AI-Based Plagiarism Detection	Turnitin introduced AI-based plagiarism detection to improve academic integrity.	Ensuring accuracy and reliability of the AI in identifying plagiarism.	Continuous algorithm updates, validation processes, and human oversight for complex cases.	Improved accuracy, reduced false positives/negatives, and upheld academic integrity.
Adaptability in Khan Academy's AI Tools	Khan Academy developed AI tools for personalized learning experiences.	Adapting AI tools to different learning styles and educational levels.	Used adaptive algorithms and feedback loops to adjust content difficulty in real-time.	Enhanced tool adaptability, improving personalized learning outcomes for diverse students.

8. THE ROLE OF TEACHERS AND EDUCATORS IN AI ASSESSMENTS

Teachers are key stakeholders in the decision, use, implementation, success and effectiveness of Intelligent Adaptive Assessment with AI. Although the AI technology provides many effective and individualized assessment strategies, teachers play decisive roles in supervising and interceding these analysis outcomes (Diliberti et al., 2024). They play a crucial role in deciding which AI tools should be used in education and how these tools can support instead of overcome the presented goals. Instructors explain the outcome of AI-based feedback to learners to assist them in making better sense of it. Furthermore, the role of teachers in checking the bias and accuracy of the AI in completing the tasks as well as modifying the procedures in response to the students' performance. Such inclusion of the AI tools by teachers can help in ensuring that the assessments that are given are more meaningful and supportive to learners. When speaking of an AI environment teaching plays a different role as the definition above has mentioned it. AI can do job such as grading, providing feedback and marking which creates time for teacher to ensure deeper learning takes place such as project based and group work.

9. THE FUTURE OF AI IN EDUCATIONAL ASSESSMENT

The future of the AI in assessment of students has the potential to revolutionise education in terms of better, faster and more insightful assessment models. We are thus expecting new generations of AI technology capable of delivering real-time feedback that meets individual learning capabilities and interests. Such changes will most probably result in enhancing the flexibility and interactivity of the assessment methods, as well as the extent of educators' understanding of students' achievements and needs. AI use of large datasets increases its predictive capabilities, which will enable pro-active actions to be taken, as well as support (Shaik et al., 2022). What is promising about this is that it can open a new era in making evaluations not only more engaging, but also fair and more in tune with the needs of multimodal learners. Thus, there are several key trends in AI technology which will further define the future of educational assessment. With the help of Natural Language Processing (NLP) AI will be able to evaluate new and more complicated skills like writing, speaking and critical thinking. The notion of Explainable AI (XAI) learned from works in this paper's literature review to enhance transparency for educators to comprehend AI algorithms and augment trust. Higher personalisation and dynamism of the algorithms will address learning style diversities, and a learning analytics multimodal approach will include a broad range of student performance aspects.

10. CONCLUSION

This results in the emergence of a new age of assessment which is student centered, data informed and flexible enough to meet the needs of diverse learners as fuel by artificial intelligence. As this chapter has detailed, traditional forms of assessment, which many consider to be biomechanistic and standardized, are now up for some new experiences facilitated by AI which comprise flexibility, individualization, and immediacy. New generation adaptive learning platforms based on artificial intelligence can significantly change the Approach to assessment. These platforms involve the adjustment of the level of difficulty depending on the learners' responses to the questions and this makes the students to be challenged enough resulting to an effective assessment activity. Furthermore, AI's data issue capability can be used to identify the learning patterns and can provide suggestions and feedback information to students and teachers/educators. AI is not a threat to teachers but should be seen as an assistant, an ally that can help teachers to do more and distribute their time between administrative and creative endeavours which include the first and direct interaction with the learners. Finally, for AI to be implemented successfully in educational assessments, it must be approached strategically and with the participation of many stakeholders. It is possible to continue to enhance and improve, to build open dialog and lively debate, and to prioritise the incorporation of relevant and important ethical factors, that future of AI and of assessments can be one where formative, good and informative, value-adding assessments are seen as an essential part of the learning process.

REFERENCES

Abdamia, N., Puteh, F., & Jantan Anua Jah, N. (2023). Investigating Learning Modalities among Diploma Students. *International Journal of Academic Research in Progressive Education and Development, 12*(2). Advance online publication. DOI: 10.6007/IJARPED/v12-i2/16552

Academy, K. (2023). Khan Academy's approach to the responsible development of AI. Khan Academy Blog. https://blog.khanacademy.org/aiguidelines/

Afzal, S., Shashidhar, V., Sindhgatta, R., & Sengupta, B. (2018). Impact of tutor errors on student engagement in a dialog based intelligent tutoring system. In Intelligent Tutoring Systems: 14th International Conference, ITS 2018, Montreal, QC, Canada, June 11–15, 2018 [Springer International Publishing.]. *Proceedings, 14*, 267–273.

Afzal, S., Dhamecha, T., Mukhi, N., Sindhgatta Rajan, R., Marvaniya, S., Ventura, M., & Yarbro, J. (2019). Development and deployment of a large-scale dialog-based intelligent tutoring system. In *Proceedings of the 2019 Conference of the North American Chapter of the Association for Computational Linguistics: Human Language Technologies*, Volume 2 (Industry Papers) (pp. 114-121). Association for Computational Linguistics.

Agrawal, A., & Reed, B. (2022). A Survey On Grading Format Of Automated Grading Tools For Programming Assignments. ICERI Proceedings. DOI: 10.21125/iceri.2022.1912

Ahn, L. V. (2012). *Proceedings of the 10th Conference of the Association for Machine Translation in the Americas: Keynote Presentations*. Association for Machine Translation in the Americas., https://www.aclweb.org/anthology/2012.amta-keynotes.4/

AL-Roomy, M. A. (2023). The Relationship Among Students' Learning Styles, Health Sciences Colleges, and Grade Point Average (GPA). *Advances in Medical Education and Practice, 14*(14), 203–213. DOI: 10.2147/AMEP.S395720 PMID: 36909353

Ayala-Pazmiño, M. (2023). Artificial Intelligence in Education: Exploring the Potential Benefits and Risks. 593 Digital Publisher CEIT, 8(3), 892–899. DOI: 10.33386/593dp.2023.3.1827

Brdesee, H., Alsaggaf, W., Aljohani, N. R., & Hassan, S.-U. (2022). Predictive Model Using a Machine Learning Approach for Enhancing the Retention Rate of Students At-Risk. *International Journal on Semantic Web and Information Systems, 18*(1), 1–21. DOI: 10.4018/IJSWIS.299859

Challis, D. (2005). Committing to quality learning through adaptive online assessment. *Assessment & Evaluation in Higher Education, 30*(5), 519–527. DOI: 10.1080/02602930500187030

Chen, J., Whittinghill, D. C., & Kadlowec, J. (2006). Using Rapid Feedback to Enhance Student Learning and Satisfaction. Proceedings. Frontiers in Education. 36th Annual Conference, 13-18. DOI: 10.1109/FIE.2006.322306

Chen, Z. (2023). Ethics and Discrimination in Artificial intelligence-enabled Recruitment Practices. *Humanities & Social Sciences Communications, 10*(1), 1–12. DOI: 10.1057/s41599-023-02079-x

Choi, S., McMaster, K. L., Kohli, N., Shanahan, E., Birinci, S., An, J., Duesenberg-Marshall, M. K., & Lembke, E. S. (2024). Longitudinal effects of data-based instructional changes for students with intensive learning needs: A piecewise linear–linear mixed-effects modeling approach. *Journal of Educational Psychology*, *116*(4), 608–628. DOI: 10.1037/edu0000853

Chow, S.-M., Lee, J., Park, J., Kuruppumullage Don, P., Hammel, T., Hallquist, M. N., Nord, E. A., Oravecz, Z., Perry, H. L., Lesser, L. M., & Pearl, D. K. (2024). Personalized Education through Individualized Pathways and Resources to Adaptive Control Theory-Inspired Scientific Education (iPRACTISE): Proof-of-Concept Studies for Designing and Evaluating Personalized Education. *Journal of Statistics and Data Science Education : An Official Journal of the of the American Statistical Association*, *32*(2), 1–42. DOI: 10.1080/26939169.2024.2302181

Collett, D. (2023). FeedbackFruits. Learning Management System. https://lms.unimelb.edu.au/learning-technologies/feedbackfruits

Diliberti, M. K., Schwartz, H. L., Doan, S., Shapiro, A., Rainey, L. R., & Lake, R. J. (2024). *Using Artificial Intelligence Tools in K–12 Classrooms*. RAND Corporation., https://www.rand.org/pubs/research_reports/RRA956-21.html

Erickson, J. A., Botelho, A. F., McAteer, S., Varatharaj, A., & Heffernan, N. T. (2020). The automated grading of student open responses in mathematics. *Proceedings of the Tenth International Conference on Learning Analytics & Knowledge*. DOI: 10.1145/3375462.3375523

Gao, R., Merzdorf, H. E., Anwar, S., Cynthia Hipwell, M., & Srinivasa, A. (2024). Automatic assessment of text-based responses in post-secondary education: A systematic review. Computers & Education. *Artificial Intelligence*, *6*, 100206–100206. DOI: 10.1016/j.caeai.2024.100206

Gernsbacher, M. A., Soicher, R. N., & Becker-Blease, K. A. (2020). Four Empirically Based Reasons Not to Administer Time-Limited Tests. *Translational Issues in Psychological Science*, *6*(2), 175–190. DOI: 10.1037/tps0000232 PMID: 32582819

Ghufron, M. A., & Rosyida, F. (2018). The Role of Grammarly in Assessing English as a Foreign Language (EFL) Writing. *Lingua Cultura*, *12*(4), 395. DOI: 10.21512/lc.v12i4.4582

Glaser, R., & Silver, E. (1994). Chapter 9: Assessment, Testing, and Instruction: Retrospect and Prospect. *Review of Research in Education*, *20*(1), 393–419. DOI: 10.3102/0091732X020001393

Hacker, S. B. H. (2014). Duolingo: Learning a language while translating the web (Doctoral dissertation, Doctoral Dissertation. Carnegie Mellon University).

Hahn, M. G., Navarro, S. M. B., De La Fuente Valentin, L., & Burgos, D. (2021). A Systematic Review of the Effects of Automatic Scoring and Automatic Feedback in Educational Settings. *IEEE Access : Practical Innovations, Open Solutions*, *9*, 108190–108198. DOI: 10.1109/ACCESS.2021.3100890

Hasnine, M. N., Nguyen, H. T., Tran, T. T. T., Bui, H. T. T., Akçapınar, G., & Ueda, H. (2023). A Real-Time Learning Analytics Dashboard for Automatic Detection of Online Learners'. *Affective Science*, *23*(9), 4243–4243. DOI: 10.3390/s23094243 PMID: 37177447

Hooda, M., Rana, C., Dahiya, O., Rizwan, A., & Hossain, M. S. (2022). Artificial Intelligence for Assessment and Feedback to Enhance Student Success in Higher Education. *Mathematical Problems in Engineering*, *2022*(5215722), 1–19. DOI: 10.1155/2022/5215722

How, M. L. (2019). Future-ready strategic oversight of multiple artificial superintelligence-enabled adaptive learning systems via human-centric explainable AI-empowered predictive optimizations of educational outcomes. *Big Data and Cognitive Computing*, *3*(3), 46.

Huang, L. (2023). Ethics of Artificial Intelligence in Education: Student Privacy and Data Protection. *Science Insights Education Frontiers*, *16*(2), 2577–2587. DOI: 10.15354/sief.23.re202

Ira., & Assessment, N J T F O. (1995). Standards for the Assessment of Reading and Writing. National Council of Teachers of English, 46(1), 125-125. DOI: 10.2307/358885

Joshi, N. (2020). Assessments: Different Types, Importance, & More. https://www.evelynlearning.com/what-are-assessments/

Kamalov, F., Calonge, D. S., & Gurrib, I. (2023). New Era of Artificial Intelligence in Education: Towards a Sustainable Multifaceted Revolution. *Sustainability (Basel)*, *15*(16), 12451. DOI: 10.3390/su151612451

Kamalov, F., & Gurrib, I. (2023). New Era of Artificial Intelligence in Education: Towards a Sustainable Multifaceted Revolution. Cornell University. https://doi.org//arxiv.2305.18303DOI: 10.48550

Karacı, A., Piri, Z., İbrahim, H., & Bilgici, G. (2018). Student Perceptions of an Intelligent Tutoring System: A Technology Acceptance Model Perspective. *International Journal of Computer Applications*, *182*(22), 31–36. DOI: 10.5120/ijca2018918025

Kerimbayev, N., Umirzakova, Z., Shadiev, R., & Jotsov, V. (2023). A student-centered approach using modern technologies in distance learning: A systematic review of the literature. *Smart Learning Environments*, *10*(1), 61. Advance online publication. DOI: 10.1186/s40561-023-00280-8

Kim, K. H., & Zabelina, D. (2015). Cultural bias in assessment: Can creativity assessment help? *The International Journal of Critical Pedagogy*, *6*(2). https://libjournal.uncg.edu/ijcp/article/download/301/856

Klobucar, A., Elliot, N., Deess, P., Rudniy, O., & Joshi, K. (2013). Automated scoring in context: Rapid assessment for placed students. *Assessing Writing*, *18*(1), 62–84. DOI: 10.1016/j.asw.2012.10.001

Koedinger, K. R., & Aleven, V. (2007). Exploring the Assistance Dilemma in Experiments with Cognitive Tutors. *Educational Psychology Review*, *19*(3), 239–264. DOI: 10.1007/s10648-007-9049-0

Langenfeld, T., Burstein, J., & von Davier, A. A. (2022). Digital-First Learning and Assessment Systems for the 21st Century. *Frontiers in Education*, *7*, 857604. Advance online publication. DOI: 10.3389/feduc.2022.857604

Liang, W., Yuksekgonul, M., Mao, Y., Wu, E., & Zou, J. (2023). GPT detectors are biased against non-native English writers. *Patterns (New York, N.Y.)*, *4*(7), 100779–100779. DOI: 10.1016/j.patter.2023.100779 PMID: 37521038

Littenberg-Tobias, J., & Reich, J. (2020). Evaluating access, quality, and equity in online learning: A case study of a MOOC-based blended professional degree program. *The Internet and Higher Education, 47*, 100759. DOI: 10.1016/j.iheduc.2020.100759

Liu, M. (2023). Exploring the Application of Artificial Intelligence in Foreign Language Teaching: Challenges and Future Development. SHS Web of Conferences, 168, 03025–03025. DOI: 10.1051/shsconf/202316803025

Loewen, S., Crowther, D., Isbell, D. R., Kim, K. M., Maloney, J., Miller, Z. F., & Rawal, H. (2019). Mobile-assisted language learning: A Duolingo case study. *ReCALL, 31*(3), 293–311. DOI: 10.1017/S0958344019000065

Ludwikowska, K. (2022). Competency-Based Tests as a Tool for Teacher Evaluation in Higher Education Institutions. *Central European Management Journal, 30*(3), 85–111. DOI: 10.7206/cemj.2658-0845.83

Ma, X., & Jiang, C. (2023). On the Ethical Risks of Artificial Intelligence Applications in Education and Its Avoidance Strategies. *Journal of Education Humanities and Social Sciences, 14*, 354–359. DOI: 10.54097/ehss.v14i.8868

Maghsudi, S., Lan, A., Xu, J., & van der Schaar, M. (2021). Personalized Education in the Artificial Intelligence Era: What to Expect Next. *IEEE Signal Processing Magazine, 38*(3), 37–50. DOI: 10.1109/MSP.2021.3055032

Matos, G. (2023). Demystifying Artificial Intelligence: Understanding its Evolution, Key Areas, and Fundamentals. Medium; Share! por Ateliê de Software. https://share.atelie.software/demystifying-artificial-intelligence-understanding-its-evolution-key-areas-and-fundamentals-2dd875364ea3

Méndez-Ortega, M. G., Herrera-Granda, E. P., Malte, A. E. P., & Enríquez, R. B. H. (2021). Supervision and Control of Students during Online Assessments Applying Computer Vision Techniques: A Systematic Literature Review. *Universal Journal of Educational Research, 9*(5), 1000–1013. DOI: 10.13189/ujer.2021.090513

Millikin, C. C. (2023). Future-Proof your Instructional Design with Universal Design for Learning and Translanguaging. *Literacy Information and Computer Education Journal, 14*(1), 3709–3720. DOI: 10.20533/licej.2040.2589.2023.0488

Mohammed-Marzouk, M. R. (2012). Teaching and Learning in Iraq: A Brief History. *The Educational Forum, 76*(2), 259–264. DOI: 10.1080/00131725.2011.653869

Murphy, D. H., Little, J. L., & Bjork, E. L. (2023). The Value of Using Tests in Education as Tools for Learning—Not Just for Assessment. *Educational Psychology Review, 35*(3), 89. Advance online publication. DOI: 10.1007/s10648-023-09808-3

Murphy, R., Gallagher, L., Krumm, A., Mislevy, J., & Hafter, A. (2023), Khan Academy in Schools. SRI Education https://s3.amazonaws.com/KA-share/impact/khan-academy-implementation-report-2014-04-15.pdf

Nettles, M. T. (2019). History of Testing in the United States: Higher Education. *The Annals of the American Academy of Political and Social Science, 683*(1), 38–55. DOI: 10.1177/0002716219847139

Nguyen, N. (2022) FeedbackFruits Impact Report 2022. https://feedbackfruits.com/blog/infographic-feedbackfruits-impact-report-2022

Pearson Results Team. (2021) Enhance student success with Revel. https://www.pearson.com/ped-blogs/meaningful-outcomes/2021/05/enhance-student-success-with-revel.html

Phuoc Khai, M.A., T., & Thi Nam Thi M.A., N. (. (2021). THE APPLICATION OF GOOGLE CLASSROOM TO MOTIVATE ENGLISH NON-MAJORED STUDENTS. *International Journal of Advanced Research*, *9*(03), 47–55. DOI: 10.21474/IJAR01/12552

Reilly, E. D., Stafford, R. E., Williams, K. M., & Corliss, S. B. (2014). Evaluating the validity and applicability of automated essay scoring in two massive open online courses. *International Review of Research in Open and Distance Learning*, *15*(5). Advance online publication. DOI: 10.19173/irrodl.v15i5.1857

Renz, A., & Hilbig, R. (2020). Prerequisites for artificial intelligence in further education: Identification of drivers, barriers, and business models of educational technology companies. *International Journal of Educational Technology in Higher Education*, *17*(1), 14. Advance online publication. DOI: 10.1186/s41239-020-00193-3

Revel - Interactive Content Learning Tool. (2023). https://www.pearson.com/uk/educators/higher-education-educators/products-and-services/course-resources-and-content/revel.html

Ritter, S., Anderson, J. R., Koedinger, K. R., & Corbett, A. (2007). Cognitive Tutor: Applied research in mathematics education. *Psychonomic Bulletin & Review*, *14*(2), 249–255. DOI: 10.3758/BF03194060 PMID: 17694909

Rupali, M., & Amit, P. (2017). A Review Paper on General Concepts of "Artificial Intelligence and Machine Learning.". *IARJSET*, *4*(4), 79–82. DOI: 10.17148/IARJSET/NCIARCSE.2017.22

Scarfe, P., Watcham, K., Clarke, A., & Roesch, E. (2024). A real-world test of artificial intelligence infiltration of a university examinations system: A "Turing Test" case study. *PLoS One*, *19*(6), e0305354–e0305354. DOI: 10.1371/journal.pone.0305354 PMID: 38923941

Shaik, T., Tao, X., Li, Y., Dann, C., McDonald, J., Redmond, P., & Galligan, L. (2022). A Review of the Trends and Challenges in Adopting Natural Language Processing Methods for Education Feedback Analysis. *IEEE Access : Practical Innovations, Open Solutions*, *10*, 56720–56739. DOI: 10.1109/ACCESS.2022.3177752

Steiss, J., Tate, T., Graham, S., Cruz, J., Hebert, M., Wang, J., Moon, Y., Tseng, W., Warschauer, M., & Olson, C. B. (2024). Comparing the quality of human and ChatGPT feedback of students' writing. *Learning and Instruction*, *91*, 101894–101894. DOI: 10.1016/j.learninstruc.2024.101894

Sun, S., Wu, X., & Xu, T. (2023). A Theoretical Framework for a Mathematical Cognitive Model for Adaptive Learning Systems. *Behavioral Sciences (Basel, Switzerland)*, *13*(5), 406–406. DOI: 10.3390/bs13050406 PMID: 37232643

Swiecki, Z., Khosravi, H., Chen, G., Martinez-Maldonado, R., Lodge, J. M., Milligan, S., Selwyn, N., & Gašević, D. (2022). Assessment in the age of artificial intelligence. *Computers and Education: Artificial Intelligence*, *3*(3), 100075. DOI: 10.1016/j.caeai.2022.100075

Sze, V., Chen, Y.-H., Yang, T.-J., & Emer, J. S. (2017). Efficient Processing of Deep Neural Networks: A Tutorial and Survey. *Proceedings of the IEEE, 105*(12), 2295–2329. DOI: 10.1109/JPROC.2017.2761740

Taylor, D. L., Yeung, M., & Bashet, A. Z. (2021). Personalized and Adaptive Learning. Innovative Learning Environments in STEM Higher Education, 17–34. DOI: 10.1007/978-3-030-58948-6_2

Walker, E., Rummel, N., & Koedinger, K. R. (2009). Integrating Collaboration And Intelligent Tutoring Data In The Evaluation Of A Reciprocal Peer Tutoring Environment. *Research and Practice in Technology Enhanced Learning, 04*(03), 221–251. DOI: 10.1142/S179320680900074X

Wong, S. S. H. (2023). Deliberate Erring Improves Far Transfer of Learning More Than Errorless Elaboration and Spotting and Correcting Others' Errors. *Educational Psychology Review, 35*(1), 16. Advance online publication. DOI: 10.1007/s10648-023-09739-z PMID: 36776579

Zhai, X., Chu, X., Chai, C. S., Jong, M. S. Y., Istenic, A., Spector, M., Liu, J.-B., Yuan, J., & Li, Y. (2021). A Review of Artificial Intelligence (AI) in Education from 2010 to 2020. *Complexity, 2021*(8812542), 1–18. DOI: 10.1155/2021/8812542

Zheng, C., Yuan, K., Guo, B., Hadi Mogavi, R., Peng, Z., Ma, S., & Ma, X. (2024, May). Charting the future of AI in project-based learning: a Co-design exploration with students. In *Proceedings of the 2024 CHI Conference on Human Factors in Computing Systems* (pp. 1-19).

Chapter 12
ChatGPT as an Automated Essay Scoring System in Comparison With Human Raters in Malaysia

Marwan Abd Jal
Universiti Teknologi Malaysia, Malaysia

Si Na Kew
https://orcid.org/0000-0001-6648-6806
Universiti Teknologi Malaysia, Malaysia

Ghazali Bunari
Universiti Teknologi Malaysia, Malaysia

ABSTRACT

This research compares ChatGPT, known as AI chatbot, with human raters to assess its capability as an automated scoring system in grading essays. The objective is to determine whether ChatGPT can effectively evaluate elements such as grammar, coherence, and organisation in essays comparable to human raters. To ensure the evaluation aligns with the Malaysia's education system, this research has utilised written essays from an English university course as a sample. This approach helps the researchers understand how well ChatGPT performs within Malaysian's education context. Data were collected using ChatGPT and human rater. The findings of this study revealed that ChatGPT can be used as an automated scoring system because there is no significant difference between human raters in assessing grammar and organization. However, monitoring from humans is needed as there are significant differences in assessing coherence. It is believed that the findings from this study can help the university and the Ministry of Education to be clear about the ChatGPT as an automated scoring system.

INTRODUCTION

In Malaysia, written essays are essentially graded by human raters who always consider important factors such as grammar, coherence, and organization. These evaluators asses quality and adherence to academic standards, which is quite a rigorous, time-consuming and potentially biased task. In response

DOI: 10.4018/979-8-3693-9062-7.ch012

to changes in the education system, there is a growing need for more efficient and accurate essay grading systems (Barritt et al., 1986). As a result, various methods have been considered to facilitate this process each offering their own approaches and possibilities.

There have been significant transformations in educational practices, particularly in the assessment of written text, following the advent of information and communication technology (ICT). Among these changes, the introduction of Automated Essay Scoring (AES) systems stands out. These systems utilize advanced algorithms and artificial intelligence to evaluate written essays (Abdullah, 2017). For instance, ChatGPT, an AI language model developed by OpenAI, exemplifies this innovation. According to Piarulli et al. (2023), ChatGPT demonstrates remarkable potential in understanding and generating human-like text.

However, there is still an issue that depends on the efficiency of AES such as ChatGPT, which is the reliability and authenticity of the given system compared to human raters in Malaysian educational context. The following hypothesis is formulated as the aim of this study: The scoring of written essays by ChatGPT is equivalent to the scoring by human raters. This study aims to investigate whether there is a significant difference between ChatGPT and the evaluation by human raters. This is to answer the research question of whether automated scoring is both effective and feasible in the Malaysian context.

Background of study

Automated essay scoring is one of the new innovations in the teaching and interaction process that seeks to ease the process of grading of essays and at the same time eliminating evaluative prejudice and differential treatment. AES systems analyzed in this research include both standalone software and distributed services designed to evaluate and score written essays (Shermis & Burstein, 2003). Likewise, ChatGPT has a role in natural language processing and artificial intelligence schemes as well. Still, it is indeed for specific use in creating human-like informal or casual responses to conversational input, as well as creating texts, translating languages, creating other forms of creative content, and many others. This shows that there are numerous applications and approaches one can incorporate in language processing and communication among the many technologies that are available.

The continuity of carrying out artificial intelligence symbolize a new age for the Malaysian education system as it highlights new changes in different aspects of learning. This transformation is referred to in the literature as datafication, as defined in detail by Mayer et. al (2014). The advent of ChatGPT means that internet assisted learning can be learner and subject centric making the level of learner participation and tutor output even higher. Hence, the process of learning is improved by integrating ChatGPT into different learning environments for better versatility in learning practices. Further, it seems when integrating ChatGPT in the future, a few of the administrative tasks like registrations and managing resources would be automated to save the educators' time spent on inculcating necessary educational knowledge. Furthermore, through ChatGPT, the educators and the students are able to have access to so many quality learning resources that can really change the research outlook as well as the curriculum planning. This feature of AI tools demonstrates the importance of such tools in the improvement of educational processes and effectiveness.

A larger issue appears in the form of a well-rounded skill set necessary for proper communications and academic achievement that writing essays serves. Proficiency in grammar such as sentence structure, punctuation, verb agreement (Ramineni et al., 2013). With AES systems like ChatGPT, the elements pf communication above can be accurately evaluated using natural language processing and allows educators to provide constructive feedback that helps to improve student's writing mechanics. In addition, cohesion helps in improving the quality of arguments or ideas that one reads is essay writing, poor organization often results in waterfall effects on reader. Written coherence is the logical flow and connectivity of ideas within an essay, typically assessed by AES systems through evaluation of word choice that results in lexical cohesion and analysis for discourse markers (Shermis & Hamner, 2012). In the meantime, good organization goes beyond that and means to create cohesive paragraph with proper introduction, body, and conclusion. Organizational skills are assessed in an AES system to determine whether students have the ability to structure their writing appropriately, so they make claims or arguments persuasively.

In the traditional model, essay evaluation requires human raters to evaluate essays in terms of content and organization as well as coherence and execution based on their own established standards and personal judgement (Burstein et al., 2003). Human raters provide expert, nuanced feedback reflecting the complexity of students' writing abilities. Yet this could be time consuming, subject to bias and possibly inconsistently applied approach across raters (Shermis & Hamner, 2012). Information and communication technology reverted the traditional assessment practices by launching automated, semi-automated agents like AES. Moreover, AI models such as ChatGPT most clearly represent these systems, using algorithms to evaluate essays quickly and objectively in order for students to receive real time feedback on their writing (Brown et al,. 2020). Even though assessment that is driven by ICT makes it efficient, adaptable, upscaling and as a consequence face issue of deployment of AI models across teaching (Myint & Adams, 2019), the transferability between vast linguistic contestant were applied. Finally, critics worry about the capability of AES to recognize above the word aspects associated with writing creating and critical analysis (Perelman, 2021).

The adoption of ChatGPT as an Automated Essay Scoring system is a huge leap for the education sector in Malaysia regarding how they grade essays. This study seeks to see if there are any significant difference of ChatGPT in assessing the grammar, coherence and organization of essays done by students competing to the human raters. While the human raters are resourceful, they also have limitations as they might not be as consistent. According to Hussein et al,. (2019), there are a number of problems that can arise when assessing essays by humans, which can make the procedure unreliable. In comparison, ChatGPT applies the latest technology in providing accurate feedback in a consistent and objective manner, using natural language processing. This research is explicitly aimed at establishing the noted differences, and the findings will guide the stakeholders in understanding how such AI's can help in the grading of essays in Malaysia education.

Problem Statement

The use of artificial intelligence methods related to learning analytics and educational technology has been topic undertaking research in academic literature as well as numerous industry forums since 1970s (Rudolph et al, 2023). Automated essay scoring systems like ChatGPT could serve as valid educational evaluation tools, yet whether they can be relied upon and how accurate they have remained an important question that is much relative to human raters. As such, questioning has been aroused in whether or not the examination at this scale and subtlety will be replicated by algorithms as proficiently because it is through human raters related to limitations of AI within interpretative assessment (Jones, 2020). While educational institutions are now starting to leverage these technologies within their grading systems, it is imperative for ChatGPT's performance against human raters to be extensively tested and compared.

This study addresses a key research gap: the reliability of ChatGPT as an Automated Essay Scoring (AES) system within the Malaysian education system. While AI-based scoring has been explored in other contexts, there is limited research on its effectiveness compared to human raters in Malaysia. Even though this constructed AI system has been the focus of many research efforts, most focused on their ability to produce text content, generate ideas about it or distribute information which is novel. According to Per Yeadon (2023), ChatGPT output lowest scoring first-grade writings at approximately the same level as student essays from grade 1. Moreover, the extended general English writing skills enhancement system is not available because due to the fact that most of the researchers are commercialize, typically through systems such as Criterion and My Access! (Li et al., 2015). Hence, this gap in studies stresses the importance of a comprehensive review about how well AI technology may work, including automated grading and its exact overlap with Malaysia's evolving educational landscape.

This problem statement also touches on the fundamental gaps in understanding of how these systems use and work with such constructs as language, context or subjective assessment. In the educational field, improvements are carried out to predicate if they can be equally tested or substitutable for human grading (Doe, 2021). Also, it is important to examine the differences in scores and how this influences the outcome of students so that adequate integration can be organized fairly towards educational practices.

Comparing ChatGPT as an Automated Essay Scoring (AES) system with human raters is also crucial for addressing accuracy, efficiency, and educational equity in Malaysia. Human raters may exhibit inconsistencies and biases (Attali, 2013), while AES can provide objective and consistent scoring (Zhai, 2023), reducing grading workloads and offering faster feedback. This study is particularly relevant to Malaysian education, where teachers face increasing grading demands. It supports the Malaysia Education Blueprint 2013-2025 by promoting technology integration and exploring scalable assessment methods. Understanding ChatGPT's alignment with human scoring can guide policy decisions on AI adoption for fair and efficient essay evaluation (Ke & Ng, 2022).

While past research has indicated the potential use of Automated Essay Scoring and artificial intelligence in conducting writing assessments, there remains a lack of clarity in studies, particularly in the context of AI, such as ChatGPT evaluating essays when compared to human raters. Therefore, the primary objective of this study is to investigate the performance of ChatGPT as an AES with human rater.

Objectives of Study

This research consists of three research objectives shown below:

1. To compare the accuracy of ChatGPT as an automated essay scoring system against human raters in evaluating the grammar of written essays.
2. To compare the accuracy of ChatGPT as an automated essay scoring system against human raters in evaluating the coherence of written essays.
3. To compare the accuracy of ChatGPT as an automated essay scoring system against human raters in evaluating the organization of written essays

CONCEPTUAL FRAMEWORK

Three key aspects from the conceptual framework to assess ChatGPT as an automated essay scoring system to compare with human raters. The goal is to see how ChatGPT stacks up against human raters in scoring essays based on grammar, coherence and organization of writing essays. This framework informs the evaluation and comparison of these key dimensions, as well as provide some insights into how human or automated scoring system might be implemented within each construct in essay scoring.

Figure 1. Conceptual framework

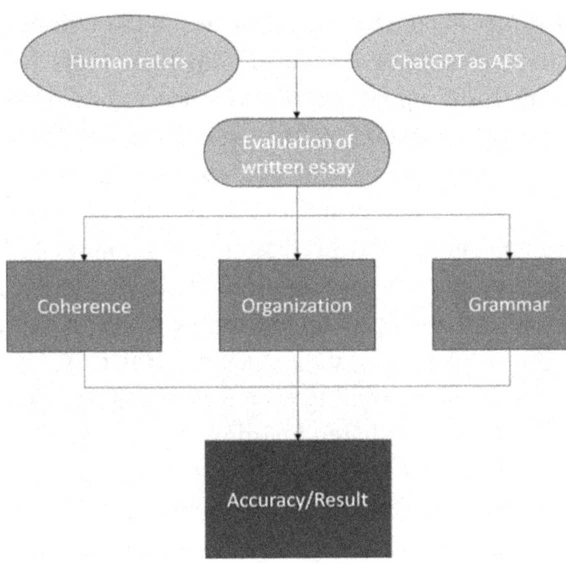

LITERATURE REVIEW

Writing Skills in Malaysia and Writing Essays

In its simplest form, the aforementioned writing skills are fundamental to success in both academia and business, serving as one of the cornerstones of Malaysian education system. As a multiracial and multicultural nation, writing proficiency in Bahasa Malaysia (BM) and English have been emphasized from primary school to tertiary level of education (Hassan et al., 2021). The course incorporates writing skills in unrelated topic areas to enhance students' conceptualizing, creativity, and expressive abilities (Arshad, 2018). However, even with these initiatives in place, skill sets for written communication still vary across populations, and the quality of writing instruction is not yet universal. In addition to the intracohort challenges mentioned above, disparities in educational resources between urban and rural schools further exacerbate these issues, leading to unequal writing competency among students (Ahmad, 2018). There is also an urgent need for continuous professional development for teachers, equipping them with effective writing strategies, especially in catering to learners of diverse proficiency levels

(Othman, 2017). To address these challenges, it may be beneficial to explore technological integration as a potential solution. This approach could help bridge gaps in resources and teaching quality, ensuring more equitable outcomes for all students.

However, we are progressing beyond traditional grammar instruction by leveraging real-time tools for automatic feedback on student writing through AI-driven technologies such as ChatGPT (Umar et al., 2021). These tools have potential to support and/or augment traditional writing instruction, reduce the burden of grading, and provide instant feedback to students. While some studies highlight the significant contributions of AI tools like ChatGPT-3 to the advancement of writing instruction (Deane, 2013), others caution that their integration into teaching must be carefully managed to ensure they complement, rather than replace, human judgment. Further research is needed to explore how these technologies impact writing skills and their potential role in addressing disparities in the writing proficiency among Malaysians (Yunus, 2016). By effectively managing and developing these tools, Malaysia aims to enhance the overall quality of student writing, fostering both academic success and professional readiness.

Essay writing is a cornerstone of education, as it assesses a student's ability to articulate thoughts, develop logical reasoning, and present coherent statements. Writing involves organizing information, constructing evidence-based arguments, and ensuring clarity and coherence of thought, skills that are essential for academic success and subsequent professional development.. Effective essay instruction focuses on fostering a coherent argument structure, appropriate language use, and logical organization of ideas. Teachers employ strategies such as explicitly teaching writing processes, modeling good writing practices, and providing specific feedback to guide students (Harris & Graham, 1996). Additionally, incorporating peer review and collaborative writing exercises into the curriculum helps deepen students' abilities through constructive criticism and shared learning (Vygotsky, 1978). Cognitive and metacognitive strategies play a critical role in the writing process (Flower & Hayes, 1981). These strategies encompass all stages of writing, from the fluid prewriting phase of brainstorming to drafting, revising, and finalizing the text. They also include planning, monitoring, and evaluating one's work, ensuring a comprehensive approach to developing strong writing skills.

When taught to students, these strategies become integral components of self-regulatory writing models, significantly enhancing their ability to produce well-organized and coherent essays (Zimmerman & Risemberg, 1997). However, essay writing remains challenging for many students, as the often struggle to organize their thoughts, maintain coherence and master mechanics such as grammar and syntax. Compounding these problems is the fact that a deficiency in motivation or self-efficacy for writing, background knowledge, and language proficiency can contribute to reluctance about composing (Graham, 2006). Another difficulty lies in the assessment of essay writing, which typically involves a formative evaluation. This process requires examining multiple dimensions of student's essays such as relevance, organization, coherence, and language use simultaneously, reflecting the complexity inherent in producing high-quality writing.

Components of Writing Essays

For centuries, essay writing has been a cornerstone of academic scholarship and intellectual discourse. Essays allow individuals to express their opinions and present arguments on a wide range of topics. A substantial body of academic literature has explored the essential components of effective essay writing, many of which have been well-documented. Among these, the introduction plays a critical role, as it sets the stage for the reader by providing a clear overview of the essay's content. Swales and Feak

(2012) suggest that a strong introduction accomplishes three key tasks: it establishes context, present the central argument or thesis, and outlines the structure of the essay. Additionally, techniques such as starting with an engaging opening like a story, question, or quote can effectively draw readers into the paper (Lunsford, 2013). However, Hacker and Sommers (2016) argue that essay writing should prioritize a clear interpretive conclusion statement, which demonstrates how evidence supports it the central argument.

Grammar

At its core, grammar serves as a foundation of writing, providing rules and structure necessary for coherent communication. When grammar is well understood, it enables the construction of correct and stylistically effective sentences, ensuring clarity and eliminating ambiguity (Weaver, 1996). A strong grasp of grammar is essential for producing well-structured and coherent writing. As Salsbury et al. (2006) emphasize, explicit grammar instruction has been shown to enhance writing skills by drawing attention to grammatical elements and the mechanics of constructing accurate sentences. Additionally, conjunctions play a crucial role in creating grammatical cohesion, while reference and substitution words contribute to the logical flow and development of ideas for readers (Halliday & Hasan, 1976). In the context of second language (L2) acquisition, grammar is indispensable for achieving writing proficiency, and effective instruction should be contextualized to support learners (Celce-Murcia & Larsen-Freeman, 1999).

In addition, modern grammar teaching methods integrate grammar instruction with writing practice, marking a significant shift from the traditional memorization techniques that have been long used. Research has shown that this approach is more meaningful and effective in teaching grammar as a component of literacy (Elley et al., 1976). By combining grammar and writing practice, this method has proven to be more successful in helping students achieve clarity and purpose in their writing. As a result, grammar is essential for high-quality writing, as it ensures clarity and coherence. The contemporary educational approach, which merges grammar instruction and writing practice, has emerged as a successful methodology for fostering strong writing skills.

Coherence

Coherence is a key element of good writing, ensuring that ideas follow logically and flow well from one to another. It enhances readability and helps readers follow the arguments or narrative presented. According to Witte and Faigley (1981), coherence can be achieved effective organization, such as logical structuring, clear topic sentences, and the use of transition words or conjunctions to connect ideas. Without these connections between sentences and topics, reader are likely to lose track of the writer's intended message. Halliday and Hasan (1976) further emphasize that coherence relies on cohesive ties within text, including reference, substitution, ellipsis, and conjunction. Additionally, lexical cohesion plays a significant role in creating coherence. Together, these elements act as the 'glue' that binds sentences and paragraphs into unified and cohesive pieces of writing.

Bae and Lee (2012) highlight the importance of clear development of ideas, where each paragraph transitions logically to the next. This progression is often guided by the use of topic sentences, which explicitly state the main idea of each paragraph, followed by related sentences that elaborate on these ideas. Moreover, it is related to one of the foundational principles in writing, which involves unity and coherence. According to Oshima and Hogue (2007), unity means that no piece of the text detracts from a single central idea or thesis. If not, a good text is one that remains coherent, and it does so by returning to the central idea of never departing from what adds nothing relevant. In the context of second language (L2) writing, achieving coherence presents unique challenges. L2 learners often struggle with coherence due to limited vocabulary and unfamiliarity with cohesive devices. (Lee, 2002). To address this, learners can benefit from practicing strategies such as logically sequencing ideas and using appropriate cohesive devices. these mid-level writing strategies provide practical ways to teach coherence to L2 learners, helping them develop stronger writing skills.

Organization

Organization is a critical aspect of effective writing. It involves arranging ideas in a logical and direct manner so that reader can easily follow and understand the writer's message. This includes the ordering of paragraphs, which may vary depending on whether the essay follows a linear structure where ideas are presented sequentially or non-linear where ideas are introduced in a less sequential or thematic order. A well-structured essay typically begins with an introduction that provides context and thesis statement, followed by body paragraphs that develop the argument, and concludes summary or call-to-action point (Smith, 2013). In addition, the Literature review posits that writing clarity and persuasiveness are influenced by clear organization. Swales and Feak (2012) argue that sections of an essay or paper must serve a clear purpose to aid in the overall flow of the text.

Organizational patterns like chronology, cause and effect, comparison and contrast, or problem-solution are particular formats of pieces that the writers use to address school papers. The patterns provide a structure that enables the authors of the paper to logically present their ideas and arguments, making it way more reader-friendly (Bailey, 2018). The organization of ideas can be especially difficult in second-language writing. However, as Hyland (2003) reports, it is common in academic writing and harder for second language learners to have their essays organized exponentially. Teaching organizational strategies (i.e., outlines and graphic organizers) can help these learners organize their writing more efficiently.

Challenges of using ICT in writing skills class

ICT integration in writing skills classes has its advantages and disadvantages. The Digital Divide is one of the most challenging aspects accompanied by online learning and facility technologies, which might increase educational inequalities. Students from underprivileged background may not have access to equipment and the internet, thus limiting their ability to fully participate in ICT-based writing activities. Moreover, both students and teachers could experience significant friction when onboarding new technologies. Wilson et al. (2007) agree that providing teachers with sufficient training and encouragement is indispensable for the effective use of ICT tools to support their teaching practices. However, in many regions that are sharper economically and geographically, the effective implementation of these resources and methods can be particularly challenging. Without a well-trained team, integrating ICT into writing instruction may prove problematic, further widening the gap in educational opportunities.

A third challenge also exists, one of distraction. Internet-based ICT tools can distract students from their writing tasks. (Kay & Lauricella, 2011). Furthermore, social media, games and other online options distract students from paying their proper attention to writing. Secondly, there are practical concerns regarding the need for sufficient infrastructure and technical support when higher education institutions use ICT to facilitate writing classes. A necessary condition for using computers in teaching is network connectivity, often accompanied by expensive software and human resources required to implement technology (Law et al., 2008). Also, there is a problem with old-fashioned writing skills. Students' development of editing and proofreading skills can be impaired as over-reliance on ICT tools (e.g., spell-checkers and grammar checkers) may have devastating effects on their learning (McVey, 2008). When students use this tool and begin to depend on it, they may not be learning important skills in recognizing mistakes or how those errors can be fixed by themselves. Moreover, this leaves one running the risk of committing academic dishonesty. Since the widespread adoption of technology and availability of information online, there is a significant risk that learners will choose (consciously or not) 'to copy and paste' by accessing content without appropriate reference, which may generate concerns about plagiaristic conduct (Selwyn, 2010).

Ways to evaluate Written Essays

Reading an essay takes a multi-layered approach to assess reading tons of literary devices, written essays, and so much more. The most common way is to use a holistic approach where an essay receives only one overall score based on your impression of the whole writing piece. According to Charney (1984), this type of rating assesses coherence, organization, content, and language use, but scores do not break these things down into little elements. Holistic scoring is both efficient and compatible with standardized testing but may leave out feedback on specific student strengths or areas of improvement.

A second technique is the analytical approach, where the evaluation will be divided into different criteria and scored separately. Content, organization, vocabulary, grammar, and mechanics are frequently used as evaluation criteria (Weigle, 2002). This method gives specific feedback, which makes it clear to the students where they need improvement. Overall, analytic scoring is slower but gives the most accurate description of where an essay excels or needs improvement.

Automated Essay Scoring System

Automated grading systems are among the tools that help grade assignments, tests, and essays without human intervention. According to Shermis and Burstein (2003), Automated Essay Scoring is a computer program that can be used independently or with other services to score and analyze written prose. They use cutting-edge technologies such as artificial intelligence and machine learning to assess the quality or accuracy of something by applying previously learned rules and patterns. Additionally, critics argue that despite its effectiveness, AES may be unable to traits in student writing and thus requires human intelligence which limits the grading quality. According to Williamson, Xi and Breyer (2012), AES is especially challenging because a key question empirical researchers face when it comes to them is the extent to which they actually capture what we expect them to. There are also concerns about hacking, test taker behaviors and the risk that implementations do not follow the guidelines. It is essential to evaluate and discriminate these attributes while assessing agreement with human raters, when it comes to automated assessments (Williamson et al., 2012).

Artificial intelligence has given rise to conversational agents that can now interact like humans. According to Altmae et al., (2023), AI chatbots were very well acknowledged tools for scientific writing. That is where AI chat comes into the picture which is an amazing entity that uses sophisticated language models to understand and give logical responses in natural language. In addition, AI chat presents their ability by assisting in text organizing, correction of spelling errors and semantics checks according to grammatical rules while drafting and summarizing content (Altmae et al., 2023). Moreover, AI chat systems use machine learning and natural language processing to understand lookups made by the user, sustain contexts that are inherent in a conversation and give responses as human (Fuchs, 2023). Thus, technology is being used in different areas such as customer service, virtual assistants and educational tools to easily fit into every communication stream. Hence, modern AI tools need to be trained as close to the lower limits of human performance.

Human Rater

Human raters are a critical part of many assessment contexts. For example, they grade tasks like essays or conversational interactions against predetermined criteria. However, human raters in automated essay scoring also introduce a subjective element as their own experiences, attitudes and interpretive styles contribute to their judgements. Furthermore, while they may adhere to certain guidelines or rubric and rank a response in areas including content understanding, language skills, and following instructions can still vary. According to Wang et al. (2011), they speculate that differences in how the essays are scored and if graders require lesson can make student capabilities look different than they actually are. It might also make them less valid test scores. Human rater played a crucial role in this process to ensure that thereby highlighting the connection between human judgement and our system effectiveness. Moreover, Bejar (2011) stated that human raters are all limited by cognitive capacities and it is very hard or impossible to measure biases which could result from systematic effects on the final scores. As a result, acknowledging the subjectivity of human raters also underscores that an evaluation system should strike balance between the unique qualities afforded by humans and processing efficiency gained form automation to build assessment mechanisms securing both accuracy and fairness.

Related Works on Marking Written Essays

According to Page (1994), research into automatic essay scoring began in the early 1960s. Automated Essay Scoring has good points, such as more consistent scoring across major assessments, saving time, and standardizing things using the same criteria for all answers. However, there are also challenges. According to Chung and O'Neil (1997), AES may consider things that are not important in grading, and it needs many examples from which to learn. Another study on AES shows that using this system means that students do not have a personal relationship with the people grading their work (Hamp-Lyons, 2001). Numerous AES systems were developed during the year, such as E-Rater, Project Essay Grader (PEG), and Intelligent Essay Assessor (IEA). Previous research has found that these systems have built-in correlation and machine learning to grade an essay (Dikli et al., 2006). As for the ChatGPT, most previous research focuses on how the AI can generate human-like text and respond to queries. Pavlik (2003), for example, examines the advantages and disadvantages of using ChatGPT for text generation in media and journalism. However, not many studies examined the differences between ChatGPT as an automated essay scoring system and human raters in evaluating the written essay.

METHOD

Research Design

To explore the effectiveness of ChatGPT as an Automated Essay Scoring (AES) system, this study employed a structured evaluation process. Essays were assessed by both human raters and ChatGPT to determine differences in grading patterns, particularly in grammar, coherence, and organization. The goal was to understand whether AI can reliably replicate human judgment in essay evaluation. The outcomes from the assessments were analysed and compared. The researcher then interpreted the results. Moreover, in quantitative research suppositions are tested using statistics, experimental techniques, and logical positivism (Hoepfl, 1997). It also emphasizes 26 quantifying and examining the causal connections between various elements (Denzin & Lincoln, 2008). Quantitative research was used to achieve the objectives of this study. The goals were to determine how accurate the AI chatbot, ChatGPT, is as an automated essay compared to human raters in assessing written essays regarding grammar, coherence, and organization.

The researcher uses a selective selection process when selecting the population for this study. The researcher also purposefully chose a population of 20 based on specific criteria, a process known as purposive sampling. According to Tyrer and Heyman (2016), the sampling method should be as rigorous as possible to ensure minimum error and bias and to enhance maximum representativeness. In addition, this study also utilises the Krejcie and Morgan table to determine the required number of essays. This table assists the researcher in choosing an appropriate number of essays to review, considering the total number of students and the accuracy of this study's desired results. According to Krejcie and Morgan's (1970) sample size table, a sample size of 19 would be required to represent a cross-section of the population in a given population of 20. Nonetheless, a researcher must consider whether the sample size is sufficient to offer sufficient accuracy for confidently making decisions based on the results.

Research Instrument

The detailed selection of the research sample of this study, which is Written Essays, focuses explicitly on UHLB 2122 written essays of second-year TESL students. The essay was chosen based on its compatibility with the study's objectives, ensuring a focused analysis of essay grading within this specific academic subject. The essays covered various topics and writing styles found in UHLB 2122 coursework to comprehensively understand the grading process in this distinctive educational setting. The sample included UHLB level 2 written essays, which were used to compare the performance of AI chatbots ChatGPT with human raters in the context of automated essay scoring.

The adapted written essay rubric used in this study is from the UHLB 2122 Course subject marking rubric for response to text assessment. It is the latest marking rubric for semester 2, 2023/2024. The rubric consists of three main evaluation points: content development, language features, formal structure, and organization. Furthermore, the rubric also consists of 9 points for each main evaluation point. The points are determined through the criteria of CEFR level, with the C1 being the highest (9 points), B2 High (6-8 points), B2 Mid (3-5 points), and the last one, B2 low (2 and below).

ChatGPT 3.5, which is the free version that available on the internet has been used as research instrument in this study to do the evaluation of the writing essay from UHLB 2122 papers. Moreover, to achieve the research objectives, several prompts have been given and converted the responses from ChatGPT into evaluations by providing the adapted rubric used in this study and also the research samples.

Data Analysis

Several stages are involved in choosing human raters, particularly final-year TESL students. Three students from this course have been selected as human raters for this study. These raters have taken writing courses, such as Fundamental Grammar, English Structure, and Writing Skills, where they learned critical abilities and information on evaluating written essays. Furthermore, they have also gone through practical teaching that has given them firsthand experience assessing different kinds of writing. The selection procedure acknowledges the value of their training in the real world and their educational background in equipping them to evaluate written work efficiently. These final-year TESL students have completed the theoretical and practical components, giving them the skills to function as competent human raters when assessing written essays. In short, these final-year TESL students were chosen as human raters because they are trained in language assessment and possess sufficient background knowledge in evaluating essays. Their academic training equips them with the necessary skills to assess grammar, coherence, organization, and content accurately. This selection enhances the study's content validity, as these raters understand assessment criteria and language proficiency standards. The standardized scoring guidelines were provided to ensure consistency across evaluations, and training sessions were held to familiarize raters with the scoring rubrics and essay expectations. These measures reduce potential bias and enhance the reliability and fairness of the comparison between ChatGPT and human raters.

Several processes have been done to make ChatGPT an automated essay-scoring system. The system is first trained using an adapted essay rubric to learn scoring criteria and trends. After being introduced, the AI evaluates essays using predetermined prompts from an essay rubric. These prompts guide evaluations of the material's relevancy, structure, and compliance with the instructions. Furthermore, the AI mimics the subtle decision-making shown throughout training using sophisticated machine learning and natural language processing methods.

RESULTS

Table 1. Descriptive analysis

F N	Minimum	Maximum	Mean	Std. Deviation	
Grammar_ChatGPT	19	4.0	9.0	6.500	1.7559
Grammar_Human	19	5	8	7.00	1.054
Coherence_ChatGPT	19	4	9	7.11	1.969
Coherence_Human	19	7	9	8.32	.749
Organization_ChatGPT	19	.5	2.0	1.316	.4475
Organization_Human	19	.5	2.0	1.211	.6523

The findings revealed intriguing differences between human raters and ChatGPT in evaluating student essays. While ChatGPT demonstrated high accuracy in identifying grammatical errors, its scoring was slightly more variable than that of human raters. This suggests that while AI can efficiently detect grammatical mistakes, it may not always apply judgment with the same consistency as a trained human evaluator. To interpret in detail, for coherence, the mean score given by ChatGPT was 7.11, which is lower than the human rater's score of 8.32. ChatGPT also showed greater variability, with a standard deviation of 1.97 compared to 0.75 for the human rater. For organization, the mean scores were similar, with ChatGPT scoring 1.32 and the human rater scoring 1.21. However, ChatGPT showed less variation, with a standard deviation of 0.45 compared to 0.65 for the human rater.

There are some discrepancies between the scores given by ChatGPT and human rater. However, human rater is more likely to average higher scores for grammar and coherence than ChatGPT. Moreover, the standard deviation scores had generally more variance for ChatGPT, especially on coherence. In this sense, these results indicate ChatGPT scoring is nearer to human raters but with more inconsistency for some areas because of how different the algorithms work on ChatGPT.

Normality Test

A normality test was conducted to see whether the data distribution is normal or not. The Kolmogorov-Smirnov test and Shapiro-Wilk test was used to conduct the normality test. These tests were applied to the variables related to grammar, coherence, and organization for both ChatGPT and human rater. With the p-value set to 0.05. The result indicated that the data is not normal. The Wilcoxon Signed-Rank Test was conducted to compare the human rater ratings and ChatGPT ratings for each research question. This test is suitable for non-parametric data and provides a robust alternative to the paired t-test (Wilcoxon, 1945).

Table 2. Normality test

Variable	Shapiro-Wilk Statistic	df	Sig.	Normality
Grammar_ChatGPT	0.843	19	0.005	No
Grammar_Human	0.790	19	0.001	No
Coherence_ChatGPT	0.810	19	0.002	No
Coherence_Human	0.777	19	0.001	No
Organization_ChatGPT	0.812	19	0.002	No
Organization_Human	0.800	19	0.001	No

Wilcoxon Signed-Rank Test Results

Table 3. Wilcoxon signed-rank test results

Writing Dimension	Test Statistic (Z)	Asymp. Sig. (2-tailed)
Grammar	-1.056	0.291
Coherence	-2.303	0.021*
Organization	-0.744	0.457

Note: $p < 0.05$ indicates statistical significance.

From Table 3, the Wilcoxon Signed-Rank Test was conducted to compare the human rater ratings and ChatGPT ratings for each research question. This test is suitable for non-parametric data and provides a robust alternative to the paired t-test (Wilcoxon, 1945). In particular, the study aims to ensure rigorous comparison between AI and human assessment in order to highlight the areas where ChatGPT aligns with or deviates from human judgment. Hence, this test is used to determine if there are significant differences between two related samples which are rater ratings and ChatGPT ratings. This method also supports the book's theme of transformative education by exploring how AI can be used in the educational area, particularly traditional assessment. Thus, the findings from this chapter can provide evidence-based insights on using AI in education and contribute to the discussion on balancing technology and human expertise in higher education.

Firstly, the Wilcoxon Signed-Rank Test for the grammar yielded a test statistic $Z=-1.056$, an asymptotic significance (2-tailed) value of $p=0.291$. Since $p>0.05$, we fail to reject the null hypothesis. This indicates that there is no statistically significant difference between the scores assigned by the human rater and ChatGPT for grammar. This finding has important educational implications, particularly for automated assessment integration in Malaysian education. The absence of significant differences indicates that ChatGPT's grammar evaluation aligns closely with human judgment, suggesting its potential as a reliable supplementary tool for assessing student writing. This could reduce teacher workload by assisting with large-scale grading while maintaining consistency across evaluations

Besides that, a particularly interesting insight emerged in the evaluation of coherence. While ChatGPT could recognize surface-level sentence structure and grammar, it struggled to assess the logical flow of ideas in student writing. This limitation highlights the continued importance of human evaluation, especially for more nuanced aspects of writing such as argument development and logical transitions. This finding is supported by the Wilcoxon Signed-Rank Test for the coherence which yielded a test statistic $Z=-2.303$ and an asymptotic significance (2-tailed) value of $p=0.021$. This suggests that ChatGPT evaluates coherence differently from human raters. This has then raised important educational implications regarding the use of AI in essay assessment. While ChatGPT can efficiently analyze surface-level coherence, for example sentence transitions and basic logical flow, it may struggle to capture deeper rhetorical structures, contextual relevance, and complex argument development (Ke & Ng, 2022). This limitation implies that human judgment remains essential for assessing aspects of writing that require a nuanced understanding of ideas and argument progression.

Thirdly, the Wilcoxon Signed-Rank Test for the organization yielded a test statistic $Z=-0.744$ and an asymptotic significance (2-tailed) value of $p=0.457$. Since $p>0.05$, we fail to reject the null hypothesis. This indicates that there is no statistically significant difference between the scores assigned by the human rater and ChatGPT for the organization. This suggests that ChatGPT can assess structural elements of essays including paragraph sequencing, logical flow, and topic transitions in a manner comparable to human evaluators. This finding has important educational implications for Malaysian education, as the alignment between ChatGPT and human raters in organization implies that AI systems can reliably assist in evaluating basic structural coherence, reducing the grading burden for educators and facilitating timely feedback for students. In particular, these findings suggest that while AI-powered grading tools can be useful in large-scale assessments, teachers should still play an active role in reviewing students' essays, especially for higher-order skills such as coherence and argumentation.

DISCUSSION

Grammar Assessments

The result showed a no significant different of the evaluations for grammar between human rater and ChatGPT. This indicates that writing samples could be checked grammatical accuracy in the way human judgement would probably decide using ChatGPT. ChatGPT processes essays using advanced algorithms, such as deep learning models and natural language processing (NLP) techniques, allowing for precise grammatical error detection (Brown et al. 2020). Conversely, human raters provide years of experience and finely tuned training to their assessments. Their expertise in comprehending context, identifying subtitle linguistic mistakes and offering individual feedback is the result of experience. Moreover, they are thereby equipped to evaluate writing for correctness and style, tone as well as an overall sense of the writing papers (Smith & Jones, 2018). Nonetheless, though ChatGPT does well on the human assessment of grammar, more analysis is necessary regarding its performance across error types and writing genres. This might be something that future research can tackle by improving ChatGPT to receive a more nuanced understanding of grammatical issues and provide feedback tailored for individual.

Coherence Assessments

On the other hand, results from the coherence assessments provide an important indication of a major issue when it comes automated writing assessment which is the significant difference between human rater and ChatGPT in assessing coherence. This difference is indicating that ChatGPT perhaps having a hard time in processing the subtle, complex nature of coherence that human raters can feel quite naturally. This involves a sophisticated layer of human judgement because coherence is assessed in the context of an essay and through multiple connections among its constituent parts (Thompson et al., 2020). In contrast, ChatGPT relies on algorithms to determine scoring of writing, and these are based upon natural language processing (NLP) technologies which have been developed further but may not capture coherence in its entirety. Therefore, there is a gap to be addressed in ChatGPT towards the understanding of discourse coherence by incorporating further step like parsing and semantic level NLP techniques. Expanding the training datasets with a stronger coherence emphasis may also be had been beneficial for ChatGPT to perform better in this important aspect (Zhang et al. 2021). Perhaps such system could allow us to exploit the virtues of human raters without throwing out advanced algorithms that promise even more reliable coherence assessments.

Organization Assessments

Furthermore, the results about the organization of essays showed that the evaluations provided by human raters and ChatGPT did not significantly differ. It means that when evaluating student writing, ChatGPT appropriately interpreted organizational aspects of the text that can be attributed to coherence and structure. In practice, human raters use these aspects to understand whether a student essay is logically organized. Therefore, the AI evaluated students' writing in a proper way. Moreover, according to Smith et al,. (2021), the algorithms used by ChatGPT are already highly skilled in these tasks. Although the tool showed good results, as to the organizations of an essay, there is still room for the improvement of the algorithms. Greater scrutiny should be used to ensure that they provided consistent evaluations of organizational coherence across texts. As noted by Tugwell et al., (2018), it is possible for NLP techniques to be refined to provide such an outcome. Thus, the outcomes were identified as such that necessitated further research efforts concerning the use of NLP techniques in writing assessment with gaps identified in the use of such approaches in evaluations related to the organization, that require further consideration.

In short, the Wilcoxon Signed-Rank Test results indicate that while ChatGPT performs similarly to human raters in assessing grammar and organization, it struggles with coherence, showing a statistically significant difference. This discrepancy highlights the limitations of AI in understanding discourse markers, logical flow, and argument development. While ChatGPT can identify basic transitions, it may fail to interpret nuanced connections between ideas or track complex argument progressions across an essay. On the other hand, human raters can assess implicit reasoning and rhetorical strategies, which are crucial for evaluating academic writing. The findings suggest that while ChatGPT can assist with surface-level evaluation, it lacks the cognitive depth to capture the sophisticated structures required in academic writing (Zhai, 2023). Thus, more attentions should be paid on this aspect.

Given these limitations, ChatGPT is still regarded as a suitable supplementary grading tool rather than a primary assessor, especially for large-scale assessments where teacher workload is high. To strike a balance between AI efficiency and human judgment, Malaysian educators can adopt a blended assessment model. ChatGPT can provide immediate feedback on grammar and organization during formative assessments that can help teachers save time, as teachers can focus on higher-order writing skills like coherence in summative assessments.

CONCLUSION

The main objective of the study was to look into ChatGPT as automated scoring system in assessing grammar, coherence and organization of writing essay and comparing it with human rater. The three research objectives were: 1) to compare the accuracy of ChatGPT as an automated essay scoring system against human raters in evaluating the grammar of written essays. 2) to compare the accuracy of ChatGPT as an automated essay scoring system against human raters in evaluating the coherence of written essays. 3) to compare the accuracy of ChatGPT as an automated essay scoring system against human raters in evaluating the organisation of written essays.

Since this research has shed light on just how poorly automated essay grading systems performs, teachers should pay close attention. Having a better understanding of the system pros and cons will enable educators to make more well-informed decisions about incorporating such technology into their teaching methodologies. It hopes by providing such, it suggests that an understanding of the nuances in these areas may result in teaching more efficiently and pleasantly than traditional methods. The results would affect educators and provide a clearer perspective on how automatic scoring systems can be used in the classroom. In conclusion, with consistent assessment procedures and quicker grading times along with potential efficiency improvement, it would all benefit schools by allowing them to adhere better to the technology landscape they are surrounded in educational paradigms leading towards more efficient schooling environment.

The findings from the Wilcoxon Signed-Rank Test reveal several key insights. Firstly, in terms of grammar, the test statistic for grammar ($Z = -1.056$) yielded a p-value of 0.291. Since this p-value is greater than the significance threshold of 0.05, we fail to reject the null hypothesis. This suggests that there is no statistically significant difference between the grammar scores assigned by the human rater and ChatGPT. In other words, both raters generally agree in their assessment of grammar. Secondly, in term of coherence, the test statistic for coherence (Z = -2.303) resulted in a p-value of 0.021. Since this p-value is less than 0.05, we reject the null hypothesis. This indicates that there is a statistically significant difference between the scores assigned by the human rater and ChatGPT for coherence. It suggests a divergence in how coherence is judged by the two raters, with the human rater and ChatGPT assessing this aspect of the text differently. Thirdly, in term of organization, the test statistic for organization (Z = -0.744) gave a p-value of 0.457. Similar to the results for grammar, the p-value is greater than 0.05, leading us to fail to reject the null hypothesis. This indicates that there is no statistically significant difference between the scores assigned by the human rater and ChatGPT for organization, showing general agreement in this category.

Conclusively, this study compared ChatGPT and human raters in evaluating grammar, coherence, and organization in student essays. The Wilcoxon Signed-Rank Test results revealed no significant difference in grammar and organization but showed a statistically significant difference in coherence. These findings suggest that while ChatGPT is reliable for assessing surface-level features, it struggles with evaluating logical flow and argument development which are the areas where human judgment remains essential. This highlights the potential of using ChatGPT as a supplementary grading tool to provide efficient feedback while relying on human assessors for more complex writing aspects. Implementing a blended assessment approach can help Malaysian educators reduce grading time while maintaining evaluation quality.

In summary, while grammar and organization show no significant differences between human and AI assessments, coherence appears to be rated differently, suggesting that coherence may be more subjective or complex to evaluate consistently across raters. As a result, it can be concluded that ChatGPT can be use as automated scoring system for assessing writing paper in terms of grammar and organization. However, assessing coherence in writing essay still need to be done by the human rater as the result of this study showed there is significant different between ChatGPT and human rater in assessing coherence. Hence, there is still monitoring needed from human when using the ChatGPT to assess the writing paper. A careful consideration into looking at the outcomes given by the ChatGPT should be done to ensure the reliability and validity of the assessments is accurately aligned with human assessments.

However, there were some unavoidable limitations in this study which might be affecting the findings of this study. First, the human raters used in this study are not having years of experience in assessing writing essay as they are from final year TESL students. With the lack of experience, the outcomes from the assessment might be not accurately follows the marking rubric compares to the raters that have years of experiences. Hence, a similar future study needs to be done by using raters with lot of experiences in assessing writing essay to ensure the validity of this study.

Besides, there is limitation in searching similar previous study or related articles because not much study and research had been done in making the ChatGPT as automated scoring system and comparing it with human rater. Moreover, as the findings from this study used Wilcoxon test to achieve the research objectives, researcher cannot determine whether ChatGPT or human rater are more accurate in assessing writing essay in terms of grammar, coherence and organization. Hence, in the future study, different methodology is needed that can dig deeper into findings discussion and accuracy for both ChatGPT and human rater can be determined. Considering the limitations of the study identified above, it is recommended that future researchers should conduct similar studies involving experienced human raters who have substantial experience in essay writing evaluation. Herein, experts' inclusion would have implied a potentially more precise evaluation of the degree to which ChatGPT system's effectiveness boats a measurable difference between two assessment methods. In addition, including a wide range of essay topics and writing styles in the study would have implied that the assessment could produce multiple insights into system's shortcoming and benefits. In other words, given that the human raters would have had a range of professional background and work experiences, the data gained from their work could have made the results of the assessment significantly more nuanced.

Similarly, to improve the quality of the results and increase their validity level, future research should encompass a significantly larger sample of writing. The latter will imply a higher degree if generalizability for the study outcomes as a tool for assessing the effectiveness of the ChatGPT system across different contexts. Furthermore, future researchers should consider including all aspects of the essay's analysis, including its logical progression, coherence, ability to integrate stylistic devices, structure and originality, among other characteristics. By including these elements in future studies, one will increase the reliability and validity levels of their outcomes and the general degree of trustworthiness of the general claim about ChatGPT tool as an efficient scoring system. Finally, including a set of recommendations for the steps that educators will need to take to set up the system and polish it to match their need will enhance the study's applicability in other settings. Combined, the identified elements could have led to significantly better results concerning ChatGPT tool's efficiency as an essay scoring system.

In conclusion, it is necessary to continue this research because it has not focused on all elements required to test the quality of writing essay effectively. Besides, the downsides of this experiment, the potential bias in the collection of data and an insignificant sample size, call into question the value, dependability, and validity of the results. Therefore, one must address these drawbacks when discussing their results. In the future, the researcher will have to analyse these poorly studied and incomplete elements of writing essays and the impacts of the biases to gain a holistic view across these two assessment methods. In addition, more comprehensive assessments in terms of evaluation criteria and more rational research design will allow them to generate far more valuable proofs supporting the integration of AI systems in educational processes that the existing research.

REFERENCES

Abdullah, A. M. (2017). "Advanced encryption standard (AES) algorithm to encrypt and decrypt data." Cryptography and https://www.researchgate.net/profile/Ako Network Security, 16(1), 11.

Adams, R., & Oliver, R. (2019). *Teaching through peer interaction*. Routledge. DOI: 10.4324/9781315115696

Ahmad, M. F., & Ghapar, W. R. G. W. A. (2019). The era of artificial intelligence in Malaysian higher education: Impact and challenges in tangible mixed-reality learning system toward self-exploration education (SEE). *Procedia Computer Science, 163*, 2–10. DOI: 10.1016/j.procs.2019.12.079

Altmäe, S., Sola-Leyva, A., & Salumets, A. (2023). Artificial intelligence in scientific writing: A friend or a foe? *Reproductive Biomedicine Online, 47*(1), 3–9. DOI: 10.1016/j.rbmo.2023.04.009 PMID: 37142479

Arshad, H. (2018). The role of affective filters in oral communication: A case study of Pakistani students and teachers. *Pakistan Journal of Language Studies*, 2(1), 51–62.

Attali, Y. (2013). *Validity and reliability of automated essay scoring*. Educational Testing Service.

Bae, J., & Lee, Y. S. (2012). Evaluating the development of children's writing ability in an EFL context. *Language Assessment Quarterly, 9*(4), 348–374. DOI: 10.1080/15434303.2012.721424

Bailey, R. (2018). Student writing and academic literacy development at university. *Journal of Learning and Student Experience, 1*(7).

Barritt, L., Stock, P. L., & Clark, F. (1986). "Researching practice: Evaluating assessment essays." College Composition & Communication, 37(3), 315-327.DOI: 10.58680/ccc198611231

Brown, T., Mann, B., Ryder, N., Subbiah, M., & Associates. (2020) Language models are few-shot learners. arXiv preprint arXiv: 2005.14165. https: //arxiv.org/abs/2005.14165

Brown, T. B. (2020). Language models are few-shot learners. *arXiv preprint arXiv:2005.14165.*

Castellanos-Nieves, D., Fernández-Breis, J. T., Valencia-García, R., Martínez-Béjar, R., & Iniesta-Moreno, M. (2011). Semantic Web Technologies for supporting learning assessment. *Information Sciences, 181*(9), 1517–1537. DOI: 10.1016/j.ins.2011.01.010

Charney, D. (1984). The validity of using holistic scoring to evaluate writing: A critical overview. *Research in the Teaching of English, 18*(1), 65–81. DOI: 10.58680/rte198415687

Chung, G. K., & O'Neil Jr, H. F. (1997). Methodological Approaches to Online Scoring of Essays.

Coffie, I. S., Doe, N. G., & Tabi, J. A. (2021). Pre-Service Science Teachers' Assessment of Supported Teaching in School. *European Scientific Journal, 17*(32), 257. DOI: 10.19044/esj.2021.v17n32p257

Deane, P. (2013). On the relation between automated essay scoring and modern views of the writing construct. *Assessing Writing, 18*(1), 7–24. DOI: 10.1016/j.asw.2012.10.002

Denzin, N. K., & Lincoln, Y. S. (Eds.). (2008). *The landscape of qualitative research* (3rd ed.). Sage Publications, Inc.

Dikli, S. (2006). An overview of automated scoring of essays. *The Journal of Technology, Learning, and Assessment, 5*, 1, 5–22.

Elley, W. B., Barham, J. H., Lamb, H., & Wylie, M. (1976). The role of grammar in a secondary school English curriculum. *Research in the Teaching of English, 10*(1), 5–21. DOI: 10.58680/rte197620040

Feak, C. B., & Swales, J. (2011). *Creating contexts: Writing introductions across genres*. No Title. DOI: 10.3998/mpub.3367288

Fuchs, K., & Aguilos, V. (2023). Integrating artificial intelligence in higher education: Empirical insights from students about using ChatGPT. *International Journal of Information and Education Technology (IJIET), 13*(9), 1365–1371. DOI: 10.18178/ijiet.2023.13.9.1939

Gardiner, A., & Smith, M. A. (2021). Conversational AI as an emerging technology. In *Proceedings of the EDSIG conference ISSN* (Vol. 2473, p. 4901).

Graham, S., & Harris, K. R. (2006). Strategy instruction and the teaching of writing. *Handbook of writing research, 5*, 187-207.

Graham, S., Harris, K. R., & Macarthur, C. A. (1995). Introduction to special issue: Research on writing and literacy. *Learning Disability Quarterly, 18*(4), 250–252. DOI: 10.2307/1511232

Graham, S., & Perin, D. (2007). Writing next-effective strategies to improve writing of adolescents in middle and high schools.

Gruenewald, D. A., & Salsbury, T. L. (2006). Review of Reclaiming the local in language policy and practice. *Journal of Research in Rural Education, 21*(11), 21–11.

Hacker, D., Sommers, N. I., Huster, K., Cullick, J. S., & Zawacki, T. M. (2016). *A Writer's Reference with Writing in the Disciplines*. Bedford/St. Martin's.

Halliday, M. (1976). *A. K., & Hasan, R.* Cohesion in English.

Hamp-Lyons, L. (2006). Feedback in portfolio based writing courses. In Hyland, K., & Hyland, F. (Eds.), *Feedback in second language writing: Contexts and issues* (pp. 140–161). Cambridge University Press. DOI: 10.1017/CBO9781139524742.010

Hassan, I., Madarina Abdul Rahaman, A., & Latiff Azmi, M. N. (2021). Development of English writing skills through blended learning among ESL learners in Malaysia. *Arab World English Journal (AWEJ) Special Issue on CALL*, (7).

Hayes, J. R., & Flower, L. (1981). *Uncovering cognitive processes in writing: An introduction to protocol analysis*. ERIC Clearinghouse.

Hayes, J. R., & Flower, L. S. (2016). "Identifying the organization of writing processes." In Cognitive processes in writing (pp. 3-30). Routledge. https://www.taylorfrancis.com/chapters/edit/10.4324/9781315630274-3/identifying organization-writing-processes-john-hayes-linda-flower

Hoepfl, M. C. (1997). Choosing qualitative research: A primer for technology education researchers. *Journal of Technology Education, 9*(1), 47–63. Retrieved February 25, 1998, from https://scholar.lib.vt.edu/ejournals/JTE/v9n1/pdf/hoepfl.pdf. DOI: 10.21061/jte.v9i1.a.4

Hussein, M. A., Hassan, H., & Nassef, M. (2019). Automated language essay scoring systems: A literature review. *PeerJ. Computer Science*, *5*, e208. https://peerj.com/articles/cs-208.pdf. DOI: 10.7717/peerj-cs.208 PMID: 33816861

Hyland, K. (2003). Writing and teaching writing. *Second language writing, 1*(2), 1-30.

Ibrahim, E. H. E., Sarudin, I., Othman, K., Malik, F. A., & Muhamad, A. J. (2017). The assessment of writing within the CEFR scale: A Malaysian context. *Advanced Science Letters*, *23*(5), 4944–4947. DOI: 10.1166/asl.2017.8968

Jones, K., & Sharma, R. (2020). On reimagining a future for online learning in the post-COVID era. *Kevin Jones & Ravi Sharma (2020). Reimagining A Future For Online Learning In The Post-COVID Era. First posted on medium. com.*

Ke, Z., & Ng, V. (2022). Automated essay scoring and feedback: Advances and challenges. [Khine, M. S., & Afari, E. Engagement in English Language Learning and Self-Regulation among Students.]. *Computers & Education*, *184*, 104521.

Lazic, D., Thompson, A., Pritchard, T., & Tsuji, S. (2020). Student preferences: using Grammarly to help EFL writers with paraphrasing, summarizing, and synthesizing. *CALL for widening participation: short papers from EUROCALL, 2020*, 183-189.

Lee, I. (2002). Teaching coherence to ESL students: A classroom inquiry. *Journal of Second Language Writing*, *11*(2), 135–159. DOI: 10.1016/S1060-3743(02)00065-6

Li, J., Link, S., & Hegelheimer, V. (2015). Rethinking the role of automated writing evaluation (AWE) feedback in ESL writing instruction. *Journal of Second Language Writing*, *27*, 1–18. DOI: 10.1016/j.jslw.2014.10.004

Lunsford, A. A., Brody, M., Ede, L. S., Moss, B. J., Papper, C. C., & Walters, K. (2013). *Everyone's an Author*. WW Norton and Company.

Mayer, R. E. (2014). Incorporating motivation into multimedia learning. *Learning and Instruction*, *29*, 171–173. DOI: 10.1016/j.learninstruc.2013.04.003

Metcalfe, J. S., Perelman, B. S., Boothe, D. L., & Mcdowell, K. (2021). Systemic oversimplification limits the potential for human-AI partnership. *IEEE Access : Practical Innovations, Open Solutions*, *9*, 70242–70260. DOI: 10.1109/ACCESS.2021.3078298

Morgan, K. (1970). Sample size determination using Krejcie and Morgan table. Kenya Projects Organization (KENPRO), 38, 607-610.

Murcia, M. C., & Freeman, D. L. (1999). *The grammar book: An ESL. EFL Teacher's Course* (2nd ed.). Heinle & Heinle.

Orrù, G., Piarulli, A., Conversano, C., & Gemignani, A. (2023). Human-like problem-solving abilities in large language models using ChatGPT. *Frontiers in Artificial Intelligence*, *6*, 1199350. DOI: 10.3389/frai.2023.1199350 PMID: 37293238

Oshima, A., & Hogue, A. (2007). *Introduction to academic writing*. Pearson/Longman.

Page, E. (1994). Computer Grading of Student Prose. *Using Modern Concepts and Software Journal of Experimental Education*, *62*(2), 127–142.

Pavlik, J. V. (2023). Collaborating with ChatGPT: Considering the implications of generative artificial intelligence for journalism and media education. *Journalism & mass communication educator, 78*(1), 84-93.

Ramineni, C., & Williamson, D. M. (2013). Automated essay scoring: Psychometric guidelines and practices. *Assessing Writing*, *18*(1), 25–39. DOI: 10.1016/j.asw.2012.10.004

Rudolph, J., Tan, S., & Tan, S. (2023). War of the chatbots: Bard, Bing Chat, ChatGPT, Ernie and beyond. The new AI gold rush and its impact on higher education. *Journal of Applied Learning and Teaching*, *6*(1), 364–389. https://journals.sfu.ca/jalt/index.php/jalt/article/download/771/577/3333

Shermis, M. D., & Burstein, J. C. (2003). *Automated essay scoring: A cross-disciplinary perspective*. Routledge., DOI: 10.4324/9781410606860

Shermis, M. D., & Hamner, B. (2013). Contrasting state-of-the-art automated scoring of essays. In *Handbook of automated essay evaluation* (pp. 313–346). Routledge.

Smith, F. (2013). *Writing and the writer*. Routledge. DOI: 10.4324/9780203812075

Smith, L. R. (2018). Former professor of Linguistics. *Challenge*, *3*(1).

Swales, J. M. (2011). *Aspects of article introductions* (No. 1). University of Michigan Press.

Thirusanku, J., & Yunus, M. M. (2014). Status of english in Malaysia. *Asian Social Science*, *10*(14), 254.

Tyrer, S., & Heyman, B. (2016). Sampling in epidemiologi cal research: Issues, hazards and pitfalls. *BJPsych Bulletin*, *40*(2), 57–60. DOI: 10.1192/pb.bp.114.050203 PMID: 27087985

Umar, U. (2021). Implementation Of E-Learning on The Teaching English As Global Language In The Pandemic-Era. *Jurnal Inovasi Penelitian*, *1*(10), 2095–2098.

Vygotsky, L. S. (1978). The prehistory of written language. *Mind in society: The development of higher psychological processes*, 105-119.

Wang, J., Lin, E., Spalding, E., Odell, S. J., & Klecka, C. L. (2011). Understanding teacher education in an era of globalization. *Journal of Teacher Education*, *62*(2), 115–120. DOI: 10.1177/0022487110394334

Weaver, C. (1996). Teaching grammar in the context of writing. *English Journal*, *85*(7), 15–24. DOI: 10.58680/ej19964835

Weigle, S. C. (2002). Assessing writing. *Ernst Klett Sprachen.*

Wilcoxon, F. (1945). Individual Comparisons by Ranking Methods. *Biometrics Bulletin*, *1*(6), 80–83. DOI: 10.2307/3001968

Williamson, D. M., Xi, X., & Breyer, F. J. (2012). A framework for evaluation and use of automated scoring. *Educational Measurement: Issues and Practice*, *31*(1), 2–13. DOI: 10.1111/j.1745-3992.2011.00223.x

Witte, S. P., & Faigley, L. (1981). Coherence, cohesion, and writing quality. *College Composition and Communication*, *32*(2), 189–204. DOI: 10.58680/ccc198115912

Yeadon, W., Inyang, O. O., Mizouri, A., Peach, A., & Testrow, C. P. (2023). The death of the short-form physics essay in the coming AI revolution. *Physics Education*, *58*(3), 035027. DOI: 10.1088/1361-6552/acc5cf

Zhai, C. (2023). AI in education: Automated scoring and its impact. *Journal of Educational Technology*, *19*(3), 145–160.

Zhang, H., & Litman, D. (2021). *Essay Quality Signals as Weak Supervision for Source-Based Essay Scoring*. Grantee Submission.

Zimmerman, B. J., & Risemberg, R. (1997). Becoming a self-regulated writer: A social cognitive perspective. *Contemporary Educational Psychology*, *22*(1), 73–101. DOI: 10.1006/ceps.1997.0919

Chapter 13
The Convergence of Technology and Vocational Pedagogy and Artificial Intelligence for Driving Transformation and Creating a Sustainable Workforce

Oladiran Stephen Olabiyi
https://orcid.org/0000-0002-1319-265X
University of Lagos, Nigeria

Caleb Chiidozie Chinedu
https://orcid.org/0000-0002-0548-3297
Universiti Tun Hussein Onn Malaysia, Malaysia

ABSTRACT

Integrating Artificial Intelligence (AI) and technology-driven vocational pedagogy in Technical and Vocational Education and Training (TVET) offers transformative potential in preparing students for the modern workforce. AI enhances skill acquisition, making learning more efficient and improving employability. This chapter explores the convergence of AI and vocational pedagogy in shaping workforce development. It defines key concepts, including AI, vocational pedagogy, and TVET, while examining AI's role in enhancing learning, assessment, and workforce readiness. The chapter also discusses the impact of vocational pedagogy on skill development, the integration of technology in TVET, and AI-driven workforce transformation in Nigeria. Challenges faced by TVET educators in adopting AI and its benefits in equipping students with essential competencies are highlighted. The chapter concludes with recommendations for leveraging AI to create a sustainable, industry-relevant vocational education system.

DOI: 10.4018/979-8-3693-9062-7.ch013

INTRODUCTION

The application of Artificial Intelligence (AI) and technology vocational pedagogy in developing the future workforce through Technical and Vocational Education and Training (TVET) shows potential for transforming the educational setting by providing students with the essential competencies needed to excel in the current employment market, this allows students to receive customized learning experiences that cater to their specific needs. This enhances students' ability to acquire skills more efficiently, ultimately improving their employability and preparedness for the requirements of the modern workforce. In the twenty-first century, Technical and Vocational Education and Training (TVET) faces challenges, including training the workforce globally and improving the educational processes associated with online and face-to-face teaching. For this, teachers and students should take advantage of the potential of tools based on artificial intelligence. One of the bulging emerging challenges in education involves offering models and plans for incorporating artificial intelligence into teaching and learning technology education programmes, based on solid educational and pedagogical principles. Meeting this challenge appropriately and effectively may help to create more flexible, personalized, and sustainable learning environments (Vázquez-Cano, 2021).

The industrial development of any nation greatly hinges on the skill level of its workforce. In turn, the workforce's effectiveness is contingent upon the quality of the nation's education and training. As education and training continue to evolve, twenty-first-century workers are facing more challenges. Technical vocational education and training (TVET) institutions are tasked with providing effective training (Olabiyi, 2014). The integration of Artificial Intelligence (AI) into Technical and Vocational Education and Training (TVET) represents a transformative shift in how skills are taught and learned globally. This convergence of artificial intelligence and pedagogy is reshaping educational frameworks, improving access, and enhancing the relevance of skill training to meet the demands of the modern workforce. (Huang & Sotheran, 2021). This integration has garnered significant academic interest due to its potential to revolutionise learning practices and align skill development with industry needs. The development of technical and vocational skills is vital to economic development. Action that is planned to impart knowledge, skills (competencies), the right attitude, autonomy of identity, perseverance, character, and work ethic to learners in readiness for work and general employment. This in turn leads to productivity, social inclusion, and economic development (UNESCO-UNEVOC, 2013).

Workforce according to Olabiyi (2020) refers to people or individuals engaged in or available for work, either in a country, area, or in a particular firm or industry. It is the number of people in a country or area who are available for work. The above definitions nonetheless, need to be stressed that the workforce of a nation includes all the industrial and factory workers as well as any person or group of persons in that nation whose productive work or services satisfy some aspects of human needs. Pedagogy refers to the technique and training of teaching. It involves the strategies, techniques, and approaches used by technology and vocational educators to facilitate teaching, learning, and the acquisition of knowledge and skills by trainees. Effective technology vocational pedagogy usually involves active engagement, critical thinking, and the creation of a supportive and inclusive learning environment. Globalisation is the integration of economies and societies through cross-country flows of information, ideas, technologies, goods, services, capital, finance, and people. It is the trend toward increased economic, cultural, and social connectedness between individuals, businesses, and public organisations across international borders (Olabiyi, 2014).

The convergence of AI and pedagogy in TVET is heralding a new era of education that prioritises personalised learning, skill relevance, and accessibility. As TVET institutions around the world embrace these technologies, they are better equipped to prepare students for the dynamic demands of the global job market. (Cedefop. 2020). The convergence of artificial intelligence and vocational pedagogy refers to the integration of artificial intelligence (AI) technologies into the field of technical and vocational education and training. This convergence aims to leverage AI tools and techniques to enhance the learning experience, skill development, and workforce readiness of technology vocational education students. By integrating AI into pedagogical practices, technical vocational education institutions can personalize learning, provide real-time feedback, and adapt teaching strategies to meet the needs of individual students. Furthermore, the convergence of AI and vocational pedagogy involves exploring ethical considerations and ensuring that the use of AI robustly aligns with the principles of fairness, transparency, and accountability in education and workforce development. Integrating AI in TVET enhances instructional methods and offers immersive, hands-on training experiences that closely replicate real-world situations, ensuring students are better prepared for modern workforce demands (Abu Bakar, Ghafa & Abdullah, 2024).

DEFINITION AND MEANING OF ARTIFICIAL INTELLIGENCE

The use of artificial intelligence and technology vocational pedagogy to transform Nigerian workforce development programmes offers the opportunity to provide the workforce with the important skills needed to succeed in a rapidly evolving economy. By utilising modern technology, personalized learning, and industry collaborations, Nigeria can improve its education system and greatly enhance employability and economic growth. The key focus should be on creating inclusive, engaging, and relevant experiences that prepare individuals for the demands of the future workplace. Artificial intelligence is a broad and rapidly evolving field that seeks to imitate human cognitive functions and has significant implications across various domains of society and industry.

Artificial intelligence was originally explained as making a machine function in ways that would be called intelligent if a human were to work (McCarthy, Minsky, Rochester, & Shannon, 1955). Today, artificial intelligence encompasses systems that employ various technologies including data mining, computer vision, language recognition, natural language generation, machine learning, and deep learning to generate or use data. These technologies are employed to predict, recommend, or make decisions with varying levels of autonomy to determine the best course of action (Eurostat, 2021). Artificial intelligence refers to the ability of machines to perform tasks that usually require human intelligence, such as learning from experience, recognising patterns, and making decisions. This swiftly developing field includes various technologies and approaches including natural language processing, machine learning, computer vision, and robotics. Artificial intelligence can be broadly categorized into two types: Narrow artificial intelligence, which is designed for a specific task, and general artificial intelligence, which would possess the ability to apply intelligence to any task, much like a human.

Artificial Intelligence denotes the simulation of human reasoning processes through machines, particularly computer systems. These processes include learning, which involves assimilating information and acquiring rules for its application, as well as reasoning, which encompasses the ability to solve problems using the acquired information, and self-correction. The meaning of artificial intelligence covers not only the technology itself but also its broader implications for technology vocational education and society at large. In the context of technology vocational education and workforce development, artificial intelligence has the potential to transform learning experiences, personalise education, and enhance skill development to meet the evolving demands of the modern workforce. When considering artificial intelligence, two key principles form its foundation: firstly, autonomy, which allows the system to perform tasks in complex situations without constant guidance from the user, and secondly, adaptability, which enables the system to improve task execution by learning from experience.

These fundamental concepts play a crucial role in shaping a pedagogical paradigm that can effectively respond to current and future educational approaches based on artificial intelligence. Artificial intelligence can be based on purely software systems, such as chatbots and virtual assistants utilizing natural language processing, facial recognition systems incorporating visual or language recognition systems, software for machine translation, data analysis based on machine learning, and neural nets for deep learning, among others. (Cope, Kalantzis, & Searsmith, 2020). Artificial intelligence aims to develop systems capable of performing tasks typically requiring human intelligence. This has the potential to enhance efficiency, accuracy, and productivity across various fields, including healthcare, business, technology vocational education, and performing art. The integration of artificial intelligence into the Technical Vocational Education and Training curriculum enables the delivery of tailored and personalised learning experiences that are specifically designed to meet the individual needs of students. This educational approach enhances students' ability to acquire essential skills more effectively, thereby enhancing their employability and readiness to meet the demands of the contemporary and self-motivated workforce. (Vázquez-Cano, 2021).

Artificial intelligence raises important considerations related to its ethical, social, and economic implications, including the following aspects, firstly, automation: artificial intelligence has the potential to automate various jobs, which can significantly impact the labour market, leading to the need for workforce reskilling and adaptation to new job requirements. Secondly, ethics and bias: There are apprehensions regarding the fairness, accountability, and transparency of artificial intelligence algorithms, especially in decision-making processes that have a direct impact on people's lives. Ensuring ethical artificial intelligence development and use is crucial in addressing these concerns. Thirdly, Human- artificial intelligence collaboration: The collaboration between humans and artificial intelligence systems opens up possibilities for enhancing human capabilities, resulting in innovative solutions and improved outcomes in various domains. Finding the right balance in human-artificial intelligence collaboration is essential for maximising the potential benefits of this partnership. (Vázquez-Cano, 2021) Artificial intelligence is a wide-ranging and rapidly evolving study that seeks to replicate human reasoning purposes and has important implications across various domains of society and industry.

The fundamental components of artificial intelligence comprise machine learning, natural language processing, computer vision, and robotics. Machine learning, a subset of artificial intelligence, is responsible for constructing algorithms that enable machines to learn from data and form predictions or decisions. This field incorporates various techniques, including supervised, unsupervised, and reinforcement learning. Natural Language Processing (NLP) is a field of artificial intelligence that empowers machines to comprehend, interpret, and produce human language, facilitating more natural interactions between humans and machines. On the other hand, computer vision pertains to enabling machines to interpret and comprehend visual data from the environment, including identifying objects, faces, and scenes in images and videos. Robotics is a branch of artificial intelligence dedicated to developing and constructing robots capable of independently or collaboratively carrying out tasks. This often involves the use of artificial intelligence to enable robots to navigate and interact with their surroundings, as well as employing expert systems that imitate the decision-making capabilities of human experts in particular areas by using rules and knowledge to solve intricate problems. AI can potentially revolutionise Technical and Vocational Education and Training by providing innovative solutions for personalised learning and efficient workforce development. (Abu Bakar, Ghafa, & Abdullah, 2024)

DEFINITION AND MEANING OF TECHNICAL/TECHNOLOGY VOCATIONAL EDUCATION AND TRAINING

The primary concern confronting the nation lies in cultivating a proficient workforce to sustain economic growth in the global economy. Strategic and well-coordinated educational and training initiatives for workforce development are pivotal in advancing the well-being of individuals, employers, enterprises, and the overall economy and society within the nation. (Olabiyi, 2020). A well-organised Technical Vocational Education and Training (TVET) system is crucial for enhancing productivity, improving competitiveness, and fostering entrepreneurial activity. The primary objective of TVET is to equip individuals for self-employment and to function as a platform for the progression of individuals in the labour market, empowering them to establish a sense of identity and contribution within their communities. (Chinedu & Olabiyi, 2018). The development of technical and vocational skills according to Olabiyi (2020) is indispensable for economic advancement due to two critical reasons. Firstly, technical vocational skills are essential for enhancing enterprise productivity, and profitability, as well as national productivity and wealth creation. The absence of requisite skills and enterprise can significantly impede national growth. The demand for skilled workers is driven by technological innovation and economic growth.

The increasing need for technical and vocational skills is a result of the convergence of various factors, including technical change, changes in work organization, growing economic openness and competitiveness, and capital deepening (the increase in capital per worker). The second reason why Technical Vocational Education and Training is crucial lies in its importance for individual prosperity. The acquisition of relevant skills not only enhances individual productivity but also has a direct impact on income levels. Technical Vocational Education and Training is designed to impart knowledge, skills (competencies), the right attitude, autonomy of identity, perseverance, character, and a work ethic to learners, preparing them for work and general employment. Consequently, this process contributes to increased productivity, social inclusion, and overall economic development. (UNESCO-UNEVOC, 2013) Technical Vocational Education and Training (TVET) has been recognised as a crucial facilitator of pedagogical strategies aimed at transitioning young individuals from academic environments to the practicalities of the workforce.

TVET is an educational form characterized by its didactic nature, focusing on teaching, learning, and research directed towards various trades, occupations, and professions (Olabiyi, 2020). According to the view of the Government of Bhutan Thimphu (2014), Technical Vocational Education and Training (TVET) is defined as a form of education designed to equip individuals with the necessary skills and knowledge for employment in specific trades, crafts, occupations, and careers. It is characterized as a flexible, democratic, and inclusive form of education, allowing for the delivery of teaching and learning at the learner's convenience, often through modularization. Additionally, it encompasses content tailored for individuals at various levels of occupational qualifications. UNESCO (2002) and FRN (2004) explained Technical Vocational Education and Training as encompassing all educational processes that go beyond general education to include the study of technologies and related sciences, the acquisition of practical skills, as well as the development of attitudes, understanding, and knowledge relevant to occupations across different sectors of economic and social life. TVET also known as workforce education, is essential for adapting individuals' skills and knowledge to meet the evolving demands of society. It focuses on developing the skills of individuals in their chosen occupations.

Therefore, TVET plays a crucial role in improving the quality of work and the competency of TVET graduates. It also contributes to increasing job satisfaction, motivating workers, and enhancing their productivity. The purpose of Technical and Vocational Education and Training is multifaceted, aiming to equip individuals with the skills necessary for self-employment and to facilitate their evolution within the workforce. TVET not only imparts specific job-related skills but also instills a sense of community and belonging among individuals. Moreover, according to Hollander and Mar (2009), TVET is considered an instrumental tool for reducing extreme poverty through the empowerment of individuals and the enhancement of their employability. The utilisation of technology is crucial in contemporary workforce development. Transforming Technical Vocational Education and Training to cultivate a sustainable workforce for the constantly evolving world of work can happen through Artificial intelligence. AI has the potential to contribute to the development of learning environments that are more enriching, personalized, and accommodating of functional diversity. This can be achieved through the implementation of active methodologies that promote self-regulated learning, leveraging technologies such as learning analytics, big data, conversational agents, blockchain, multi-format content, and gamification.

Embracing AI in education presents an opportunity to enhance the quality of learning experiences and promote a more sustainable educational model that aligns with the objectives outlined in UNESCO's 2030 Agenda for Sustainable Development (SDG 4). This agenda emphasizes the importance of ensuring inclusive and equitable quality education, as well as fostering lifelong learning opportunities for all individuals. Additionally, it underscores the need to establish education systems that are inclusive, equitable, and relevant to the diverse needs of learners. The benefits of AI in TVET according to Abu Bakar, Ghafa, and Abdullah (2024) comprise enhanced engagement, improved efficiency in administrative tasks, and data-driven insights for educators. However, the integration of AI faces significant challenges, including high implementation costs, insufficient infrastructure, and ethical concerns related to data privacy and algorithmic bias, and achieved emphasises the integration of artificial intelligence in the curriculum implementation process.

EXPLANATION AND MEANING OF PEDAGOGY AND VOCATIONAL PEDAGOGY

In the twenty-first century, educational institutions are experiencing significant changes in scientific discoveries, informatisation, globalisation, and the development of astronautics, robotics, and artificial intelligence. This era is often referred to as the age of digital technologies and knowledge, signifying a remarkable shift in our interaction with and comprehension of the world around us. The learning methods twenty-first-century students adopt differ significantly from those of the twentieth century. This shift in learning approaches has been a recurring phenomenon throughout history, particularly with the advancement of technology and the widespread use of the Internet in everyday life. In the present era, the emphasis is no longer solely on acquiring knowledge, but rather on understanding how knowledge is obtained and practically implementing artificial intelligence within the context of a Competency-based Curriculum. (Vázquez-Cano, 2021) Vázquez-Cano stressed further that twenty-first-century pedagogy necessitates adaptation of its principles to contemporary social and technological landscapes. Understanding pedagogy is essential for creating a supportive and inclusive learning environment. It involves the techniques and approaches used by educators to facilitate teaching and learning, promoting active engagement and critical thinking among students.

Pedagogy according to Anand (2021), describes the art and science of teaching students. Pedagogy is not only about training, it is about critically educating people to be self-reflective, and capable of critically addressing their relationship with others and with the larger world. Pedagogy refers to the methods and principles employed in the training and teaching of students, encompassing both the theoretical framework and practical application of teaching. It represents the intersection of cultural influences and learning techniques designed to foster comprehensive development in learners. The fundamental objective of pedagogy according to Anand (2021) is to empower students with a comprehensive understanding of the subject matter and equip them with the ability to apply their learning in real-life situations beyond the traditional classroom environment. Pedagogy in TVET is referred to as a technical teacher's understanding of how their students learn. The teachers are focused on presenting the syllabus to the students in such a way that it is relevant to their needs (Anand, 2021)

Pedagogy stresses classroom interactions between the teacher and students, which significantly impact the learner's mind. It enables teachers to understand the best suitable practices for a classroom setting. It helps them to know how different students learn and grasp information so that they can tailor their lessons to satisfy those needs. It is likely to improve the quality of teaching and how it is received by the students (Christine, 2024). Christine added that pedagogy is important in helping teachers understand the best ways to conduct a classroom. It gives them insights into how students learn differently in different topics so that they can conduct lessons to suit these needs. It aims to improve the quality of education for students. Effective pedagogy is crucial for creating engaging and meaningful learning experiences that cater to the diverse needs of learners. In the context of technology vocational education, pedagogy plays a vital role in shaping the delivery of knowledge and skills to prepare students for the demands of the modern workforce.

Vocational pedagogy according to Vázquez-Cano (2021) includes the practices, techniques, and approaches employed by teachers in vocational technical education to facilitate the process of teaching and learning, as well as the acquisition of knowledge and skills by students. It involves the practical application of teaching and instructional methods that are specifically tailored to vocational and technical training, aiming to equip students with the necessary competencies for particular occupations or trades. Successful vocational pedagogy frequently entails fostering active engagement, promoting critical thinking, and establishing a supportive and inclusive learning environment that is customised to meet the requirements of the workforce. Vocational pedagogy encompasses various meanings and connotations that mirror different educational traditions and influences. These differences often stem from national interpretations of the extent of a teacher's decision-making. For instance, in Slovenia, vocational pedagogy is described in the literature as a pedagogical discipline that addresses broader issues within technical vocational education and training, including the organisation, principles, and financing of TVET, as well as the collaboration between the realms of work and education (Muršak 2004).

Moreover, according to Benedek (2003 and 2006), vocational pedagogy encompasses a broad concept that includes fundamental principles and funding concerns of TVET, the relationship between TVET and the economy, strategies for cultivating occupation-specific competencies, substantive and methodological considerations in TVET, approaches for addressing learners with special educational needs and providing remedial education for learners who are falling behind their peers. Understanding the impacts of vocational pedagogies, particularly learner-centered approaches, holds significant importance in informing policy formulation. This understanding facilitates the development of models and tools that can assist technical vocational education teachers and trainers in effectively aligning teaching and learning methods with the specific needs of their students and the contexts in which they operate. Consequently, vocational pedagogies can have a direct influence on the quality of teaching and learning, thereby contributing to the attainment of technical vocational education broader objectives (Cedefop, 2015).

Therefore, it is imperative to reconsider the instructional and pedagogical model that supports the integration of technology, both within and outside the classroom. Simply incorporating technology into education does not inherently lead to improvement without a robust instructional component. As a result, initiatives based on artificial intelligence will necessitate substantial instructional and pedagogical adjustments. In 2010, UNESCO put forth a set of recommended teaching strategies for the twenty-first century, including experiential learning, storytelling, values education, inquiry-based learning, appropriate assessment, future problem solving, outside classroom learning, and community problem solving among others (UNESCO, 2010). It is essential for teachers to actively incorporate innovative teaching methods in their practice. The more diverse and engaging the strategies and methods used in teaching, the more effectively they can motivate students' cognitive activity, foster problem-solving skills, and facilitate in-depth learning and practical skill acquisition. A Dedicated teacher continually enhances their teaching skills and seeks out and develops new methods and technologies for teaching. The main types include:

Competency-based training (CBT) is an educational approach that focuses on equipping learners with specific skills and competencies required for a particular job or profession. CBT is an approach to technical and vocational education and training that underscores what a person can do in the workplace as a result of completing a training programme. Competency-based training programmes are often comprised of modules broken into segments called learning outcomes, which are based on standards set by the industry, and assessment is designed to ensure each student has achieved all the outcomes (skills and knowledge) required by each module. Ideally, progress within a competency-based training programme is not based on time. Some competency-based training modules have two assessment components.i.e. On-the-job and Off-the-job. (Commonwealth of Learning, n.d., ILO, 2020). The main characteristics of CBT among others include outcome-oriented; individualized learning; real-world relevance; assessment-focused; and flexibility. CBT is widely used in vocational education and training programmes, as it helps ensure that graduates are ready for work and meet employers' expectations.

Project-based learning (PBL) is a learning method that is based on the theory of constructivism through the principles of learning by doing founded by John Dewey (Bender, 2012). Based on this principle, William Heard Kilpatrick further developed the idea of teaching and learning through a method known as project-based learning (Beckett, & Slater, 2019). PBL method allows students to engage in learning situations through the application of ideas and the production of a project (Guo, Saab, Post, & Admiraal, 2020; Kaldi, Filippatou, Govaris, 2011; Krajcik, Blumenfeld, Marx & Soloway, 1994). Students work on projects that simulate real-world tasks relevant to their field. PBL is interpreted as a model of activity that differs from ordinary classroom practice and involves a broad range of disciplines. In addition, PBL is said to be an active and student-centered method of learning that is believed to enable students to gain deeper knowledge through active exploration of real-world challenges and problems. Project-based learning is a learning method that differs from ordinary classroom practice as it is a hands-on project, actively engaged and student-centered, and involves the process of exploring for deep knowledge and thus producing individuals with problem-solving skills as well as the challenges facing the real world. PBL is highly relevant in Technical and Vocational Education and Training (TVET) as it enhances practical skills, encourages critical thinking, and fosters collaborative work. PBL engages students in real-world projects that are closely aligned with industry standards, allowing them to apply theoretical knowledge in practical scenarios. PBL not only increases student engagement but also prepares them for the workforce by developing essential competencies. PBL offers numerous benefits, particularly in TVET. Here are some key advantages: enhanced critical thinking, practical application, collaboration skills, engagement and motivation, creativity and innovation, self-directed learning, interdisciplinary learning, preparation for the workforce, and development of soft skills.

Experiential learning is a process that develops knowledge, skills, and attitudes based on consciously thinking about an experience. Thus, it involves direct and active personal experience combined with reflection and feedback. (UNESCO, 2010). Experiential learning engages students in critical thinking, problem-solving, and decision-making in contexts that are personally relevant to them. This approach to learning also involves making opportunities for debriefing and consolidation of ideas and skills through feedback, reflection, and the application of the ideas and skills to new situations. Experiential learning is personal and effective, influencing both feelings and emotions as well as enhancing knowledge and skills. Experiential learning is particularly relevant in Technical and Vocational Education and Training (TVET) for several reasons: Experiential learning emphasizes active participation, allowing students to engage directly with tools, technologies, and real-world scenarios, essential for mastering vocational skills, it provides learning opportunities within the specific context of the industry, enabling students to understand how their skills apply in actual work environments,

Furthermore, experiential learning equips students with the competencies needed to transition smoothly into the workforce, making them more attractive candidates to employers, it promotes continuous improvement through reflection on experiences and constructive feedback, helping students to identify areas for growth, engaging in experiential learning fosters critical soft skills, such as teamwork, communication, and problem-solving, which are crucial for success in any professional setting, students are often more motivated and engaged when learning through experience, as it connects academic concepts to real-life applications and challenges, bridges the gap between theoretical knowledge and practical application, reinforcing understanding and retention of information. Also, dealing with unpredictable workplace situations, students learn to adapt and develop strong problem-solving abilities, essential skills in today's dynamic job market.

Work-integrated learning (WIL) is a component of technical and vocational education and training. One of the main purposes of TVET institutions is to prepare students for the world of work. TVET practitioners thus need to get regular workplace experience to keep abreast of developments in the industry. Industry-based WIL is described as learning in and from workplaces through industry visits, placements, and other interactions with the industry. (Petrina, & Carver, 2019) The Council of Higher Education (CHE, 2011) defines WIL as an educational pedagogy comprising curricula, as well as pedagogic, and assessment practices across a range of academic disciplines that integrate formal learning and workplace concerns. WIL comes in many forms thus Jackson (2013) describes it as it is a flexible creature that can be adapted to different disciplines and organizational contexts. These forms may include sandwich programmes, apprenticeships, credit-bearing WIL programs, teaching practice, and industry-based WIL, amongst others. Industry-based WIL in the South African context has therefore come to be understood as a new form of workplace learning in TVET programmes in which practitioners' practice to teach and learn the skills, techniques, and practices of a specific subject from industry placements.

WIL provides students with real-world experiences, enhances their employability, and equips them with the necessary competencies that employers seek. This type of learning fosters collaboration between educational institutions and industries, ensuring that the curriculum is aligned with market demands and industry standards. WIL offers numerous benefits for students, educational institutions, and employers. The benefits for students include providing practical, hands-on experiences that enhance their understanding of theoretical concepts, students can developing essential technical and soft skills that are highly valued in the workforce, through industry experience, students become more attractive to potential employers, improving their job prospects, and WIL allows students to build professional connections, which can lead to job offers or mentorship and also gain insights into various career paths, helping them make informed decisions about their future. TVET Institutions also benefit through WIL in the areas of collaboration with industry so that the curriculum remains up-to-date and aligned with labour market needs, real-world applications of knowledge can lead to higher student motivation and engagement, and through WIL TVET institutions can develop strong relationships with local businesses and industries, benefiting from shared resources and expertise. Employers also benefit by identifying and nurturing potential candidates for future employment through internships and placements, students bring fresh ideas and knowledge to the workplace, contributing to innovation and improvement, and engaging students through WIL can be a cost-effective way for companies to assess talent before making full-time hiring decisions.

IMPORTANCE OF VOCATIONAL PEDAGOGY IN TEACHING TVET PROGRAMMES

The industrial development of any country depends to a great extent on the level of skills its workforce possesses, and the skills and effectiveness of the workforce, in turn, depend upon the quality of the nation's education and training. Education and training are undergoing continuous change, which poses more challenges to workers in the twenty-first century, and TVET institutions that are responsible for their training. (Olabiyi, 2019). Technology Education students of the twenty-first century do not learn in the same way as those of the twentieth century. Whilst this phenomenon has occurred at all stages of history and society's educational development, this has become even more prominent considering the irruption of technology and the Internet in human daily life. (Vázquez-Cano, 2021) A pedagogy approach in technology education refers to the methods and strategies used to teach and learn skills, knowledge, competencies, and attitudes required to secure and progress in occupation and new emerging occupation. Pedagogy is defined simply as the method, and practice, of teaching. It encompasses teaching approaches, teaching theory, and feedback and assessment.

When discussing the pedagogy of teaching, it refers to the way teachers deliver the content of a technology education programme to a class, pedagogy extends beyond merely delivering content; it involves understanding the complexities of the learning process and adapting to the diverse needs of students. It reflects the philosophy of education, values, and beliefs that educators hold regarding learning and teaching (Horn & Chavez, 2022). In technology education, various pedagogical approaches are used to teach students the skills and knowledge needed for a specific occupation or trade for effective workforce development. The dynamic landscape of technology education has witnessed a profound shift from traditional to modern pedagogical paradigms over the years. Pedagogy plays a pivotal role in education by providing a constructive framework for teachers to effectively impart theoretical knowledge and practical skills. Educators' pedagogical approaches, influenced by their teaching philosophies and cultural awareness, are instrumental in catering to diverse learning styles. Establishing meaningful classroom relationships is crucial for students as it catalyzes leveraging previous learning experiences. These relationships create an enabling environment for students to expand upon their existing knowledge, thereby fostering continuous cognitive growth and development.

The concept of vocational pedagogy in the opinion of Cedefop (2015) encompasses the wide range of instructional decisions made by vocational teachers and trainers. It involves adapting teaching methods to meet the needs of learners and aligning with the specific context in which they are operating. Vocational pedagogy involves a wide range of deliberate choices made by vocational teachers and trainers as they deliver instruction, tailoring their methods to meet the needs of learners and align with the specific context in which they are teaching. (Shulman, 2005), this concept pertains to the instructional strategies that shape the fundamental approaches through which future professionals are being prepared for their future careers.

The science, art, and craft of teaching and learning vocational education encompass the complex processes, methodologies, and skills employed by vocational educators to impart knowledge and facilitate learning in vocational education settings. It involves the deliberate decisions made by vocational teachers as they engage in teaching, continuously adapting their instructional approaches to accommodate the diverse learning needs of their students and to align with the specific contextual factors present within their educational environment. This holistic approach ensures that vocational teachers can effectively meet the unique needs of their students and create a supportive and inclusive learning environment. (UNESCO-UNEVOC 2014)

Pedagogy involves an all-inclusive approach to teaching, integrating both theoretical principles and practical applications. It involves the exploration of optimal frameworks and techniques to enhance the quality of teaching and learning experiences. The execution of pedagogy is influenced by educators' teaching philosophies, incorporating an appreciation of diverse cultural backgrounds and various learning styles. Additionally, pedagogy draws upon scientific theories of learning and the philosophy of education to guide its implementation. This holistic perspective underscores the pivotal role of pedagogy in fostering enriching educational interactions and experiences. The advancement of education is greatly enhanced by the field of Pedagogical Innovation, which plays a pivotal role in developing, implementing, and sharing new teaching practices. Innovation encompasses new essences, methods, techniques, technologies, and content, driving positive change within the educational landscape. According to Taubaeva and Laktionova (2001), the innovative process in education is a multifaceted endeavour that shapes educational content and establishes new organisational frameworks. Innovative teaching methods empower educators to foster novel interactions with students, introducing innovative practical activities that enhance the mastery of educational material.

In the field of TVET, there has been a shift towards emphasizing the development of competencies rather than just the acquisition of knowledge. Competencies are not easily acquired in a single lesson; instead, they are the result of consistent knowledge formation over time. This process involves the implementation of learning strategies over a certain period. These strategies integrate various approaches, development directions, instructional methods, and types. They are designed to achieve the desired educational outcomes. By employing active, innovative, project-based, and playful teaching strategies, educators can effectively apply the concepts of constructivism and connectivism. The following are some of the specific importance of using appropriate vocational pedagogy.

The implementation of a well-considered pedagogy in classrooms can lead to a significant improvement in the quality of education. This improvement can positively impact students by enhancing their understanding of educational material, ultimately resulting in improved learning outcomes. The application of a well-considered pedagogy in classrooms unequivocally leads to a significant improvement in the quality of TVET programs. This improvement undeniably benefits students by enhancing their understanding of educational material, ultimately resulting in markedly improved learning outcomes.

Firstly, it improves the quality of teaching: The application of a well-considered pedagogy in classrooms unequivocally leads to a significant improvement in the quality of education. This improvement undeniably benefits students by enhancing their understanding of educational material, ultimately resulting in markedly improved learning outcomes.

Also, it encourages a cooperative learning environment: The incorporation of pedagogy in technical and vocational education and training encourages collaborative efforts among students aimed at accomplishing shared tasks and engaging in collective learning. This practice enhances their cognitive skills by fostering the exchange of perspectives and insights, thereby facilitating their adaptation to cooperative learning environments and nurturing their potential to emerge as proficient workforce in the future.

Furthermore, the application of a well-considered pedagogy in classrooms Eliminates monotonous learning: Pedagogy and child development are closely intertwined, serving to expand students' cognitive capacities beyond conventional memorization and basic comprehension. This approach engenders sophisticated cognitive processes, encompassing analysis, creative ideation, and critical evaluation. Moreover, it makes students more receptive to what the teacher is teaching.

Moreover, through the application of a well-considered pedagogy in classrooms students can follow their ways of learning: A well-designed pedagogy plays a crucial role in facilitating students' comprehension of educational content through diverse approaches. It accommodates the varying learning styles and capabilities of individual students, allowing them to engage with their preferred modes of learning. Consequently, this tailored approach fosters a deeper understanding of the subject matter, thereby enhancing students' skills and overall learning achievements.

Convenient learning approach for all students: Students with diverse learning needs, including those with physical, cognitive, or emotional challenges, require personalized instructional strategies to effectively access and engage with educational content. The implementation of differentiated pedagogical approaches, such as multisensory learning techniques and individualized education plans, is crucial to promoting their academic success and fostering their inclusion within the mainstream educational environment.

The application of a well-considered pedagogy in classrooms improves teacher-student communication: Understanding the student better allows the teacher to identify areas for improvement and provide constructive guidance, leading to academic progress. This personalized approach to education can significantly enhance the learning experience and help students reach their full potential.

TECHNOLOGY IN TECHNICAL AND VOCATIONAL EDUCATION AND TRAINING

The historical context of technology in vocational training can be traced back to various key developments. In the early twentieth century, vocational education began to formalize, focusing on providing skills for specific trades. The introduction of industrial machines necessitated training programmes that could teach workers the operation and maintenance of these tools. Post-World War II, the expansion of technological advances led to the integration of more sophisticated equipment, requiring updated training methods. In recent decades, the rise of digital technology has revolutionized vocational training, introducing online learning platforms, simulations, and virtual reality, making training more accessible and efficient. These changes reflect the continuous evolution of technology in the educational sector, aimed at meeting the demands of the job market. It's important to consult multiple sources and current research for comprehensive information.

The technology influences all aspects of TVET delivery, from the integration of new digital skills and competencies into teaching and learning processes to the implementation of learning itself. Learners, both young and adult, must be equipped with the technology skills needed for new and old jobs and to become digitally competent, capable, literate, intelligent citizens. TVET institutions are under pressure to utilize digital technology to be more accessible, affordable, and individually tailored while improving their quality and labour market relevance. (UNESCO, 2023) TVET teachers need to understand the characteristics of technology tools to be able to choose the right ones for use in technology-supported pedagogical models. The integration of technologies in TVET can support learning processes because they reflect situations similar to the ones faced by learners in real work settings. Technology plays a crucial role in Technical and Vocational Education and Training by enhancing the learning experience, improving education delivery, and equipping students with relevant skills for the job market.

The ability of teachers to use digital technologies is crucial for their successful integration into the learning process. This starts with the design of a clear instructional plan to enhance TVET delivery with the use of technologies, and it results ultimately in the creation of an environment that is conducive to achieving the intended learning outcomes (Dwayi, 2017). However, teachers who lack the necessary competencies often fail to realise what can be achieved in the curriculum with technology in comparison to what is achieved without technology. The integration of technology artificial intelligence (AI) and specialised pedagogy enhances student learning experiences. It is clear that AI has broad implications for the whole of humanity, and therefore for the technical and vocational education and training institutions that equip lifelong learners with the skills to navigate both work and society. Therefore, there is a need for institutions and other stakeholders to rise to the challenge through research and innovative programmes, paving the way for a better understanding of AI's potential – and its pitfalls. Artificial intelligence (AI) according to UNESCO-UNEVOC (2021) is changing the way we work, live, communicate, learn, and play.

Individuals are increasingly encountering advanced technologies such as AI in their everyday lives, some of which may have a profound impact on their lives. UNESCO- UNEVOC stressed further that in the early years of the twenty-first century, many occupations have been influenced by human creativity and innovation, allowing for the increased extraction of value from emerging technologies. The integration of AI into industrial and agricultural processes, services, value chains, and workplace structures has become a focal point of many national policies. While AI has the potential to enhance the quality of life, it also introduces significant policy, ethical, and social considerations, such as job creation and obsolescence. Consequently, it has emerged as a source of social and political tension and has the potential to exacerbate disparities both within and between nations. AI is making an impact on labour markets that is significant and far-reaching. A report from the McKinsey Global Institute suggested that nearly half of the tasks currently performed by human workers possibly will be automated using existing technology by the year 2055 (Manyika et al., 2017). This trend is expected to contribute to the increasing prevalence of higher-skill jobs in the workforce. Furthermore, a mounting body of research indicates that factors such as technological advancements and globalisation are leading to a polarisation of the labour market, with a growing divide between high-skilled and low-skilled jobs, a phenomenon often referred to as raising out of the workforce. (Autor 2010; Bárány & Siegel, 2015; Brown, 2016; Goos, Manning & Salomons, 2014). Workers with intermediate skills are at particular risk because of the routine nature of the tasks they often perform and the fact that the technologies that can replace them, such as AI and robotics, can create considerable cost savings for employers. However, an important caveat is that this refers to intermediate skills as we currently know them. Analyses conducted by occupation rather than wage percentile reveal the persistence of intermediate occupations, thereby highlighting 'the changing nature of intermediate jobs' (McIntosh, 2013). Therefore, while the skills needed by the labour market may be changing, intermediate-level education such as technical and vocational education and training (TVET) remains far from obsolete in the digital age.

IMPACT OF VOCATIONAL PEDAGOGY ON TVET STUDENT LEARNING AND SKILL DEVELOPMENT

Skill is an organized sequence of actions, proficiency executed and usually displaying a flexible but systematic, temporal patterning. Flexibility describes the ability to free oneself from the rigidity of attitude and procedure associated with pre-conceived tradition. Skill is the capability of accomplishing a task with precision and certainty, practical knowledge in combination with ability, cleverness, and expertness (Olabiyi, 2019). Skill, therefore, is a well-established habit of carrying out a task easily and well. It involves the acquisition of performance capability, to perform acquired skills learned with practice. Skill development is the ability to do or perform an activity that is related to some meaningful actions, works, or jobs. Olabiyi (2019) points out that to develop a particular skill is to show the habit of thinking, acting, and behaving in a specific activity in such a way that the process becomes natural to an individual through constant practice. Skill development requires actual muscular movements of fingers, hands, arms, and other parts of the body, coordinated with the eyes and sometimes the ear. Such movements are involved in the use of tools, instruments, machines, and consumable materials.

Skill development according to Olabiyi (2004) varies with the nature, complexity, and type of activity that is involved. For instance, skills needed in woodwork will be different from the skills required in battery charging or machining. Skill development requires intelligent humans. Indeed, most learned or developed skills present great challenges to TVET institutions on the integration of practical work and theoretical fields, common sense, a good power of observation, and courage. An individual who opts for skill development should among other things, possess qualities such as interest, ability, aptitude, patience, personality characteristics, and other human qualities that would enable them to succeed in it. It is important to point out that before any skill is developed, it is important to ascertain that the skill needed. Olabiyi (2004) observed that it is not enough to assume that because somebody fails to achieve the desired results, there is a need to train people to acquire skills as a result of failure, which might be due to a variety of other causes. A lot of resources could have been wasted on skills developed just because the skills and students' needs have not been identified. Therefore, there is a need for skill development when efficiency and effectiveness are being sacrificed and also, where there is a change in technology, methods, or required behavior rendering the current skill obsolete.

Across the globe, technical and vocational education and training (TVET) is widely acknowledged for its key role in fostering economic and socio-economic development, enhancing productivity, empowering individuals, and mitigating poverty. However, the quality of TVET, concerning both learner outcomes and teaching inputs, exhibits notable variations. In certain nations, this detrimental disparity is being tackled through the implementation of accountability frameworks aimed at corroborating the quality of provision, while in others, efforts are focused on enhancing the professionalization and training of the TVET workforce. (Majumdar, 2014). To enhance skill development in TVET, according to Majumdar it's essential to allocate resources towards the transformation of infrastructure and equipment, actively engage employers in the development of curricula, leverage smart technologies, and integrate formative assessment strategies to achieve the best possible outcomes. Essentially, TVET institutions require a strong vocational pedagogy model that expresses the science, art, and craft of teaching and learning vocational education. It's crucial to articulate with clarity and assurance the most effective teaching and learning methods for various learners striving to acquire skills, competencies, and dispositions across diverse contexts.

Understanding vocational pedagogy is critical to the improvement of learner outcomes in TVET and can help to improve the status and quality of TVET. Vocational education pedagogy significantly impacts student learning and skill development by providing practical, hands-on training that aligns with industry needs. (UNESCO, 2014) This approach fosters critical thinking, problem-solving, and technical skills essential for occupation readiness. Furthermore, vocational education emphasizes experiential learning, which enhances student engagement and knowledge retention, leading to better employment outcomes. Vocational pedagogy enables us to develop models and tools that can help TVET teachers match teaching and learning methods more effectively to their students' needs and contexts. Through such means, vocational pedagogy can directly impact the quality of teaching and learning (Gamble, 2013). To be a great TVET teacher requires a model of virtue, knowledge, and skill. It is arguably an even more challenging role than being a general education teacher in schools because its contexts are more varied. It requires expertise in both a vocational field and in vocational pedagogy. This combination, in turn, requires TVET teachers to have a confident and expansive view of the full range of outcomes that their teaching can release from their students. (Lucas, 2014)

Vocational pedagogy enables TVET teachers to match teaching and learning methods to their students' needs and contexts, it directly impacts the quality of teaching and learning., and provides an alternative to the traditional method of education. It also plays a critical role in skill development and employability and helps people in better performance of their jobs as they acquire a great learning experience. Vocational pedagogy underscores student-centered learning, encouraging active participation, critical thinking, and collaboration among students. It often incorporates technology, experiential learning, and individualized instruction tailored to students' needs. TVET expands and transforms when new ideas, methods, and practices occur in the classroom. Vocational pedagogy incorporates strategies to enhance the overall education experience. Blended/ hybrid learning are two key elements that have recently contributed to developing vocational pedagogy. With so much transformation in the education space, it can take time to see a clear picture of modern pedagogy and what it means, especially for schools with limited resources and availability to implement change.

Olabiyi (2019) observed that skill development will be effective if the trainers and trainees can participate fully in the process. This implies that learners and teachers must have a clear idea of what they want to achieve by the time training is completed. The basic purpose of skill development is to shape or reshape the behavior patterns of learners. This desired behavior is about learning. To achieve the desired objective, emphasis must be placed on practical knowledge that expresses what learners will be able to do with the theoretical, practical, and attitude that has been changed; these will influence self-reliance and sustainable development for industrial and technological development. Olabiyi suggested that the first step in planning for skill development is to identify the skill needed and develop the skill objectives from the skill needed. Olabiyi explained further that it is important to establish whether the person or persons to be trained can already perform the activities identified in the objectives and to what level. Also, the trainer needs to be informed about what prior knowledge or experiences the teachers have or better still, arrange for the students to meet with the students. Also, careful attention should be to modern pedagogy relevant to the skills, the physical arrangement of the environment, and workshop facilities, and through investigation of those specific skills that are realistically unique to each student a survey of employment opportunities will also determine the skill to be developed.

Good teachers are just as critical for TVET. TVET teachers have a distinctive role to play: not only do they need to be experts in their subject with a sound understanding of its pedagogy, but they also need to have practical and up-to-date vocational expertise relevant to the workplace. Quality TVET teachers are those with expert knowledge in their field who can transfer it to their students.

ROLES OF ARTIFICIAL INTELLIGENCE IN SHAPING WORKFORCE DEVELOPMENT IN THE TWENTY-FIRST CENTURY

Artificial Intelligence (AI) is increasingly reshaping the workforce, making it more sophisticated and future-proof. However, concerns about job displacement and unemployment are growing. How can organizations address these concerns and encourage workforces to embrace AI? The rapid global integration of AI technology is outpacing the speed at which workforces are embracing AI as a driving force for change. This presents a significant opportunity for organizations international to proactively assist and equip their workforce for the evolving corporate landscape. Considering the profound and transformative impact of AI on industries, society, and everyday life, it is essential for organizations to gradually and decisively prepare themselves and their employees for this transformation. Dealing with occupational, and professional growth demands necessitates an appreciation of workforce development as an integral role of TVET. The role of TVET in developing workforce skills by promoting the use of artificial intelligence learning opportunities in TVET institutions and workplaces is widely acknowledged. The global economic crisis and high unemployment levels among youth and adults illustrate the need to concentrate more on workplace skill growth. The need to develop vocational skills through AI has gotten much help from UN organisations like the ILO and UNESCO. (Olabiyi, 2022).

Workforce training in the opinion of Olabiyi should be competency-based, learner-centered, versatile, and closely oriented to organisational activities that benefit from carefully selected competencies. The workforce in the twenty-first century will be required to possess a broad set of knowledge, skills, work habits, and traits acknowledged by educational professionals, school administrators, teachers, employers, and organized private sectors to be critically important to success in the world of work. The twenty-first-century skills are abilities that learners must acquire to succeed in the modern age of knowledge and information. It is a detailed collection of work habits, skills, expertise, and personality characteristics identified by stakeholders as systematically crucial to business performance across industries (Awofala & Olabiyi, 2019). The acquisition of twenty-first-century skills is imperative for individuals to adeptly navigate the evolving requisites of the labour market, technological progress, and global competitiveness. These skills encompass critical thinking, creativity, collaboration, communication, information literacy, media literacy, technology literacy, flexibility, leadership, initiative, productivity, and social skills. As such, the development and integration of these skills into educational curricula and vocational training programmes are vital to preparing individuals for the challenges and opportunities of the future workforce.

Leading organizations are actively moving towards adopting AI in the workplace, incorporating virtual personal assistants, speech recognition, machine learning, and natural language processing. Those that have already embraced AI are poised to experience substantial long-term growth and success. However, it's important to address the concerns surrounding AI adoption's impact on employees. Many understandably fear potential job displacement and unemployment, particularly in fields like software development, data science, manufacturing, and engineering. Employees in these sectors perceive AI as a looming threat to their roles and express apprehension about potentially becoming secondary resources in the face of AI's capabilities. The recent advancements in AI technology have provided an opportunity for TVET institutions to offer highly personalized training tailored to the unique learning needs of diverse learners. As learners within the TVET framework often have distinct learning preferences and aptitudes, with some benefiting from traditional instructor-led training (ILT) or blended learning while others may require alternative delivery modes, AI can effectively discern and analyze the individual learning behaviours of each student. By harnessing this capability, AI can provide personalized insights and targeted recommendations aimed at optimizing the learning experience for each TVET learner. This personalized approach to training delivery not only holds significant promise for enhancing learning outcomes but also for catering to the diverse learning needs within TVET institutions.

It is important for TVET institutions when planning for workforce development in the twenty-first century, to recognize the more positive counter-effect of AI adoption, despite the initial apprehensions. One significant outcome is the heightened awareness among organizations regarding the critical need for employee training and development. The adoption of AI necessitates substantial investments in supporting technologies and the implementation of learning and development programmes and platforms for employees. Consequently, organizations cannot overlook the imperative of investing in ancillary technology and the development of their human workforce when embracing AI. Integrating AI into TVET institutions' programmes offers a multitude of benefits. Addressing the persistent challenge of worker engagement and its impact on productivity, the integration of advanced AI techniques such as AI-powered chatbots, personalized learning modules, real-time feedback mechanisms, and comprehensive learning analytics has demonstrated significant usefulness. These AI-powered tools can enhance the learning experience, improve knowledge retention, and provide valuable insights to educators and administrators, ultimately contributing to the overall advancement of TVET institutions in developing the workforce. The use of AI-powered chatbots empowers organizations to harness the capabilities of natural language processing and machine learning, thereby enhancing learning outcomes in the TVET institutions for developing workforce skills. Moreover, advanced chatbots can serve as effective teaching assistants, facilitating the timely and proficient resolution of learners' inquiries within the TVET framework.

The emergence of learning analytics has significantly influenced how TVET institutions can approach workforce development. Through AI-powered analytics, TVET institutions can increase a deeper understanding of their students' needs, enabling them to make well-informed decisions that positively impact learning outcomes through Learning and development (L&D) AI, Learning and Development Artificial Intelligence, refers to the use of artificial intelligence technologies in the field of learning and development. AI technology plays a pivotal role in shaping the future workforce. Organizations are currently developing AI platforms that will become essential components of workplaces shortly. (Newsroom, 2018) Consequently, the future workforce will need the necessary skills and expertise to effectively collaborate with advanced AI systems, and this can only be achieved through learning and development. L&D involves leveraging AI and machine learning algorithms to augment different facets of employee training, skill development, and knowledge acquisition within organizations. These advanced technologies can be harnessed to tailor learning experiences, suggest pertinent training resources, streamline administrative responsibilities, and deliver instantaneous feedback and evaluation. These technologies can be utilized to personalize learning experiences, recommend relevant training materials, automate administrative tasks, and provide real-time feedback and assessment. L&D AI has the potential to revolutionize traditional training methods and significantly improve the effectiveness and efficiency of learning programs within corporate and educational settings.

CONVERGENCE OF TECHNOLOGY, VOCATIONAL EDUCATION PEDAGOGY, AND ARTIFICIAL INTELLIGENCE

The AI age has now given rise to significant changes in the way people interact with each other and their environment. So far, the rate of innovation has exceeded the rate of policy development, and certainly the rate of curriculum reform, thus creating new challenges, some of which are already in the process of being solved through the use of AI. The integration of AI into technical and vocational education and training programmes holds great promise for addressing these challenges and creating more flexible, personalized, and sustainable learning environments. It's essential to continue improving and integrating AI technologies into educational settings to better prepare students for the demands of the modern workforce. The utilization of Artificial Intelligence (AI) is anticipated to increase and astonish in the near term. The involvement of TVET institutions with AI must be immediate and comprehensive. With the evolving demands of the labour force, TVET institutions need to be prepared and equipped to promptly address both job-specific skills and the cross-cutting skills essential for adapting to new work methodologies and the renewed emphasis on lifelong learning and continuous upskilling. Anticipated trends in automation are likely to displace numerous workers, necessitating the need for reskilling. As the interactions and intersections between humans and machines continue to expand, TVET institutions must ensure that students can comprehend and navigate these interactions, to avoid exclusion or, worse, exploitation.

The integration of Artificial Intelligence (AI) with TVET is multifaceted and holds significant potential. AI can enrich TVET by facilitating tailored learning experiences, streamlining administrative responsibilities, and refining assessment procedures. Furthermore, AI can contribute to curriculum development by analysing job market demands and projecting future skill prerequisites. Additionally, AI technologies can be assimilated into training initiatives to furnish learners with essential proficiencies for burgeoning industries. In the ever-evolving landscape of technology and workforce, the field of Technical and Vocational Education and Training finds itself at a crucial juncture. The integration of Artificial Intelligence (AI) into TVET holds the promise of propelling it into the future, ensuring the relevance, adaptability, and inclusivity of the workforce of tomorrow. At its core, TVET serves as the vital link between the realms of education and employment by providing the necessary theoretical knowledge and practical skills tailored to meet the demands of various professions. Beyond the significant economic benefits and its impact on a country's GDP, TVET also plays a pivotal role in fostering the social inclusion of marginalized individuals, offering them a clear pathway to empowerment and upward career mobility. The dawn of AI in TVET has been pivotal since its inception. Not only does it present tools and approaches that, beyond doubt, elevate the quality of vocational training by a notch. In addition, AI has the potential for the adaptability of educational material and the vastness of TVET programmes to match today's demands and the future demands of the jobs market. AI makes TVET a continuously changing educational landscape, which is not only adjustable but exclusively centered on the person.

OPPORTUNITIES FOR CREATING A SUSTAINABLE WORKFORCE

Artificial intelligence (AI) is indeed a core aspect of the fourth industrial revolution, alongside the transformation of mechanical technology, electric power technology, and information technology, and plays a crucial role in promoting the transformation and upgrading of the digital economy industry. The rapid iteration and cross-border integration of general information technology in the era of the digital economy have significantly contributed to stabilizing employment and promoting growth. However, it's important to note that this is primarily due to the employment effect resulting from ongoing technological progress and the development of the times in the field of social production. As digital technology advances, it will inevitably replace some tasks that were previously performed by human labour. (Hen, & Zhang, 2024). AI technology represents significant progress in productivity, and it is essential to objectively examine its dual effects of substitution and employment creation in the era of artificial intelligence. Actively integrating change and adapting to development is crucial for enhancing comprehensive competitiveness and better qualifying workers for current and future work. Technology should ideally be used to enhance the quality of work and productivity, rather than solely focusing on extending working hours and accelerating the pace of work. This perspective aligns with the idea that technology should be leveraged to improve the overall work experience and outcomes for employees. (Spencer, 2023).

The integration of Artificial Intelligence with Technical and Vocational Education and Training holds the potential to cultivate a sustainable and adaptable workforce by enhancing skill development, fostering job readiness, and ensuring responsiveness to dynamic market changes. AI technology can facilitate the customization of training programmes to cater to the individual needs of learners, broaden access to education through online platforms, and automate administrative functions within educational institutions. Concurrently, TVET programmes can furnish individuals with practical competencies that align with industry requisites, particularly in the realm of green technologies and environmentally sustainable practices. Collectively, the amalgamation of AI and TVET can nurture a workforce that not only possesses relevant skills but also demonstrates the capability to confront forthcoming challenges sustainably. It is advisable to conduct a comprehensive exploration of specific programmes and collaborative initiatives within a geographic region to gain insights into the practical implementation of these transformative opportunities. (Omeh, Olelewe, & Hu, 2024)

The impact of AI on employment is distinct from that of previous industrial revolutions, and it is exceptional in that machines are no longer straightforward mechanical tools but have assumed more of a worker role, just as people who can learn and think tend to do (Boyd & Holton, 2018). AI-related technologies continue to advance, the industrialization and commercialization process continues to accelerate, and the industry continues to explore the application of AI across multiple fields.

By properly investing in educational frameworks that allow for new avenues of learning and skills-gathering, we can make flexible education systems an intrinsic part of the cultural norm and arm employees with the complementary skillsets they'll inevitably need for sustainable careers. Today, many colleges are focused on honing one's hard tech skills, but in this digitally native culture, success is built on possessing myriad talents. It's therefore critical we advocate for curriculums that include both hard and soft skills, such as emotional intelligence, and self-efficacy. TVET institutions must work to dispel long-held cultural beliefs that education ends at a person's commencement ceremony. Implement fluid and seamless learning opportunities. The modern workplace will continuously require students to learn new solutions for a variety of fresh challenges and successful organisations will be those that both recognize and cater to employee needs for lifelong learning.

However, TVET institutions need to go beyond simply making education and training available. Instead, TVET institutions and employers must meet employees on the platforms that best align with their habits – encouraging them to pursue skills development programmes that are right for them, at their own pace, and through mediums that are best suited to their learning style. Whether it is webinars, online games, or in-person mentor programmes, we must find ways to seamlessly integrate organic reskilling moments at work, so it does not feel like a "chore," but rather becomes a fluid and natural aspect of the holistic work experience. Adopting a top-down approach to learning can significantly enhance development within organizations. TVET institutions and business leaders have a unique opportunity to lead by example in reskilling workforces whose roles are set to evolve, thereby nurturing a culture of curiosity and continuous learning. By implementing change from the top down, leaders can effectively cultivate a sustainable workforce. When leaders actively participate in training alongside their teams, they not only showcase their commitment to growth but also inspire their employees to engage in their development. Research shows that learners often discover the skills they need to improve through specific guidance and hands-on support from their managers. Moreover, CEOS need to foster an environment of inquiry by asking questions and learning from those around them. This willingness to be vulnerable and curious can contribute to a company culture that encourages employees to adopt trainable and inquisitive mindsets. By participating in regular skill development and retraining programs, everyone can feel more prepared to embrace the challenges of the evolving workplace.

Utilize artificial intelligence and machine learning to enhance reskilling strategies. In the current era of artificial intelligence, the success of businesses increasingly depends on the dynamic between individuals and machines, and employee reskilling plays a crucial role in this context. Research indicates that a substantial proportion of workers—80%—are open to acquiring new skills that will enable them to leverage artificial intelligence within their existing roles. As AI and machine learning technologies continue to transform job functions, these same innovations can be employed to develop effective training systems and tools designed to facilitate efficient reskilling of employees. Reskilling solutions driven by these technologies are accessible, user-friendly, and highly cost-efficient.

THE POTENTIAL OF AI IN TVET

Integrating AI with TVET presents an opportunity to make vocational training more effective and responsive to labour market demands. AI can help clients identify jobs in the future and skills they will require. One of the studies by UNESCO, 'Artificial Intelligence in Education: Challenges and Opportunities for Sustainable Development', has realised the benefits of using AI. Hence, they have revised their strategies, focusing on the AI aspect. AI can offer personalised and dynamic learning scripts, which factor in their prospects. It can also evaluate their probable underperformance areas before they enter employment. Equally, it will help individuals develop adaptive behaviours, given that the highly technological hemisphere remains ambiguous. AI can develop dynamic educational surroundings that adjust to individual learning needs. Through personalised pathways, trainees can work on their concerns and hence become adjustable to the market sooner. AI can improve learners problem-solving competencies to enable them to do well in the business environment.

Integrating AI with TVET offers a significant opportunity to enhance the effectiveness and responsiveness of vocational training to labour market demands. AI can assist individuals in identifying future job prospects and the skills they will need. A study by UNESCO titled Artificial Intelligence in Education: Challenges and Opportunities for Sustainable Development highlights the benefits of leveraging AI, prompting a revision of strategies to place greater emphasis on its role. AI can provide custom-made and adaptive learning experiences tailored to individual prospects. It can also identify potential areas of underperformance before individuals enter the workforce. Moreover, AI will help learners develop adaptive behaviours in an ever-evolving technological landscape. By creating dynamic educational environments that cater to individual learning needs, AI enables trainees to address their specific challenges, increasing their adaptability to the market. Ultimately, AI can enhance problem-solving competencies, equipping learners to thrive in the business environment.

The AI era presents an array of exciting opportunities despite the challenges at hand. Embracing technological advancements such as AI provides access to a diverse set of tools previously inaccessible, offering novel perspectives on data and the world, innovative means of connectivity and exploration, and fresh approaches to resolving longstanding issues. Although the COVID-19 crisis has laid bare the digital gap, a commendable proportion of TVET institutions demonstrated remarkable adaptability through the provision of distance learning, thereby paving the way for more adaptable pedagogical approaches in the future. This is of particular significance considering the strategic advantages often held by TVET institutions, including cost efficiency and industry affiliations, which have the potential to benefit both working professionals and students.

Artificial intelligence offers a significant opportunity to enhance educational quality by fostering the creation of more engaging, personalized, and adaptable learning environments. This encompasses the use of active methodologies that encourage self-regulated learning, utilizing tools such as learning analytics, big data, conversational agents, blockchain, multi-format content, and gamification. Integrating artificial intelligence into education aligns with the goals outlined in UNESCO's 2030 Agenda for Sustainable Development (SDG 4), which aims to ensure inclusive, equitable, and high-quality education while promoting lifelong learning opportunities for everyone. By focusing on developing education systems that are inclusive, equitable, and relevant to all learners, AI contributes to the pursuit of a more sustainable educational framework. (Cope, Kalantzis, & Searsmith, 2020).

It will take a concerted effort by international bodies, governments, institutions, and employers, but with considerable and targeted investments in infrastructure, human capital, ethical design, and values-based deployment of AI, the future could be a world in which the recognition of prior learning, continuous lifelong learning opportunities, ICT and industry-academia collaborations give rise to high-quality skilling opportunities and significant progress towards inclusive growth and development. It will require a collaborative effort from international organisations, governments, educational institutions, and employers. However, with substantial and focused investments in infrastructure, human capital, ethical design, and value-driven implementation of AI, there is potential for a future where the acknowledgment of previous learning, continuous lifelong learning prospects, ICT integration, and industry-academia partnerships lead to high-caliber skill development opportunities and substantial advancements toward inclusive growth and development.

DIVERSITY OF TVET CONTEXTS

TVET institutions operate within a range of contexts. Some operate in upper-middle-income and higher-income societies where AI is already deeply embedded in legislation and governance, policy, state expenditure, the private sector, and the national economy. Many of the TVET institutions in these societies are already playing a leading role in the 'hollowing out' of intermediate-level skills and the integration of flexible learning pathways and AI directly into education and training. In other countries, governments without the resources or industrial base to develop AI will become clients of governments and private sector companies that own and provide AI goods and services – a second iteration of the 'export raw, import refined' paradigm, whereby developing countries in particular export raw materials such as cotton and import processed or value-added goods such as clothing (Kasahara, 2004). Countries that stick to this routine will likely hire AI consultants and service providers to apply AI to the sectors that need it intending to ensure that local production conforms to international value chains. In some contexts, the degree to which AI is currently embedded in governments and businesses is limited, and even more so when it comes to civil society; the impacts of AI remain less comprehensive and far-reaching, and its role as a driver of change in TVET has not yet been established.

Even in these countries, however, it is not a matter of if, but when the change will come about. The transformation timeline may vary considerably between regions and countries but, as the AI industry continues to expand and the uses of AI continue to multiply, countries are likely to increase their engagement. TVET systems that are not proactive in considering the impact of these shifts on their curricula and training programmes run the risk of becoming irrelevant. Current research indicates that many TVET institutions have yet to form meaningful or robust responses to the changes occurring in the era of AI. It is imperative that TVET institutions, regardless of the context, understand the current and future importance of AI and begin to incorporate AI into their development and planning processes. Forward-thinking and, where possible, pre-emptive action will position TVET institutions and their graduates to thrive in the AI era and make a positive contribution to economic, social, and individual goals. Failure to do so will have the opposite effect; TVET graduates will be poorly prepared for the labour market and TVET as a whole will lose its status when precisely the opposite is needed.

CHALLENGES FACED BY TVET EDUCATORS IN UTILIZING ARTIFICIAL INTELLIGENCE

Considering the growing interest in and relevance of artificial intelligence in developing the workforce, there is an urgent desire to understand the challenges and obstacles to developing and adopting artificial intelligence towards preparing the workforce. Challenges as viewed by Pearson (2009) in Olabiyi (2014) are difficulties in an undertaking; that is stimulating for one engaged in it. Something that, by its nature or character, serves as a call to battle, a tasking activity, or a special effort is a challenge. Challenges in preparing TVET students for the future workforce via artificial intelligence cannot be avoided but can be managed and improved for the effective functioning of TVET programs, there will be qualified workers for industries. As such, the need for preparing STEM graduates for an effective workforce remains a great challenge. Preparing students to succeed in a completely different job market is a responsibility we cannot ignore even though it may feel impossible to keep up with such rapid change, what makes this task particularly challenging is that today's youth will likely face challenges that the adults around them can barely imagine, it is, therefore, critical to prepare our students to navigate a world that is volatile, uncertain, complex and ambiguous.

Artificial intelligence has the potential to reshape skill demands, career opportunities, and the distribution of workers among industries and occupations. However, researchers and policymakers are underequipped to forecast the labour trends resulting from specific cognitive technologies, such as artificial intelligence. Typically, technology is designed to perform a specific task which alters the demand for specific workplace skills. The resulting alterations to skill demand diffuse throughout the economy, influencing occupational skill requirements, career mobility, and societal well-being (e.g., impacts on workers' social identity). Identifying the specific pathways of these dynamics has been constrained by coarse historical data and limited tools for modeling resilience. This challenge can be overcome by prioritizing data collection on workforce development required for different careers that are detailed, responsive to real-time changes in the labour market, and respect regional variability (Scheinkman, 2019)

Furthermore, TVET institutions that are saddled with the responsibilities of developing the workforce must develop better access to data that are not structured on skills from resumes and job posting along with new indicators for technological change and models for direct change that will enable new and promising techniques and forecasting the future of work, improved data collection will enable the use of new data-driven tools, including machine learning applications and systemic modeling that more accurately reflects the complexity of workplace systems. New data will lead to new research that enriches our understanding of the impact of technology on modern labour markets. UNESCO-UNEVOC (2020) observed that TVET institutions that train workers to possess valuable skills that lead to higher wages must have data that will reflect the need for the workforce required in workplaces. Kirchhoff added that looking at education and wages alone is not enough to explain the lack of technical skills required by the workforce.

TVET educators teach students who have access to powerful computer hardware and software. The challenge for the instructors is that they must update their knowledge and skills in adopting artificial intelligence to be relevant in carrying out their responsibilities. Management and manipulation of data will likely replace the use of textbooks as the foundation of vocational curriculum materials. (Royh & McEwing, 1985) Furthermore, technical vocational educators need to accept the fact that technologies will be packaged in powerful and different forms and this technology will have relevant applications for different vocational areas. TVET educators will, therefore, need to reposition themselves, their students, and the programs to work with the state-of-the-art of artificial intelligence to achieve the objective of workplaces. (King & Persily, 2018) TVET programs must support the use of artificial intelligence. TVET instructors must develop aggressive attitudes toward technological developments by learning about new technology systems, which will have an impact on their vocational disciplines. The challenge of teaching learners with limited literacy and numeracy: Many learners have difficulties with reading and writing yet still need to be supported to develop skills and expertise. Sometimes it is a case of not mastering the language of instruction, in which case ICT translating software can help.

More fundamentally when learners have limited basic literacy it calls upon great skill and creativity on the part of the teacher. Methods such as practical hands-on demonstration, and the use of annotated pictures, simple forms, videos, and storyboards were suggested. It is therefore essential to offer solutions and recommendations aimed at enhancing teaching-learning processes and fostering the acquisition of skills and knowledge required by contemporary technology vocational education students to thrive in their personal, professional, and civic endeavours. In the twenty-first century, teachers encounter a multitude of challenges related to pedagogy and instructional approaches, particularly in the context of both physical and virtual teaching settings, as the distinction between the two continues to diminish. Rising to these challenges will necessitate continuous investment in infrastructure, the professional development of teachers and other staff, curriculum reviews, and multi-stakeholder institutional and departmental governance. Individual institutions and entire systems may encounter financial and human capital shortages, have to navigate competing priorities, or potentially alter established ways of working.

REFERENCES

21Vital Chatbot Statistics. (https://outgrow.co/blog/vital-chatbot-statistics) *Originally published onJuly7,2019*

Abu Bakar, M. H., Ghafa, N. H. M., & Abdullah, F. (2024). Exploring the Integration of Artificial Intelligence in Technical and Vocational Education and Training (TVET): Applications, Benefits, Challenges, and Future Prospects. *Borneo Engineering & Advanced Multidisciplinary International Journal (BEAM)3* (Special Issue (ICo- ASCNITech 2024), 57-63. https://beam.pmu.edu.my/index.php/beam/article/view/189

Anand, S. (2021) What is Pedagogy? Importance of Pedagogy in the Teaching and Learning Process October 7, 2021.

Autor, D. (2010). The Polarization of Job Opportunities in the U.S. Labor Market: Implications for Employment and Earnings. The Center for American Progress and The Hamilton Project. Retrieved from: https://economics.mit. Edu/files/5554

Bárány, Z., & Siegel, C. (2015). Job Polarization and Structural Change. Presented at the American Economic Association Annual Meeting, Jan 3-5, 2016. https://www.aeaweb.org/conference/2016/retrieve.php?pdfid=906

Beckett, G., & Slater, T. (2019). *Global Perspectives on Project-Based Language Learning, Teaching, and Assessment: Key Approaches, Technology Tools, and Frameworks.* Routledge. DOI: 10.4324/9780429435096

Bender, W. N. (2012). *Project-Based Learning: Differentiating Instruction for the 21st Century.* Corwin Press.

Boyd, R., & Holton, R. J. (2018). Technology, innovation, employment and power: Does robotics and artificial intelligence really mean social transformation? *Journal of Sociology (Melbourne, Vic.)*, *54*(3), 331–345. DOI: 10.1177/1440783317726591

Brown, A. (2016). 'Key findings about the American workforce and the changing job market'. Pew Research Center. Accessed: http://www.pewresearch.org/fact- tank/2016/10/06/key-findings-about-the-american-workforce and-the-changing-job- market/

Chinedu, C. C., & Olabiyi, O. S. (2015). Empowering Nigerian youths through technical vocational education and training for enhancing national security. *Journal of Technical Education and Training*, *7*(1), 10–22.

Chinedu, C. C., Olabiyi, O. S., & Kamin, Y. (2015). Strategies for improving higher order thinking skills in teaching and learning of design and technology education. *Journal of Technical Education and Training*, *7*(2), 35–43.

Christine Persaud (2024). 9 Pedagogical Approaches for Higher Ed Explained [Plus: 40+ Free Strategies to Implement in Your Classroom] | Top Hat May 16, 2024.

Commonwealth of Learning, TVET Professional Development Toolkit for the Pacific, Commonly used terms, n.d.

Cope, B., Kalantzis, M., & Searsmith, D. (2020). Artificial intelligence for education: Knowledge and its assessment in AI-enabled learning ecologies. *Educational Philosophy and Theory*. Advance online publication. DOI: 10.1080/00131857.2020.1728732

Derijan, I., & Valchev, G. (2012). Spiritual and moral development of the child in Bulgaria— Traditions and modern projection. In *Yearbook of Burgas Free University* (p. 165). BRU.

Federal Republic of Nigeria. (2004). *National Policy of Education* (4th ed.). NERDC.

Gamble, J. (2013). *Why improved formal teaching and learning are important in TVET. Revisiting global trends in TVET*. UNESCO.

Goos, M., Manning, A., & Salomons, A. (2014). 'Explaining job polarization: Routine-biased technological change and offshoring'. *The American Economic Review, 104*(8), 2509–2526. DOI: 10.1257/aer.104.8.2509

Guo, P., Saab, N., Post, L. S., & Admiraal, W. (2020). A review of project-based learning in higher education: Student outcomes and measures," International Journal of Educational Research, vol. 102, Hen, Y., & Zhang, X. (2024). The impact of artificial intelligence on employment: the role of virtual agglomeration. *Humanities & Social Sciences Communications, 11*(1), 122. DOI: 10.1057/s41599-024-02647-9

Hollander, A., & Mar, N. Y. (2009). Towards Achieving TVET for All: The Role of the UNESCOUNEV-OC International Centre for Technical and Vocational Education and Training. International Handbook of Education for the Changing World of Work, 41– 57. DOI: 10.1007/978-1-4020-5281-1_3

Horn, M. & Chavez, A. (2022). The Future of Education: What is Modern Pedagogy and What Does it Mean? The future of education. November 21, 2022

ILO (2020). Competency-Based Training (CBT): An Introductory Manual for Practitioners.

Jackson, E. (2013) Choosing a Methodology: Philosophical Underpinning, Practitioner Research in *Higher Education Journal, 7(1)*, October. Available at: http://194.81.189.19/ojs/index.php/prhe (Accessed 15 October. Kaldi, S. Filippatou, D. and Govaris, C. (2011). Project-based learning in primary schools: Effects on pupils' learning and studies," Education Journal, vol. 39, no. 1, pp. 35-47

Kamalov, F., Santandreu Calonge, D., & Gurrib, I. (2023). New Era of Artificial Intelligence in Education: Towards a Sustainable Multifaceted Revolution. *Sustainability (Basel), 15*(16), 12451. DOI: 10.3390/su151612451

Kasahara, S. (2004). The flying geese paradigm: a critical study of its application to East Asian regional development. United Nations Conference on Trade and Development. Online at https://mpra.ub.uni-muenchen.de/21881/ MPRA Paper No. 21881, posted 07 Apr 2010 13:40 UTC

Krajcik, J. S., Blumenfeld, P. C., Marx, R. W., & Soloway, E. (1994). A collaborative model for helping middle grade science teachers learn project-based instruction. *The Elementary School Journal, 94*(5), 483–497.

Lucas, B. (2014). Vocational pedagogy: what it is, why it matters and how to put it into practice; Report of the UNESCO-UNEVOC online conference, 12-26 May 2014

Majumdar, S. (2014). Vocational pedagogy: what it is, why it matters and how to put it into practice; Report of the UNESCO-UNEVOC online conference, 12-26 May 2014

Manyika, J., Lund, S., Chui, M., Bughin, J., Woetzel, J., Batra, P., Ko, R., & Sanghvi, S. (2017). *Jobs lost, jobs gained: Workforce transitions in a time of automation. McKinsey Global Institute*. McKinsey and Company.

McCarthy, J., Minsky, M. L., Rochester, N., & Shannon, C. E. (1955). A proposal for the Dartmouth summer research project on artificial intelligence. *AI Magazine*, *27*(4), 12–14. DOI: 10.1609/aimag.v27i4.1904

McIntosh, S. (2013). *Hollowing-out and the Future of the Labour Market. BIS Research Paper No.134*. Department for Business Innovation and Skills., https://assets.publishing.service.gov.uk/government/uploads/system/ uploads/ attachment_data/file/250206/bis-13-1213-hollowing-out-and-future-of-the-labour- market.pdf

Muršak, K. A. (2004). The Fourth Industrial Revolution: Potential of Artificial Intelligence Technology in TVET education. In LIS International Conference (Vol. 8, No. September, pp. 70-78).

Newsroom (https://www.gartner.com/en/newsroom/press-releases/2018-02-19-gartner-says- 25-percent-of-customer-service-operations-will-use-virtual-customer-assistants-by- 2020)

Oksana, C. (2024). Bridging the Gap: Traditional vs. Modern Education (A Value-Based Approach for Multiculturalism). In Lifelong Learning - Education for the Future World in Filippo Gomez Paloma (Eds) DOI: DOI: 10.5772/intechopen.114068

Olabiyi, O. S. (2004) Relevance of Student Industrial Work Experience Scheme among Technical College Students in Lagos State. (Unpublished M.Ed. Thesis) Submitted to the Department of Vocational Teachers Education, University of Nigeria, Nsukka.

Olabiyi, O. S. (2009). Assessment of Skill Development Programme offered to special needs learners in vocational rehabilitation centres in South West Nigeria (Unpublished Ph.D. Thesis) Submitted to the Department of Vocational Teachers Education, University of Nigeria, Nsukka.

Olabiyi, O. S. (2021). Convergence of artificial intelligence and technical vocational education. In Oladipo, S. A., Adeosun, A. O., Owoyemi, T. E., Anyikwa, E. B., Ogunsemore, M. A., & Adeniyi, S. O. (Eds.), *Education in a rapidly changing world* (pp. 315–333). University of Lagos Press and Bookshop.

Olabiyi, O. S. (2021). The role of lifelong learning in developing workplace skills and challenges of technical vocational education and training. In *contemporary issues in education and learning*. Ed. Abiona, A., Afonja, A., Ojo, R., Aitokhuehi, O., & Olafare, F. University of Lagos Press and Bookshop. (pp 281-291).

Olabiyi, O. S. (2022). Sustainable innovative teaching strategies for enhancing effective engagement of woodwork technology students in vocational skills. *Journal of TVET Transformation*, *1*(1), 38–49.

Olabiyi, O.S. (2022). Assessing effectiveness of teaching practice towards quality preparation of pre-service technical teachers. *Journal of Technological and Vocational Education* 28(2), 01-13. https://doi.org/DOI: 10.21831/jptk.v28i1.45519

Olabiyi, O. S., & Awofala, A. O. A. (2019). Effect of co-operative learning strategy on senior secondary school students' achievement in woodwork technology. *Acta Didactica Napocensia, 12*(2), 171–182. DOI: 10.24193/adn.12.2.13

Olabiyi, O. S & Chinedu, C. C (2018). Perception of employers' in transforming technical and vocational education and training vis-a-vis emerging technology tools for sustainable workforce development in Nigeria. *Path of Science: International Electronic Scientific Journal. Traektoriâ Nauki = Path of Science, 4*(4), 5001-5010.

Olabiyi, O. S., & Olafare, F. O. (2022). Utilization of Work-Based Learning Program to Develop Employability Skill of Workforce (Craftsmen) In Construction Industry Towards Industrial Development. *Indonesian Journal of Educational Research and Technology, 2*(3), 179–188. https://ejournal.upi.edu/index.php/IJERT/. DOI: 10.17509/ijert.v2i3.43970

Omeh, C. B., Olelewe, C. J., & Hu, X. (2024). (2024). Application of artificial intelligence (AI) technology in TVET education: Ethical issues and policy implementation. *Education and Information Technologies*. Advance online publication. DOI: 10.1007/s10639-024-13018-x

Petrina, B., & Carver, P. (2019). Enablers of work-integrated learning in technical vocational education and training teacher education. *International Journal of Work-Integrated Learning, Special Issue, 20*(2), 147–159.

Shulman, L. (2005). Signature pedagogies in the professions. *Daedalus, 134*(3), 52–59. DOI: 10.1162/0011526054622015

Stanley, J. (2015). *CEDEFOP: Vocational Pedagogies and Benefits for Learners: Practices and Challenges in Europe*. Publications Office of the European Union.

Taubayeva, Sh. T, & Laktionova, S.N. (2001). Pedagogical Innovation as a Theory and Practice of Innovations in the Education System. Алмату: Gylym; 2001.

The Deloitte Millennial Survey. https://www2.deloitte.com/us/en/pages/about-deloitte/articles/millennial-survey.html

The Replacement for Annual Reviews. (https://www.gallup.com/services/192827/organization-greatest-potential-unlocked.aspx) (UNESCO, (2023). Enhancing TVET through digital transformation in developing countries.

UNESCO. (2014). *Teaching and learning: Achieving quality for all. Education for all Global Monitoring Report 2013/14*. UNESCO.

UNESCO 2010: Teaching and Learning for a sustainable future, a multimedia education programme. UNESCO- UNEVOC (2021). Understanding the impact of artificial intelligence on skills development

UNESCO-UNEVOC International Centre. (2020). Trends in New Qualifications and Competencies for TVET Perspectives of the European UNEVOC Network. UNESCO- UNEVOC. https://unevoc.unesco.org/pub/bilt_ trends_mapping_study.pdf

United Nations Educational Scientific and Cultural Organization. (2002). Technical and Vocational Education and Training in the 21st Century: New Roles and Challenges for Guidance and Counselling. Retrieved from https://unesdoc.unesco.org/images/0013/001310/131005e.pd

Vázquez-Cano, E. (2021). Artificial intelligence and education: A pedagogical challenge for the 21st century. Educational Process. *International Journal (Toronto, Ont.)*, *10*(3), 7–12.

Chapter 14
The Role of Artificial Intelligence Autonomy in Higher Education in India

Chirag Khandelwaal
https://orcid.org/0009-0000-6368-3783
Christ University, India

Pankaj Dhaundiyal
Christ University, India

Abhinav Kataria
Christ University, India

ABSTRACT

To leverage the benefits of artificial intelligence applications for experiential learning, many higher education institutes have started using artificial intelligence by adopting many artificial intelligence-driven technologies. Some of them are chatbots, generative AI, concepts of virtual tutors, and providing students with various automated assessment tools for their own assessment, which might change the traditional teaching methodology. This chapter examines the role of artificial intelligence autonomy in higher education in India, deep-diving into AI's impact on students' learning outcomes by leveraging AI-driven technologies in education. This research will specifically have five major variables that will be examined and measured. These variables are usage intention, thought autonomy, action autonomy, sensing autonomy, and culture. This study will examine the five main dimensions of AI autonomy: usage intention, thought autonomy, action autonomy, sensing autonomy, and culture.

1. INTRODUCTION

To leverage the benefits of applications of artificial intelligence for providing experiential learning, many higher education institutes have started the usage of artificial intelligence by adopting many artificial intelligences driven technologies. Some of them are chatbots, generative AI, concepts of virtual tutors and providing students with various automated assessment tools for their own assessment which

DOI: 10.4018/979-8-3693-9062-7.ch014

might change the traditional teaching methodology. Niu et al. (2024) find out that advancement and increasing applications of AI technology in higher education not only provide more efficient tools for teachers in long-term and focused teaching, but also provide new active and independent spaces for sustainable self-motivated learning for college students. Learning can be customised by AI as per student need as stated by Chatterjee & Bhattacharjee (2020). AI played a crucial role in redefining the Indian education by making their educational journey more personalized and shifting the charge of learning from teachers to students but role of AI in higher education is still very limited sited by Surugiu et al. (2023). This needed because there is generally high student- teachers ratio makes student interaction minimal as stated by Chen et al. (2023)

This study will look forward for examining the role of artificial intelligence autonomy in higher education in India, deep diving into the impact that AI made on students learning outcomes by leveraging AI driven technologies in field on education. This research will specifically have 5 major variables which will be examined and measured. These variables are usage intention, thought autonomy, action autonomy, sensing autonomy, and culture. Salinas-Navarro (2024) investigates how GenAI can enhance teaching and learning by constructively addressing study situations beyond conventional learning approaches and cultivating high-order skills and knowledge acquisition.AI raises question of academic integrity. Academic integrity is defined as "being honest in academic work and taking responsibility" (East &Donnelly 2012). "The many facets of academic integrity, from plagiarism to contract cheating"This unit will cover the concept Artificial intelligence and its various autonomous dimensions and implications of integrating AI in education

This study will study and examine the five main dimensions of AI autonomy: usage intention, thought autonomy, action autonomy, sensing autonomy, and culture. These variables or five specific dimensions are taken in to consideration of assessing the role of artificial intelligence in influencing autonomous learning in higher education. Niu et al. (2024) says that when people believe that a machine or algorithm can independently sense the external environment, think about reasons, plan, and take action to solve problems.

1.1 Opportunities and challenges with AI integration in Higher education

If we talk about Indian education systems, artificial intelligence offers plethora of opportunities and set of challenges when we talk specifically about adoption of AI driven technologies in the field of education. In India, due to pandemic covid-19, acceptance of AI amongst students have accelerated a lot. Students and teachers are understanding how to use AI rationally to get benefits in the field of education to maximize learning outcome. Now a days government is also promoting the same by coming up with NEP (new education policy). How ever, adopting Artificial intelligence can impose several challenges which might be difficult in tackling and finding solutions. Some of those challenges are limitations of tech infrastructure in India, privacy is a major concern and who to integrate ethics with AI is also a concern. Despite all these challenges, Artificial intelligence Is considered an asset for all stakeholders of educational institutions. AI is beneficial because of is capacity of making autonomous decisions and fostering an autonomous learning environment.

2. LITERATURE REVIEW

(Berente et al. 2021) Artificial Intelligence technologies are advance technologies that solves complex decision-making problems including machine learning models, natural-language processing techniques, computer vision, robotics, algorithms, etc. Past Literatures delt with understanding of role of artificial intelligence in higher education and its integration. They also delt with integration of AI with learning modules and its potential challenges like cheating, hindering integrity of assignments and learning outcomes.

Success of AI educators could only be determined by how independently they could take decisions minimizing the human interactions. "The success of AI educators would thus potentially be highly dependent on whether AI educators can meet students' intrinsic needs." (Niu et al. 2024). Some scholars were very much interested in how AI benefits can be leveraged in Education. (Guilherme 2019) with the integration of AI in education we can make learning process more effective, while it will reduce the important connectivity between teachers and students, that interaction which is required. (Cope et al.2021) examined that AI will never replace the traditional teaching style but it will increase education for students and other people. Some learned scholars examined how teachers are readily accepting integration of AI in the field of education. (Wang et al.2023) found the relationship between AI enhanced innovation and AI readiness of teachers. Both positive and negative results were concluded. (Kim et al. 2022) examined that due to technology overload some tutors are resisting AI assistance in the field of education. Some scholars examined the role of Artificial intelligence in maximizing achievements in education. (Ouyang and Jiao 2021) examines how AI plays a role in these paradigm - AI-directed, AI-supported, and AI-empowered paradigms. Most of the scholars have invested their time in examining and analysing the ways of integration of AI in education. They mainly focused on how tools of AI can be incorporated in the field of education, focusing how AI can potentially influence the achievements in the field of education. Very few have examined how students' achievements are highly influenced by motivation to take leverage of AI in field of education. (Kim et al. 2022) examined and found higher level of presence amongst students when they found their AI instructors have human like voice, leading higher trust and credibility. (Xia et al.2022) examined that both students and teachers' attributes are important and both traits influences the achievements of students in education.

Now if we talk about student perspective academic integrity is an issue which is defined as "being honest in academic work and taking responsibility" (East and Donnelly 2012). (Evering and Moorman 2012, p.35) suggested that due to high change in digital environment, challenge of plagiarism and the concept of academic integrity needed concept of re-examination. Various studies suggest (Howard and Davies 2009; Williams 2007) that due to abrupt use of AI in education people tend to present somebody else idea as their own idea after making changes in it, basically misrepresenting somebody else's original idea. After this change in the digital environment the concept of academic integrity became widespread making it a common challenge. It has become a problem for institutions as they cannot rely on a few traditional plagiarism detection tools who fails to recognize "the act of a student obtaining their assignment from another party" (Awdry 2020). Peer to peer sharing sites and many paraphrasing tools available online are now a threat to institutions as they fail to detect plagiarism through their old software which ultimately compromises academic integrity. (Rogerson and McCarthy 2017) examines that AI tools are problematic especially in case of academic integrity and due to this act of copying, students' ability to write, present ideas get affected. (Harrison et al. 2020) examines and draws clear distinction between students' perception on paying somebody else for writing for them and copying essays from some sites where peers upload assignments which is not considered dishonest by them and they feel that doing this involves lesser risk as compared to other dishonest methods.Other problematic area which is being discussed less is changing characteristics of students attending universities. We have change lot of change in availability of new AI tools and generative AI applications. Especially these so-called generation Z have wide range of opportunities ad many AI tools are now readily available and they have different thinking patters and have different working style as compared to rest generations. (Polakova and Klimova 2019) new generation like gen Z have very much limited attention span, they want to skim through whole text quickly and just end up reading only 20% of the text which they skim through. (Szymkowiak et al. 2021) also explains the same argument and says that these generation want everything before time, making them impatient and due to this attitude, they want to use such applications which are multi-tasking and can do their tasks instantly. This impatient attitude causes cheating. Due to this what happen is, generation Z do not see the process or method they just focus on end-result. Due to this cheating has now become very socially acceptable (Flom et al. 2021) says this. (Amigud 2019) examines what are the min reasons which makes students to take such step of cheating and they are willing to outsource their assignments harming the academic integrity and university plagiarism norms. Through extensive research they found that "perseverance was the top reason for outsourcing work" they felt very much tired, bored and monotony while doing their assignments and get frustrated by the level of efforts required to put in in to assignments. This happens due to concept of "academic aptitude" which means that the level of skills and knowledge required in completing the given assignment, students do not possess which makes completion of that assignment difficult and they struggle in completion of assignment. Some of the other reasons which also contribute in the same are lack of motivation, some medical issues and they often lack discipline. (Brimble 2016, p.378) also examines and finds all these above are reasons for students to outsource their assignment. (Bretag et al. 2018) also gave a big reason for this outsourcing of assignment which they call as "contract cheating". It happens due to dissatisfaction between students for the course which is being taught in their institutions as they lack proficiency in English language as many students do not have this language as there first language. (Cotton et al.2023) are the first to list down various issues like essay generation, which can be generated using free software like ChatGPT which had millions of downloads within few days of their release. They also list down potential opportunities which are generated with the usage of this software in field of higher education. (Javed et al. 2023) also came with potential benefits of using this software in higher education. For example, this software can act as a "virtual teaching assistant" which will aid students in clarifying the important concepts, jargonish words and much more. In fact (Yu 2023) went ahead and suggested that students should be taught how to use these generative AI applications so they can have an edge in job market. With the evolution in the technology of Artificial intelligence, AI systems are highly expected to serve as an independent agent which can accomplish all the tasks automatically without any human intervention (Niu et al.2024). Artificial autonomy which is also referred as "AI autonomy" (Mezrich and J.L. 2022) and termed as "machine autonomy" (Etzioni et al. 2016) simply means degree or extent up to which it can perform tasks without any human intervention, operating much of the tasks independently (Rijsdijk et al. 2007). Only a few pieces of literature talk about autonomy.

Talking specifically, many research scholars examined the difference between AI agents and human agents. (Kim and Duhachek 2020) shows that due to lack of autonomous intention in human agents they are different from AI agent who have the capability of performing tasks autonomously. In conclusion, through the literature review we can conclude that there are many theories regarding the AI technologies, their challenges and their opportunities related to their integration in higher education but impact of AI autonomy and their usage intention in higher education is still not clear.

3. THEORETICAL FRAMEWORK

3.1 Theoretical Framework for AI Autonomy in Higher Education

The role of AI autonomy in higher education is the name of chapter of book and its theoretical framework will constitute of several key concepts related to it and various dimensions related to AI autonomy, just to explore how AI related technologies can enhance student autonomy and how it can enhance and enrich learning experiences and outcomes. Theory which is being formulated below will be based on existing established theories in the field of education, AI autonomy to guide overall research and analysis regarding AI autonomy in education.

Key concepts

a) Technology Acceptance Model (TAM) - TAM model commonly known as technology acceptance model elaborates how users that is students and teachers come to accept and use AI driven technology. It mainly focuses on two main factors of TAM.

Perceived usefulness: - Perceived usefulness means how users will perceive the usage of AI. It means how users perceive that role of AI will enhance their learning outcomes.

Perceived ease of use: - This means degree to which users like students and teachers perceive how effort free the AI integration will be in the field of education. AI integration or adoption in the field of higher education depends on perceived usefulness and perceived ease of use. (Abdullah et al. 2016)

b) Self-determination Theory (SDT) - This theory is inclined towards motivation and self-drive especially regarding integrating technologies like AI autonomy in education. This theory suggests that how autonomy will lead to more inner motivation and enhanced learning experiences and outcomes.

AI enabled systems support some dimensions of AI autonomy like though and action autonomy as AI integration in education make students to make decisions independently, creating personalised experience and engaging students in self-directed activities (Ryan and Deci 2017).

c) Constructive Learning Theory - This theory is inclined towards making or constructing own knowledge by gaining experiences and going through the learning material.

This theory deals with the dimension of sensing autonomy. AI driven technologies like Virtual tutors, personalised learning systems enable this dimension from where its easy for students to get personalized learning material and personalized feedback based on student's performance (Holmes et al. 2019).

d) Cultural Adaptation Framework - This framework deals with how cultural norms should be kept in mind while integrating AI driven technologies in the field of education and how it should align with culture and values of institutions where its integrated.

Alignment of AI driven technologies in education is highly influenced by cultural expectations, student teacher dynamics, institutions beliefs, values and how institution readily accept technology. All these factors determine the success of AI integration in higher education in India (Straub et al. 2016).

3.2 Dimensions of AI Autonomy

This study will study and examine the five main dimensions of AI autonomy: usage intention, thought autonomy, action autonomy, sensing autonomy, and culture. These variables or five specific dimensions are taken in to consideration of assessing the role of artificial intelligence in influencing autonomous learning in higher education

1) Usage intension: - Usage intention simply means readiness (Oliveira et al. 2016) or willingness or intention towards adopting AI driven tools by educational institutions which will foster an environment for personalized learning. Here based of TAM MODEL usage intention measures willingness to adopt by teachers, students and by whole academic institution. In reference in Indian education, AI driven tools and its usage intention or its willingness to adopt might be influenced by some key important factors like AI ready infrastructure, awareness about how to leverage benefits of artificial intelligence in education, and majorly impacted by strict policies of educational institutions.
2) Thought Autonomy: - This dimension means autonomy that students have in personalized learning experience. As discussed in Self-Determination Theory (SDT), this means that independent thinking and decision making of students without asking their peers or teachers. This makes them independent and give them autonomy to create a vibrant learning experience. AI driven tools can offer though autonomy by providing personalized tutors, dynamic learning systems which will be tuned as per students learning pace.
3) Action autonomy: - This dimension of autonomy means taking actions autonomously. It means that giving students autonomy that without asking anyone they have the leverage to perform educational tasks autonomously without any intervention of teachers or pears (Jeno and Diseth 2019). AI driven systems are capable for providing students with real time support reducing teachers' intervention.
4) Sensing Autonomy: - AI systems collect data based on all the performances made by students. Then based on that data, analyses are made and then AI adjusts itself autonomously to the students learning pace. Constructive Learning theory throws light of this concept. This kind of autonomy where AI uses data and makes personalized learning module is called sensing autonomy and provide personal feedback (Bond et al. 2018.
5) Culture: - This factor is most important factor amongst all the dimensions. Culture plays an essential role in acceptance of artificial intelligence by educational institutions in India. Cultural attitudes like teaching style, learning styles, student and teacher relationship should also be tried to be integrated in this AI systems. Theory of cultural Adaptation framework explains this dimension and examines in context to Indian education, Artificial intelligence should be aligned with the cultural and societal norms in providing personalized learning so that AI acceptance could be increased (Straub et al. 2016).

4. VISUAL REPRESENTATION OF MODEL

This is the visual model of my framework which shows Usage intention as a dependent variables and dimensions related of Autonomy like Though Autonomy, action autonomy, sensing autonomy, sensing autonomy, and culture are all independent variables.

4.1. Thought autonomy and usage intention

4.1.1. Introduction to Thought autonomy

Autonomy means independently. Thought autonomy means thinking independently, making decisions independently and it involves evaluating and analyzing the information without external interference or without any guidance of someone. In reference with AI driven technologies or systems in education, it becomes essential for students as it makes students more empower to get engaged with the content on their own will. The relationship between usage intention (dependent variable) and thought autonomy (independent variable) impacts how frequently and with how much efficiency students are using AI driven tools in the field of the education. This theory is more relevant in higher education, as it involves more engagement, In-depth learning. Various studies have examined that AI though autonomy in higher education can enhance student's usage intention to use more AI driven tools with efficiency, because it matches with the goals of the students of being independent and being self-motivated (Surugiu et al., 2024).

4.1.2. The role of Thought autonomy in higher education

Various studies have shown and have examined that when students are given an opportunity to have control on their own process of learning in education, they tend to feel a sense of responsibility and ownership towards their education or their learning process (Smith et al., 2023). This thought autonomy makes students encouraged to use more and more AI driven tools as a part of educational resource more actively and with greater self-inner motivation. This autonomy gives students full freedom to question the assumptions, participating or actively engaging in critical thinking and dive deep in the topic instead of learning it from surface level (Chen et al., 2023). AI driven tools and systems which are used in higher education and which fosters thought autonomy, encourages students to go through all the course material or modules themselves, which encourages them to choose paths that suits them and which challenge their critical thinking.

For example, AI driven learning platforms can give or allow students of higher education to pick tough exercise or to choose level of difficulty on their own, engaging them with the content which is adaptive in nature based on performance showed by children on the platform during exercises. This dimension of autonomy will be a great advantage as through the AI driven systems, students can get feedbacks regarding their regular performance in AI driven platform while learning or giving exercise and tests.

Through above characteristics, AI driven platform who are responsible in higher education, is trying to create such an environment where student will feel that they are having the control of their learning process and education, this will ultimately increase students' willingness to learn more through these AI driven platform. (Johnson et al., 2023).

4.1.3. How Usage intention is impacted by thought autonomy in higher education

There are several deciding factors which decides the usage intention of a particular AI driven tool usage in higher education, one such primary factor is autonomy in AI. Various studies have examined that students feel more motivated to use the AI driven platforms that supports and foster environment for self -determined learning (Patel & Zhang, 2024). Students feel more engaged, self-motivated and are motivated to achieve their academic learning goals when AI driven learning platforms are supported by feature of thought autonomy. The inner motivation of students is the power driver of usage intention of students, as it reduces resistance to usage and adoption of AI driven technologies and encourages students to use these AI technologies more frequently.

Students who perceive a particular technology having greater thought autonomy, they are more inclined towards usage of AI technologies for their self-driven learning and they tend to perceive that resource more valuable for their learning process in higher education. Various research has examined and showed that AI tools which offers more personalization and a concept of adaptive learning, have more inclination of students as it offers them to explore the learning process at their own pace (Park & Lee, 2024).

There are various famous theories which are in the fields of technology acceptance and educational psychology which presents the role and importance of thought autonomy in enhancing usage intention and engagement of students in higher education. Various researchers have justified that through the concept of self-Determination Theory (SDT) that motivation and engagement in any activity enhances when autonomy is present as it is important and fundamental psychological need (Ryan & Deci, 2000). As per the theory of SDT, this dimension of autonomous behaviour which is considered self-motivated, students generally engage themselves with their learning with AI driven platforms as these technologies align with students' interest (Vallerand, 2023).

Students are generally more inclined towards AI driven technologies for learning this is so because it gives students an autonomy and a sense of liberation on how to take your educational journey rather than being a restrictive tool and these tools also align with students' high curiosity to learn and know new things (Hsu et al., 2023).

AI driven platform who fosters a learning environment incorporates thought autonomy through various ways to enhance the usage intention amongst students. One approach is these AI driven learning platforms can have options for adaptive learning, they should have personalised content as per the pace of the student's learning. This will make sure that students will feel unique as there learning process is personalized with the usage of AI driven platforms (Sharma & Gupta, 2023). Furthermore, AI driven technologies which creates this kind of environment where every performance is being tracked, feedback is given can enhance usage intention amongst students towards these AI driven technologies as they are fostering thought autonomy. Additionally, these technologies are also helping students to apply their classroom theoretical knowledge in practical real-world challenges by motivating them to do it on their own which fosters thought autonomy (Chang & Kim, 2024).

Thought autonomy is useful and increases usage intention but this dimension of autonomy also offer some challenges in learning process. Too much thought autonomy can confuse students and they may struggle in managing their time, assignments which will ultimately reduce their inner motivation to use these AI driven platforms for higher education (Wang & Zhang, 2024). One suggestion is, AI should me designed in such a way that it only helps the students when it is required and just to make sure that student's learning process is on the right track (Saito et al., 2024).

4.2. Action autonomy and Usage intention

Action autonomy in the field of education refers to student's capacity to act independently by making choices and having behavior and actions that can help them towards achieving their desired goal. For example, student's ability to make choices and act without any human intervention in their learning process. It enables the students to make choices and let them decide how, when and what to learn instead of somebody else controlling their educational journey. This dimension of autonomy offers students to make autonomous decisions which allows their greater interaction with the AI driven platform and it also increases student's inner motivation for using these AI technologies (Luo & Wang, 2024). Overall, this means that when students experience action autonomy while using AI driven platforms for their education, they start navigating content related to education and make independent decisions to achieve their learning goals or outcomes.

4.2.1. Role of Action autonomy in education

In AI driven platforms, role of action autonomy is very much crucial especially for creating a learning environment because it fosters student's engagement and satisfaction when this dimension is playing a role in AI based learning (García et al., 2024). These AI driven learning platforms who offers action autonomy allows students to decide themselves about setting their educational goals and can customize the whole learning platform. This kind of pedagogy provides students with sense of responsibility and students get more motivated to use these AI driven platform. Studies have examined and studies that AI driven platforms which are offering these types of tailored solutions are more likely to develop the interest of students to use those platforms and feels that this platform is more valuable for their learning process (Li et al. 2023). Due to this perception of platform being valuable, students use these platforms more regularly. Studies have examined and have found that when these AI driven platforms grant more action autonomy to students, they are more able to get benefits as they are able to align their educational experience with their needs which makes their learning more effective (Martinez & Cooper, 2023). This degree of action autonomy is important in AI driven platforms so that they can provide students with the opportunity to prioritize some specific topics, focusing on weak topics or they can even have advance material to challenge themselves. This dimension of autonomy is provided in learning platforms to make education and learning process more personalized and more effective for students as this type of autonomy caters vast learning styles (Rodriguez & Chan, 2024).

4.2.2. How usage intention is influenced by action autonomy

Usage intention or chances of students keep using these AI driven platforms for their education depends upon level of action autonomy being provided by the platform. In other words, it means that degree of action autonomy will influence the usage intention amongst students towards usage of AI driven technologies for educational journey. When students get to make choices and to make decisions independently about their own learning activities, they tend to use AI related technologies more as their commitment towards those AI driven technologies increases (Moreno et al., 2023). Various researches have examined and concluded that this dimension of autonomy tends to increase the adoption rates of that AI driven platform for education which have demonstrated autonomy and it led to reduction in resistance in usage of that AI driven technology as well (Santiago & Yoon, 2024). This increases the frequency to use these platforms because of students develop a sense of ownership and students feel more empowered. In the research of (Grant and Phillips 2023) they examined and showed a comparison that students who have experienced action autonomy were more motivated, more engaged to use these AI driven platforms then those students who perceived the platform's structure more rigid instead of autonomy. Through there research, one thing can be concluded that autonomy enhances emotional response towards the AI driven learning platforms. Several very famous theories like the theory of self-determination theory (SDT) and the theory of planned behaviour (TPB) explains the importance of action autonomy. The theory of TPB explains that when individual feels that they are having control on their own actions and are independent to take decisions and choose how to act, they are more likely to involve in any behaviour (Ajzen, 1991). Studies have examined and showed that when AI powered earning platforms aligns with action autonomy, students have choices to make and they feel for motivated or empowered to use that AI driven platform means increase in usage intention (Lin et al., 2024). Studies have also found out that when the AI technologies are made keeping in mind of action autonomy, it increases student's inner motivation to use it which helps in building an effective learning environment which ultimately increases the usage intention (Zhao & Chiu, 2023). If we consider what can be the practical applications of action autonomy in AI powered learning platforms for higher education, it would be giving students a choice to set own goals, adjust their own level of difficulty and can alter the paths of learning.

4.3. Sensing autonomy and usage intention

Sensing autonomy in content to educational environment fostered by AI driven educational platforms means that ability of these platforms to gather the data, then based on gathered data and information about students through their performance in assignments, it analyses, interpret and take decisions using data of student's performance without any human intervention. This feature of AI based platforms is that without any human intervention, it can give personalized education to students just with the help of data interpretation. This is the top most reason why dimension of sensing autonomy is very important as it allows customization in learning process as per the need for an individual and this ultimately increases the engagement of students over these AI powered platforms which increases usage intention. If we talk more in context to usage intention, various studies have examined that due to sensing autonomy students feel that the platforms align with their education needs so automatically their usage intention or probability of their adoption of AI powered platform increases (Chen et al., 2023).

4.3.1. Role of sensing autonomy

Sensing autonomy plays a major or crucial role in imparting a personalized education with the help of AI powered platform. In this, through recommending various other sources to students, giving recommendations and various feedbacks based on students' performance makes the AI powered platform a tool for imparting personalised education. This kind of providing feedbacks and recommendations make platform more adaptable and beneficial for students because every student generally have different patterns or learning styles and different progress made in learning process which these platforms respond personally by adapting to student's style of learning (Zhou & Lee, 2024). For instance, lets understand by taking a practical example of an AI powered learning platform which is also adaptable in nature. Dream Box is an application which monitors and tracks the performance of each student, list down their strength and weakness and give them recommendations and personalised support. This not only helps students to help them to learn at their own pace but also it providing tailored support. Various researches have examined and have showed that these AI based platforms who fosters and environment adaptive learning through the feature of this dimension of autonomy gives students a perspective of sense of mastery which will going to make positive impact on the adoption or usage intention of students towards these AI powered platforms (Johnson & Wang, 2024).

4.3.2. How usage intention is affected by sensing autonomy

Usage intention of using AI powered platforms in education is greatly influenced by the student's perception related to how much these AI technologies are relevant to their usage and their needs and how its responses are relevant to students. Various studies have examined and showed that when individuals especially students use these AI driven platforms and perceive them as they are providing them personalized recommendations and based on their performance providing them with feedback are mostly become the reason for increased engagement and their frequency of using the platform (Brown et al., 2023). Studies have examined and showed that students who are getting more personalised and tailored feedback from the AI powered adaptive learning platforms are more likely influences positively on usage intention and increased frequency of usage in comparison to students who were not getting that tailored feedback and getting just generic feedbacks and recommendations (Li and Liu, 2023). This research also examined and concluded that usage intention of students using a platform not only depends on that platform's functionalities, but it also depends upon how much platform is able and successful to create and foster a learning environment which feels students that the platform is engaging, supportive and relevant to their educational needs. Dimension of this AI autonomy successfully does that by provides a sense of personalisation in education which fosters a sense of commitment amongst students towards usage to the AI driven platforms. Various theories like Technology Acceptance Model (TAM) and the Unified Theory of Acceptance and Use of Technology (UTAUT) are deemed successful in portraying positive relationship between sensing autonomy and usage intention of students. As per the theory of TAM model, technology acceptance is greatly influenced by the technology's ease of use and its perceived usefulness. AI powered platform have sensing autonomy which is highly adaptable to the needs of students which make it easy and convenient for them to use the platform which increase their usage and frequency to use that platform (Venkatesh and Bala, 2008). AI driven learning platforms offers adaptability and adjust to the needs of the students, this dynamic and real time adjustments make these platforms more conducive to sensing autonomy, and due to this real time adaptability and feedbacks, they can meet the student's education need and expectations from the platforms which increase their engagement on the platforms ultimately increasing the usage intention (Venkatesh et al., 2003).

4.3.3. Practical applications of sensing autonomy AI driven platforms

There are many AI-driven learning platforms which depicts the benefits of having sensing autonomy in it. For example, take any platform like Coursera, Udemy and khan Academy they are having the assignments and have that platform which is adaptable which gets adapted as per the student's performance, needs, and based on the various responses received by the student. There is a famous theory which is being proved in a research paper that when you challenge students with the assignments more especially beyond their capacity and their skill sets, they feel more engaged and learners feel more benefited (Vygotsky, 1978).

4.4. Culture and Usage Intention

There is a significant relationship between usage intention and culture in education especially where educational environment is AI based, this area of research throws light on engagement, motivation, and usage intention is impacted by cultural norms and cultural setting of students. Culture in this field refers to values, believes that will impact their interaction with the AI powered learning-based platforms and their adoption. Examining this kind of relationship is important as cultural setting impacts how students are perceiving the technologies and it will further impact their usage intention and their adoption of AI powered learning platforms in their education. As mentioned in cultural dimensional theory, various dimensions like individualism vs collectivism, uncertainty avoidance and power distance also became the major factors for affecting adoption of technology as mentioned by (Hofstede, 1984). Let us take an example. Suppose any country or region where there is collectivist culture, then societal norms, social acceptance will play a major role in adoption of AI technologies but if any country or any region is having individualistic cultures, then in this case, personal preferences and personal choices will impact the adoption of AI technologies. This is so because they feel more confident as there are having the culture of individualism so they want independence and greater autonomy so they get more attracted towards adoption of AI technology. Various studies have also examined and proves that various cultural values impact or affects the perception of students to use technology (Tarhini et al., 2014).

Details of how cultural dimensions affect usage intention

a. **Individualism vs collectivism –** In areas or societies where culture is of collectivism, your usage intention of adoption of technology not only depends on your choice but its greatly influenced by your peer's influence on you and people endowering that technology around you. For instance, if any one in your society or a community member endorses you about any AI driven platforms for education, students will feel using it and they are more likely to get inclined towards it (Shin & Kim, 2010). In contrast, scenario is completely different in societies or communities where culture is more individualistic. In this student's intention of adoption of using AI technology is more influenced by their own perception about technology, their own individual choices, and their inner motivation to use that technology.
b. **Power distance - In** societies where there is a culture of high-power distance, there hierarchy is valued more and scope of autonomy is less, take example of countries like India. So, in these societies' instructor-based platforms are valued and preferred more in comparison to AI driven platforms which have high degree of autonomy and offering independence in making choices and taking decisions. To make AI platforms align with this culture, it is required to make platform more structured to align with students need (Elbeltagi et al., 2013). In contrast, in societies or communities where there is less power distance, take example of USA, then culture is more self-paced, so AI platforms which have autonomy, provides learning environment where there is power to make decisions and choose more autonomously are more aligned with students need. Basically, students from communities having culture of less power distance are more engaged and willingly adopt AI technologies.
c. **Uncertainty avoidance –** In societies or communities where culture of uncertainty avoidance is higher, there students are more hesitant to adopt AI based technologies due to issue of privacy, trust, reliability, usage intention (Srite & Karahanna, 2006). So, AI driven platform should align with their

need by integrating privacy, reliability and security and clarity and built trust amongst students for the same which will ensure their adoption of these technologies for their education. In contrast, in societies or communities where degree of uncertainty avoidance is low, students are more motivated to use the technologies are likely have new innovate experiment. They adopt these technologies without much assistance or extensive guidance.

4.4.1. Cultural Fit and Usage intention

Here the term "cultural fit" refers to how AI driven technology in higher education will be able to fit or align with the cultural values of the societies or communities being practiced as this will be influencing student's perception on technology which will affect their adoption and usage intention. For instance, studies have examined and showed that positive perception with positively impact the usage intention (Lee et al., 2013). As also discussed earlier, suppose in society where collaborative learning is more promoted or more valued there AI adoption or usage intention will be influenced by peers. Then AI tools that align with student's need of being more structured and guided are more fit into the culture where power distances culture are high. So, for instance, if you want to make AI based learning more appealing and engaging in collectivism culture, them promote peer education (Wong et al., 2013) give group assignments, make environment of education more peer friendly to increase AI powered platform's usage intention amongst students.

4.4.2. Practical applications on culture, AI in education

a. Some of the strategies are recommended by many researchers to make AI technologies more culturally fit as culture in India is much diverse, so developers can keep certain things in mind so that these technologies can be integrated in educational institutions.
b. **Learning paths should be customizable** – AI platforms can make paths flexible and make sure that students have that autonomy to customize their own learning paths. This kind of flexibility should keep one thing in mind that it is respected by both collectivist and individualist culture and at the same time ensure that students are getting that comfort in adopting these AI technologies for education (Jung et al., 2016).
c. **Language options and more localized content** – Cultural aspect and language options should be integrated to enhance students' intention of use AI technologies more. What happens is when students find the learning content or their course material more aligned with the culture being practiced, they are more motivated and influenced to use the AI driven technology for education (Lai, Li, & Gong, 2016)
d. **Trust building –** Developers should build trust by integrating privacy, and transparency and customer support to enhance adoption of AI based learning technologies in culture where there is high Uncertainty-Avoidance. This should be done to make students more motivated and comfortable to use that AI platform, thus increasing the adoption of usage intention amongst students (Gefen et al., 2003).

5. IMPLICATIONS AND FUTURE DIRECTION OF STUDY

This study has many practical implications. You all know that AI technology is not something very new and many of you might me using AI tools knowingly or unknowingly but still the concepts related to artificial intelligence and its applications in higher education is still needs to be popular as many academicians, students and staffs have not explored its all dimensions. Still a big challenge for academicians, policy makers and for designers, the problem is how the AI educators should be designed so that in institutions and student's usage intention or their adoption of these AI technologies are still a challenge. Due to increasing demand for AI tools, it is important for higher institutions to integrate the AI technologies with a very sustainable perspective for enhancing students learning process, but for that it is important or very crucial to understand the student perspective of how they perceiving these technologies and how they associate these technologies with their learning styles.This study will offer a plethora of viewpoints of student's perspective of using or adopting artificial intelligence technologies in higher education and how they are perceiving the AI educators and what are their reactions, whether they are resistant to change or they are reacting positively with different dimensions of autonomy of AI. This paper also presents the important dimensions or features of AI autonomy. This study examines that how action autonomy is positively related and can influence the usage of AI by students in higher education. It examines that whether after adopting the technologies of AI and using AI educators, are students feeling that they have technologies which have the capability and power to make independent decisions without much human intervention and are students getting that real time support. This study also examines how usage of AI by students are giving them opportunity of personalized learning experience, this is measured by examining the other dimension of AI autonomy which Is Though autonomy. Examining whether they are getting that vibrant learning experience and personalized learning which means that whether the AI educators or virtual learning tools are adjusting their pace of teaching as per learning pace of students and as per their need and their learning capacity. Our study how culture and dimension of sensing autonomy positively influences the usage intention of AI related tools and technology in higher education. In this, study examines how AI have independent capability of collecting data of students learning pace, analysing their assignments and how they are adjusting them for students, making a personalize learning module. Our study also examines how factor of culture is very much important in usage intention. As, culture plays a very crucial role especially in India in integration of AI technologies in higher education, it is because there is no standards or benchmarking related to education or in any field, due to diverse practices and different teaching pedagogy, cultural factors are key drivers which influences AI usage intention in the field of education. Cultural factors like attitude of students, societal norms, student teachers' relations, teaching and learning style highly influence the usage of AI in education. AI should also align with societal norms as they are also a major deciding factor in adoption of technologies.

Our research has several limitations and which will give an opportunity for future research in this direction. First, our study has taken 300 responses from questionnaire being circulated in universities in India. Future research in this domain is highly recommended to take societal norms into considerations. Second, this research was conducted through questionnaire for examining role of AI autonomy in higher education through a student's perspective. Future study could examine the high and low level of autonomy impact on student usage intention and their adoption of AI educators. Limitation was sometimes respondents are themselves not aware of AI educators so before making them fill any questionnaire, a short video could be shown to give them a context about this domain and how it is being used in the field of education. In future, research could be conducted by choosing any one specific AI educator tool and analysing their usage by gathering students' data who have used that application in their learning process. This study also does not distinguish their respondents as college students, graduate students, post graduate students and PHD students. Future research could distinguish them as per their level of education and then gather the student's data to know more specific about does the level of education also impacts the usage intention of students or not. Future research could also target impact of artificial intelligence on motivating students and their academic success. In this, research could examine how AI could actually increase students' motivation in attending and learning the lectures regular and how it will be increasing students' engagement and through integration of AI in their learning whether they are getting that academic success means whether they could improve their scores and their performance In academics after using AI tutors or educators could also examine how AI educators could help students in setting goals and achieving it. Next future research related to this domain could be examining how AI tools or AI educators could help in bridging gaps in education. They should examine that whether the AI tools and applications could bridge the gaps which are there in education. Future study should examine the ethical and privacy concerns related to usage of artificial intelligence in the field of education. They should address challenges like privacy related to sensitive information of students that AI could leak out and could be misused by institutions. Second major challenge they can address is ethical issues. AI could generate and responds to answers which may not be ethical or inappropriate for students. They should also address the transparency of algorithms which can be used in enhancing the students experience in education. Future study could work on formulating policies for institutions related to usage of artificial intelligence for maintain ethics, transparency, and academic integrity and examine how AI autonomy could align with these institutions policies.

6. CONCLUSION

This book chapter successfully examines and presented how usage intention of using AI driven learning platforms can be impacted by the AI autonomy in higher education. For examining this, this book chapter have explored the various dimensions of AI autonomy - Thought Autonomy, Action Autonomy, Sensing Autonomy, and Culture- presented the in depth understanding that how the education can be imparted with thee help of AI driven platforms making the education more personalized, outcome based and more adaptive to our culture. All the dimensions discussed in the book chapter presents how it positively affects the inner motivation of students to use the apps, which increases the student's engagement which ultimately increases the adoption of these AI driven platforms. In our chapter through our model, we explained how thought autonomy, action autonomy, sensing autonomy and culture affects the usage intention and various relevant studies have been cited to make the study more authentic and to provide the concrete evidence to prove the credibility and reliability of the things being discussed in explaining the dimensions of autonomy and their potential impact on usage intention. Thought autonomy, the very first dimension of the AI autonomy which we discussed in the beginning. We came on the conclusion that yes, thought autonomy greatly influences the usage intention, increase the student engagement and frequency of using the AI driven platforms by giving the opportunity to students to take decisions independently related to their learning process which also kind of enhances their inner motivation to use the AI driven platforms. Action autonomy, is the second dimension of the AI autonomy which was discussed in this chapter. After exploring this dimension, conclusion can be derived that yes, action autonomy greatly influences the usage intention. This dimension give opportunity for thinking and making choices independently without any human intervention. Then we have cited that various studies have examined and have proved that students who perceive that they are having the greater control of their own learning path, feels motivated and engages more with the AI driven platforms. Sensing autonomy, is the third dimension of the AI autonomy which was discussed in this chapter. Through this, we have concluded that sensing autonomy positively impacts the usage intention. Sensing autonomy means how independently the AI driven learning platforms can gather the data, analyse it, and can provide the tailored recommendations and feedbacks to the students based on their showcased performance.

Cultural fit or cultural alignment is the most important amongst all the dimensions discussed in this book chapter. It greatly influences the usage intention. If the specific contents or modules are aligned with the culture of the society or the community, then engagement increase which ultimately increase the usage intention.

REFERENCES

Abdullah, F., Ward, R., & Ahmed, E. (2016). Investigating the influence of the most commonly used external variables of TAM on students' perceived ease of use and perceived usefulness of e-portfolios. *Computers in Human Behavior, 63*, 75–90. DOI: 10.1016/j.chb.2016.05.014

Ajzen, I. (1991). The theory of planned behavior. *Organizational Behavior and Human Decision Processes, 50*(2), 179–211. DOI: 10.1016/0749-5978(91)90020-T

Amigud, A., & Lancaster, T. (2019). 246 reasons to cheat: An analysis of students' reasons for seeking to outsource academic work. *Computers & Education, 134*, 98–107. DOI: 10.1016/j.compedu.2019.01.017

Aronson, J., & Davis, C. (2024). Gamification and autonomous learning in AI-based education. *Journal of Educational Technology and Learning, 15*(3), 100–115.

Awdry, R. (2021). Assignment outsourcing: Moving beyond contract cheating. *Assessment & Evaluation in Higher Education, 46*(2), 220–235. DOI: 10.1080/02602938.2020.1765311

Berente, N., Gu, B., Recker, J., & Santhanam, R. (2021). Managing artificial intelligence. *Management Information Systems Quarterly, 45*, 1433–1450.

Bond, M., Marín, V. I., Dolch, C., Bedenlier, S., & Zawacki-Richter, O. (2018). Digital transformation in German higher education: Student and teacher perceptions and usage of digital media. *International Journal of Educational Technology in Higher Education, 15*(1), 1–20. DOI: 10.1186/s41239-018-0130-1

Brown, T., Lee, K., & Wilson, R. (2023). Adaptive learning in higher education: The role of personalization in student engagement. *Journal of Learning Analytics, 10*(3), 165–178.

Chatterjee, S., & Bhattacharjee, K. K. (2020). Adoption of artificial intelligence in higher education: A quantitative analysis using structural equation modelling. *Education and Information Technologies, 25*(5), 3443–3463. DOI: 10.1007/s10639-020-10159-7

Chen, L., Jensen, P., & Albert, S. (2023). AI and personalization in education: Fostering engagement through autonomous learning. *Educational Technology Research and Development, 71*(2), 231–250.

Chen, Y., Jensen, S., Albert, L. J., Gupta, S., & Lee, T. (2023). Artificial intelligence (AI) student assistants in the classroom: Designing chatbots to support student success. *Information Systems Frontiers, 25*(1), 161–182. DOI: 10.1007/s10796-022-10291-4

Cheng, H., & Kim, S. (2024). Autonomy in AI learning environments: The role of intrinsic motivation. *Educational Psychology Review, 29*(1), 78–96.

Chong, A., & Tan, M. (2024). Balancing autonomy and guidance in adaptive learning. *Computers & Education, 190*, 104639.

Cope, B., Kalantzis, M., & Searsmith, D. (2021). Artificial intelligence for education: Knowledge and its assessment in AI-enabled learning ecologies. *Educational Philosophy and Theory, 53*(12), 1229–1245. DOI: 10.1080/00131857.2020.1728732

Davis, F. D. (1989). Perceived usefulness, perceived ease of use, and user acceptance of information technology. *Management Information Systems Quarterly*, *13*(3), 319–340. DOI: 10.2307/249008

East, J., & Donnelly, L. (2012). Taking responsibility for academic integrity: A collaborative teaching and learning design. *Journal of University Teaching & Learning Practice*, *9*(3).

Elbeltagi, I., McBride, N., Hardaker, G., & Magd, H. A. E. (2013). Examining the factors that affect intention to use mobile learning in a collaborative context. *Computers & Education*, *63*, 191–206.

Ertmer, P. A., Ottenbreit-Leftwich, A. T., Sadik, O., Sendurur, E., & Sendurur, P. (2012). Teacher beliefs and technology integration practices: A critical relationship. *Computers & Education*, *59*(2), 423–435. DOI: 10.1016/j.compedu.2012.02.001

Etzioni, A., & Etzioni, O. (2016). AI assisted ethics. *Ethics and Information Technology*, *18*(2), 149–156. DOI: 10.1007/s10676-016-9400-6

Evering, L. C., & Moorman, G. (2012). Rethinking plagiarism in the digital age. *Journal of Adolescent & Adult Literacy*, *56*(1), 35–44. DOI: 10.1002/JAAL.00100

Flom, J., Green, K., & Wallace, S. (2023). To cheat or not to cheat? An investigation into the ethical behaviors of generation Z. *Active Learning in Higher Education*, *24*(2), 155–168. DOI: 10.1177/14697874211016147

García, M.. (2024). Autonomy-supportive AI platforms in secondary education. *Computers & Education*, *167*, 104193.

Gonzalez, J.. (2023). Data privacy concerns in personalized learning environments: Implications for AI in education. *Computers in Human Behavior*, *137*, 107402.

Grant, S., & Phillips, R. (2023). Autonomy and agency in digital education. *Journal of Learning and Technology*, *12*(2), 43–55.

Guilherme, A. (2019). AI and education: The importance of teacher and student relations. *AI & Society*, *34*(1), 47–54. DOI: 10.1007/s00146-017-0693-8

Harrison, D., Patch, A., McNally, D., & Harris, L. (2021). Student and faculty perceptions of study helper websites: A new practice in collaborative cheating. *Journal of Academic Ethics*, *19*(4), 483–500. DOI: 10.1007/s10805-020-09373-2

Hofstede, G. (1984). *Culture's consequences: International differences in work-related values*. SAGE Publications.

Holmes, W., Bialik, M., & Fadel, C. (2019). *Artificial Intelligence in Education: Promises and Implications for Teaching and Learning*. Center for Curriculum Redesign.

Howard, R. M., & Davies, L. J. (2009). Plagiarism in the Internet age. *Educational Leadership*, *66*(6), 64–67.

Jeno, L. M., & Diseth, Å. (2019). A self-determination theory perspective on autonomy support, autonomous self-regulation, and perceived school performance. *International Journal of Educational Research*, *94*, 1–12.

Johnson, S., & Wang, T. (2024). Exploring the impact of adaptive learning on student engagement in higher education. *Journal of Educational Technology*, *35*(1), 45–61.

Johnston, H., Wells, R. F., Shanks, E. M., Boey, T., & Parsons, B. N. (2024). Student perspectives on the use of generative artificial intelligence technologies in higher education. *International Journal for Educational Integrity*, *20*(1), 2. DOI: 10.1007/s40979-024-00149-4

Kim, J.. (2024). Self-reflection tools in AI education: Empowering autonomous learning. *International Journal of Artificial Intelligence in Education*, *34*(1), 53–69.

Kim, J., Merrill, K.Jr, Xu, K., & Kelly, S. (2022). Perceived credibility of an AI instructor in online education: The role of social presence and voice features. *Computers in Human Behavior*, *136*, 107383. DOI: 10.1016/j.chb.2022.107383

Kim, J. H., Kim, M., Kwak, D. W., & Lee, S. (2022). Home-tutoring services assisted with technology: Investigating the role of artificial intelligence using a randomized field experiment. *JMR, Journal of Marketing Research*, *59*(1), 79–96. DOI: 10.1177/00222437211050351

Kim, T. W., & Duhachek, A. (2020). Artificial intelligence and persuasion: A construal-level account. *Psychological Science*, *31*(4), 363–380. DOI: 10.1177/0956797620904985 PMID: 32223692

Lai, F., & Cheng, R. (2024). Personalization and critical thinking: Balancing AI-driven learning. *The Journal of Higher Education*, *76*(2), 119–135.

Lee, M. K., Cheung, C. M., & Chen, Z. (2013). Acceptance of Internet-based learning medium: The role of extrinsic and intrinsic motivation. *Information & Management*, *50*(4), 218–227.

Li, Y., & Liu, Z. (2023). The impact of tailored feedback on student engagement in online platforms. *Interactive Learning Environments*, *31*(4), 555–571.

Lin, T.. (2024). Planned behavior and technology adoption in education. *Educational Technology Research Journal*, *56*(4), 567–588.

Maheshwari, G. (2021). Factors affecting students' intentions to undertake online learning: An empirical study in Vietnam. *Education and Information Technologies*, *26*(6), 6629–6649. DOI: 10.1007/s10639-021-10465-8 PMID: 33686331

Mezrich, J. L. (2022). Is artificial intelligence (AI) a pipe dream? Why legal issues present significant hurdles to AI autonomy. *AJR. American Journal of Roentgenology*, *219*(1), 152–156. DOI: 10.2214/AJR.21.27224 PMID: 35138133

Moore, C., & Lee, A. (2024). Balancing autonomy and guidance in AI education. *Journal of Educational Research and Innovation*, *45*(3), 221–233.

Moreno, F.. (2023). Autonomy and usage intention in AI learning platforms. *Journal of Educational Technology & Society*, *23*(4), 56–73.

Nguyen, A.. (2024). Motivational effects of adaptive language learning platforms: A Duolingo case study. *Language Learning & Technology*, *28*(1), 80–95.

Niu, W., Zhang, W., Zhang, C., & Chen, X. (2024). The Role of Artificial Intelligence Autonomy in Higher Education: A Uses and Gratification Perspective. *Sustainability (Basel), 16*(3), 1276. DOI: 10.3390/su16031276

Oliveira, T., Thomas, M., Baptista, G., & Campos, F. (2016). Mobile payment: Understanding the determinants of customer adoption and intention to recommend the technology. *Computers in Human Behavior, 61*, 404–414. DOI: 10.1016/j.chb.2016.03.030

Ouyang, F., & Jiao, P. (2021). Artificial intelligence in education: The three paradigms. *Comput. Educ. Artif. Intell., 2*, 100020. DOI: 10.1016/j.caeai.2021.100020

Poláková, P., & Klímová, B. (2019). Mobile technology and Generation Z in the English language classroom—A preliminary study. *Education Sciences, 9*(3), 203. DOI: 10.3390/educsci9030203

Rijsdijk, S. A., Hultink, E. J., & Diamantopoulos, A. (2007). Product intelligence: Its conceptualization, measurement and impact on consumer satisfaction. *Journal of the Academy of Marketing Science, 35*(3), 340–356. DOI: 10.1007/s11747-007-0040-6

Rogerson, A. M., & McCarthy, G. (2017). Using Internet based paraphrasing tools: Original work, patchwriting or facilitated plagiarism? *International Journal for Educational Integrity, 13*(1), 1–15. DOI: 10.1007/s40979-016-0013-y

Ryan, R. M., & Deci, E. L. (2017). *Self-determination theory: Basic psychological needs in motivation, development, and wellness.* Guilford Press. DOI: 10.1521/978.14625/28806

Salinas-Navarro, D. E., Vilalta-Perdomo, E., Michel-Villarreal, R., & Montesinos, L. (2024). Using generative artificial intelligence tools to explain and enhance experiential learning for authentic assessment. *Education Sciences, 14*(1), 83. DOI: 10.3390/educsci14010083

Santiago, A., & Yoon, K. (2024). Student motivation in autonomous learning environments. *Journal of Educational Motivation Studies, 19*(2), 143–158.

Shin, D. H., & Kim, W. Y. (2010). Applying the Technology Acceptance Model and flow theory to cyworld user behavior: Implication of the web2.0 user acceptance. *Cyberpsychology, Behavior, and Social Networking, 13*(4), 405–411.

Singh, V., & Patel, L. (2024). Scaffolding and action autonomy in AI platforms. *Learning and Instruction, 70*, 102–118.

Smith, T., & Wang, F. (2023). Autonomy and motivation in AI-based learning environments. *Learning and Instruction, 65*, 101–115.

Srite, M., & Karahanna, E. (2006). The role of espoused national cultural values in technology acceptance. *Management Information Systems Quarterly, 30*(3), 679–704. DOI: 10.2307/25148745

Straub, D. W., Loch, K. D., & Hill, C. E. (2016). Transfer of information technology to the Arab world: A test of cultural influence modeling. *Journal of Global Information Technology Management, 19*(2), 3–29.

Surugiu, C., Grădinaru, C., & Surugiu, M. R. (2024). Artificial Intelligence in Business Education: Benefits and Tools. *Amfiteatru Economic, 26*(65), 241–258. DOI: 10.24818/EA/2024/65/241

Szymkowiak, A., Melović, B., Dabić, M., Jeganathan, K., & Kundi, G. S. (2021). Information technology and Gen Z: The role of teachers, the internet, and technology in the education of young people. *Technology in Society, 65*, 101565. DOI: 10.1016/j.techsoc.2021.101565

Tarhini, A., Hone, K., & Liu, X. (2014). A cross-cultural examination of the impact of social, organizational and individual factors on educational technology acceptance between British and Lebanese university students. *British Journal of Educational Technology, 45*(4), 739–755. DOI: 10.1111/bjet.12169

Vallerand, R. J. (2023). Intrinsic and extrinsic motivation in education. *Contemporary Educational Psychology, 68*, 241–255.

Venkatesh, V., & Bala, H. (2008). Technology Acceptance Model 3 and a research agenda on interventions. *Decision Sciences, 39*(2), 273–315. DOI: 10.1111/j.1540-5915.2008.00192.x

Venkatesh, V., Morris, M. G., Davis, G. B., & Davis, F. D. (2003). User acceptance of information technology: Toward a unified view. *Management Information Systems Quarterly, 27*(3), 425–478. DOI: 10.2307/30036540

Vygotsky, L. S. (1978). *Mind in Society: The Development of Higher Psychological Processes.* Harvard University Press.

Wang, X., Li, L., Tan, S. C., Yang, L., & Lei, J. (2023). Preparing for AI-enhanced education: Conceptualizing and empirically examining teachers' AI readiness. *Computers in Human Behavior, 146*, 107798. DOI: 10.1016/j.chb.2023.107798

Wong, S. L., Teo, T., & Russo, S. (2013). Influence of gender and computer teaching efficacy on computer acceptance among Malaysian student teachers: An extended Technology Acceptance Model. *Australian Journal of Educational Technology, 29*(3), 394–412.

Xia, Q., Chiu, T. K., Lee, M., Sanusi, I. T., Dai, Y., & Chai, C. S. (2022). A self-determination theory (SDT) design approach for inclusive and diverse artificial intelligence (AI) education. *Computers & Education, 189*, 104582. DOI: 10.1016/j.compedu.2022.104582

Zhao, L., & Chiu, W. (2023). Self-determination theory in AI-driven education. *Journal of Educational Computing Research, 61*(2), 104–121.

Compilation of References

Abdamia, N., Puteh, F., & Jantan Anua Jah, N. (2023). Investigating Learning Modalities among Diploma Students. *International Journal of Academic Research in Progressive Education and Development*, *12*(2). Advance online publication. DOI: 10.6007/IJARPED/v12-i2/16552

Abdullah, A. M. (2017). "Advanced encryption standard (AES) algorithm to encrypt and decrypt data." Cryptography and https://www.researchgate.net/profile/Ako Network Security, 16(1), 11.

Abdullah, F., Ward, R., & Ahmed, E. (2016). Investigating the influence of the most commonly used external variables of TAM on students' perceived ease of use and perceived usefulness of e-portfolios. *Computers in Human Behavior*, *63*, 75–90. DOI: 10.1016/j.chb.2016.05.014

Abu Bakar, M. H., Ghafa, N. H. M., & Abdullah, F. (2024). Exploring the Integration of Artificial Intelligence in Technical and Vocational Education and Training (TVET): Applications, Benefits, Challenges, and Future Prospects. *Borneo Engineering & Advanced Multidisciplinary International Journal (BEAM)3* (Special Issue (ICo- ASCNITech 2024), 57-63. https://beam.pmu.edu.my/index.php/beam/article/view/189

Abulibdeh, A., Zaidan, E., & Abulibdeh, R. (2024). Navigating the confluence of artificial intelligence and education for sustainable development in the era of industry 4.0: Challenges, opportunities, and ethical dimensions. *Journal of Cleaner Production*, *437*, 140527. DOI: 10.1016/j.jclepro.2023.140527

Academy, K. (2023). Khan Academy's approach to the responsible development of AI. Khan Academy Blog. https://blog.khanacademy.org/aiguidelines/

Adams, R., & Oliver, R. (2019). *Teaching through peer interaction*. Routledge. DOI: 10.4324/9781315115696

Afzal, S., Dhamecha, T., Mukhi, N., Sindhgatta Rajan, R., Marvaniya, S., Ventura, M., & Yarbro, J. (2019). Development and deployment of a large-scale dialog-based intelligent tutoring system. In *Proceedings of the 2019 Conference of the North American Chapter of the Association for Computational Linguistics: Human Language Technologies*, Volume 2 (Industry Papers) (pp. 114-121). Association for Computational Linguistics.

Afzal, S., Shashidhar, V., Sindhgatta, R., & Sengupta, B. (2018). Impact of tutor errors on student engagement in a dialog based intelligent tutoring system. In Intelligent Tutoring Systems: 14th International Conference, ITS 2018, Montreal, QC, Canada, June 11–15, 2018 [Springer International Publishing.]. *Proceedings*, *14*, 267–273.

Agrawal, A., & Reed, B. (2022). A Survey On Grading Format Of Automated Grading Tools For Programming Assignments. ICERI Proceedings. DOI: 10.21125/iceri.2022.1912

Ahmad, M. F., & Ghapar, W. R. G. W. A. (2019). The era of artificial intelligence in Malaysian higher education: Impact and challenges in tangible mixed-reality learning system toward self-exploration education (SEE). *Procedia Computer Science*, *163*, 2–10. DOI: 10.1016/j.procs.2019.12.079

Ahmad, S., Tahar, R. M., Muhammad-Sukki, F., Munir, A. B., & Rahim, R. A. (2015). Role of feed-in tariff policy in promoting solar photovoltaic investments in Malaysia: A system dynamics approach. *Energy*, *84*, 808–815. DOI: 10.1016/j.energy.2015.03.047

Ahmad, T., Madonski, R., Zhang, D., Huang, C., & Mujeeb, A. (2022). Data-driven probabilistic machine learning in sustainable smart energy/smart energy systems: Key developments, challenges, and future research opportunities in the context of smart grid paradigm. *Renewable & Sustainable Energy Reviews*, *160*, 112128. DOI: 10.1016/j.rser.2022.112128

Ahmad, T., Zhang, D. D., & Huang, C. (2021). Methodological framework for short-and medium-term energy, solar and wind power forecasting with stochastic-based machine learning approach to monetary and energy policy applications. *Energy*, *231*, 120911. DOI: 10.1016/j.energy.2021.120911

Ahmad, T., Zhang, D., Huang, C., Zhang, H., Dai, N., Song, Y., & Chen, H. (2021). Artificial intelligence in sustainable energy industry: Status Quo, challenges and opportunities. *Journal of Cleaner Production*, *289*, 125834. DOI: 10.1016/j.jclepro.2021.125834

Ahmed, Z., Mohamed, K., Zeeshan, S., & Dong, X. (2020). Artificial intelligence with multi-functional machine learning platform development for better healthcare and precision medicine. *Database : The Journal of Biological Databases and Curation*, *2020*, baaa010. DOI: 10.1093/database/baaa010 PMID: 32185396

Ahn, L. V. (2012). *Proceedings of the 10th Conference of the Association for Machine Translation in the Americas: Keynote Presentations*. Association for Machine Translation in the Americas., https://www.aclweb.org/anthology/2012.amta-keynotes.4/

Ajzen, I. (1991). The theory of planned behavior. *Organizational Behavior and Human Decision Processes*, *50*(2), 179–211. DOI: 10.1016/0749-5978(91)90020-T

Akbaş, M. (2024). EXPLORING ACTIVE LEARNING METHODS FOR EFFECTIVE NURSING EDUCATION. *International Journal of Pedagogics*, *4*(12), 8–13.

Aldhafeeri, F. M., & Alotaibi, A. A. (2022). Effectiveness of digital education shifting model on high school students' engagement. *Education and Information Technologies*, *27*(5), 6869–6891. DOI: 10.1007/s10639-021-10879-4 PMID: 35103044

Alenezi, M., Wardat, S., & Akour, M. (2023). The need of integrating digital education in higher education: Challenges and opportunities. *Sustainability (Basel)*, *15*(6), 4782. DOI: 10.3390/su15064782

Alina, K. R. U. K. (2022). The benefits of Virtual Learning Environment (VLE) in teaching ESP. АКТУАЛЬНІ ПИТАННЯ ГУМАНІТАРНИХ НАУК, 2022171.

Al-Masri, R. A., Chenoweth, J., & Murphy, R. J. (2019). Exploring the status quo of water-energy nexus policies and governance in Jordan. *Environmental Science & Policy*, *100*, 192–204. DOI: 10.1016/j.envsci.2019.06.012

Almeida, T. D. F. S., & Sartori, J. (2012). A relação entre desmotivação e o processo ensino-aprendizagem. Revista Monografias Ambientais, 1870-1886.

Al-Raeei, M. (2024). Artificial intelligence for climate resilience: Advancing sustainable goals in SDGs 11 and 13 and its relationship to pandemics. *Discover Sustainability*, *5*(1), 513. DOI: 10.1007/s43621-024-00775-5

Al-Raeei, M. (2024). The smart future for sustainable development: Artificial intelligence solutions for sustainable urbanization. *Sustainable Development.*

AL-Roomy, M. A. (2023). The Relationship Among Students' Learning Styles, Health Sciences Colleges, and Grade Point Average (GPA). *Advances in Medical Education and Practice*, *14*(14), 203–213. DOI: 10.2147/AMEP.S395720 PMID: 36909353

Al-Sharafi, M. A., Al-Emran, M., Arpaci, I., Iahad, N. A., AlQudah, A. A., Iranmanesh, M., & Al-Qaysi, N. (2023). Generation Z use of artificial intelligence products and its impact on environmental sustainability: A cross-cultural comparison. *Computers in Human Behavior*, *143*, 107708. DOI: 10.1016/j.chb.2023.107708

Altmäe, S., Sola-Leyva, A., & Salumets, A. (2023). Artificial intelligence in scientific writing: A friend or a foe? *Reproductive Biomedicine Online*, *47*(1), 3–9. DOI: 10.1016/j.rbmo.2023.04.009 PMID: 37142479

Alzoubi, Y. I., & Mishra, A. (2024). Green artificial intelligence initiatives: Potentials and challenges. *Journal of Cleaner Production*, *468*, 143090. DOI: 10.1016/j.jclepro.2024.143090

American Psychological Association. (2022). *Dictionary of Psychology*. APA Dictionary of Psychology. https://dictionary.apa.org/motivation

Amigud, A., & Lancaster, T. (2019). 246 reasons to cheat: An analysis of students' reasons for seeking to outsource academic work. *Computers & Education*, *134*, 98–107. DOI: 10.1016/j.compedu.2019.01.017

Anand, S. (2021) What is Pedagogy? Importance of Pedagogy in the Teaching and Learning Process October 7, 2021.

Anderson, J., Rainie, L., & Luchsinger, A. (2018). Artificial intelligence and the future of humans. *Pew Research Center, 10*(12).

Anderson, P. (2020). Experiential Learning in Sustainability Education: Challenges and Innovations. *Sustainability Education Journal*, *15*(2), 45–63.

Ando, H., Cousins, R., & Young, C. (2014). Achieving saturation in thematic analysis: Development and refinement of a codebook. *Comprehensive Psychology*, *3*, 03.CP.3.4. DOI: 10.2466/03.CP.3.4

Angela, W. (2014). Virtual Classrooms in the Workplace: an Implementation Study. DOI: 10.21427/D71M8R

Anthonysamy, L., Koo, A. C., & Hew, S. H. (2020). Self-regulated learning strategies in higher education: Fostering digital literacy for sustainable lifelong learning. *Education and Information Technologies*, *25*(4), 2393–2414. DOI: 10.1007/s10639-020-10201-8

Anurogo, D., La Ramba, H., Putri, N. D., & Putri, U. M. P. (2023). Digital Literacy 5.0 to enhance multicultural education. *Multicultural Islamic Education Review, 1*(2), 109–179. DOI: 10.23917/mier.v1i2.3414

Arends, R. (2008). *Aprender a Ensinar*. MacGraw Hill.

Aronson, J., & Davis, C. (2024). Gamification and autonomous learning in AI-based education. *Journal of Educational Technology and Learning, 15*(3), 100–115.

Arshad, H. (2018). The role of affective filters in oral communication: A case study of Pakistani students and teachers. *Pakistan Journal of Language Studies, 2*(1), 51–62.

Assembleia da República Portuguesa. (2005). *Constituição da República Portuguesa*. https://www.parlamento.pt/Legislacao/Paginas/ConstituicaoRepublicaPortuguesa.aspx

Attali, Y. (2013). *Validity and reliability of automated essay scoring*. Educational Testing Service.

Autor, D. (2010). The Polarization of Job Opportunities in the U.S. Labor Market: Implications for Employment and Earnings. The Center for American Progress and The Hamilton Project. Retrieved from: https://economics.mit. Edu/files/5554

Awdry, R. (2021). Assignment outsourcing: Moving beyond contract cheating. *Assessment & Evaluation in Higher Education, 46*(2), 220–235. DOI: 10.1080/02602938.2020.1765311

Ayala-Pazmiño, M. (2023). Artificial Intelligence in Education: Exploring the Potential Benefits and Risks. 593 Digital Publisher CEIT, 8(3), 892–899. DOI: 10.33386/593dp.2023.3.1827

Ayeni, O. O., Al Hamad, N. M., Chisom, O. N., Osawaru, B., & Adewusi, O. E. (2024). AI in education: A review of personalized learning and educational technology. *GSC Advanced Research and Reviews, 18*(2), 261–271. DOI: 10.30574/gscarr.2024.18.2.0062

Bacich, L., & Moran, J. (2018). *Metodologias ativas para uma educação inovadora - uma abordagem teórico-prática* (de Oliveira, P. A., Ed.). PENSO EDITORA LTDA.

Badr, H. S., Zaitchik, B. F., & Guikema, S. D. (2020). Machine learning for precipitation and streamflow forecasting in the western United States. *Environmental Modelling & Software, 126*, 104660.

Bae, J., & Lee, Y. S. (2012). Evaluating the development of children's writing ability in an EFL context. *Language Assessment Quarterly, 9*(4), 348–374. DOI: 10.1080/15434303.2012.721424

Bailey, R. (2018). Student writing and academic literacy development at university. *Journal of Learning and Student Experience, 1*(7).

Baker, R. S., & Siemens, G. (2014). *Educational data mining and learning analytics*. Cambridge Handbook of the Learning Sciences, 253-272.

Baker, R. S., Martin, T., & Rossi, L. M. (2016). Educational data mining and learning analytics. *The Wiley handbook of cognition and assessment: Frameworks, methodologies, and applications*, 379-396.

Baker, R. S. (2016). Adaptive Learning Technologies: The Next Generation of Education. *AI & Society, 31*(4), 275–290.

Bansal, M., Goyal, A., & Choudhary, A. (2022). A comparative analysis of k-nearest neighbor, genetic, support vector machine, decision tree, and long short term memory algorithms in machine learning. Decision Analytics Journal, 3, Article 100071.

Barak, M., & Assal, M. (2018). Robotics and STEM learning: Students' achievements in assignments according to the P3 Task Taxonomy—practice, problem solving, and projects. *International Journal of Technology and Design Education*, *28*(1), 121–144. DOI: 10.1007/s10798-016-9385-9

Bárány, Z., & Siegel, C. (2015). Job Polarization and Structural Change. Presented at the American Economic Association Annual Meeting, Jan 3-5, 2016. https://www.aeaweb.org/conference/2016/retrieve.php?pdfid=906

Barbosa, E., & Moura, D. (2013). Metodologias ativas de aprendizagem na Educação Profissional e Tecnológica. *Boletim Técnico Do Senac*, *39*(2), 48–67. DOI: 10.26849/bts.v39i2.349

Barlas, P., Lanning, I., & Heavey, C. (2015). A survey of open source data science tools. *International Journal of Intelligent Computing and Cybernetics*, *8*(3), 232–261. DOI: 10.1108/IJICC-07-2014-0031

Barritt, L., Stock, P. L., & Clark, F. (1986). "Researching practice: Evaluating assessment essays." College Composition & Communication, 37(3), 315-327.DOI: 10.58680/ccc198611231

Barrows, H. S., & Tamblyn, R. M. (1980). *Problem-based learning: An approach to medical education.* Springer Publishing Company.

Barth, M., Godemann, J., Rieckmann, M., & Stoltenberg, U. (2007). Developing key competencies for sustainable development in higher education. *International Journal of Sustainability in Higher Education*, *8*(4), 416–430. DOI: 10.1108/14676370710823582

Bauerlein, M. (2009). *The Dumbest Generation: How the Digital Age Stupefies Young Americans and Jeopardizes Our Future (Or, Don 't Trust Anyone Under 30)* (1st ed.). TarcherPerigee.

Beard, C., & Wilson, J. P. (2006). *Experiential Learning: A Best Practice Handbook for Educators and Trainers*. Kogan Page.

Beardsley, M., Albó, L., Aragón, P., & Hernández-Leo, D. (2021). Emergency education effects on teacher abilities and motivation to use digital technologies. *British Journal of Educational Technology*, *52*(4), 1455–1477. DOI: 10.1111/bjet.13101

Becker, F. (2009). O que é Construtivismo? *Desenvolvimento e Aprendizagens Sob o Enfoque Da Psicologia II*, 1–8.

Beckett, G., & Slater, T. (2019). *Global Perspectives on Project-Based Language Learning, Teaching, and Assessment: Key Approaches, Technology Tools, and Frameworks*. Routledge. DOI: 10.4324/9780429435096

Bed, P. Dhakal., Lekhnath, Sharma. (2016). Virtual Learning Environment (VLE). *The Mathematics Educator*. Advance online publication. DOI: 10.11648/j.edu.20160506.11

Bello, O. W., Ehira, D. N., Ayeni, J. K., Faruk, N., & Balogun, N. A. (2014). Towards the Design of a Synchronous Virtual Learning System [CJICT]. *Covenant Journal of Informatics and Communication Technology*, *2*(2), 59–74.

Bender, W. N. (2012). *Project-Based Learning: Differentiating Instruction for the 21st Century*. Corwin Press.

Bereczki, E. O., & Kárpáti, A. (2021). Technology-enhanced creativity: A multiple case study of digital technology-integration expert teachers' beliefs and practices. *Thinking Skills and Creativity*, *39*, 100791. DOI: 10.1016/j.tsc.2021.100791

Berente, N., Gu, B., Recker, J., & Santhanam, R. (2021). Managing artificial intelligence. *Management Information Systems Quarterly*, *45*, 1433–1450.

Berland, M., & Wilensky, U. (2016). Integrating AI and data science tools into classroom settings: A means of enhancing critical analysis and environmental awareness. *Learning, Media and Technology*, *41*(3), 370–389.

Bezzina, S., & Dingli, A. (2024). The transformative potential of Artificial Intelligence for Education. *Networked Learning Conference, 14*(1). https://doi.org/DOI: 10.54337/nlc.v14i1.8077

Biasutti, M., & Frate, S. (2017). A conceptual framework for the sustainability of education for sustainable development. *Journal of Cleaner Production*, *168*, 144–152.

Bibri, S. E. (2019). On the sustainability of smart and smarter cities in the era of big data: An interdisciplinary and transdisciplinary literature review. *Journal of Big Data*, *6*(1), 25. DOI: 10.1186/s40537-019-0182-7

Biletska, I. O., Paladieva, A. F., Avchinnikova, H. D., & Kazak, Y. Y. (2021). The use of modern technologies by foreign language teachers: Developing digital skills. *Linguistics and Culture Review*, *5*(S2), 16–27. DOI: 10.21744/lingcure.v5nS2.1327

Bilotta, E., Bertacchini, F., Gabriele, L., Giglio, S., Pantano, P. S., & Romita, T. (2021). Industry 4.0 technologies in tourism education: Nurturing students to think with technology. *Journal of Hospitality, Leisure, Sport and Tourism Education*, *29*, 100275. DOI: 10.1016/j.jhlste.2020.100275

Binagwaho, A., Bonciani Nader, H., Brown Burkins, M., Davies, A., Hessen, D. O., Mbow, C., & Tong, S. (2022). *Knowledge-driven actions: transforming higher education for global sustainability: independent expert group on the universities and the 2030 agenda*. UNESCO Publishing.

Binns, R., & Gallo, G. (2021). Addressing biases and ethics in AI education: A framework for responsible integration. *Journal of Technology and Society*, *19*(2), 123–139.

Birol, F. (2022). *World Energy Outlook 2022 (Technical)*. International Energy Agency., Available at https://iea.blob.core.windows.net/assets/830fe099-5530-48f2-a7c1-11f35d510983/WorldEnergyOutlook2022.pdf

Bisen, V. S. (2020). *What is Human in the Loop Machine Learning: Why & How Used in AI?* Medium. https://medium.com/vsinghbisen/what-is-human-in-the-loop-machine-learning-why-how-used-in-ai-60c7b44eb2c0

Bond, M., Marín, V. I., Dolch, C., Bedenlier, S., & Zawacki-Richter, O. (2018). Digital transformation in German higher education: Student and teacher perceptions and usage of digital media. *International Journal of Educational Technology in Higher Education, 15*(1), 1–20. DOI: 10.1186/s41239-018-0130-1

Bonwell, C. C., & Eison, J. A. (1991). Active Learning: Creating Excitement in the Classroom. 1991 ASHE-ERIC Higher Education Reports. In *ASHE-ERIC Higher Education Report.*

Bonwell, C. C., & Eison, J. A. (1991). ASHE-ERIC Higher Education Report: Vol. 1. *Active learning: Creating excitement in the classroom.* The George Washington University.

Borenstein, J., & Howard, A. (2021). Emerging challenges in AI and the need for AI ethics education. *AI and Ethics, 1*(1), 61–65. DOI: 10.1007/s43681-020-00002-7 PMID: 38624388

Bower, M., & Stavenhagen, C. (2021). Empowering students to innovate: AI-driven problem-solving in sustainability education. *Journal of Computer Assisted Learning, 37*(1), 43–55.

Boyd, R., & Holton, R. J. (2018). Technology, innovation, employment and power: Does robotics and artificial intelligence really mean social transformation? *Journal of Sociology (Melbourne, Vic.), 54*(3), 331–345. DOI: 10.1177/1440783317726591

Braunerhjelm, P., & Hepburn, C. (2023). Climate change, complexity, and policy design. *Oxford Review of Economic Policy, 39*(4), 667–679. Advance online publication. DOI: 10.1093/oxrep/grad047

Braun, V., & Clarke, V. (2006). Using thematic analysis in psychology. *Qualitative Research in Psychology, 3*(2), 77–101. DOI: 10.1191/1478088706qp063oa

Brdesee, H., Alsaggaf, W., Aljohani, N. R., & Hassan, S.-U. (2022). Predictive Model Using a Machine Learning Approach for Enhancing the Retention Rate of Students At-Risk. *International Journal on Semantic Web and Information Systems, 18*(1), 1–21. DOI: 10.4018/IJSWIS.299859

Brenner, B. (2018). Transformative sustainable business models in the light of the digital imperative—A global business economics perspective. *Sustainability (Basel), 10*(12), 4428. DOI: 10.3390/su10124428

Brookfield, S. D. (2012). *Teaching for critical thinking: Tools and techniques to help students question their assumptions.* John Wiley & Sons.

Brown, A. (2016). 'Key findings about the American workforce and the changing job market'. Pew Research Center. Accessed: http://www.pewresearch.org/fact- tank/2016/10/06/key-findings-about-the-american-workforce and-the-changing-job- market/

Brown, T. B. (2020). Language models are few-shot learners. *arXiv preprint arXiv:2005.14165.*

Brown, T., Mann, B., Ryder, N., Subbiah, M., & Associates. (2020) Language models are few-shot learners. arXiv preprint arXiv: 2005.14165. https: //arxiv.org/abs/2005.14165

Brown, T., Lee, K., & Wilson, R. (2023). Adaptive learning in higher education: The role of personalization in student engagement. *Journal of Learning Analytics, 10*(3), 165–178.

Buchanan, J., Pressick-Kilborn, K., & Maher, D. (2018). Promoting environmental education for primary school-aged students using digital technologies. *Eurasia Journal of Mathematics, Science and Technology Education, 15*(2), em1661.

Buckingham, D. (2020). Epilogue: Rethinking digital literacy: Media education in the age of digital capitalism. *Digital Education Review*, (37), 230–239. DOI: 10.1344/der.2020.37.230-239

Buhl, A., Schmidt-Keilich, M., Muster, V., Blazejewski, S., Schrader, U., Harrach, C., Schäfer, M., & Süßbauer, E. (2019). Design thinking for sustainability: Why and how design thinking can foster sustainability-oriented innovation development. *Journal of Cleaner Production*, *231*, 1248–1257. DOI: 10.1016/j.jclepro.2019.05.259

Burch, G. F., Giambatista, R., Batchelor, J. H., Burch, J. J., Hoover, J. D., & Heller, N. A. (2019). A meta-analysis of the relationship between experiential learning and learning outcomes. *Decision Sciences Journal of Innovative Education*, *17*(3), 239–273. DOI: 10.1111/dsji.12188

Büyükbaykal, C. I. (2015). Communication technologies and education in the information age. *Procedia: Social and Behavioral Sciences*, *174*, 636–640. DOI: 10.1016/j.sbspro.2015.01.594

Bynum, T., & Rogerson, S. (2022). *Computer Ethics and Professional Responsibility*. John Wiley & Sons.

Cao, K. Y., Xu, X. P., Wu, Q., & Zhang, Q. P. (2017). Optimal production and carbon emission reduction level under cap-and-trade and low carbon subsidy policies. *Journal of Cleaner Production*, *167*, 505–513. DOI: 10.1016/j.jclepro.2017.07.251

Capra, F. (2005). *Systems thinking as a framework for sustainability education*. Center for Ecoliteracy.

Castellanos-Nieves, D., Fernández-Breis, J. T., Valencia-García, R., Martínez-Béjar, R., & Iniesta-Moreno, M. (2011). Semantic Web Technologies for supporting learning assessment. *Information Sciences*, *181*(9), 1517–1537. DOI: 10.1016/j.ins.2011.01.010

Castrillón-Mendoza, R., Rey-Hernández, J. M., & Rey-Martínez, F. J. (2020). Industrial decarbonization by a new energy-baseline methodology. Case study. *Sustainability (Basel)*, *12*(5), 1960. DOI: 10.3390/su12051960

Cath, C. (2018). Governing artificial intelligence: Ethical, legal and technical opportunities and challenges. *Philosophical Transactions. Series A, Mathematical, Physical, and Engineering Sciences*, *376*(2133), 20180080. DOI: 10.1098/rsta.2018.0080 PMID: 30322996

Cave, S., & Dihal, K. (2019). Hopes and fears for intelligent machines in fiction and reality. *Nature Machine Intelligence*, *1*(2), 74–78. DOI: 10.1038/s42256-019-0020-9

Chai, C. S., Lin, P. Y., Jong, M. S. Y., Dai, Y., Chiu, T. K. F., & Huang, B. Y. (2020) Factors influencing students' behavioral intention to continue artificial intelligence learning. In Proceedings of the International Symposium on Educational Technology, (ISET020), Bangkok, Thailand, 24–27 August.

Chai, C. S., Lin, P. Y., Jong, M. S. Y., Dai, Y., Chiu, T. K. F., & Qin, J. J. (2020). Primary school students' perceptions and behavioral intentions of learning artificial intelligence. *Journal of Educational Technology & Society*.

Challis, D. (2005). Committing to quality learning through adaptive online assessment. *Assessment & Evaluation in Higher Education*, *30*(5), 519–527. DOI: 10.1080/02602930500187030

Chan, Y. T. (2020). On the impacts of anticipated carbon policies: A dynamic stochastic general equilibrium model approach. *Journal of Cleaner Production*, *256*, 120342. DOI: 10.1016/j.jclepro.2020.120342

Charney, D. (1984). The validity of using holistic scoring to evaluate writing: A critical overview. *Research in the Teaching of English*, *18*(1), 65–81. DOI: 10.58680/rte198415687

Chassignol, M., Khoroshavin, A., Klimova, A., & Bilyatdinova, A. (2018). Artificial Intelligence trends in education: A narrative overview. *Procedia Computer Science*, *136*, 16–24. DOI: 10.1016/j.procs.2018.08.233

Chatterjee, S., & Bhattacharjee, K. K. (2020). Adoption of artificial intelligence in higher education: A quantitative analysis using structural equation modelling. *Education and Information Technologies*, *25*(5), 3443–3463. DOI: 10.1007/s10639-020-10159-7

Chauhan, D., Bahad, P., & Jain, J. K. (2024). Sustainable AI: Environmental Implications, Challenges, and Opportunities. Explainable AI (XAI) for Sustainable Development, 1-15.

Chen, J., Whittinghill, D. C., & Kadlowec, J. (2006). Using Rapid Feedback to Enhance Student Learning and Satisfaction. Proceedings. Frontiers in Education. 36th Annual Conference, 13-18. DOI: 10.1109/FIE.2006.322306

Cheng, H., & Kim, S. (2024). Autonomy in AI learning environments: The role of intrinsic motivation. *Educational Psychology Review*, *29*(1), 78–96.

Chen, L., Jensen, P., & Albert, S. (2023). AI and personalization in education: Fostering engagement through autonomous learning. *Educational Technology Research and Development*, *71*(2), 231–250.

Chen, Y., Jensen, S., Albert, L. J., Gupta, S., & Lee, T. (2023). Artificial intelligence (AI) student assistants in the classroom: Designing chatbots to support student success. *Information Systems Frontiers*, *25*(1), 161–182. DOI: 10.1007/s10796-022-10291-4

Chen, Z. (2023). Ethics and Discrimination in Artificial intelligence-enabled Recruitment Practices. *Humanities & Social Sciences Communications*, *10*(1), 1–12. DOI: 10.1057/s41599-023-02079-x

Chetty, K., Qigui, L., Gcora, N., Josie, J., Wenwei, L., & Fang, C. (2018). Bridging the digital divide: Measuring digital literacy. *Economics*, *12*(1), 20180023. DOI: 10.5018/economics-ejournal.ja.2018-23

Chinedu, C. C., & Olabiyi, O. S. (2015). Empowering Nigerian youths through technical vocational education and training for enhancing national security. *Journal of Technical Education and Training*, *7*(1), 10–22.

Chinedu, C. C., Olabiyi, O. S., & Kamin, Y. (2015). Strategies for improving higher order thinking skills in teaching and learning of design and technology education. *Journal of Technical Education and Training*, *7*(2), 35–43.

Chiu, T. K. F., & Churchill, D. (2015). Exploring the characteristics of an optimal design of digital materials for concept learning in mathematics: Multimedia learning and variation theory. *Computers & Education*, *82*, 280–291. DOI: 10.1016/j.compedu.2014.12.001

Chiu, T. K. F., & Churchill, D. (2016). Adoption of mobile devices in teaching: Changes in teacher beliefs, attitudes and anxiety. *Interactive Learning Environments, 24*(2), 317–327. DOI: 10.1080/10494820.2015.1113709

Chiu, T. K. F., & Churchill, D. (2016). Design of learning objects for concept learning: Effects of multimedia learning principles and an instructional approach. *Interactive Learning Environments, 24*(6), 1355–1370. DOI: 10.1080/10494820.2015.1006237

Chiu, T. K. F., & Mok, I. A. C. (2017). Learner expertise and mathematics different order thinking skills in multimedia learning. *Computers & Education, 107*, 147–164. DOI: 10.1016/j.compedu.2017.01.008

Chiu, T. K., Jong, M. S. Y., & Mok, I. A. (2020). Does learner expertise matter when designing emotional multimedia for learners of primary school mathematics? *Educational Technology Research and Development, 68*(5), 2305–2320. DOI: 10.1007/s11423-020-09775-4

Chiu, T. K., & Lim, C. P. (2020). *Strategic Use of Technology for Inclusive Education in Hong Kong: A Content-Level Perspective*. ECNU Rev. Educ.

Choi, S., McMaster, K. L., Kohli, N., Shanahan, E., Birinci, S., An, J., Duesenberg-Marshall, M. K., & Lembke, E. S. (2024). Longitudinal effects of data-based instructional changes for students with intensive learning needs: A piecewise linear–linear mixed-effects modeling approach. *Journal of Educational Psychology, 116*(4), 608–628. DOI: 10.1037/edu0000853

Chong, A., & Tan, M. (2024). Balancing autonomy and guidance in adaptive learning. *Computers & Education, 190*, 104639.

Chow, S.-M., Lee, J., Park, J., Kuruppumullage Don, P., Hammel, T., Hallquist, M. N., Nord, E. A., Oravecz, Z., Perry, H. L., Lesser, L. M., & Pearl, D. K. (2024). Personalized Education through Individualized Pathways and Resources to Adaptive Control Theory-Inspired Scientific Education (iPRACTISE): Proof-of-Concept Studies for Designing and Evaluating Personalized Education. *Journal of Statistics and Data Science Education : An Official Journal of the of the American Statistical Association, 32*(2), 1–42. DOI: 10.1080/26939169.2024.2302181

Christine Persaud (2024). 9 Pedagogical Approaches for Higher Ed Explained [Plus: 40+ Free Strategies to Implement in Your Classroom] | Top Hat May 16, 2024.

Chung, G. K., & O'Neil Jr, H. F. (1997). Methodological Approaches to Online Scoring of Essays.

Clayton, T., & Radcliffe, N. (2018). *Sustainability: a systems approach*. Routledge. DOI: 10.4324/9781315070711

Climate Interactive. (2020). *En-ROADS: Climate Solutions Simulator.* Climate Interactive. Retrieved from https://www.climateinteractive.org/tools/en-roads

Climate, A. I. (2021). *Climate Risk Analytics for a Resilient Future*. ClimateAI. Retrieved from https://climate.ai

Coffie, I. S., Doe, N. G., & Tabi, J. A. (2021). Pre-Service Science Teachers' Assessment of Supported Teaching in School. *European Scientific Journal, 17*(32), 257. DOI: 10.19044/esj.2021.v17n32p257

Cofino, C. L., Atillo, G. N. A., & Velos, S. P. (2021). E-xtension: A virtual learning environment (vle) system for a state university. *International Journal of Computing Sciences Research*, *5*, 663–678.

Collett, D. (2023). FeedbackFruits. Learning Management System. https://lms.unimelb.edu.au/learning-technologies/feedbackfruits

Collins, A., & Halverson, R. (2018). *Rethinking education in the age of technology: The digital revolution and schooling in America*. Teachers College Press.

Commonwealth of Learning, TVET Professional Development Toolkit for the Pacific, Commonly used terms, n.d.

Cope, B., Kalantzis, M., & Searsmith, D. (2020). Artificial intelligence for education: Knowledge and its assessment in AI-enabled learning ecologies. *Educational Philosophy and Theory*. Advance online publication. DOI: 10.1080/00131857.2020.1728732

Crivosoft, M. D. L. (2023). *Plataforma Virtual First*. Youtube. https://www.youtube.com/watch?v=h69cEQYxw_s

Danish, M. S. S., Elsayed, M. E. L., Ahmadi, M., Senjyu, T., Karimy, H., & Zaheb, H. (2020). A strategic-integrated approach for sustainable energy deployment. *Energy Reports*, *6*, 40–44. DOI: 10.1016/j.egyr.2019.11.039

Danish, M. S. S., Senjyu, T., Funabashia, T., Ahmadi, M., Ibrahimi, A. M., Ohta, R., & Sediqi, M. M. (2019). A sustainable microgrid: A sustainability and management-oriented approach. *Energy Procedia*, *159*, 160–167. DOI: 10.1016/j.egypro.2018.12.045

Davies, M. (2015). A Model of Critical Thinking in Higher Education. In Paulsen, M. B. (Ed.), *Higher Education: Handbook of Theory and Research* (pp. 41–82). Springer. DOI: 10.1007/978-3-319-12835-1_2

Davis, F. D. (1989). Perceived usefulness, perceived ease of use, and user acceptance of information technology. *Management Information Systems Quarterly*, *13*(3), 319–340. DOI: 10.2307/249008

De Jong, T., & Van Joolingen, W. R. (2019). AI tools as interdisciplinary bridges in education: From biology to earth sciences. *Educational Research Review*, *29*, 100309.

Deane, P. (2013). On the relation between automated essay scoring and modern views of the writing construct. *Assessing Writing*, *18*(1), 7–24. DOI: 10.1016/j.asw.2012.10.002

Dede, C. (2009). Immersive interfaces for engagement and learning. *Science*, *323*(5910), 66–69. DOI: 10.1126/science.1167311 PMID: 19119219

DeepMind. (2021). Deep Learning for Precipitation Nowcasting. *Nature*, *597*, 672–677.

Deka, D., Backhaus, S., & Chertkov, M. (2018). Structure learning in power distribution networks. *IEEE Transactions on Control of Network Systems*, *5*(3), 1061–1074. DOI: 10.1109/TCNS.2017.2673546

Denzin, N. K., & Lincoln, Y. S. (Eds.). (2008). *The landscape of qualitative research* (3rd ed.). Sage Publications, Inc.

Derijan, I., & Valchev, G. (2012). Spiritual and moral development of the child in Bulgaria— Traditions and modern projection. In *Yearbook of Burgas Free University* (p. 165). BRU.

Digital, P. (2020). Plano de Ação para a Transição Digital de Portugal. In *Economia e Transição Digital.* https://www.portugal.gov.pt/gc22/portugal-digital/plano-de-acao-para-a-transicao-digital-pdf.aspx

Dikli, S. (2006). An overview of automated scoring of essays. *The Journal of Technology, Learning, and Assessment*, *5*, 1, 5–22.

Diliberti, M. K., Schwartz, H. L., Doan, S., Shapiro, A., Rainey, L. R., & Lake, R. J. (2024). *Using Artificial Intelligence Tools in K–12 Classrooms.* RAND Corporation., https://www.rand.org/pubs/research_reports/RRA956-21.html

DRE. (2009, August 27). *DL n.º 85/2009 - Estabelece o regime da escolaridade obrigatória para as crianças e jovens que se encontram em idade escolar e consagra a universalidade da educação pré-escolar para as crianças a partir dos 5 anos de idade.* Diário Da República n.º 166/2009, Série. *Ide (São Paulo).*

DRE. (2022). *Código do Trabalho.* Diário Da República n.º 30/2009, Série I de 2009-02-12. https://dre.pt/dre/legislacao-consolidada/lei/2009-34546475

Dwivedi, D. N., Mahanty, G., & nath Dwivedi, V. (2024). Intelligent Conservation: A Comprehensive Study on AI-Enhanced Environmental Monitoring and Preservation. In The Convergence of Self-Sustaining Systems With AI and IoT (pp. 215-226). IGI Global.

Dwivedi, Y. K., Hughes, L., Ismagilova, E., Aarts, G., Coombs, C., Crick, T., Duan, Y., Dwivedi, R., Edwards, J., Eirug, A., Galanos, V., Ilavarasan, P. V., Janssen, M., Jones, P., Kar, A. K., Kizgin, H., Kronemann, B., Lal, B., Lucini, B., & Williams, M. D. (2021). Artificial Intelligence (AI): Multidisciplinary perspectives on emerging challenges, opportunities, and agenda for research, practice and policy. *International Journal of Information Management*, *57*, 101994. DOI: 10.1016/j.ijinfomgt.2019.08.002

Dwivedi, Y. K., Hughes, L., Kar, A. K., Baabdullah, A. M., Grover, P., Abbas, R., Andreini, D., Abumoghli, I., Barlette, Y., Bunker, D., Chandra Kruse, L., Constantiou, I., Davison, R. M., De', R., Dubey, R., Fenby-Taylor, H., Gupta, B., He, W., Kodama, M., & Wade, M. (2022). Climate change and COP26: Are digital technologies and information management part of the problem or the solution? An editorial reflection and call to action. *International Journal of Information Management*, *63*, 102456. DOI: 10.1016/j.ijinfomgt.2021.102456

Easouh, F. Y. J., Oweis, T. E., & Makahleh, H. A. (2024). A Bibliometric Lens on the Future: How AI continues to transform education institutions. Human Systems Management, (Preprint), 1-20.

East, J., & Donnelly, L. (2012). Taking responsibility for academic integrity: A collaborative teaching and learning design. *Journal of University Teaching & Learning Practice*, *9*(3).

Eden, C. A., Adeleye, O. O., & Adeniyi, I. S. (2024). A review of AI-driven pedagogical strategies for equitable access to science education. *Magna Scientia Advanced Research and Reviews, 10*(2), 044-054.

Edeni, C. A., Adeleye, O. O., & Adeniyi, I. S. (2024). The role of AI-enhanced tools in overcoming socioeconomic barriers in education: A conceptual analysis. *World Journal of Advanced Research and Reviews*, *21*(3), 944–951. DOI: 10.30574/wjarr.2024.21.3.0780

Edwards-Fapohunda, M. O., & Adediji, M. A. (2024). Sustainable Development of Distance Learning in Continuing Adult Education: The Impact of Artificial Intelligence. *Iconic Research and Engineering Journals*, *8*(1), 113–114.

Eggleston, J. (2018). *School-Based Curriculum Development in Britain: A Collection of Case Studies.* Routledge. DOI: 10.4324/9780429454622

Eguchi, A., Okada, H., & Muto, Y. (2021). Contextualizing AI education for K-12 students to enhance their learning of AI literacy through culturally responsive approaches. *Kunstliche Intelligenz*, *35*(2), 153–161. DOI: 10.1007/s13218-021-00737-3 PMID: 34376922

Eilermann, S., Wehmeier, L., Niggemann, O., & Deuter, A. (2023, July). KIAAA: An AI assistant for teaching programming in the field of automation. In 2023 IEEE 21st International Conference on Industrial Informatics (INDIN) (pp. 1-7). IEEE.

Elbeltagi, I., McBride, N., Hardaker, G., & Magd, H. A. E. (2013). Examining the factors that affect intention to use mobile learning in a collaborative context. *Computers & Education*, *63*, 191–206.

Ellen MacArthur Foundation. (2014). Towards the Circular Economy Vol.3: Accelerating the scale-up across global supply chains. *Ellen MacArthur Foundation*, (January), 1–64. DOI: 10.1162/108819806775545321

Elley, W. B., Barham, J. H., Lamb, H., & Wylie, M. (1976). The role of grammar in a secondary school English curriculum. *Research in the Teaching of English*, *10*(1), 5–21. DOI: 10.58680/rte197620040

El-Swaify, M. A. (2022). The global nexus: Bridging science, technology, and business in the international landscape. International Multidisciplinary Journal of Science. *Technology & Business*, *1*(01), 22–28.

Entezari, A., Aslani, A., Zahedi, R., & Noorollahi, Y. (2023). Artificial intelligence and machine learning in energy systems: A bibliographic perspective. Energy Strategy Reviews, 45, Article 101017.

Erickson, J. A., Botelho, A. F., McAteer, S., Varatharaj, A., & Heffernan, N. T. (2020). The automated grading of student open responses in mathematics. *Proceedings of the Tenth International Conference on Learning Analytics & Knowledge*. DOI: 10.1145/3375462.3375523

Ernst, D., Glavic, M., & Wehenkel, L. (2004). Power systems stability control: Reinforcement learning framework. *IEEE Transactions on Power Systems*, *19*(1), 427–435. DOI: 10.1109/TPWRS.2003.821457

Ertmer, P. A., Ottenbreit-Leftwich, A. T., Sadik, O., Sendurur, E., & Sendurur, P. (2012). Teacher beliefs and technology integration practices: A critical relationship. *Computers & Education*, *59*(2), 423–435. DOI: 10.1016/j.compedu.2012.02.001

Etzioni, A., & Etzioni, O. (2016). AI assisted ethics. *Ethics and Information Technology*, *18*(2), 149–156. DOI: 10.1007/s10676-016-9400-6

Evering, L. C., & Moorman, G. (2012). Rethinking plagiarism in the digital age. *Journal of Adolescent & Adult Literacy*, *56*(1), 35–44. DOI: 10.1002/JAAL.00100

Facione, P. A. (2015). *Critical Thinking: What It Is and Why It Counts.* Insight Assessment.

Fadel, C., Holmes, W., & Bialik, M. (2019). *Artificial intelligence in education: Promises and implications for teaching and learning.* Centre for Curriculum Redesign.

Faias, J. (2021). *Active Methodologies for Learning*. Ukrothe. https://www.ukrothe.eu/en/blog/active-methodologies-learning

Falloon, G. (2020). From digital literacy to digital competence: The teacher digital competency (TDC) framework. *Educational Technology Research and Development, 68*(5), 2449–2472. DOI: 10.1007/s11423-020-09767-4

Fan, Z., Yan, Z., & Wen, S. (2023). Deep learning and artificial intelligence in sustainability: A review of SDGs, renewable energy, and environmental health. *Sustainability (Basel), 15*(18), 13493. DOI: 10.3390/su151813493

Feak, C. B., & Swales, J. (2011). *Creating contexts: Writing introductions across genres*. No Title. DOI: 10.3998/mpub.3367288

Federal Republic of Nigeria. (2004). *National Policy of Education* (4th ed.). NERDC.

Fernandes, D. (2007). A avaliação das aprendizagens no Sistema Educativo Português. *Educação e Pesquisa, 33*(3), 581–600. DOI: 10.1590/S1517-97022007000300013

Ferrario, M. (2024), The Challenges of Artificial Intelligence In Online Learning, DynDevice, https://www.dyndevice.com/en/news/the-challenges-of-artificial-intelligence-in-online-learning-ELN-1883/

Figueiredo, P., & Joaquim, A. F. (2023). The impact of artificial intelligence and intergenerational diversity. In Ince, F. (Ed.), *Leadership Perspectives on Effective Intergenerational Communication and Management* (pp. 72–90). IGI Global., DOI: 10.4018/978-1-6684-6140-2.ch005

Flom, J., Green, K., & Wallace, S. (2023). To cheat or not to cheat? An investigation into the ethical behaviors of generation Z. *Active Learning in Higher Education, 24*(2), 155–168. DOI: 10.1177/14697874211016147

Floridi, L., & Cowls, J. (2022). A unified framework of five principles for AI in society. *Machine learning and the city: Applications in architecture and urban design*, 535-545.

Foong, Y. P., Pidani, R., Sithira Vadivel, V., & Dongyue, Y. (2024). Singapore smart nation: journey into a new digital landscape for higher education. In *Emerging Technologies in Business: Innovation Strategies for Competitive Advantage* (pp. 281–304). Springer Nature Singapore. DOI: 10.1007/978-981-97-2211-2_13

Fuchs, K., & Aguilos, V. (2023). Integrating artificial intelligence in higher education: Empirical insights from students about using ChatGPT. *International Journal of Information and Education Technology (IJIET), 13*(9), 1365–1371. DOI: 10.18178/ijiet.2023.13.9.1939

Gabr, A. Z., Helal, A., & Abbasy, N. (2020). Economic evaluation of rooftop grid-connected photovoltaic systems for residential building in Egypt. *International Transactions on Electrical Energy Systems, 30*(6), e12379. DOI: 10.1002/2050-7038.12379

Gamble, J. (2013). *Why improved formal teaching and learning are important in TVET. Revisiting global trends in TVET*. UNESCO.

Gao, R., Merzdorf, H. E., Anwar, S., Cynthia Hipwell, M., & Srinivasa, A. (2024). Automatic assessment of text-based responses in post-secondary education: A systematic review. Computers & Education. *Artificial Intelligence*, *6*, 100206–100206. DOI: 10.1016/j.caeai.2024.100206

García, M.. (2024). Autonomy-supportive AI platforms in secondary education. *Computers & Education*, *167*, 104193.

Gardiner, A., & Smith, M. A. (2021). Conversational AI as an emerging technology. In *Proceedings of the EDSIG conference ISSN* (Vol. 2473, p. 4901).

Gernsbacher, M. A., Soicher, R. N., & Becker-Blease, K. A. (2020). Four Empirically Based Reasons Not to Administer Time-Limited Tests. *Translational Issues in Psychological Science*, *6*(2), 175–190. DOI: 10.1037/tps0000232 PMID: 32582819

Ghufron, M. A., & Rosyida, F. (2018). The Role of Grammarly in Assessing English as a Foreign Language (EFL) Writing. *Lingua Cultura*, *12*(4), 395. DOI: 10.21512/lc.v12i4.4582

Gladysz, P., Strojny, M., Bartela, Ł., Hacaga, M., & Froehlich, T. (2022). Merging climate action with energy security through CCS-a multi-disciplinary framework for assessment. *Energies*, *16*(1), 35. DOI: 10.3390/en16010035

Glaser, R., & Silver, E. (1994). Chapter 9: Assessment, Testing, and Instruction: Retrospect and Prospect. *Review of Research in Education*, *20*(1), 393–419. DOI: 10.3102/0091732X020001393

Glatthorn, A. A., Boschee, F., Whitehead, B. M., & Boschee, B. F. (2018). *Curriculum Leadership: Strategies for Development and Implementation*. SAGE.

Gleason, B., & Von Gillern, S. (2018). Digital citizenship with social media: Participatory practices of teaching and learning in secondary education. *Journal of Educational Technology & Society*, *21*(1), 200–212.

Goh, A., & Sanders, D. (2019). Using AI to Improve Student Learning: A Critical Look at AI-Driven Feedback Systems. *Journal of Educational Technology*.

Gokhale, A. A. (1995). Collaborative learning enhances critical thinking. *Journal of Technology Education*, *7*(1), 22–30. DOI: 10.21061/jte.v7i1.a.2

Gonzalez, J.. (2023). Data privacy concerns in personalized learning environments: Implications for AI in education. *Computers in Human Behavior*, *137*, 107402.

Goos, M., Manning, A., & Salomons, A. (2014). 'Explaining job polarization: Routine-biased technological change and offshoring'. *The American Economic Review*, *104*(8), 2509–2526. DOI: 10.1257/aer.104.8.2509

Gorelick, N., Hancher, M., Dixon, M., Ilyushchenko, S., Thau, D., & Moore, R. (2017). Google Earth Engine: Planetary-scale geospatial analysis for everyone. *Remote Sensing of Environment*, *202*, 18–27. DOI: 10.1016/j.rse.2017.06.031

Graesser, A. C., Conley, M. W., & Olney, A. (2018). Intelligent Tutoring Systems: Past, Present, and Future. *Educational Psychology Review*, *30*(1), 109–128.

Graham, S., & Harris, K. R. (2006). Strategy instruction and the teaching of writing. *Handbook of writing research, 5*, 187-207.

Graham, S., & Perin, D. (2007). Writing next-effective strategies to improve writing of adolescents in middle and high schools.

Graham, S., Harris, K. R., & Macarthur, C. A. (1995). Introduction to special issue: Research on writing and literacy. *Learning Disability Quarterly*, *18*(4), 250–252. DOI: 10.2307/1511232

Grant, S., & Phillips, R. (2023). Autonomy and agency in digital education. *Journal of Learning and Technology*, *12*(2), 43–55.

Gray, L., & Kneale, P. (2014). Interdisciplinary learning through AI: Engaging students in environmental science projects. *Journal of Science Education and Technology*, *23*(5), 715–728.

Green, R., & Petty, T. (2019). Student engagement through AI simulations in environmental science courses. *The Journal of Environmental Education*, *50*(3), 237–249.

Gruenewald, D. A., & Salsbury, T. L. (2006). Review of Reclaiming the local in language policy and practice. *Journal of Research in Rural Education*, *21*(11), 21–11.

Guilherme, A. (2019). AI and education: The importance of teacher and student relations. *AI & Society*, *34*(1), 47–54. DOI: 10.1007/s00146-017-0693-8

Guillermo, M.-R. (2022). Asynchronous learning: Evaluation of virtual classroom metrics according to the perception of university students. *Indonesian Journal of Electrical Engineering and Computer Science*, *28*(2), 1058–1058. DOI: 10.11591/ijeecs.v28.i2.pp1058-1066

Guo, P., Saab, N., Post, L. S., & Admiraal, W. (2020). A review of project-based learning in higher education: Student outcomes and measures," International Journal of Educational Research, vol. 102, Hen, Y., & Zhang, X. (2024). The impact of artificial intelligence on employment: the role of virtual agglomeration. *Humanities & Social Sciences Communications*, *11*(1), 122. DOI: 10.1057/s41599-024-02647-9

Gustian, D., Marzuki, M., Nukman, N., Purnama, Y., & Abdurrahman, D. (2024). Synergies In Education: Integrating Character, Literacy, And Technology For Enhanced Outcomes: Current Perspectives From Global Education Experts. *International Journal Of Teaching And Learning*, *2*(2), 498–512.

Hacker, S. B. H. (2014). Duolingo: Learning a language while translating the web (Doctoral dissertation, Doctoral Dissertation. Carnegie Mellon University).

Hacker, D., Sommers, N. I., Huster, K., Cullick, J. S., & Zawacki, T. M. (2016). *A Writer's Reference with Writing in the Disciplines*. Bedford/St. Martin's.

Hahn, M. G., Navarro, S. M. B., De La Fuente Valentin, L., & Burgos, D. (2021). A Systematic Review of the Effects of Automatic Scoring and Automatic Feedback in Educational Settings. *IEEE Access : Practical Innovations, Open Solutions*, *9*, 108190–108198. DOI: 10.1109/ACCESS.2021.3100890

Halliday, M. (1976). *A. K., & Hasan, R.* Cohesion in English.

Hamp-Lyons, L. (2006). Feedback in portfolio based writing courses. In Hyland, K., & Hyland, F. (Eds.), *Feedback in second language writing: Contexts and issues* (pp. 140–161). Cambridge University Press. DOI: 10.1017/CBO9781139524742.010

Haoyang, You. (2024). (1) Application of English Online Learning System Based on Artificial Intelligence. DOI: 10.1109/ICICACS60521.2024.10498680

Harrison, D., Patch, A., McNally, D., & Harris, L. (2021). Student and faculty perceptions of study helper websites: A new practice in collaborative cheating. *Journal of Academic Ethics, 19*(4), 483–500. DOI: 10.1007/s10805-020-09373-2

Hasnine, M. N., Nguyen, H. T., Tran, T. T. T., Bui, H. T. T., Akçapınar, G., & Ueda, H. (2023). A Real-Time Learning Analytics Dashboard for Automatic Detection of Online Learners'. *Affective Science, 23*(9), 4243–4243. DOI: 10.3390/s23094243 PMID: 37177447

Hassan, I., Madarina Abdul Rahaman, A., & Latiff Azmi, M. N. (2021). Development of English writing skills through blended learning among ESL learners in Malaysia. *Arab World English Journal (AWEJ) Special Issue on CALL*, (7).

Hayes, J. R., & Flower, L. S. (2016). "Identifying the organization of writing processes." In Cognitive processes in writing (pp. 3-30). Routledge. https://www.taylorfrancis.com/chapters/edit/10.4324/9781315630274-3/identifying organization-writing-processes-john-hayes-linda-flower

Hayes, J. R., & Flower, L. (1981). *Uncovering cognitive processes in writing: An introduction to protocol analysis*. ERIC Clearinghouse.

Heidari, A., Navimipour, N. J., Jamali, M. A. J., & Akbarpour, S. (2023). A green, secure, and deep intelligent method for dynamic IoT-edge-cloud offloading scenarios. *Sustainable Computing : Informatics and Systems, 38*, 100859. DOI: 10.1016/j.suscom.2023.100859

Helbing, D. (2019). *Societal, economic, ethical and legal challenges of the digital revolution: from big data to deep learning, artificial intelligence, and manipulative technologies*. Springer International Publishing.

Helmers, E., & Ilchmann, F. (2019). Sustainability Subjects in University Education - Development of a Comprehensive Indicator System and Quantitative Analysis of Degree Programs at German Universities. *European Journal of Sustainable Development Research, 3*(4), em0092. Advance online publication. DOI: 10.29333/ejosdr/5771

Henriksen, D., Mishra, P., & Stern, R. (2024). Creative Learning for Sustainability in a World of AI: Action, Mindset, Values. *Sustainability (Basel), 16*(11), 4451. DOI: 10.3390/su16114451

Herden, C. J., Alliu, E., Cakici, A., Cormier, T., Deguelle, C., Gambhir, S., . . . Edinger-Schons, L. M. (2021, March). "Corporate Digital Responsibility" New corporate responsibilities in the digital age. In Sustainability Management Foruml NachhaltigkeitsManagementForum (Vol. 29, No. 1, pp. 13-29). Berlin/Heidelberg: Springer Berlin Heidelberg.

Hettiarachchi, H., & Kshourad, C. (2019). Promoting waste-to-energy: Nexus thinking, policy instruments, and implications for the environment. In Kumar, S., Kumar, R., & Pandey, A. (Eds.), *Current developments in biotechnology and bioengineering* (pp. 163–184). Elsevier. DOI: 10.1016/B978-0-444-64083-3.00009-9

Hider, U., & Saleem, K. (2024). Sustainable Strategies for Education Enhancement: The Role of AI in Curriculum Development.

Higgins, K., Calvert, A., Thompson, A. S., & Galvin, T. (2024). *Sustainable food systems: Embedding education for sustainable development (ESD) in a food science module*. Open Scholarship of Teaching and Learning., DOI: 10.56230/osotl.77

Hines, A., Schutte, J., & Romero, M. (2019). Transition scenarios via backcasting. *Journal of Futures Studies*, *24*, 1–14.

Hmelo-Silver, C. E. (2004). Problem-based learning: What and how do students learn? *Educational Psychology Review*, *16*(3), 235–266. DOI: 10.1023/B:EDPR.0000034022.16470.f3

Hmelo-Silver, C. E., & Azevedo, R. (2017). Using AI to simulate real-world problem-solving in sustainability education. *Cognitive Science and Education*, *42*(2), 230–245.

Hoepfl, M. C. (1997). Choosing qualitative research: A primer for technology education researchers. *Journal of Technology Education*, *9*(1), 47–63. Retrieved February 25, 1998, from https://scholar.lib.vt.edu/ejournals/JTE/v9n1/pdf/hoepfl.pdf. DOI: 10.21061/jte.v9i1.a.4

Hofstede, G. (1984). *Culture's consequences: International differences in work-related values*. SAGE Publications.

Hollander, A., & Mar, N. Y. (2009). Towards Achieving TVET for All: The Role of the UNESCOUNEVOC International Centre for Technical and Vocational Education and Training. International Handbook of Education for the Changing World of Work, 41– 57. DOI: 10.1007/978-1-4020-5281-1_3

Holmes, W., Bialik, M., & Fadel, C. (2021). Artificial intelligence in education: Promises and implications for teaching and learning. Center for Curriculum Redesign. https://curriculumredesign.org/wp-content/uploads/AIED-Book-Excerpt-CCR.pdf

Holmes, W., Bialik, M., & Fadel, C. (2019). *Artificial Intelligence in Education: Promises and Implications for Teaching and Learning*. Center for Curriculum Redesign.

Hooda, M., Rana, C., Dahiya, O., Rizwan, A., & Hossain, M. S. (2022). Artificial Intelligence for Assessment and Feedback to Enhance Student Success in Higher Education. *Mathematical Problems in Engineering*, *2022*(5215722), 1–19. DOI: 10.1155/2022/5215722

Horn, M. & Chavez, A. (2022). The Future of Education: What is Modern Pedagogy and What Does it Mean? The future of education. November 21, 2022

Howard, R. M., & Davies, L. J. (2009). Plagiarism in the Internet age. *Educational Leadership*, *66*(6), 64–67.

How, M. L. (2019). Future-ready strategic oversight of multiple artificial superintelligence-enabled adaptive learning systems via human-centric explainable AI-empowered predictive optimizations of educational outcomes. *Big Data and Cognitive Computing*, *3*(3), 46.

Huang, L. (2023). Ethics of Artificial Intelligence in Education: Student Privacy and Data Protection. *Science Insights Education Frontiers*, *16*(2), 2577–2587. DOI: 10.15354/sief.23.re202

Husain, N. (2023). Educational Renaissance: Unleashing the Potential of Interdisciplinary AI Integration. *Journal of Environmental Science and Technology*, *2*(1), 159–166.

Hussein, M. A., Hassan, H., & Nassef, M. (2019). Automated language essay scoring systems: A literature review. *PeerJ. Computer Science*, *5*, e208. https://peerj.com/articles/cs-208.pdf. DOI: 10.7717/peerj-cs.208 PMID: 33816861

Hutson, J., & Ceballos, J. (2023). Rethinking education in the age of AI: The importance of developing durable skills in the Industry 4.0. *Journal of Information Economics*, *1*(2), 26–35. DOI: 10.58567/jie01020002

Hyland, K. (2003). Writing and teaching writing. *Second language writing, 1*(2), 1-30.

Ibrahim, E. H. E., Sarudin, I., Othman, K., Malik, F. A., & Muhamad, A. J. (2017). The assessment of writing within the CEFR scale: A Malaysian context. *Advanced Science Letters*, *23*(5), 4944–4947. DOI: 10.1166/asl.2017.8968

ILO (2020). Competency-Based Training (CBT): An Introductory Manual for Practitioners.

Indicators, O. C. D. E. (2021). *Education at a Glance 2020*. OECD Publishing. https://doi.org/https://doi.org/10.1787/69096873-en

Inoue, N., & Matsumoto, S. (2019). An examination of losses in energy savings after the Japanese Top Runner Program? *Energy Policy*, *124*, 312–319. DOI: 10.1016/j.enpol.2018.09.040

Ioannou, A. (2019). A Model of Gameful Design for Learning Using Interactive Tabletops: Enactment and Evaluation in the Socio-emotional Education Classroom [J]. *Educational Technology Research and Development*, *67*(2), 277–302. DOI: 10.1007/s11423-018-9610-1

Ira., & Assessment, N J T F O. (1995). Standards for the Assessment of Reading and Writing. National Council of Teachers of English, 46(1), 125-125. DOI: 10.2307/358885

Islam, A., Ali, R., Singh, G., Islam, B., Islam, A., & Hossain, S. (2024, May). An Evaluation of AI-Enhanced Collaborative Learning Platforms. In 2024 International Conference on Communication, Computer Sciences and Engineering (IC3SE) (pp. 207-211). IEEE.

Islam, M. E., Polas, M. R. H., & Rahman, M. M. (2025). Sustainability and AI in Transnational Higher Education. In Bridging Global Divides for Transnational Higher Education in the AI Era (pp. 379-400). IGI Global Scientific Publishing.

Iyer, L. (2019). Critical Thinking and it's Importance in Education. *Cognitive, Psychological and Behavioural Perspectives in Education*. https://www.researchgate.net/publication/339433132_Critical_Thinking_and_it's_Importance_in_Education

Jackson, E. (2013) Choosing a Methodology: Philosophical Underpinning, Practitioner Research in *Higher Education Journal, 7(1)*, October. Available at: http://194.81.189.19/ojs/index.php/prhe (Accessed 15 October. Kaldi, S. Filippatou, D. and Govaris, C. (2011). Project-based learning in primary schools: Effects on pupils' learning and studies," Education Journal, vol. 39, no. 1, pp. 35-47

Jafari, H., Safarzadeh, S., & Azad-Farsani, E. (2022). Effects of governmental policies on energy-efficiency improvement of hydrogen fuel cell cars: A game-theoretic approach. *Energy*, *254*, 124394. DOI: 10.1016/j.energy.2022.124394

James, Hutson., Daniel, Plate. (2024). (3) Leveraging AI to Personalize and Humanize Online Learning. Advances in mobile and distance learning book series, DOI: 10.4018/979-8-3693-0762-5.ch011

Javaid, M., Haleem, A., Vaishya, R., Bahl, S., Suman, R., & Vaish, A. (2020). Industry 4.0 technologies and their applications in fighting COVID-19 pandemic Diabetes & Metabolic Syndrome. *Clinical Research & Reviews*, *14*(4), 419–422. PMID: 32344370

Jawaid, A., Batool, M., & Arshad, W. (2025). *AI and English Language Learning Outcomes*. Contemporary Journal of Social Sciences, 12(1), 55–71. Retrieved from https://contemporaryjournal.com/index .php/14/article/view/387

Jeno, L. M., & Diseth, Å. (2019). A self-determination theory perspective on autonomy support, autonomous self-regulation, and perceived school performance. *International Journal of Educational Research*, *94*, 1–12.

Jewitt, K. E. (2018). Using virtual reality to enhance informal learning in small and medium enterprises (Doctoral dissertation, University of Glasgow).

Jiang, Y., & Zhao, C. H. (2022). Attention classification-and-segmentation network for micro-crack anomaly detection of photovoltaic module cells. *Solar Energy*, *238*, 291–304. DOI: 10.1016/j.solener.2022.04.012

Jia, X. H., & Tu, J. C. (2024). Towards a New Conceptual Model of AI-Enhanced Learning for College Students: The Roles of Artificial Intelligence Capabilities, General Self-Efficacy, Learning Motivation, and Critical Thinking Awareness. *Systems*, *12*(3), 74. DOI: 10.3390/systems12030074

Joaquim, A. F. (2018). *O papel do trabalho de projeto no ensino profissional da disciplina de área de integração (Relatório de Prática de Ensino Supervisionada. Mestrado em Ensino de Economia e de Contabilidade)* [Instituto de Educação da Universidade de Lisboa]. http://hdl.handle.net/10451/34940

Joaquim, A. F., & Figueiredo, P. (2023). Entrepreneurship in teaching: The teaching of Economics A with the application of Active Methodologies: Case Study. In Bilodeau, J., & Hughes, L. (Eds.), *Creating Motivational Online Environments for Students*. IGI Global., DOI: 10.4018/978-1-6684-4533-4.ch009

Joaquim, A. F., & Figueiredo, P. (2024). Entrepreneurial Leadership Development in the Digital Age. *European Conference on Management Leadership and Governance, 20*(1), 210–219. DOI: 10.34190/ecmlg.20.1.2942

Jófili, Z. (2002). Piaget, Vygotsky, Freire e a construção do conhecimento na escola. *Educação: Teorias e Práticas, 2*(2), 191–208. https://www.maxwell.vrac.puc-rio.br/7560/7560.PDF

Johnson, S., & Wang, T. (2024). Exploring the impact of adaptive learning on student engagement in higher education. *Journal of Educational Technology*, *35*(1), 45–61.

Johnston, H., Wells, R. F., Shanks, E. M., Boey, T., & Parsons, B. N. (2024). Student perspectives on the use of generative artificial intelligence technologies in higher education. *International Journal for Educational Integrity*, *20*(1), 2. DOI: 10.1007/s40979-024-00149-4

Jones, K., & Sharma, R. (2020). On reimagining a future for online learning in the post-COVID era. *Kevin Jones & Ravi Sharma (2020). Reimagining A Future For Online Learning In The Post-COVID Era. First posted on medium. com.*

Joshi, N. (2020). Assessments: Different Types, Importance, & More. https://www.evelynlearning.com/what-are-assessments/

Juarez, A., Rabago, J., Pliego, L., Salazar, G., & Gonzalez, P. (2024). INTEGRATING AI AND VR IN GLOBAL CLASSROOM: ENHANCING DESIGN COMPETENCIES THROUGH MULTICULTURAL COLLABORATION. In EDULEARN24 Proceedings (pp. 89-97). IATED.

Kaack, L. H., Donti, P. L., Strubell, E., Kamiya, G., Creutzig, F., & Rolnick, D. (2022). Aligning artificial intelligence with climate change mitigation. *Nature Climate Change*, *12*(6), 518–527. DOI: 10.1038/s41558-022-01377-7

Kalton, G., & Flores-Cervantes, I. (2003). Weighting methods. *Journal of Official Statistics*, *19*, 81–97.

Kamalov, F., & Gurrib, I. (2023). New Era of Artificial Intelligence in Education: Towards a Sustainable Multifaceted Revolution. Cornell University. https://doi.org//arxiv.2305.18303DOI: 10.48550

Kamalov, F., Calonge, D. S., & Gurrib, I. (2023). New Era of Artificial Intelligence in Education: Towards a Sustainable Multifaceted Revolution. *Sustainability (Basel)*, *15*(16), 12451. DOI: 10.3390/su151612451

Kanipriya, M., Sugumaran, D., Pandiyarajan, V., Yogananda, B. S., Selvakumar, P., & Mohan, S. (2024, January). Analysis of Electromyography Signals for Control of Mechanical Prosthesis using Machine Learning Techniques. In 2024 2nd International Conference on Intelligent Data Communication Technologies and Internet of Things (IDCIoT) (pp. 1059-1067). IEEE.

Karacı, A., Piri, Z., İbrahim, H., & Bilgici, G. (2018). Student Perceptions of an Intelligent Tutoring System: A Technology Acceptance Model Perspective. *International Journal of Computer Applications*, *182*(22), 31–36. DOI: 10.5120/ijca2018918025

Karagiannopoulos, S., Aristidou, P., & Hug, G. (2019). Data-driven local control design for active distribution grids using off-line optimal power flow and machine learning techniques. *IEEE Transactions on Smart Grid*, *10*(6), 6461–6471. DOI: 10.1109/TSG.2019.2905348

Kasahara, S. (2004). The flying geese paradigm: a critical study of its application to East Asian regional development. United Nations Conference on Trade and Development. Online at https://mpra.ub.uni-muenchen.de/21881/ MPRA Paper No. 21881, posted 07 Apr 2010 13:40 UTC

Kaswan, K. S., Dhatterwal, J. S., & Ojha, R. P. (2024). AI in personalized learning. In *Advances in Technological Innovations in Higher Education* (pp. 103–117). CRC Press. DOI: 10.1201/9781003376699-9

Kayyali, M. (2025). The Future of AI in Education: Predictions and Emerging Trends. Next-Generation AI Methodologies in Education, 367-406.

Kayyali, M. (2024). Future possibilities and challenges of AI in education. In *Transforming education with generative AI: Prompt engineering and synthetic content creation* (pp. 118–137). IGI Global. DOI: 10.4018/979-8-3693-1351-0.ch006

Kerimbayev, N., Umirzakova, Z., Shadiev, R., & Jotsov, V. (2023). A student-centered approach using modern technologies in distance learning: A systematic review of the literature. *Smart Learning Environments, 10*(1), 61. Advance online publication. DOI: 10.1186/s40561-023-00280-8

Ke, Z., & Ng, V. (2022). Automated essay scoring and feedback: Advances and challenges. [Khine, M. S., & Afari, E. Engagement in English Language Learning and Self-Regulation among Students.]. *Computers & Education, 184*, 104521.

Khan, N., Sarwar, A., Chen, T. B., & Khan, S. (2022). Connecting digital literacy in higher education to the 21st century workforce. *Knowledge Management & E-Learning, 14*(1), 46–61.

Kim, J. H., Kim, M., Kwak, D. W., & Lee, S. (2022). Home-tutoring services assisted with technology: Investigating the role of artificial intelligence using a randomized field experiment. *JMR, Journal of Marketing Research, 59*(1), 79–96. DOI: 10.1177/00222437211050351

Kim, J.. (2024). Self-reflection tools in AI education: Empowering autonomous learning. *International Journal of Artificial Intelligence in Education, 34*(1), 53–69.

Kim, J., Merrill, K.Jr, Xu, K., & Kelly, S. (2022). Perceived credibility of an AI instructor in online education: The role of social presence and voice features. *Computers in Human Behavior, 136*, 107383. DOI: 10.1016/j.chb.2022.107383

Kim, K. H., & Zabelina, D. (2015). Cultural bias in assessment: Can creativity assessment help? *The International Journal of Critical Pedagogy, 6*(2). https://libjournal.uncg.edu/ijcp/article/download/301/856

Kim, T. W., & Duhachek, A. (2020). Artificial intelligence and persuasion: A construal-level account. *Psychological Science, 31*(4), 363–380. DOI: 10.1177/0956797620904985 PMID: 32223692

Klobucar, A., Elliot, N., Deess, P., Rudniy, O., & Joshi, K. (2013). Automated scoring in context: Rapid assessment for placed students. *Assessing Writing, 18*(1), 62–84. DOI: 10.1016/j.asw.2012.10.001

Koedinger, K. R., & Aleven, V. (2007). Exploring the Assistance Dilemma in Experiments with Cognitive Tutors. *Educational Psychology Review, 19*(3), 239–264. DOI: 10.1007/s10648-007-9049-0

Kolb, D. A. (1984). *Experiential Learning: Experience as the Source of Learning and Development.* Prentice Hall.

Konopka, C. L., Adaime, M. B., & Mosele, P. H. (2015). Active Teaching and Learning Methodologies: Some Considerations. *Creative Education, 06*(14), 1536–1545. DOI: 10.4236/ce.2015.614154

Kosaretsky, S., Zair-Bek, S., Kersha, Y., & Zvyagintsev, R. (2022). *General education in Russia during COVID-19: Readiness, policy response, and lessons learned Primary and Secondary Education During covid 19.* Springer.

Koul, R., Wang, T., & Yu, H. (2022). *Artificial Intelligence in Education: Emerging Technologies, Models and Applications* (Cheng, E. C., Ed.). Springer.

Krajcik, J. S., Blumenfeld, P. C., Marx, R. W., & Soloway, E. (1994). A collaborative model for helping middle grade science teachers learn project-based instruction. *The Elementary School Journal*, *94*(5), 483–497.

Kryukov, V., & Gorin, A. (2017). Digital technologies as education innovation at universities. *Australian Educational Computing*, *32*(1), 1–16.

Kuhn, D. (2010). *Education for thinking*. Harvard University Press.

Kuhn, D. (2020). *Education for Thinking*. Harvard University Press.

Kumar, A., Agrawal, R., Wankhede, V. A., Sharma, M., & Mulat-Weldemeskel, E. (2022). A framework for assessing social acceptability of industry 4.0 technologies for the development of digital manufacturing. *Technological Forecasting and Social Change*, *174*, 121217.

Lai, F., & Cheng, R. (2024). Personalization and critical thinking: Balancing AI-driven learning. *The Journal of Higher Education*, *76*(2), 119–135.

Lalima, K. L. D., & Lata Dangwal, K. (2017). Blended Learning: An Innovative Approach, Universal. *The Journal of Educational Research*, *5*(1), 129–136. DOI: 10.13189/ujer.2017.050116

Langenfeld, T., Burstein, J., & von Davier, A. A. (2022). Digital-First Learning and Assessment Systems for the 21st Century. *Frontiers in Education*, *7*, 857604. Advance online publication. DOI: 10.3389/feduc.2022.857604

Lazic, D., Thompson, A., Pritchard, T., & Tsuji, S. (2020). Student preferences: using Grammarly to help EFL writers with paraphrasing, summarizing, and synthesizing. *CALL for widening participation: short papers from EUROCALL, 2020*, 183-189.

Leão, D. M. M. (1999). Paradigmas Contemporâneos de Educação: Escola Tradicional e Escola Construtivista. *Cadernos de Pesquisas*, *107*(107), 187–206. https://www.scielo.br/j/cp/a/PwJJHWcxknGGMghXdGRXZbB/?format=pdf&lang=pt. DOI: 10.1590/S0100-15741999000200008

Lee, I. (2002). Teaching coherence to ESL students: A classroom inquiry. *Journal of Second Language Writing*, *11*(2), 135–159. DOI: 10.1016/S1060-3743(02)00065-6

Lee, M. K., Cheung, C. M., & Chen, Z. (2013). Acceptance of Internet-based learning medium: The role of extrinsic and intrinsic motivation. *Information & Management*, *50*(4), 218–227.

Lee, V. R., & Wilkerson, M. H. (2018). Data use by middle and secondary students in the digital age: A status report and future prospects. *British Journal of Educational Technology*, *49*(5), 848–863.

Lemarchand, P., McKeever, M., MacMahon, C., & Owende, P. (2022). A computational approach to evaluating curricular alignment to the united nations sustainable development goals. *Frontiers in Sustainability*, *3*, 909676. DOI: 10.3389/frsus.2022.909676

Lesage-Landry, A., & Taylor, J. A. (2018). Setpoint tracking with partially observed loads. *IEEE Transactions on Power Systems*, *33*(5), 5615–5627. DOI: 10.1109/TPWRS.2018.2804353

Li, J. H., & Xu, G. C. (2022). Circular economy towards zero waste and decarbonization. Circular Economy, 1, Article 100002.

Liang, W., Yuksekgonul, M., Mao, Y., Wu, E., & Zou, J. (2023). GPT detectors are biased against non-native English writers. *Patterns (New York, N.Y.)*, *4*(7), 100779–100779. DOI: 10.1016/j.patter.2023.100779 PMID: 37521038

Li, J., Link, S., & Hegelheimer, V. (2015). Rethinking the role of automated writing evaluation (AWE) feedback in ESL writing instruction. *Journal of Second Language Writing*, *27*, 1–18. DOI: 10.1016/j.jslw.2014.10.004

Lima, A. R., Cavalcante, A. A., Torquato, C. B., & Vanzella, E. (2020). A correlação entre desmotivação e redução do rendimento escolar: Um estudo da 3ª série do ensino médio no município de Parambu – CE. *Série Educar- Volume 24 – Ensino Fundamental e Médio*. DOI: 10.36229/978-65-86127-39-3.CAP.16

Lima, V., & Gaspar, F. C. (2024). Inbound learning: Revolutionizing educational paradigms. *Brazilian Journal of Business*, *6*(2), e69276. DOI: 10.34140/bjbv6n2-010

Lim, C. P., Wang, T., & Tan, S. C. (2021). The Role of AI in Collaborative Learning. *Computers & Education*, *168*, 104–118.

Lim, M. M., Jørgensen, P. S., & Wyborn, C. A. (2018). Reframing the sustainable development goals to achieve sustainable development in the Anthropocene—A systems approach. *Ecology and Society*, *23*(3), art22. DOI: 10.5751/ES-10182-230322

Lin, T.. (2024). Planned behavior and technology adoption in education. *Educational Technology Research Journal*, *56*(4), 567–588.

Littenberg-Tobias, J., & Reich, J. (2020). Evaluating access, quality, and equity in online learning: A case study of a MOOC-based blended professional degree program. *The Internet and Higher Education*, *47*, 100759. DOI: 10.1016/j.iheduc.2020.100759

Liu, M. (2023). Exploring the Application of Artificial Intelligence in Foreign Language Teaching: Challenges and Future Development. SHS Web of Conferences, 168, 03025–03025. DOI: 10.1051/shsconf/202316803025

Li, Y., & Liu, Z. (2023). The impact of tailored feedback on student engagement in online platforms. *Interactive Learning Environments*, *31*(4), 555–571.

Loewen, S., Crowther, D., Isbell, D. R., Kim, K. M., Maloney, J., Miller, Z. F., & Rawal, H. (2019). Mobile-assisted language learning: A Duolingo case study. *ReCALL*, *31*(3), 293–311. DOI: 10.1017/S0958344019000065

Long, D., & Magerko, B. (2020). What is AI literacy? Competencies and design considerations. *Proceedings of the 2020 CHI Conference on Human Factors in Computing Systems*, 1-16. DOI: 10.1145/3313831.3376727

Lopes, M. A. da S. (2023). *Metodologias ativas vs. passivas: afinal qual a diferença no ensino de Geografia?* (Issue 3) [Mestrado, Universidade do Porto]. https://hdl.handle.net/10216/152679

Lucas, B. (2014). Vocational pedagogy: what it is, why it matters and how to put it into practice; Report of the UNESCO-UNEVOC online conference, 12-26 May 2014

Ludwikowska, K. (2022). Competency-Based Tests as a Tool for Teacher Evaluation in Higher Education Institutions. *Central European Management Journal*, *30*(3), 85–111. DOI: 10.7206/cemj.2658-0845.83

Lunsford, A. A., Brody, M., Ede, L. S., Moss, B. J., Papper, C. C., & Walters, K. (2013). *Everyone's an Author*. WW Norton and Company.

Luse, A., & Rursch, J. (2021). Using a virtual lab network testbed to facilitate real-world hands-on learning in a networking course. *British Journal of Educational Technology*, *52*(3), 1244–1261. DOI: 10.1111/bjet.13070

Macal, C. M., & North, M. J. (2010). Tutorial on agent-based modelling and simulation. *Journal of Simulation*, *4*(3), 151–162. DOI: 10.1057/jos.2010.3

Maghsudi, S., Lan, A., Xu, J., & van der Schaar, M. (2021). Personalized Education in the Artificial Intelligence Era: What to Expect Next. *IEEE Signal Processing Magazine*, *38*(3), 37–50. DOI: 10.1109/MSP.2021.3055032

Mahadev Madgule, N., Vinayaka, Y., Sonkhaskar, Y. M., Patel, D. R., Karthikeyan, P., & Selvakumar, P. (2023). Mechanical properties and microstructure of activated TIG welded similar joints of Inconel alloys by desirability approaches. *Materials Today: Proceedings*, *77*, 528–533. DOI: 10.1016/j.matpr.2022.12.250

Maheshwari, G. (2021). Factors affecting students' intentions to undertake online learning: An empirical study in Vietnam. *Education and Information Technologies*, *26*(6), 6629–6649. DOI: 10.1007/s10639-021-10465-8 PMID: 33686331

Mahmoud, C. F., & Sørensen, J. T. (2024). Artificial Intelligence in Personalized Learning with a Focus on Current Developments and Future Prospects. *Research and Advances in Education*, *3*(8), 25–31. DOI: 10.56397/RAE.2024.08.04

Majeed, A., Ahmad, M., Rasheed, M. F., Khan, M. K., Popp, J., & Oláh, J. (2022). The dynamic impact of financial globalization, environmental innovations and energy productivity on renewable energy consumption: Evidence from advanced panel techniques. *Frontiers in Environmental Science*, *10*, 10. DOI: 10.3389/fenvs.2022.894857

Majumdar, S. (2014). Vocational pedagogy: what it is, why it matters and how to put it into practice; Report of the UNESCO-UNEVOC online conference, 12-26 May 2014

Manyika, J., Lund, S., Chui, M., Bughin, J., Woetzel, J., Batra, P., Ko, R., & Sanghvi, S. (2017). *Jobs lost, jobs gained: Workforce transitions in a time of automation. McKinsey Global Institute*. McKinsey and Company.

Mao, J., Chen, B., & Liu, J. C. (2024). Generative artificial intelligence in education and its implications for assessment. *TechTrends*, *68*(1), 58–66. DOI: 10.1007/s11528-023-00911-4

Marcos-Sánchez, R., Ferrández, D., & Morón, C. (2022). Systems thinking for sustainability education in building and business administration and management degrees. *Sustainability (Basel), 14*(19), 11812. DOI: 10.3390/su141911812

Margot, K. C., & Kettler, T. (2019). Teachers' perception of STEM integration and education: A systematic literature review. *International Journal of STEM Education, 6*(1), 2. DOI: 10.1186/s40594-018-0151-2

Martin, A. (2020). How to optimize online learning in the age of coronavirus (COVID-19): A 5-point guide for educators. *Journal of Chemical Information and Modeling, 53*(9), 1689–1699.

Martínez-Bravo, M. C., Sádaba Chalezquer, C., & Serrano-Puche, J. (2022). Dimensions of digital literacy in the 21st century competency frameworks. *Sustainability (Basel), 14*(3), 1867. DOI: 10.3390/su14031867

Martin, F., & Parker, M. A. (2014). Use of Synchronous Virtual Classrooms: Why, Who, and How? *Journal of Online Learning and Teaching, 10*(2), 192–210.

Massey, A. P., Montoya, M. M., & Wu, P. F. (2013, January). 3D virtual environments and corporate learning: An empirical investigation of benefits. In 2013 46th Hawaii International Conference on System Sciences (pp. 893-902). IEEE.

Matos, G. (2023). Demystifying Artificial Intelligence: Understanding its Evolution, Key Areas, and Fundamentals. Medium; Share! por Ateliê de Software. https://share.atelie.software/demystifying-artificial-intelligence-understanding-its-evolution-key-areas-and-fundamentals-2dd875364ea3

Ma, X., & Jiang, C. (2023). On the Ethical Risks of Artificial Intelligence Applications in Education and Its Avoidance Strategies. *Journal of Education Humanities and Social Sciences, 14*, 354–359. DOI: 10.54097/ehss.v14i.8868

Mayer, R. E. (2014). Incorporating motivation into multimedia learning. *Learning and Instruction, 29*, 171–173. DOI: 10.1016/j.learninstruc.2013.04.003

McCarthy, J., Minsky, M. L., Rochester, N., & Shannon, C. E. (1955). A proposal for the Dartmouth summer research project on artificial intelligence. *AI Magazine, 27*(4), 12–14. DOI: 10.1609/aimag.v27i4.1904

McDougall, J., Readman, M., & Wilkinson, P. (2018). The uses of (digital) literacy. *Learning, Media and Technology, 43*(3), 263–279. DOI: 10.1080/17439884.2018.1462206

McGinley, T., & Karlshøj, J. (2022). A Circular Education System for the AEC. In *Proceedings of the 2022 European Conference on Computing in Construction European Council on Computing in Construction*. https://doi.org/DOI: 10.35490/EC3.2022.216

McIntosh, S. (2013). *Hollowing-out and the Future of the Labour Market. BIS Research Paper No.134.* Department for Business Innovation and Skills., https://assets.publishing.service.gov.uk/government/uploads/system/ uploads/ attachment_data/file/250206/bis-13-1213-hollowing-out-and-future-of-the-labour- market.pdf

MEC. (2017). Perfil Dos Alunos À Saída da Escolaridade Obrigatório. *Editorial Do Ministério Da Educação e Ciência*, 1–30. http://www.dge.mec.pt/sites/default/files/Curriculo/Projeto_Autonomia_e_Flexibilidade/perfil_dos_alunos.pdf

Meetaverse (2024), Virtual Learning Environments Unveiled: A Path to Digitial Education, https://meetaverse.com/blog/virtual-learning-environments/

Mehta, A., Shah, T., & Thomas, R. J. (2023). Strategies to address environmental degradation in developing nations: A multifaceted approach. *Journal of Intelligent Connectivity and Emerging Technologies*, *8*(2), 17–34.

Méndez-Ortega, M. G., Herrera-Granda, E. P., Malte, A. E. P., & Enríquez, R. B. H. (2021). Supervision and Control of Students during Online Assessments Applying Computer Vision Techniques: A Systematic Literature Review. *Universal Journal of Educational Research*, *9*(5), 1000–1013. DOI: 10.13189/ujer.2021.090513

Menezes, S. K. de O., & Francisco, D. J. (2020). Educação em tempos de pandemia: Aspectos afetivos e sociais no processo de ensino e aprendizagem. *Revista Brasileira de Informática Na Educação*, *28*, 985–1012. DOI: 10.5753/rbie.2020.28.0.985

Meola, A. (2022). *Generation Z: Latest Gen Z News, Research, Facts*. Insider Intelligence | EMarketer. https://www.insiderintelligence.com/insights/generation-z-facts/

Mesquita, L., & de-Lima-Santos, M. F. (2024). Google news initiative innovation challenge in Latin America: Business models between path dependence and power relations. *Journal of Media Business Studies*, •••, 1–26. DOI: 10.1080/16522354.2024.2402630

Metcalfe, J. S., Perelman, B. S., Boothe, D. L., & Mcdowell, K. (2021). Systemic oversimplification limits the potential for human-AI partnership. *IEEE Access : Practical Innovations, Open Solutions*, *9*, 70242–70260. DOI: 10.1109/ACCESS.2021.3078298

Mezrich, J. L. (2022). Is artificial intelligence (AI) a pipe dream? Why legal issues present significant hurdles to AI autonomy. *AJR. American Journal of Roentgenology*, *219*(1), 152–156. DOI: 10.2214/AJR.21.27224 PMID: 35138133

Middleton, P. (2018). Sustainable living education: Techniques to help advance the renewable energy transformation. *Solar Energy*, *174*, 1016–1018. DOI: 10.1016/j.solener.2018.08.009

Miettinen, R. (2000). The Concept of Experiential Learning and John Dewey's Theory of Reflective Thought and Action. *International Journal of Lifelong Education*, *19*(1), 54–72. DOI: 10.1080/026013700293458

Miller, E., & Madsen, L. (2015). Educating the 21st-century global citizen: How AI simulations develop systems thinking and environmental literacy. *The Journal of Environmental Education*, *46*(2), 95–111.

Millikin, C. C. (2023). Future-Proof your Instructional Design with Universal Design for Learning and Translanguaging. *Literacy Information and Computer Education Journal*, *14*(1), 3709–3720. DOI: 10.20533/licej.2040.2589.2023.0488

Minocha, S., & Tilling, S. (2019). The Use of Augmented Reality in Environmental Education: Opportunities and Challenges. *Journal of Interactive Learning Research*, *30*(2), 123–140.

Misha, A. (2024), How AI Can Foster Creative Thinking in the Classroom and Beyond, EdSurge, https://www.edsurge.com/news/2024-09-18-how-ai-can-foster-creative-thinking-in-the-classroom-and-beyond

Mohamed, A. Z. Z. O. U. A. Z. I. (2023). Fostering sustainable Development Through Artificial Intelligence in Education (ESD): A Comprehensive Evaluation Framework and Key Criteria Analysis.

Mohammed-Marzouk, M. R. (2012). Teaching and Learning in Iraq: A Brief History. *The Educational Forum*, *76*(2), 259–264. DOI: 10.1080/00131725.2011.653869

Moller, S. J., & Herrick, T. (2020). Overcoming barriers to AI integration in K-12 science education. *International Journal of Education Technology*, *38*(4), 569–585.

Mollick, E. (2024), Using AI Tutors to Flip Your Classroom, Edutopia, https://www.edutopia.org/article/using-ai-tutors-flipped-classroom/

Monica, W. (2018). *Nirase, Fathima, Abubacker.* Effective Utilisation of VLE with Joint Multinational Postgraduate Programme., DOI: 10.1109/NCG.2018.8593057

Moon, J. A. (1999). *Reflection in learning and professional development: Theory and practice.* Kogan Page.

Moore, C., & Lee, A. (2024). Balancing autonomy and guidance in AI education. *Journal of Educational Research and Innovation*, *45*(3), 221–233.

Moran, J. (2015). Mudando a educação com metodologias ativas. In: Souza C A, Morales OET (organizadores). *Coleção Mídias Contemporâneas. Convergências Midiáticas, Educação e Cidadania: Aproximações Jovens*, 180. https://www2.eca.usp.br/moran/?p=543

Moreno, F.. (2023). Autonomy and usage intention in AI learning platforms. *Journal of Educational Technology & Society*, *23*(4), 56–73.

Morgan, K. (1970). Sample size determination using Krejcie and Morgan table. Kenya Projects Organization (KENPRO), 38, 607-610.

Murcia, M. C., & Freeman, D. L. (1999). *The grammar book: An ESL. EFL Teacher's Course* (2nd ed.). Heinle & Heinle.

Murphy, R., Gallagher, L., Krumm, A., Mislevy, J., & Hafter, A. (2023), Khan Academy in Schools. SRI Education https://s3.amazonaws.com/KA-share/impact/khan-academy-implementation-report-2014-04-15.pdf

Murphy, D. H., Little, J. L., & Bjork, E. L. (2023). The Value of Using Tests in Education as Tools for Learning—Not Just for Assessment. *Educational Psychology Review*, *35*(3), 89. Advance online publication. DOI: 10.1007/s10648-023-09808-3

Muršak, K. A. (2004). The Fourth Industrial Revolution: Potential of Artificial Intelligence Technology in TVET education. In LIS International Conference (Vol. 8, No. September, pp. 70-78).

Mutambik, I. (2024). The Use of AI-Driven Automation to Enhance Student Learning Experiences in the KSA: An Alternative Pathway to Sustainable Education. *Sustainability (Basel)*, *16*(14), 5970. DOI: 10.3390/su16145970

Neshat, N., Amin-Naseri, M., & Danesh, F. (2014). Energy models: Methods and characteristics. *Journal of Energy in Southern Africa*, *25*(4), 101–111. DOI: 10.17159/2413-3051/2014/v25i4a2243

Nettles, M. T. (2019). History of Testing in the United States: Higher Education. *The Annals of the American Academy of Political and Social Science*, *683*(1), 38–55. DOI: 10.1177/0002716219847139

Newsroom (https://www.gartner.com/en/newsroom/press-releases/2018-02-19-gartner-says- 25-percent-of-customer-service-operations-will-use-virtual-customer-assistants-by- 2020)

Nguyen, N. (2022) FeedbackFruits Impact Report 2022. https://feedbackfruits.com/blog/infographic-feedbackfruits-impact-report-2022

Nguyen, A.. (2024). Motivational effects of adaptive language learning platforms: A Duolingo case study. *Language Learning & Technology*, *28*(1), 80–95.

Nhi Nguyen. (2023), Opportunities and Challenges of AI in Higher Education, Feedback Fruits, https://feedbackfruits.com/blog/opportunities-and-challenges-of-ai-in-higher-education#existing-challenges

Niemiec, C. P., & Ryan, R. M. (2009). Autonomy, competence, and relatedness in the classroom: Applying self-determination theory to educational practice. *Theory and Research in Education*, *7*(2), 133–144. DOI: 10.1177/1477878509104318

Nishant, R., Kennedy, M., & Corbett, J. (2020). Artificial intelligence for sustainability: Challenges, opportunities, and a research agenda. *International Journal of Information Management*, *53*, 102104. DOI: 10.1016/j.ijinfomgt.2020.102104

Niu, W., Zhang, W., Zhang, C., & Chen, X. (2024). The Role of Artificial Intelligence Autonomy in Higher Education: A Uses and Gratification Perspective. *Sustainability (Basel)*, *16*(3), 1276. DOI: 10.3390/su16031276

Nonet, G. A. H., Gössling, T., Van Tulder, R., & Bryson, J. M. (2022). Multi-stakeholder engagement for the sustainable development goals: Introduction to the special issue. *Journal of Business Ethics*, *180*(4), 945–957. DOI: 10.1007/s10551-022-05192-0 PMID: 36065323

Nost, E., & Colven, E. (2022). Earth for AI: A political ecology of data-driven climate initiatives. *Geoforum*, *130*, 23–34. DOI: 10.1016/j.geoforum.2022.01.016

Obracht-Prondzyńska, H., Duda, E., Anacka, H., & Kowal, J. (2022). Greencoin as an AI-based solution shaping climate awareness. *International Journal of Environmental Research and Public Health*, *19*(18), 11183. DOI: 10.3390/ijerph191811183 PMID: 36141452

OCDE. (2023). PISA 2022 Results: The State of Learning and Equity in Education. In *Pisa 2022: Vol. I*. OCDE. DOI: 10.31244/9783830998488

OECD. (2018). *Education GPS - Portugal*. Teachers and Teaching Conditions, Lower and Upper Secondary Education. https://gpseducation.oecd.org/CountryProfile?primaryCountry=PRT&treshold=10&topic=TA

OECD. (2019a). PISA 2021 creative thinking framework. *OECD Future of Education and Skills 2030, 53*(9), 1689–1699. https://www.oecd.org/pisa/publications/PISA-2021-creative-thinking-framework.pdf

OECD. (2019b). Skills for 2030. *OECD Future of Education and Skills 2030*, 16. https://www.oecd.org/education/2030-project/teaching-and-learning/learning/skills/Skills_for_2030_concept_note.pdf

Okada, A. (2025). *CARE-KNOW-DO: Mapping Knowledge in Education and AI Applications*. Springer. Retrieved from https://link.springer.com/chapter/10.1007/978-3-031-54677-8_4

Oksana, C. (2024). Bridging the Gap: Traditional vs. Modern Education (A Value-Based Approach for Multiculturalism). In Lifelong Learning - Education for the Future World in Filippo Gomez Paloma (Eds) DOI: DOI: 10.5772/intechopen.114068

Olabiyi, O. S & Chinedu, C. C (2018). Perception of employers' in transforming technical and vocational education and training vis-a-vis emerging technology tools for sustainable workforce development in Nigeria. *Path of Science: International Electronic Scientific Journal. Traektoriâ Nauki = Path of Science, 4*(4), 5001-5010.

Olabiyi, O. S. (2004) Relevance of Student Industrial Work Experience Scheme among Technical College Students in Lagos State. (Unpublished M.Ed. Thesis) Submitted to the Department of Vocational Teachers Education, University of Nigeria, Nsukka.

Olabiyi, O. S. (2009). Assessment of Skill Development Programme offered to special needs learners in vocational rehabilitation centres in South West Nigeria (Unpublished Ph.D. Thesis) Submitted to the Department of Vocational Teachers Education, University of Nigeria, Nsukka.

Olabiyi, O. S. (2021). The role of lifelong learning in developing workplace skills and challenges of technical vocational education and training. In *contemporary issues in education and learning.* Ed. Abiona, A., Afonja, A., Ojo, R., Aitokhuehi, O., & Olafare, F. University of Lagos Press and Bookshop. (pp 281-291).

Olabiyi, O.S. (2022). Assessing effectiveness of teaching practice towards quality preparation of pre-service technical teachers. *Journal of Technological and Vocational Education* 28(2), 01-13. https://doi.org/DOI: 10.21831/jptk.v28i1.45519

Olabiyi, O. S. (2021). Convergence of artificial intelligence and technical vocational education. In Oladipo, S. A., Adeosun, A. O., Owoyemi, T. E., Anyikwa, E. B., Ogunsemore, M. A., & Adeniyi, S. O. (Eds.), *Education in a rapidly changing world* (pp. 315–333). University of Lagos Press and Bookshop.

Olabiyi, O. S. (2022). Sustainable innovative teaching strategies for enhancing effective engagement of woodwork technology students in vocational skills. *Journal of TVET Transformation, 1*(1), 38–49.

Olabiyi, O. S., & Awofala, A. O. A. (2019). Effect of co-operative learning strategy on senior secondary school students' achievement in woodwork technology. *Acta Didactica Napocensia, 12*(2), 171–182. DOI: 10.24193/adn.12.2.13

Olabiyi, O. S., & Olafare, F. O. (2022). Utilization of Work-Based Learning Program to Develop Employability Skill of Workforce (Craftsmen) In Construction Industry Towards Industrial Development. *Indonesian Journal of Educational Research and Technology, 2*(3), 179–188. https://ejournal.upi.edu/index.php/IJERT/. DOI: 10.17509/ijert.v2i3.43970

Oliveira, P., Cunha, C., & Nakayama, M. (2016). Learning Management Systems (LMS) and e-learning management: An integrative review and research agenda. *Journal of Information Systems and Technology Management, 13*(2), 157–180. DOI: 10.4301/S1807-17752016000200001

Oliveira, T., Thomas, M., Baptista, G., & Campos, F. (2016). Mobile payment: Understanding the determinants of customer adoption and intention to recommend the technology. *Computers in Human Behavior, 61*, 404–414. DOI: 10.1016/j.chb.2016.03.030

Omeh, C. B., Olelewe, C. J., & Hu, X. (2024). (2024). Application of artificial intelligence (AI) technology in TVET education: Ethical issues and policy implementation. *Education and Information Technologies*. Advance online publication. DOI: 10.1007/s10639-024-13018-x

Omitaomu, O., & Niu, H. R. (2021). Artificial intelligence techniques in smart grid: A survey. *Smart Cities, 4*(2), 548–568. DOI: 10.3390/smartcities4020029

Orrù, G., Piarulli, A., Conversano, C., & Gemignani, A. (2023). Human-like problem-solving abilities in large language models using ChatGPT. *Frontiers in Artificial Intelligence, 6*, 1199350. DOI: 10.3389/frai.2023.1199350 PMID: 37293238

Oshima, A., & Hogue, A. (2007). *Introduction to academic writing*. Pearson/Longman.

Ossiannilsson, E. (2022), Seamless Learning Reflection, In the Book Seamless Learning in Higher Education2, Pressbooks, https://pressbooks.pub/seamlesslearning2/chapter/chapter-8-seamless-learning-reflection/

Ouyang, F., & Jiao, P. (2021). Artificial intelligence in education: The three paradigms. *Comput. Educ. Artif. Intell., 2*, 100020. DOI: 10.1016/j.caeai.2021.100020

Page, E. (1994). Computer Grading of Student Prose. *Using Modern Concepts and Software Journal of Experimental Education, 62*(2), 127–142.

Pandey, N., de Coninck, H., & Sagar, A. (2022). Beyond technology transfer: Innovation cooperation to advance sustainable development in developing countries. *Wiley Interdisciplinary Reviews. Energy and Environment, 11*(2), e422. DOI: 10.1002/wene.422

Pane, J. F., Griffin, B. A., McCaffrey, D. F., & Karam, R. (2017). *Effectiveness of Cognitive Tutor Algebra I at Scale*. RAND Corporation.

Pane, J. F., Steiner, E. D., Baird, M. D., & Hamilton, L. S. (2015). *Continued progress: Promising evidence on personalized learning*. RAND Corporation. DOI: 10.7249/RR1365

Patil, V. (2024). The Potential of AI in Enhancing Education Access and Quality.

Patrick, H., & Canevello, A. (2011). Methodological overview of a self-determination theory-based computerized intervention to promote leisure-time physical activity. *Psychology of Sport and Exercise, 12*(1), 13–19. DOI: 10.1016/j.psychsport.2010.04.011 PMID: 21103069

Pattison, P., Bridgeman, A., Bulmer, A., McCallum, P., & Miles, R. (2023). Renewing the Sydney undergraduate curriculum. *Higher Education, 86*(6), 1489–1506. DOI: 10.1007/s10734-022-00982-x PMID: 36536882

Paul, R., & Elder, L. (2007). *The miniature guide to critical thinking: Concepts and tools*. Foundation for Critical Thinking.

Pavitra, M. (2024), How to Use AI for Brainstorming (Use Cases and Tools), Click Up, https://clickup.com/blog/how-to-use-ai-for-brainstorming/

Pavlik, J. V. (2023). Collaborating with ChatGPT: Considering the implications of generative artificial intelligence for journalism and media education. *Journalism & mass communication educator, 78*(1), 84-93.

Pearson Results Team. (2021) Enhance student success with Revel. https://www.pearson.com/ped-blogs/meaningful-outcomes/2021/05/enhance-student-success-with-revel.html

Pedaste, M., Mäeots, M., Siiman, L. A., de Jong, T., van Riesen, S. A., Kamp, E. T., Manoli, C. C., Zacharia, Z. C., & Tsourlidaki, E. (2015). Phases of inquiry-based learning: Definitions and the inquiry cycle. *Educational Research Review, 14*, 47–61. DOI: 10.1016/j.edurev.2015.02.003

Pena-Ayala, A. (2014). Educational Data Mining: A Survey and a Data Min- ing-based Analysis of Recent Works [J]. *Expert Systems with Applications, 41*(4), 1432–1462. DOI: 10.1016/j.eswa.2013.08.042

Pereira, P., & Lima, V. (2021). INBOUND LEARNING: CONTRIBUTO PARA UMA NOVA METODOLOGIA DE ENSINO Inbound Learning: contribution to a new Learning Methodology Inbound Learning: contribución a una nueva Metodologia de Aprendizaje. In *Rev UI_IPSantarém* (Vol. 9, Issue 4).

Petrina, S. (2004). Sidney Pressey and the Automation of Education, 1924-1934. *Technology and Culture, 45, n.º 2*, 305–330. https://www.jstor.org/stable/40060743

Petrina, B., & Carver, P. (2019). Enablers of work-integrated learning in technical vocational education and training teacher education. *International Journal of Work-Integrated Learning, Special Issue, 20*(2), 147–159.

Phuoc Khai, M.A., T., & Thi Nam Thi M.A., N. (. (2021). THE APPLICATION OF GOOGLE CLASSROOM TO MOTIVATE ENGLISH NON-MAJORED STUDENTS. *International Journal of Advanced Research, 9*(03), 47–55. DOI: 10.21474/IJAR01/12552

Piniel, K., & Csizér, K. (2013). L2 motivation, anxiety and self-efficacy: The interrelationship of individual variables in the secondary school context. *Studies in Second Language Learning and Teaching, 3*(4), 523. DOI: 10.14746/ssllt.2013.3.4.5

Pinkwart, N., & Liu, S. (Eds.). (2020). *Artificial intelligence supported educational technologies*. Springer. DOI: 10.1007/978-3-030-41099-5

Poláková, P., & Klímová, B. (2019). Mobile technology and Generation Z in the English language classroom—A preliminary study. *Education Sciences, 9*(3), 203. DOI: 10.3390/educsci9030203

Porayska-Pomsta, K., Holmes, W., & Nemorin, S. (2023). The ethics of AI in education. In *Handbook of Artificial Intelligence in Education* (pp. 571–604). Edward Elgar Publishing. DOI: 10.4337/9781800375413.00038

Portugal, O. N. U. (2022). *Objetivos de Desenvolvimento Sustentável.* https://unric.org/pt/objetivos-de-desenvolvimento-sustentavel/

Postigo, G. Z., Foster, C., & Hardy, J. (2015). An Introduction to Critical Thinking and Logic. In *With Good Reason: A Guide to Critical Thinking*. Bridge point Education. DOI: 10.2307/j.ctt1t89436

Power School. (2023). [Personalized Learning: A Whole Child Approach, https://www.powerschool.com/blog/personalized-learning-crash-course/]. *Future, K-12*, •••.

Pratyush, Banerjee. (2022). Corporate E-Learning Initiatives: A New Paradigm for Employee Development. NHRD Network journal, DOI: 10.1177/26314541221088043

Prince, M. (2004). Does active learning work? A review of the research. *Journal of Engineering Education, 93*(3), 223–231. DOI: 10.1002/j.2168-9830.2004.tb00809.x

Priya, A. K., Devarajan, B., Alagumalai, A., & Song, H. (2023). Artificial intelligence enabled carbon capture: A review. *The Science of the Total Environment, 886*, 163913. DOI: 10.1016/j.scitotenv.2023.163913 PMID: 37150463

Qureshi, M. I., Khan, N., Raza, H., Imran, A., & Ismail, F. (2021). Digital Technologies in Education 4.0. Does it Enhance the Effectiveness of Learning? A Systematic Literature Review. *International Journal of Interactive Mobile Technologies, 15*(4), 31. DOI: 10.3991/ijim.v15i04.20291

Radesky, J., & Hiniker, A. (2022). From moral panic to systemic change: Making child-centered design the default. *International Journal of Child-Computer Interaction, 31*, 100351. DOI: 10.1016/j.ijcci.2021.100351 PMID: 35340408

Radovanović, D., Holst, C., Belur, S. B., Srivastava, R., Houngbonon, G. V., Le Quentrec, E., Miliza, J., Winkler, A. S., & Noll, J. (2020). Digital literacy key performance indicators for sustainable development. *Social Inclusion (Lisboa), 8*(2), 151–167. DOI: 10.17645/si.v8i2.2587

Raftery, D. (2018). Ubiquitous mobile use: Student perspectives on using the VLE on their phone. *Irish Journal of Technology Enhanced Learning, 3*(2), 47–57.

Rahman, M. R. (2023). Students' class participation and creative thinking: Basis for class engagement framework. https://doi.org/DOI: 10.54097/hiaad.v3i3.11289

Rajendran, D. P. D., & Sundarraj, R. (2021). Using topic models with browsing history in hybrid collaborative filtering recommender system: Experiments with user ratings. *International Journal of Information Management Data Insights, 1*(2), 100027. DOI: 10.1016/j.jjimei.2021.100027

Ramakrishnan, T., Mohan Gift, M. D., Chitradevi, S., Jegan, R., & Jose, P. S.H.; Nagaraja; Sharma, H.N.R.; Selvakumar, P.; Mekuria Hailegiorgis, S. (2022) Study of Numerous Resins Used in Polymer Matrix Composite Materials. Advances in Materials Science and Engineering, vol. 2022, Article ID 1088926, 8 pages. DOI: 10.1155/2022/1088926

Ramakrishnan, T., Mohan Gift, M. D., Chitradevi, S., Jegan, R., Hency Jose, P. S., Nagaraja, H. N., & Hailegiorgis, S. M. (2022). Study of numerous resins used in polymer matrix composite materials. *Advances in Materials Science and Engineering, 2022*(1), 1088926.

Ramineni, C., & Williamson, D. M. (2013). Automated essay scoring: Psychometric guidelines and practices. *Assessing Writing*, *18*(1), 25–39. DOI: 10.1016/j.asw.2012.10.004

Ranson, H., & Zhang, J. (2021). AI-ASSISTED RESPONSIBLE MANAGEMENT EDUCATION. Principles of Responsible Management Education (PRME) in the Age of Artificial Intelligence (AI): Opportunities, Threats, and the Way Forward, 43.

Rebedea, T., Dascalu, M., Trausan-Matu, S., & Crossley, S. A. (2020). Exploring students' argumentative discourse through natural language processing: Implications for science education. *International Journal of Artificial Intelligence in Education*, *30*(1), 1–27.

Reiddagnvy. (2022). Students' perception of Synchronous (virtual chat) or Asynchronous learning (Discussion board). DOI: 10.14293/S2199-1006.1.SOR-.PPSIDGD.v1

Reilly, E. D., Stafford, R. E., Williams, K. M., & Corliss, S. B. (2014). Evaluating the validity and applicability of automated essay scoring in two massive open online courses. *International Review of Research in Open and Distance Learning*, *15*(5). Advance online publication. DOI: 10.19173/irrodl.v15i5.1857

Reinhardt, K. S., & Elwood, S. (2019). Promising practices in online training and support: Microlearning and personal learning environments to promote a growth mindset in learners. In *Handbook of research on virtual training and mentoring of online instructors* (pp. 298–310). IGI Global. DOI: 10.4018/978-1-5225-6322-8.ch013

Rene, E. R., Sethurajan, M., Ponnusamy, V. K., Kumar, G., Dung, T. N. B., Brindhadevi, K., & Pugazhendhi, A. (2021). Electronic waste generation, recycling and resource recovery: Technological perspectives and trends. *Journal of Hazardous Materials*, *416*, 125664. DOI: 10.1016/j.jhazmat.2021.125664 PMID: 33838506

Renz, A., & Hilbig, R. (2020). Prerequisites for artificial intelligence in further education: Identification of drivers, barriers, and business models of educational technology companies. *International Journal of Educational Technology in Higher Education*, *17*(1), 14. Advance online publication. DOI: 10.1186/s41239-020-00193-3

Repo, P., Anttonen, M., & Mykk, Ã. (2018). Lack of congruence between European citizen perspectives and policies on circular economy. *European Journal of Sustainable Development*, *7*(1), 249–249. DOI: 10.14207/ejsd.2018.v7n1p249

Revel - Interactive Content Learning Tool. (2023). https://www.pearson.com/uk/educators/higher-education-educators/products-and-services/course-resources-and-content/revel.html

Rick Fiene. (2024), Linear and Circular Thinking, https://medium.com/@rickfiene/linear-and-circular-thinking-

Rijsdijk, S. A., Hultink, E. J., & Diamantopoulos, A. (2007). Product intelligence: Its conceptualization, measurement and impact on consumer satisfaction. *Journal of the Academy of Marketing Science*, *35*(3), 340–356. DOI: 10.1007/s11747-007-0040-6

Ritter, S., Anderson, J. R., Koedinger, K. R., & Corbett, A. (2007). Cognitive Tutor: Applied research in mathematics education. *Psychonomic Bulletin & Review*, *14*(2), 249–255. DOI: 10.3758/BF03194060 PMID: 17694909

Rodrigues, A. L. (2017). *A Formação Ativa de Professores com Integração Pedagógica das Tecnologias Digitais* [Instituto de Educação - Universidade de Lisboa]. https://repositorio.ul.pt/handle/10451/28329

Rodrigues, A. L., & Cabrito, B. (2022). *Metodologias de ensino, avaliação e aprendizagem Didática da Economia e Contabilidade* (Coleção Caderno de Mertrado | e-book, Ed.). EDUCA - Associação de Estudos e Publicidade.

Rogerson, A. M., & McCarthy, G. (2017). Using Internet based paraphrasing tools: Original work, patchwriting or facilitated plagiarism? *International Journal for Educational Integrity*, *13*(1), 1–15. DOI: 10.1007/s40979-016-0013-y

Roll, I., & Wylie, R. (2016). Evolution and revolution in artificial intelligence in education. *International Journal of Artificial Intelligence in Education*, *26*(2), 582–599. DOI: 10.1007/s40593-016-0110-3

Rolnick, D., Donti, P., & Kaack, L. (2019). Tackling climate change with machine learning. *Nature Machine Intelligence*, *1*(3), 144–153. arXiv1906.05433 PMID: 31161156

Romero, M. (2024). Collaborative Design of AI-Enhanced Learning Activities. arXiv preprint arXiv:2407.06660.

Romero, C., & Ventura, S. (2020). Educational data mining and learning analytics: An updated survey. *Wiley Interdisciplinary Reviews. Data Mining and Knowledge Discovery*, *10*(3), e1355. DOI: 10.1002/widm.1355

Romy Frederick. (2024), AI-Enhanced Collaborative Learning: Fostering Teamwork in the Digital Age, iLeaf Solutions Pvt. Ltd., https://www.ileafsolutions.com/ai-enhanced-collaborative-learning-fostering-teamwork-in-the-digital-age

Rosenberg, A., & Holm, S. (2021). AI and Critical Thinking in Education: Opportunities and Challenges. *Learning, Media and Technology*, *46*(3), 271–284.

Rudolph, J., Tan, S., & Tan, S. (2023). War of the chatbots: Bard, Bing Chat, ChatGPT, Ernie and beyond. The new AI gold rush and its impact on higher education. *Journal of Applied Learning and Teaching*, *6*(1), 364–389. https://journals.sfu.ca/jalt/index.php/jalt/article/download/771/577/3333

Rumpagaporn, M. W. (2007). Students' Critical Thinking Skills, Attitudes To ICT and Perceptions of Ict Classroom Learning Environments Under the ICT Schools Pilot Project in Thailand [University of Adelaide]. In *Development*. https://digital.library.adelaide.edu.au/dspace/bitstream/2440/37896/8/02whole.pdf

Rupali, M., & Amit, P. (2017). A Review Paper on General Concepts of "Artificial Intelligence and Machine Learning.". *IARJSET*, *4*(4), 79–82. DOI: 10.17148/IARJSET/NCIARCSE.2017.22

Ryan, R. M., & Deci, E. L. (2000). Self-determination theory and the facilitation of intrinsic motivation, social development, and well-being. *The American Psychologist*, *55*(1), 68–78. DOI: 10.1037/0003-066X.55.1.68 PMID: 11392867

Ryan, R. M., & Deci, E. L. (2017). *Self-determination theory: Basic psychological needs in motivation, development, and wellness*. Guilford Press. DOI: 10.1521/978.14625/28806

Sabory, N. R., Senjyu, T., Momand, A. H., Waqfi, H., Saboor, N., Mobarez, R., & Razeqi, F. (2021). LEED scores of residential buildings in poor cities: Kabul city case. *Sustainability (Basel), 13*(12), 6959. DOI: 10.3390/su13126959

Sachs, J. D., Lafortune, G., Fuller, G., & Drumm, E. (2023). *Sustainable Development Report 2023: Implementing the SDG Stimulus Includes the SDG Index and Dashboards*. DOI: 10.25546/102924

Sajja, R., Sermet, Y., Cikmaz, M., Cwiertny, D., & Demir, I. (2024). Artificial intelligence-enabled intelligent assistant for personalized and adaptive learning in higher education. *Information (Basel), 15*(10), 596. DOI: 10.3390/info15100596

Salinas-Navarro, D. E., Vilalta-Perdomo, E., Michel-Villarreal, R., & Montesinos, L. (2024). Using generative artificial intelligence tools to explain and enhance experiential learning for authentic assessment. *Education Sciences, 14*(1), 83. DOI: 10.3390/educsci14010083

Samaranayake, P. N. (2024). Navigating The Moral Prospect: Ethical Consideration in The Digital Age. *Journal of Ethics and Emerging Technologies, 34*(1), 1–13. DOI: 10.55613/jeet.v34i1.144

Sanabria Zepeda, J. C., Olivo Montaño, P. G., Artemova, I., & Argüelles Cruz, A. J. (2024). Prospective narratives on global issues: An AI-based pedagogical model for assessing complex thinking. JOTSE. *Journal of Technology and Science Education, 14*(1), 184–199. DOI: 10.3926/jotse.2445

Sandhu, R., Channi, H. K., Ghai, D., Cheema, G. S., & Kaur, M. (2024). An Introduction to Generative AI Tools for Education 2030. Integrating Generative AI in Education to Achieve Sustainable Development Goals, 1-28.

Santiago, A., & Yoon, K. (2024). Student motivation in autonomous learning environments. *Journal of Educational Motivation Studies, 19*(2), 143–158.

Santos, P., & Castro, F. (2019). Simulation-Based Learning and AI Applications in STEM Education. *Computers in Human Behavior*.

Sarkar, D., & Gilman, M. (2018). AI in climate education: Using machine learning to teach about environmental impacts. *International Journal of Climate Education, 12*(1), 30–45.

Scarfe, P., Watcham, K., Clarke, A., & Roesch, E. (2024). A real-world test of artificial intelligence infiltration of a university examinations system: A "Turing Test" case study. *PLoS One, 19*(6), e0305354–e0305354. DOI: 10.1371/journal.pone.0305354 PMID: 38923941

Schleicher, A. (2018). Educating learners for their future, not our past. *ECNU Review of Education, 1*(1), 58–75. DOI: 10.30926/ecnuroe2018010104

Schön, D. A. (1983). *The reflective practitioner: How professionals think in action*. Basic Books.

Selvakumar, P. (2023). Biomedical applications of polymers in biosensors, cancer vaccines and drug delivery systems. *Biopolimery i Kletka, 39*(4), 245–256. DOI: 10.7124/bc.000AA0

Selvakumar, P. (2024, July 26). Mariappan; Petchiammal; Shunmugam; Sivagami; Samuel Jabez, R.P. (2024) Removal of chemicals from effluent using photobioreactor technology to improve environmental and health impacts. *Zeitschrift für Physikalische Chemie*, *238*(7), 1295–1302. Advance online publication. DOI: 10.1515/zpch-2023-0450

Selvakumar, P. (2025, January 29). Palanisamy; Satheesh Kumar; Cinthaikinian; Selvamurugan; Vigneshkumar; Mariappan; Raja; Palani Kishore, S. (2024) Biosensors and its diverse applications in healthcare systems. *Zeitschrift für Physikalische Chemie*, *239*(1), 37–43. Advance online publication. DOI: 10.1515/zpch-2023-0406

Selvam, A. A. A. (2024). Exploring the Impact of Artificial Intelligence on Transforming Physics, Chemistry, and Biology Education. *Science Education*, *2*. Advance online publication. DOI: 10.21428/a70c814c.747297aa

Selwyn, N. (2019). Should Robots Replace Teachers? AI and the Future of Education. *Policy Futures in Education*, *17*(1), 10–27.

Shah, P. (2023). *AI and the Future of Education: Teaching in the Age of Artificial Intelligence*. John Wiley & Sons.

Shaik, T., Tao, X., Li, Y., Dann, C., McDonald, J., Redmond, P., & Galligan, L. (2022). A Review of the Trends and Challenges in Adopting Natural Language Processing Methods for Education Feedback Analysis. *IEEE Access : Practical Innovations, Open Solutions*, *10*, 56720–56739. DOI: 10.1109/ACCESS.2022.3177752

Shakir, F., Naz, A., & Ahmed, S. M. Z. (2024). Exploring teachers' perceptions and practices in education for sustainable development (ESD) in public schools of Karachi. Pakistan. *Journal of the Humanities and Social Sciences*, *12*(1), 902–914. Advance online publication. DOI: 10.52131/pjhss.2024.v12i1.2090

Shapiro, J. (2018). Digital Play for Global Citizens: A Guide from the Joan Ganz Cooney Center at Sesame Workshop. In Joan Ganz Cooney Center at Sesame Workshop. Joan Ganz Cooney Center at Sesame Workshop. 1900 Broadway, New York, NY 10023.

Shephard, K. (2015). *Higher education for sustainable development*. Springer. DOI: 10.1057/9781137548412

Shermis, M. D., & Burstein, J. C. (2003). *Automated essay scoring: A cross-disciplinary perspective*. Routledge., DOI: 10.4324/9781410606860

Shermis, M. D., & Hamner, B. (2013). Contrasting state-of-the-art automated scoring of essays. In *Handbook of automated essay evaluation* (pp. 313–346). Routledge.

Shin, D. H., & Kim, W. Y. (2010). Applying the Technology Acceptance Model and flow theory to cyworld user behavior: Implication of the web2.0 user acceptance. *Cyberpsychology, Behavior, and Social Networking*, *13*(4), 405–411.

Shulman, L. (2005). Signature pedagogies in the professions. *Daedalus*, *134*(3), 52–59. DOI: 10.1162/0011526054622015

Shwedeh, F., Salloum, S. A., Aburayya, A., Fatin, B., Elbadawi, M. A., Al Ghurabli, Z., & Al Dabbagh, T. (2024). AI Adoption and Educational Sustainability in Higher Education in the UAE. In *Artificial Intelligence in Education: The Power and Dangers of ChatGPT in the Classroom* (pp. 201–229). Springer Nature Switzerland.

Siemens, G., & Baker, R. S. (2012). Learning analytics and educational data mining: Towards communication and collaboration. *Proceedings of the 2nd International Conference on Learning Analytics and Knowledge*, 252–254. DOI: 10.1145/2330601.2330661

Siemens, G., & Long, P. (2011). Penetrating the Fog: Analytics in Learning and Education. *EDUCAUSE Review*, *46*(5), 30–40.

Siham, E. K. (2024). Tech-Enhanced Ties: AI's Role in Cross-Cultural Peer Education. PROCEEDINGS BOOK, 671.

Silva, J. M., & Salinas, A. (2020). The role of AI in fostering innovation in sustainability education. *Sustainability in Higher Education*, *15*(3), 189–205.

Silver, D., Schrittwieser, J., Simonyan, K., Antonoglou, I., Huang, A., Guez, A., Hubert, T., Baker, L., Lai, M., Bolton, A., Chen, Y., Lillicrap, T., Hui, F., Sifre, L., van den Driessche, G., Graepel, T., & Hassabis, D. (2017). Mastering the game of Go without human knowledge. *Nature*, *550*(7676), 354–359. DOI: 10.1038/nature24270 PMID: 29052630

Singh, E., Vasishta, P., & Singla, A. (2024). AI-enhanced education: Exploring the impact of AI literacy on generation Z's academic performance in Northern India. *Quality Assurance in Education*.

Singh, V., & Patel, L. (2024). Scaffolding and action autonomy in AI platforms. *Learning and Instruction*, *70*, 102–118.

Sintov, N., Kar, D., Nguyen, T., Fang, F., Hoffman, K., Lyet, A., & Tambe, M. (2017). Keeping it Real: Using Real-World Problems to Teach AI to Diverse Audiences. *AI Magazine*, *38*(2), 35–47. DOI: 10.1609/aimag.v38i2.2733

Smith, F. (2013). *Writing and the writer*. Routledge. DOI: 10.4324/9780203812075

Smith, L. R. (2018). Former professor of Linguistics. *Challenge*, *3*(1).

Smith, T., & Wang, F. (2023). Autonomy and motivation in AI-based learning environments. *Learning and Instruction*, *65*, 101–115.

Sonetti, G., Brown, M., & Naboni, E. (2019). About the triggering of UN sustainable development goals and regenerative sustainability in higher education. *Sustainability (Basel)*, *11*(1), 254. DOI: 10.3390/su11010254

Southworth, J., Migliaccio, K., Glover, J., Reed, D., McCarty, C., Brendemuhl, J., & Thomas, A. (2023). Developing a model for AI Across the curriculum: Transforming the higher education landscape via innovation in AI literacy. *Computers and Education: Artificial Intelligence*, *4*, 100127. DOI: 10.1016/j.caeai.2023.100127

Sparks, C., Dimmock, J., Lonsdale, C., & Jackson, B. (2016). Modeling indicators and outcomes of students' perceived teacher relatedness support in high school physical education. *Psychology of Sport and Exercise*, *26*, 71–82. DOI: 10.1016/j.psychsport.2016.06.004

Spillane, J. P., Blaushild, N. L., Neumerski, C. M., Seelig, J. L., & Peurach, D. J. (2022). Striving for coherence, struggling with incoherence: A comparative study of six educational systems organizing for instruction. *Educational Evaluation and Policy Analysis*, *44*(4), 567–592. DOI: 10.3102/01623737221093382

Sreenivasulu, A., Manimozhi, T., Satheesh Kumar, P., Selvakumar, P., & Singh, P. (2022) The Model of Smart Sensing Device For Sensitive Nanoclusters Modification in Sensing Properties. 2022 2nd International Conference on Advance Computing and Innovative Technologies in Engineering (ICACITE), Greater Noida, India, pp. 1043-1047. DOI: 10.1109/ICACITE53722.2022.9823846

Srite, M., & Karahanna, E. (2006). The role of espoused national cultural values in technology acceptance. *Management Information Systems Quarterly*, *30*(3), 679–704. DOI: 10.2307/25148745

SS, V. C., Hareendran, A., & Albaaji, G. F. (2024). Precision farming for sustainability: An agricultural intelligence model. Computers and Electronics in Agriculture, 226, 109386.

Stanley, J. (2015). *CEDEFOP: Vocational Pedagogies and Benefits for Learners: Practices and Challenges in Europe*. Publications Office of the European Union.

Stecyk, A., & Miciuła, I. (2024). Artificial Intelligence Integrated Energy Education Framework. A Holistic Approach.

Steinmayr, R., Weidinger, A. F., Schwinger, M., & Spinath, B. (2019). The importance of students' motivation for their academic achievement-replicating and extending previous findings. *Frontiers in Psychology*, *10*(JULY), 1730. Advance online publication. DOI: 10.3389/fpsyg.2019.01730 PMID: 31417459

Steiss, J., Tate, T., Graham, S., Cruz, J., Hebert, M., Wang, J., Moon, Y., Tseng, W., Warschauer, M., & Olson, C. B. (2024). Comparing the quality of human and ChatGPT feedback of students' writing. *Learning and Instruction*, *91*, 101894–101894. DOI: 10.1016/j.learninstruc.2024.101894

Sterling, S. (2013). Learning for resilience, or the resilient learner? Towards a necessary reconciliation in a paradigm of sustainable education. In *Resilience in social-ecological systems* (pp. 45–62). Routledge.

Straub, D. W., Loch, K. D., & Hill, C. E. (2016). Transfer of information technology to the Arab world: A test of cultural influence modeling. *Journal of Global Information Technology Management*, *19*(2), 3–29.

Subramaniam, R., & Nakkeeran, S. (2019). Impact of corporate e-learning systems in enhancing the team performance in virtual software teams. In Smart Technologies and Innovation for a Sustainable Future: Proceedings of the 1st American University in the Emirates International Research Conference—Dubai, UAE 2017 (pp. 195-204). Springer International Publishing.

Sugumaran, K. M., Pandiyarajan, V., & Selvakumar, P. (2024) Analysis of Electromyography Signals for Control of Mechanical Prosthesis using Machine Learning Techniques. 2024 2nd International Conference on Intelligent Data Communication Technologies and Internet of Things (IDCIoT), Bengaluru, India, pp. 1059-1067. DOI: 10.1109/IDCIoT59759.2024.10467707

Sun, A. Y., & Scanlon, B. R. (2019). How can Big Data and machine learning benefit environment and water management: A survey of methods, applications, and future directions. *Environmental Research Letters, 14*(7), 073001. DOI: 10.1088/1748-9326/ab1b7d

Sun, S., Wu, X., & Xu, T. (2023). A Theoretical Framework for a Mathematical Cognitive Model for Adaptive Learning Systems. *Behavioral Sciences (Basel, Switzerland), 13*(5), 406–406. DOI: 10.3390/bs13050406 PMID: 37232643

Surugiu, C., Grădinaru, C., & Surugiu, M. R. (2024). Artificial Intelligence in Business Education: Benefits and Tools. *Amfiteatru Economic, 26*(65), 241–258. DOI: 10.24818/EA/2024/65/241

Suryanarayana, K. S., Kandi, V. P., Pavani, G., Rao, A. S., Rout, S., & Krishna, T. S. R. (2024). Artificial Intelligence Enhanced Digital Learning for the Sustainability of Education Management System. *The Journal of High Technology Management Research, 35*(2), 100495. DOI: 10.1016/j.hitech.2024.100495

Swales, J. M. (2011). *Aspects of article introductions* (No. 1). University of Michigan Press.

Swanson, D.M.; Pashby, K. (2016) Towards a critical global citizenship? A comparative analysis of GC education discourses in Scotland and Alberta. J. Res. Curric. Instr.

Swiecki, Z., Khosravi, H., Chen, G., Martinez-Maldonado, R., Lodge, J. M., Milligan, S., Selwyn, N., & Gašević, D. (2022). Assessment in the age of artificial intelligence. *Computers and Education: Artificial Intelligence, 3*(3), 100075. DOI: 10.1016/j.caeai.2022.100075

Sywelem, M. M. G. (2024). Artificial Intelligenc and the Sustainability of Educational Services: An Overview. *WORLD (Oakland, Calif.), 10*(1), 8–17.

Sze, V., Chen, Y.-H., Yang, T.-J., & Emer, J. S. (2017). Efficient Processing of Deep Neural Networks: A Tutorial and Survey. *Proceedings of the IEEE, 105*(12), 2295–2329. DOI: 10.1109/JPROC.2017.2761740

Szymkowiak, A., Melović, B., Dabić, M., Jeganathan, K., & Kundi, G. S. (2021). Information technology and Gen Z: The role of teachers, the internet, and technology in the education of young people. *Technology in Society, 65*, 101565. DOI: 10.1016/j.techsoc.2021.101565

Tagliagambe, S. (2023). Phenomenology and the Digital World: Problems and Perspectives. *Foundations of Science, 28*(4), 1157–1174. DOI: 10.1007/s10699-022-09863-z

Talebkhah, M., Sali, A., Gordan, M., Hashim, S. J., & Rokhani, F. Z. (2023). Comprehensive review on development of smart cities using industry 4.0 technologies. *IEEE Access : Practical Innovations, Open Solutions, 11*, 91981–92030. DOI: 10.1109/ACCESS.2023.3302262

Tao, F., Zhang, H., Liu, A., & Nee, A. Y. C. (2018). Digital twin in industry: State-of-the-art. *IEEE Transactions on Industrial Informatics, 15*(4), 2405–2415. DOI: 10.1109/TII.2018.2873186

Tapalova, O., & Zhiyenbayeva, N. (2022). Artificial intelligence in education: AIEd for personalised learning pathways. *Electronic Journal of e-Learning, 20*(5), 639–653. DOI: 10.34190/ejel.20.5.2597

Tarhini, A., Hone, K., & Liu, X. (2014). A cross-cultural examination of the impact of social, organizational and individual factors on educational technology acceptance between British and Lebanese university students. *British Journal of Educational Technology, 45*(4), 739–755. DOI: 10.1111/bjet.12169

Tarmanini, C., Sarma, N., Gezegin, C., & Ozgonenel, O. (2022). Short term load forecasting based on ARIMA and ANN approaches. *Energy Reports*, *9*, 550–557. DOI: 10.1016/j.egyr.2023.01.060

Tarrête, A. (2022). *Navigating difference in inter- & transdisciplinary learning*. https://doi.org/DOI: 10.5463/thesis.14

Taubayeva, Sh. T, & Laktionova, S.N. (2001). Pedagogical Innovation as a Theory and Practice of Innovations in the Education System. Алматy: Gylym; 2001.

Taylor, D. L., Yeung, M., & Bashet, A. Z. (2021). Personalized and Adaptive Learning. Innovative Learning Environments in STEM Higher Education, 17–34. DOI: 10.1007/978-3-030-58948-6_2

Tebenkov, E., & Prokhorov, I. (2021). Machine learning algorithms for teaching AI chat bots. *Procedia Computer Science*, *190*, 735–744. DOI: 10.1016/j.procs.2021.06.086

The Deloitte Millennial Survey. https://www2.deloitte.com/us/en/pages/about- deloitte/articles/millennial-survey.html

The Replacement for Annual Reviews. (https://www.gallup.com/services/192827/organization- greatest-potential-unlocked.aspx) (UNESCO, (2023). Enhancing TVET through digital transformation in developing countries.

Thinger, C., Verma, A. S., Thakore, A. K., Purohit, P., Kalyanwat, B., & Sikarwal, P. (2024). AIED-Artificial Intelligence in Education World-Opportunities, Challenges, and Future Research. Challenges, and Future Research (November 14, 2024).

Thirusanku, J., & Yunus, M. M. (2014). Status of english in Malaysia. *Asian Social Science*, *10*(14), 254.

Tilbury, D. (2011). *Education for sustainable development: An expert review of processes and learning*. UNESCO.

Tongco, M. D. C. (2017). Purposive sampling as a tool for informant selection. *Ethnobotany Research and Applications*.

Tyrer, S., & Heyman, B. (2016). Sampling in epidemiologi cal research: Issues, hazards and pitfalls. *BJPsych Bulletin*, *40*(2), 57–60. DOI: 10.1192/pb.bp.114.050203 PMID: 27087985

Umar, U. (2021). Implementation Of E-Learning on The Teaching English As Global Language In The Pandemic-Era. *Jurnal Inovasi Penelitian*, *1*(10), 2095–2098.

UNESCO 2010: Teaching and Learning for a sustainable future, a multimedia education programme. UNESCO- UNEVOC (2021). Understanding the impact of artificial intelligence on skills development

UNESCO. (2014). *Teaching and learning: Achieving quality for all. Education for all Global Monitoring Report 2013/14*. UNESCO.

UNESCO. (2017). *Education for sustainable development goals: Learning objectives*. United Nations Educational, Scientific and Cultural Organization.

UNESCO. (2020). *Education for sustainable development: A roadmap*. United Nations Educational, Scientific and Cultural Organization.

UNESCO-UNEVOC International Centre. (2020). Trends in New Qualifications and Competencies for TVET Perspectives of the European UNEVOC Network. UNESCO- UNEVOC. https://unevoc.unesco.org/pub/bilt_ trends_mapping_study.pdf

United Nations Educational Scientific and Cultural Organization. (2002). Technical and Vocational Education and Training in the 21st Century: New Roles and Challenges for Guidance and Counselling. Retrieved from https://unesdoc.unesco.org/images/0013/001310/131005e.pd

Vakaliuk, T. A., Spirin, O. M., Lobanchykova, N. M., Martseva, L. A., Novitska, I. V., & Kontsedailo, V. V. (2021, March). Features of distance learning of cloud technologies for the quarantine organisation's educational process. *Journal of Physics: Conference Series, 1840*(1), 012051. DOI: 10.1088/1742-6596/1840/1/012051

Valle-Cruz, D., Criado, J. I., Sandoval-Almazán, R., & Ruvalcaba-Gomez, E. A. (2020). Assessing the public policy-cycle framework in the age of artificial intelligen From agenda-setting to policy evaluation. *Government Information Quarterly, 37*(4), 101509. DOI: 10.1016/j.giq.2020.101509

Vallerand, R. J. (2023). Intrinsic and extrinsic motivation in education. *Contemporary Educational Psychology, 68*, 241–255.

Van Haneghan, J. P., Pruet, S. A., Neal-Waltman, R., & Harlan, J. M. (2015). Teacher beliefs about motivating and teaching students to carry out engineering design challenges: Some initial data. *Journal of Pre-College Engineering Education Research, 5*(2). Advance online publication. DOI: 10.7771/2157-9288.1097

Van Wynsberghe, A. (2021). Sustainable AI: AI for sustainability and the sustainability of AI. *AI and Ethics, 1*(3), 213–218. DOI: 10.1007/s43681-021-00043-6

Vázquez-Cano, E. (2021). Artificial intelligence and education: A pedagogical challenge for the 21st century. Educational Process. *International Journal (Toronto, Ont.), 10*(3), 7–12.

Venkatesh, V., & Bala, H. (2008). Technology Acceptance Model 3 and a research agenda on interventions. *Decision Sciences, 39*(2), 273–315. DOI: 10.1111/j.1540-5915.2008.00192.x

Venkatesh, V., Morris, M. G., Davis, G. B., & Davis, F. D. (2003). User acceptance of information technology: Toward a unified view. *Management Information Systems Quarterly, 27*(3), 425–478. DOI: 10.2307/30036540

Vijayakumar, G., Rajkumar, M., Chandar, N. R., Selvakumar, P., & Duraisamy, R. (2024). Environmentally friendly TDS removal from waste water by electrochemical ion exchange batch-type recirculation (EIR) technique. *Environmental Science. Water Research & Technology, 10*(4), 826–835. DOI: 10.1039/D3EW00793F

Vinuesa, R., Azizpour, H., Leite, I., Balaam, M., Dignum, V., Domisch, S., & Nerini, F. F. (2020). The role of artificial intelligence in achieving the Sustainable Development Goals. *Nature Communications, 11*(1), 1–10. DOI: 10.1038/s41467-019-14108-y PMID: 31932590

Vygotsky, L. S. (1978). The prehistory of written language. *Mind in society: The development of higher psychological processes*, 105-119.

Vygotsky, L. S. (1978). *Mind in Society: The Development of Higher Psychological Processes*. Harvard University Press.

Walker, E., Rummel, N., & Koedinger, K. R. (2009). Integrating Collaboration And Intelligent Tutoring Data In The Evaluation Of A Reciprocal Peer Tutoring Environment. *Research and Practice in Technology Enhanced Learning*, *04*(03), 221–251. DOI: 10.1142/S179320680900074X

Wang, J., Lin, E., Spalding, E., Odell, S. J., & Klecka, C. L. (2011). Understanding teacher education in an era of globalization. *Journal of Teacher Education*, *62*(2), 115–120. DOI: 10.1177/0022487110394334

Wang, K., & Zhu, C. (2019). MOOC-based flipped learning in higher education: Students' participation, experience and learning performance. *International Journal of Educational Technology in Higher Education*, *16*(1), 1–18. DOI: 10.1186/s41239-019-0163-0

Wang, X., Li, L., Tan, S. C., Yang, L., & Lei, J. (2023). Preparing for AI-enhanced education: Conceptualizing and empirically examining teachers' AI readiness. *Computers in Human Behavior*, *146*, 107798. DOI: 10.1016/j.chb.2023.107798

Wang, Y. (2023). Synergy in Silicon: The Evolution and Potential of Academia-Industry Collaboration in AI and Software Engineering. *Authorea Preprints*.

Wang, Y. D. (2014). Building Trust in E-Learning. *Athens Journal of Education*, *1*(1), 9–18.

Wang, Y. Y., & Wang, Y. S. (2019). Development and validation of an artificial intelligence anxiety scale: An initial application in predicting motivated learning behavior. *Interactive Learning Environments*.

Weaver, C. (1996). Teaching grammar in the context of writing. *English Journal*, *85*(7), 15–24. DOI: 10.58680/ej19964835

Wei, C. C., Zhang, C. G., Vardar, O., Watson, J., & Canbulat, I. (2022). Quantitative assessment of energy changes in underground coal excavations using numerical approach. *Geohazard Mechanics*, *1*(1), 58–68. DOI: 10.1016/j.ghm.2022.11.003

Weigle, S. C. (2002). Assessing writing. *Ernst Klett Sprachen*.

Westwood, P. (2018). *Inclusive and adaptive teaching: Meeting the challenge of diversity in the classroom*. Routledge. DOI: 10.4324/9781351061261

Wiek, A., Withycombe, L., & Redman, C. L. (2011). Key competencies in sustainability: A reference framework for academic program development. *Sustainability Science*, *6*(2), 203–218. DOI: 10.1007/s11625-011-0132-6

Wilcoxon, F. (1945). Individual Comparisons by Ranking Methods. *Biometrics Bulletin*, *1*(6), 80–83. DOI: 10.2307/3001968

Williamson, B., & Eynon, R. (2020). AI in Education: Opportunities and Challenges. *Learning, Media and Technology*, *45*(3), 251–264.

Williamson, D. M., Xi, X., & Breyer, F. J. (2012). A framework for evaluation and use of automated scoring. *Educational Measurement: Issues and Practice*, *31*(1), 2–13. DOI: 10.1111/j.1745-3992.2011.00223.x

Willis, V. (2024). The role of artificial intelligence (AI) in personalizing online learning. *Journal of Online and Distance Learning*, *3*(1), 1–13.

Wing, J. M. (2020). The data life cycle as an organizing principle for big data research. *Harvard Data Science Review*, *2*(2).

Witte, S. P., & Faigley, L. (1981). Coherence, cohesion, and writing quality. *College Composition and Communication*, *32*(2), 189–204. DOI: 10.58680/ccc198115912

Wong, S. L., Teo, T., & Russo, S. (2013). Influence of gender and computer teaching efficacy on computer acceptance among Malaysian student teachers: An extended Technology Acceptance Model. *Australian Journal of Educational Technology*, *29*(3), 394–412.

Wong, S. S. H. (2023). Deliberate Erring Improves Far Transfer of Learning More Than Errorless Elaboration and Spotting and Correcting Others' Errors. *Educational Psychology Review*, *35*(1), 16. Advance online publication. DOI: 10.1007/s10648-023-09739-z PMID: 36776579

Wright, W. (1990). *SimEarth: The Living Planet.* Maxis Software.

Wu, Y. (2024). Revolutionizing Learning and Teaching: Crafting Personalized, Culturally Responsive Curriculum in the AI Era. *Creative Education*, *15*(8), 1642–1651. DOI: 10.4236/ce.2024.158098

Xia, Q., Chiu, T. K., Lee, M., Sanusi, I. T., Dai, Y., & Chai, C. S. (2022). A self-determination theory (SDT) design approach for inclusive and diverse artificial intelligence (AI) education. *Computers & Education*, *189*, 104582. DOI: 10.1016/j.compedu.2022.104582

Xia, Y., Shin, S. Y., & Kim, J. C. (2024). Cross-cultural intelligent language learning system (cils): Leveraging ai to facilitate language learning strategies in cross-cultural communication. *Applied Sciences (Basel, Switzerland)*, *14*(13), 5651. DOI: 10.3390/app14135651

Yang, Y. Y., Sun, X. L., Zhu, X. Q., & Xie, Y. J. (2013). Scenario simulation and policy analysis on energy development in Qinghai Province. *Procedia Computer Science*, *17*, 720–728. DOI: 10.1016/j.procs.2013.05.093

Yeadon, W., Inyang, O. O., Mizouri, A., Peach, A., & Testrow, C. P. (2023). The death of the short-form physics essay in the coming AI revolution. *Physics Education*, *58*(3), 035027. DOI: 10.1088/1361-6552/acc5cf

Yekollu, R. K., Bhimraj Ghuge, T., Sunil Biradar, S., Haldikar, S. V., & Farook Mohideen Abdul Kader, O. (2024, February). AI-Driven Personalized Learning Paths: Enhancing Education Through Adaptive Systems. In International Conference on Smart Data Intelligence (pp. 507-517). Singapore: Springer Nature Singapore.

Yellu, R. R., Maruthi, S., Dodda, S. B., Thuniki, P., & Reddy, S. R. B. (2021). AI Ethics-Challenges and Considerations: Examining ethical challenges and considerations in the development and deployment of artificial intelligence systems. *African Journal of Artificial Intelligence and Sustainable Development*, *1*(1), 9–16.

Yuan, F., Shen, Z., Wei, X., Sun, C., & Li, M. (2018). Machine learning approaches for geospatial big data analysis: A review. *Big Earth Data*, *2*(3), 276–296.

Zahid, H. (2024). Educational Renaissance: Unleashing the Potential of Interdisciplinary AI Integration.

Zawacki-Richter, O., Marín, V. I., Bond, M., & Gouverneur, F. (2019). Systematic review of research on artificial intelligence applications in higher education – where are the educators? *International Journal of Educational Technology in Higher Education*, *16*(1), 1–27. DOI: 10.1186/s41239-019-0171-0

Zeng, L. T., Qiu, D. W., & Sun, M. Y. (2022). Resilience enhancement of multi-agent reinforcement learning-based demand response against adversarial attacks. *Applied Energy*, *324*, 119688. DOI: 10.1016/j.apenergy.2022.119688

Zh, A. M. (2024). ARTIFICIAL INTELLIGENCE IN EDUCATION: POSSIBILITIES FOR PERSONALIZING LEARNING. Экономика и социум, (11-1 (126)), 1317-1323.

Zhai, C. (2023). AI in education: Automated scoring and its impact. *Journal of Educational Technology*, *19*(3), 145–160.

Zhai, X., Chu, X., Chai, C. S., Jong, M. S. Y., Istenic, A., Spector, M., Liu, J.-B., Yuan, J., & Li, Y. (2021). A Review of Artificial Intelligence (AI) in Education from 2010 to 2020. *Complexity*, *2021*(8812542), 1–18. DOI: 10.1155/2021/8812542

Zhang, H., & Litman, D. (2021). *Essay Quality Signals as Weak Supervision for Source-Based Essay Scoring*. Grantee Submission.

Zhao, L., & Chiu, W. (2023). Self-determination theory in AI-driven education. *Journal of Educational Computing Research*, *61*(2), 104–121.

Zheng, C., Yuan, K., Guo, B., Hadi Mogavi, R., Peng, Z., Ma, S., & Ma, X. (2024, May). Charting the future of AI in project-based learning: a Co-design exploration with students. In *Proceedings of the 2024 CHI Conference on Human Factors in Computing Systems* (pp. 1-19).

Zimmerman, B. J., & Risemberg, R. (1997). Becoming a self-regulated writer: A social cognitive perspective. *Contemporary Educational Psychology*, *22*(1), 73–101. DOI: 10.1006/ceps.1997.0919

Zmire, Z., & Chen, X. (2024). AI's Role in Enhancing Cross Cultural Competence and Leadership through Online Education Programs. In *Proceedings of the International Conference on New Findings in Humanities and Social Sciences* (Vol. 1, No. 1, pp. 1-16). DOI: 10.33422/hsconf.v1i1.268

Василишина, Н. М. (2020). Benefits of digital learning application at universities. Вісник Житомирського Державного Університету Імені Івана Франка. *Педагогічні Науки*, (103), 61–68.

About the Contributors

Caleb Chidozie Chinedu is a distinguished senior lecturer at the Faculty of Technical and Vocational Education, Universiti Tun Hussein Onn Malaysia (UTHM). With a Ph.D., M.Ed., and a bachelor's degree in Technical and Vocational Education, Dr. Chinedu brings over a decade of teaching, research, and administrative experience in TVET and teacher education research. His extensive research interests encompass a variety of critical areas, including Education for Sustainable Development, green skills, higher-order thinking skills (HOTS), curriculum development and pedagogy, leadership and management in TVE, TVET student enrolment, TVET marketability, lifelong learning, Industrial Revolution 4.0, and the digital transformation of TVET systems. Moreover, he is deeply invested in exploring the evolving impact of Generative AI on education. As a passionate educator with exceptional leadership skills in Technical and Vocational Education, Dr. Chinedu is committed to advancing sustainability education. He currently serves as a Principal Research Fellow at the Malaysian Research Institute for Vocational Education & Training (MyRIVET) at UTHM. In this role, he leads high-quality research projects focused on sustainability education, fosters relationships with key TVET stakeholders, disseminates research findings through publications and presentations, and contributes to research funding proposals and strategy development. Dr. Chinedu also holds several key leadership positions, including the; • Managing Editor of the Journal of Technical Education & Training, Faculty of Technical and Vocational Education, UTHM. • Editor of TVET Prospect, a quarterly publication of MyRIVET. • Dissertation Coordinator for the Doctor of Education (EdD) Program at the Faculty of Technical and Vocational Education, UTHM. His involvement in numerous national and international grant-funded projects has been instrumental in examining the relationship between sustainability education and the employability of TVET graduates, assessing the quality of education for migrant children in Malaysia, and developing green TVET frameworks.

Nofouz Mafarja (Ph.D.) is a Senior Lecturer at the Department of Mathematics and Science Education in the Faculty of Education at the Universiti Malay. Her research focuses on physics education, scaffolding in education, collaborative learning (specifically the Reciprocal Teaching strategy), word problem-solving in physics, critical thinking skills, STEM education, academic self-concept, attitude towards learning physics, and reading comprehension in science. She is also actively involved in research workshops, statistical data analysis (using SPSS, AMOS, and Smart-PLS), and research methodology. Currently, she is engaged in several research projects on industrial revolution 4.0, lifelong learning, teaching innovation, learning support, virtual reality, Hybrid Learning System PjBL Model, society 5.0, critical thinking skills, Generative AI tools, and teaching practices. She has experience in teaching sciences, curriculum development, lesson planning, educational technology, tutoring, educational leadership, and science teacher training.

Mahmood H. Hussein (Ph.D.) is a postdoctoral research fellow at the Faculty of Technical and Vocational Education, Tun Hussein Onn University of Malaysia. He has a Ph.D. in educational technology from the University of Malaya. His research interests include Digital Game-Based Learning, Generative Artificial Intelligence in Education, Human-Computer Interactions, and STEM education. Dr. MH. Hussein has published several articles in leading education journals.

***

C.Tamilarasi has a strong sense of dedication and devotion to teaching, research, and the academic community. She is having 5 years of experience in teaching and presently working as an Assistant Professor at B.S Abdur Rahman Crescent institute of science and technology. Her teaching philosophy emphasizes hands-on learning and real-world applications, aiming to prepare students for both academic and industry careers. She integrates project-based learning into her courses, allowing students to work on the recent technologies. Her passion for teaching is to empower students with the latest knowledge and skills in technology, aimed at their overall development and success.

Yiming Chen With nearly 20 years of experience in innovation and entrepreneurship education, I has dedicated their career to empowering students to adapt to the rapid evolution of science and technology. A key focus of their work has been integrating emerging technologies and efficiency tools into educational practices, enabling students to excel academically and acquire the practical skills necessary for employment. Their research and efforts consistently center on enhancing students' learning experiences by leveraging new tools and methodologies to equip them for the challenges of the modern workforce.

Nurul Ain Chua Binti Abdullah is a Senior Lecturer at Universiti Malaysia Terengganu (UMT), where she focuses on teaching Mandarin as a foreign language to non-native learners. She is actively involved in research related to Mandarin language acquisition and educational technology in language learning. Dr. Nurul Ain has over 30 years of experience in education and has taught at various levels, from primary to tertiary. She has presented her research at numerous national and international conferences. Her research interests include technology-enhanced language learning, language pedagogy, and differentiated instruction.

Swathi Chundru, a QA Automation Engineer and Technical Lead with over 13 years of experience specializing in ETL Testing, Data Warehousing, Functional Testing, and Automation. My expertise spans a range of tools, including Informatica, AbInitio, DataStage, and SSIS, along with databases like Teradata, MySQL, MS SQL Server, and Oracle. I currently work at Motivity Labs, where I've had the opportunity to lead large-scale projects in the banking and insurance sectors, collaborating with clients like Santander Consumer USA and Blue Cross Blue Shield. I hold a Bachelor's degree in Electronics and Communications from JNT University and am ISTQB Foundation Level certified. In addition to my professional work, I've co-authored two peer-reviewed research papers published in EDAS, and I've presented my research on Artificial Intelligence (AI) at the 3rd International Conference on Research in Multidisciplinary Studies and a Faculty Development Program. I've completed peer reviews for IGI Global and CMT, and had the honor of serving as a judge for the QS Reimagine Education Awards. I thrive in both Agile and Waterfall environments, and I enjoy mentoring teams in SQL, ETL testing, and automation. Innovation and problem-solving are the key drivers in my career, and I'm always looking for ways to enhance technology and improve processes.

Vignesh G. D. is a young and dynamic individual with a strong academic background in Electronics & Communication Engineering. Currently working as an Assistant Professor in the Department of Electronics & Communication Engineering, St Joseph's College of Engineering (Autonomous), affiliated to Anna University, Chennai. He is passionate about research, believes in learning and is striving to enhance his skills. Currently, his research area includes Machine Learning & AI, Internet of Things (IoT) and Cognitive Radio (CR) based Wireless Sensor Networks (CR-WSNs). He has 7 years of teaching experience. His research findings have been published in ESCI/SCOPUS/WOS/Google-indexed international journals. He has attended and presented many research articles at international conferences.

Soumya Sankar Ghosh Experienced Linguist by profession with almost 10 years of research and job experience in both the field of academics and the IT industry. Skilled in Discourse Analysis, Data Analysis, Semantics, Text-to-Speech, and Pragmatics. In December 2019, I obtained my PhD in Linguistics from Jadavpur University, Kolkata. Currently working as, an Assistant Professor, at VIT Bhopal University Madhya Pradesh, India.

Rituraj Jain is currently working in the Department of Information Technology at Marwadi University, Rajkot - India. He has published many papers in International Journals and Conferences. He is an Oracle Database SQL Certified Expert. He is associated with professional bodies like IEEE, the Indian Society of Technical Education (ISTE), Computer Science Teachers Association (CSTA), Academy & Industry Research Collaboration Center (AIRCC), International Association of Computer Science and Information Technology (IACSIT), International Association of Engineers (IAENG). His research interests include Cloud Computing, Machine Learning, Deep Learning, Fuzzy Logic, IoT, Genetic Algorithms, Big Data and Software Engineering.

Ana Filipa Vieira Joaquim PhD student and researcher in Global Studies. Her research focuses on disinformation and propaganda. With a master's degree in economics and accounting teaching and a bachelor's in marketing, she has laid a solid academic foundation for her professional journey. Lecturer in secondary and higher education. She has worked as a consultant and trainer for various institutions. She has published several articles and papers and has participated in numerous conferences and lectures.

K. Sowmiya is an Assistant Professor in the Department of Computer Science and Engineering at B.S. Abdur Rahman Crescent Institute of Science and Technology. With a strong research focus on deep learning, she has published several papers in prominent conferences, contributing to advancements in her field. Mrs. K. Sowmiya is dedicated to guiding and mentoring students, having supervised numerous projects works. Her commitment to both research and education reflects her passion for fostering innovation and academic growth in computer science.

Mustafa Kayyali I am an ardent advocate for excellence in higher education, driven by a relentless pursuit of quality, recognition, and innovation. My journey in academia started with a Master's in Quality Management and Evaluation in Higher Education from Universitat Oberta de Catalunya, followed by a Ph.D. in Quality Management from Azteca

University. These academic pursuits have laid a strong foundation for my expertise in Accreditation, Quality Assurance, and Higher Education Rankings. As an entrepreneur, researcher, translator, and publisher, I am deeply involved in various facets of the academic world. My diverse interests encompass Management, Translation, Interpretation, and Academic consulting, contributing to a well-rounded understanding of the industry. Throughout my career, I have made significant contributions to academic literature, with more than 20 published papers and 7 book chapters to my name. Additionally, I take pride in having translated 5 books, bridging language gaps, and promoting knowledge exchange on a global scale. I am committed to fostering positive change in higher education and contributing to its continuous improvement.

Kew Si Na is a senior lecturer at Universiti Teknologi Malaysia, Malaysia. Her research interests are teaching and learning, Teaching English as a Second Language (TESL), Technology Enhanced Language Learning (TELL), Computer Assisted Language Learning (CALL), Online Teaching and Learning, Learning Analytics (LA), etc

Mohanarajesh Kommineni a Master of Computer Science and engineering with 11 years of experience, is a Senior Data Engineer specializing in the Healthcare insurance, Life insurance, Construction, Restaurant and Supply chain industries. With expertise in architecting, designing, developing, automating, and testing. Throughout my career, I have actively contributed to the advancement of Software Engineering demonstrating a commitment to innovation and excellence. My technical expertise spans Leading project with onshore and offshore model solving migration issues for reporting and architecting Azure services for non-cloud clients to capture data processing from external vendors and I have a proven track record of leadership in handling team to contribute for company benefits which fits with certification career advancement in technologies. Working as Principal Engineer and Senior Data Engineer adding value to life insurance client as data Modeler (ER Studio) to design model for warehouse and API. Using ER Studio data Architect and ER Studio Business Architect tools to design Logical and Conceptual data models for business purpose. Added all entities and relationships for common model which helps in processing analytical data and improve business needs. Worked as Principal Engineer and participated in Architecting solution on Azure cloud for client during POC. Designed Azure architecture to convert 3rd party input data and transform the analytical data to warehouse for behavioral health client. Implementing warehouse and processing complete data in client's database. Designed data model using Erwin and created the Datawarehouse structure and updated existing MDH model to eliminate duplicates in data processing from legacy system integration with current system. Migrated reports and implemented solutions by converting functions from Teradata to snowflake and upgraded all existing reports for PowerBI and SSRS and deployed to production validating and comparing with existing reports data. Worked on Water fall model and migrated to Agile model with daily Scrum, sprint reviews and sprint planning. I have been actively involved in publishing a research book on cloud computing titled as "Risk Analysis For Exploring the Opportunities In Cloud Outsourcing" with LAP LAMBERT Academic Publishing while working on the research in 2013 where there was big scope in cloud computing area to address. I have authored paper; Develop New Techniques for Ensuring Fairness in Artificial Intelligence and ML Models to Promote Ethical and Unbiased Decision-Making; in International Journal of Innovations in Applied Sciences & Engineering(ijiase) Participated in 3rd International Conference on Research in Multidisciplinary studies. Presented paper titled "Developing generative models that protect data privacy while producing meaningful synthetic data train the models" in

Conference Artificial Intelligences Impact on Transforming Software, Robotics, Electrical, Electronics; Mechanical Fields - Series – 2. My dedication to advancing technology and mentoring the next generation of engineers aligns with interest in becoming member of IEEE, IGI and Inder science. I am committed to fostering technological innovation and excellence in engineering education.

Vitor Lima is a Graduate in Marketing and Consumer MBA Coordinator in Digital Marketing and ISLA Santarém e-commerce. Inbound Learning Active Methodology Mentor.

Praveen Kumar Maroju is a seasoned data science professional with over 16 years of experience in the banking and retail sectors. As a Master of Computer Science, he specializes in architecting and implementing innovative automation solutions. A pioneer in automation technology, Praveen Kumar Maroju successfully spearheaded the creation of a groundbreaking fifth-generation scriptless automation tool. This revolutionary tool has significantly streamlined operations for clients, such as the State Bank of Mauritius, by dramatically reducing setup time and complexity. By eliminating the need for manual intervention, Praveen Kumar Maroju has enabled rapid implementation and basic sanity checks within just two months—a substantial improvement over the industry standard of two years. Praveen Kumar Maroju has presented his work on these innovative ideas at multiple conferences, where he has consistently received positive feedback from industry experts and peers. His research papers have been published in reputable journals and are widely available on platforms like ResearchGate and Google Scholar. With a comprehensive understanding of the project lifecycle, Praveen Kumar Maroju excels in managing projects from inception to completion. Their expertise extends to collaborating with stakeholders to define requirements, allocating resources, and ensuring timely delivery within an Agile framework.

Mimi Mohaffyza Mohamad (PhD) is Associate Professor at Faculty of Technical and Vocational Education, Universiti Tun Hussein Onn Malaysia. She is specializing in learning style, Problem solving skills, TVET curriculum development, TVET Teacher Education, lifelong learning, innovation of teaching and learning for TVET and integrating teaching and workplace requirement and technology

NehruP is an esteemed Assistant Professor at B.S Abdur Rahman Crescent Institute of Science and Technology. With a strong academic background and a passion for education, Nehru has been inspiring and guiding students in the field of Generative AI and Blockchain. His research interests include Plant disease prevention and he has published several papers in renowned journals and conferences. Nehru's dedication to teaching and research has made a significant impact on the academic community, and he continues to be a valuable asset to the institution.

P. Selvakumar is currently an Associate Professor in the Department of Science and Humanities at Nehru Institute of Technology, Coimbatore, Tamil Nadu, India. Since 2023, he has served as the Department IQAC Coordinator at the institute. Prior to joining Nehru Institute of Technology, he held positions as an Assistant Professor in the Department of Science and Humanities various engineering colleges in Coimbatore, Tamil Nadu, India, spanning from 2011 to 2023. Dr.P. Selvakumar's academic and research interests lie primarily in the field of phytochemistry. He has made significant contributions to his field, with an impressive record that includes 30 journal publications, 12 patents, and 20 conference papers. Additionally, he has organized 5 seminars and conferences, further demonstrating his commitment to academic and scientific exchange. Throughout his career, Dr. P.Selvakumar has been recognized for his dedication and excellence in teaching, having been honored with several awards, including the Best Teacher Awards. He holds a prominent position in the academic community, contributing actively to research.

Damodharan Palaniappan works as an Associate Professor & Head in the Department of Information Technology, Marwadi University, Rajkot, Gujarat. He completed his Ph.D. at Anna University, Chennai, M.E. in Computer Science and Engineering at C.I.E.T, Coimbatore and B.E. in Computer Science and Engineering at CSI College of Engineering, Ketty, Nilgiri. He has 19 years' experience of teaching and research. Currently, he guides 6 Ph.D. research scholars. He has authored 8 book chapters, and he has published research papers in reputed journals. His interested areas of research are Data Mining, Image Processing, Software, Machine Learning and Deep Learning.

Kumar Parmar I am an Assistant Professor with a strong foundation in Computer Science and Engineering, currently pursuing my PhD at Marwadi University. With a Master's in Computer Engineering and extensive teaching experience across various institutions, I am dedicated to fostering a dynamic and innovative learning environment. My expertise spans Operating Systems, Linux Administration, Cybersecurity, IoT, and Software Engineering, Machine Learning, Deep learning. In addition to teaching, I have contributed to research with multiple publications and patents, and I am actively involved in guiding projects, mentoring students, and coordinating academic clubs. My professional journey is driven by a passion for continuous learning and collaboration

R. L. Jasmine is currently working as a Teaching Fellow in College of Engineering, Guindy, Anna University, Chennai India. Her research interests include big data Analytics, database systems, image processing, software testing, and computational intelligence algorithms.

Oladiran Stephen Olabiyi is an Associate Professor at the University of Lagos, Faculty of Education, Department of Science and Technology Education. He holds a Nigerian Certificate in Education (Technical) in Woodwork/Technical Drawing from Emmanuel Alayande College of Education (1993), a BTech Ed in Woodwork Technology Education from the Federal University of Technology, Minna (1999), and an MEd and PhD in Industrial Technical Education from the University of Nigeria, Nsukka (2005, 2009). He is the author of several books and has published widely in national and international journals. A member of professional associations such as NATT, NAEC, and NVA, he also serves as an editorial member of NATT. He is happily married with children.

Premavathi T, working as Assistant Professor in the Department of Computer Engineering – Artificial Intelligence, Marwadi University, Rajkot, Gujarat. I did B.E in Computer Science and Engineering at Dhanalakshmi Srinivasan Engineering College, Perambalur, TamilNadu and I did her M.E in Software Engineering with Distinction in Anna University. I am currently pursuing Ph.D. at the Marwadi University. I am having 14+ years of experiences in teaching. My area of interests are Machine Learning, Deep Learning, Big data analystics, etc.

Wang Jing (female, born in 1990) is a lecturer at Bingtuan Xingxin Vocational and Technical College, China, and a Ph.D. candidate at the School of Business and Economics, Universiti Putra Malaysia, Malaysia. She can be identified via her ORCID: https://orcid.org/0009-0003-6647-9923.

Tie Xiaoyao, male, born in 1989, is a member of the Communist Party of China and a doctoral candidate. He inherits the classic tradition of oil painting and is committed to inheriting and carrying forward the art of oil painting. He has rich teaching experience and solid painting skills. He has been invited to participate in overseas academic lectures many times, to explain and demonstrate the methodology of research papers. He has several academic papers and art reviews published in journals such as the International Journal of Education & Technology and the Journal of Academic Research (CUeJAR). He is an associate professor at the School of Art of Qilu Institute of Technology, a member of the Xinxiang Artists Association, the second doctoral supervisor of the Amity Global Institute's EdD program with TEESSIDE University, and the training program assistant at Shenzhen University.

Goh Ying Soon is a senior lecturer and he currently teaches Mandarin as the third language to non-native learners in MARA University of Technology, Malaysia. He is a member of the International Society for Chinese Language Teaching. He has experiences in teaching Mandarin at primary, secondary and tertiary level for more than 25 years. He has been actively presenting papers in national and international conferences. His research interests are on the use of educational technology in Mandarin teaching and learning, web-based instruction, translation, and etc. Updated resume: click here (dropbox). Google Scholar record. researchgate, academia.edu, cnki, scopus (Author ID: 25925392000), book publication, http://www.researcherid.com/rid/U-7238-2017, https://orcid.org/0000-0002-6654-2887, http://myrid .gov.my/2014-1221-3221.

Hutkemri Zulnaidi (Ph.D) is Associate Professor at the Department of Mathematics and Science Education, Faculty of Education, Universiti Malay. He is specializes in mathematics education, technology in education, problem solving, assessment and measurement, statistics and quantitative research method. He is presently involved in several research projects on industrial revolution 4.0, lifelong learning, teaching innovation, learning support, burnout, soft skill, and teaching practices. He is also actively involved in research workshops statistical data analysis (SPSS, AMOS and Smart-PLS) and Research Methodology.

Index

A

Action Autonomy 307, 308, 311, 312, 313, 315, 316, 320, 321, 326
Active Methodologies 93, 94, 95, 96, 97, 98, 99, 107, 108, 282, 297
Adaptive Learning 2, 4, 6, 15, 22, 39, 41, 42, 43, 45, 53, 59, 63, 66, 67, 69, 70, 71, 72, 74, 76, 77, 78, 79, 82, 83, 84, 85, 86, 90, 113, 122, 148, 154, 156, 157, 159, 161, 166, 170, 171, 174, 182, 183, 190, 204, 211, 230, 232, 233, 237, 238, 244, 248, 250, 251, 297, 314, 317, 323, 325
AI 1, 2, 3, 4, 5, 6, 7, 8, 9, 10, 11, 12, 13, 14, 15, 17, 18, 19, 20, 21, 22, 23, 24, 25, 26, 27, 28, 29, 30, 31, 32, 33, 37, 38, 39, 41, 42, 43, 44, 45, 46, 47, 48, 49, 50, 51, 53, 54, 56, 57, 58, 59, 63, 66, 67, 68, 69, 71, 72, 73, 74, 75, 76, 77, 78, 79, 80, 81, 82, 83, 85, 86, 87, 88, 89, 90, 93, 101, 102, 106, 107, 111, 112, 118, 119, 120, 121, 122, 123, 124, 125, 126, 127, 128, 129, 130, 133, 134, 135, 136, 137, 138, 139, 140, 141, 142, 143, 144, 145, 146, 147, 148, 151, 153, 154, 155, 156, 157, 158, 159, 160, 161, 162, 163, 164, 165, 166, 167, 168, 169, 170, 171, 173, 174, 175, 176, 177, 178, 179, 180, 181, 182, 183, 184, 185, 189, 190, 191, 192, 193, 194, 195, 197, 198, 199, 200, 201, 202, 203, 204, 205, 206, 207, 209, 210, 211, 212, 213, 214, 215, 216, 218, 220, 221, 222, 223, 227, 228, 229, 230, 231, 232, 233, 234, 236, 237, 238, 239, 240, 241, 242, 243, 244, 245, 246, 248, 251, 253, 254, 255, 256, 258, 261, 262, 263, 264, 266, 267, 268, 269, 270, 272, 273, 274, 275, 277, 278, 279, 281, 282, 289, 290, 292, 293, 294, 295, 296, 297, 298, 302, 303, 304, 307, 308, 309, 310, 311, 312, 313, 314, 315, 316, 317, 318, 319, 320, 321, 322, 323, 324, 325, 326, 327
AI-Enhanced 2, 3, 4, 5, 6, 8, 10, 11, 12, 13, 37, 38, 43, 46, 49, 53, 54, 56, 57, 58, 59, 129, 148, 170, 173, 176, 190, 191, 203, 205, 327
AI-enhanced Education 4, 54, 58, 59, 148, 190, 327
AI in Education 4, 11, 13, 15, 18, 22, 43, 45, 49, 56, 57, 58, 67, 68, 69, 72, 74, 75, 87, 88, 89, 155, 156, 160, 166, 167, 168, 169, 171, 184, 191, 220, 230, 266, 275, 282, 308, 309, 319, 320, 324
AI in Sustainable 17, 18, 26, 27, 29, 31, 175, 199
Algorithmic Transparency 153, 164
Artificial Autonomy 310
Artificial Intelligence 1, 4, 6, 9, 12, 15, 18, 20, 21, 22, 29, 30, 34, 36, 37, 39, 41, 44, 45, 51, 53, 54, 56, 57, 58, 59, 63, 66, 69, 71, 72, 73, 75, 79, 86, 87, 88, 91, 108, 111, 112, 127, 128, 130, 134, 135, 136, 137, 138, 140, 142, 144, 149, 151, 153, 154, 156, 158, 160, 165, 171, 173, 174, 175, 177, 179, 182, 183, 184, 192, 194, 195, 197, 198, 203, 209, 215, 217, 218, 219, 220, 221, 222, 223, 227, 228, 230, 231, 232, 233, 235, 236, 237, 239, 240, 241, 242, 243, 244, 246, 247, 248, 249, 250, 251, 254, 255, 256, 261, 271, 272, 273, 274, 277, 278, 279, 280, 282, 284, 289, 292, 293, 294, 295, 296, 297, 298, 299, 301, 302, 303, 304, 305, 307, 308, 309, 310, 312, 320, 321, 323, 324, 325, 326, 327
Automated Essay Scoring System 253, 255, 256, 257, 261, 262, 268
Automated Grading 230, 233, 236, 238, 246, 247, 256, 261

C

ChatGPT 58, 59, 250, 253, 254, 255, 256, 257, 258, 262, 263, 264, 265, 266, 267, 268, 269, 270, 272, 273, 274, 310
Circularity 111, 122, 123, 126
Continuous Assessment 142, 239
Critical Thinking Skills 40, 94, 109, 115, 173, 174, 181, 188, 189, 191, 229
Cultural Dimensions 27, 37, 38, 53, 54, 55, 59, 318
Culture 26, 32, 39, 40, 47, 48, 49, 59, 109, 114, 127, 147, 166, 211, 229, 295, 296, 307, 308, 311, 312, 313, 318, 319, 320, 321, 322, 324
Curriculum Design 38, 54, 154, 156, 183, 190

D

Development Pedagogy 11, 17, 18, 27, 28, 29, 31, 32
Digital Equity 8, 11
Digital Literacy 17, 18, 20, 22, 94, 95, 96, 98, 99, 197, 198, 200, 201, 202, 204, 205, 206, 207, 208, 209, 212, 213, 214, 215, 216, 217, 218, 219, 220, 221, 223

E

Education 1, 2, 3, 4, 5, 6, 7, 8, 9, 11, 12, 13, 14, 15, 18, 20, 22, 25, 26, 27, 28, 30, 31, 32, 34, 35, 36, 37, 38, 39, 40, 41, 42, 43, 44, 45, 46, 47, 48, 49, 50, 51, 53, 54, 55, 56, 57, 58, 59, 60, 63, 64, 65, 66, 67, 68, 69, 70, 71, 72, 73, 74, 75, 76, 78, 79, 80, 81, 82, 85, 87, 88, 89, 90, 91, 93, 94, 95, 96,

97, 98, 99, 100, 101, 102, 103, 104, 105, 106, 107, 108, 109, 111, 112, 113, 118, 120, 121, 122, 124, 125, 126, 127, 128, 129, 130, 133, 134, 141, 142, 143, 144, 145, 146, 147, 148, 150, 153, 154, 155, 156, 157, 158, 159, 160, 164, 165, 166, 167, 168, 169, 170, 171, 172, 173, 174, 175, 177, 179, 180, 181, 182, 183, 184, 185, 186, 187, 189, 190, 191, 192, 193, 194, 195, 197, 198, 199, 200, 201, 202, 203, 204, 205, 206, 207, 208, 209, 210, 211, 212, 213, 214, 215, 216, 217, 218, 219, 220, 221, 222, 223, 228, 230, 231, 232, 235, 238, 239, 241, 242, 244, 246, 247, 248, 249, 250, 251, 253, 254, 255, 256, 257, 258, 260, 266, 271, 272, 273, 274, 275, 277, 278, 279, 280, 281, 282, 283, 284, 285, 286, 287, 288, 289, 290, 291, 294, 295, 296, 297, 298, 299, 301, 302, 303, 304, 305, 307, 308, 309, 310, 311, 312, 313, 314, 315, 316, 317, 318, 319, 320, 321, 323, 324, 325, 326, 327
Educational Assessments 227, 228, 229, 230, 235, 245
Educational Technology 34, 46, 56, 91, 127, 193, 195, 219, 220, 222, 250, 255, 275, 323, 325, 327
Ethical AI 8, 9, 18, 19, 20, 21, 23, 24, 25, 28, 29, 30, 31, 153, 156, 168, 223
Ethical Considerations 2, 3, 5, 11, 12, 17, 18, 19, 20, 23, 29, 30, 31, 51, 54, 90, 142, 145, 154, 155, 156, 157, 158, 160, 164, 169, 181, 184, 185, 190, 191, 200, 204, 211, 212, 230, 238, 241, 279
Ethical Implications 17, 19, 49, 118, 144, 145, 157, 159, 160, 163, 185, 190, 202, 203, 209, 211, 213
Experiential learning 1, 2, 3, 4, 5, 6, 7, 8, 9, 11, 12, 13, 14, 15, 43, 52, 53, 72, 170, 214, 218, 284, 285, 291, 307, 326

G

Global Learner Community 37, 59

H

Higher Education 15, 57, 58, 59, 65, 94, 107, 129, 171, 185, 192, 193, 194, 195, 197, 198, 212, 213, 214, 217, 218, 219, 220, 221, 222, 246, 248, 249, 250, 251, 260, 266, 271, 272, 274, 285, 302, 307, 308, 309, 310, 311, 312, 313, 314, 316, 319, 320, 321, 323, 324, 325, 326
Human Raters 253, 254, 255, 256, 257, 261, 262, 263, 264, 265, 266, 267, 268, 269, 270

I

Inbound Learning 93, 95, 96, 99, 100, 101, 103, 104, 105, 106, 108, 109
Intelligent Tutoring 4, 7, 15, 39, 45, 59, 72, 112, 125, 126, 154, 156, 159, 174, 204, 230, 231, 232, 238, 246, 248, 251

L

Learning 1, 2, 3, 4, 5, 6, 7, 8, 9, 10, 11, 12, 13, 14, 15, 17, 18, 21, 22, 26, 27, 28, 29, 30, 31, 32, 34, 35, 36, 37, 38, 39, 40, 41, 42, 43, 44, 45, 46, 47, 48, 49, 50, 51, 52, 53, 54, 55, 56, 57, 58, 59, 60, 63, 64, 65, 66, 67, 68, 69, 70, 71, 72, 73, 74, 75, 76, 77, 78, 79, 80, 81, 82, 83, 84, 85, 86, 87, 88, 89, 90, 91, 93, 94, 95, 96, 97, 98, 99, 100, 101, 102, 103, 104, 105, 106, 107, 108, 109, 111, 112, 113, 114, 115, 116, 117, 118, 119, 120, 121, 122, 123, 124, 125, 126, 127, 128, 129, 130, 133, 134, 135, 136, 138, 139, 140, 141, 142, 143, 144, 145, 146, 147, 148, 149, 150, 151, 152, 153, 154, 155, 156, 157, 158, 159, 160, 161, 162, 163, 164, 165, 166, 167, 168, 169, 170, 171, 172, 174, 175, 176, 177, 178, 179, 180, 181, 182, 183, 184, 185, 187, 188, 189, 190, 191, 192, 193, 194, 195, 199, 200, 201, 202, 203, 204, 205, 207, 208, 209, 210, 211, 212, 213, 214, 215, 216, 217, 218, 219, 220, 221, 222, 223, 227, 228, 229, 230, 231, 232, 233, 234, 235, 236, 237, 238, 239, 240, 241, 242, 243, 244, 245, 246, 247, 248, 249, 250, 251, 254, 255, 258, 260, 261, 262, 264, 267, 271, 272, 273, 274, 277, 278, 279, 280, 281, 282, 283, 284, 285, 286, 287, 288, 289, 290, 291, 292, 293, 294, 295, 296, 297, 298, 299, 301, 302, 303, 304, 307, 308, 309, 311, 312, 313, 314, 315, 316, 317, 318, 319, 320, 321, 322, 323, 324, 325, 326

P

Pedagogy 1, 11, 17, 18, 27, 28, 29, 31, 32, 45, 95, 97, 99, 141, 142, 157, 173, 185, 186, 248, 277, 278, 279, 282, 283, 285, 286, 287, 288, 289, 290, 291, 292, 294, 299, 301, 302, 303, 315, 320
Personalization 6, 7, 13, 22, 42, 45, 46, 59, 126, 155, 157, 162, 165, 170, 234, 239, 314, 323, 325
Personalized Learning 7, 11, 17, 18, 22, 29, 38, 41, 42, 43, 44, 45, 50, 56, 57, 58, 66, 67, 68, 69, 70, 71, 72, 73, 74, 76, 77, 78, 79, 80, 83, 84, 85, 86, 87, 89, 113, 114, 117, 118, 122, 123, 124, 126, 129, 153, 155, 156, 160, 162, 163, 165, 170, 171,

174, 189, 190, 203, 204, 211, 236, 238, 239, 243, 279, 293, 311, 312, 320, 324
Predictive Analytics 7, 11, 13, 69, 73, 135, 139, 140, 148, 153, 154, 155, 156, 157, 158, 159, 160, 161, 164, 165, 167, 168, 169, 170, 175, 180, 233

R

Real-world experiences 145, 286
Renewable Energy Education 133, 134, 141, 142, 143, 144, 145, 146, 147, 148

S

Science Education 173, 174, 179, 180, 182, 183, 189, 190, 191, 193, 194, 222, 247
sensing Autonomy 307, 308, 311, 312, 313, 316, 317, 320, 321, 322
Student Engagement 2, 42, 43, 46, 51, 64, 76, 78, 79, 81, 82, 86, 89, 96, 99, 114, 154, 174, 193, 223, 246, 285, 291, 321, 323, 325
Sustainability 1, 2, 3, 4, 5, 6, 7, 8, 9, 10, 11, 12, 13, 14, 15, 17, 18, 19, 20, 21, 22, 24, 29, 31, 32, 37, 38, 39, 42, 43, 44, 45, 46, 47, 48, 49, 52, 53, 54, 55, 56, 57, 58, 59, 65, 66, 85, 87, 91, 111, 122, 125, 126, 128, 134, 136, 138, 139, 140, 144, 145, 146, 147, 149, 151, 153, 154, 155, 156, 157, 158, 159, 160, 161, 163, 164, 165, 166, 167, 168, 169, 170, 173, 174, 175, 176, 177, 178, 179, 180, 181, 185, 186, 189, 190, 191, 192, 193, 194, 195, 197, 198, 199, 200, 201, 202, 205, 206, 207, 208, 209, 210, 211, 212, 213, 214, 215, 216, 217, 218, 219, 220, 221, 222, 223, 248, 302, 326
Sustainability Education 1, 2, 3, 4, 5, 6, 8, 9, 11, 12, 13, 14, 15, 37, 38, 39, 42, 43, 44, 46, 47, 48, 49, 53, 54, 55, 59, 66, 91, 125, 153, 154, 155, 156, 157, 158, 159, 160, 164, 165, 166, 167, 168, 169, 170, 174, 175, 177, 185, 191, 192, 193, 194, 197, 198, 208, 209, 210, 211, 212, 215, 216
Sustainable Futures 200, 201, 202, 212
Sustainable Power Systems 133, 148
Sustainable workforce 277, 282, 295, 296, 304

T

Teaching 11, 15, 17, 18, 19, 22, 27, 34, 35, 36, 38, 39, 40, 41, 44, 45, 51, 53, 54, 55, 58, 59, 65, 66, 67, 68, 69, 70, 71, 72, 73, 74, 75, 76, 78, 79, 80, 81, 82, 83, 85, 86, 87, 88, 91, 93, 94, 95, 96, 97, 98, 99, 100, 101, 102, 103, 104, 105, 108, 109, 111, 112, 113, 114, 116, 117, 118, 121, 123, 124, 125, 126, 127, 128, 133, 141, 142, 143, 145, 147, 151, 154, 156, 168, 171, 174, 180, 181, 184, 186, 187, 190, 192, 201, 204, 206, 207, 208, 209, 211, 213, 214, 216, 219, 222, 223, 228, 230, 231, 234, 235, 237, 239, 240, 241, 244, 249, 254, 255, 258, 259, 260, 264, 268, 271, 272, 273, 274, 278, 279, 281, 283, 284, 285, 286, 287, 288, 289, 290, 291, 293, 299, 300, 301, 302, 303, 304, 307, 308, 309, 310, 312, 320, 324, 327
Teaching-Learning Process 95, 96, 98, 101, 104, 112, 113, 116, 117, 121, 126
Teaching the Future 133
Technology 1, 5, 12, 15, 17, 18, 19, 21, 22, 29, 30, 31, 32, 34, 35, 36, 37, 42, 43, 46, 47, 48, 49, 50, 51, 54, 56, 58, 59, 66, 67, 68, 69, 70, 71, 72, 75, 76, 80, 81, 82, 84, 85, 87, 88, 89, 90, 91, 98, 99, 101, 102, 105, 106, 109, 111, 112, 113, 116, 117, 118, 119, 121, 127, 129, 133, 134, 139, 140, 142, 144, 147, 151, 153, 154, 155, 157, 158, 159, 164, 166, 167, 168, 169, 170, 180, 185, 192, 193, 194, 195, 197, 198, 200, 201, 202, 203, 204, 205, 206, 207, 208, 209, 210, 211, 212, 213, 214, 215, 216, 217, 218, 219, 220, 222, 223, 227, 228, 230, 231, 233, 236, 237, 241, 242, 243, 244, 248, 250, 251, 254, 255, 256, 261, 262, 266, 268, 272, 275, 277, 278, 279, 280, 281, 282, 283, 284, 286, 288, 289, 290, 291, 292, 293, 294, 295, 299, 301, 303, 304, 308, 309, 310, 311, 312, 314, 315, 317, 318, 319, 320, 323, 324, 325, 326, 327
Thought Autonomy 307, 308, 312, 313, 314, 321

V

Virtual 2, 3, 4, 6, 8, 10, 11, 13, 39, 45, 49, 50, 66, 72, 89, 99, 101, 106, 107, 111, 112, 113, 114, 115, 116, 117, 118, 119, 121, 124, 126, 127, 128, 129, 133, 134, 142, 174, 176, 183, 189, 214, 220, 221, 238, 262, 280, 289, 293, 300, 302, 303, 307, 310, 311, 320

www.ingramcontent.com/pod-product-compliance
Lightning Source LLC
LaVergne TN
LVHW062119300926
849161LV00010B/2490